Religion in Japanese History

LECTURES ON THE HISTORY OF RELIGIONS
SPONSORED BY THE
AMERICAN COUNCIL OF LEARNED SOCIETIES
NEW SERIES, NUMBER SEVEN

Religion in Japanese History

JOSEPH M. KITAGAWA

COLUMBIA UNIVERSITY PRESS
New York

Columbia University Press
New York   Oxford
Copyright © 1966, 1990 Columbia University Press
All rights reserved

Library of Congress Cataloging-in-Publication Data

Kitagawa, Joseph Mitsuo, 1915–
Religion in Japanese history / Joseph M. Kitagawa.
p.   cm.
(Lectures on the history of religions ; new ser., no.7)
Includes bibliographical references.
ISBN 0-231-02834-2
ISBN 0-231-02838-5 (pbk)
1. Japan—Religion.
I. Title.
II. Series.
BL2202.K5   1990
291'.0952—dc20
90-37727
CIP

Casebound editions of Columbia University Press books are Smyth-sewn and printed
on permanent and durable acid-free paper

Printed in the United States of America

c 10 9 8 7 6 5 4 3 2 1

p 10 9 8 7 6 5 4 3

TO THE MEMORY OF MY PARENTS

Kitagawa Chiyokichi († *1939*)

AND

Kitagawa Nozaki Kumi († *1945*)

This volume is the seventh to be published in the series of Lectures on the History of Religions for which the American Council of Learned Societies, through its Committee on the History of Religions, assumed responsibility in 1936.

Under the program the Committee from time to time enlists the services of scholars to lecture in colleges, universities, and seminaries on topics in need of expert elucidation. Subsequently, when possible and appropriate, the Committee arranges for the publication of the lectures. Other volumes in the series are Martin P. Nilsson, *Greek Popular Religion* (1940), Henri Frankfort, *Ancient Egyptian Religion* (1948), Wing-tsit Chan, *Religious Trends in Modern China* (1953), Joachim Wach, *The Comparative Study of Religions,* edited by Joseph M. Kitagawa (1958), R. M. Grant, *Gnosticism and Early Christianity* (1959), Robert Lawson Slater, *World Religions and World Community* (1963), and Joseph L. Blau, *Modern Varieties of Judaism* (1966), Morton Smith, *Palestinian Parties and Politics That Shaped the Old Testament* (1971), Philip H. Ashby, *Modern Trends in Hinduism* (1974), Victor Turner and Edith Turner, *Image and Pilgrimage in Christian Culture* (1978), Annemarie Schimmel, *As Through a Veil: Mystical Poetry in Islam* (1982), Peter Brown, *The Body and Society: Men, Women, and Sexual Renunciation in Early Christianity* (1988), and W. H. McLeod, *The Sikhs: History, Religion, and Society* (1989).

Contents

Preface to the Paperback Edition

I must admit that I have mixed feelings at the prospect of having a paperback edition of *Religion in Japanese History*. On the one hand, I am naturally delighted to learn that the volume has met, at least to a certain extent, the needs of readers since its publication. On the other hand, I know only too well that a variety of illuminating new studies on various phases of Japanese religion have appeared over the past two decades, even though a thorough revision of the contents of this volume in light of these new studies is not a feasible option at this time. Thus, the paperback edition is substantially the same as the hardcover volume, except of course for the addition of a very brief account to update it on recent developments. But I have high hopes that the particular concerns which had originally motivated me to work on this subject are still relevant today. What concerned me then—and what has continued to concern me all these years—is not the accumulation of more data, important though they are, but rather the well-balanced perspectives from which to approach Japanese religion, culture, and history.

In this connection, Mircea Eliade often reminded us that the discovery of non-Western religions and cultures after the Renaissance was as significant an experience for the West as the invention of the telescope; both radically altered the way the West perceived its place in the universe. As might be expected, Europeans' initial response to non-Western traditions was to measure them against their own inherited value system in keeping with the accepted Western pattern which had always tried to absorb and integrate new and alien features and elements into its ever-expanding synthetic unity, e.g., Hellenism, Near Eastern religion, Roman jurisprudence, etc. Meanwhile, some European intellectuals began to feel that it was important to interpret non-Western traditions on their own terms, and not through the frameworks of Western civilization and Christianity. Even then it remained the case that from the time of the Enlightenment in the seventeenth and eighteenth centuries to World War II, it was often assumed that non-Westerners should present their religions and cultures primarily as data for Westerners to analyze and interpret from Western perspectives, perspectives which were claimed to be unbiased, neutral, objective, and universal. Subsequently, impressive superstructures developed, constituting "Oriental" (including Indological, Sinological, and Japanological) Studies and "African" Studies, and dealing with a variety of non-Western languages, arts, economic systems, social and political orders, religions and cultures, analyzed and interpreted, however, by means of Westernized models, concepts, and logic. (In this particular reflection, we intend to deal especially with Japanological studies.)

Today, many followers of Western-inspired Oriental Studies may be surprised to learn that some of their forefathers had agreed with Hegel's daring thesis, as explicated by W. Halbfass:

The "phenomenology" or self-manifestation of the absolute merges into man's work in history, into human self-fulfillment. Man becomes "present God" (*präsent Gott*) and continues the divine process in his own worldly presence, in taking charge of his world and discovering the dignity of the absolute *in* it. (Wilhelm Halbfass, *India and Europe*, Albany: S.U.N.Y. Press, 1988, p. 93)

In a similar vein, E. Husserl, the father of modern phenomenology, asserted:

Europe alone can provide other traditions with a *universal framework of meaning and understanding*. They will have to "Europeanize themselves, whereas we . . . will never, for example, Indianize ourselves." The "Europeanization of all foreign parts of mankind" . . . is the destiny of the earth. (*Ibid.*, p. 437, my italics)

Three remarks might be made in this connection. First, we must give due credit to the pioneers of the West-inspired Oriental Studies for plunging into an unknown territory and initiating a new academic enterprise, however one-sided it may seem in retrospect, and leaving behind such great monuments as the *Sacred Books of the East* (edited by Friedrich Max Müller) and the *Encyclopaedia of Religion and Ethics* (edited by James Hastings). Second, to make matters more complicated, during the nineteenth and even in the twentieth century up to World War II, under the strong impact of the Westernization of the whole world, many Asian thinkers naively swallowed the West's questionable and self-authenticating claim *à la* Hegel that "Asian thought is comprehensible and interpretable within European thought, but not vice versa . . . *European thought has to provide the context and categories* for the exploration of all traditions of thought" (*Ibid.*, p. 96, my italics). It should be noted that in those days, to adopt *in toto* the Western mode of scholarship was an easy—and often the only— way for Asian scholars to gain entrée into the global academy. Once the predominantly Westernized approach to Asian religions and cultures became accepted in Asia, however, it has continued to exert gentle tyranny on some Asian, to say nothing of many Western, scholars of Asian subjects even after the erosion of Western colonialism in Asia. Third, thus ironically today there are far too many thinkers and scholars both in the West and in the non-Western world who are under the happy illusion that the only and the most adequate way to study, say, Japanese religion and culture is by following the perspectives and methods of the traditional West-inspired Oriental (or Japanological) Studies.

I hope the above account about the confusing state of the study of non-Western traditions may explain, at least in part, why in the early 1960s I both as a student of Japanese culture and as a stu-

dent of the history of religions (*Religionswissenschaft*)—born and
educated through college in Japan, but received graduate education and subsequently taught in the U.S.—aspired simultaneously
to bring to bear the insight of *Religionswissenschaft* to the study of
Japanese religion, while utilizing Japanese religion as a case study
to refine and improve the structure and contour of the general
discipline of the history of religions. In short, to me the study of
Japanese religion and the study of the history of religions dove-
tailed very closely, demanding for me to hold in balance both my
dual (Eastern and Western) backgrounds and double (Japanology
and *Religionswissenschaft*) vocations. As far as the original volume
of *Religion in Japanese History* was concerned, developing an adequate, well-balanced perspective was more a matter of aspiration
than achievement on my part, but the experience of working on
the subject opened my vista in many respects.

Inasmuch as I was born and raised in Japan, it was fairly natural for me to be "autobiographically" interested in the "inner"
meaning of Japanese religion, and since I studied and have taught
in the field of *Religionswissenschaft* in the West, you can readily
understand that I study Japanese religion "biographically" (in contradistinction to "autobiographically"), that is, objectively, as an
outsider-examiner, as well. My dual background does not mean,
however, that I am critical of Japanese scholars who approach
Japanese religion autobiographically—primarily but, of course, not
exclusively—just as I am in no way critical of non-Japanese scholars who regard Japanese religion ostensibly as an object of study,
perceiving it empathetically but still as an outsider. I have also
realized that autobiographical and biographical approaches repre-
sent two different, and equally legitimate, perspectives. And, in
this sense, having a dual background implies a heavy emotional
strain on me, in spite of certain advantages.

In sharp contrast to the West-inspired "Oriental" or "Japanological" studies, which tend to analyze and interpret Japanese data
through Western perspectives and by means of Westernized methods, the advantage of an insider's autobiographical perception is to
be able to draw out the inner meaning of, say, Japanese religion,

even though it often entails uncritical acceptance of the self-authenticating circularity of the inherited Japanese tradition, e.g., the so-called "self-evident" notions of truth, of justice, or right or wrong. Also, implict in the autobiographical mind-set is something like a "mental prism," which sorts significant items from a mass of data and relates historical realities to the realm of fantasy and imagination. More often than not, insiders seem to be inclined to accept the "givenness" of inherited doctrines, mores, and other religious practices, whereas outsiders—even when they depend heavily on the insiders' autobiographical statements for their (i.e. outsiders') assessment of, say, Japanese religion—tend to exercise principles of selectivity and discrimination in accordance with their own mental prisms.

In reference to the subject matter of "religion," I must admit that although I am greatly indebted to the history of religions, a discipline developed in the last century in the West, I have been uneasy about the notion of religion as a separate or separable domain of human activity. I believe that it is a peculiar Western convention to divide human experience into such semi-autonomous pigeonholes as religion, philosophy, ethics, aesthetics, culture, society, etc. No doubt this type of convention has been useful in the West, but some people naively assume that this provincial Western mode has universal validity, partly because they do not know other, that is, non-Western ways of dividing human experience. With that in mind, in writing on *Religion in Japanese History,* I made every effort to retrieve the traditional Japanese mode of perceiving the texture of reality and human experience. In so doing, I discovered that in Japan, as much as it was true in many other parts of the world, what we tend to isolate as religion in the history of religions is very much a part of what might be termed, for a lack of better description, the religious-cultural-social-political synthesis, e.g., the Ritsuryō ("imperial rescript") synthesis in the seventh and eighth centuries, the Tokugawa synthesis 1603–1867, and the Meiji synthesis, which commenced in 1868 and lasted until the end of World War II. In all these cases, what we call religion provided the cosmic legitimation for the particular form of synthesis, as I tried to explicate in *Religion in Japanese History*.

It may be appropriate for me to conclude this preface with a brief reflection on recent cultural, political, and religious developments in Japan. In the mid-1960s—two decades after the end of World War II when I finished the book—I already discerned, though not very clearly, that Japan's priorities as much as the historical reality surrounding Japan were undergoing radical changes, and be it noted that these two factors then as now were inseparably interrelated. Now with the commencement of the new Heisei era, begun in 1989, certain trends have become more apparent, while new factors and wrinkles have set in and muddle the water, too.

In order to make my reflection more succinct, let us—at the expense of oversimplification—depict three crucial dates of modern Japanese history, i.e., 1868, the beginning of modern Japan, 1945, the defeat of Japan at the end of World War II, and 1989, the beginning of the Heisei era, following the demise of the Shōwa Emperor. Throughout these years, the multifaceted and contradictory features of modern Japan, like mother-of-pearl, appeared differently to different peoples and perspectives, e.g., the Japanese and foreign governments, conservative and progressive insiders, and pro- and anti-Japanese outsiders, etc. For example, the objective of modern Japan, following the "opening" of Japan to the rest of the world in the mid-nineteenth century, as far as the Meiji regime was concerned, was to achieve "economic prosperity and a strong defense," thus making Japan a modern nation-state, as rich and powerful as leading Western powers. For this purpose, the government wanted to import technology and practical knowledge from the West, while consolidating the national fabric by elevating super-religious Shinto and the emperor cult as patriotic duties for all Japanese citizens regardless of their personal beliefs. Meanwhile, Japan's relentless determination to dominate other Asian nations by emulating Western-style imperial colonialism, from the turn of the century till 1945, gave the erroneous impression to some people in the West and in Asia that Japan had given up her

inherited tradition in favor of "Westernism," even though there is
a grain of truth in such a characterization.

In 1945 the defeated Japan, under the Allied military occupation, was destined to confront an ambiguous future. Deprived of
its military power and former colonial possessions, Japan chose
industrialization as its only, and the most feasible, option, which
ushered in rapid social changes of great magnitude. For example,
at the end of World War II, 70 percent of the total population
resided in rural areas; twenty years later, the ratio between urban
and rural populations became almost the reverse. The recovery
and growth of cities and industries that began around 1950 was
further expedited by the development of mass communication media and the transportation system. These in turn disseminated urban values and the urban ways of life.

The dazzling social, economic, and political changes, however,
inevitably left dark shadows on the psyche of the populace, who
had already suffered from the loss of the cozy self-authenticating
worldview of the pre-war Japan. It came as a shock to many Japanese men and women that they now had to live in a strange new
world, very different from what they had known or expected—a
new world shaped by science, technology, industry, and business,
all of which tend to repudiate the sacred pieties, morals, and rituals of their inherited traditions. Besides, the religious topography
of the Japanese was transformed directly or indirectly by a series
of world events, such as the end of Western colonialism, the growth
of world communism, which propelled such Asian communist states
as China, North Korea, and Vietnam, the increasing seculariza-
tion of cultures in various continents, and the rise of many new
Eastern religions.

In 1989 the long Shōwa era, covering an eventful six decades,
came to an end with the death of the emperor bearing the era's
name. By then Japan had become one of the financial powerhouses
in the world, as testified by the fact that dignitaries from over 160
nations attended the imperial funeral in February that year. Ironically, the government's primary preoccupation with economic
success at the expense of other pursuits of life has made Japan

culturally weightless; many people, including sensitive Japanese intelligentsia, worry that Japan as a national community is bound to experience a "rich but desolate" isolation in the near future unless its priorities are radically altered soon. By this I don't mean that people are against Japan's commitment to international trade, industry, and technology as such, but that they think economic prosperity alone will not be enough for the well-being of Japan as a national community or for its people. Some people are also worried about Japan's naiveté and ineptness in global political affairs, which are in such sharp contrast to its shrewd business acumen. At any rate, Japan's lack of understanding of, and rapport with, its Asian neighbors and its misjudgment of political realities in the West, Middle East, Africa, and Latin America have already brought to Japan a series of major and minor crises caused by such events as the triumph of communism in China, Nixon's opening of China, a Muslim revolution that affected oil production, insensitivities to Korean and Chinese reaction to Japanese school texts' account of the Pacific War, unexpected developments in Afghanistan, Eastern Europe, Beijing, Latin America, and South Africa, to say nothing about her own peoples' impatience with corruption in high places.

In retrospect, it becomes evident that the rapid rise of modern Japan from its feudal past in the mid-nineteenth century revolved around two parallel and simultaneous processes, namely the "modernization of tradition" and the "traditioning of modernity." From 1868 until 1945 these two processes were cleverly manipulated by the government, which superimposed its own newly-created traditions, including state Shinto, the emperor cult, financial prosperity, and militarism, as national priorities. Again from 1945 until 1989, the government created new traditions and advocated new national priorities stressing financial development at the expense of other objectives, for example, by providing businesses with export subsidies, trade barriers to protect the home market and low cost credit, etc., thus facilitating what some people regard as the economic miracle of post-war Japan. But, lamentably, compared to the government individuals and individual initiatives have been ignored and sacrificed. I remember very well that shortly after World War II Hajime Nakamura lamented the fact that the general populace in Japan did not grasp the importance of "the individual as a social entity" (see H. Nakamura, *Ways of Thinking of Eastern Peoples,* ed. P. P. Weiner, Honolulu: East-West Center Press, 1964, p. 145; Nakamura's original Japanese version—on which my ideas were based—was published in 1948). And the cultivation of "the individual as a social entity" in men and women, instead of remaining as "corporate beings, political, economic, or religious," may be one of the most urgent needs for the new religious-social-cultural-political synthesis in the Heisei era of Japan.

Preface

The present book is based on a series of lectures given in 1962–63 under the auspices of the Committee on the History of Religions of the American Council of Learned Societies. The purpose of these lectures was neither to give a general survey of Japanese religion to the uninitiated nor to discuss technical minutiae of interest primarily to a few learned scholars. What was intended was to delineate both for a general audience and for scholars the significance, inner logic, and patterns of religious phenomena in Japan both historically and structurally from the perspective of *Religionswissenschaft,* the discipline variously known as History of Religions, Phenomenology of Religions, and the Comparative Study of Religions.

The complexity of the historic interactions of various religious systems in Japan is such that it would have been easier, for readers as well as for the author, if the study had concentrated either on the religious developments of one historical period, or on one of the major religious systems, such as Shinto, Buddhism, or Japanese Confucianism. However, the scarcity of works, especially in Western languages, dealing with Japanese religion as a whole has challenged me to undertake the present task. It might also be added in this connection that for me personally it has been a rewarding experience to write on the religious heritage of my ancestors, who, distant though they may be in time, space, and memory, have nurtured my thinking and being. It is my sincere hope that this study will in some way make a modest contribution to the discipline of *Religionswissenschaft*.

The general plan of this book is conditioned by the fact that the material was originally organized to form six lectures based on a conventional periodization of Japanese history. Because of the nature of the assignment, each lecture had to be more or less autonomous and independently coherent without losing the organizational idea of the entire series. Thus readers will find that each chapter emphasizes some specific motif: religious leadership (Chapter I), modes of religious apprehension (Chapter II), religious societies (Chapter III), the relationship between the feudal regime and religious systems (Chapter IV), and the problem of "modernity" (Chapter V). Chapter VI is devoted to the portrayal of the religious situation in the post-Second World War period. For the most part, the doctrine of the various religious traditions has not been stressed. Rather, emphasis has been placed on delineation of the intricate relationships that have existed between the various religious systems of Japan and the coeval social, political, and cultural developments. Parenthetically, it might be added that any discussion of Japanese religion can ill afford to neglect its prehistory. An additional chapter on this subject was prepared, but I have not included it in this volume for reasons of space. Those who are interested, however, are referred to my article, "The Prehistoric Background of Japanese Religion," *History of Religions, II* (No. 2, Winter, 1963), 292–329.

Throughout the book all Japanese names are written with the family name preceding the given name, except in the notes, where the Western custom is followed. With regard to place names, personal names, and the titles of Japanese works, I have not strictly followed any one established system of transliteration. For instance, diacritical marks have been omitted from such familiar names as Bukkyo, Kyoto, Kyushu, Osaka, Shinto, and Tokyo. When two vowels appear successively, such as *u* and *e*, the letter *y* is sometimes added. *Ue*, for example, thus becomes *uye*. In the main, when I had to choose between consistency and simplicity, I followed the latter principle. All honorifics are eliminated, except when necessary to identify the person, e.g., the Empress Shōtoku or the Prince Regent Shōtoku.

Obviously, no one can study Japanese religion without the benefit of a host of Japanese and Western scholars. While space does not allow me to cite the names of all those to whom I owe much, I must not fail to mention my special indebtedness to Professor Hori Ichiro of Tohoku University, Sendai, Japan, not only because his works have been an invaluable source of information but also because he has taken the trouble to go over the first four chapters of the book. I must also mention the names of two scholars, Joachim Wach (1898–1955) and Kishimoto Hideo (1903–64), who for years urged me to work on this subject, and whose influence has marked various sections of this book.

Thanks are due to the Committee on the History of Religions of the American Council of Learned Societies (ACLS) which, under the chairmanship of Professor Walter Harrelson and his successor, Professor Robert M. Grant, appointed me to give these lectures. I am grateful as well to Dean Jerald C. Brauer, Professor Mircea Eliade, and Professor Charles H. Long, all of the University of Chicago Divinity School, whose encouragement and support enabled me to accept this assignment. It is also my pleasant duty to express my gratitude to Mr. D. H. Daugherty, Executive Associate of the ACLS, and to my gracious hosts at the institutions where I had the privilege of delivering these lectures —Duke University, the University of Wisconsin, Syracuse University, Harvard Divinity School (and the Harvard-Yenching Institute), Northwestern University, the University of California (Berkeley), Claremont Graduate School (and the Blaisdell Institute), the University of Pennsylvania, Haverford College, Southern Methodist University, Rice University, Columbia University, Oberlin College, and Notre Dame University.

I have received many helpful comments and suggestions both from the scholars of the various campuses I visited and from those who read parts of the manuscript, notably Professors Erwin Goodenough of Yale (Emeritus), Mircea Eliade and Eugene Soviak of Chicago, Joseph L. Blau of Columbia, Philip H. Ashby of Princeton, Jacques Duchesne-Guillemin of Liège, Mr. William

P. Woodard of the International Institute for the Study of Religions, Tokyo, Mrs. Kyoko (Motomochi) Nakamura, and Mr. H. Byron Earhart. Dr. Charles S. J. White, now with the University of Wisconsin, and the Reverend Robert S. Ellwood have not only made stylistic improvements but have also offered many valuable suggestions. The typing of the manuscript was done by Miss Gloria Valentine and by the secretarial staff of the University of Chicago Divinity School under the direction of Mrs. Minerva Bell. I also wish to express my sincere appreciation to the staff of Columbia University Press, especially to Miss Elisabeth L. Shoemaker, for assistance and encouragement.

Passages from the following books are quoted by permission of the respective publishers: Masaharu Anesaki, *History of Japanese Religion* (c. 1963, Charles E. Tuttle Co., Inc., Rutland, Vermont, and Tokyo, Japan); Kishimoto Hideo, comp. and ed., *Japanese Religion in the Meiji Era,* tr. and adapted by John F. Howes (1956, Obunsha Co., Ltd., Tokyo); Edwin O. Reischauer, *Japan: Past and Present* (1946, Alfred A. Knopf Inc., New York); Edwin O. Reischauer and John K. Fairbank, *East Asia: The Great Tradition* (Volume I of A History of East Asian Civilization) (1958, Houghton Mifflin Company, Boston); G. B. Sansom, *The Western World and Japan* (1950, Alfred A. Knopf Inc., New York); G. B. Sansom, *A History of Japan to 1334* (1958) and *A History of Japan, 1334-1615* (1961, Stanford University Press, Stanford); and Langdon Warner, *The Enduring Art of Japan* (1952, Harvard University Press, Cambridge).

The publication of the present volume would not have been possible without the opportunities given to me to visit Japan in 1958–59 and 1961–62. My research was greatly facilitated through the assistance rendered to me by many friends in Japan. Also, my wife, Evelyn M. Kitagawa, played no small part in helping me to carry out my research and writing, not only with her valuable comments and indefatigable curiosity, but also with her patience and understanding. My only regret is that my parents were no longer alive to share the joy of family reunion. Thus, to their beloved memory this book is humbly dedicated.

Religion in Japanese History

Abbreviations

ERE   *Encyclopaedia of Religion and Ethics,* ed. James Hastings. 13 vols. New York, 1928

FEQ   *The Far Eastern Quarterly* (Lancaster, Pa.)

FS   *Folklore Studies* (Peking; later Tokyo)

JAOS   *Journal of the American Oriental Society* (Philadelphia)

JAS   *The Journal of Asian Studies* (formerly *The Far Eastern Quarterly*) (Ann Arbor, Mich.)

JGZ   *Jinruigaku zasshi* (Journal of anthropology)

RGG   *Religion in Geschichte und Gegenwart* (Tübingen)

SJA   *Southwestern Journal of Anthropology* (Albuquerque, N.M.)

SKT   *Sekai kokogaku taikei* (Encyclopedia of world archeology)

TASJ   *Transactions of Asiatic Society of Japan* (Tokyo)

ZNBT   *Zusetsu Nihon bunkashi taikei* (Illustrated encyclopedia of Japanese cultural history)

ZNMZ   *Zusetsu Nihon minzokugaku zenshu* (Collected works on Japanese folklore illustrated)

ZNR   *Zusetsu Nihon rekishi* (Illustrated history of Japan)

ZSBT   *Zusetsu Sekai bunkashi taikei* (Illustrated encyclopedia of cultural history of the world)

CHAPTER I

Emperor, Shaman, and Priest

RELIGIOUS LIFE OF THE EARLY JAPANESE

(ca. third–eighth centuries)

There are many different approaches to the study of Japanese religion. One could certainly take up different religious systems, such as Shinto, Buddhism, or the new religions of the period since the Second World War, and study them separately. Or one could approach the subject topically and delineate the relevance of the myths and symbols, doctrines and dogmas, or ethical systems and ecclesiastical organizations of one or more religions. In this study, however, I shall approach Japanese religion historically, not only in the sense of studying its involvement in the social and political life of the nation in the various historic periods, but also to show how the universal phenomenon called "religion" has unfolded itself in the drama of Japanese history.

In the first chapter, I shall attempt to give a bird's-eye view of the religious development in Japan from its obscure beginning to the end of the eighth century A.D. This was in a real sense Japan's formative period. Not only did the people in Japan learn the crafts of reading and writing during this period, but they also began to be self-conscious about themselves as a people and about their destiny in the universe, political, cultural, and religious. In the study of the Japanese religion of this period, I shall place special emphasis on the problem of religious leadership, especially charismatic leadership, which is an important and often neglected dimension.

The term *charisma* is usually translated as "spiritual gift" or "gift of grace." [1] While it is not possible to discuss here the intricate relationship between charisma and human pneuma, or between charisma and the human psyche, we can safely assume that persons endowed with some quality of *charis* have been known in every religious tradition. Thanks to Max Weber, the term *charisma* has become an important concept in religio-scientific study, denoting the extraordinary quality which dwells in a person, leader, or ruler who exercises authority over others.[2] Weber was particularly careful in differentiating "personal charisma" from the "charisma of office," both of which have played important roles in the history of all religions. It is my contention that one way to understand the nature and development of Japanese religion during its early period is to examine the three-fold relationship that existed among three types of charismatic leadership, namely, that of emperor, of shaman, and of priest. Before entering upon this discussion, however, we must glance briefly at the structure of the historical development of the early period in Japan.

Yamatai and Yamato

The smooth transition from mythology to history that characterizes the official chronicles of Japan does not assist us in our attempt to square the legendary account of the founding of the Japanese nation with historical evidence. The earliest written record concerning Japan is the Chinese document, the *Wei Chih,* or "History of the Kingdom of Wei," written in the third century A.D. According to this book, the land of the Wa (the Japanese people) was located in the middle of the ocean, and was over five thousand li long. There were many principalities, chief among them the state of Yamatai (or Yabadai), which in some sense had dominion over the others. The Chinese chronicler describes the customs and manners of the people of Wa, and then portrays the

[1] See *ERE*, III, 368–72.
[2] See Wach, *Sociology of Religion,* pp. 337–41, and Max Weber, *The Sociology of Religion,* pp. xxxiv and 2–3.

female ruler Pimiko or Himiko as a shamanic diviner or medium.[3] Piecing together available Chinese records, we also learn that some of these principalities in Japan sent envoys to China in A.D. 57, 107, 239, 240, 245, 247, 265, and 266.[4] These envoys are described as emissaries who paid tribute to the Chinese monarchs as all the satellite nations of China were expected to do in those days. It is interesting to note, as far as the Chinese sources are concerned, that the sending of Japanese envoys was abruptly terminated for over a century, from A.D. 266 onward until tribute was sent again in 413, followed by similar missions in 421, 478, and 503.[5]

One of the most intriguing questions to ponder is the geographical location of the state of Yamatai. The seventh-century Chinese record states that the capital of Japan (Wa-kuo) "is Yamato, known in the Wei history as Yamadai," thus equating Yamatai and Yamato.[6] For centuries, traditional Japanese historians accepted this view, and some able scholars in recent years have also argued, on the basis of very convincing archaeological evidence, that Yamatai was located somewhere in or around the Yamato district. On the other hand, many other contemporary Japanese scholars, as well as Western Japanologists, including Sansom and Reischauer, seem to hold that Yamatai and Yamato were two different states with similar sounding names, and that Yamatai was

[3] Tsunoda, *Japan in the Chinese Dynastic Histories,* pp. 8–16.

[4] In the *Hou Han Shu* (History of the later Han dynasty), we read: "In the second year of the Chien-wu Chung-yüan era [A.D. 57] the Wa country Nu sent an envoy with tribute who called himself *ta-fu.* This country is located in the southern extremity of the Wa country. Kang-wu bestowed on him a seal." (Tsunoda, *Japan in the Chinese Dynastic Histories,* p. 2.) The golden *inju* (seal) discovered in 1789 on Shiga island in northern Kyushu reads "King of Nu of Wa [vassal of] Han." (ZSBT, *Nihon,* I, 168–69.) Whether or not Nu was a small *kuni* (state) situated in northern Kyushu, it was mentioned in the *Wei Chih* as one of the principalities belonging to Yamatai. In A.D. 238 the Chinese court conferred upon Pimiko the title "Queen of Wa Friendly to Wei" and presented to her the decoration of the gold seal with purple ribbon. (Tsunoda, *Japan in the Chinese Dynastic Histories,* p. 14.)

[5] Enoki, *Yamatai-koku,* p. 26.

[6] Tsunoda, *Japan in the Chinese Dynastic Histories,* p. 28.

located in northern Kyushu.[7] While this controversy cannot be
easily resolved, I am inclined to side with the "Kyushu theory" on
the historical ground that Yamatai prospered before the unification
by the Tennō clan of the Yamato district, as well as on the ground
that the geographical description of Yamatai and other principalities as recorded in the "History of the Kingdom of Wei" seems to
suit Kyushu more than the Yamato district.

At any rate, the "History of the Kingdom of Wei" gives us a
fairly realistic picture of the very early stage of Japanese history.
We are told that men tattooed their faces and decorated their
bodies with designs, and that their clothing was fastened loosely
around the body while women wore dresses, little more than single pieces of cloth, and wore their hair in loops. The people were
familiar with agriculture and sericulture, and they produced fine
linen and silk fabrics. They enjoyed liquor and believed in divination; and they created and observed strict social distinctions. We
are also told that, while the earlier Yamatai had been ruled by a
man, Pimiko, a woman, was accepted as their ruler after a long
period of constant warfare. When she died, a great mound was
raised in her honor. Thereafter a male succeeded to the throne but
was rejected by the populace, whereupon a relative of Pimiko
named Iyo or Ichiyo, a girl of thirteen, became the queen and
order was restored. She was subsequently proclaimed by the Chinese monarch to be the ruler of Yamatai. The new queen sent a
delegation to the Chinese capital, offering slaves, carved jade, and
brocades as tribute.[8] After that, nothing was heard about the State
of Yamatai.

Meanwhile, the decline of the Wei dynasty in China in A.D.
265 resulted in the loosening of Chinese control over Korea, the
result of which was to give rise to competing principalities on the
peninsula. Also, we learn from the Korean sources that the Japa-

[7] See J. Young, *The Location of Yamatai: A Case History in Japanese
Historiography, 720–1945*; Sansom, *A History of Japan to 1334*, p. 16;
Reischauer and Fairbank, *East Asia: The Great Tradition*, p. 468. For
more recent theories, see Mitsusada Inouye, *Nihon kokka no kigen*, pp.
40–69, and Kazuo Enoki, *Yamatai-koku*, pp. 5–100.

[8] Tsunoda, *Japan in the Chinese Dynastic Histories*, pp. 10–16.

nese were importing iron from Korea. In 366 a Japanese envoy was dispatched to one of the Korean principalities called Paekche. In 367 an envoy of Paekche visited Japan, and in 369 Japanese forces fought side by side with the army of Paekche against a rival principality called Silla. Japan not only continued to exchange envoys with Paekche in 370, 371, and 372, but also established a small colony called Mimana at the southern tip of the Korean peninsula. We also learn from the inscription on a monument dedicated to one of the kings of a northern Korean principality, called Koguryŏ, that Japanese expeditionary forces crossed the sea in 391, and fought against the Koguryŏ army several times over a period of ten years or more. Even though the Koguryŏ records claimed an overwhelming victory over the Japanese, the Japanese military base at Mimana lasted until as late as 562 when it was destroyed by Silla.[9]

It may be recalled that until A.D. 266 Yamatai was regarded as nothing more than an insignificant country ruled by a queen who had some kind of political influence over other principalities in western Japan. But one hundred years later Japan appears to have acquired sufficient political and military power to invade Korea and establish a colony there. Significantly, this period of one hundred years corresponds roughly to the early phase of the so-called Kofun (tumulus) period that marked a new cultural achievement in Japan. And it is quite plausible to conjecture that the unification of Japan, however nominal, by the Tennō clan took place starting from the Yamato district sometime between 266 and 366.

Unfortunately, the accounts of the first ten or more emperors, to say nothing of the founding of the Japanese nation, in both the *Kojiki* (Records of ancient matters) and the *Nihonshoki* or *Nihongi* (Chronicles of Japan) are notoriously unreliable historically, though they are exceedingly valuable in religious terms. Actually, these accounts portray the earthly counterpart and extensions of the mythical events in the heavenly domain, according

[9] Enoki, *Yamatai-koku,* pp. 101–14. Enoki (pp. 117–20) also compares accounts of Japanese campaigns in Korea with the accounts of the *Nihon-shoki.*

to which Amaterasu (the Sun Goddess) sent her grandson, Ninigi, to rule the earth, and it was Ninigi's great-grandson who became the first legendary emperor, Jimmu. Jimmu, so we are told, led his clan from the island of Kyushu and moved eastward, pacifying the various tribes on the way, until he reached the Yamato region where he established his dynasty in the year 660 B.C. Following Jimmu, so the legendary genealogy informs us, was a series of emperors with unusually long reigns of one hundred years or more. Curiously, the *Nihonshoki* describes the long and eventful career of the tenth emperor Sujin in much the same way as it does that of the first emperor Jimmu, and both Jimmu and Sujin are called the "Hatsukunishirasu-sumera-mikoto" (The Emperor, the August Founder of the Nation).[10] The similarity of their careers as unifiers of the nation has caused many scholars to speculate that the accounts of the two emperors, Jimmu and Sujin, in the *Nihonshoki* actually refer to the same person.[11]

Following the description of Sujin, the *Nihonshoki* also records the colorful careers of Prince Yamatotakeru, who singlehandedly pacified rebellious tribes, and of the Empress Jingō, who allegedly led an armada to invade Korea. Most scholars agree that the accounts of emperors beginning with Ōjin, who is regarded as the

[10] W. G. Aston, in *Nihongi: Chronicles of Japan from the Earliest Times to A.D. 697*, translated this title properly in connection with Sujin (I, 161), but distorted the significance by not translating it as a title in connection with Jimmu (I, 133). According to Aston, "The name of the Emperor [Jimmu] *who thus began to rule the Empire* was . . ." (my italics). He should have translated thus: "He was called 'The Emperor, the August Founder of the Nation.' " See also Kisaburo Ichimura, "Nihon kenkoku-irai no nensu ni tsuite," in *Takigawa hakase kanreki kinen ronbun-shū*, vol. II, *Nihonshi hen*, pp. 367–89.

[11] See Uyemura, *Jimmu Tennō*, pp. 68–77, for the problem of the identity of the Emperor Sujin. Concerning this, Egami Namio argues that the real founder of the Yamato kingdom was Sujin, who began his career as a king of the dynasty, originally of Tungusic ancestry, in charge of the Korean principality called Mimana. From Korea, Sujin invaded Kyushu and then moved to the Yamato district. Egami characterizes the imperial clan as the *kiba-zoku* (tribe of mounted warriors). See Oka, et al., *Nihon minzoku no kigen*, pp. 249–53, and Inouye, *Nihon kokka no kigen*, pp. 199-204.

fifteenth emperor according to the legendary genealogy, can be trusted even though their posthumous names, such as Nintoku, Richū, Hansei, Ingyō, Ankō, and Yūryaku, for example, may have been concocted by later court historians. Meanwhile, the sixth-century Chinese record, the "History of the Liu Sung Dynasty" (*Sung Shu*) mentions the five Japanese rulers—San, Chin, Sai, Kō, and Bu (or Ts'an, Chēn, Sai, Kō, and Wu)—who dealt with the Sung Court during the fifth and sixth centuries. There is a strong suggestion that Sai, Kō, and Bu corresponded to the emperors Ingyō, Ankō, and Yūryaku, but the identities of the first two, namely, San and Chin, cannot be established accurately.[12] Two things are pertinent in this connection. First, these Japanese rulers claimed not only to be kings of Wa (Japan) but also suzerains of parts of Korea, such as Paekche, Silla, Imna, Chin-han, and Mok-han; and the Chinese Court recognized their claims. Second, the last of the five, Bu, in his letter to the Chinese monarch in 478, describes how his "forebears" had pacified fifty-five countries of hairy men in the east, sixty-six countries of barbarians in the west, and ninety-five countries in the north, and had unified Japan. Bu also admits that Japanese influence in Korea was greatly threatened by the rising power of Koguryŏ.[13]

Although scholars have not agreed specifically as to who Bu's "forebears" were, we may safely assume that they were the emperors Ōjin and Nintoku, mentioned in the Japanese official chronicles. Some scholars are persuaded that Ōjin was the founder of a new dynasty which arose after the decline of the previous imperial line. It is an interesting coincidence that the custom of building grand tombs was ascribed to him; this certainly implies that a new cultural impetus was gathering force.[14] While we have

[12] See Sansom, *A History of Japan to 1334*, pp. 42–43; Enoki, *Yamataikoku*, pp. 164–75; and Tsunoda, *Japan in the Chinese Dynastic Histories*, pp. 24–25.

[13] See Tsunoda, *Japan in the Chinese Dynastic Histories*, pp. 23–24.

[14] According to one version cited in the *Nihonshoki*, Ōjin's predecessor, the Emperor Chūai, "having gone to smite the Kumaso [a tribe in Kyushu], was hit by an enemy's arrow and slain." (Aston, *Nihongi*, I, 222.) Ōjin, whose birth story is full of miraculous elements, is said to have married Nakatsu-hime, a princess from the previous dynasty, as

no way of reconstructing with accuracy the early history of Japan, it is not impossible to speculate that the matrilineal line of the Yamatai (the Pimiko and Ichiyo line) was taken over by the patrilineal line of Sujin ("The Emperor, the August Founder of the Nation") around the turn of the third century; and that when Sujin's line declined, or was defeated, the new dynasty of Ōjin, Nintoku, and the five kings mentioned in the "History of the Liu Sung Dynasty" became the ruling house of Japan.[15] When and how the regime moved from Kyushu to the Yamato district cannot be ascertained, but either Sujin or one of his successors might have moved to Yamato. Ōjin and Nintoku probably came from families of Kyushu origin, or at least maintained rapport with Kyushu barons.

The important thing, however, is not the instability of the ruling house but the homogeneity of the people and culture, existing already in the early stage of the historic period. Most people were engaged in farming, their legacy from the beginning of the Yayoi period (*ca.* 250 B.C.-A.D. 250), with some hunting and fishing on the side. The use of bronze, copper, and iron had been introduced from the Asiatic continent; and immigrants from Korea and China who had started settling in Japan from the middle of the Yayoi period brought new and better methods in farming, casting, weaving, and other craftsmanship. Japanese society in the early historic period was based on independent clans (*uji*), which began to be consolidated under the Tennō (imperial) clan beginning sometime around the turn of the fourth century. Although the position of the ruling dynasty was not

---

though he wanted to legitimatize his accession to the throne. It might also be mentioned that Iwanaga-hime, another wife of Ōjin, was the daughter of Katsuragi Sotsuhiko (literally, a "man of Kumaso"), who is recorded as the Japanese commander in Korea in the campaign against Silla. Also, Ōjin's successor, Nintoku, married Kaminaga-hime, daughter of a local magnate of Hiuga (where Amaterasu's grandson, Ninigi, is alleged to have descended from heaven), in Kyushu. We are reminded by archaeologists that the tomb of Nintoku is by far the grandest of all tombs constructed in the Kofun (tumulus) period. For various theories on Ōjin and Nintoku, see Enoki, *Yamatai-koku,* pp. 201–8.

[15] See Enoki, *Yamatai-koku,* pp. 207–8.

always secure, political stability was maintained through a balance of power among the great clan chieftains. Meanwhile, the ever-increasing demand for iron and other materials drove Japan to establish a foothold in Korea. Through this channel many features of Sino-Korean civilization reached Japan in the fifth and sixth centuries.

Early Shinto

The history of early Japan gives the impression that what mattered was the affairs of the ruling families and not the life of the ordinary people. However, it seems necessary to attempt at least to reconstruct an image of the common man. Fortunately for us, the diverse cultural and ethnic elements that made up the population of the Japanese islands during the prehistoric period had achieved something of a common ethos by the dawn of the historic period as a result of exposure to the same physical environment and of sharing a common destiny for a period of centuries. Underlying the peculiar ethos of the early Japanese was their attitude toward life and the world and their religious outlook, not so much in a systematic philosophical sense as with respect to what Anesaki once called the "sympathetic response of the heart." [16]

Because of the lack of a better term, I resort to the expression "early Shinto" to refer to the religion of the Japanese people of this period.[17] The term Shinto, literally "the Way of the kami or gods," has many meanings. It could mean the magico-religious beliefs and practices of the Japanese, derived from the kami. Sometimes this term is used to designate a certain ideology or theology, which implies some normative principles for ethics and other aspects of individual and communal life.[18] Here I use the term loosely to refer to the not too well systematized, indigenous

[16] Anesaki, *History of Japanese Religion,* p. 5.

[17] This is what Sir Ernest M. Satow called "pure Shin-tau," which was the religion of the Japanese people prior to the introduction of Buddhism and Confucian philosophy into Japan. See Satow, "The Revival of Pure Shin-Tau," *TASJ, III* (Part I, 1874), 1–87.

[18] For a different usage of the term *Shinto,* see Tsuda, *Nihon no Shinto,* pp. 1–18.

religious tradition of the early Japanese. The main characteristic
of early Shinto was its cosmic orientation, in the sense that no
object or human act has autonomous intrinsic value, for, as Eliade
astutely points out: "Objects or acts acquire a value, and in so
doing become real, because they participate . . . in a reality
[called kami] that transcends them. . . . The object appears as
the receptacle of an exterior force [i.e., kami] that differentiates it
from its milieu and gives it meaning and value." [19] Central to
this simple cosmic religion was the notion of kami, which is
usually translated as gods, deities, or spirits, but also means
"above," "superior," or the "numinous or sacred nature."

While early Shinto was not interested in speculating on the
metaphysical meaning of the world, the early Japanese took it for
granted that they were integrally part of the cosmos, which they
saw as a "community of living beings," all sharing the kami
(sacred) nature. The Japanese myths mention the existence of
eight hundred myriads of kami, a metaphor employed to express
belief in the sacredness of the whole universe. In such a world
view, people did not consider themselves in any way separated
from cosmic existence and the rhythm of nature. They felt a
deep kinship with the world of nature, so that "no tree could be
marked for felling, no bush tapped for lacquer juice, no oven
built for smelting or for pottery, and no forge fire lit without appeal to the *Kami* residing in each." [20] In other words, farmers,
hunters, artists, and those engaged in other occupations were
regarded as instruments of the kami who worked through them,
for they knew that without the invisible creative aid of the kami
they could not perform anything.[21] The meaning of human life

[19] Eliade, *The Myth of the Eternal Return*, pp. 3–4.

[20] Langdon Warner, *The Enduring Art of Japan*, pp. 18–19. This is
the notion of hierophany, to use Eliade's term. "This force [of kami]
may reside in the substance of the object or in its form; a rock reveals
itself to be sacred because its very existence is a hierophany: incom-
pressible, invulnerable, it is that which man is not. It resists time; its
reality is coupled with personality." (Eliade, *The Myth of the Eternal
Return*, p. 4.)

[21] Nishida, *"Yosashi"—A Fundamental Concept of Japanese Religion*,
tr. Donald L. Philippi, pp. 13–14.

was understood in terms of man's relation to the kami, who would "enable" (*yosasu*) men to act in their behalf. Herein lies the early Shinto conception of correspondence between the realm of kami and that of man.

At the expense of oversimplification, we may now consider two characteristics of early Shinto. First of all, there was a sense of gratitude toward the kami. Sorrows there were, and also a feeling of fear toward evil kami and malevolent *mono* (spirits); but, all in all, life was good (*yoshi*) and beautiful; and human beings had reason to be thankful for their lot in this world. Second, there was an emphasis upon purification, reported, incidentally, by a third-century Chinese historian as one of the cultural features of the Japanese.[22] What concerned the early Japanese was not moral sins but physical and mental defilements, which had to be cleansed ceremonially by exorcism and abstention. One of the *Norito* (ritual prayers), however, lists two categories of sins.[23] Nevertheless, there was a general tendency to regard *tsumi* (sin) or *ashi* (evil) as something which was caused primarily by external factors. In effect, evil was not viewed as a reality; rather, evil was a lack of harmony and beauty, and could be corrected and redressed by purificatory ceremonies (*haraye*) performed by the ablutionist.

Turning to the myths, we find early Shinto accepting a three-dimensional universe: the highest realm (*Takama-no-hara* or "The Plain of the High Sky") where male and female kami reside; the

[22] See Tsunoda, *Japan in the Chinese Dynastic Histories,* p. 11: "When death occurs, mourning is observed for more than ten days. . . . When the funeral is over, all members of the whole family go into the water to cleanse themselves in a bath of purification."

[23] The category of "heavenly sins" includes breaking down the ridges, covering up the ditches, releasing the irrigation sluices, double planting, setting up stakes, skinning animals alive or backward, and defecation. The category of "earthly sins" includes cutting living flesh, cutting dead flesh, white leprosy, skin excrescences, violation of one's own mother, violation of one's own child, violation of a mother and her child, and transgression with animals. See Philippi, tr., *Norito,* pp. 46–47: "Great Exorcism of the Last Day of the Sixth Month—Minazuki-tsugomori no oho-haraye."

lowest realm (*Yomotsu-kuni* or "The Nether World"), the habi-
tation of unclean and malevolent spirits; and the middle domain
(*Utsushi-yo* or "The Manifested World") where men and other
animate and inanimate beings reside. In actual practice, however,
the early Japanese seemed to have only a vague notion of the
difference between these three dimensions of the universe. There
is good reason to believe that they envisaged both the heavenly
domain and the nether region as being in the "other world,"
which was frequently associated with certain mountains, or in
some instances with islands believed to exist beyond the sea. Many
old Shinto rituals, signifying the "welcoming" and "seeing off"
of kami, imply that the kami were believed to come from and return to the mountains or islands.[24] Also, the spirits (*tama*) of
the dead, especially those of noblemen, were believed to become
kami and return to the other world.

There were all kinds of kami, benevolent and malevolent,
strong as well as weak. A further nuance is provided by the
word *tama* (spirit, or soul). Traditionally, Shinto acknowledged
four kinds of spirits—*ara-mi-tama,* those which rule with authority
and power; *nigi-mi-tama,* those which bring about union, harmony, and recollection; *kushi-mi-tama,* those which cause mysterious transformation; and *saki-mi-tama,* those which impart
blessings. There are suggestions that one and the same kami might
have more than one *tama*.[25] Spirits of enemies and those who
might have met an unfortunate death, later known as *go-ryō,* were
also believed to have potency. Moreover, the *mono* or *mononoke*
(sometimes spirits of animals) were widely feared and venerated.
All those kami and spirits could "possess" men and women, and
those who were thus possessed were called *kami-gakari* (kami-
possessed) and *mono-tsuki* (*mono*-possessed), respectively.

The gradual stratification of Japanese society and the unification of the nation inevitably resulted in changes in the religious

---

[24] Some of these rituals are explained in Matsumoto, *Nihon no Shinwa,*
pp. 1–44.

[25] See Aston, *Nihongi,* I, 237. Amaterasu herself admonished the Empress Jingō by saying: "My rough spirit [*ara-mi-tama*] may not approach
the imperial residence."

sphere, as exemplified by a tendency to obliterate the distinctions among the regional, communal, and national kami. It is widely believed among scholars that early Shinto did not have fixed liturgies, ecclesiastical organizations, or elaborate rituals. Most religious functions, except for those in the homes, took place around a *himorogi* (holy tree), *iwasaka* (holy rock), or in the paddy field.[26] The kami thus worshiped had no individual names, for they were related to specific regions, so that they were regarded simply as the *ubusuna-kami* (the kami of the region where one is born) or *chinju-no-kami* (the kami who protects the region) of such and such a geographical area. Also, in farming and fishing communities, the kami of agriculture and those of the sea were celebrated according to agricultural and fishing seasons, respectively.[27]

Side by side with the regional kami there also existed communal kami who were to protect, and who were venerated by, specific kinship and communal groups. And, since communal and regional ties often overlapped, regional kami and communal kami coalesced in many instances. Although the social unit called *uji* (the clan) or *dōzoku* (literally, those who belong to the same lineage) was not based on the strict principle of consanguinity, the blood relationship, real or fictitious, was considered important for communal cohesion, so that *uji-gami* (kami of the clan) and the *uji* shrine were superimposed on regional communities.[28] Thus community festivals, such as the *kinen-sai* or *toshi-goi-no-matsuri* (the festival for praying for good harvest) and *shin-jō-sai* or *niiname-matsuri* (harvest festival) in many cases invoked the *uji-gami*, which had incorporated within them the qualities of regional kami. In the course of time the *uji-gami* took on the char-

[26] Even today, some of the old shrines, such as the Ōmiwa shrine in Nara prefecture and the Suwakami shrine in Nagano prefecture, do not have halls for the kami. People go to these shrines but worship the mountains which are believed to be saturated with the kami nature.

[27] For rituals of rice production, see Haga, *Ta no kami,* pp. 17–80.

[28] For the development of the family, kinship, *dōzoku,* and *uji* systems in the early period of Japan, see Aruga, *Nihon kazoku-seido to kosaku-seido,* pp. 94–144; Fukuo, *Nihon kazoku-seido-shi,* pp. 7–34; Hori, *Minkan shinkō,* pp. 119–68; and Ōta, *Nihon jōdai ni okeru shakai-soshiki no kenkyū.*

acteristics of the deified ancestor of the *uji* and later, under Chinese influence, the *uji* shrine came to be dedicated to the ancestor.[29] In general, the unity of the clan was maintained by: (a) a paternal community organization with *honke* (the main family) as the center, (b) residence in the same locality, and (c) claiming the same *uji-gami* (the kami of the clan). The *uji-no-kami* (the clan chieftain) also acted as the priest, serving the welfare of the kami of the clan. The *uji-bito* (clansmen) were divided into several vocational units (*be*); and employees and slaves, who had no blood relationship with the clan, were also regarded as integral parts of the clan structure. When the clan became too large, so that parts of the clan membership had to settle elsewhere, they established branch shrines of the *uji-gami*. This practice was known as *bun-rei* (literally, dividing the spirit [of the kami]).[30]

Among all the clans the Tennō (imperial) clan had the strongest military power, and it began to impose its political power as well as religious tradition upon others early in the historic period. Unification of Japan by the imperial clan was reflected in the increasing systematization of the religious practices and myths of various other clans, whereby the "national kami," originally the kami merely of the imperial clan, began to make their presence felt in the life of those clans which developed rapport with the emperor. Nevertheless, the kami mentioned in the *Kojiki* and the *Nihonshoki* hardly touched the lives of the common people, for, as Harada points out, "the descriptions of the mythological age [in the official chronicles of Japan] were the products of a special idea peculiar to the then high class, and their deities were completely different from the ones of communities, or *uji-gami* born from the actual daily life of the people." [31]

[29] For the subject of ancestor worship, see Takeda, *Sosen sūhai*. It is significant to note in this connection that in the oldest anthology of poems, called *Manyōshū*, ancestors as such are hardly mentioned, whereas the kami of mountains are mentioned thirty-six times and the kami of the sea are mentioned twenty-two times. See Toshiaki Harada, *Jinja*, p. 104.

[30] Nishitsunoi, "Social and Religious Groups in Shinto," in The Japanese Association for Religious Studies, *Religious Studies in Japan*, p. 224.

[31] Harada, "The Origin of Community Worship," in The Japanese

Charisma of the Emperor

The exact chronology and activities of the early Yamato sovereigns are, as I have mentioned earlier, clouded in mystery. Judging from the alleged biographies of some of the early emperors, even in the *Nihonshoki,* which was designed to uphold the imperial dignity, we discover that the Yamato monarchs did not aspire to be exemplary in moral character. They did, however, claim that the imperial clan was the only legitimate ruling family of the nation on religious grounds, even though in actual practice great clan chieftains, who accumulated wealth and power in competition with the imperial clan, had a great deal to say about the administration and often settled succession disputes among the quarrelsome royal members.[32]

Nevertheless, in principle, the emperor possessed both the "imperial" charisma, by virtue of his direct descent from Amaterasu Ō-mi-kami, the kami of the imperial clan, and also the "priestly"

Association for Religious Studies, *Religious Studies in Japan,* p. 216. It must be mentioned, however, that the kami of other clans and new territories were gradually incorporated into the framework of the imperial clan myths by a skillful reinterpretation based on the motif of "descent." For example, the brother of Amaterasu is said to have descended to Izumo Province, and the grandson of Amaterasu allegedly descended to Kyushu—the two important regions in Japan. A special point was made of the descent of the *tama* (soul) of Amaterasu to Ise Province, and of the descent of the mythological hero, Yamato-takeru, to the eastern and western provinces to pacify the local kami and clans. For this hero, see Uyeda, *Yamato-takeru-no-Mikoto.* Furthermore, Ō-kuni-nushi, the mythological ruler of the Izumo Province, and Ō-mono-nushi-no-Ōkami, the regional kami of the Yamato Province, came to be thought of as one and the same figure. Eventually, Ō-mono-nushi-no-Ōkami is said to have married Princess Yamato-to-to-hi-momoso, the aunt of the emperor Sujin and a shamanic diviner. Such a "naturalization" of earthly kami into the pantheon of the imperial clan must have taken a long time.

[32] Sansom, *A History of Japan to 1334,* p. 43. It was the great chieftains, the Ō-omi and the Ō-muraji, "who chose the heir, at times in defiance of the sovereign's testament, and the position of legitimate heirs was often dangerous, for more than one of them fled to a distant province to escape assassination."

charisma as head of the dominant clan.[33] The fact that he had both spiritual and political authority is nothing exceptional in the history of religions, for in many societies a king or a supreme chief was often regarded as the "spiritual, legal, and economic head of the tribe by virtue of his ancestry, position, and sacred attributes."[34] In Japan, as elsewhere, the charisma of the imperial office was carefully safeguarded, for example, by strict taboos placed upon the throne and the minute observance of rites in connection with the succession of the imperial regalia: the sacred jewels, the mirror, and the divine sword.[35] Also, strict observance of many rituals was demanded of the emperor for the successful administration of political duties both in normal times and in times of crisis.

The emperor was expected to obey the divine words of the kami (*mi-koto*), communicated to him through dreams and the state of ecstasy known as kami-possession, which was often induced by the playing of the *koto* and other musical instruments. In some cases, tortoise shell divination was also used to determine the will of the kami. The emperor claimed that the divine word was given to him as the representative of the nation; so that "those who receive this command, from the highest gods [kami], the Heavenly Deities, to the Emperor, and down to the common people, are all charged with the sacred mission."[36] Related to the notion of *mi-koto* (divine words of the kami) was the belief in *koto-dama* (the potency of the spirit of *tama* residing in the spoken words). Beautifully phrased speech and correctly uttered words were believed to bring about good results, while carelessly phrased speech and incorrectly pronounced words were believed to bring about evil results.[37]

[33] On the etymology of Amaterasu, see Ōbayashi, *Nihon shinwa no kigen*, pp. 131–32.

[34] Wilfrid D. Hambly, *Source-Book for African Anthropology* (Field Museum of Natural History Publications, Anthropological Series), XXVI (Chicago, 1937), 508.

[35] These three symbols of the imperial authority were used by other chieftains in Kyushu. See Enoki, *Yamatai-koku*, pp. 139–46.

[36] Nishida, *Yosashi*, p. 9.

[37] See Anesaki, *History of Japanese Religion*, pp. 44–45, for an example of an elaborate ritual prayer taken from the Nakatomi Ritual.

It was taken for granted that the Yamato court was modeled after the heavenly court as described in the myths. For instance, the heavenly court of Amaterasu included such figures as Ame-no-koyane, the prototype of the priest; Futo-dama, the prototype of the ablutioner; and Ame-no-uzume, the prototype of the shamanic diviner. Correspondingly, the Yamato court included Nakatomi-no-muraji, the family of the priests; Imbe-no-obito, the family of the ablutioners; and Sarume-no-kami, the family of the diviners. The early Japanese did not draw a line of demarcation between the sacred and the profane dimensions of life, or between *matsuri* (religious rituals) and *matsuri-goto* (political administration), both of which were ultimately under the authority of the emperor who himself was directed by the divine will.[38] Understandably, the emperor delegated political responsibilities to his ministers and shared his priestly office with the religious dignitaries, with the ablutioner, the supplicator, and the liturgist in the court. In the course of time the positions of ministers and of religious functionaries became hereditary in certain families, which provided continuity in the court and maintained the stability of the nation.

And yet, the significance of the Japanese pattern is that the proper function of the "charisma of the imperial office" was understood to depend heavily on the "personal charisma" of the shamanic diviner.

Charisma of the Shaman

The charisma of the imperial office was, of course, the gift of Amaterasu, bestowed exclusively upon the head of the imperial

[38] According to the *Nihonshoki* (chap. III), the first legendary emperor, Jimmu, acted as though he were a puppet of the heavenly kami. Once, when he had difficulty in pacifying his enemies, he was given a divine message in his dream "to take clay from inside the shrine of Mount Kagu and make of it eighty platters and sacred urns with which to make sacrifice to the heavenly and earthly kami, and then to pronounce incantation." This he did, and his enemies were easily subdued. Also, in the fourth year after he established his court in Kashiwara of the Yamato district, Jimmu erected a shrine at Mount Tomi in honor of Amaterasu in grateful acknowledgment of her *mi-tama* (august spirit), which had descended from heaven above in order to guide and assist the emperor. See Uyemura, *Jimmu tennō*, pp. 7–10.

clan. Such a charisma was believed to be received by the emperor with the sacred regalia at the time of his enthronement. Conversely, it was the exclusive duty and prerogative of the emperor to maintain a special rapport with Amaterasu, the kami of the imperial clan, and even the empress and the heir apparent were usually not allowed to worship Amaterasu without the explicit permission of the emperor. With the expansion of the power of the imperial clan, the other clans were gradually integrated into the framework of the Yamato kingdom, and the emperor as sovereign and chief priest was expected to propitiate the kami of other clans, as well as the kami of regions which came under the imperial influence. It is important to note in this connection that the potency of the imperial charisma did not enable the emperor to develop rapport with other kami. For this he needed the service of a shamanic diviner (miko), who functioned as his medium with kami of other clans and with various kinds of spirits.

The important role played by the shamanic diviners during the early period of Japan was succinctly described by a Chinese reporter who said that the people in Japan "have profound faith in shamans, both male and female." [39] Significantly, both the *Kojiki* and the *Nihonshoki* tell us that the mother of the first legendary emperor Jimmu was called Tama-yori-hime, a very common name given to a female shamanic diviner. The name in question literally means "a woman (*hime*) in whom dwelled (*yori*) the spirit (*tama*) of the kami." [40] Equally important is the account of the Emperor Sujin in the *Nihonshoki*,[41] for he was ably assisted by two charismatic persons. One was his own aunt, Princess Yamato-to-to-hi-momoso, who was a shamanic diviner exclusively for the imperial family. The other was Ōtataneko, a person of humble origin who happened to be endowed with a charismatic personality.

The Emperor Sujin, who was most conscientious in serving

[39] Tsunoda, *Japan in the Chinese Dynastic Histories*, p. 31.

[40] Yanagita, *Imōto no chikara*, pp. 51–76.

[41] As stated earlier, both Jimmu and Sujin were officially called "The Emperor, the August Founder of the Nation."

the kami of the imperial clan, could not understand why his reign was troubled by epidemics and rebellion. Then the emperor's aunt became kami-possessed, and through her the kami of the Yamato region, Ō-mono-nushi-no-Ōkami, communicated to the emperor that order would be restored if the emperor duly worshiped him. Following the oracle, the emperor venerated the kami of the Yamato region, but peace still did not prevail. So the emperor cleansed himself, practiced abstinence, and prayed for a further oracle. That night, in a dream, the kami instructed the emperor to find Ōtataneko, who would serve the kami properly. This the emperor did, and peace was immediately restored and prosperity came to his reign. This account is interesting for many reasons. First, Ō-mono-nushi-no-Ōkami, the regional kami of Yamato, refused the intercession offered by the shamanic diviner of the imperial household. Instead, he specified that Ōtataneko, whom he claimed to be "his child," be chosen to serve him.[42] Evidently, some of the shamanic diviners came from hereditary diviners' families, while others were charismatic individuals without any training, special preparation, or other professional qualifications. Whether they were of noble birth or of humble origin, they were usually maidens or women of a certain psychological habitude, possessing a high degree of excitability, and the capacity to be kami-possessed.

The enormous prestige of such charismatic women in the early period of Japan is evidenced by the legendary account of the Empress Jingō, shamanic diviner *par excellence,* who also ruled the nation after the death of her husband, the Emperor Chūai.[43] Many scholars today are of the opinion that the legendary account

[42] Ōtataneko was located in an obscure village in Suye, in the district of Chinu. See Aston, *Nihongi,* I, 153.

[43] She was reputed to have the magical power of pacifying the kami and the spirits. When a tribe called Kumaso on Kyushu island ignored the imperial authority, the emperor sought divine guidance through the kami-possession of the Empress Jingō. The emperor is said to have played upon a musical instrument called the koto, while Takeshi-uchino-sukune, a minister, supplicated. Takeshi-uchino-sukune was probably a male shaman, or a medium who deciphered the message uttered by the female

of the Empress Jingō was modeled after that of Pimiko, herself
a shamanic diviner and the queen of Yamatai.[44] Nevertheless,
there must have been cases of shamanic diviners who played the
important role of imperial consort. In fact, some of the imperial
consorts (*kisaki* or *Ō-kisaki*) were given the title *nakatsu-sumera-
mikoto*, which could mean either "the one who carries on the
imperial duty between the death of her husband and the accession
of the next emperor" or "the august medium who transmits the
mi-koto (divine word) of the heavenly kami." [45]

From Asuka to Nara

The historical situation in the sixth and seventh centuries
brought about a series of social, cultural, political, and religious
changes in Japan under the influence of Chinese thought and
institutions, and of Buddhism. During much of this period the

---

shaman in her state of kami-possession. See Kenji Okamoto, *Jingō kōgō*,
pp. 145–46.

At any rate, the kami spoke to the emperor through the empress,
stating that a Korean principality, Silla, was backing the rebellious tribe
in Kyushu, and that the emperor was advised to conquer Silla, which
was full of gold, silver, and other dazzling treasures. The emperor, however, questioned the authenticity of the oracle, whereupon the kami
recanted the promise, and the emperor died suddenly. (In another version,
it is said that the emperor was slain in the battle against the rebellious
Kumaso.)

After the death of her husband, the empress ruled the nation on behalf
of her yet unborn child. Having performed a great purification rite, she
entered the sacred ground and sought the divine oracle. Receiving the
kami's assurance of victory in the contemplated Korean campaign, Jingō
commanded the armada herself and defeated the Korean force. Upon her
return, her child was born; he became the Emperor Ōjin, or so the
chroniclers tell us.

[44] On Jingō and Pimiko, see Okamoto, *Jingō kōgō*, pp. 148–68.

[45] *Ibid.*, pp. 124–25. Both interpretations of this title are plausible, and
one and the same woman can combine both functions. The so-called
Empress Jingō probably did not exist, for the chroniclers seem to have
projected the image of Pimiko as a prelude to the account of the Emperor
Ōjin. Nevertheless, the portrayal of Jingō is an ideal type of those imperial consorts who were shamanic diviners and who also carried on
imperial duties in the absence of the emperor.

Yamato sovereigns resided in various spots of the Asuka area, roughly the central part of the Yamato basin. Hence the designation "Asuka era." Actually, there was no permanent national center to speak of until A.D. 710 when the capital city was established in Nara, situated in the northern part of the Yamato basin.

The introduction of Chinese civilization does not imply that the people on the continent suddenly "discovered" Japan, much as Columbus "discovered" the new world. Chinese civilization had been infiltrating Japan over a long period of time through the sporadic migration of *kika-jin* (naturalized people from Korea and China).[46] The chieftains of the imperial and other great clans depended heavily on these naturalized Koreans and Chinese as instructors, interpreters, clerks, and technicians. Around the turn of the fifth century, the Emperor Ōjin is said to have appointed Confucian scholars from Korea to tutor his children.[47] Meanwhile, as mentioned earlier, Japan lost Mimana, its foothold in south Korea, to Silla in 562, during the reign of the Emperor Kimmei. It is interesting to note that just before the fall of Mimana, Japan's ally in Korea, the king of Paekche, is said to have presented Buddhist images and scriptures to the Japanese court.[48] The date, which is given as 552 in the *Nihonshoki*, but

[46] On this important subject, see Seki, *Kika-jin.*

[47] We are told that upon the death of the Emperor Ōjin, the crown prince who had been given Confucian ethical training refused the throne on the grounds that he lacked "virtue and learning," and requested his brother to ascend the throne. His brother, too, declined the kingship, saying it would violate his sense of "filial piety" to act counter to his father's wishes. Here the question of imperial succession was not discussed in terms of the charisma. Both brothers considered the office of the emperor in the Confucian terms of virtue, learning, and filial piety. In the end, the crown prince took his own life, so that his brother was compelled to be enthroned. The new emperor, known as Nintoku, was portrayed as a sage, in the manner of the ancient sage kings of China. This allegedly benevolent emperor remitted taxes, built ditches, pools, and canals, constructed highways, and cultivated rice fields in remote areas. In comparing the *Kojiki* and the *Nihonshoki*, we find that the latter, which was more deeply influenced by Chinese thought, presented more moralized accounts than the former.

[48] For the introduction of Buddhism into Japan, see Anesaki, *History of Japanese Religion*, pp. 51–56.

might be 538, is significant only to the extent that it pinpoints
the official introduction of Buddhism into the Japanese court;
however, many naturalized Chinese and Koreans had undoubtedly been Buddhists prior to this date. More pertinent questions
for us concern the aspects of Chinese civilization and of Buddhism
that were adopted and the way in which they were understood
by the Japanese.

The sixth century was a turbulent period in Japan, both internally and externally. Sansom observes that Japanese policy in
Korea failed not for military reasons, but "because the central
government in Yamato could not depend upon the obedience of
the great territorial chieftains in western Japan, especially in
Kyushu, or upon the loyalty of its representatives in Korea, or
indeed upon the integrity of its Great Ministers at Court."[49]
Moreover, across the ocean, the powerful Sui dynasty reunited
China in 589. In this situation, the imperial clan allied itself, by
marriage or otherwise, with the rising Soga clan that succeeded
in eliminating the influence of the other great clans by skillful
intrigue. Incidentally, it was the chief of the Sogas who became
the advocate of the doctrine of the Buddha as a new kami
over the protests of others who feared the potency of this unknown deity.[50] The Soga chief also arranged the nomination of
the Empress Suiko (r. 592–628) as the first female to receive the
charisma of the imperial office. The real administrative responsibility, however, fell upon a young nephew of the empress, Prince
Regent Shōtoku. Thus began the separation of the two imperial

[49] Sansom, *A History of Japan to 1334,* p. 47.

[50] The Soga clan built the first Buddhist temple on its family estate. A
certain Keibin, a naturalized Japanese who had been a Buddhist priest in
Korea but had since renounced the cloth, was persuaded to resume the
priesthood, and it was he who "ordained" the three nuns. It is to be noted
that these three nuns were young maidens, ranging from eleven to seventeen years of age, and that they were children of Korean immigrants to
Japan. Their age was not sufficient for ordination according to the requirement of the Buddhist *Vinaya.* They must have been chosen to attend to
the spirit of the Buddha, just as young maidens were usually chosen for
similar duties in connection with the kami. See Nishida, *Nihon shūkyō-
shisō-shi no kenkyū,* pp. 489–90.

prerogatives, namely, the priestly function and administrative duties.

Prince Shōtoku (573–621) was determined to uphold the throne as the central authority over the traditional clan chieftains and local magnates. In this attempt he looked upon the Chinese empire as his model for the new political order to be established in Japan. Externally, he hoped to regain Japan's foothold in Korea through sending an expeditionary force there, but this project collapsed upon the death of the commanding general. Shōtoku also tried to establish a "multi-religious system," not dissimilar to the system adopted by Wen Ti of the Sui dynasty in China.[51] Shōtoku made every effort to maintain a proper balance among Shinto, Confucianism, and Buddhism. In the main, he accepted the Chinese concept of the emperor as "Son of Heaven," who was to rule the nation with the help of his bureaucratic officials, and not on the basis of the unpredictable divine oracles transmitted through shamanic diviners. This led him to transform the hereditary ministers, who were *de facto* chieftains of powerful clans, into bureaucrats, divided into twelve "cap-ranks."[52] It was his intention to recruit talented officials, and he sought to create a new class of literate gentry somewhat analogous to the *ju* in China. To this end he sent a number of promising younger officials, scholars, and Buddhist priests to China for further training. He is credited with envoying Ono-no-Imoko to the Sui court in 607.[53] Regarding the "Seventeen Article Constitution," supposed to have been promulgated by Shōtoku in 604 and often called the first constitution of Japan, many scholars are inclined to hold that it was the work of a later period, dedicated to the memory of Shōtoku.[54] Nevertheless, the spirit of the Constitu-

[51] Arthur F. Wright, "The Formation of Sui Ideology, 581–604," in Fairbank, ed., *Chinese Thought and Institutions*, p. 104.

[52] See Aston, *Nihongi*, II, 127–28.

[53] This mission had more cultural than diplomatic significance. See Mori, *Kentō-shi*, p. 6.

[54] Sansom, *A History of Japan to 1334*, pp. 51–52. Sansom also states (pp. 52–53): "It is curious, in the light of Prince Shōtoku's posthumous fame, that we have very little exact information about his activities. His

tion reflects something of Shōtoku's intention. For example, we read in the second article: "Sincerely revere the Three Treasures. The Three Treasures, i.e., Buddha, Dharma, and Samgha, are the supreme refuge of all beings, and are objects of veneration in all nations." This emphasis on Buddhism is balanced by the Confucian ideas hinted at in the third article. Shōtoku is also said to have sent forth another proclamation in 607, advocating the veneration of the kami.[55]

Prince Shōtoku seemed to be attracted to Buddhism not only through his own personal faith but because of its force as the bearer of a great civilization. He was instrumental in building many temples, each one of which was in effect a composite of religious, educational, and philanthropic units served by a group of monks or nuns. His own peculiar attitude toward Buddhism, reflected in his indifference to doctrinal and ecclesiastical divisions; in his dependence on the Lotus Sūtra, especially because of its soteriological universalism; and in his stress on the path of the lay devotee left lasting marks on the subsequent development of Buddhism in Japan. Furthermore, the significance of his religious policy must be seen to lie in the fact that the Buddhism that was introduced as a religion of certain clans was now transformed into the religion of the throne and the empire.[56] Thus, in 623, the year following Shōtoku's death, the first imperial edict was issued for the regulation of the classes of the Buddhist hierarchy. It was reported, then, that there were forty-six Buddhist edifices, 816 monks, and 569 nuns. Outside the religious sphere, notwithstanding the high ideals and reforms implicit in the edicts and injunctions attributed to Shōtoku, it is more accurate to say that he merely prepared the way for future reforms.

While the Soga clan continued to be important, after Prince Shōtoku's death the balance of power was suddenly shifted by

---

chief interest seems to have been the study of Buddhist literature and the Chinese classics."

[55] See Aston, *Nihongi*, II, 128–33.

[56] On Shōtoku's contribution to Japanese Buddhism, see Watsuji, *Nihon seishin-shi kenkyū*, pp. 1–49, and Futaba, *Kodai Bukkyō shisō-shi kenkyū*, pp. 304–86.

Kamatari, chief of the traditionally priestly family of the Nakatomi (later renamed Fujiwara), who, in collaboration with the ambitious Prince Naka-no-ōye (later the Emperor Tenchi), successfully carried out *coups d'état* and eliminated the influence of the Soga clan. Thus began the so-called Taika Reform of 645, which was subsequently revised and modified due to the issuance of the Taihō Code of 701–2.[57] The latter half of the seventh century, known as the "Reform Era," was marked by internal disorder, exemplified by the burning of the imperial palace on several occasions. Despite the opposition of traditional local magnates, Prince Naka-no-ōye was ruthless in executing reform measures, mercilessly destroying all who opposed him. In order to safeguard the northern borders, he sent expeditionary forces to subjugate the Ainu tribes. (Incidentally, two Ainus accompanied the Japanese ambassador to the T'ang court in 659.) The prince also persuaded the aged empress to command the Korean campaign,[58] but the Japanese forces were disastrously defeated by the combined military power of the Koreans (Silla) and the Chinese (T'ang) in 663. This marked the end of the token influence of Japan over the Korean peninsula.[59] The defeat in Korea necessitated the modification of the reform policy, and the prince, now the Emperor Tenchi, had to concern himself with internal problems of peace and order.[60]

Following the death of Tenchi, the throne held by Prince Ōtomo (known as the Emperor Kōbun) was usurped by Temmu in 672.[61] The combined reign of the Emperor Temmu (d. 686)

[57] For details, see Tsunoda, *et al.*, *Sources of Japanese Tradition*, pp. 70–92.

[58] On the road the Empress Saimei died in Kyushu in 661. From that year until he was officially enthroned in 668, Naka-no-ōye reigned as the crown prince. This system of rule is called *sho-sei*. See Naoki, *Jitō tennō*, p. 82.

[59] From that time on, Japan had to concentrate on a defensive policy, hence the establishment of defense headquarters at the Dazaifu in Kyushu.

[60] See Naoki, *Jitō tennō*, pp. 92–98.

[61] Historians have never agreed as to whether or not Prince Ōtomo was officially enthroned. The *Nihonshoki* does not recognize Ōtomo, and thus counts 672 as the first year of Temmu's reign, although Temmu was enthroned officially in 673.

and the Empress Jitō witnessed an extreme concentration of power in the imperial family. The wife of Temmu, Empress Jitō, who was the daughter of Tenchi, remained officially on the throne until 697, but continued until her death in 702 as the power behind her grandson, the Emperor Mommu. During this time, Japanese society became increasingly stratified according to Chinese influence. A type of Confucianism, which was not the classical teaching of the sages but an eclectic system developed during the Han period, provided Japan with the first rational norm for interhuman relationships. The ambiguity of the ancient cosmological system was reinterpreted according to the Taoist and Confucian ideologies. The kami, for example, were reformed into ethical divine beings, closely identified with Heaven. The spirit of the Taika and Taihō eras also resulted in a series of sweeping changes in the government, both central and provincial, in the registration of households, and in the taxation system. Inevitably, Chinese influence divided the Japanese populace into two strata—the upper class, which was influenced by continental thought and customs, and the lower class, which remained untouched by the new civilization except for various kinds of obscure witchcraft, magic, and astrology that infiltrated from China.

In one sense, the reform era turned out to be a period of bloodshed and intrigue among the ever growing numbers of royalty, bureaucrats, traditional clan chieftains, and local magnates who were determined to preserve their wealth, power, and prerogatives. The Emperor Temmu complained in desperation: "The deference paid by government officials to *miyahito* [or untitled mistresses of the palace] is far too great. Sometimes they go to their doors and address their plaints to them, sometimes they pay court at their houses by offerings of presents." [62] Actually, the

---

[62] See Aston, *Nihongi*, II, 351. Aston's translation of *miyahito* as "Palace officials (female)" is misleading. In the old days all wives of the emperor were called *kisaki* and the chief wife was called *Ō-kisaki*. By the seventh century, imperial wives were classified into several grades: the queen, followed by *hin*, who were *kisaki* of noble origin, and then by *miyahito* (also called *kyūjin* or *meshi-onna*), who were daughters of local magnates. See Naoki, *Jitō tennō*, pp. 14–18. Not all *miyahito* were im-

stability of the Yamato court was maintained by the power of the Fujiwara clan. After the death of Kamatari in 669, his son Fujiwara Fubito exerted unprecedented influence as the father-in-law of two sovereigns and the grandfather of another. Due to the gradual rise of the Fujiwara and other families politically, the reform measures that were supposedly modeled after the Chinese system were inevitably modified to fit into the Japanese situation.[63] It is even questionable whether this legislation was understood, let alone obeyed, in the countryside away from Yamato. Nevertheless, the prestige of the government increased, to the extent that even the islands of Tane, Yaku, and Dokan became tributaries to the Yamato court toward the end of the seventh century.

One of the most important projects undertaken by the government in the early eighth century was the establishment of a capital city modeled after the Chinese capital, in Nara, which was selected no doubt for a number of political, cultural, and religious reasons. The greater part of the eighth century, from 710 to 781, is called the Nara period. During this time, the reform measures of the Taika and Taihō era virtually collapsed because of repeated revisions made for the benefit of the former clan chieftains and local magnates, now forming a group of tightly knit court nobility. Most of them enjoyed the privilege of keeping the imperially exempted manors (*shōen*) in the countryside. Outside the manors, taxes were becoming prohibitive, and the government had no power to enforce police or military duties on the manors. Farmers abandoned their rice fields for new territories in order to avoid tax collectors. In general the new state of affairs enhanced the prosperity of the upper classes, but increased the exploitation of the lower, and left their misery deeper. The

perial concubines, however. One such woman, Agata-no-Inugai Michiyo, married the son of Fujiwara Kamatari, Fubito, and became the mother of the Empress *Kōmyō*, consort of the Emperor Shōmu.

[63] For a detailed historical description of the reform era, see Sansom, *A History of Japan to 1334*, pp. 67–81; Takekoshi, *The Economic Aspects of the History of the Civilization of Japan*, I, 11–63; and Tsuda, *Nihon jōdaishi no kenkyū*, pp. 153–295. On the so-called Yōrō Code of 718, see Dettmer, *Die Steuergesetzgebung der Nara-Zeit*.

government continued to invest unusually large sums of money for the construction of the capital and costly Buddhist temples. Thus, "while courtiers and dignitaries of the church rode splashingly by in splendid robes of brocade, . . . peasants went in breechcloths for several months of the year, barefoot or straw sandaled." [64]

Much has been written about the splendor of the arts and architecture of the Nara period. In addition, the eighth century also produced a number of important written documents, such as the *Kojiki* (Records of ancient matters), the *Fudoki* (Records of local surveys), the *Nihonshoki* (Chronicles of Japan), the *Kaifūsō* (Fond recollection of poetry), and the *Manyōshū* (Anthology of myriad leaves), as well as copies of a number of Buddhist scriptures.[65] Undoubtedly the great underlying inspiration of the Nara culture was Buddhism, for in a true sense eighth century Japan developed what might be called a Buddhist "ecclesiastification of culture."

Institutionalization of the Priesthood

The religious situation in Japan during the sixth, seventh, and eighth centuries witnessed the gradual emergence of the priestly "privileged class," in both the Shinto and Buddhist folds, often competing in power and wealth with the greedy court nobility. It may be recalled that before the introduction of Buddhism, Shinto had no fixed ecclesiastical organization. People belonged to a particular "liturgical community" that had special rapport with certain kami. Membership in such a community was based on "givenness" in terms of one's clan or place of birth; and, more often than not, communal and regional bonds were closely interrelated. In principle, the clan chieftain (*uji-no-kami*) was also

---

[64] Warner, *The Enduring Art of Japan*, p. 12.

[65] A record of special interest is the *Shinsen shōjiroku* (The new compilation of the register of families), completed in 815. It divides the aristocracy of the Nara period into three categories: *shin-betsu* (descendants of heavenly and earthly kami), *kō-betsu* (descendants of imperial and other royal families), and *ban-betsu* (descendants of naturalized Chinese and Koreans).

in charge of religious functions in connection with the kami of his clan. In other words, the sociological unit of the clan (*uji*) was in effect the basic unit of religious solidarity, so that clansmen maintained an exclusive relationship with their own kami.

While the clan chieftain was ultimately responsible for religious functions, the actual performance of rituals was often undertaken by designated members of the clan. We read in the *Nihonshoki* that the Emperor Sujin made Nagochi of the Yamato clan "master of worship of *Yamato no Oho-kuni-dama no Kami*." [66] The "master of worship," be it noted, was not merely superior to other priestly functionaries such as the *negi* (supplicator), whose role was to invoke the kami's actual presence during the ceremonies, and the *hafuri* or *hō-ri* (ablutioner) who was expected to purify the sacred compound and the participants of various kinds of defilements. The "master of worship" was called the *kan-nushi* (*kami-nushi*, literally, the kami-master), *iwai-nushi*, or *iwai-no-ushi*, which implies that during the ceremony, at least, he became more than a mere human being; for the kami was believed to enter the physical being of the *kan-nushi* to transform him. In other words, the "master of worship" was the temporary kami or at least the kami's representative and not the representative of the people. Evidently, there were several kinds of *kan-nushi*, however. Some of them were hereditary, while others were chosen for a certain period from among the charismatic clansmen; the one from among the latter is often called the *ichinen-kan-nushi* (the master of worship for one year only). Some of them, of the charismatic type, were capable of becoming kami-possessed, while others depended on shamanic diviners (*miko*) to speak in behalf of the kami.[67]

[66] Aston, *Nihongi*, I, 155.

[67] Yanagita, *Minzokugaku jiten*, pp. 124–26. According to the legendary accounts of the Empress Jingō, she acted as the *kan-nushi*, while Nakatomi Ikatsu-omi acted as *saniwa* (supplicator and interpreter of the divine oracle) and Takeshi-uchino-sukune played a musical instrument. This story leads us to believe that a common pattern in the old days was for a shamanic diviner (*miko*) to become the *kan-nushi*, as is still the usual pattern in Okinawa today. With the institutionalization of the Shinto priesthood, however, the functions of the *kan-nushi* and that of the *miko*

The rapid centralization of the government in the seventh century, requiring the cooperation of the kami, resulted in the institutionalization of the charisma of the Shinto priesthood. Even Prince Shōtoku, himself an ardent Buddhist, urged his ministers to do reverence to the heavenly and earthly kami.[68] The Emperor Kōtoku, who was accused of being an extreme Buddhist, "despising the Way of the kami," [69] was nevertheless instrumental in elevating Kamatari (or Kamako) from the traditionally Shinto priestly clan of the Nakatomi to be the ruling minister of the court. By this time the emperor dared to proclaim that "Heaven covers us; Earth upbears us; the Imperial way is but one." As such, the throne adopted that most pretentious title, *Akitsu-mikami-to Amenoshita-shiroshimesu Yamato-no-sumeramikoto* (the living kami, the ruler of the world, and the emperor of the Yamato kingdom).[70] Such an exalted monarch, however, needed desperately to have the cooperation of the *taifu* (*mayetsu-kimitachi*) or local Shinto priests for the execution of the Taika reform measures.[71] Evidently this meant that the privileges and prerogatives of the Shinto priesthood had to be recognized by the government.[72] At the turn of the eighth century a department of Shinto

---

were separated, and the latter acquired a lower position in the Shinto hierarchy. See Yanagita, *Nihon no matsuri*, pp. 134–63.

[68] Aston, *Nihongi*, I, 135–36.

[69] *Ibid.*, II, 195. What angered the court historians is the fact that the emperor ordered the cutting down of the trees at the shrine of Iku-kuni-dama.

[70] See Aston, *Nihongi*, II, 197–98.

[71] *Ibid.*, II, 199–200. In 645 the Emperor Kōtoku inquired after the opinion of the *taifu* and the provincial government officials as to the method of using the people's services for government programs. One of the ministers advised the throne: "First of all the kami of heaven and earth should be propitiated by worship; thereafter affairs of the government ought to be considered." Accordingly, the imperial messengers were sent to the provinces of Owari and Mino to levy offerings (*mitegura*) for the kami.

[72] Aston, *Nihongi*, II, 336. In 677 the Emperor Temmu gave orders to the effect that the tax collected for the "shrines of heavenly and earthly kami" should be divided into three shares, one of which was to be set apart for the offerings to the kami and the other two given to the *kan-*

affairs was established side by side with the great council of state. Chieftains of the hereditary Shinto priestly families thus became bureaucratic government officials with graded court rank and prescribed duties.

A similar development took place regarding the Buddhist priesthood. As has been mentioned earlier, Buddhism was initially accepted as the religion of certain clans (*uji*), and Buddhist temples were regarded as *uji-dera* (temples of the clan) somewhat analogous to the Shinto shrines of the clan. Many temples, such as the Asuka Temple by the Soga and the Kume Temple by the Kume, were built and maintained by the prominent *uji*. Those who thus adhered to Buddhism were primarily interested in acquiring mundane benefits. The statues and paintings of Shaka (Sākyamuni), Amida (Amitābha or Amitāyus), Yakushi (Bhaisajyaguru), Kannon (Avalokiteśvara), Miroku (Maitreya), and Shi-tennō (the four Deva kings) were believed to have special potencies; and they became objects of popular devotion. The scriptures (sutras) used in the seventh century, such as the *Myōhō-Rengekyō* (*Saddharma-puṇḍarīka*, or the *Lotus Sutra*), the *Konkōmyōkyō* (*Suvarṇa-prabhāsa*, or the *Golden Light Sutra*), and the *Ninnō-hannyakyō* (the *Sutra of Prajñāpāramitā Our Benevolent King*), were recited primarily for their supposedly magical power to bring wealth, health, good fortune, and longevity.[73]

It may be well for us to remember that the Buddhism that was

---

nushi (priests). We also learn from the *Nihonshoki* that in 673 (during the reign of Temmu), "with the view of sending the Imperial Princess Ohoki to attend upon the Shrine of Amaterasu Ōmikami, she was made to dwell in the Abstinence-palace of Hatsuse. This was that she might first purify herself before she approached the presence of the kami later." (See Aston, *Nihongi*, II, 322.) The princess left the Abstinence-palace the next year and proceeded to the shrine of Ise. (*Ibid.*, p. 326.) Amaterasu was originally worshiped within the palace compound; during the reign of the Emperor Sujin her *locus* was moved to Kasanui where the *himorogi* (sacred tree) was planted in her honor. (*Ibid.*, I, 152.) Amaterasu is said to have been enshrined at Ise under the reign of Suinin. (*Ibid.*, I, 176–77.) These accounts are not altogether reliable. It is most likely that the lofty status of the shrine of Ise, dedicated to Amaterasu, was acknowledged for the first time in 673–74.

[73] De Visser, *Ancient Buddhism in Japan*, I, 3–26.

transplanted to Japan in the sixth and seventh centuries was no longer the simple religion of Indian ascetics and mendicants. By that time Buddhism had had a long history in India, Central Asia, and China, where it had developed art, architecture, rituals, philosophies, and a voluminous scripture called the Tripitaka. All these religious and cultural aspects of Buddhism attracted the clan chieftains as much as they did the Yamato court. Undoubtedly Prince Shōtoku's interest in Buddhism, at least in part, was on account of its potentiality for becoming the common faith of diverse clans that had hitherto been divided politically and religiously. On the other hand, Shōtoku accepted the Confucian premise that society had to be stratified according to intelligence, ability, and morality. Besides, his own upbringing led him to take for granted certain social gradations based on birth and lineage. Therefore Shōtoku's understanding of Buddhism tended to deemphasize the horizontal differences of the traditional clan system as well as the sectarian divisions of Buddhism, but encouraged the vertical gradation of society even among the Buddhist clerics, as exemplified by the ecclesiastical ranks of *sōjō, sōzu,* and *hōzu.* According to the edict of 623, it was up to the throne to "appoint a *sōjō* and a *sōzu* for the supervision of the priests and nuns." [74] This policy of government control of clerical status and jurisdiction, which was followed by subsequent rulers, greatly determined the development of Buddhism in Japan. That is, the Buddhist community (*samgha*), as such, had no opportunity to develop its own integrity and coherence, because from the time of Prince Shōtoku onward "the state functioned not as a patron (*Schutz-patronat*) but as the religious police (*Religions-polizei*) of Buddhism." [75]

The Taika and Taihō eras (645–702) witnessed a decline in the importance of the clan-sponsored temples and an increase in the prestige of state-sponsored temples.[76] In 685 orders were sent

[74] Aston, *Nihongi,* II, 153.

[75] Nakamura, *The Ways of Thinking of Eastern Peoples,* p. 455.

[76] In the edict of 680, we read: "Henceforth, let all temples, with the exception of the two or three great national temples, cease to be administered by officials. But for those which hold a sustenance-fief, a limit

to all the provinces from the throne that "in every house a Buddhist altar should be established, and an image of Buddha with Buddhist scriptures placed there. Worship was to be paid and offerings of food made at these altars." [77] State sponsorship also meant the reciting and copying of various sutras, especially the *Konkōmyōkyō* (*The Sutra of the Golden Light*) which provided a Buddhistic rationale for exalted kingship. [78] The *Konkōmyōkyō*, the *Hokkekyō* (*Lotus Sutra*), and the *Ninnōkyō* (*Benevolent King's Sutra*) were regarded as the "Three Scriptures Protecting the State." In the Nara period the Emperor Shōmu went further by proclaiming in 741 that in every province there was to be one state-supported official temple (*kokubunji*). [79] About ten years later, Tōdaiji (The Eastern Great Temple) in Nara was made the national cathedral (*sō-kokubunji*, "the chief temple" among all the state-supported official temples), while Hokkeji (The Lotus Nunnery) was made the chief national nunnery (*sō-kokubun-niji*). [80]

Clearly, the aim of the government in sponsoring Buddhism was not the salvation of the people but the protection of the state. [81] For this purpose, the government was not discriminatory, so long as the cult or religion was willing to be at its service. For example, an official Confucian festival was celebrated in 701 side by side with Shinto and Buddhist services. The government also

---

from first to last of thirty years is fixed. This will be discontinued when, upon calculating the years, the number of thirty is completed." (Aston, *Nihongi*, II, 346.)

[77] *Ibid.*, II, 369.

[78] De Visser, *Ancient Buddhism in Japan*, I, 14–16.

[79] To be more exact, in each province there was to be one temple, connected with the pagoda, and one nunnery. All these temples were called *Konkōmyō-Shitennō-gokokuji* (The temple for the protection of the nation by the four Deva kings), while the nunneries were called *Hokke-Metsuzai no Tera* (Temples for the extinction of sins by means of the *Lotus Sutra*). Both were supported by a sustenance-fief from the government treasury.

[80] Ishida, *Tōdaiji to Kokubunji*, pp. 4–26.

[81] Nakamura points out that the Japanese utilized Buddhism "as a means and an instrument to realize a certain socio-political end. They were not converted to Buddhism. They converted Buddhism to their own tribalism." (*The Ways of Thinking of Eastern Peoples*, p. 457.)

held Onmyōdō (Yin-yang school) geomancy and astrology in high esteem. The Taihō edicts specified the appointment of seven Yin-yang masters, one doctor, one astrologer, and one "doctor of the calendar" as regular members of the central government. Monarchs were particularly sensitive to natural calamities, which implied a lack of virtue on the part of the Son of Heaven. In order to avert the consequences of evil omens such as eclipses, the *musha-daiye* (literally, great limitless meeting), *hōjō-ye* (meeting for liberating living beings), and other magico-religious rites were sponsored by the court. Shinto, Buddhism, Confucianism, and other religious movements were thus regarded as means for upholding the cause of the ruling regime. The court frequently summoned Shinto and Buddhist functionaries to "pray" for rain, relief from pestilence, and other practical benefits; and in return for these services, large estates were donated to Shinto shrines and Buddhist temples, and the clergy were showered with honors and favors by the court.

During the Nara period Buddhism enjoyed royal favor, over-shadowing that extended to Shinto, for the government depended on Buddhism as the chief civilizing agency which would help solidify the nation. In turn, the court generously offered donations to the Buddhist temples in the form of land allotments (*fuko*). Also, in order to cultivate new land in the distant provinces, the government encouraged wealthy temples to invest money. Such a policy resulted in a rapid increase in the number of powerful temples.[82] With such thorough backing from the court, Buddhism was destined to prosper during the Nara period. Learned priests welcomed and studied different doctrinal and philosophical systems, such as the Jōjitsu (Satyasiddhi, a Hinayanistic negativism), the Sanron (Mādhyamika, a Mahayanistic negativism), the Hossō

---

[82] For the economic aspects of the national cathedral, Tōdaiji, see Hiraoka, *Tōdaiji no Rekishi*, pp. 128–41. We are told that between the middle of the sixth century and the middle of the seventh century there were only six temples built, but in less than fifty years after 645, which was the beginning of the Taika era, over 110 temples were erected. During the Nara period there were 361 temples constructed. All these temples were provided with *fuko*.

(Yogācāra, a Mahayanistic idealism), the Kusha (Abhidharma-kośa, a Hinayanistic realism), and the Kegon (Avatamsaka, a Mahayanistic totalism).[83] These schools are usually known as "sects," but actually they were little more than philosophical traditions based on different scriptures. Unfortunately, these philosophical differences became symbols for ecclesiastical-political divisions between powerful temples. At first the most prominent of these was the Hossō school, transmitted by Dōshō (d. 700), a Japanese priest who had studied in China under Hiuen-tsang.[84] The prestige of the Hossō school was gradually eclipsed by the newly transmitted Kegon school, of which Rōben (d. 773) was the chief spokesman; he was also counselor to the Emperor Shōmu.

Another school which was important during the Nara period was the Ritsu (Vinaya) school, based on the seventh-century Chinese monk Tao-hsuan's teachings on monastic· disciplines. Since Japanese Buddhists accepted the orthodox view that the charismatic authority of Gautama Buddha had been superseded by the charisma of ecclesiastical offices, they became preoccupied with the question of "validity of ordination" which the Ritsu school claimed to transmit, tending to place less emphasis on morality and the monastic disciplines that were the primary aims of Tao-hsuan.[85] During the Nara period Ganjin (Chien-chien),

[83] For a general description of these Buddhist schools of the Nara period, see such standard works as August Karl Reischauer, *Studies in Japanese Buddhism;* Eliot, *Japanese Buddhism;* Yamakami, *Systems of Buddhist Thought;* and Takakusu, *The Essentials of Buddhist Philosophy.*

[84] See Waley, *The Real Tripitaka,* pp. 105–6. Dōshō's tradition was known as the Southern School of Hossō, with its headquarters at the Gangō Temple at Nara. Dōshō did not have much aptitude for philosophy, and spent much of his time in philanthropic works. The other tradition, the Northern School of Hossō, with its headquarters at Kōfuku Temple, originally the Fujiwara clan temple, was transmitted by Gembō (d. 746). Gembō was a learned man, but was also very ambitious and immoral; he was later relegated to a minor temple in Kyushu.

[85] Buddhism has two kinds of ordination—one for the initiation of a novice receiving the five disciplinary rules and another involving five additional rules for the priesthood. Records reveal that previously in Japan there had been some kind of informal initiation rite that was not

a Chinese Vinaya master, was invited to the Japanese court; he introduced the orthodox Vinaya school of Tao-hsuan, and many members of the imperial family received their "lay ordination" from him. Although Ganjin trained many disciples, the Japanese Ritsu school was preoccupied with external formalities and lacked concern for moral discipline.

Charisma of the Shamanistic Buddhist

The rapprochement between Buddhism and Shinto, the unique feature of Japanese religion, developed primarily from two sources during the Nara period. First there was a sociological factor. While Buddhism made great advances during the seventh and the eighth centuries, Shinto was far from being dead. In 737 there were over 3,000 Shinto shrines of various sizes and degrees of importance. Meanwhile, wealthy Buddhist temples that owned land found that their tenants derived their sense of solidarity and belonging from the kami and cults of Shinto. Buddhist institutions realized quickly that if they allowed Shinto shrines on their properties their lands would be protected by the taboo respected by the superstitious masses. Thus Shinto shrines found their way into the sacred premises of Buddhist institutions so that the kami could protect the latter, and in turn Buddhist altars were built near Shinto shrines in order to afford the protection of Shinto by the Buddha. As though to symbolize this new spirit, in 783 the kami Hachiman was named *Daijizaiten-bosatsu*, thus equating him with a Buddhist *bodhisattva*.[86] Buddhism was so powerful during this period that Shinto had nothing to lose by religious alliance.

Second there was the role of the shamanistic Buddhist, called *ubasoku-zenji* (*upasaka*-ascetic, magician, healer, and medium), that bridged the gap between Shinto and Buddhism. The origin

the full ordination prescribed by the Vinaya. The latter requires three *wajō* (masters) and seven witnesses as well as a proper ordination hall (*kaidan*).

[86] See Taijō Tamamuro, "Nihon Bukkyō-shi gaisetzu," in Hajime Nakamura, Fumio Masutani, and J. M. Kitagawa, eds., *Gendai Bukkyō meicho zenshū*, Vol. III, *Nihon no Bukkyō*, pp. 60–62.

of the *ubasoku* is obscure, but it is safe to state that many rustic magicians, healers, and shamanic diviners of the mountain districts and the countryside who came under the nominal influence of Buddhism during the seventh and eighth centuries were known by this general designation. The *ubasoku* had no formal training in Buddhist doctrines; although they were known for unusual spiritual power, they were not recognized by orthodox Buddhist schools as regular clergy. In most cases their relationship with Buddhism was very tenuous. But they were greatly influenced by Shinto, Taoism, and the shamanistic folk piety of the pre-Buddhist period. The term *ubasoku* does not refer to any organized movement, at least within the context of the Nara period. There were various types of men in this category. One of the earliest shamanistic Buddhists was En-no-Shōkaku, who came to be regarded as the founder of the Shugen-dō, a special order of mountain priests, in the later period.[87] It is said that he came from a family of hereditary shamanic diviners that served *Hitokoto-nushi* (the kami of One Word, or the kami who blesses or curses with a word), the kami of Mount Katsuragi. Never ordained to the regular Buddhist priesthood, En-no-Shōkaku acquired superhuman power as the result of austere mental and physical disciplines on the mountain. He claimed that in his previous existences he had been a direct disciple of Buddha and also an emperor of Japan. The orthodox Buddhist hierarchy were jealous of En-no-Shōkaku's popularity, and consequently he was banished to the island of Izu around the turn of the eighth century by the order of the Emperor Mommu.[88]

There were many reasons for the popularity of shamanistic Buddhists during the Nara period. First, many people who em-

[87] Wakamori, *Shugen-dō-shi kenkyū*, pp. 18–50.

[88] Another strange Buddhist of this period was Hōdō, an Indian monk who was said to have come to Japan by way of China and Korea, riding on a purple cloud. He led a solitary and austere life on Mount Hokke in Kyushu. A devotee of the Thousand-Armed Avalokiteśvara, he was noted for his healing ability and was credited with having cured the Emperor Kōtoku of illness in 649. For a brief period, he played an important role as the presiding priest over several Buddhist festivals. See De Visser, *Ancient Buddhism in Japan*, I, 195.

braced Buddhism during this period, with the exception of
learned priests and intelligentsia, accepted Buddha in the traditional Japanese religious context. For instance, in the famous
"Songs on the Buddha's Foot-Prints" of the eighth century
Buddha was portrayed as a great healer, a holy man, and a *marahito* (*marebito,* a traditional Shinto term for a kami who visits
villages from a far-off place at the time of harvest and other
important seasons).[89] Most Buddhists were primarily interested in
invoking the new kami for a variety of practical benefits and an
assurance of well-being in the life to come. Second, both the
Buddhist and Shinto priests were *de facto* government officials,
closely identified with the cause of the throne and of the upper
strata of society. No doubt these "official" priests knew which
sutra (Buddhist scripture) or *norito* (Shinto prayer) to recite, to
what Buddha image or kami to pray for help, and which charms
or incantations to use for all kinds of needs of the government
and of the government leaders, but they paid little attention to
the soteriological needs of the masses. In fact, a vocation to the
religious life was open only to the children of the aristocratic
gentry in those days. Third, the oppressed peasantry needed some
sort of spiritual guidance which they could not get from the
"official" priests. The glorious culture of the Nara period brought
little benefit or consolation to those who had barely enough to eat
and lacked adequate clothing. It should also be remembered
that they lived close to the world of nature which was permeated
by the kami nature. Thus, it was but fitting and understandable
that the peasants welcomed and supported the *ubasoku,* who in
many ways played the same important role as the traditional
shamanic diviner. These *ubasoku* wandered from village to village,
comforting the sick and the oppressed, and offering divination
and prayer, in the name of Buddha, the supreme miracle worker.

The government and orthodox Buddhist hierarchy were alarmed
at the increasing influence of the *ubasoku,* so that edicts were
issued in 701, 717, 729, and 764, admonishing the priests and

[89] See Philippi, tr., "Songs on the Buddha's Foot-Prints," *Nihonbunka-
Kenkyusho-Kiyō* (Tokyo, Kokugakuin University), No. 2 (March, 1958),
p. 153.

nuns to conform to the *Sō-ni Ryō* (Regulations for priests and nuns). What concerned the authorities was not only the moral laxity of some of the clerics but also black magic and possible conspiracy on the part of the unauthorized priests. Such edicts, however, were not effective in restricting the ever-growing activities of the *ubasoku*. Not all the *ubasoku* represented undesirable elements, of course. Many of them were noted not only for their charismatic power in shamanistic divination but also for community leadership in such enterprises as building bridges, digging irrigation ponds and ditches, and constructing roads. Their influence was conspicuously strong among people in distant places during the eighth century. Some of the *ubasoku* were critical of the corruption of the ecclesiastical dignitaries in the capital and asserted that their own path, later called *Bosatsu-dō* (the path to bodhisattvahood) or *Hijiri-dō* (the path to holy manhood), was the only true way to salvation.[90]

The problem was not so much a question of orthodoxy versus unorthodoxy, valid ordination versus irregular priesthood, or official religion versus popular religion, as of two diametrically opposed ways of understanding the nature of charisma, soteriology, and eschatology. The orthodox Buddhists, the inheritors of the "charisma of the ecclesiastical offices," were convinced that the soteriological path was integrally related to the orthodox Buddhist community (*Samgha*), which alone provided proper instruction and propagation of the faith, administration of the cult, and the care of the poor, sick, and neglected—all within the framework of a transcendent eschatology. Thus they stressed the importance of valid ordination and transmission of authority, and they viewed the imperial government as the necessary protector of the Samgha. On the other hand, the *ubasoku*, who had maintained the spirit and forms of pre-Buddhist shamanic diviners in Japan, understood the gospel of Buddhism in terms of creative spirituality and immanental eschatology, disregarding the validity of ordination and transmission of ecclesiastical authority. Even though many of them underwent austere disciplines, basically

[90] See Hori, "On the Concept of Hijiri (Holy-Man)," *Numen,* V (1958), 128–60; 199–232.

they were more concerned with a predisposition to respond to spiritual stimuli and a susceptibility to supernatural influences. To them, therefore, the importance was not the "charisma of office" but "personal charisma," even though the latter might be accompanied by certain personal abnormalities and eccentricities. When they found their principle of "personal charisma" and the "path of sanctification" in irreconcilable opposition to governmental regulation or the policies of the orthodox Buddhist hierarchy, they were willing to undergo persecution and hardship because of their religious convictions. Thus it is readily understandable that to reconcile these two opposed approaches to religion presented a crucial problem to Japanese religion in the eighth century.

The reconciliation of the orthodox Buddhist hierarchy and the *ubasoku,* of the state religion and the religion of the masses, was achieved largely through the combined roles played by the Emperor Shōmu and Gyōgi Bosatsu (670–749), the leader and spokesman for the unaffiliated shamanistic Buddhists. Little need be said about the Emperor Shōmu, who sponsored the erection of a colossal image of Lochana Buddha in Nara. In his proclamation we read: "Having respectfully succeeded to the throne through no virtue of Our own, out of a constant solicitude for all men, We have been ever intent on aiding them to reach the shore of the Buddha-land." He goes on to say: "It is We who possess the wealth of the land; it is We who possess all power in the land. With this wealth and power at Our command, We have resolved to create this venerable object of worship [the image of Lochana Buddha]." [91] Shōmu thereby added to the traditional charisma of the imperial office the new element of being the head of the state religion, defined in Buddhist terms. He hopefully envisaged the establishment of a grand commonwealth, guided by Buddha's law, reflecting the heavenly tranquillity of which the Lochana Buddha would be the earthly symbol.

[91] "Proclamation of the Emperor Shōmu on the Erection of the Great Buddha Image," *Shoku Nihongi,* in *Rikkokushi,* III, 320–21; English translation taken from Tsunoda, *et al., Sources of Japanese Tradition,* pp. 106–7.

But the emperor's pious proclamation did not inspire the populace in the distant provinces to contribute money or labor, and it looked as though the image of Buddha would not be built. In this situation, the emperor had to turn to Gyōgi, whom he appointed to the position of archbishop. Not much is known about Gyōgi's background, except that he was at one time a follower of the Hossō school and that he was arrested in 717 by the government because of his activities in preaching the doctrine of meritorious works (*punya*) among the peasants. He is also said to have been a worshiper of Amida (Amitābha) as well as a devotee of the Miroku (Maitreya) cult and a believer in the doctrine of rebirth in the Tushita heaven.[92] At any rate, the orthodox ecclesiastics discredited the path of sanctification (*Hijiri-dō*) advocated by Gyōgi, but the pious masses called him "Bosatsu" (Bodhisattva) in recognition of his good works. His preaching was direct and personal, combining the motifs of meritorious works and faith in Amida. The fact that Gyōgi, who had neither training abroad nor ecclesiastical standing in the Buddhist hierarchy, was suddenly elevated to the position of archbishop, bypassing all ecclesiastical dignitaries, indicates how eager the court was to secure the cooperation and support of the masses for the project of erecting the image of the Lochana Buddha. According to legend, Gyōgi was sent to the Grand Shrine of Ise, carrying a Buddhist relic as an offering to Amaterasu, the kami of the imperial clan. There he received a favorable oracle concerning the construction of the Buddha statue, whereupon he traveled about the countryside collecting offerings from the people for this project. Thus, through the combined initiative of the Emperor Shōmu and Gyōgi, and the cooperation of Shinto priests and shamanistic Buddhists, the great image of the Lochana Buddha was completed in 749 and dedicated in 752 with due splendor and glory.[93]

[92] De Visser, *Ancient Buddhism in Japan*, I, 333–34. See also Futaba, *Kodai Bukkyō shisō-shi kenkyū*, pp. 388–543; and Kaoru Inouye, *Gyōgi*.

[93] It is reported that the kami Usa Hachiman in Kyushu, who also delivered an oracle favoring the construction of the Lochana Buddha statue, was escorted to Nara and enshrined within the compound of the Tōdaiji

Following in the footsteps of Gyōgi, some of the *ubasoku* of
his time joined the orthodox Buddhist hierarchy; but there were
others who continued to remain apart, seeking salvation outside
the state-sponsored Buddhist community. In the meantime, the
Emperor Shōmu, who considered himself the "servant of the
Three Treasures," abdicated in 749 to take priestly vows. His
daughter, who succeeded to the throne as Empress Kōken, herself
abdicated in 758 in favor of a young prince who became the
Emperor Junnin. The retired empress became involved roman-
tically, according to legends, with Dōkyō, the court chaplain.
This priest had acquired healing power at Mount Katsuragi, the
home of En-no-Shōkaku and the center of training for shamanistic
Buddhists. Being politically ambitious, Dōkyō persuaded the retired empress to oust the young emperor, whom she banished and
later had strangled. When the empress, now called the Empress
Shōtoku, returned to power, Dōkyō, after being appointed successively "chief minister and master" and "king of the law"
(*hō-ō*), soon attempted to usurp the throne. His conspiracy was
shattered by a divine oracle from the kami Usa Hachiman in
Kyushu.[94] The empress died in 770 and an elderly emperor,
Kōnin, ascended the throne. In 781 Kōnin was succeeded by the
Emperor Kammu, and the colorful Nara period came to an end.

The religious situation in Japan had undergone many changes.
The earlier pattern of interplay between the emperor's charisma
and the charisma of the shamanic diviner had to undergo a series
of transformations under the impact of Chinese civilization and
of Buddhism. The advocates of a centralized empire envisaged a
unified nation, based on a multireligious policy. Inevitably,
Shinto, Confucianism, and Buddhism were closely identified with
the causes of the court and nobility, while the spiritual welfare
of the masses who thus had to turn to the *ubasoku*, the shamanistic Buddhists, for religious leadership was ignored. For a num-

---

where Buddhist priests recited sutras before him. The emperor conferred on
the kami Usa Hachiman a "cap of honor," as a token of his esteem. The
Shinto priests and priestesses who served the kami were likewise honored
by the court.

[94] See Yokota, *Dōkyō*.

ber of reasons, Gyōgi Bosatsu; the shamanistic Buddhist *par excellence,* had been elevated to the position of archbishop. But
the gap between the Buddhist orthodoxy and the followers of
ubasoku was not closed completely.

The "ecclesiastification" of culture, as envisaged by the Nara
monarchs, brought neither heavenly peace to the nation nor
prosperity and happiness to the people. While nobles and high
ecclesiastics enjoyed the elegant products of the Nara culture, the
masses huddled in misery.[95] To be sure, some pious Buddhists
were motivated by their sense of compassion to help the needy
and cure the sick.[96] But for the most part, the nation suffered
from overtaxation, political intrigue, and general apathy. In this
situation, religious vitality was maintained not by ecclesiastical
dignitaries in the court but by the crude and superstitious shamanistic Buddhists who undertook an austere training in the
sacred mountains and presented to the masses a doctrine of simple
and direct faith in the kami and the Buddha. It was from this
tradition, the Buddhist fusion with primitive shamanism and
divination, that the creative impulse was elicited in the Heian
period as well as in the subsequent history of Japanese religion.

[95] See Iyanaga, *Nara-jidai no kizoku to nōmin.*
[96] For the charitable work of the Empress Kōmyō, see Hayashi, *Kōmyō
kōgō.*

CHAPTER II

Kami, Amida, and Jizō

RELIGIOUS DEVELOPMENT

DURING THE HEIAN PERIOD

(ca. ninth–twelfth centuries)

When the Emperor Kammu ascended the throne in 781, he inherited a nation that was threatened by financial bankruptcy, political corruption, and internal disunity. He followed the policy of his predecessor, the Emperor Kōnin, who had been compelled to withdraw the government subsidy of Buddhist establishments in order to balance the national budget. Also, with a great deal of courage and determination, Kammu and his advisers moved the capital from Nara, first to Nagaoka in 784 and then to Kyoto in 794, in order to be freed from the interference of the powerful aristocracy and ecclesiastical hierarchy which had controlled the political life of the old capital. The new capital in Kyoto was called the Heian-kyō or the "Capital of Peace and Tranquility." Although the imperial family lived in this city until 1868, the center of political power moved to Kamakura toward the end of the twelfth century. Thus the designation "Heian period" refers only to the period roughly from the ninth to the twelfth centuries. The political development of the Heian period resolved itself into three different phases: the first was the era of court rule (794–858), which permitted a semblance of imperial initiative in national affairs; the second was the era of the Fujiwara Regency (858–1068), in which the Fujiwara oligarchy was in effect the ruling power of the nation; and the third was the era of *inzei* (cloistered rule) (1069–1190) by retired emperors.[1]

For the most part, the Heian period was, despite its name, far from being peaceful and tranquil. During the reign of Kammu (781–806), the heir apparent, Prince Sawara, was murdered by conspirators at court.[2] Moreover, a large number of men had to be mobilized to subjugate the northern borders where the descendants of the Ainu and others flaunted their independence against the imperial authority.[3] Kammu's son, the Emperor

[1] See Yoshimura, *Inzei.*

[2] Although Kammu appointed Sawara, his brother by a different mother, as crown prince, their relationship was not harmonious. Kammu depended on Fujiwara Tanetsugu, who was related to the rich Hata family settled in the Kyoto region. Prince Sawara, on the other hand, was supported by Saegi Imagehito. The balance of power between the two parties—Kammu and Fujiwara Tanetsugu versus Sawara and Saegi Imagehito—was broken when Tanetsugu banished Imagehito. In 784 a commission under Tanetsugu began construction of the new capital at Nagaoka. The following year Tanetsugu was assassinated by someone believed to be Prince Sawara's confidant. Sawara and his men were therefore banished, and the prince was murdered on the island of Awaji. Throughout Kammu's reign Sawara's ghost was said to have haunted the throne, as a consequence of which the emperor offered the dead prince the posthumous title of "Emperor Sudō" in 800.

[3] Opinions still vary about the ethnic affiliation of the people in the northern borders of Japan during this period. Hasebe Kotondo asserts that those in the northern part of Honshū island during the Nara and Heian periods were mostly of Japanese origin and had migrated there in order to avoid taxation, etc. See Hasebe, "Ezo," in Nihon Jinruigaku-kai, ed., *Nihon minzoku*, pp. 135–36. See also Kitagawa, "Ainu Bear Festival," *History of Religions*, I (No. 1, 1961), 111. At any rate, the subjugation of the northern borders was a consistent policy of the government during the Nara and Heian periods. It involved a considerable expenditure difficult to manage, since the national budget of the early Heian period had dwindled as a result of the construction of the capital and the increase of tax-exempt manors. In 788 Ki-no-Kosami was appointed "General of the East" (*seitō taishi*), but he turned out to be incompetent. In 791 Sakanouye-no-Tamuramaro was made deputy commander of the imperial forces. He was later given the title of Barbarian-subduing Generalissimo (*Sei-i Tai-shōgun*). This title was later appropriated by the rulers of the feudal regime. See Takahashi, *Sakanouye-no-Tamuramaro.*

Heizei (r. 806–9), became involved with Lady Kusuriko, who persuaded the emperor to banish Prince Iyo under suspicion of rebellion.[4] When Heizei abdicated the throne to his brother, Saga (r. 806–24), Kusuriko plotted to overthrow the new emperor to bring back Heizei. The ex-emperor's party made Nara their headquarters, and some of the local chieftains, including Abe-no-Kiyotsugu, supported him. The emperor's party, however, outsmarted and defeated Heizei, whereupon Kusuriko committed suicide. Heizei was persuaded to devote the rest of his life to Buddhism.[5] The Emperor Saga chose Kachiko of the Tachibana family as his consort; and his children were given the surname Minamoto-no-Ason. From this time onward, the families of Tachibana and Minamoto played important roles in the life of the court.

Most important and powerful among all the Heian nobility, however, was the Fujiwara clan, which intermarried frequently with the imperial family.[6] The Fujiwaras, moreover, possessed

[4] Kusuriko was the daughter of Fujiwara Tanetsugu, who had been Kammu's confidant. Though it was Kusuriko's own daughter who was the Emperor Heizei's concubine, Kusuriko herself charmed the emperor. She thus exercised political power through the emperor himself and her own brother, Fujiwara Nakanari. The unfortunate Prince Iyo and his mother were imprisoned in Kawara Temple, where they committed suicide. Prince Iyo's tutor, Ato Ōtari, happened to be the uncle of Kūkai, better known as Kōbō Daishi; Ato Ōtari fled to Shikoku island.

[5] The emperor's party managed to persuade Sakanouye-no-Tamuramaro to stay on their side. The emperor also secured the support of Kōbō Daishi, who held a Shingon votive service for "the prolongation of the throne and the safety of the nation" (*hōso chōkyū, kokudo an-on*). The ex-Emperor Heizei's son, the Crown Prince Takaoka, became Kōbō Daishi's disciple and later attempted to visit India, but died on his way.

[6] Nakatomi Kamatari, the chief architect of the Taika reform, was given the new family name of Fujiwara. His son, Fubito, the chief architect of the Taihō Code, had four sons who established the four Fujiwara families—Nanke (the Southern Fujiwara family), Hokke (the Northern Fujiwara family), Shikike (the Shiki Fujiwara family), and Kyōke (the Kyō Fujiwara family). Fubito's daughter, Miyako, was the consort of the Emperor Mommu and mother of the Emperor Shōmu. Fubito's other daughter, Kōmyō, became the consort of Shōmu and mother of the Empress Kōken. Fubito's sons, however, died before they could exert political influence. The power was in the hands of the Tachibana clan, and for a

great wealth and influence in the provinces, derived primarily from their estates; as Sansom points out, "their domains grew because they could afford protection to small landowning families who would 'commend' their fields to Fujiwara manorial lords." [7] When the Emperor Seiwa ascended the throne in 858 at the age of nine, his maternal grandfather, Fujiwara Yoshifusa, became the *sesshō* (a form of regent), the first man of nonroyal blood ever to hold such a dominant position. When Seiwa abdicated in 876 to the Emperor Yōzei, who also was nine years of age at the time of accession, Yoshifusa's adopted son, Fujiwara Mototsune, was appointed regent.[8] It was Mototsune who was given the official title of both *sesshō* and *kampaku,* a combination which implied that he was to serve as permanent regent, regardless of the age of the emperor. After the death of Mototsune, it looked as though the throne, with the assistance of Sugawara Michizane and able members of other noble families, could resist the influence of the Fujiwara family. However, the latter was so powerful and shrewd that its rivals were systematically ousted from the court after the turn of the tenth century. In 930 Fujiwara Tadahira became the regent. In fact, the political destiny of Japan was completely in the hands of the Fujiwara oligarchy during the

---

time in the hands of the priest, Dōkyō. After Dōkyō was banished through the combined efforts of the Shikike and the Hokke of the Fujiwara clan, the Emperor Kōnin ascended the throne. Kōnin's son, the Emperor Kammu, married Otomuro, a Fujiwara, and they begot the emperors Heizei and Saga. Kammu had another consort, Tabiko, also one of the Fujiwara, by whom he had another son, the Emperor Junna (r. 823–33). Fujiwara Fuyutsugu, the "Minister of the Left" under the Emperor Junna, married off his daughter Junko to the Emperor Nimmyō (r. 833–50); Junko's son became the Emperor Montoku (r. 850–58). Besides, Fuyutsugu's son, Yoshifusa, married Minamoto-no-Kiyohime, daughter of the Emperor Saga. Yoshifusa's daughter, Akira-keiko, became the consort of Montoku and mother of the Emperor Seiwa (r. 858–76). See Fujiki, *Heian jidai no kizoku no seikatsu,* pp. 31–34.

[7] Sansom, *A History of Japan to 1334,* p. 139. See also Fujiki, *Heian jidai no kizoku no seikatsu,* pp. 56–70.

[8] Mototsune did not get along with the child emperor and refused to go to the court. Therefore, government officials had to go to his residence (*mandokoro*) to secure his decisions on political affairs.

tenth century and much of the eleventh, even though the Fujiwara clan suffered from internal disunity every now and again.

By far the most colorful and successful among all the Fujiwara
dictators was Michinaga (966–1027). He was blessed with influential family contacts and had many eligible daughters who
were married off to would-be emperors at crucial moments. He
was merciless in eliminating his rivals, including his own nephew,
Fujiwara Korechika, from court circles. With the help of his
sister, Senshi, who was the mother of the Emperor Ichijō (r.
986–1011), Michinaga climbed quickly to the position of *nairan,*
the deputy of the throne in examining all official documents regarding affairs of state. His own daughter, Shōshi (Akiko), consort of the Emperor Ichijō, bore a son, who later became the
Emperor Go-Ichijō. Michinaga retired from the regency in 1017.
Although he took priestly vows two years later, he remained the
most powerful man in the kingdom until his death. His son,
Yorimichi, served as dictator (*kampaku*) during the reigns of
the emperors Go-Ichijō (r. 1016–36), Go-Suzaku (r. 1036–45),
and Go-Reizei (r. 1045–68). Under Michinaga and Yorimichi,
the Fujiwara clan enjoyed unrivaled prestige, wealth, and power,
far surpassing that of the imperial family. After the retirement of
Yorimichi in 1068, however, the influence of the Fujiwara oligarchy steadily declined; even though important positions were
usually filled by the members of the Fujiwara family for another
century or so, they had less real power in controlling important
affairs of state.[9]

The excessive use of dictatorial power by the Fujiwara regents
resulted in frustration and dissatisfaction on the part of emperors
and court nobles who were suppressed by the Fujiwara oligarchy.
Inevitably, their dissatisfaction had to erupt. The eruption took
shape in the form of the *inzei* or "rule by retired monarchs."[10] It

----

[9] Kawasaki, *Kizoku bunka no seijuku* (ZNR 3), pp. 85–106.

[10] The term *in* simply means a house or living quarters. In this case, it is
an abbreviation of *go-in* which literally means "living quarters in the
rear of the imperial residence." When the head of a family retired from
active household duties, he was often given living quarters (*in-kyo*) behind
the main quarters within the family compound. Similarly, when the em-

may be recalled that the power of the Fujiwara regents derived from the fact that they were the relatives on the maternal side of the nominally reigning emperors. Even Michinaga, at the height of his power, would say, "Great as are our power and prestige, nevertheless they are those of the Sovereign, for we derive them from the majesty of the Throne." [11] The *inzei,* on the other hand, operated on the patriarchal principle that, even though an emperor might turn over the "charisma of the imperial office" to his son or brother, an abdicated emperor still controlled the affairs of the court as the legitimate chieftain of the patriarchal imperial clan (*uji*).

The architect of the *inzei* system was the Emperor Go-Sanjō, whose mother, Teishi, was not a Fujiwara woman but the daughter of the late Emperor Sanjō. When Go-Sanjō was enthroned in 1069 he did not, therefore, have to depend on a Fujiwara regent as had been the case with his predecessors. By chance, the daughters and granddaughters of Fujiwara Yorimichi, who was then in power, failed, much to the relief of the emperor, to bear male children to the royal princes to whom they were married. Go-Sanjō abdicated in 1072 with the intention of controlling the affairs of the nation from behind the throne, but he was soon taken ill and died.[12] The actual rule of the *inzei,* in the full sense, began when the Emperor Shirakawa (r. 1072–86), after abdication, continued to rule the nation during the reigns of

---

peror abdicated, he was offered special quarters (*go-in*) within the palace compound. Incidentally, an abdicated emperor was given the title, *dajō-tennō* or *jō-kō; should such a person take priestly vows, he was called *hō-kō* or *hō-ō* which meant "abdicated monarch in priestly clothes." Naturally, abdicated monarchs needed money. Thus, when the Emperor Reizei abdicated in 969, he was given a piece of land in the province of Musashi. This was the beginning of the so-called *go-in-ryō* (property for the support of the retired emperor's residence). Initially, the *go-in* was simply a living space, staffed with a small number of servants and attendants. Later, when the retired monarchs became *de facto* rulers, they established the *go-in-chō* (court or administrative offices within the rear palace), well staffed with court officials (*in-shi*). See Yoshimura, *Inzei,* pp. 2–7.

[11] Quoted in Sansom, *A History of Japan to 1334,* p. 157.

[12] Scholarly opinions vary widely regarding the intention of Go-Sanjō. See Yoshimura, *Inzei,* pp. 42–74.

Horikawa, Toba, and Sutoku. When Shirakawa died in 1129 he
was followed by Toba (r. 1107–26), who continued *inzei* rule
until his death in 1156, while the titular emperors Sutoku,
Konoye, and Go-Shirakawa ascended to the throne successively.
The last powerful *inzei* ruler was Go-Shirakawa (r. 1156–59),
who ruled the nation for over thirty years until he died in 1192,
dominating the national scene during the nominal reigns of the
emperors Nijō, Rokujō, Takakura, Antoku, and Go-Toba.[13] The
situation became very complex as two abdicated emperors often
remained alive simultaneously, for instance, Shirakawa and Toba,
Toba and Sutoku, and Sutoku and Go-Shirakawa.[14] For the most
part, the *inzei* era was characterized by an ugly power struggle
among competing ex-emperors or between the ex-emperor and the
titular emperor, abuse of authority by ex-emperors in power and
their subordinates, extreme nepotism, administrative inefficiency,
and indifference to human decency and morality.[15] Moreover, the
fact that three ex-emperors took priestly vows resulted in the involvement of the *inzei* in the expanding area of ecclesiastical
politics.

Politics during the eleventh and twelfth centuries centered
around the imperial and the Fujiwara and other aristocratic families in Kyoto. Meanwhile, a new factor appeared on the horizon,
an increase in prominence of the warrior class in the provinces
away from the capital. The emergence of the warrior class can be
traced back to the turn of the tenth century when large manors

[13] Go-Toba (r. 1184–98) also claimed the *inzei* until he died in 1239.
However, the real political power had shifted by that time from the palace
of the abdicated emperor to the court of the feudal government.

[14] In the thirteenth century there was a time when three ex-emperors—
Go-Toba, Tsuchimikado, and Juntoku—lived simultaneously. The most
extreme case was that in which five ex-emperors—Go-Fukakusa, Kameyama,
Go-Uda, Fushimi, and Go-Fushimi—overlapped. The abdicated emperors
after the time of Go-Shirakawa, however, had no real power to rule the
nation.

[15] For example, it is widely believed that the Emperor Sutoku was
fathered by ex-Emperor Shirakawa, even though officially he is listed as
the son of the Emperor Toba and his consort, Fujiwara Akiko, and as the
grandson of Shirakawa. See Kawasaki, *Kizoku bunka no seijuku* (ZNR 3),
p. 140.

(*shōen*) in the countryside had to be defended by private warriors who were in the service of provincial lords. The gradual decline of central authority encouraged the rise of the warriors, who accumulated their own prestige, power, and wealth. Some of the warrior families, such as the Taira and the Minamoto, served the court of the Fujiwara clan in the capital. Others, like the Abe and the Fujiwara (no relation to the Fujiwara clan of Kyoto) in the northeastern provinces, became in effect autonomous rulers of their territories.[16]

The year 1156 marked a turning point in the history of the Heian period. There were three important figures who for different reasons formed an alliance—the ex-Emperor Sutoku, who wanted to eliminate the power of the Emperor Go-Shirakawa; Fujiwara Yorinaga, who not only competed with his own brother Tadamichi, then holding the position of *kampaku,* but also tried to restore the past glory of the Fujiwara oligarchy; and Minamoto Tameyoshi, who considered the rising Taira family to be the archenemy. On the other side, the emperor, supported by Taira Kiyomori and some members of the Minamoto warrior clan, put down the insurrection, called the *Hogen no ran.* Three years later, rivalry between the Taira and Minamoto clans caused another insurrection, the *Heiji no ran,* resulting in the phenomenal rise of the Taira clan at the expense of the Minamoto. It also precipitated the end of the influence of the Fujiwara clan and the emergence of a new social order under the dominance of the warrior class. The story of the rival warrior clans, the Taira (or Heike) and the Minamoto (or Genji), provides us with a series of colorful events "dictated not by the mind but by the passions of jealousy, anger, pride, rapacity, and cruelty." [17]

Culture and Religion

The transfer of the capital from Nara to Kyoto toward the end of the eighth century marked also the beginning of a new phase in the development of Japanese culture and religion. During the

[16] See Takahashi, *Ōshū Fujiwara-shi yondai.*
[17] Sansom, *A History of Japan to 1334,* p. 256.

Nara period the elite classes were too busy importing culture, art, and learning from China to develop their own fully. Those were the days when the talented son of a minor official, such as Kibi-no-Makibi (695–775), who spent nineteen years of study in China, could be elevated to the lofty position of "Minister of the Right," in recognition of his contribution to the introduction of Chinese art and learning, including astronomy, mathematics, jurisprudence, music, and calligraphy, into Japan.[18] The orthodox Buddhist schools of the Nara period, likewise, were nothing more than direct transplantations of Chinese Buddhist schools into Japan.

The picture was quite different in the Heian period. During the early Heian period cultural and religious influences continued to flow in from China, but they were quickly indigenized. The Heian period for its part produced, in addition to poetry and prose by Japanese in the Chinese language, a wide variety of Japanese-language poetry, novels, diaries, essays, historical literature, and moralistic novels.[19] No doubt, the invention of the

[18] See Toshihiko Miyata, *Kibi-no-Makibi*. Incidentally, one of his fellow Japanese students, Abe-no-Nakamaro, who was well versed in Chinese learning, remained in China for the rest of his life, serving as a government official in the court of the T'ang dynasty.

[19] Notable among Chinese writings by Japanese during the Heian period are the *Ryōun-shū* (A collection of poems in Chinese) and the *Honchō monzui* (Chinese prose by Japanese). Two important collections of Japanese poems are the *Kokin-shū* (Anthology of poems, ancient and modern) and the *Kinyō-wakashu* (A collection of golden leaves). Among the well-known novels of the Heian period are the *Ise monogatari* (Tales of Ise), the *Taketori monogatari* (Tale of the old bamboo-cutter), and, best of all, the *Genji monogatari*, by Lady Murasaki, which has been translated by Arthur Waley as *The Tale of Genji*. One of the late pieces of Heian literature, the *Tsutsumi Chūnagon monogatari*, has been translated jointly by Joseph K. Yamagiwa and Edwin O. Reischauer. See *Translations from Early Japanese Literature* by Reischauer and Yamagiwa, pp. 139–267. Among the well-known diaries of the Heian period are the *Tosa nikki* (The diary of Tosa), the *Murasaki-shikibu nikki* (Diaries of Lady Murasaki), and the *Izumi-shikibu nikki* (Diaries of Lady Izumi). See Imai, *Heian-jidai nikki bungaku no kenkyū*. The best essay of this period was the *Makura-no-sōshi* (The pillow book) by Lady Seishōnagon. Among historical writings, the *Eiga monogatari* (Tales of power and glory) has a pro-Fujiwara slant,

hirakana—a form of Japanese alphabet, created by abbreviating Chinese characters selected to stand for Japanese sounds—facilitated literary creation, even though the Chinese language continued to be used for important religious and secular instruction and writing. In art and architecture the Heian period also achieved unprecedented richness, elaboration, and delicacy, as exemplified by the *yamato-e* (a form of scroll painting), simple but elegant urban gardens, and such architectural monuments as the Shinto shrine at Itsukushima, commonly referred to as Miyajima or "Shrine Island," and the Hō-ō-dō (Phoenix Hall) of the Byōdōin Temple at Uji.

From the sociological point of view, the line of demarcation between the upper and lower strata that characterized society during the Nara period continued to exist in the Heian period. The aristocrats and clergy were the two main "bearers of culture," even though they did not always see eye to eye on specific issues. The Heian aristocracy was determined by four factors: (1) lineage, (2) court rank, (3) economic power, and (4) learning. While there was constant rivalry among them, the aristocrats all cooperated to maintain their privileged status. Thus, in 815 the *Shinsen shōjiroku* (The new compilations of the register of families) was drawn up "to sift the gold from the pebbles," in the words of the preface to this social register. It seems that the aristocrats had come to resent the fact that some commoners pretended to be scions of the ancient nobility. As to the court ranks, despite the intentions of the earlier reformers to confer them upon men according to their merit and ability, in actuality only the descendants of influential aristocratic families were eligible for consideration, so that lineage and court ranks complemented

---

while the *Ō-kagami* (The great mirror) takes a more critical view. Incidentally, "The Section on Michinaga and the Stories of the Fujiwara Clan" of the *Ō-kagami* is included in Reischauer and Yamagiwa, *Translations from Early Japanese Literature*, pp. 271–374. By far the most important source for the understanding of the religious ethos of the Heian period is the *Konjaku monogatari* (Tales of long ago). Most of these works are cited in Kokusai bunka shinkōkai, ed., *Introduction to Classic Japanese Literature*. Those who read Japanese are advised to consult Igarashi, *Heian-chō bungaku-shi*, 2 vols., and Suzuki, *Heian-makki monogatari no kenkyū*.

each other. Those who had court rank, moreover, were entitled
to various kinds of economic privilege. They received lands, silk,
cotton, horses, carriages, and servants according to their grades.
They were also exempted from certain taxes, and their penalties
for crime were lighter. Furthermore, children of men of higher
rank upon reaching the age of twenty-one were exempted from
national examinations and given appropriate ranks.[20] The land
laws, which had attempted to make the government the sole authority in allotting lands to each household, collapsed in the
eighth century; the result was the phenomenal growth during the
Heian period of manors (*shōen*) owned by aristocratic families
and religious institutions. As far as education was concerned, it
was regarded primarily as a means for qualifying for government
service on the part of aristocratic families. In addition to the
daigaku (academies) supported by the government, some of the
influential families established their own schools, for example, the
Bunshō-in was set up by the Sugawara family, the Kangaku-in
by the Fujiwara family, the Gakkan-in by the Tachibana family,
the Shōgaku-in by the Ariwara family, and the Kōbun-in by the
Wake family.

Ironically, the Heian period, introduced by a protest against
the "ecclesiastification" of culture in Nara, quickly developed its
own form of extreme clericalism.[21] The clergy were the only
class of men who had as much standing as the aristocrats in terms
of court rank, economic power, and learning, without necessarily
having the same high family background. In principle, the clergy
were men of religious faith and training, and their prestige was
not derived from the historic causality of lineage. But the situation
during the Heian period made the priesthood the only available
channel of upward social mobility, so that many men "entered
temples not in search for the truth but in quest for worldly riches
and privileges." [22] Actually, religious institutions became more
and more influential as they acquired status as great landowners.
One factor in this development can be traced to the ancient Shinto

[20] See Fujiki, *Heian jidai no kizoku no seikatsu*, pp. 10–27.
[21] See Hori, *Nihon Bukkyō-shi-ron*, pp. 322–47.
[22] Nakamura, *The Ways of Thinking of Eastern Peoples*, p. 453.

idea of keeping sickness and death from sacred places. Toward the end of the seventh century the government urged Buddhist temples to secure private living quarters outside the temple compounds for the housing of sick and aged priests and nuns. Gradually this became the common pattern, and those priests who had private means made it a habit to keep private residences from which they commuted daily to their temples. In the course of time it became difficult to draw a line between what belonged to the temples and what belonged to these private residences. The private quarters of the priests became known as *inke* or *monzeki*. Many aristocratic families donated quarters to the clergy as well as land to temples in order to maintain *de facto* control over properties ostensibly set aside for pious purposes.[23] In other words, the aristocracy and the clergy needed each other for their mutual benefit, and they supported each other.

Heian society accepted indiscriminately the religious practices of Shinto, the Yin-yang system, Confucianism, and Buddhism—although Buddhism was by far the most influential among them. In the main, the Confucian tradition was regarded as the norm of education. Shinto developed elaborate services for ancestors. Some of the shrines were dedicated to the ancestors of Korean and Chinese immigrant families.[24] Many Chinese magico-religious practices infiltrated Japan, such as the sacrifice of oxen, the worship of Heaven, and the veneration of the Pole Star. The government issued an edict in 807, for instance, forbidding sorcerers, diviners, and priests to seduce the superstitious masses, but the government was powerless to control the abuse of religious rites by practitioners of Onmyōdō (the Yin-yang and Taoistic magic) and other occult systems. In fact, some of these practitioners were called upon even by the court in time of pestilence, or to aid in the selection of the heir apparent.

The two most significant religious movements during the early

[23] Tamamuro, "Nihon Bukkyō-shi gaisetsu," pp. 30–31.

[24] For example, the Taiheki shrine at Uzumasa, Kyoto, and the Keiman shrine at Ashiwara were dedicated to the ancestors of the Hata family (Chinese), while the Shirahige shrine in Musashi was dedicated to a Korean pioneer.

Heian period were the Tendai school, systematized by Dengyō
Daishi, and the Shingon school formulated by Kōbō Daishi. Both
stressed the monastic discipline, "esoteric" (*mikkyō*) cults, and
alliance with Shinto, and both considered it their primary duty
to support the throne and the government. Shortly after the time
of Dengyō Daishi and Kōbō Daishi, however, both schools de-
generated into magico-religious cults, offering appropriate rituals
for all conceivable occasions. Both the Tendai monastery at Mt.
Hiei and the Shingon monastery at Mt. Kōya kept mercenaries
who fought ruthlessly for the advantage of their masters, and
the clergy of these organizations competed with aristocrats for
extralegal benefits and secular power. A famous passage from the
Shin-sarugaku-ki portrays a typical cleric of the Heian period:
"Gorō is a scholar and great high priest of the Tendai sect. He
is a great master in Indian logic and Buddhist philosophy. . . .
No clerical position, high or low, is good enough for him. *He
aspires only to be chief abbot of the Tendai order."* [25] Related to
this development was the order of mountain ascetics (*shugen-dō*),
heirs of the shamanistic Buddhism of the Nara period. During
the Heian period these mountain ascetics became allies of the
Tendai and Shingon schools and came to be known as the Tendai
Shugen-dō and the Shingon Shugen-dō respectively.

Under the influence of the Tendai and the Shingon schools,
Shinto and Buddhism developed a unique pattern of coexistence,
known as the Ryōbu-Shinto in the Shingon tradition or Sannō-
Ichijitsu-Shinto in the Tendai tradition. Accordingly, Shinto
kami were robbed of their distinctiveness and were now interpreted to be manifestations of Buddhas and bodhisattvas in Japanese form.

Around the middle of the Heian period the Amida (Amitabha)
cult came into vogue. Faith in the mercy of Amida had not been
unknown to Buddhists both in China and Japan before that time.
What was unique in the Heian period was that pleasure-loving
aristocrats invoked the holy name of Amida not for deliverance
from the chain of existences but for the prolongation of luxury,

[25] Quoted in Nakamura, *The Ways of Thinking of Eastern Peoples*,
p. 453. (My italics.)

pomp, and comfort into the next world. On the other hand, the oppressed and the downtrodden, having little comfort in this life, did not wish to have similar experiences in the life to come. The only thing they could hope for was that Jizō (Bodhisattva Ksitigarbha) would relieve them of suffering in hell-fire.

In short, one way to understand the religious situation during the Heian period is to study the types of religious affirmations that developed and the types of divinities that were venerated during this period.

Esoteric Buddhism (Mikkyō)

In the early Heian period new religious attitudes and teachings were demanded. Two prominent men appeared to contribute to their formation—each in his own way. They were men of different types, but common to both were the aims of establishing a united center for Japanese Buddhism and a policy of securing support from the aristocracy formulating national policy. They attempted to derive their knowledge of Buddhist teaching from China directly rather than by accepting what was known in the established Buddhist schools of the Nara period. Both of them erected headquarters on sacred mountains and emphasized learning, monastic disciplines, esoteric cults, and mysteries. They were Saicho and Kūkai, better known by their posthumous names, Dengyō Daishi and Kōbō Daishi; their teachings and organizations were to dominate the religious and social life of the coming centuries. They dreamed of a grand union of religion and state, and they were concerned with all phases of national life. Their religious convictions made it possible for them to transcend their immediate surroundings, yet they were both children of their age. They were both caught in the intertwining of the fortune and fate of the aristocracy and the clergy.

DENGYŌ DAISHI AND THE TENDAI SCHOOL: Dengyō Daishi or Saicho (766–822) was the descendant of a Chinese immigrant family.[26] Although early in his life he was trained in the Sanron

---

[26] On the life of Dengyō Daishi, see Yamamoto, *Dengyō Daishi*.

(Mādhyamika), Hossō (Yogācāra), and Kegon (Avatamsaka) doctrines, and was ordained in the *kaidan* (ordination hall) of Tōdaiji at Nara when he was nineteen years old, he left the old capital to become a hermit at Mt. Hiei near his home. There he came across the writings of Chih-i, the formulator of the Chinese school of T'ien-t'ai. Slowly a group of seekers gathered around him, and he was invited to the court of the Emperor Kammu shortly after the new capital was established in Kyoto. His monastery at Mt. Hiei was called the "chief seat of religion for ensuring the safety of the nation" (*chingo kokka no dōjō*). Early in the ninth century Saicho was sent to China, where he received the bodhisattva ordination from Tao-sui, the mystical Mantra (*Mikkyō*) doctrines from Shun-chiao, and the secret of Zen meditation from Hsiu-jan. He was also trained there in the Vinaya (*Ritsu*). He returned to Japan in 805, and attempted to systematize the Tendai school, incorporating (1) moral precepts, (2) monastic disciplines, (3) esoteric cults, and (4) Zen (Ch'an) practices within the framework of the *Lotus Sutra*. He followed the main tenets of Chih-i (531–97), who had classified the Buddhist scriptures according to the five periods of Sākyamuni's life. Chih-i approved the cult of Amida, and is said to have died invoking the holy name of Amida. Saicho was attracted by the T'ien-t'ai (Tendai) system which found meaning and value in the world of appearance and also taught that Buddhahood was accessible not only to a select few but to every creature.[27]

[27] In a sense, the T'ien-t'ai or Tendai system restored an "absolute" to Buddhist metaphysics by recognizing the "absolute nature of Buddha" (*Buddha-Tathatā*) in all beings. Also, this system identified causal origination (*pratītya-samutpāda*), void (*sūnyatā*), and the Middle Path. The nature of dharma is both void and relative. Material existence is not different from void. Nonexistence and temporary existence are simply contrasts, and the middle between them is identical with both. Based on this understanding of dharma, the Tendai philosophy concludes that the worldly state is permanent. See Takakusu, *The Essentials of Buddhist Philosophy*, pp. 126–41; Shimaji, *Tendai kyōgaku-shi*; Ishizu, *Tendai jissō-ron no kenkyū*; Sekiguchi, "Tendai shikan no seiritsu to sono tenkai," in Miyamoto, ed., *Bukkyō no kompon shinri*, pp. 841–70; and Ui, "A Study of Japanese Tendai Buddhism" in Japanese National Commission for UNESCO, comp., *Philosophical Studies of Japan*, I, 33–74.

Saicho was warmly supported by the court at first, but after the death in 806 of the Emperor Kammu, who had been Saicho's patron, his younger contemporary, Kūkai, became more popular in the circle of the court. Saicho sought Kūkai's cooperation, but for personal and doctrinal reasons their friendship did not endure.[28] Thereafter, Saicho singlehandedly fought for his two aims. One was the defeat of the Hossō doctrine, the standard philosophical system during the Nara period.[29] The other was the establishment of the independent Tendai ordination. Respecting this, his request to the court for official recognition of the Tendai ordination was not granted until after his death. During his lifetime he took a conciliatory attitude toward Shinto, as evidenced by his veneration of *Sannō* (the King of the Mountain), the Shinto kami of Mt. Hiei.[30] Following his example, subsequent followers of Tendai developed the theory of the *Sannō Ichijitsu Shinto* that aimed at a doctrinal synthesis of Shinto and Buddhism.

After Saicho's time, the Tendai school produced a number of able leaders, such as Ennin (794–864), Enchin (814–91), Ryōgen (912–85), Jakushō (952–1034), Jōjin (1011–81), Chōgo (1049–1133), and Chūjin (1065–1138).[31] Among them, Ennin was credited with the systematization of "Tendai Esotericism" (Taimitsu) and with the transmission of the "cult of *nembutsu*" (invocation of Buddha's name) from China.[32] En-

[28] The Tendai was eclectic enough to agree with the Shingon on many points of doctrinal interpretation. Thus, while holding the *Lotus Sutra* and the person of Sākyamuni in the utmost reverence, it did not hesitate to recognize Mahāvairocana ("the Great Sun Buddha" of the Shingon) as representing the Dharmakāya. Shingon too was tolerant and comprehensive, but ultimately it considered itself alone to be the true esoteric system.

[29] The Hossō emphasized hierarchical degrees of spiritual attainment in both theory and practice; and the result was an aristocratic religion, as evidenced by the Hossō school in the Nara period. Saicho, who advocated the universality of salvation, was attacked by many learned priests, notably by a Hossō priest, Tokuichi. Saicho wrote the *Hokke-shūku* (Book to explain the superiority of the Lotus) in defense of the Tendai doctrine.

[30] Katsuno, *Hiei-san to Kōya-san*, pp. 1–17.

[31] See Tamamuro, "Nihon Bukkyō-shi gaisetsu," pp. 46–49.

[32] On Ennin, see E. O. Reischauer, *Ennin's Travels in T'ang China*,

chin, the nephew of the founder of the Japanese Shingon school, Kūkai, was also an advocate of "Tendai esotericism." In contrast to the Sanmon sect which incorporated the tradition of Ennin, Enchin's tradition became known as the Jimon sect of the Tendai school, with semi-independent headquarters at Mii temple on the shore of Lake Biwa. Thus, not long after the death of Saicho, the Tendai school came to be known as *Mikkyō* (esoteric Buddhism) side by side with the Shingon school. In the tenth century violent disputes over appointment to the abbotship of the Tendai monastery broke out between the Sanmon and Jimon sects; by the eleventh century both factions depended on armed bands of priests (*sōhei* or "warrior priests") to fight against each other. These "warrior priests" had formerly been unordained mercenaries; later on, ordained priests also took arms, and their ruthless activities were feared by the government and the people alike.[33] Nevertheless, the Tendai monastery at Mt. Hiei continued to attract both pious and learned men throughout the Heian period.[34]

---

and his translation of Ennin, *Diary: The Record of a Pilgrimage to China in Search of the Law.* On Tendai esotericism (Taimitsu), see Kyōjun Shimizudani, *Tendai no mikkyō.*

[33] Usually in large temples there were two kinds of low ranking members —"student priests," who were trained for Buddhist learning, and "working priests," who were responsible for the maintenance of the establishment. These two were called *gakushō* and *dōshū* at the Tendai monastery of Mt. Hiei, *gakuryō* and *gyōnin* at the Shingon monastery at Mt. Kōya, and *gakuryō* and *dōshū* at Kōfuku temple at Nara. It was generally understood that only children of good families were "student priests" and that they alone were considered for higher ranks in the hierarchy. The "working priests" included various kinds of men who before entering the temples had had no religious interests; they often caused trouble for the "student priests." The so-called warrior priests developed from the "working priests," and were referred to, for example, as *yama-hōshi* (warrior priests from the mountain, i.e., Mt. Hiei) and *Nara-hōshi* (warrior priests from Nara, i.e., Kōfuku temple at Nara), respectively. *Yama-hōshi* usually carried the "portable shrine" of the Hiye-Sannō shrine of Mt. Hiei, while *Nara-hōshi* carried with them the divine tree (*shinboku*) of the Kasuga shrine, the clan (*uji*) shrine of the Fujiwara. In so doing, they could threaten the court and the Fujiwara family with divine punishments. See Takanobu Katsuno, *Sōhei*, pp. 1–10.

[34] Moreover, many of the Buddhist leaders in the subsequent period, in-

KŌBŌ DAISHI AND THE SHINGON SCHOOL: Kōbō Daishi or Kūkai (773–835) was originally trained for government service. While in the academy (*daigaku*) he experienced a change of heart and left the capital. Whether he spent long years in austere mental and physical training in the tradition of the shamanistic Buddhists cannot be verified, despite many legends that point in that direction. In his work, the *Sangō-Shiiki* (A treatise on three teachings) written in 797, Kūkai attempted to harmonize Taoism and Confucianism with Buddhism.[35] Somewhere along the line, he came across the Great Sun Sutra (*Mahāvairocana Sutra*), which led him to become a follower of esoteric Buddhism.[36] While in China, 804–6, he studied under Hui-kuo, who was the direct disciple of the famous esoteric Buddhist master, Amoghavajra.[37] Upon his return to Japan, Kūkai represented the Shingon (Chen-yen in Chinese) doctrine in such a way that the established schools at Nara did not react so strongly against him as they had against Saicho. Kūkai was often invited to court, and was given a seat in the Tōdai temple, Nara. He also attempted to conciliate Saicho for the time being. He and the Emperor Saga, moreover, were re-

---

cluding Genkū (d. 1212) of the Pure Land school, Shinran (d. 1262) of the True Pure Land school, Chishin (d. 1289) of the Ji sect, Ryōnin (d. 1132) of the Yūzū-Nembutsu sect, Eisai (d. 1215) of the Rinzai Zen sect, Dōgen (d. 1252) of the Sōtō Zen sect, and Nichiren (d. 1282) of the Nichiren school, had all studied at Mt. Hiei.

[35] See Takarada, *Sangōshiiki kanchū;* and Kanshō Mori, *Sangōshiiki kōgi.*

[36] See Tajima, *Etude sur le Mahāvairocana-Sūtra.*

[37] Kūkai also learned Sanskrit from an Indian monk, Prajna, who is said to have worked with the Nestorian priest, Adam. See Takakusu, tr., *I-Tsing, A Record of the Buddhist Religion as Practiced in India and the Malay Archipelago,* p. 224. Kūkai is credited with the introduction into Japan of the slightly altered form of the Devanagari letters called *Shittan,* which are written in vertical columns and are much used in Shingon books. But the fact that Kūkai had studied under Prajna cannot be taken to mean that Kūkai came in contact with Syrian Christianity, as has been asserted by several scholars. At the same time, the lack of concrete evidence must not close our eyes to the possible influence Kūkai could have received from such a syncretistic sect as the *Chin-tan-chiao* (Golden Pill Sect) which has certain affinities with the Shingon school. See Reichelt, *Religion in Chinese Garments,* pp. 169–70.

ported to have received Shinto *abhiseka*, a form of initiation.[38] In light of this it is not surprising that the Emperor Saga, who was well known for his interest in literature and calligraphy, became a patron of Kūkai, who was also gifted in the arts and literature. As a mark of his recognition of Kūkai's school, the emperor received the Shingon initiation rite from Kūkai himself. Kūkai established his monastic center at Mt. Kōya, and the Tōji (eastern temple) of Kyoto was also handed over to him, under the title *Kyō-ō-gokoku-no-tera,* or "temple for the protection of the nation." Kūkai offered various rites at the request of the court, and was well repaid with honor and prestige. Besides promoting the arts and learning generally, he established the *Shugei-shuchi-in,* a school that offered both religious and secular education.[39] After the death of Saicho in 822 Kūkai undoubtedly became the dominant religious figure in Japan, while Shingon became, to all intents and purposes, a national religion. Kūkai left many important writings, including the *Jūjūshinron* (The ten stages of religious consciousness), and *Sokushin-jōbutsugi* (The doctrine of becoming a buddha with one's body during one's earthly existence).

The Shingon school considers the Great Sun Buddha (Mahāvairocana) to be the central deity and metaphysical principle. According to its teaching, all the doctrines of Sākyamuni, a manifested Buddha, were temporal, the absolute truth being delivered only by the Dharmakāya (Truth body), Mahāvairocana, through the three secrets, "the body, speech, and thought" of Buddha. In order to "become Buddha in this very body," one has

---

[38] This was a form of initiation rite unknown in earlier Shinto but adopted by Ōnakatomi-no-Kiyomaro. It became a popular rite in the Miwa school of Shinto. On this occasion, Kūkai is said to have written a poem:

> Among various ways to become a Buddha
> The most potent way is
> Kami-no-michi [the way of the kami].

See Matsumoto, *Kōbo Shinran Nichiren,* p. 161.

[39] Kōyasan-daigaku Mikkyō-kenkyūkai, ed., *Kōbō Daishi no risō to geijutsu.*

to depend on *mudrās* (devotional gestures made with the hands and fingers), *dhāranī* (mystical verse), and *yoga* (concentration).[40] The Shingon school, with its use of rich symbols, rituals, *mandalas* (diagrammatic pictures of the universe), and iconography, met the spiritual needs of people of all walks of life. Besides, Shingon, known as the *Tōmitsu* (eastern esotericism) in contrast to the *Taimitsu* of the Tendai school, provided a philosophical basis for the pattern of coexistence between Buddhism and Shinto called *Ryōbu Shinto*.

The great ecclesiastical structure created by Kūkai was, however, destined to develop internal tensions, as between Tōji (The eastern temple) of Kyoto and the monastery in Mt. Kōya, as well as among the various subsects which mushroomed.[41] Some of the outstanding Shingon priests during the Heian period were Kanchō (d. 998), founder of the Hirosawa sect of Shingon; Ninkai (d. 1046), founder of the Ono sect of Shingon; Kanjō (d. 1125), who was highly respected by the court, and Kakuban (d. 1143), founder of the Shingi-Shingon sect. During the tenth century Tōji prospered at the expense of Mt. Kōya. It was Fujiwara Michinaga, the most powerful dictator of the eleventh century, who by a personal visit initiated the restoration of the glory of Mt. Kōya. Ex-Emperors Shirakawa, Toba, and others also paid personal visits to this holy mountain.

For the most part, the two schools of esoteric Buddhism (*Mikkyō*)—the Tendai (*Taimitsu*) and the Shingon (*Tōmitsu*)—prospered through the support of the court and the aristocratic families, especially the Fujiwara. Sad to say, while there were no doubt sincere clergy, many of the *Mikkyō* priests were corrupt, specializing in offering *kaji-kitō* (magico-religious rites and prayers) for the healing of the sick, for exorcising ghosts, for safe delivery at childbirth, and for every conceivable personal advantage. The temple treasuries fattened as these ecclesiastical or-

---

[40] Tajima, *Les deux grands mandalas et la doctrine de l'ésotérisme Shingon*; Takagami, *Mikkyō gairon*; Kambayashi, *Kōbō Daishi no shisō to shūkyō*. See also Saunders, *Mudrā: A Study of Symbolic Gestures in Japanese Buddhist Sculpture*.

[41] Ui, *Nihon Bukkyō gaishi*, pp. 52–59.

ganizations developed *de facto* "states within the state" with lucrative manors.[42]

Transmutation of Shinto

The eclectic spirit of magico-religious culture plus the phenomenal development of the cults of esoteric Buddhism (*Mikkyō*)
did not leave Shinto untouched during the Heian period. While,
in the main, Buddhism was more influential than Shinto, the
latter continued to hold its own, as evidenced by the prosperity
of such shrines as Kamo, Matsuo, Hirano, Umemiya, Kasuga,
and Iwashimizu.[43] Throughout the Heian period, there were two
contradictory trends within Shinto. One might be characterized
as "nostalgia for the golden past," while the other grew from a
spirit of accommodation with new religious and cultural beliefs
and practices. The former was represented by *Semmyō* (imperial
edicts) contained in the *Shoku-Nihongi* (Chronicles of Japan
continued) compiled in 797.[44] One of the leading motifs of
Semmyō was *akaki-naoki-kokoro* (the bright and pure mind) or
akaki-kiyoki-naoki-makoto-no-kokoro (the bright, pure, upright,
and sincere mind) which was presented as the moral, political,
and judicial principle of the "Way of *kannagara*" (in accordance
with the kami). This resurgence of Shinto ideals was an understandable reaction against the Nara period during which national policies were greatly influenced by Buddhism. Self-con-
sciousness on the part of the Shinto priesthood of the early Heian
period was exemplified by Imbe-no-Hiromichi, who compiled a
work on history—as transmitted in the traditionally priestly family
of the Imbe—known as the *Kogoshūi* (Gleanings from ancient
accounts), in 807.[45]

With the compilation of the *Engishiki* (Rules and regulations

---

[42] Takekoshi, *Economic Aspects of the History of the Civilization of
Japan*, I, 84–91; and Hosokawa, *Jiryō shōen no kenkyū*.

[43] Miyaji, *Jingi-shi taikei*, pp. 44–70, and appendix, pp. 3–24.

[44] Herbert, *Semmyō, die Kaiserlichen Erlasse des Shoku-Nihongi*; Snellen,
tr., "Shoku-Nihongi: Chronicles of Japan Continued," *TASJ*, 2d series,
Vols. XI (1934) and XIV (1937).

[45] Katō and Hoshino, trs., *The Kogoshūi: Gleanings from Ancient Stories*.

collected during the Engi era) in 927, both the status of Shinto shrines and the system of Shinto priesthood were minutely regulated and institutionalized, not only in the capital city but in distant provinces as well.[46] In the eleventh century the government designated twenty-two important shrines—Ise, Iwashimizu, Kamo, Matsuo, Hirano, Inari, Kasuga, Ōharano, Ōmiwa, Isonokami, Yamato, Hirose, Tatsuta, Sumiyoshi, Hiye, Umemiya, Yoshida, Hirota, Gion, Niu, Kibune, and Kitano—as "specially privileged." They were to receive offerings from the court on their regular festivals. In each province various shrines were classified by rank according to their degree of importance, *ichi-no-miya* (shrines of first rank), *ni-no-miya* (shrines of second rank), and *san-no-miya* (shrines of third rank). Usually the provincial officials were held responsible for their maintenance. Some of the old shrines continued to be supported by specific aristocratic families, and a few wealthy shrines even kept mercenaries for protection. During the power struggle between the Minamoto and the Taira warrior clans, the mercenaries of the Kumano shrine supported the Minamoto, while those of the Usa shrine in Kyushu sided with the Taira.

Notwithstanding the external prosperity of the Shinto shrines, Shinto as such began to change noticeably from within. Even Imbe-no-Hiromichi, traditional Shintoist *par excellence,* appropriated Confucian notions into his interpretation of the meaning of Shinto rituals.[47] Many Shinto priests utilized Chinese geomancy, the Yin-yang system, and Taoistic ideas, and the kami were often referred to as *shinmei* or *myōjin,* words of unmistakably Chinese origin referring to gods.[48] By far the greatest influence was exerted on Shinto by Buddhism, especially by the two esoteric schools of

[46] During this period some of the shrines which had no fixed priesthood, such as Futara shrine near Nikkō, began to adopt the system of priesthood. The institutionalization of the Shinto priesthood implied that the *kannushi* (master of worship) became *gūji* (priest in charge of the shrine). Under the *gūji* served the *negi* (supplicating priest). For details, see Yanagita, *Minzokugaku Jiten,* pp. 124–26.

[47] Tsuda, *Nihon no Shinto,* pp. 39–40.

[48] *Ibid.,* pp. 49–57, for the etymological study of *shin-mei* and *myō-jin.*

Shingon and Tendai. As noted earlier, the trend toward the
alliance and coexistence of Shinto and Buddhism can be traced
to the Nara period. At first the kami were considered to be the
"protectors of Buddha's Law" (*gohō-shin*), and as such the kami
of the Usa Hachiman shrine in Kyushu had been invited to Nara
and enshrined within the compound of Tōdai temple, the national cathedral of Buddhism. Soon, however, this belief was
reversed so that the kami were considered to be in need of salvation through the help of the Buddha. Hence, Buddhist scriptures
were recited before the altar of the kami, and *jingū-ji* (Buddhist
chapels for Shinto shrines) were established. Some of the honored
kami also received the Buddhist title of *bosatsu* (bodhisattva).[49]
During the early Heian period, both Saicho of the Tendai school
and Kūkai of the Shingon school took a conciliatory attitude toward Shinto, although they did not articulate a theory equating
kami and the Buddha. The idea that the kami's original nature,
Honji, was nothing but the Buddhahood gradually developed
around the middle of the Heian period, replacing the notion that
the kami required the help of the Buddha for their own salvation
or deliverance.[50] Thus, inasmuch as they were manifestations of
buddhas, the kami came to be regarded as worthy objects of
worship and adoration.

The theoretical formula for the "coexistence of Shinto and
Buddhism" was later designated either as *Ryōbu* (Two-sided)
Shinto in the tradition of the Shingon school, or as *Sannō Ichijitsu*
(Mountain-king One-truth) Shinto in the Tendai tradition. But
practical coexistence between the two religions was well estab-
lished during the Heian period.[51] Buddhism absorbed the optimis-

---

[49] Ōyama, *Shin-Butsu kōshō-shi*, pp. 1–20. According to the *Semmyō*
(imperial edict) of 765, the heavenly and earthly kami were to be respected
in the same way as the Three Treasures (that is, Buddha, Dharma, and
Samgha).

[50] The theoretical formulation of this was not completed until the Kamakura period, in spite of the widely held view that so-called Ryōbu (two-
sided) Shinto was systematized by Kūkai. The legend of Ryōbu Shinto,
attributed to Kūkai, must have arisen after the middle of the Kamakura period or later. See Kiyohara, *Shintō-shi*, p. 220.

[51] Ōyama, *Shin-Butsu kōshō-shi*, pp. 31–209.

tic world-affirming attitude of Shinto so that the traditional motifs of Buddhism, a quietistic view of Nirvana and a negative outlook regarding life and the world, were greatly modified.[52] On the other hand, Shinto underwent a slow process of transmutation during the Heian period under the influence of syncretistic esoteric Buddhism. For example, the traditional concept that the kami and clansmen (*uji-bito*) shared an exclusive mutual interrelationship gave way before the notion that some kami, noted for *reigen* (marvelous efficacy) in healing the sick, prolonging life, and giving happiness, could be worshiped by whoever might have need of them. Thus the three shrines at Kumano in the present Wakayama prefecture and the Hiye shrine on Mt. Hiei attracted many devotees, to the extent that "branch shrines"—the Ima-Kumano (new Kumano) shrine and the Shin-Hiye (new Hiye) shrine—were established in Kyoto by the ex-Emperor Go-Shirakawa. Also attractive to many pilgrims from distant places was the Itsukushima shrine, now known as Miyajima. Many Shinto shrines accepted Buddhistic features, the most conspicuous example being the Iwashimizu Hachiman shrine, which performed Buddhist-like rituals with Buddhist ceremonial ornaments and was served by married *sha-sō* (literally, "Buddhist priests serving in the Shinto shrines").[53]

One of the important factors that accelerated the growth of coexistence between Shinto and Buddhism, as well as the transmutation of Shinto, was the *ubasoku-dō*, the tradition of shamanistic Buddhism which can be traced to the *ubasoku* (*upasaka*) of the Nara period. Those who followed this tradition were simultaneously lay Buddhists and occult Shintoists. These *ubasoku* usually underwent austere training in the mountains and acquired mysterious powers of healing, divination, and exorcism. There were two main types of *ubasoku*—those who traveled the countryside (*junrei* or "pilgrims") and *yama-no-hijiri* or "holy men of the

---

[52] Muraoka, *Shintō-shi*, pp. 42–43. According to Muraoka, the *Genji monogatari* (Tale of Genji) shows an interesting admixture of world-affirming and world-negating attitudes, as exemplified by its hero, Genji, as well as by a secondary figure, Akashi Nyūdō.

[53] Miyaji, *Jingi-shi taikei*, pp. 59–67.

mountains." The latter were also commonly known as *yama-bushi* or "those who sleep among mountains."[54] During the Heian period, it was taken for granted among the esoteric Buddhist priests that they had to spend some time as *yama-bushi* in order to sharpen their magical power, and many of them chose for this purpose the mountain range of Yoshino, which had been a sacred place of the kami.[55] It was widely believed that the legendary shamanistic diviner, En-no-Shōkaku, had taken his training in this region. It was a Shingon patriarch, Shōbō (832–909), founder of the Daigo temple, who was instrumental in systematizing the training program of *yama-bushi* at Yoshino and also in popularizing this cult. Later, however, the sacred mountain of Yoshino was taken over by the *yama-bushi* of the Tendai tradition. In addition to Yoshino, there were other mountains, such as Kumano, Tateyama, Hakusan, and Daisen, that also attracted many *yama-bushi*.

In addition to the Buddhist priests who took temporary mountain training, there were those who were, so to say, professional *yama-bushi*. They were mostly married, and lived among the people, but they regularly spent some time in the mountains, often serving as "guides" for pious laymen and priests who were not accustomed to the dangerous conditions of travel. In the course of time, these professional *yama-bushi* developed their own cults and

[54] Anesaki, *History of Japanese Religion*, p. 139: "They were, as a rule, men of lower caste representing the crude side of religion, and they exercised a great influence upon the people by appealing directly to vulgar ideas and superstition." "They also conducted young men at the time of adolescence to sacred mountains and initiated them into mysteries—a system of religious 'Boy Scouts' of the olden times . . ." (*ibid.*, p. 140). For a systematic discussion of "the holy man of the mountain," see Hori, *Wagakuni minkan-shinkō-shi no kenkyū*, II, 89–152.

[55] There are several famous mountain peaks in the region of Yoshino. The best known is the Kane-no-mitake, also known as Kogane-no-mine or Mitake. The training at this mountain peak is referred to as *Mitake-sōji*. For details, see Murakami, *Shugen-dō no hattatsu*, pp. 72–91. At Yoshino there were two Shinto shrines—Mikumari (water-dividing) and Yamaguchi (mouth of the mountain). These shrines were dedicated to the kami who were in charge of rivers, mountains, and agriculture. Women were not allowed to enter the sacred zone of Yoshino.

their own brotherhood. Briefly stated, their cults combined some features of esoteric Buddhism, such as *goma* (*homa*) sacrifice, and some of Shinto, such as *haraye* (purification), and *shōji* (*shōjin*, that is, "abstinence"). Their *dōjō* (places where discipline is practiced) were usually sacred mountains of the Shinto tradition.[56] Although there was at first no rigid organizational structure for these *yama-bushi*, many of them belonged to informal brotherhoods and venerated En-no-Shōkaku as the legendary founder of their tradition. Gradually, some of the able *yama-bushi* who had "mastered the magical power" (*shu-gen*) were employed by superstitious aristocrats in the capital for healing and exorcism.

The vogue of the *yama-bushi* coincided with the rise of an obsessive concern for the Pure Land during the middle of the Heian period. Many ex-emperors, members of the Fujiwara clan, and other aristocrats then aspired to have a foretaste of the life to come by making pilgrimages to the sacred mountains of Kumano and Yoshino which were believed to be the "pure land on this earth." [57] In this situation, the importance of *yama-bushi* as guides (*sendatsu* or *sendatsu-shōnin*) came to be recognized. The Shinto shrines at Kumano had been served by the three priestly families of the Ui, Suzuki, and Enomoto. Buddhist influence penetrated Kumano during the Nara period, and the kami enshrined at the shrines at Kumano were believed to be manifestations (*gongen*) of such important Buddhist divinities as Yakushi Nyorai (Bhaiṣajyaguru), Kanzeon or Kannon Bosatsu (Avalokiteśvara), Jizō Bosatsu (Kṣitigarbha), and Amida-butsu (Amitābha).[58] Meanwhile, the ex-Emperor Shirakawa paid a visit to Kumano in 1090, accompanied by a Tendai patriarch, Zōyo, who

[56] Miyaji, *Jingi-shi taikei*, pp. 67–68.

[57] The three sacred mountains of Kumano were visited by the ex-Emperor Uda as early as 907, followed by the ex-Emperor Hanayama in 986 and 999, and by the ex-Emperors Shirakawa and Toba in 1125. In fact, Shirakawa paid nine visits, Toba twenty-one visits, Go-Shirakawa thirty-three visits, and Go-Toba thirty-one visits to Kumano alone. See Murakami, *Shugen-dō no hattatsu*, p. 119.

[58] According to a legend, Ippen, the founder of the Ji sect, was enlightened when he made a pilgrimage to Kumano. *Ibid.*, p. 116.

served as his chaplain. Pleased by his service, Shirakawa created
the position of *sanzan-kengyō* (ecclesiastical supervisor of the three
mountains of Kumano) for Zōyo, and this position was inherited
by Zōyo's Tendai successors. Through this initial connection,
one school of the mountain ascetics later came to be affiliated with
the Tendai school, while another school came to be affiliated with
the Shingon school.[59]

The popularization of pilgrimages was not confined to sacred
mountains, visits to which involved a considerable amount of
hardship and inconvenience. Many pious priests, laymen, and
laywomen considered it meritorious to visit less hazardous holy
places, as exemplified by the account of the aged mother and sister
of the vicar-general (*sōzu*) of Yogawa in *The Tale of Genji*. Both
his mother, who was well over eighty, and his sister, a woman of
about fifty, set out on a pilgrimage to a holy place called Hatsuse
"in fulfilment of a long-standing vow." [60] Such a pilgrimage was
an attempt to "experience" salvation physically as an alternative
to mental discipline and meditation. It was also believed that by
undergoing the inconveniences and hardships of the pilgrimage,
one might nullify one's sins and be assured of rebirth in the Pure
Land after one's death. The fact that so many people of various
walks of life made pilgrimages to mountains and distant places
was significant, in the sense that the religious beliefs and practices of Shinto and Buddhism, as well as those of the aristocrats
and the masses, influenced each other.[61]

Shinto shrines continued to survive throughout the Heian period, and in times of crisis the government and people made frequent and generous offerings to the kami. However, the nature

[59] For the development of the Tendai Shugen-dō (more strictly known as
the Honzan-ha Shugen-dō) and the Shingon Shugen-dō (Tōzan-ha Shugen-dō), see Wakamori, *Shugen-dō-shi kenkyū*, pp. 183–203.

[60] See Waley, tr., *The Tale of Genji*, by Lady Murasaki, II, 1083.

[61] Hori, *Waga-kuni minkan-shinkō-shi no kenkyū*, II, 105–10. Out of
this tradition, there developed various courses of pilgrimages, designating
holy places—thirty-three in Western Japan, eighty-eight in the island of
Shikoku, and others, which have been followed by the faithful to this
day. On the problem of "directional taboos" and other related subjects, see
Frank, *Kata-imi et kata-tagae*.

and character of the shrines had changed through Buddhist, Chinese, and other influences. The kami lost their own independent qualities, and were equated with buddhas, bodhisattvas, and sometimes with *goryō* (the spirits of those who had had an unfortunate death), believed to haunt their enemies. Thus, in supposedly Shinto shrines, Buddhist and other non-Shinto cults operated, including *goryō-ye*, a special ritual designed to pacify the spirits with *sumō* (wrestling), dances, and other entertainments.[62] People no longer were bound by the specific kami of their own families and clans; they could invoke any one of the Shinto or Buddhist divinities according to their needs and inclinations.

Amida and Jizō

The complex religious situation of the Heian period was dramatically reflected in the various kinds of divinities venerated in accordance with different types of religious affirmations on the part of the people. Among these divinities were Amida (Amitābha, "the Buddha of Infinite Light," or Amitāyus, "the Buddha of Infinite Life"), who was the favorite Buddha among the aristocrats, and Jizō (Ksitigarbha, the bodhisattva who saves the souls of the dead from suffering in hell), who found many devotees among the masses.

It may be recalled that when Buddhism was first introduced into Japan, before the Nara period, Japanese Buddhists venerated indiscriminately the statues of Shaka (Sākyamuni), Miroku (Maitreya), Yakushi (Bhaisajyaguru), Kannon (Avalokiteśvara), and Amida, because at first very few, if any, knew the differences in nature and function of these divinities. During the Nara period, it was the influence of the Hossō (Yogācāra) school that popularized the Maitreya cult, wherein many people prayed to the future Buddha Maitreya, who was believed to reside in the Tushita (Contentment) Heaven. People soon learned, however, that there

---

[62] Hori, *Waga-kuni minkan-shinkō-shi no kenkyū*, II, 457–70. Incidentally, the famous Gion Festival in Kyoto arose as a *goryō-ye* (ritual for the pacification of haunting spirits) in 876. It became an annual festival from 970 onward.

was another and more glamorous paradise, Sukhāvatī or the Pure Land, which was the abode of Amida, so that there was a gradual shift in popularity from Maitreya to Amida. In 760 the Empress Dowager Shōtoku distributed paintings of Amida's Pure Land and copies of the *Sutra in Praise of the Pure Land (Shōsan-Jōdo-kyō)* to all the provincial temples; and in 782 the Hossō priest, Shōkai of Kofuku temple, Nara, celebrated the first *Amida-keka* (Rites of repentance addressed to Amida).[63] The spread of the cult also resulted in the building of temples dedicated to Amida, such as the *Amida-dō* (Amida chapel) in Tōdai temple and the *Jōdo-in* (temple of the Pure Land) in Hokke temple. However, during the Nara period there was no indication that people prayed to Amida for their own deliverance. Rather, people dedicated the Amida temples and used the Amida cult ostensibly for the "repose" of deceased parents or spouses; in this sense the Amida cult of the Nara period failed to comprehend the unique nature and function of Amida. Certainly the pessimistic outlook regarding the present world that underlies belief in Amida's Pure Land was totally lacking in those days.[64]

Early in the Heian period the Amida cult waned for a time; Saicho of the Tendai school emphasized faith in Shaka (Buddha Sākyamuni) as it is taught in the *Lotus Sutra*, while Kūkai of the Shingon school stressed Dainichi (Mahāvairocana, the "Great Sun Buddha" or the "Cosmic Buddha") as his doctrine is taught in the *Great Sun Sutra*.[65] It must be mentioned in this connection that Saicho was interested in a method of mystic contemplation, known as *Hokke-zammai* (contemplation on the Lotus), as a means for experiencing the truth of the *Lotus Sutra*, and

[63] De Visser, *Ancient Buddhism in Japan*, I, 318. The close connection between Maitreya and Amitābha was noted in China, too, because both of them stood for "easy ways" toward Nirvana instead of the "difficult way" of the Aryas. Both were based on "the power of another" for the salvation of beings, and not on one's own ability to deliver oneself.

[64] This important observation is well documented in Inouye, *Nihon Jōdo-kyō seiritsu-shi no kenkyū*, pp. 15–40. For the influence of the Amida cult on the Buddhist schools of the Nara period, see pp. 41–81.

[65] In addition to Dainichi, the Shingon school introduced many divinities from its rich pantheon.

established the Hokke-Zammai-in (Lotus contemplation chapel) for this purpose. However, this chapel was used mostly as a lecture hall and not as a meditation center during Saicho's lifetime. Following his death, the Tendai school quickly developed as an esoteric Buddhist school, and only in this atmosphere did mystic contemplation come to be taken seriously. This trend led to the emergence of the Amida cult and the belief in the Pure Land within the Tendai school. It was Ennin (794–864) who introduced *jōgyō-zammai* (literally, a "perpetually moving concentration" on Amida) from China to Mt. Hiei.[66] The *jōgyō-zammai* consists of ninety days of uninterrupted ceremony, constant invocation of the holy name of Amida, and visualization of the image of Amida. For this reason, it is also called *Nembutsu-zammai* (contemplation that invokes the name of the Buddha Amida). While Ennin's younger contemporary, Enchin (814–91), stressed the *Hokke-zammai,* Ennin's followers continued to advocate the Amida cult.

The *nembutsu* (invocation of Amida's name) began to be an important motif of the Tendai school in the middle of the tenth century, a time of social and political disorder as the result of the decline of the power of the central government. In the provinces

---

[66] Saicho developed his mystical-philosophical system based on the "Three Great Works" of the Chinese T'ien-t'ai school—the *Words and Phrases of the Lotus* (*Fa-hua wen-chü*), *Profound Meaning of the Lotus* (*Fa-hua hsüan-i*), and *Great Concentration and Insight* (*Mo-ho chih-kuan*), all ascribed to Chih-i (or Chih-k'ai, 538–597). Chih-i's method of concentration aims at gaining religious insight into the nature of the universe, which, according to the T'ien-t'ai, consists of a single absolute mind known as *Bhūtatathatā* (Genuine Thusness) or *Tathāgata-garbha* (Storehouse of Thus Come). See Fung Yu-lan, *A History of Chinese Philosophy*, II, 360–83. Chih-i, being a skillful syncretist, devised various methods of mental concentration known in his time under four main types. One of them was the *Pratyutpanna-samādhi*, a hybrid of the *dhyana* and the Amida cult, developed early in the fifth century by Hui-yüan at Mt. Lu for the "White Lotus Society," which was organized by him. See Zürcher, *The Buddhist Conquest of China*, I (Text), 219–23. Chih-i incorporated the *Pratyutpanna-samādhi* by calling it the "perpetually moving concentration" (*jōgyō-zammai* in Japanese). Saicho, himself a mystic, took to *Hokke-zammai* (Lotus contemplation) but not to the *jōgyō-zammai*.

ambitious governors and strong men took up arms and fought among themselves. In 939 a disgruntled nobleman, Taira-no-Masakado, established a "kingdom" in the Kantō region and declared himself the "new emperor," while in the western part of Japan another frustrated nobleman, Fujiwara Sumitomo, commanding a sizable naval force in the Inland Sea, rebelled against the government in Kyoto. Although these rebellions were successfully subdued after some fighting and much praying to Shinto and Buddhist divinities, difficult social conditions caused by drought, famine, epidemic, and great fires, plus a sudden increase in robbery, murder, and suicide, convinced many people that the end of the present world period, which was anticipated on the basis of Buddhist cosmic history, might be approaching soon.[67] In this atmosphere a group of serious-minded men, mostly young intellectuals and minor aristocrats in Kyoto, formed in 964 a devotional society called *Kangaku-ye*, centered on belief in Amida.[68] At the same time, in the Tendai monastery on Mt. Hiei, the Abbot Ryōgen (912–85) instilled an ardent faith in Amida into his disciples.

One of Ryōgen's followers, Genshin (942–1017) not only structured a theoretical basis for faith in Amida's Pure Land in his famous work, *The Essentials of Salvation* (*Ōjō-yōshū*, written in 985), but also depicted the blissful splendor of the Pure Land in paintings and poems. Although he was not an active propagandist, he was instrumental in creating in 986 a new kind of religious society unknown in Japan before his time. It was called the "Samadhi Group of Twenty-five" (*Nijūgo-zammai-*

---

[67] The belief in the millennium was based on the Buddhist legend that divides the period after Buddha's death into three parts. The first thousand years were to be the period of the "Perfect Law" (*Sad-dharma* or *shō-bō*), the second thousand were the period of the "Copied Law" (*Prati-rūpa-dharma; zō-hō* or *zō-bō*), and the third thousand were the period of the "End of the Law" (*Paschima-dharma* or *mappō*) which was the period of degeneration. Both Saicho and Kūkai accepted this view of cosmic history. According to one interpretation of this theory, the year 1052 was the beginning of the period of the "End of the Law." See Anesaki, *History of Japanese Religion*, pp. 149–50.

[68] See Inouye, *Jōdo-kyō seiritsu-shi no kenkyū*, pp. 150–51.

kesshū) and was composed of Amida devotees, including priests, nuns, and laity. It existed for the purpose of mutual edification in the religious life and more especially for mutual assistance at the time of the deaths and funerals of its members.[69] It is significant that Genshin and his followers were very critical of the social, political, cultural, and religious conditions of their times. Yet, instead of involving themselves in active social or political reforms, they became introspective, contemplating the meaning of the transitoriness (*mujō*) of life and the world; in the words of Genshin: "Fifty years of human life is equivalent to one day and night in the realm of the Four Deva Kings." [70] Such an intense realization of the nature of human existence drove the forerunners of Japanese Pure Land Buddhists to seek refuge not only from the disturbing elements of society but also from corporate life in the temples. Thus developed the private cottages (*bessho*) of these individual "holy men" (*hijiri* or *shōnin*) in the proximity of, but away from, temple compounds. In the course of time a number of such private cottages were established, thanks to the donations of wealthy laymen, in the suburbs of Kyoto. Many laymen, as well as spiritually disquieted priests and nuns, were attracted to these informal religious centers, and there sought spiritual instruction. The embryonic beginning of Amida pietism was in these loosely organized fraternities which might be termed *collegia pietatis*, "limited in numbers and united in common enthusiasm, peculiar convictions, intense devotion and rigid discipline." [71]

We will see in the next chapter how full-fledged Amida pietism

[69] Unlike the Amidists of the Kamakura period, Genshin accepted the importance of traditional meditation and other paths as helpful to salvation, except of course that in his view reciting the holy name of Amida was more effective than other ways. In this sense, he was a pioneer of the Pure Land tradition in Japan, but his view cannot be equated with those of Hōnen and Shinran. See Inouye, *Jōdo-kyō*, pp. 112–20.

[70] This translation is taken from Tsunoda, *et al.*, *Sources of Japanese Tradition*, p. 200. On the meaning of *mujō* or *mono-no-aware*, which was an important motif during the Heian period, see Watsuji, *Nihon seishin-shi kenkyū*, pp. 217–35.

[71] Wach, *Sociology of Religion*, p. 175.

developed in the thirteenth century through independent ecclesiastical organizations. During the Heian period, however, Amida pietism had no intention of seceding from the traditional schools of Japanese Buddhism. Admittedly there was an element of protest on the part of Amida pietists against the laxity, corruption, and spiritual aridity of the established temples of their time. But the followers of Amida did not wish to split the ecclesiastical structure but to develop "a core of spiritual elite within the larger religious group" (*ecclesiola in ecclesia*). But, as might be expected, the influence of the Amida pietist movement began to be felt in many areas, three in particular being of concern to this discussion.

The first was the influence of the Amida pietist movement upon the established schools of Buddhism. Little needs to be said about Tendai, which served as the womb of Amida pietism in Japan. Externally, the Tendai school prospered under its abbots of aristocratic origin, through the lucrative income of its manors, and through the powerful arms of the "warrior priests" (*sōhei*). But spiritually and morally it steadily declined, for monastic discipline and philosophical learning were neglected, and internal factionalism increased. Understandably, some of the minor priests, who were serious about their religious vocations, were attracted to Amida pietism. One such man, Ryōnin (1072–1132), started the Yūzū-Nembutsu (All-permeating faith of the Buddha Amida) sect, synthesizing the tenets of the Lotus and Amida doctrines. Although it was short-lived, his movement greatly influenced the religiously serious priests of the Tendai school.[72] Belief in the Pure Land also penetrated Mt. Kōya, the sacred mountain of the Shingon school.[73] The most conspicuous advocate of the Pure

[72] On Ryōnin and the Yūzū-Nembutsu sect, see Saitō, *Jōdo-kyō-shi*, pp. 477–83. His motto was: "One in all, all in one; one acts for all, all act for one." What Ryōnin advocated was a collective path for salvation, and the salvation of society at large. Although in his devotional aspect he was an ardent Amida pietist, his scriptural basis was derived from the *Kegon* (*Avatamsaka*) *sutra* as much as from the *Lotus Sutra*. See Takakusu, *The Essentials of Buddhist Philosophy*, p. 169.

[73] There were several factors that brought about the rise of the Amida cult at Mt. Kōya. The first was political. In order to satisfy the needs of

Land in the Shingon school was Kakuban (1095–1143), the founder of the Shingi-Shingon (New doctrine-Shingon) sect. Being a skillful syncretist, Kakuban combined the invocation of Amida's name with the Shingon cult. He considered the mystery of "invoking the holy name" as one of the "three secrets" of traditional Shingon practice—*go-mitsu* or the "secret of speech"— and equated Amida's Pure Land with Dainichi's paradise (*mitsugon-jōdo*). While his system incorporated the devotional intensity of the Amida cult, Kakuban's theoretical framework remained substantially that of Shingon.[74] The influence of the Amida cult was felt even in Nara, especially by the Sanron (Mādhyamika) priests at Tōdai temple, such as Eikan (d. 1111), Kakuju (d. 1125), and Jūyo (d. *ca.* 1145). It is to be noted that these men and their followers resided in Kōmyōsan temple, which was a rest home for priests of the Tōdai temple. The principal characteristics of the Amida cult in Nara were its pluralistic qualities, incorporating within it Sanron, Shingon, and Amida beliefs and practices.[75]

The second important area in which the Amida cult exerted great influence was upon the religious outlook of the aristocrats

the aristocrats, the Shingon school developed such rites as the *Amida-Goma* (Homa sacrifice for Amida) and other funerary rites based on the Amida cults. See Hori, *Waga-kuni minkan shinkō-shi no kenkyū*, II, 296– 98. Also the government often appointed to the abbacy of Mt. Kōya prelates from Nara and Kyoto who were not genuine followers of the Shingon doctrines; some of them were personally devotees of the Amida cult. The second was geographical. Since Mt. Kōya was situated on the mountain away from Kyoto, many contemplative persons and semireligious refugees sought peace and quiet there. Many of them established private quarters in the proximity of the temples but led their own religious life. Those who were devotees of the Amida cult were called *Kōya-hijiri* (holy men of Mt. Kōya). Kakuban was supported by such men, and when he had to flee from Kōya and establish his own temple at Negoro, many of the *Kōya-hijiri* followed him. The third was cultic. That is to say, Mt. Kōya had had the tradition of the Maitreya cult, which had typological affinities with the Amida cult. Even today, Kūkai is believed only to be asleep, and he is expected to return again to this earth.

[74] See Inouye, *Jōdo-kyō seiritsu-shi no kenkyū*, pp. 335–66.

[75] *Ibid.*, pp. 382–401.

during the middle and the later Heian period. Here, however, sincerity in seeking salvation was totally emasculated, so that the Pure Land of Amida was interpreted purely from aesthetic and sentimental viewpoints without any reference to its ethical, doctrinal, and philosophical content. Never before, nor after, was there such a period as the Fujiwara era wherein the society of the Japanese elite was governed by what Sansom calls a "rule of taste." There were such exceptions as Yoshishige-no-Yasutane and Fujiwara Michinaga's own son, Akinobu, who deserted life in the court and entered the priesthood, but such cases were rare. Most courtiers were concerned with elegant pastimes, of which there were many. In the words of Warner: "The court of King Louis of France was never more delightfully decadent or so utterly given over to the pursuit of butterflies. It is worth reminding one's self that these were the days when Harold's uncouth thanes were harried by William the Conqueror newly landed in England." [76]

The aristocrats of the Fujiwara period were notoriously superstitious, and they enjoined every incantation and magico-religious rite. The Hōjō temple, dedicated by Fujiwara Michinaga to the repose of his own soul, enshrined all possible Buddhist divinities. Michinaga, according to his own admission, had nothing more to desire in this world: "My aspiration is fully satisfied like a full moon in the sky." Such a man and others like him were not driven to faith in the Pure Land by their experience of the misery and suffering of this life. Rather, they wanted to "actualize" the Pure Land and enjoy it while they were on this earth. The *Eiga monogatari* (Tales of power and glory) vividly describe the splendor of Michinaga's temple, which was designed to reproduce the brilliance of paradise. "Jewelled nets were suspended from the branches of the plants fringing the pond. . . . Boats adorned with gems idled in the shade of trees, and peacocks strutted on the island in the middle. . . ." [77] Michinaga's son, Fujiwara Yorimichi, was equally extravagant in building the Phoenix Hall of the Byōdō temple at Uji. In these magnificent temples, aristocrats

[76] Warner, *The Enduring Art of Japan*, p. 32.
[77] Quoted in Sansom, *History of Japan to 1334*, p. 175.

sponsored Buddhist ceremonies which were as lavish as their banquets. Very popular was a ritual called "Welcoming the Amida" in which twenty-five handsome priests wearing jeweled crowns offered sweet-smelling incense to the golden statues of Amida. Such a use of the Amida cult encouraged a glorious Buddhist art and architecture, but made a mockery of the faith and practice of Amida pietism.

In sharp contrast to the Amida cult among the aristocrats, Amida pietism also merged with the tradition of the shamanistic Buddhists of the previous period. A conspicuous example of the shamanistic Amidist was Kūya or Kōya (903–72). According to legends, he was the son of an imperial prince, but this is very doubtful. He had been a Tendai priest for a while, but before going to Mt. Hiei he had wandered among the mountains and in the countryside and was called a *shami* (unordained priest). It is not clear whether he was influenced by the Tendai or Nara tradition of Amida pietism. But his biographers portray him as a spiritual heir to Gyōgi, the shamanistic Buddhist *par excellence* of the Nara period.[78] Indeed, Kūya was one of the *hijiri* (holy men) whose charismatic qualities made them real religious leaders among the masses. Many of the *hijiri*, syncretistic though they were, came under the influence of the Amida cult. Kūya, for example, taught people to invoke the holy name of Amida, using a popular melody, wherever they happened to be—in the paddy field or market place.[79] The significance of the Amida cult among the lower strata of Heian society was its acceptance as a form of magical incantation (*Nembutsu* or "reciting the Buddha's name" magic). It was the intention of Kūya and others to offer the oppressed masses a glimpse of hope in the life to come by assuring them of rebirth in Amida's Pure Land. However, the masses,

[78] For the discussion of Kūya's life and work, see Hori, *Waga-kuni min-kanshinkō-shi no kenkyū*, II, 260–78.

[79] On "Kūya Wasan" (chanting ascribed to Kūya), see Iba, "Bukkyō ongaku," pp. 200–1. Kūya was called the "holy man of the market place," for he led people around him in dancing and chanting "Namu Amida Butsu." He, like Gyōgi before him, engaged in many philanthropic activities, and traveled to Hokkaido to preach the gospel of Amida to the Ainus.

who had never experienced comfort and happiness in this world, had no aptitude for imagining a land of bliss in the hereafter, just as the Heian aristocrats had no gift for feeling the misery and suffering of this life. Thus, many poor people began to fear suffering in hell rather than to anticipate the joy of rebirth in the Pure Land; this psychological twist in popular piety resulted in the sudden popularity of another Buddhist divinity of obscure origin, Jizō (Bodhisattva Ksitigarbha, known as Ti-tsang in Chinese) who was believed to stand between this world and the next and to save those who were on their way to hell.

Jizō was not a prominent bodhisattva originally, even though he was mentioned in the Sutra on the Buddha Names, in which Buddha enumerates Buddhas, bodhisattvas, and pratyekabuddhas, to the number of 11,093.[80] Jizō became important as he came to be closely affiliated with Amida in China where he was known as Ti-tsang (the Treasure-chamber of the world). According to the Scripture Concerning Ti-ts'ang's Vows (Ti-ts'ang Pen-yüan Ching), he made a vow, much as Amida did, not to attain Buddhahood until the last soul in hell might be redeemed. In fact, Amida expresses his compassion through the mediation and vicarious atonement of Jizō. During the T'ang dynasty esoteric Buddhism stressed Jizō's importance as the gracious bodhisattva of the lower world in many elaborate votive rituals for the deceased.[81]

In Japan, Jizō made his first appearance in the form of a statue in the lecture hall of Tōdai temple, Nara, but then he was relegated to the minor position of being an attendant to Senju Kannon (One-thousand-armed-Avalokiteśvara). One legend says that Gyōgi carved a statue of Jizō in the Ise district for the pur-

---

[80] Buddhabhāsita-buddhanāma-sūtra (Bussetsu Butsumyōkyō, in Japanese), No. 44 in the Nanjio Catalogue. See Nanjio, comp., A Catalogue of the Chinese Translation of the Buddhist Tripitaka, p. 99.

[81] For the importance of Ti-tsang (Jizō) in China, see Reichelt, Truth and Tradition in Chinese Buddhism, pp. 82–111. For a comprehensive treatment of Jizō, see "Jizō Bosatsu" in Mochizuki, Bukkyō daijiten, IV, 3595–3601; Manabe, Jizō Bosatsu no kenkyū; and de Visser, The Bodhisattva Ti-Tsang (Jizō) in China and Japan.

pose of driving away epidemics. Actually, Jizō's importance was recognized only after Kūkai founded the Shingon school early in the Heian period. Jizō found some prominent devotees, including the Emperor Seiwa and some of the court ladies, and there were occasional celebrations of the *Jizō-keka* (Repentance rites addressed to Jizō) in the tenth century. With the rise of the Amida cult, his popularity as one of the five central buddhas became noticeable.[82] In Genshin's famous painting known as *Raigō* (Welcome), Amida is pictured descending from heaven to welcome the holiest of the nine classes of believers in accordance with his vow. Amida is preceded by Kannon and Seishi and followed by Jizō, portrayed as a priest holding a blazing pearl and the *abhaya-mudrā*.[83] Indeed, Jizō was the personification of Amida's boundless compassion.

More important from our standpoint is the fact that this versatile Buddhist divinity managed to take on the role and function of the old kami for the people in the lower strata of Japanese society through the influence of the shamanistic Amidists. In the *Konjaku monogatari* (Tales of long ago), a voluminous collection of over one thousand popular stories, probably the most valuable source regarding the religious beliefs and practices of the masses during the Heian period, there are a number of accounts of Jizō.[84] Many of these stories are based on the simple motif of retribution, except that Jizō appears in the form of a young boy and either rescues people from their predicaments or restores life to a dead

[82] The so-called *Amida Gobutsu* (Five Buddhas of the Amida Circle) include Amida Sanzon—Amida, Kannon, and Seishi—accompanied by Jizō and Nāgārjuna. Incidentally, the Pure Land school accepted Nāgārjuna and Aśvaghosha as two patriarchs of its tradition.

[83] De Visser, *Ancient Buddhism in Japan*, I, 334–35. On the iconographic representation of Jizō in the Shingon tradition, see Toganoo, *Mandara no kenkyū* (*Toganoo zenshū* IV), 86–87, 95–97, 102–4, 358, 366, and Plates 67, 68, and 70.

[84] Yamada, *et al., Konjaku monogatari*, Vol. III, *Nihon koten bungaku taikei*, No. 24, pp. 502–49. Also see Katayose, *Konjaku monogatarishū-ron*, pp. 432–61; Tsukakoshi, tr., *Konjaku: Altjapanische Geschichten aus dem Volk zur Heian-Zeit;* and Jones, tr., *Ages Ago: Thirty-Seven Tales from the Konjaku Monogatari Collection.*

person. Usually Jizō explains in dreams the reasons behind his actions, and adds a simple exhortation to the people to the effect that they should take heed of the Buddha's way.

As the divinity of the poor, Jizō took over the role of the traditional "kami of the road" (*Sae-no-kami* or *Sai-no-kami*) who was believed to guard the turning points of highways. Jizō enriched the cult of the "kami of the road" by adding the notion that he was also the guardian of those who finish the course of this life and are about to enter the life to come. People had a great fear of the sufferings they might undergo in hell, which were realistically described in moralistic tales of retribution. The masses looked toward Jizō as a potent mediator on behalf of souls destined to descend to the lower world. Even today the Japanese countryside is dotted with stone statues of Jizō, either at the roadside or in the neighborhood of *akago-zuka* (infant mounds). Evidently in the old days dead infants were buried in those unpretentious mounds, in the belief that they would be born again soon. In the course of time, Jizō came to be regarded as the special protector of infants and children who had died—a function for which he was never held responsible in China.[85] Many of these statues of Jizō are covered with votive offerings in the form of pebbles placed there by passers-by: probably a pre-Buddhist practice in connection with the "kami of the road." After these kami were transformed into Jizō, people continued the custom on the ground that "each of those pebbles meant one pebble less to be heaped up on the beach of the river in hell by the souls of the children, who stood under Jizō's protection." [86]

[85] Yanagita, *Minzokugaku jiten*, pp. 1–2 and 257–58.

[86] De Visser, *Ancient Buddhism in Japan*, I, 103. He tends to equate the "kami of the road" with phallicism. While some of them undoubtedly were phallic gods, most were free from phallic connotations. Even Buckley, who overly stressed the phallic motif of Japanese religion, noted the apparent absence of phallicism from the great highway called the Tōkaidō. See Buckley, *Phallicism in Japan*, p. 32. According to Fenellosa, "one of the most striking of these early Jizōs is cut, life-size and in high relief, out of a mountain ledge on the little path across the Hakone mountain from Ashinoyu to Hakone." The local legend says that this was carved by Kūkai. See Fenollosa, *Epochs of Chinese and Japanese Art*, I, 149.

In retrospect it becomes apparent that all kinds of magico-religious traditions influenced the Japanese people during the Heian period. In spite of all the divinities thus introduced, however, there were actually only two or three types of divinities that enjoyed a large number of followers. Furthermore, these divinities—the kami, Amida, and Jizō—were eclectic and interchangeable except as separate symbols for the types of religious affirmation on the part of the people in the higher and lower strata of society. Some people hold that Japan became a Buddhist country during the Heian period when Buddhism in effect absorbed Shinto. Yet, is it not equally true that Buddhism surrendered to the ethos of that nebulous religion of Japan, which lay deeper than the visible religious structure, commonly referred to as Shinto?

CHAPTER III

The Pure Land, Nichiren, and Zen

RELIGIOUS MOVEMENTS IN MEDIEVAL JAPAN

(ca. thirteenth–sixteenth centuries)

The medieval period began in Japan toward the end of the twelfth century. In 1192 the last important figure of the "cloistered rule" (*inzei*), the ex-Emperor Go-Shirakawa, died, while in the same year the first great military ruler, Minamoto Yoritomo, established his feudal regime (*bakufu*) at Kamakura, not far from the present Tokyo. Thus began the so-called Kamakura era which lasted until 1333. Following the decline of the *bakufu* at Kamakura, there was a short-lived period of "imperial rule" under the Emperor Go-Daigo. But the misguided and unrealistic policies of greedy courtiers, who actually were in control of power, drove the dissatisfied warriors to side with rebellion under the leadership of Ashikaga Takauji, the founder of the Ashikaga *bakufu*. Since most of the Ashikaga shogun (warrior rulers) made their headquarters in a section of Kyoto called Muromachi, the period of their rule, 1338–1573, is often referred to as the Muromachi era.

The shift in political center from Kyoto to Kamakura, or "from the chrysanthemum to the sword," to use Ruth Benedict's phrase, meant more than a decline in the status of the refined courtiers who had manipulated the throne, coupled with the rise of rough and boisterous warriors who became tired of being pushed around by the effete court circle. While there is much truth in this perspective, there is also something more fundamental to note. The history of medieval Japan, like its counterpart in other parts of the world, has been written as though the only actors in the drama were the elite of society. However, a radical event, such as the establishment of the feudal regime, was not possible unless there was a general feeling of approval on the part of the people toward the necessary correction of what was basically wrong with the previous form of government.

We may recall that the guardians and transmitters of culture during the Heian period were the aristocracy and the clergy. It was they who dominated the political, social, economic, cultural, and religious life of the nation by introducing into Japan various aspects of Chinese civilization together with Chinese Buddhism. Even today, one has only to visit remains of temples or villas of the Heian period, either in Kyoto or at Uji, to feel the grandeur of the culture of former times. There one experiences among other things the poignant beauty expressed in highly stylized landscaping. The typical garden of the Heian period utilized pond, stream, bridge, rock, and trees in such a way as to reproduce in miniature the real mood of nature, so that, as Lafcadio Hearn once remarked, the garden was at once a picture and a poem; perhaps even more a poem than a picture. One can best understand the spirit of Heian culture when one sits quietly in one of these gardens, viewing the arrangement of artificial waterfalls and strangely shaped rocks brought in from the mountains. In such surroundings men and women "illuminated the holy books of an imported Indian religion with delicate drawings and webs of beaten gold leaf. . . . and there they played the game of floating wine cups down the meandering rills, with a forfeit due from the gallant or the lady whose craft foundered on the way." [1] Artificial landscaping was but one example of the lacy refinement of Heian culture nurtured by aristocracy and clergy. It was all

[1] Warner, *The Enduring Art of Japan*, p. 31. Incidentally, even the meandering stream was so designed that it flowed from east to west, or from north to south, but never from west to east, or from south to north, for it was believed that the four quarters of the world were ruled by four deities, and that the east was the source of purity whereas the west was the outlet of all impurities, etc. See Tatsui, *Japanese Gardens*, p. 13.

elegant and exquisite, but, like a dainty artificial flower, the aristocratic culture of Kyoto lacked a certain measure of real life.

In a definite way, the Kamakura period was marked by the rejection of artificial culture delicately concocted by courtiers and clergy, in favor of a more natural spirit and indigenous forms of culture and society. Whether the warriors realized it or not, they were destined to play a key role as spokesmen and agents of this nostalgia for the indigenous tradition which, ironically, had to be implemented by a new form of political and social order.[2] It is understandable, therefore, that the warriors sensed an inner contradiction, caught as they were between the urge to go forward looking for novelty and the opposite sentiment of looking backward toward an idealized past. Yet the leaders of feudal society failed to understand the degree to which they and the masses had been influenced by the historical experiences of Japan during the Nara and Heian periods. As a consequence they had to make a series of compromises both with the residual features of the previous regime and with the new demands of the general populace. Many features of the Kamakura period, including its art, literature, and religious movements, were characterized by a passionate search for meaning, certainty, and coherence in a new society that was emerging from a combination of influences from diverse, and often contradictory, forces at work.

Take, for example, the peculiar make-up and ethos of the warrior class. Of the origin and gradual development of the warriors during the Heian period, I have taken note above. Here I mention only that the warriors grew in strength in the eastern provinces where the influence of the central government was never strongly felt, and that their solidarity was based on the ancient Japanese pattern of the clan (*uji* and *dōzoku*) system. In the course of time warrior clans as such developed. Then, based on kinship and regional ties, a larger solidarity group, called the *tō*, came into existence. Some of these *tō* again formed informal confederations under grand chieftains (*tōryō*), much as the semiautonomous clans formed confederations during the early

---

[2] See Nishida, *Nihon bunka-shi josetsu,* pp. 373–437.

days of the Yamato kingdom.[3] But unlike the early emperor whose authority was based, at least in part, on charisma, the patriarchal chief of a confederation of warrior clans could exercise his autocratic power only in so far as he had the consent of the chieftains within the federation. Of course, Minamoto Yoritomo held the title of shogun, but although he actually obtained this position by the support of local powers, he had to ask the court, which alone could speak in the name of the "charisma of the imperial office" to confer the title on him.[4] The power of the Minamoto clan was based on its holding of reclaimed lands and manors, but there were many influential clans, such as the Hōjō, the Wada, and the Miura, that were also holders of their own manors, even though they pledged allegiance to the Minamoto chief. In such a situation, rights, interests, fidelity, and obligation were intricately interrelated, and the conflicts of these elements threatened the otherwise efficient and seemingly tightly knit pyramid structure of warrior society. In fact the Minamoto shogun was soon eliminated by the Hōjō chiefs, who, however, as the *shikken* (regents for the shogun) maintained the same administrative structure at Kamakura.[5]

[3] The famous confederation in the Kanto region, known as the "Seven Tō of Musashi" (*Musashi-shichi-tō*), was composed of the following: Tan-tō, Kisai-tō, Kodama-tō, Inomata-tō, Nishino-tō, Yokoyama-tō, and Murayama-tō. Each *tō* consisted of many clans (*dōzoku-dan*); for example, the Kodama-tō had fifty-eight clans within it. See Kobata and Wakamori, *Nihonshi kenkyū*, p. 121.

[4] This attitude toward the "charisma of the imperial office" was not simply based on practical efficiency. When Yoritomo's wife, Lady Masa (daughter of the Hōjō family and called the "Female Shogun" on account of her ruthless use of power) was in Kyoto in 1218, she was invited to visit the ex-Emperor Go-Toba. However, she declined the honor on the ground that a country woman of humble origin should not be received by the ex-sovereign. She packed her luggage and returned home immediately. See Takekoshi, *The Economic Aspects of the History of Japan*, I, 185–86.

[5] The Hōjō chiefs, who usurped the power of the Minamoto family, had to invite Kujō Yoritsune (1218–56), then only a two-year-old infant, to become the titular shogun. This cumbersome arrangement caused many complications later on. The list of "Hōjō Regents in the Thirteenth

Much has been written about the organizational structure of the feudal regime and about the development of Kamakura as the new political center of the nation.[6] Here we are concerned only with the fact that the gigantic administrative machine of the Kamakura regime was based on a very few simple principles derived from the tradition of family or clan rule. Sansom rightly observes that the feudal institution at Kamakura was founded not on a coherent political theory but on "a series of political afterthoughts." The only consistent principle was the relationship of the vassal to his lord, defined so rigidly in terms of loyalty, fidelity, and honor, that it became a pseudoreligious code in the subsequent period.[7] Otherwise, principles and policies were simple, realistic, and flexible. Fifty-one such principles were compiled in 1232 as the *Jōei shikimoku* (Legislation of the Jōei era).[8] In principle, the Taihō code, handed down from the eighth century, was still in effect within the sphere of influence of the court. However, even some of the courtiers began to favor the simplicity of the Kamakura code over the cumbersome Taihō code. Actually, there were many borderline matters which could be handled either through Kyoto or through Kamakura, and many cases were referred to the shogun's court. For example, in the thirteenth-century literary work entitled the *Izayoi nikki* (Diary of the waning moon), the heroine writes concerning a succession dispute between the eldest son of her husband and herself, as stepmother. She wished to have some of the patrimony for her

---

Century" and the list of "Titular and Cloistered Emperors after Go-Shirakawa's death in 1192" are given in Sansom, *A History of Japan to 1334,* p. 370.

[6] *Ibid.,* pp. 339–69 and 387–408. Regarding the city of Kamakura, see Yazaki, *Nihon toshi no hatten katei,* pp. 71–76. See also Shinoda, *The Founding of the Kamakura Shōgunate, 1180–1185,* and des Longrais, *Age de Kamakura.*

[7] On the "Code of Warriors," see Sansom, *A History of Japan to 1334,* pp. 358–69; Suzuki, *Zen and Japanese Culture,* pp. 61–214; and Nitobe, *Bushidō.*

[8] It was otherwise known as the *Goseibai shikimoku* (Principles for the shogun's court decisions). After its compilation many articles were added, so that eventually the New Appendix had 362 articles.

young sons, while the eldest son felt that the major portion of his father's property should be bequeathed to him. The step-mother went all the way from Kyoto to Kamakura, traveling from the sixteenth day to the twenty-ninth day of the tenth moon of 1277, in order to have the shogun's court settle the matter for her, even though this was a civilian issue.[9] The upshot was that there were two sets of legal, social, economic, and political principles operating during the Kamakura period.

[9] See the section on "The *Izayoi Nikki*," in Reischauer and Yamagiwa, *Translations from Early Japanese Literature*, pp. 1–135. In comparing the two codes that were in use during the Kamakura period, we note that the Taihō is based on the nationalization of land, even though it never worked well, while the Jōei affirms the private ownership of land—a pre-Taihō custom of Japan. The Jōei code rejects the Taihō civil service admin-istration—which again did not work out well—in return for paternal-istic control through clan chiefs. Actually, the Jōei formula in regard to marriage, for example, reflected the prevailing practice among the middle and lower classes, so that men and women were permitted to marry at any age, whereas the Taihō gave a normative statement concerning the marriageable age. According to the Kamakura formula those who wished to marry were not required to be registered in the provincial office, which was the Taihō requirement, but needed only the consent of their respective parents or guardians. Social stability was maintained therefore not through the administrative office but by means of the kinship system, which again was an ancient Japanese form. In regard to divorce, the Jōei follows Taihō principles almost entirely except that new regulations were introduced to control the effects of divorce. There were many other minor differences between the two codes, of course, but the basic difference was not so much a matter of legal opinions and theory as one of attitude toward jurisprudence. In the main, the Jōei code sanctioned what was going on in practice, without imposing the legal red tape that had been adopted from the Chinese legal systems. This does not mean that the Jōei code attempted to turn the clock back to the ancient clan days. While the Jōei code took it for granted that the welfare and honor of the clan (*ichizoku* or *ichimon*) were to be controlled by the clan chieftain, the "head of each household" (*katoku*) was given more authority and power over his children than were given to his counterpart in ancient days. If the children did not obey the *katoku*, they were subject to "excommunication" (*gisetsu* or *kandō*). See Asakawa, *The Early Institutional Life of Japan*; Fukuo, *Nihon kazoku-seido-shi*; and Munroe Smith, "The Japanese Code and the Family," in his *A General View of European Legal History and Other Papers.*

There were two developments that presented serious problems for the Kamakura regime. The first was an internal "rebellion" known as the Shōkyū or Jōkyū War, initiated in 1221 by the ambitious ex-Emperor Go-Toba (r. 1184–98). It was his hope to restore the power and prestige of "cloistered rule," which now had become an ornamental institution. He managed to secure the support of courtiers, disgruntled warriors in the western provinces, and great religious establishments, and declared war on Kamakura. In this, Kyoto underestimated the strength and determination of the Kamakura regime. The Kyoto forces were quickly defeated, and Go-Toba and two other retired emperors were sent into exile, while important rebel leaders were put to death.[10] Although later historians often disparage the action of the Kamakura regime in exiling ex-emperors, one has to remember that the corruption and degeneration of the court was such that the masses did not support the Kyoto forces.[11]

A second major event, the Mongol invasion, was much greater in scope and more serious in nature, for the survival of the whole nation was at stake. It is to be noted that since 894, when the sending of envoys to China was terminated, Japanese authorities

[10] For details of this war, see Sansom, *A History of Japan to 1334*, pp. 376–84. Behind the political struggle between Kyoto and Kamakura, there was a personal factor, too. Go-Toba gave certain manors to his favorite dancing girl Kamegiku, also known as Iga-no-Tsubone. But the land steward of these manors, who had been appointed by the Kamakura regime, did not recognize her authority. Go-Toba sent word to Kamakura to dismiss the guilty steward, but Kamakura refused. Go-Toba felt slighted, of course. The ex-Emperor Tsuchimikado suggested that this was a minor incident and tried to pacify Go-Toba, but in vain. See Takekoshi, *The Economic Aspects of the History of the Civilization of Japan*, I, 184–85.

[11] In his reply to the saintly priest Myōye, Hōjō Yasutoki, then the *shikken* of the Kamakura regime, explained why drastic measures had to be taken against the court "for the sake of the people." He cited instances of injustice in the areas of Japan where the court had authority. "There were *rōnin* [warriors without masters] everywhere, and robbery and piracy were rife. Therefore, the people could enjoy no peace of mind, and the highways were almost deserted by travellers. . . . If the court had all the country under its control, unhappiness would become universal. . . ." (*Ibid.*, pp. 187–88.)

had not been much concerned with what was happening in China, even though informal trade continued, and Japanese students, especially Buddhist priests, occasionally visited the continent. Meanwhile, in the twelfth and thirteenth centuries, the Mongols swept out of the steppes and conquered most of the known world. Khubilai (1215–94), the great Mongol khan and emperor of all China, sent word to Japan urging her to pay tribute; but Hōjō Tokimune (1251–84), then the *shikken* of the Kamakura regime, refused the honor, although it may have been rather foolhardy for him to take such action. In 1274 a combined force of Chinese and Korean troops in 450 warships invaded Kyushu. Obviously, the Japanese were not prepared to compete with the invading force, which had superior arms; in consequence, they suffered heavy losses. However, a tempest, believed by the Japanese to be a *kamikaze* (divine wind), caused great hardship to the invaders and destroyed many of their vessels. Again, in 1281, another expedition 140,000 strong in 4,000 ships invaded Kyushu, and again the Japanese losses were tremendous. But the determined fighters resisted the landing of the Chinese troops, and again a storm, divine or otherwise, drove the invaders away.

The extraordinary national crisis caused by the Mongol invasion helped to create a heightened sense of national consciousness on the part of the general populace in Japan. Even the aristocrats no longer retained the attitude of a few centuries before of intoxication with the superior culture of China. On the other hand, the Kamakura regime completely exhausted its political vitality and financial resources because of the Mongol threat that lasted until the death of Khubilai Khan two decades later. The national defense had to be maintained. While the expenditures mounted, the economic conditions of the people went from bad to worse.[12] The warriors expected and demanded a reward for

[12] In 1297 the debts owed by Kamakura retainers were canceled by the order of the regime. This order, known as *tokusei* (virtuous administration), backfired because merchants would no longer loan money or goods to warriors. Thus, warriors had to depend on the chieftains of some of the prosperous military families.

their services, and when they did not receive it, they were disgruntled. With the decline of the authority of the Kamakura regime, some of the chieftains of the powerful military clans in the provinces began to develop semiautonomous power. They were called *shugo-daimyō* or "feudal lords who protect others," [13] and with their emergence the foundation of the Kamakura regime was greatly weakened.

Taking advantage of the decline of the Kamakura regime, the Emperor Go-Daigo (r. 1318–39) plotted to regain by force from the feudal regime power for the throne, and also to keep the succession on his own side of the imperial family, known as the Daikakuji line.[14] Thus, supported by great religious establishments and by warriors who were persuaded to uphold the royal cause, he launched a military campaign against Kamakura in 1331. It is to be noted, however, that the Kamakura regime took the step of "enthroning" Prince Kazuhito, son of Go-Fushimi (r. 1298–1301), who was a member of a line rival to Go-Daigo's, called the Jimyōin, as the "Emperor" Kōgon. The Kamakura view was that its claim was legitimate.[15] Despite much hardship and frustration as an exile in an isolated island, the determined Emperor Go-Daigo managed to stage an unexpected comeback in

---

[13] The term *daimyō* literally means "great name" and was derived from the "name fields," one of the categories of private property in the make-up of the manors. See Reischauer and Fairbank, *East Asia*, p. 552.

[14] At that time there were two lines within the imperial family, both going back to Go-Saga's children. The line of Go-Fukakusa was called the Jimyōin family, while that of Kameyama was called the Daikakuji family. The Kamakura regime tried to keep both families happy, and also to keep the imperial family divided, by alternating the emperorship between them, the length of reign being limited to ten years per emperor. Go-Daigo, who was from the Daikakuji family, succeeded Hanazono (r. 1308–18) of the Jimyōin family. On this complicated problem, see Sansom, *A History of Japan to 1334*, pp. 478–84.

[15] Actually, such succession disputes were common in the history of Japan. Go-Daigo's claim was justified on the ground that he held the three symbols of the charisma of the imperial office, the sacred jewel, the mirror, and the sword. Even when the imperial authority was at its lowest ebb, and individual emperors were often manipulated, ignored, and banished, the charisma of the imperial office was respected.

1333 with the help of the loyalists, while even the residual power of the Kamakura regime collapsed because of defections. During the next three years Go-Daigo and his advisers attempted to restore the "imperial rule." This in itself was a noble idea, and there were no doubt some who sincerely believed in this as a cause. But among those who sided with Go-Daigo there were many whose motives were mixed, and in the end the mismanagement and injustice that characterized the imperial regime drove many warriors to side with Ashikaga Takauji who claimed the title of shogun for himself in 1335. Takauji secured the support of Kōgon who had been earlier made "emperor" by the Kamakura regime. In 1336 Takauji's forces defeated the government armies, and thus ended the "imperial rule" which had had a certain symbolic value but was able to accomplish nothing.

Ashikaga Takauji spent the rest of his life trying to restore peace and order to the war-torn nation. He managed to coerce Go-Daigo into turning the throne over to the "Emperor" Kōmyō of the Jimyōin line, but Go-Daigo slipped away from Kyoto with the sacred regalia which represented the imperial charisma and established a rival court at Mt. Yoshino.[16] Disunity within the

---

[16] In 1336, when Go-Daigo escaped to Mt. Hiei, he tried to take the "Emperor" Kōgon with him, but the latter, who had been siding with Ashikaga Takauji, refused to go on the ground that he was sick. As soon as Takauji's forces captured Kyoto, however, Kōgon established his "cloistered rule" (*inzei*). In the summer of the same year, Kōgon's younger brother was declared to be the "Emperor" Kōmyō. In the autumn, Takauji persuaded Go-Daigo to return to Kyoto from Mt. Hiei where he was protected by the strong arm of the Tendai monasteries. As soon as Go-Daigo returned, he was held in house arrest in Kyoto and had to surrender the sacred regalia to Kōmyō on the second of the eleventh month in 1336. Evidently Go-Daigo had been prepared for this turn of events and had had an imitation set of the sacred regalia made, and this set was conferred on the "Emperor" Kōmyō. In this drama are involved many difficult problems that are not too dissimilar to the question of the "validity" of sacerdotal succession in some religious traditions. Obviously Go-Daigo, under coercion to be sure, went through the ceremony of transferring the imperial charisma by means of a set of sacred regalia which were then accepted by others, who participated in the rite, as genuine items. There was "intention" on the part of Kōmyō to accept the imperial office. Given these factors, the

Ashikaga family plus a power struggle among his followers haunted Takauji and his successor Yoshiakira. Stability in the Ashikaga feudal regime did not come until the tenure of the third shogun, Ashikaga Yoshimitsu (1358–1408; ruled as shogun 1368–94). In the main the Ashikaga regime was modeled after the Kamakura regime. The guiding principle of the new government was the *Kemmu shikimoku* (Rules issued during the Kemmu era) consisting of seventeen articles adopted by Ashikaga Takauji.[17] Unlike the Kamakura regime which considered all warriors to be directly controlled by the shogun, the Ashikaga regime was designed to control local feudal lords who claimed the loyalty of their own retainers. Inevitably, the local feudal lords (daimyo) accumulated wealth and power, which gradually

question has not been answered as to whether or not Kōmyō was a "valid" emperor. Even Ashikaga Takauji waited until after this ceremony to begin his feudal regime (*bakufu*), and he was careful to be officially appointed to the position of shogun by the new "emperor" Kōmyō. Meanwhile, Go-Daigo took the genuine set of regalia and escaped to Yoshino, which was one of the important centers of the *shugen-dō* (Order of Mountain Ascetics). Actually, Go-Daigo wished to go to Mt. Kōya, the center of Shingon Buddhism, for he was counting on the help of the Shingon monasteries to support his cause. However, the monasteries at Mt. Kōya did not welcome the fugitive monarch, and thus he had to set up his court, known as *Nanchō* ("Southern dynasty" in contrast to the *Hokuchō* or "Northern dynasty" of Kyoto) at Yoshino. For these and other complex problems involved in the period of the Two Dynasties, see Murata, *Nambokuchō-ron*, pp. 85–100. In the "Southern dynasty," Go-Daigo was succeeded by Go-Murakami, Chōkei, and Go-Kameyama. (Incidentally, the Emperor Chōkei's existence was not recognized until 1926 when a famous historian, Yashiro Kuniharu, proved that such an emperor actually lived. *Ibid.*, pp. 120–21.) There was a temporary unification of the two dynasties in 1351 when the Southern Emperor Go-Murakami was persuaded to return to Kyoto as the only monarch. Only then did the Southern dynasty reveal that the set of sacred regalia which had been given to the Northern monarchs was not genuine. Go-Murakami and his followers were also determined to destroy the Ashikaga regime *in toto*, but their forces were defeated in 1352, and the Southern dynasty again became a government in exile. Not until 1392, when the Southern monarch Go-Kameyama surrendered the sacred regalia to the Northern monarch Go-Komatsu, were the two imperial lines reunited.

[17] See Sansom, *A History of Japan 1334–1615*, pp. 57–58.

undercut the authority of the shogun. Among the retainers, too, there developed a tendency to change allegiance from one daimyo to another, due to economic necessity and political instability. Those who were more adventurous and reckless made a career as soldiers of fortune by joining groups of pirate-traders known as *Wakō* or "Japanese Marauders" who invaded Korean and Chinese coastal towns.[18]

Economic necessity made Ashikaga Takauji turn to foreign trade, and he permitted the Tenryū temple in Kyoto to send ships to China. Evidently Japanese goods, especially swords and sulphur, were in great demand in those days; the Tenryū trade was a profitable business not only to the Tenryū temple but also to the regime. This type of informal commerce came to an end with the collapse of the Mongol dynasty in China. With the rise of the Ming dynasty, a mission was dispatched to Japan in 1369, asking the Japanese authorities to control the depredations of the *Wakō* and proposing legal trade which would be beneficial to both sides. In 1401 Ashikaga Yoshimitsu, who had already retired from the position of shogun, paid tribute to the Ming court, and thus began the Tally trade (*kangō bōyeki*).[19] The resumption of official relations with China also brought in many cultural influences, including Zen Buddhism and the cult of tea, as well as Neo-Confucianism and ink painting. The combination of Chinese and Japanese elements produced among other things an exquisite and simple ink painting which manages "in a flick to show a curving surface and an edge. . . . It omits just as the eye omits in looking at a landscape, and the spectator brings to the scene his own image-making faculty that we all share, no

---

[18] Actually, there were many Chinese and Koreans among the *Wakō*. On their activities, see Tanaka, *Wakō to kangō bōyeki;* see especially pp. 217–26 for reference materials on the subject. See also Delmar E. Brown, *Money Economy in Medieval Japan.*

[19] Reischauer and Fairbank, *East Asia,* p. 562: "The strong influence at the Ashikaga court of Zen monks who were in close contact with China had helped to build up a feeling of great respect for Chinese culture. Consequently, the acceptance of China's nominal suzerainty was probably not so distasteful to the Ashikaga as to the political leaders who preceded and followed them."

two of us alike, the exercise of which is the highest creative delight." [20] Within Japan the economic and population growth plus the rise of competing daimyo resulted in the development of cities and towns, such as the "temple and shrine town," the "port town," and the "castle town." Many of these towns later developed systems of self-rule and self-defense.[21]

The eventful Muromachi era also witnessed a gradual social revolution that produced various kinds of new social groupings. The manorial system, the basis of feudal society during the Kamakura era, collapsed and was taken over by a territorial system under the control of daimyo. The clan (*uji*), which constituted the solidarity group during the Kamakura era, also collapsed; and the household became the new solidarity unit of society. The term *sōryō*, which originally referred to the chieftain or manager of the clan, became the designation of the head of the household, who came to assume an amount of responsibility and authority greater than ever before. In a time of social, economic, and political insecurity, it was desirable to keep household property intact instead of distributing it among the children; thus a single heir was chosen to inherit the household property. The property was identified under the household name, and whoever was representing the household came to be known as *myōdai* or "name representative." The daimyo demanded allegiance of various households, both civilian and military, in their territories. They also interfered with the property inheritance of the households within their sphere of influence.[22] The principle of primogeniture was not only advocated by the daimyo for political reasons, but was welcomed by the eldest sons of each household as well, for many of them resented the shift in a father's preference to the children of a later marriage. With the rise of the

[20] Warner, *The Enduring Art of Japan*, p. 57.

[21] Yazaki, *Nihon toshi no hatten katei*, pp. 89–123.

[22] See Fukuo, *Nihon kazoku seido-shi*, p. 146. For example, the daimyo discouraged the practice of the *niwaka-yōshi* (sudden adoption of a son from outside the family as the inheritor of the household headship) because the daimyo felt that each household head should be trained from childhood for the honor of serving the daimyo interest.

household system, however, the position of women declined. In addition, merchants and artisans developed various kinds of societies known as *za*, which were often connected with Shinto shrines or Buddhist temples for the purpose of avoiding certain taxes in return for offering services for the maintenance of these religious establishments and participating in cultic affairs. Some of the powerful *za* managed to enter into contractual relationships with the daimyo. Even the farmers, who for centuries had been regarded virtually as serfs, began to organize their own societies called *sō*. These *sō* were managed by their leaders, known variously as *bantō, otona, satanin,* or *tone,* who negotiated with authorities regarding taxes and other matters. When the authorities made unreasonable demands, farmers often staged *do-ikki* (farmers' uprisings).[23]

Meanwhile, a bloody power struggle continued among influential daimyo. The most devastating conflict was the ten-year war of Ōnin, 1467–77, that divided the nation into two armed camps. Following the Ōnin war, there was a century of internal warfare throughout the nation, referred to as the *sengoku jidai* (the era of incessant warfare), even though the nominal Ashikaga shogunate lasted until 1573. The social and political chaos came to an end with the emergence of three strong men—Oda Nobunaga (1534–82), Toyotomi Hideyoshi (1536–98) and Tokugawa Iyeyasu (1542–1616)—who restored unity and order to the life of the nation.

In looking over the medieval period, what is most interesting to us is the fact that the religious movements reflected the ethos of the new social order that was in the making. For example, Buddhist groups manifested the strong characteristics of "societies,"

---

[23] In 1429 farmers rising up in Harima defeated the regular army of the daimyo Akamatsu Mitsusuke, and in 1485 a similar uprising at Yamashiro put to flight the crack army of Hatakeyama Masanaga. In Yamashiro male members of the age group between fifteen and sixty elected thirty-six (or thirty-eight) representatives; based on democratic processes, self-rule persisted for nearly ten years. See Kobata and Wakamori, *Nihon-shi kenkyū,* pp. 169–70, for a list of "uprisings" that took place between 1426 and 1580.

centering around the intense religious experience of their charismatic leaders. Some of these new religious groups became involved in a series of "uprisings," such as the *Ikkō-ikki* (uprising of the Honganji followers) and the *Hokke-ikki* (uprising of the Nichiren followers). Let us first turn to Shinto and see how it developed during the medieval period.

Shinto, Old Buddhism, and Shugen-dō

The medieval period witnessed a complex development in Shinto along both doctrinal and practical lines, due to the influence of Buddhism, the policies of the feudal regimes, and political as well as social changes. The Kamakura regime stressed the solidarity of the warrior clans, and this policy encouraged clan-centered Shinto cults. Although Minamoto Yoritomo was a pious Buddhist and restored many temples during his tenure, he paid supreme homage to the Tsurugaoka Hachiman, the kami of the Minamoto clan.[24] Doctrinally, Shinto accepted the main tenets of the theories of *Ryōbu-Shinto,* formulated by the Shingon Buddhists, and *Sannō-Ichijitsu-Shinto,* formulated by the Tendai Buddhists, both of which stressed the coexistence of Shinto and Buddhism in Buddhistic terms. For example, even the two shrines at Ise—the holy place of the kami of the imperial clan, Amaterasu—were interpreted in terms of the two realms of Mahāvairocana, the Cosmic Buddha of the Shingon school.[25] The Mongol

[24] In fact, the city of Kamakura was built around the Tsurugaoka Hachiman shrine which still holds the commanding position of the city. Regarding the religious policy of Minamoto Yoritomo, see Tsuji, *Nihon Bukkyō-shi: Chūsei-hen,* I, 1–36.

[25] Thus, the Inner Shrine (*Nai-kū*) of Ise was interpreted as the manifestation of the Womb-store realm of Mahāvairocana, while the Outer Shrine (*Ge-kū*) of Ise was the manifestation of the Diamond realm of Mahāvairocana. On these two realms of the Mahāvairocana, see Takakusu, *The Essentials of Buddhist Philosophy,* pp. 149–51. A historical work called the *Gukanshō* (Humble opinions), ascribed to the Tendai priest Jien, or Jihen, written about 1220 in order "to enlighten people who find it hard to understand the vicissitudes of life," interprets the Prince Regent Shōtoku and Sugawara-no-Michizane to be incarnations of Avalokiteśvara (*Kannon*). See Muraoka, *Nihon-shisō-shijō no shomondai,* p. 171.

invasions of 1274 and 1281 turned national attention to Shinto shrines and Buddhist temples, where prayers for victory were recited during crises and thanksgivings were offered for the felicitous outcome of events. The Shinto shrines, as much as the Buddhist temples, claimed credit for the supernatural aid that brought the "divine wind" to chase away the invaders, and they received vast quantities of rice and money both from the authorities and from the people.

Following the decline of the Kamakura regime, the short-lived "imperial rule" also gave further impetus to the revitalization of Shinto, which then began to develop its own doctrines in an attempt to become emancipated from Buddhist influences.[26] This effort was undertaken by Watarai Tsuneyoshi (d. 1339) and Watarai Iyeyuki (d. *ca.* 1355) of the priestly family of the Outer Shrine of Ise that has given the name "Ise Shinto" to this school of thought.[27] In spite of a serious effort to the contrary, Ise Shinto was far from being free from Chinese and Buddhist concepts. Nevertheless, Ise Shinto exerted significant influences upon Kitabatake Chikafusa (1293–1354), who was one of the architects of "imperial rule" under Go-Daigo. He wrote the *Records of the*

[26] The first attempt along this line was made by an unknown author in his work, *Shintō Gobusho,* which has been referred to as the "Shinto Pentateuch" by Katō. This work was probably compiled around the middle of the thirteenth century. According to Hirai, the *Shintō Gobusho* is based on five main concepts. First, the kami, *michi* ("the way" or *tao*), and man are essentially three in one. Second, "chaos" is the ultimate reality according to Shinto, and the kami are not manifestations of the Buddha-nature. Third, the kami of the Outer Shrine of Ise and the kami of the Inner Shrine of Ise share the same kami-nature which is what the ancient Japanese scriptures refer to as the "chaos." Fourth, the unique quality of Shinto is purity, and thus purification ceremonies are emphasized. Fifth, cultivation of the virtue of honesty should be the religious path for a Shinto believer. See Hirai, The Concept of Man in Shinto, pp. 33–34.

[27] Watarai Iyeyuki wrote a fifteen-volume work, *Ruiju-jingi-hongen* (Origins of the Shinto cults). Ise Shinto is also known as Watarai Shinto or Deguchi Shinto, so called from the family name of these priests, who previously were called the Deguchi and then changed their name to Watarai. On Ise Shinto, see Hirata, *Shintō no hongi to sono tenkai,* pp. 37–70.

Legitimate Succession of the Divine Sovereigns (*Jinnō-shōtō-ki*) in 1339, and stressed the unique quality of Japan as a divine nation. Holding that the sacred regalia of the charisma of the imperial authority—the mirror, the jewel, and the sword—were the symbols of the national virtues—truth, mercy, and justice—of Japan, Kitabatake acknowledged that Buddhism had supplied a metaphysical basis for the Shinto-inspired form of Japanese life, while Confucianism had also made contributions in providing ethical structures and principles.[28] Similar Shinto apologetics were taken up by Ichijō Kanera (1402–81), a nobleman whom Anesaki characterized as "an idealistic monist," and Yoshida Kanetomo (1435–1511), the founder of the tradition known variously as Yoshida, Urabe, or Yuiitsu Shinto.[29]

Equally significant was the transformation of the membership of the Shinto community from *uji-bito* (clansmen) to *uji-ko* (children of the kami). Although the traditional structure of the Shinto community was based on the given relationship between the clansmen and their kami (*uji-gami*), in many instances the *uji-gami* was also considered the regional kami, and thus the membership of the Shinto community was often defined as much in regional as in kinship terms. It is also to be remembered that during the medieval period the basic solidarity unit of society gradually shifted from the clan to the household. This was partly due to the fact that the larger grouping of *ichimon* or *ichizoku* (literally, "those who share one and the same gate" or "one tribal group") by necessity had to include households of different clan affiliation, even though a substantial number of them belonged to the same clan. Such a development might be explained in

[28] See Tsunoda, *et al.*, *Sources of Japanese Tradition*, pp. 273–82.

[29] In his book, *Yuiitsu Shintō myōhō yōshū* (The teachings of the one and the only Shinto), Yoshida Kanetomo cites three trends within Shinto: first, the transmission of the ancient Shinto teachings and practice as handed down in many shrines (*Honjaku Engi Shinto*), second, the Buddhistic Shinto (*Ryōbu Shinto*), last, the unique Shinto transmitted in his own family (*Gempon Sōgen Shinto* or the "Fundamental Shinto"). The last is divided into esoteric and exoteric divisions, and Yoshida stresses the importance of the esoteric side. See Hirai, The Concept of Man in Shinto, pp. 42–45; and Hirata, *Shintō no hongi to sono tenkai*, pp. 71–85.

terms of the practical needs of self-defense, of those who resided in the same locality, against enemies during a period of political disorder. A more plausible explanation might be derived from the unique Japanese custom of "adoption," that had prevailed from early times.[30] Furthermore, among the warriors, it was common for a certain adult to become the *eboshi-oya* (cap father) of a boy and present him with the cap (*eboshi*) when he was initiated before the kami. The initiation took place when the boy became fifteen years of age; from that day on he was regarded as the *eboshi-go* (cap child), and became the *de facto* son of the *eboshi-oya*. In non-warrior circles, a similar custom of "pseudo-adoption" was common, and the children thus adopted were known as *yū-shi* or *yashinai-go* (child who is to be cared for).[31]

In a real sense, the concept of *uji-ko* was based on the same notion of "pseudo-adoption" wherein the kami (*uji-gami*) was believed to enter into a pseudo-kinship relationship with those who joined the liturgical community. They were accepted as *uji-ko* (children of the kami).[32] Connected with this development was that of *za* or *miya-za*, professional guilds affiliated with the Shinto shrines, as mentioned earlier. The "members of *za*" (*za-nin*) held meetings at the shrine to settle their practical and cultic matters. The leaders of *za* were responsible for both the liturgical activities of the shrine and the welfare of its members.[33] Eventually, Shinto also developed the organizational structure called *kō*, consisting of devotees of the kami of certain shrines, which were not necessarily confined to the circle of *uji-ko*.[34] Thus Shinto, which had already been transmuted during the

[30] Adoption was encouraged during the medieval period, more in order to maintain the strength of the *ichizoku* than to secure the lineage of each household. Adoption could be arranged from wider circles than those of blood relationship, even though the latter type was more frequent. See Fukuo, *Nihon kazoku-seido-shi*, p. 105. See also Tsugaru, *Die Lehre von der Japanischen Adoption*.

[31] On the other hand, the legally adopted child was called *yō-shi*.

[32] Wakamori, *Chūsei kyōdōtai no kenkyū*, pp. 5–105. See also Yanagita, *Minzokugaku jiten*, pp. 55–58.

[33] See Yanagita, *Minzokugaku jiten*, pp. 189–91.

[34] *Ibid.*

Heian period, underwent a further process of transformation during the medieval period.

The advent of the feudal regime, with the decline of the aristocracy and the collapse of the manorial system, caused serious difficulties for the old Buddhist schools. This was true of those which had been established during the Nara period, especially the Hossō (Yogācāra), Kegon (Avatamsaka), and Ritsu (Vinaya), as well as of the two schools founded during the Heian period, namely, the Tendai and Shingon. Many of the difficulties they faced, such as the corruption of the clergy, catering to vested interests, cumbersome rituals, and incomprehensible doctrinal formulations, were undoubtedly of their own making. Having been accustomed to the generous support of the aristocracy and lucrative incomes from their land holdings, the old schools neglected the laymen and laywomen who, as a result, were driven to the simple teachings and cults of Amida pietism. More fundamentally, the leaders of the old schools failed to understand the nature of the society that was emerging before their eyes. As Anesaki points out, "the Buddhist hierarchies lost their prestige to a large extent, together with their political supporters at court; ceremonies and mysteries were much discredited, while undercurrents of unrest and aspiration manifested themselves in various ways." [35]

In the main, the religious policy of the Kamakura regime was fair, though firm, and social and political revolution served as a cleansing and stimulating experience for the complacent religious establishments. Other factors that assisted the reawakening of the old schools were the renewed influence of Chinese Buddhism, the prevailing "eschatological" belief in the coming end of the present world-period, and competition from the new schools of Buddhism which will be discussed later. Historians tend to overstress the importance of the new schools of the Kamakura period at the expense of the old schools, but we should not overlook such outstanding priests of the old traditions as Jōkei (1155–1213) of the Hossō school; Kōben, better known as Myōye-Shō-

---

[35] Anesaki, *History of Japanese Religion*, p. 167.

nin (1173–1232), Sōshō (1202–92), and Gyōnen (1230–1321) of the Kegon school; and Eizon (1201–90) and Ninshō (1217–1303) of the Shingon-Ritsu school. Some of the new features that characterized the old schools during the Kamakura era were (1) the *Shaka-Nembutsu* (Recitation of the name of Sakyamuni), an effort to counteract the popularity of the *Amida-Nembutsu* (Recitation of the name of Amida); (2) the cult of Maitreya, the future Buddha, also an effort to compete with the Amida cult; (3) simplification of doctrines, as exemplified by the teachings of Kōben; (4) renewed emphasis on monastic disciplines which were rejected by the new schools; and (5) emphasis on philanthropic activities as illustrated by the works of Eizon and Ninshō.[36] It is also to be remembered that many of the leaders of the new schools came out of the reform tradition of the old schools, especially the Tendai.

Unfortunately, these efforts on the part of a small number of the clergy hardly touched the old monastic establishments, especially those at Mt. Hiei, Mt. Kōya, and Nara. In addition to the fact that the power struggle among them continued, they were still deeply involved in the political affairs of the nation.[37] The Mongol invasions provided occasions for the old schools, particularly the Shingon and Tendai, to offer their magico-religious incantations, which made them again wealthy and powerful in a worldly sense. While the Kamakura regime came under the influence of Zen Buddhism, the court in Kyoto was still under the spell of esoteric Buddhism. The Emperor Go-Uda (r. 1274–87; retired, 1287–1324), for example, devoted his energy to the restoration of the Shingon school, and entered the Shingon priesthood in 1276.[38] It has been noted already that Go-Uda's son,

---

[36] On Jōkei, see Iyenaga, *Nihon Bukkyo shisō no tenkai*, pp. 95–116. Regarding the general situation of the old schools of Buddhism during the Kamakura era, see ZNBT, VI, *Kamakura jidai*, pp. 186–97, and Tsuji, *Nihon Bukkyō-shi: Chūsei-hen*, I, 194–287.

[37] It is to be noted that the principal support for the ex-Emperor Go-Toba in his "rebellion" against Kamakura in 1221 came from warrior priests of Kumano and Mt. Hiei.

[38] See Tsuji, *Nihon Bukkyō-shi: Chūsei-hen*, II, 395–428.

Go-Daigo, in his military campaign against Kamakura, depended heavily on the temples of Mt. Hiei, Daisen, Yoshino, and Mt. Kōya. In fact, the first move of the "imperial rule" was richly to reward the religious establishments for their services to the court.[39]

The Muromachi regime under the Ashikaga shogun took a cautious attitude toward religious establishments. One of its guiding principles was that "the claims and petitions of shrines and monasteries must be carefully scrutinized, since the professed motives are not always the true ones." [40] The third Ashikaga shogun, Yoshimitsu, nevertheless, made Mansai or Manzei (1378–1435), the abbot of the Shingon temple, Daigoji, in Kyoto, his political adviser; this fact indicates the influence of the clergy that developed increasingly during the Muromachi era.[41] Among sects, the one in the forefront during the Muromachi era, however, was the Rinzai Zen school, considered to be *de facto* the state religion. The powerful monasteries at Nara (Hossō temple, Kōfukuji), at Mt. Hiei (Tendai), at Mt. Kōya (Shingon), and at Negoro (Shingi-Shingon) held their own because of their wealth and military strength. But as organized religious groups among the general populace these old schools failed to compete with the new schools. The only rapport they had with the masses was indirectly through the Shugen-dō (Order of Mountain Ascet-

---

[39] Kobata and Wakamori, *Nihonshi kenkyū*, p. 153. Many of the land properties of the Kamakura regime were distributed among larger religious establishments. In one instance, the farmers of the Wakasa province which became the property of the Shingon temple in Kyoto, called Tōji, bitterly complained about the prohibitive tax imposed by the Tōji administrators. They stated that the administration under the Kamakura regime was far better for their welfare. See Kuwata, *Kizoku bunka kara Buke bunka ye* (ZNR, 4), p. 72.

[40] Cited in Sansom, *A History of Japan, 1334–1615*, p. 57.

[41] Mansai, or Manzei, was the son of a court official of high rank, and reached in 1425 the highest ecclesiastical dignity. "He became extremely rich, acquiring estates in twenty provinces. His advice was constantly sought by Yoshimitsu, who was his uncle, and in time by Yoshimochi. He has been described as the Black-robed Prime Minister." (Sansom, *A History of Japan, 1334–1615*, p. 160.)

ics), which maintained its contact with the Tendai and Shingon schools on the one hand and with the masses on the other.

Previously, we traced the origin of the Shugen-dō to the tradition of the shamanistic Buddhists of the Nara period. The main strength as well as the weakness of the Shugen-dō was its nondoctrinal, practical, and "adhesive" character. While never being considered an organized sect or denomination, the mountain ascetics (*yama-bushi*) and their spiritual cousins in the countryside, known as *hijiri* or *shōnin* (holy men), gained influence and prestige among both the upper and the lower stratum of society during the Heian period. During the late Heian period the mountain ascetics at Kumano developed an affiliation with the Tendai school and came to be known as the Honzan tradition.[42] The mountain ascetics at Kimpu, on the other hand, became affiliated with the Shingon school, and came to be known as the Tōzan tradition.[43] The former was under the jurisdiction of the *Shōgo-in monzeki* (the prince-abbot of the Shōgo temple), while the latter was under that of the *Sambō-in monzeki* (the prince-abbot of the Sambō-in at Daigo).

With the advent of feudal society, the mountain ascetics lost their aristocratic patrons and thus turned their attention primarily toward the masses.[44] In this situation, the mountain ascetics, as such, began to organize themselves, at first as informal brotherhoods but gradually as well-defined societies, never, however, repudiating completely their precarious affiliation with the Tendai and Shingon schools as well as with Shinto.[45] The order of

[42] The mountain of Kumano was regarded as the "main mountain" (*honzan*) of this tradition.

[43] The mountain of Kimpu (Kimpu-sen) was the "primary mountain" (*tōzan*) of this tradition.

[44] During the later Heian era, many ex-emperors and courtiers made pilgrimage to Kumano and other holy places. During the Kamakura era, only the ex-Emperors Go-Saga (twice) and Kameyama (once) could afford such a costly undertaking. Likewise, courtiers were no longer able to spend money on pilgrimages.

[45] For example, many mountain ascetics made it a habit to congregate at the Shinto shrine of Ima-kumano, which was a branch shrine of the Kumano shrines, in Kyoto. They were technically under the jurisdiction of

mountain ascetics under this organization was known as the Shugen-dō (the path of acquiring magical power by means of austere training). In contrast to the Tendai and the Shingon schools, both of which were based on lofty philosophical doctrines, the Shugen-dō stressed nondoctrinal austere disciplines on the mountains and advocated the magical potency of the mystic syllables (*dhāranī*) for the masses.[46] The two main traditions of the mountain ascetics, the Honzan and the Tōzan, became "sects" of the Shugen-dō. While both regard En-no-Shōkaku, the shamanistic ascetic of the Nara period, as the legendary founder of the Shugen-dō, the Tōzan sect venerated Shōbō (d. 909) as its systematizer. In addition there were minor differences between the two sects. For example, the ascetics of the Honzan do not cut their hair, while those of the Tōzan sect have the head shaved. Also, the routes of their mountain pilgrimages are exactly opposite. That is to say, while the Honzan sect follows a course starting from Kumano, proceeding to Ōmine, and ending at Yoshino, the Tōzan sect starts from Yoshino and ends at Kumano.[47] The prominent holy mountains of the Shugen-dō are Mt. Katsuragi, Mt. Kimpu (Kogane-no-mine), Mt. Ōmine, the three mountains of Kumano, Mt. Fuji, Mt. Haku, and Mt. Tate of the Hokuriku area, Mt. Haguro of the Tohoku district, Mt. Dai (Daisen) of the San-in district, and Mt. Hiko of Kyushu. Later, Mt. Ontake of the Shinano district also became an important center for ascetic training.[48]

During the Muromachi era, the Shugen-dō was further institutionalized and came to be regarded as the *Shugen-shū*, an inde-

---

the prince-abbot of the Shōgo (Tendai) temple. See Wakamori, *Shugen-dō-shi kenkyū*, p. 188.

[46] For the popularity of the *dhāranī* during the medieval period, see Tamamuro, "Nihon Bukkyō-shi gaisetsu," pp. 154–56.

[47] On other differences between the two sects of the Shugen-dō, see Wakamori, *Shugen-dō-shi kenkyū*, pp. 183–203.

[48] See Tamamuro, "Nihon Bukkyō-shi gaisetsu," pp. 161–65. In addition to the Honzan and the Tōzan, two other prominent sects of the Shugen-dō were the Hiko-san (which seceded from the Honzan sect during the Tokugawa period) and the Haguro sect which dominated the scene in the northern part of Japan. See Togawa, *Haguro yama-bushi to minkan shinkō*.

pendent religious system, or the *Zatsu-shū*, an eclectic school related both to Shinto and Buddhism. Although the mountain ascetics were required to go through initiation rites, they were not considered "ordained priests" in the sense that Buddhist and Shinto clergy were. Variously known as *yama-bushi, hō-in,* and *gyō-nin,* these ascetics were in constant demand among the masses as well as among some of the leading families. Many of them served as professional guides for the pious in their pilgrimages to holy places, and developed a kind of "pastoral relation" with certain families and villagers. Some of the mountain ascetics accumulated lands and properties, and they even acted as deputies (*daikan*) for provincial officials. In many districts there developed devotional fraternities (*kō-sha*) for the reciting of the mystic syllables (*dhāraṇī*); in the course of time members of these fraternities became "parishioners" (*danka*). On the other hand, some of the ascetics served as semiprofessional messengers from one place to another, or as traveling salesmen. Since the *yama-bushi* were permitted to bear swords on their persons, they even acted as mercenaries in time of war. It is altogether difficult to assess the influence of these elusive ascetics, but there is no doubt that they preserved the shamanistic tradition of Japanese religion in areas where other religious bodies failed to penetrate.[49] In this sense, the Shugen-dō or Shugen-shū was the most persistent rival of new Buddhist schools that arose during the Kamakura era.

The Pure Land, Nichiren, and Zen

The new social order that emerged during the medieval period under the leadership of the warriors inspired new types of Buddhist schools. "The Buddhist religion of the new age," says

[49] Tarō Wakamori suggests that the legend of Shōbō who is said to have killed the snake on the mountain is significant in the sense that the snake was feared and venerated as the kami of the mountain in accordance with folk belief. (*Shugen-dō-shi kenkyū,* p. 201.) He also suggests that the *saitō* ritual, a fire-burning rite, can be traced to the *saitō-yaki,* a fire-burning ceremony at the holy place of a kami who protects a road. Under the influence of the Shugen-dō, this ancient ritual was transformed into the *saitō-goma* (Homa sacrifice) introduced by Shingon esotericism. (*Ibid.,* pp. 241–42.)

Anesaki, "was not one of ceremonies and mysteries but a religion of simple piety or of spiritual exercise. Dogma gave way to personal experience, and ritual and sacerdotalism to piety and intuition. . . ." [50] The new Buddhist movements were led by five figures who were very different in their outlook and temperament. They were Hōnen (1133–1212) of the Pure Land school, Shinran (1173–1262) of the True Pure Land school, Nichiren (1222–82) of the Nichiren school, Eisai (1141–1215) of the Rinzai Zen school, and Dōgen (1200–53) of the Sōtō Zen school. These men were instrumental in the transformation of "Buddhism in Japan" into "Japanese Buddhism," whether or not they were conscious of the roles they were playing in such a process.

For the most part, the many schools of Buddhism in Japan prior to the Kamakura era took for granted the soteriological dualism that divided the path of the clergy and that of the laity. Their orthodoxy was not determined by doctrinal formulations but rather by the validity of the transmission of the charisma of the ecclesiastical office.[51] The fact that these Buddhist schools all willingly served the interests of the temporal authority was undoubtedly due to the fact that Buddhism entered Japan as a religion of the aristocracy and the court. More basically, Buddhism in Japan had always equated its own sphere with that of the state so that, in principle, outside the national community there was no meaningful framework for the sociological expression of Buddhism. Thus there were monastic communities and there were lay devotees, but there never developed an independent Buddhist community which would nurture Buddhist normative principles concerning the social, political, and cultural dimensions of human life and society. In other words, Buddhism, despite its otherworldly beliefs, prospered in Japan as a religion of this world, and more specifically as a religion of the Japanese nation.[52]

[50] Anesaki, *History of Japanese Religion*, p. 168.

[51] Even the Tendai school, which originally had trouble in securing the authorization of the court for its "ordination hall," later took a formalistic attitude in regard to the question of ordination.

[52] See Nakamura, *The Ways of Thinking of Eastern Peoples*, pp. 337–55. I agree with Nakamura's description of ultranationalism as one of the

In contrast to the older Buddhist schools, the new schools that came into existence during the Kamakura era attempted to develop their own "specifically religious societies," embracing within them both the clergy and laity. The functional difference between the clergy and laity was recognized, but it had nothing to do with the question of salvation. The focal point of each of these religious societies was the religious experience of its founder. Authenticity in religious leadership was determined by the quality of the personal charisma and not by the transmission of the charisma of the ecclesiastical office. The central motif of these religious movements was not the attainment of Buddhahood by means of spiritual discipline or the magical power of the divinities, but an experiencing of the certainty of salvation.

HŌNEN AND THE PURE LAND MOVEMENT: Like many of the new Buddhist leaders of the Kamakura era, Hōnen took his training as a Tendai priest at Mt. Hiei.[53] In the late Heian period the Tendai monastic center at Mt. Hiei prospered externally but suffered from an internal power struggle among the prince-abbots. While many of the high ecclesiastics led a life of leisure in their private residential quarters in Kyoto, some of the serious-minded young clergy came under the influence of the Amida cult. There also developed several schools of "oral transmission" of the mystical truth which fostered a close relationship between the master and the disciple within the Tendai framework.[54] Among several

---

characteristics of the way of thinking of the Japanese, and his opinion that it has conditioned Japanese Buddhism historically. He says: "Just as religion was the basis of the ethical thinking of the Indians, family the basis of the practical morals of the Chinese, so the state was the basis of all thought in the Japanese." (*Ibid.,* p. 352.) In this sense one might go so far as to say that Buddhism did not convert the Japanese but rather that it was transmuted into a Japanese religion.

[53] There have been many good works on the life of Hōnen. One of the best is Tamura, *Hōnen shōnin den no kenkyū.* The only important work in English on Hōnen's life is Coates and Ishizuka, *Hōnen the Buddhist Saint.* When Hōnen was a small boy, his warrior father was attacked and killed by bandits. The dying father instructed Hōnen not to spend his life trying to avenge him but to enter the priesthood.

[54] See Inouye, *Nihon Jōdo-kyō seiritsu-shi no kenkyū,* pp. 288–91.

teachers who instructed Hōnen, there was one Higo Ajari, a shamanistic Tendai priest who according to legends "drowned himself" in order to wait for the appearance of the future Buddha Maitreya.[55] Hōnen also studied at Nara but was not satisfied with the traditional teachings of Buddhism. Thereafter, he became a disciple of a charismatic holy man (*shōnin*) and devotee of the Amida cult, called Eikū, who resided at Kurodani.[56] In time he realized that the path of sanctification and enlightenment by means of precepts, meditation, and knowledge was theoretically possible but practically impossible.[57] He came to realize, in reading Genshin's *Essentials of Salvation* (*Ōjō Yōshū*), that he was to seek not "enlightenment" but "salvation in the Pure Land."[58] Based on this faith, Hōnen wrote the *Senchaku Hongan Nembutsu-shū* (Collection of passages on the original vow of Amida in which the Nembutsu is chosen above all ways of achieving rebirth).[59]

Hōnen, thus convinced of the certainty of salvation through

[55] See Tamura, *Hōnen shōnin den no kenkyū*, pp. 273–75.

[56] Coates and Ishizuka, *Hōnen the Buddhist Saint*, p. 85. Eikū's master was Ryōnin (1073–1132), who advocated the *Yūzū-Nembutsu*, a corporate cult for reciting the holy name of Amida.

[57] The path to enlightenment presented three questions to the mind of Hōnen. First, in what way does the right knowledge arise? Second, without the right knowledge, how can one be freed from the chain of evil passion whence comes evil conduct? Third, unless one is freed from evil conduct and evil passions, how can one obtain deliverance from the bondage of birth and death? See Coates and Ishizuka, *Hōnen*, p. 186.

[58] It is to be noted that through Genshin's writing Hōnen was led to the Chinese Pure Land writing. The *Commentary on the Meditation Sutra* by Zendō (Shan-tao) states: "Whether walking or standing, sitting or lying, only repeat the name of Amida with all your heart. Never cease the practice of it even for a moment. This is the very work which unfailingly issues in salvation, for it is in accordance with the Original Vow (*hongan*) of that Buddha." See Coates and Ishizuka, *Hōnen*, p. 187.

[59] The term *senchaku* (choosing) does not mean mere "shopping around." It implies the willingness to take a risk in faith. With this motif of man's "choosing," Hōnen's Pure Land movement became qualitatively different from the earlier Pure Land cults. The difference between the earlier Pure Land belief and Hōnen's motif was clearly seen in iconographical expressions. See Ishida, *Jōdo-kyō bijutsu*.

the mercy of Amida, established his headquarters in the midst of the secular society of Kyoto and gathered together disciples, including Shinran. Hōnen's followers felt, as he did, that, in view of the impending end of the present world-period, the surest way open for them was to trust wholeheartedly in Amida and invoke his holy name, the "name" being the mysterious embodiment of his saving power.[60] Hōnen's popularity inevitably aroused jealousy, opposition, and persecution from the old schools of Buddhism, to the extent that he was banished from Kyoto in 1207. Stripped of clerical status, Hōnen, now a layman with the name of Fujii Motohiko, still attracted many followers. His exile was abrogated in 1211, and he died the next year at the age of eighty.

There is no evidence to support the view that Hōnen attempted to establish a new sect or school. He neither built a temple nor tried to organize his followers into ecclesiastical groups. However, his disciples, who at first formed only an informal fellowship or confraternity, developed gradually into a religious society. At a time when the old order of society was disintegrating, his followers discovered that faith could provide a basis for group cohesion, transcending kinship, class, and all other natural factors that usually divide human society.[61] In this sense, Hōnen left a great legacy to the subsequent history of Japanese Buddhism, namely, faith as the basis for the development of an independent religious society.

After the death of Hōnen, persecution of the Pure Land followers continued. In 1227 Hōnen's disciples were again banished from the capital, and Hōnen's grave was desecrated. Nevertheless, in spite of or because of these persecutions, the Pure Land movement spread in the Hokuriki, Tōkaidō, and Kyushu areas; the Pure Land devotees contributed money for the establishment of a great statue of Amida in Kamakura in 1238. Meanwhile, the

[60] Anesaki, *History of Japanese Religion*, p. 173: "The formula provided for the purpose of this name calling is *Namu Amida Butsu*, that is, 'Adoration to the Buddha of Infinite Life and Light.' Faith is of course the fundamental requisite on the part of those to be saved, in repeating his holy name."

[61] See Inouye, *Nihon Jōdo-kyō seiritsu-shi no kenkyū*, pp. 319–33.

leaders of the Tendai school at Mt. Hiei and of the Hossō school at Kōfukuji, Nara, staged a series of persecutions of the Pure Land followers that lasted until the time of the Ōnin War (1467–77). But the persecution only helped to solidify the group consciousness of the Pure Land devotees. Among all the subgroups of this movement, the one developed in Kyushu became most influential. Its tradition known as the Chinzei-ha (tradition of Kyushu) gradually penetrated both Kamakura and Kyoto. It was Chinzei-ha which established itself in Kyoto as the Jōdo-shū (Pure Land sect) around the middle of the fourteenth century; by the end of the fifteenth century it became sufficiently strong to rival the power of the Tendai school.[62]

SHINRAN AND THE TRUE PURE LAND SCHOOL: Among all the able disciples of Hōnen, the one who was destined to be most influential was Shinran.[63] He was only eight years old when he was sent to the Tendai monastery at Mt. Hiei, where he stayed twenty years. Little is known about his activities at Mt. Hiei except that he was a minor monk in the Jōgyō Zammai-dō.[64] When he was twenty-nine years of age, he became a disciple of Hōnen. It was then that Shinran dared to risk his whole existence on Amida's saving power. Shinran stated that he did not know, and he did

---

[62] Tamura, *Hōnen shōnin den no kenkyū*, p. 222.

[63] There are many works on Shinran's life and thought. The most definitive biographical study of Shinran is Matsuno, *Shinran—Sono shōgai to shisō no tenkai katei*. Among the English works are Lloyd, *Shinran and His Work: Studies in Shinshu Theology*; Gesshō Sasaki, *A Study of Shin Buddhism*; Takahashi and Izumida, *Shinranism in Mahayana Buddhism and the Modern World*; Kōshō Yamamoto, *The Private Letters of Shinran Shōnin*; Nakai, *Shinran and His Religion of Pure Faith*; and D. T. Suzuki, *A Miscellany on the Shin Teachings of Buddhism*. I wish to acknowledge my special indebtedness to Yoshinori Takeuchi, "Shinran's Religious Philosophy" (mimeographed lecture notes). See also Ryōsetsu Fujiwara, *The Tanni shō*. For a sociological study of the True Pure Land sect, see Morioka, *Shinshū kyōdan to Iye-seido*.

[64] This was the chapel of the *jōgyō-zammai* (a method of *samadhi* or contemplation by means of constantly walking around the statue of Amida reciting his name).

not care, whether the *Nembutsu* (recitation of Amida's name) was really the means to rebirth in the Pure Land or the road to Hell. "Even though, having been persuaded by Hōnen Shōnin, I should go to Hell through the Nembutsu, I should not regret it." [65] This thoroughgoing faith of Shinran came out of a soul-searching that made him realize the utter helplessness of the human being. Men outwardly pretend to speak truth, but inwardly their hearts are filled with greed, anger, and deceitfulness. Try though he might, Shinran could not overcome his sense of human depravity. Thus, after testing all other paths and disciplines, there was nothing left for him except to believe in the mercy of Amida. Accordingly he believed it is not man who "chooses" Amida, but rather it was Amida's Original Vow (*hongan*) which "chose" all beings to be saved.[66] Thus, even our faith is really the gift of Amida. "Shameless though I be and having no truth in my soul, yet the virtue of the Holy Name, the gift of Him that is enlightened, is spread throughout the world through my words, although I am as I am." [67] No one realized as acutely as Shinran did the subtle danger that one's faith can degenerate into "faith in one's own faith." In his view, faith in the "other power" (Amida) is the most difficult way.[68]

No one among the believers in the Pure Land was as much "possessed" by Amida's mercy as Shinran. It was but logical, then, that he should reject all the traditional cults and methods of spiritual exercise and completely eliminate the distinctions between clergy and laity. He married and had children. He, too, was

[65] Takeuchi, *Kyōgyō shinshō no tetsugaku*, pp. 110–11. The *Kyōgyō shinshō* literally means "Testimony (*shō*) for the true teaching (*kyō*), true practice (*gyō*), and true faith (*shin*)" of the Pure Land.

[66] Furuta, *Nihon Bukkyō shisō-shi*, p. 91.

[67] Shinran, *Buddhist Psalms*, tr. by Yamabe and Beck, p. 86.

[68] Hōnen taught that "even a bad man will be saved, how much more a good man!" Shinran reversed it and said that "even a good man will be received, how much more a bad man!" That is to say, neither good nor bad counts, only the saving act of Amida. Thus, according to Shinran, the *Nembutsu* must not be practiced "in order to be saved," but as the expression of gratitude toward the one who has chosen to redeem us whatever we happen to be.

banished from Kyoto in 1207. Unlike earlier Buddhists in Japan who obediently succumbed to the temporal power, Shinran dared to raise a prophetic voice against the emperor and officials for inflicting punishment on Hōnen Shōnin and his disciples in a manner "against the Dharma," the eternal Law of Buddha.[69] Thus, following the Buddha's Law rather than the law of the land, Shinran proceeded to preach in exile the gospel of the Pure Land to the oppressed and downtrodden among the masses, as well as among the warriors. After staying in the eastern provinces for nearly two decades, he returned to Kyoto. He continued to preach and write until he died in 1262 at the age of ninety.

Shinran never intended to found a new sect. In fact, he refused to call anyone his disciple; he called his followers *dō-gyō* (fellow believers). But his disciples formed informal local fellowships called *monto* (believers of the Jōdo-mon). They were so fervently dedicated to the *Nembutsu* that they were called the *ikkō-shū* (the "one direction" or "single minded" sect). In 1274 Shinran's daughter, Kakushin-ni (1222–81), established her father's mausoleum in the Ōtani section of Kyoto, with the understanding that her descendants were to be its hereditary wardens. This was the beginning of the institutionalization of the True Pure Land group. Under Kakushin-ni's grandson, Kakunyo (d. 1351), Shinran's mausoleum was called the Hongan-ji (Temple of the Original Vow of Amida). The Hongan-ji maintained a nominal affiliation with the Tendai monastic center at Mt. Hiei until the time of Rennyo (1415–99), the eighth patriarch of the temple. With rare courage, Rennyo destroyed all the ornaments and scriptures that had Tendai connotations, thus declaring the full independence of the True Pure Land sect. The forces of Mt. Hiei retaliated in 1465 by burning the Hongan-ji.[70] During the Ōnin War, while the feudal lords (daimyo) were brawling and the established older schools of Buddhism declined, the True Pure Land sect grew together as a tightly knit religious-political society under the leadership of Rennyo. They were ready to fight with arms against

---

[69] This passage from the *Kyōgyō Shinshō* is explicated in Yoshinori Takeuchi, "Shinran's Religious Philosophy," pp. 26–27.

[70] Tamamuro, "Nihon Bukkyō-shi gaisetsu," pp. 149–50.

rival powers, religious, military, or civil. The uprising of the followers of this sect was called the *Ikkō-ikki* (Uprising of the Ikkō Believers). Such uprisings took place in the Hokuriku district in 1473, 1474, 1487, and 1488. In the sixteenth century nearly twenty major Ikkō uprisings took place, involving fighting against the professional soldiers of the feudal lords. Even the strong man, Oda Nobunaga (1534–82) failed to defeat the Ikkō followers who defended their temple in Osaka with the slogan: "The mercy of Buddha should be recompensed even by pounding flesh to pieces. One's obligation to the Teacher should be recompensed even by smashing bones to bits!" [71] Ironically, the followers of Shinran, who had rejected the institutionalization of religion, sacerdotalism, and temporal power, developed the most militant religious-political society, with a hierarchy based on hereditary principles. This sect accumulated power that rivaled any feudal lord's toward the end of the Muromachi era.

It may be worth while for us to recall that the tradition of Shinran was one of the four major types of Amida pietism that prospered in Japan. The first was the belief in Amida as taught by the Nara schools, according to which Amida is one of the five Wisdom Buddhas (*Dhyani-Buddhas*). The second was the tradition of the shamanistic Amidist, Kūya (903–972), who taught the communal Nembutsu (recitation of Amida's name). His short-lived movement was restored by another shamanistic Amidist, Ippen-Shōnin (1239–89) who advocated the rule of reciting the hymn of Shan-tao six times every day. Thus Ippen's movement was known as the Ji (Times) sect. Ippen followed the pattern of the shamanistic holy men (*hijiri*) and spent his life as an itinerant sage (*yugyō shōnin*), traveling in many parts of Japan. He claimed that he received his revelation at Kumano, the ancient Shinto center and one of the holy places of the Shugen-dō (Order of Mountain Ascetics). His followers took a conciliatory attitude toward Shinto. Later, his disciples formed an informal brotherhood (*kessha*), which eventually became institutional-

---

[71] Cited in Tsunoda, *et al., Sources of Japanese Tradition,* p. 211. On the subject of the *Ikkō* uprising, see Kasahara, *Ikki-ikki*.

ized.[72] The third tradition of Amida pietism in Japan was Hōnen's Pure Land school; the fourth was Shinran's True Pure Land school. The importance of the last two schools, according to Takakusu, is that "in both Jōdo and Shin the Buddha Amida is more than one of the five Buddhas, although his land is laid in the Western Quarter; instead, he is the one central Buddha."[73] Equally significant was the fact that faith in the Pure Land became instrumental in establishing independent "religious societies" which provided a new basis for social solidarity in Japan.

NICHIREN AND THE NICHIREN SCHOOL: Nichiren, the founder of the unique Buddhist school bearing his name, was one of the most charismatic personalities in the religious history of Japan.[74] It has been rightly said that Nichirenism is half the man and half the *Lotus Sutra*.[75] Nichiren, son of a humble fisherman in what is now Chiba prefecture, probably led the most eventful life among

[72] See Hori, *Waga-kuni minkan-shinkō-shi no kenkyū*, II, 337–52; and Inaba, "Ippen Shōnin no shisō ni tsuite," *Nihon Bukkyō shigaku*, II (No. 2, April, 1943), 60–75.

[73] Takakusu, *The Essentials of Buddhist Philosophy*, p. 175. The basic difference between them lies in the fact that while Hōnen taught the faith in Amida's Three Vows in accordance with the three *Sukhāvatī* texts of the Pure Land school, Shinran based his teaching on the One Vow, namely the eighteenth vow, of Amida as described in the larger *Sukhāvatī* text. On Shinran's novel reinterpretation of Shan-tao's teachings, based no doubt on Shinran's unique and intense religious experience, see Nakamura, *The Ways of Thinking of Eastern Peoples*, pp. 419–20.

[74] Nichiren's colorful life and passionate teachings have been portrayed in many books. In my opinion, the following are important: Anesaki, *Hokke-kyō Gyōja Nichiren*; Masutani, *Shinran, Dōgen, Nichiren*; Yamakawa, *Hokke shisō-shi-jō no Nichiren Shōnin*; Miyazaki, *Nichiren-shū-shi kenkyū*, Vol. 1; and Ōno, *Nichiren*. English publications on Nichiren include the following: Anesaki, *Nichiren, the Buddhist Prophet*; Sansom, "Nichiren," in Eliot, *Japanese Buddhism*, pp. 416–31; and Satomi, *Japanese Civilization: Its Significance and Realization, Nichirenism and the Japanese National Principles*.

[75] The *Lotus (Saddharma-pundarīka) Sutra*, known as *Myōhō-renge-kyō* in Japanese, was first translated into Chinese by Dharmaraksa in the Western Tsin dynasty (265–316), and was again translated by Kumarajiva in 407. Nichiren preferred the second translation and read it with the Tendai exegesis.

all the leaders of the new Buddhist movements during the Kamakura era. As a young man, Nichiren was haunted by two questions. One was personal: how could he experience the certainty of salvation? The second was historical: why were the imperial forces defeated by the Kamakura regime in 1221 in spite of the prayers and incantations offered by the Tendai and Shingon ecclesiastics on behalf of the imperial cause? These two problems —the salvation of man and the religious meaning of empirical history—preoccupied him throughout his life. In 1242, when he was twenty-one, he went to Mt. Hiei, where he stayed until 1253. There he came to be convinced that the key to his two fundamental problems was contained in the *Lotus Sutra.*

In 1253 Nichiren began his prophetic mission, urging the whole nation to return to the teaching of the *Lotus Sutra.* A series of natural calamities that plagued the nation at that time was a sure sign, in his mind, that the period of *mappō* (the degeneration of Buddha's Law) had come. In 1260 he presented his biting essay on "the establishment of righteousness and the security of the nation" (*Risshō ankoku ron*) to the authorities, prophesying that the nation would not only suffer from natural calamities but would be invaded by foreign enemies. Nichiren's foes attempted to kill him, but he escaped. In 1261 he returned to Kamakura, and thereafter was promptly banished to a desolate section of the Izu peninsula. Two years later he was released. He renewed his violent attack against the Pure Land and Shingon schools and again barely escaped assassination in 1264. When the messenger of the Mongol Khan arrived in 1268, demanding tribute from Japan, Nichiren reminded the authorities of his earlier warning. As the result of his continued attack on the leaders of the regime and established Buddhism, he was exiled in 1271 to the distant island of Sado.[76] In 1274 he was released; again he

[76] Nichiren's life was full of miraculous events. In 1271 he was tried for high treason. On his way to Tatsu-no-kuchi, where he was to be executed, he called on Hachiman, the patron kami of the Minamoto clan, to rescue him. According to his own account, as he sat on a straw mat, waiting for the executioner to strike him, bright light from heaven blinded the soldiers, so that they became panic-stricken and ran away. This convinced Nichiren all the more of his divine mission.

warned the authorities of the coming invasion. When his advice
was not taken seriously, he left Kamakura and retired to Mt.
Minobu. In the autumn of that year the first Mongol invasion
took place. At Minobu, Nichiren spent his time instructing his
disciples and writing essays and books, constantly urging the nation and the people to turn to the truth of Buddhism. However,
Japan managed to survive the second Mongol invasion in 1281,
and Nichiren decided not to discuss this matter again. He died the
following year.

From every indication, Nichiren wanted to restore and reform
the Tendai school. He accepted *in toto* the Tendai doctrine of
ichinen-sanzen, holding that all the three thousand spheres of the
living creatures are embraced in one thought.[77] In one sense,
Nichiren's was a reform movement within the Tendai school. In
another sense, however, his novel approach to religious and temporal matters was such that his movement had more affinities with
other new schools of Buddhism. For example, he disregarded the
validity of the transmission of the charisma of ecclesiastical offices.
To him, the transmission of the *Lotus Sutra* was based on a
"spiritual succession" from one charismatic person to the next,
even though there might be a long time span between them. Thus
Nichiren considered himself, on one hand, the successor to the
transmission of the "Sākyamuni-Chi-hi [founder of the T'ien-t'ai
school in China]-Dengyō" line, and, on the other, also the in-
carnation of Viśistacāritra Bodhisattva (Jōgyō, in Japanese, to
whom Sākyamuni is said to have entrusted the *Lotus Sutra*). He
was intent on destroying the Pure Land, Shingon, Ritsu (Vinaya), and Zen schools. His famous maxim was: "Those who
practice invocation to Amitābha are due to suffer continuous
punishment in Hell; the Zen sect is the devil; the Shingon sect
is the ruiner of the country; the Ritsu sect is the enemy of the
country." [78] Yet he shared with the Shingon school the use of the

---

[77] On Nichiren's understanding of *honkaku* (original enlightenment),
which he had inherited from the Tendai school, see Tamura, "Nihon
Tendai honkaku-shisō no keisei-katei," *Journal of Indian and Buddhist
Studies,* X (No. 2, March, 1962), 661–72.

[78] Quoted in Nakamura, *The Ways of Thinking of Eastern Peoples,* p.
398.

mandala and the belief in *sokushin jōbutsu* (becoming a buddha with one's body during one's earthly existence). He shared with the Pure Land believers the doctrine of the redeemability of the man of evil nature, and the superiority of faith over knowledge. Although he denounced the *Nembutsu* (recitation of Amida's name), he virtually substituted for it the recitation of the title of the *Lotus Sutra* in the form of *Namu Myō-hō Renge-kyō* (Adoration be to the Sutra of the Lotus of the Perfect Truth). His establishment of the *kaidan* (ordination hall) was no doubt influenced by the example of Dengyō Daishi, but by the tradition of the Ritsu (Vinaya) school as well. He was also in agreement with the leaders of other new Buddhist schools concerning the redeemability of women.[79]

Nichiren was also a patriot, considering himself the pillar, the eyes, and the great vessel of Japan.[80] He was convinced that the nation prospers only when the truth of Buddhism is revered. Yet his was not an emotional nationalism. He respected the throne but felt that the throne should be subservient to religious authority. He dared to state that the ex-Emperors Go-Toba and Juntoku died in exile "because of the bad karma of having despised the Buddha Sākyamuni and having neglected the *Lotus Sutra*."[81] What Nichiren envisaged was the establishment of the great Buddha land in Japan. His charismatic personality was such that he attracted many dedicated disciples, who were willing to suffer hardship and persecution with their master.[82] After Nichiren's death in 1282 his

[79] This was one of the most significant, innovative motifs of the new Buddhist schools during the Kamakura era. See Matsuno, "Kamakura Bukkyo to josei," *Journal of Indian and Buddhist Studies*, X (No. 2, March, 1962), 648–60.

[80] In his commentary on the passage in the *Lotus Sutra* which says "the Buddha appeared in the world," Nichiren says "by 'world' Japan is meant. . . ." See Nakamura, *The Ways of Thinking of Eastern Peoples*, p. 346.

[81] "Reply to Sister Myōhō," cited *ibid.*, p. 395, footnote 28.

[82] Nichiren on his part reciprocated with tender friendship toward his followers. In his letter to his disciple Kingo, he recalled how Kingo had followed him on his way to the miraculously prevented beheading. "Over and over I recall to mind that you came following me when I was going to be beheaded, and that you cried and wept, holding the bridle of my horse. How can I forget that as long as I may live? If you should fall to the hells . . . I would not follow the call of my Lord Sakya, however he

six closest disciples continued to propagate the faith of the Lotus, directing the affairs of the local congregations (*shū*), scattered mostly in the eastern provinces.

The year 1294 marked the beginning of the spread of the Nichiren sect to Kyoto; it continued to grow during the fourteenth century in spite of persecution by the forces of Mt. Hiei. In the past the animosity of the Tendai hierarchy was no doubt due to the fact that many Tendai clergy were converted to the teaching of the Lotus. During the fifteenth century, with the disintegration of the social order, the followers of Nichiren began to equip themselves with arms. Their uprising, known as the *Hokke-ikki* (Uprising of the *Hokke* or Lotus followers), was just as effective and devastating as the *Ikkō-ikki* (Uprising of the Ikkō-shū or the followers of the True Pure Land school). The military victory of the followers of Nichiren over the followers of the True Pure Land in 1532 made the former the strongest religious group in Kyoto. But the tables were again turned in 1536 when twenty-one of its temples were destroyed by the armed forces of Mt. Hiei; it is said that 58,000 of Nichiren's followers were killed in action.[83] However, the simple teaching and militant faith that characterized the Nichiren school continued to attract warriors and simple folks in the provinces. Ironically, this school, based on the *Lotus Sutra* that teaches universal salvation, developed into the most exclusivistic religious, social, and political society in Japan.

EISAI AND THE RINZAI ZEN SCHOOL: Although meditation (*dhyana* or the "concentration of mind") has been practiced by Buddhism from its inception, the "Meditation school" with its special forms of training and transmission was the product of Chinese Buddhism. In China, however, Ch'an (Zen in Japanese) existed side by side with other Buddhist traditions. This type of Zen was introduced to Japan by a Japanese Hossō priest, Dōshō, and a Chinese Vinaya (Ritsu, in Japanese) master, Tao-hsüan

---

might invite me to Buddhahood, but I would surely be in the hell where you are." Cited in Anesaki, *Nichiren, the Buddhist Prophet*, p. 58.

[83] Kōza Bukkyō Series, No. V, *Nihon no Bukkyō*, ed. Yūki, et al., p. 221.

(Dōsen in Japanese) during the Nara period. In the early Heian period Saicho—or Dengyō Daishi—incorporated Zen, as one of the important ingredients, into his Tendai system. It was only during the medieval period that Zen developed into independent Buddhist schools. The three Zen schools in Japan that arose during the Kamakura era were (1) the Rinzai sect, introduced from China by Eisai in 1191, (2) the Sōtō sect introduced from China by Dōgen in 1227, and (3) the Fuke sect founded by Kakushin in 1255.[84] A fourth tradition, known as the Ōbaku sect, was established by a Chinese priest, Ingen, in 1654.[85] Unlike other new schools of Buddhism that developed during the Kamakura era, Zen schools were introduced from China; as such, therefore, they represented a different ethos from that of the indigenous new schools. In the main, Zen schools followed the tradition of the older Buddhist schools in the sense that they catered to the upper strata of society, and did not organize independent and self-supporting "religious societies," in the strict sense of new schools, until sometime later.

Eisai (1141–1215) combined within himself both the Heian and the Kamakura attitudes toward religion and society. As a young Tendai priest, he had become disheartened by the decline of the traditional Buddhist precepts and monastic disciplines at Mt. Hiei. His chief concern was not with a "certainty of salvation" as in the cases of Hōnen, Shinran, and Nichiren. His main preoc-

[84] Kakushin, who studied under Fu-yen in China, founded a mendicant form of Zen Buddhism, usually referred to as *komusō* (community of nothingness). "The school eventually became a community of *rōnin* (lordless warriors). . . . This was abolished after the Great Restoration in 1868." (Takakusu, *The Essentials of Buddhist Philosophy*, p. 161.)

[85] Books on Zen are numerous. Ruth Fuller Sasaki, "A Bibliography of Translations of Zen (Ch'an) Works," *Philosophy East and West*, X (Nos. 3–4, Oct., 1960–Jan., 1961), 149–66, is helpful. Among many books by D. T. Suzuki, the following are specially important: *Essays in Zen Buddhism*, Series I, II, and III; *Studies in Zen Buddhism*; *Zen and Japanese Buddhism*; and *Zen and Japanese Culture*. *The Blue Cliff Records: The Hekigan Roku*, tr. and ed. with commentary by R. D. M. Shaw, is also helpful. Probably the handiest single volume on Zen is Heinrich Dumoulin, *Zen: Geschichte und Gestalt* (English translation, *A History of Zen Buddhism*).

cupation was with the purification and restoration of the traditional glories of Buddhism in Japan. He lived at a time when high
ecclesiastics were accumulating temporal power and wealth, a
time in which pleasure-loving aristocrats considered it an enter-
tainment to invite handsome and sweet-voiced clergy to chant
sutras before them. In order to learn the true tradition of Tendai,
Eisai visited China in 1168 and there became interested in Ch'an
(Zen). Again he studied in China (1187–91), pursuing further
training in Ch'an, T'ien-t'ai and Vinaya. Upon his return, he
taught and practiced Zen, but only as one important element in
the comprehensive Tendai system. It may be that he followed this
course through practical necessity even though he really wanted
to set up a Zen school independent of the Tendai structure.[86] At
any rate, he maintained rapport with the court in Kyoto, and received favor from the feudal regime at Kamakura. His conciliatory attitude toward the warriors, who were then the new leaders
of Japanese society, helped the cause of Zen a great deal. Political
development in China under the rising Mongol dynasty, moreover, led some able Ch'an masters to come to Japan where they
were cordially welcomed by the Kamakura regime.[87]

The Rinzai tradition of Zen in Japan and its Chinese counterpart, Lin-ch'i, were quite different in ethos, however. In China,
Ch'an was noted for "No dependence upon the words and letters;
a special transmission outside the classified teachings; direct pointing to the mind of man; seeing into one's own nature." [88] Chinese

[86] In spite of his argument that Zen was an integral element of the
Tendai system, he was often criticized by his colleagues at Mt. Hiei. His
disciple Gyōyū became chaplain of the Kamakura shogunate in his capacity as the master of the Tendai esotericism (*Taimitsu*). It was Bennen
(1202–80) who laid the foundation for the independence of the Rinzai
school. Kōza Bukkyo V, *Nihon no Bukkyo*, pp. 125–30.

[87] Among them were Tao-lung (Dōryū in Japanese; founder of the
Kenchō temple), Tsu-yüan (Sogen in Japanese, founder of the Engaku
temple), and I-ning (Ichinei in Japanese). Both Hōjō Tokiyori and
Hōjō Tokimune, the *shikken* of the Kamakura regime, were interested in
Zen, and invited several Chinese Ch'an masters to Japan. Correspondingly,
many Japanese priests went to China to study Ch'an there. See *Kamakura
Jidai* (ZNBT VI), pp. 178–83.

[88] Quoted in Morgan, *The Path of the Buddha*, p. 340.

Ch'an masters did not even pay respect to kings or princes. But, in Japan, Eisai studied religious law and observed ceremonial rules, practiced Tendai, Shingon, and Zen alike, and also recommended to others the observance of *Nembutsu*.[89] He even initiated the "Esoteric Zen" (*Zenmitsu,* so called in contrast to the *Tōmitsu* or Shingon esotericism and the *Taimitsu* or Tendai esotericism) which opened the way for offering prayers and incantations. The two temples established by Eisai—Kennin-ji in Kyoto and Jufuku-ji in Kamakura—were the training centers for Zen as well as for the Tendai and Esoteric schools. The Kennin-ji was made the branch temple of the Enryaku-ji at Mt. Hiei. Eisai depended heavily on scriptures and was a firm believer in the doctrine of *mappō* (the period of degeneration of Buddha's law). He took it for granted that one of the main tasks of Buddhism was to do its share in the protection of the state, as he taught in his essay "The Propagation of Zen for the Protection of the Nation" (*Kōzen-gokoku-ron*).

While Eisai did not direct his attention toward the common people, he and his followers made great contributions to the cultural life of the nation as a whole. The introduction of tea, for instance, was credited to Eisai.[90] Far more significant was the fact that Eisai and his disciples were instrumental in transplanting the Chu Hsi tradition of Neo-Confucianism to Japan,[91] and Zen

[89] Quotation from *Shaseki-shū,* cited in Nakamura, *The Ways of Thinking of Eastern Peoples,* p. 406, footnote 16.

[90] This is a debatable problem. The Emperor Shōmu, during the Nara period, is said to have invited one hundred Buddhist priests to take tea in his palace, and Eliot thinks that Kōbō Daishi introduced tea to Japan. Tea was not appreciated until the Kamakura era, and "Eisai can at least claim the credit of making it fashionable and of inventing the tea ceremonies." (Eliot, *Japanese Buddhism,* p. 283.) For Eisai's essay "Drink Tea and Prolong Life" (*Kissa yōjō-ki*), see Tsunoda, *et al., Sources of Japanese Tradition,* pp. 243–46.

[91] On the question as to who initially introduced Neo-Confucian writings to Japan, see Spae, *Itō Jinsai,* pp. 31–39. According to Spae, Eisai came in contact with Tou-Ts'ung-chou, a disciple of Chu Hsi, and it is more than probable that Eisai returned to Japan in 1191 with a copy of one of Chu Hsi's works. But Shunjō (1166–1227) is usually considered the first Japanese monk to have introduced the *New Commentaries* of the Sung school.

temples soon functioned as schools for Neo-Confucianism.[92] Meanwhile, the trend of the followers of Rinzai Zen to become independent of the Tendai school resulted in a series of persecutions led by the forces of Mt. Hiei during the thirteenth and fourteenth centuries. But the Rinzai Zen school gained patronage among the warrior leaders so that it became to all intents and purposes the state religion during the Muromachi era, as evidenced by the establishment in each province of a Zen temple by the Ashikaga regime. Trade with China on the part of the Rinzai Zen temple, Tenryū-ji, has been mentioned earlier. Even in the period of political unrest in the sixteenth century the cultural life of Japan was maintained by Zen priests. "As the holders of land property, libraries, collections of art, belonging to their monasteries, and as the men most advanced in culture, Zen monks were not only able to maintain their own culture but worked to educate others." [93]

It was under their inspiration that the art, literature, the tea cult, and the Nō play, for example, developed.[94] The stern austerity and the meditation upon paradoxical statements (*kōan*) that were the basis of the Rinzai Zen attracted only a few serious seekers; nevertheless, the spiritual mood and the artistic refinement of the entire Japanese culture were deeply influenced by Zen Buddhism.[95]

DŌGEN AND THE SŌTŌ ZEN SCHOOL: In many ways Dōgen (1200–53) was vastly different from Eisai. Born into a family of noble lineage, Dōgen experienced the tragedy of losing his father and mother at an early age. Realizing the transitoriness (*mujō*) of life, Dōgen at thirteen entered the Tendai monastery at Mt. Hiei.

---

[92] The famous Ashikaga Academy at Shimozuke had several thousand students toward the end of the fourteenth century. All the teachers and students of this school were Zen priests, and it is to be noted that students came from all parts of Japan. See Tamamuro, "Nihon Bukkyō-shi gaisetsu," p. 99.

[93] Anesaki, *History of Japanese Religion*, p. 234.

[94] See Tsunoda, *et al., Sources of Japanese Tradition*, pp. 261–66 and 283–303.

[95] See Warner, *The Enduring Art of Japan*, pp. 53–60.

His search for the "certainty" of attaining Buddhahood drove him from Mt. Hiei, first to a Pure Land teacher, and then to Myōzen, the disciple of Eisai. In 1223 Dōgen went to China, still looking for a truly enlightened person, and there by chance encountered Ju-ching, a Ch'an master, at the T'ien-t'ung monastery. It was under Ju-ching's tutelage that Dōgen experienced "enlightenment." Returning to Japan in 1227, he tried to transmit his newly gained insight without establishing a new sect. However, his tradition eventually developed into the independent Sōtō (Chinese: *Ts'ao-tung*) school.

Dōgen's career was characterized by the single-mindedness of his intense spiritual pilgrimage. For seven years he remained in the Kyoto area, trying to instruct seekers. In 1235 he established a *sōbō* (monks' living quarters for the purpose of the corporate life of Zen discipline) at Uji, a suburb of Kyoto. In order to secure the court's permission for his enterprise, Dōgen wrote an essay insisting that his approach was the truest path in Buddhism. His essay was "censored" by the ecclesiastics at Mt. Hiei, whose troops fell upon his new monastic center and destroyed it.[96] Therefore, in 1243, Dōgen moved to a remote section of Echizen province and reestablished his monastery, which was later called Eihei-ji (Temple of Perpetual Peace). There he put into practice the most stern Zen discipline, without seeking recognition, support, or favor from the temporal authorities. Even when he was given the purple robe by the ex-Emperor Go-Saga, who evidently was deeply impressed by his spirituality, Dōgen refused the honor. When in 1250 a messenger came for the third time from the court, Dōgen accepted but never wore the garment.[97] He died in 1253.

Understandably, Dōgen's strict approach to religion and life had no popular appeal. At one time he held that enlightenment

[96] Kōza Bukkyō V, *Nihon no Bukkyō*, pp. 193–99.
[97] The following poem was written by Dōgen on that occasion:
　　Though the valley below the Eihei-ji is not deep,
　　I am profoundly honored to receive the imperial command.
　　But I would be laughed at by monkeys and cranes
　　If an old monk wore the purple robe.
Cited in Nakamura, *The Ways of Thinking of Eastern Peoples*, p. 461.

could be achieved even in secular life; but gradually he moved
toward a monastic emphasis and designed rules for the corporate
life of the monastic community. Yet he always maintained that the
truth of Buddhism is "applicable to everybody" (*fukan*) regardless of intellectual capacity or social background.[98] Holding that
women had as much chance as men of achieving enlightenment,
he had several able women disciples.[99] His chief principle in the
practice of religious meditation was not thinking upon the *kōan*,
as in the Rinzai tradition, but the physical practice of "sitting
straight," without any effort at achieving enlightenment. There is
no question that Dōgen was one of the most intellectual of all the
Buddhist leaders of the Kamakura era. Instead of blindly following the tradition of the Ts'ao-tung (Sōtō) masters in China,
Dōgen followed his own line of thought based largely on his own
religious experience. He was critical of the Chinese Ch'an masters
who ignored Buddhist scriptures; on the contrary he relied heavily
on scriptural authority. In his view "the true intention of the
Buddha can be found *only in the sutras*." [100] On the other hand,
he was critical of the new Buddhist movements of his time for
their acceptance of the theory of the three world-periods—*shōbō*
(period of the Perfect Law), *zohō* (period of the Copied Law),
and *mappō* (period of the Latter Law). Thus, unlike Hōnen,
Shinran, and Nichiren, whose teachings were derived from the

[98] Evidently Dōgen did much of his writing in the *kana* syllabary. Many
of his works, which were really lecture notes, have been since touched up
by his disciples. In the original they must have been easier to comprehend
than in the versions handed down to our time. See Furuta, *Nihon Bukkyō
shisō-shi*, pp. 100–11.

[99] See Matsuno, "Kamakura Bukkyo to Josei," pp. 654–55.

[100] Nakamura, *The Ways of Thinking of Eastern Peoples*, p. 370. However, Dōgen used his own interpretation of certain scriptural passages. For
instance, the passage from the *Nirvana Sutra* to the effect that "all sentient beings have the Buddha-nature" is usually interpreted to mean that
"all sentient beings have the capacity to become Buddha in a future
world." Dōgen states, however, that "all existence is the Buddha-nature."
Here he takes the phrase "all have" as a noun meaning an "absolute one."
See Watsuji, *Nihon Seishin-shi kenkyū*, pp. 348–49. Cited also in Nakamura, *The Ways of Thinking of Eastern Peoples*, p. 303, footnote 11.

notion of *mappō*, Dōgen was persuaded that a true believer has access to the "Perfect Law" of Buddha.[101]

In the most crucial way, however, Dōgen was a child of his time, for he shared with Hōnen, Shinran, and Nichiren a special view of the significance of "faith." Although Zen traditionally taught self-realization, Dōgen realized that in the final analysis one has to have absolute faith in "the Buddha as an ideal person, and *be saved by him.*" [102] These two emphases, on scriptural authority and on faith in Buddha, led Dōgen unwittingly to sacerdotalism and authoritarianism. In practical terms, one must have faith in his master. He says: "In order to embrace Buddhism, one must abandon his own judgments of good and evil. Rather must one follow the words and examples of our Buddhist predecessors, regardless of good and evil." [103] No doubt his was a creative synthesis based on his spiritual pilgrimage, long years of study, and his own "enlightenment experience," and in this sense the Sōtō Zen school in Japan was Dōgen's unique creation.[104]

Dōgen's remarkable system, which inevitably had many contradictions within it, was destined to be formalized and distorted immediately after his death. His disciple and successor as abbot of Eiheiji, Ejō (d. 1280), instructed Gikai (d. 1309) to observe and study the monastic rules of other Zen temples in Kyoto and Kamakura, as well as in China. After years of study Gikai added many minute rules and regulations that improved Dōgen's rules in some ways but ended by losing his real spirit. Repeated "improvements" made matters worse during the Muromachi era, for the Sōtō priests began to be preoccupied with the study of Neo-Confucianism. The branch temples of the Eiheiji in the countryside competed with other Buddhist societies, such as the Shingon, Pure Land, True Pure Land, and Nichiren, on their own terms by offering prayers and incantations for the laity.[105]

[101] Ivenaga, *Nihon Bukkyō shisō no tenkai*, pp. 176–77.
[102] Nakamura, *The Ways of Thinking of Eastern Peoples*, p. 364.
[103] Cited *ibid.*, p. 358.
[104] Eto, *Shūso to shiteno Dōgen zenji*, p. 322.
[105] See Tamamuro, "Nihon Bukkyō-shi gaisetsu," pp. 110–12, and Kōza Bukkyo V, *Nihon no Bukkyō*, pp. 205–6.

Be that as it may, the Sōtō Zen school, which was founded by Dōgen, served as a necessary corrective to other new Buddhist schools during the medieval period. All these new schools arose partly because of the spiritual needs of the time and partly because of the intense religious inquiry and experience of their leaders, many of whom were charismatic personalities. It was an irony of history that these new Buddhist schools were destined to develop into religious, social, and political societies shortly after the deaths of their founders. Their institutionalization was justified on the ground of practical necessity, and many of the changes undoubtedly were introduced with good intentions. But the result was that these new, supposedly religious societies proved to be just as aggressive in worldly affairs as the old established schools. Toward the latter part of the sixteenth century Japan was divided not only among the semi-independent powerful feudal lords (daimyo) but also among equally powerful and fanatic followers of religious societies. That is why the task of unification of the nation which will be discussed in the next chapter, involved religious as well as political measures.

CHAPTER IV

Kirishitan, Neo-Confucianism,
and the Shogunate

RELIGIOUS TRENDS

DURING THE TOKUGAWA PERIOD

(ca. seventeenth–mid-nineteenth centuries)

The significance of the unification of Japan under the Tokugawa feudal regime (*bakufu*) early in the seventeenth century can best be understood if we recall the period of political and social disintegration that lasted over a century following the ten-year-long civil war of the Ōnin era, 1467–77. During this period not only did the imperial court fall into decay, but the power and prestige of the Ashikaga shogunate also steadily declined. The manors (*shōen*) that had once provided the social and economic basis for the feudal system were gradually transformed into the territories of ambitious daimyo (feudal lords) who competed among themselves for greater power. In the countryside increasing numbers of villages developed as self-governing units. The minor officials, who at one time had been agents of the centralized feudal system, became rural aristocrats—identifying their lot with that of the villagers. Also, in various parts of the country commercial and other types of towns developed with their own systems of defense and administration. For example, some of the religious societies, notably those of the True Pure Land sect (*Jōdō-shin shū*), developed self-sustaining towns, such as Yamashina Hongan-ji near Kyoto and Ishiyama Hongan-ji at Osaka.[1] Furthermore, each daimyo established a so-called castle town (*jōka-machi*) which served as both the political and the economic center of his territory. "In fact," says Reischauer, "when the Europeans first arrived in Japan, in the sixteenth century, they found political and social conditions which were completely understandable to them in terms of the sixteenth-century Europe they knew."[2]

During the second half of the sixteenth century three strong men successively rose to power and tried to unify the nation politically and thus to end the state of incessant warfare that had been the rule among the quarrelsome daimyo. The first of the unifiers was Oda Nobunaga (1534–82), who consolidated the present Nagoya district around 1560, and then proceeded to take over Kyoto in 1568. There he quickly deposed the last of the Ashikaga shoguns in 1573 and claimed control of the nation, even though many daimyo in the distant provinces refused to accept his authority. While throughout his life he had much trouble with rebellious daimyo and equally uncooperative religious groups, Nobunaga managed to introduce many new measures to unify the nation, such as the establishment of the *chigyō* system which authorized the daimyo to rule his fief by taxation, the institution of the *rakushi* (free market) and *rakuza* (open guild) in order to counteract local trade monopolies, the abolition of the *sekisho* (barrier) and barrier tax, and the adoption of currency control. Nobunaga also took a keen interest in the use of European firearms, and initiated the construction of a new type of castle in Azuchi in the present Shiga prefecture. He did much to restore the prestige of the imperial court, although this measure was calculated on his part to enhance his own authority.[3] His impul-

[1] Nishida, *Nihon bunkashi josetsu*, pp. 499–500; Yazaki, *Nihon toshi no hatten katei*, pp. 98–103.

[2] Reischauer and Fairbank, *East Asia*, p. 578.

[3] Oda Nobunaga studied under several Zen masters, such as Takugen Shūon, Nange Genkō, and Sakugen Shūryō. It is not clear how devout he was in his personal life, however. He was also interested in the Chu Hsi (*Shushi* in Japanese) school of Neo-Confucianism, and had a sense of social order. His respect for the imperial authority was not altogether motivated by political expediency. Nobunaga did not follow the policy of

sive character, lack of compassion, and harshness in dealing with enemies as well as subordinates resulted in his untimely death in 1582 during the rebellion of one of his generals.

The death of Oda Nobunaga propelled Toyotomi Hideyoshi (1537–98) to the forefront of Japanese history. Son of a poor farmer, Hideyoshi aspired to become a warrior, and served Oda Nobunaga. His faithful service, coupled with unusual shrewdness, enabled Hideyoshi to rise quickly, and in 1577 Nobunaga made him a leading general in charge of the campaign in the western provinces. Upon the death of Nobunaga, Hideyoshi returned immediately from the west, and established himself as successor to his late master. Thereafter, Hideyoshi defeated or bribed the rebellious daimyo in the Kyushu, Kantō, and Tōhoku districts, and by 1590 became unrivaled despot. Realizing his own humble origin, Hideyoshi maneuvered to become the *yūshi* (a sort of adopted son) of Konoye Sakihisa, and secured for himself the status of *kampaku* (dictator) and *dajō-daijin* (chancellor). He even persuaded the court to confer on him the family name of Toyotomi. Hideyoshi built a magnificent castle at Osaka, the town originally established by the True Pure Land sect. He did not attempt to institute a feudal regime but tried to use the prestige of the throne for the purpose of unifying the nation. With rare astuteness, he moved the daimyo around, and put into effect such measures as a national land survey for the purpose of ascertaining the yield of farm lands, the *katanagari* (sword hunt) that confiscated all arms of farmers and townsmen, a census of population, the minting of coins, and the encouragement of mining and other industries. He abolished the *za* (guilds), thus making tradesmen and merchants directly subservient to the daimyo, and forbade farmers to move from their lands. He was interested in trade with India, the Philippines, and Formosa, but was determined

---

Minamoto Yoritomo and Ashikaga Takauji in establishing the feudal regime (*bakufu*). Rather, he followed in the footsteps of Taira-no-Kiyomori in the sense that he sought court rank and attempted to unify the courtiers and warriors under his power. Significantly, he called himself Fujiwara Nobunaga earlier, but later called himself Taira-no-Nobunaga. See Kuwata, *Hōken bunka no keisei* (ZNR V), pp. 28–30.

to consolidate the national life by enforcing class distinctions among warriors, farmers, and townsmen. Being something of a megalomaniac, he was motivated to conquer not only the whole of Japan but other nations of Asia, and thus sent expeditions to Korea in 1592 and 1598. Little was gained from these campaigns except perhaps the removal of potters and other technicians from Korea to Japan.[4] Unlike Oda Nobunaga, Hideyoshi enjoyed high living and built a luxurious palace for himself in Kyoto. Under his extravagant patronage, many artists prospered. "Even the tea ceremony," says Warner, "originally conceived to be held by five cultivated cronies in a thatched hut, now used massive gold and silver and took place in half a dozen palaces and temples simultaneously over the city."[5] Despite the unusual success that characterized his life, Hideyoshi was not blessed with domestic happiness. His relatives were not dependable, or at least so he thought. His pathological love for Hideyori, his son by his mistress Yodo-gimi, endured until Hideyoshi died in 1598 when the boy was only six years old.

After Hideyoshi's death his followers were divided into two factions and fought for political control of the nation. The battle at Sekigahara in 1600 brought victory to Tokugawa Iyeyasu (1542–1616) and his followers over those who supported the child Hideyori; thereafter Iyeyasu was appointed by the court to the office of Seii-Taishōgun (military dictator) in 1603. Iyeyasu, originally the son of a minor daimyo not far from the present Nagoya, rose to power through his astuteness and determination. Early in his career he allied himself with Oda Nobunaga, and later submitted to Toyotomi Hideyoshi's authority. In following this course, he gained ground as a major daimyo in the eastern province. It was he who was destined to complete the task of national unification which Nobunaga and Hideyoshi had attempted before him. The feudal regime (*bakufu*) which Iyeyasu inaugurated at Edo (now Tokyo) in 1603 lasted until 1867 when the Emperor Meiji assumed direct imperial rule of the nation. Thus

[4] On Hideyoshi's Korean campaigns, see Sansom, *A History of Japan, 1334–1615*, pp. 352–62.
[5] Warner, *The Enduring Art of Japan*, p. 63.

the period between 1600 and 1867 is often referred to as the To-kugawa or Edo period. While it is not necessary to discuss in detail the complex bureaucratic structure of the Tokugawa regime, a few main features may be depicted.

Sansom is no doubt right in observing that Iyeyasu made no attempt to develop a coherent system of government. "He was de-termined to secure obedience, and it was his method to give direct orders, rather than to govern by legislation." [6] What Iyeyasu at-tempted was the establishment of permanent martial law, as it were. Geographically, Japan under the Tokugawa regime was divided into over 250 fiefs of different sizes and values. The Tokugawa ruler was both the shogun and the most important daimyo; as the latter he directly controlled nearly one fourth of Japan.[7] The remaining parts of Japan were divided into fiefs of two main types—inner and outer zones. For the most part, the inner zone was given to the *fudai daimyō* or hereditary lieges of the Tokugawa family who held responsible posts in the regime but had comparatively little income, while the outer zone was given to the *tozama daimyō* (literally "outside daimyo," referring to those who came under the Tokugawa's influence after 1600) who received a fairly sizable income but were excluded from posi-tions of influence.[8] In addition, the so-called *shimpan* (relatives of the Tokugawa family) were placed in key spots, for they were considered the most trustworthy allies of the shogunate.[9] The

[6] Sansom, *A History of Japan, 1334–1615*, p. 401. See also his *A History of Japan, 1615–1867*, for political development during the Tokugawa period.

[7] "The holding of the *Shōgun* was 2,500,000 *koku* in the beginning but increased gradually and became as much as 7,300,000 *koku* in 1700. . . . Of this, about 4,000,000 *koku* was under the direct control of the *Shōgun* and the remainder was divided among *hatamoto* and *gokenin*, both vas-sals in a direct line to the *Shōgun*." (UNESCO, Japan, p. 58.)

[8] For detailed lists of "fiefs and revenues" under both Toyotomi Hideyoshi and Tokugawa Iyeyasu, see Sansom, *A History of Japan, 1334–1615*, pp. 413–16. A map of "major *daimyō* domains around 1664" is given in Reischauer and Fairbank, *East Asia*, pp. 592–93.

[9] For example, such cities as Nagoya, Wakayama, Fukui, Aizu, and Mito were occupied by either Tokugawa or Matsudaira, both blood rela-tions of the shogun's family.

shogun, with the assistance of advisory bodies consisting of the elders (*toshiyori* or *rōjū*), the junior elders (*wakadoshiyori*), the bannermen (*hatamoto*), and the chamberlains (*sobashū*), ruled his territory directly, and other parts of the nation indirectly, through the daimyo. There were also many administrative posts such as those of the commissioners of temples and shrines (*jisha bugyō*), of finance (*kanjō bugyō*), and of cities (*machi bugyō*), as well as censors (*metsuke*). Each daimyo's realm (*han*), supposedly autonomous though strictly controlled by the central regime, had its own administrative machine modeled on a smaller scale after the example of the shogunate in Edo. As the Tokugawa regime imposed its system of hostages and of alternate attendance on all the daimyo, the families of the daimyo were kept in Edo, while the lords themselves were compelled to live alternately in their realms and in Edo. These measures not only kept the daimyo in line but also facilitated commerce, transportation, and communication systems on a national scale, even though the costs proved to be a hardship for many.

In the course of time certain minor changes were introduced into the administrative system of the shogunate, yet the amazing fact is that the political structure created by the Tokugawas in the early seventeenth century remained substantially intact until the middle of the nineteenth century.

Kirishitan

One of the most troublesome problems for the unifiers of Japan—Oda Nobunaga, Toyotomi Hideyoshi, and Tokugawa Iyeyasu—was that of religion. On the one hand, they met resistance from established religious centers and tightly knit religious societies, and on the other they were confronted by a vigorous missionary onslaught on the part of Roman Catholicism, then known as Kirishitan, from outside.[10] It is to be noted that the ex-

---

[10] Among the many books and articles in Western languages on the Kirishitan movement, the important ones are Anesaki, *A Concordance to the History of Kirishitan Missions*; Boxer, "Hosokawa Tadaoki and the Jesuits, 1587–1645," *Transactions of the Japan Society*, XXXII (London,

pansion of the Japanese in Southeast Asia in the sixteenth century was bound to result in an encounter with Europeans who were then beginning to establish their trade and missionary work in various parts of Asia. The first Europeans who set foot on Japanese soil were Portuguese.[11] They arrived in 1543 at a small island called Tanegashima off the southern tip of Kyushu. They were followed in 1549 by the Jesuit missionaries, Francis Xavier (1506–52) and his companions, who immediately began to evangelize the western parts of Japan. The merchants and the trade-conscious daimyo took keen interest in contacts with Europeans, while the warriors were fascinated by the efficiency of European firearms that proved to be far superior to such traditional Japanese weapons as the bow and arrow and the sword. As for Roman

---

1935), 79–119; Boxer, *The Christian Century in Japan, 1549–1650;* Delplace, *Le Catholicisme au Japon,* 2 vols.; Luis Frois, *Die Geschichte Japans, 1549–1578,* tr. into German by Schurhammer and Voretzsche; Gallagher, tr., *China in the Sixteenth Century: The Journals of Matthew Ricci, 1583–1610;* Hans Haas, *Geschichte des Christentums in Japan,* 2 vols.; Jennes, *History of the Catholic Church in Japan;* Voss and Cieslik, *Kirishitoki and Sayo-yoroku: Japanische Dokumente zur Missionsgeschichte des 71. Jahrhunderts;* Laures, *Nobunaga und des Christentum;* Laures, *The Catholic Church in Japan;* Laures, *Two Japanese Christian Heroes;* Murdoch and Yamagata, *A History of Japan during the Century of Early Foreign Intercourse, 1542–1651;* Toshihide Nakayama, *Collection of Historical Materials Connected with the Roman Catholic Religion in Japan* (*Kirishitan Shiryō-shū*); Natori, *Historical Stories of Christianity in Japan;* Paske-Smith, *Japanese Traditions of Christianity;* Schurhammer, *Shin-Tō: The Way of the Gods in Japan According to the Printed and Unprinted Reports of the Jesuit Missionaries in the Sixteenth and Seventeenth Centuries.* Among Japanese publications, the important ones are Anesaki, *Kirishitan shūmon no hakugai to sempuku;* Anesaki, *Kirishitan dendō no kōhai;* Ebisawa, *Kirishitan-shi no kenkyū;* Ebisawa, *Kirishitan tenseki sōkō;* Ebisawa, *Kirishitan no shakai-katsudō oyobi namban igaku;* Furuno, *Kakure Kirishitan;* Matsuda, *Kirishitan kenkyū;* Shimmura, *Nihon Kirishitan bunka-shi;* and Sukeno, *Kirishitan no shinkō seikatsu.* See also Gen'ichi Hiraga, "The Trend of Studies of 'Kirishitan' Literature," *Acta Asiatica* (Bulletin of the Institute of Eastern Culture, No. 4, Tokyo, 1963), pp. 97–113.

[11] Actually, the three Portuguese who arrived at Tanegashima had escaped from their ship. Although they wanted to go to South China in a small junk, they were driven by a typhoon to Japan.

Catholicism, many Japanese considered it to be not only a religion but the symbol of everything European. No doubt some of the early Kirishitan embraced Catholicism out of curiosity or for reasons of expediency, but an impressive number of people in various walks of life accepted the new faith for religious reasons.

Little needs to be said about the Jesuits—the Society of Jesus—founded by Ignatius of Loyola (1491–1556) in 1540. Loyola, a highborn Spaniard, combined within himself cultural sophistication, mystical insights, militant devotion, and organizational ability. He was reared in a country which had but a short time ago expelled its last Muslim rulers and was then fighting for the papal cause against the rising tide of the Protestant Reformation in Europe. In such an atmosphere Loyola and his friends formed their Company, a missionary order based on militaristic discipline, stressing the soldierly virtues of loyalty, fidelity, and obedience to their Master and Captain, the Lord Jesus. One of Loyola's companions was Francis Xavier of Navarre, who left Lisbon in 1541 for India. By chance Xavier met three Japanese at Malacca and became deeply interested in their country.[12] In 1549 Xavier personally initiated missionary work in Japan. Supported at first by rich Portuguese merchants, the Jesuits soon found favor with the daimyo in the western provinces. In a letter Xavier reported most enthusiastically on the honesty, courtesy, reasonableness, and sense of honor of the Japanese. "It seems to me," he wrote, "we shall never find among heathens another race equal to the Japanese." [13] Determined to secure the approval of his work from the highest authority of the land, Xavier traveled to Kyoto, but failed to see the shogun or the emperor. In 1551 he returned to Goa, leaving behind him a community of eight hundred Kirishitan.[14]

[12] One of the three Japanese was Yajirō, a warrior from Kagoshima. He was baptized with the Christian name of Paul at Goa. In 1549 Xavier, accompanied by Father de Torres, Brother Fernandez, the three Japanese, and two servants, arrived at Yajirō's old home, Kagoshima. Yajirō was credited with translations of the Gospel of St. Matthew, the Catechism, and other devotional literature.

[13] Taken from Xavier's letter, dated November 5, 1549, quoted in Boxer, *The Christian Century in Japan,* pp. 37–38, 401–5.

[14] While in Japan, Xavier observed that the Japanese depended heavily

After Xavier's departure the influence of the Kirishitan steadily increased until their numerical strength was estimated to be about 30,000 in 1570. One thing that might account for the remarkable success of the Jesuits was their willingness to adopt indigenous terminology to explain Catholic doctrines. For example, Xavier's chief interpreter, a former Shingon Buddhist, influenced him to adopt the word *Dainichi* (Mahāvairocana, the Great Sun Buddha of the Shingon school), as the designation of God. Other Buddhist terms frequently employed were *Hotoke* ("Buddha," used as another translation of the term God); *Jōdo* ("Pure Land," used for heaven); *Buppō* ("Buddha's Law," used to express the Law of God or religion in general); and *Sō* ("Buddhist monk," used as the designation of a Catholic priest).[15] More fundamentally, success climaxed the missionary zeal of the Jesuits because they firmly believed that their aim was "not only to seek with the aid of Divine grace the salvation and perfection of one's own soul but with the aid of the same earnestly to labor for the salvation and perfection of one's neighbor." [16]

It must not be forgotten, moreover, that the Jesuit-inspired Kirishitan groups followed the general pattern of tightly knit religious societies in Japan during the medieval period, like the True Pure Land sect or the Nichiren sect. Living as they did at a time when the political order and social fabric were disintegrating, people were in need of a sense of social identity and solidarity; many were also looking for the certainty of a salvation experience. The Jesuits offered both a concrete form of religious society and the sacramental assurance of salvation for souls. Although the faithful represented various professions and social classes, they were taught the doctrine of the equality of all men before the

---

on the authority of the Chinese. "Whereupon Xavier decided that he must visit the Chinese as soon as possible and convert them from their superstitious beliefs. With that done, he could more easily win over the Japanese, with the Gospel brought to them from China." (Gallagher, *China in the Seventeenth Century,* p. 118.)

[15] Cited in Jennes, *History of the Catholic Church in Japan,* p. 33.

[16] The opening declaration of the *General Examen* of the Society of Jesus, cited in "Jesus, Society of," *Encyclopaedia Britannica,* XIII (1962), 10.

Divine; their faith in the existence of Paradise compensated them for their hardships in the present life. On Sundays and holy days the faithful gathered either in the church or in the home of a believer for the celebration of the sacraments or for group devotions and instruction. High festivals, marriages, and funerals were important events for the community. Because of the shortage of clergy, lay assistants (*dōjuku*) played an important role in the church at large. The Jesuits promoted philanthropic works which were appreciated by both Kirishitan and non-Kirishitan,[17] and they introduced high ethical standards for individual, family, and social life.[18] "The members collected and took care of the donations and visited the sick and the poor in need of spiritual or material help. They informed the priests about funerals and took care of the Christians coming from other places." [19]

The cause of the Kirishitan was greatly enhanced by the religious policy of Oda Nobunaga, who obviously wanted to use this new group as a corrective to Buddhist societies that resisted his authority. The Tendai monastic center at Mt. Hiei, for example, with ample financial resources and defense forces, was far more powerful than the petty daimyo and proved to be a serious menace to Nobunaga. In 1571 Nobunaga's crack army attacked Mt. Hiei, burned its three thousand buildings, and massacred over 1,600 inmates. "The roar of the huge burning monastery, magnified by the cries of countless numbers of the old and the young, sounded and resounded to the ends of heaven and earth," wrote the biographer of Nobunaga.[20] Thus ended the political power of Mt. Hiei which for centuries had enjoyed the prerogatives and privileges of a *de facto* "ecclesiastical state," never submitting completely either to the imperial court or the feudal regime in matters both religious and non-religious.

However, Nobunaga faced another and far more stubborn ad-

[17] See Ebisawa, *Kirishitan no shakai katsudō oyobi namban igaku*, pp. 51–219.

[18] *Ibid.*, pp. 279–379.

[19] Jennes, *History of the Catholic Church in Japan*, p. 31.

[20] A passage from *Hoan Nobunaga-ki*, cited in Tsunoda, *et al.*, *Sources of Japanese Tradition*, p. 316.

versary in the followers of the True Pure Land, known then as the *Ikkō* (single-directed, or single-minded) sect. This was the school founded by the benevolent Shinran (d. 1262) and reorganized by Rennyo (d. 1499) into a well-disciplined, militant religious society based on strict feudal loyalties. Rennyo at first established a branch temple of the Hongan-ji (Temple of the original vow) at Ishiyama (the center of present-day Osaka). In 1532 Ishiyama became the headquarters of the True Pure Land sect, and developed into a full-fledged "temple town" with quarters for townsmen, surrounded by moats and walls for defense. In 1570 Nobunaga's forces attacked Ishiyama, but the *monto* (followers of the sect) came from all parts of Japan to defend their holy city, and Nobunaga's army was completely defeated. In a further attempt to eliminate the influence of this sect, Nobunaga attacked the followers of the True Pure Land in the Owari district, near Nagoya, but failed miserably in 1571, 1573, and 1574. Then the desperate Nobunaga tricked the *Ikkō* by offering peace, only to turn about and massacre nearly forty thousand believers in Owari. In 1575 he dispatched his forces to the Hokuriku district and massacred forty thousand more adherents of *Ikkō*. In 1576 Nobunaga again attacked Ishiyama; however, not only was his army defeated, but he himself was wounded. In the following year Nobunaga's forces attacked the Wakayama district which had supplied men and materials to Ishiyama. In 1577 the abbot of Ishiyama, Kennyo, also known as Kosa, promulgated an order to *Ikkō* believers throughout the country to send supplies and reinforcements to his headquarters. Only thus, he said, "could the Law of the Buddha be restored." [21] Finally, in 1580, the temple town of Ishiyama surrendered, and Kennyo and his followers escaped to Saginomori in the present Wakayama prefecture. In 1582 Nobunaga made a last attempt to eliminate *Ikkō* believers at Saginomori, but because of his own death this campaign remained uncompleted. During his lifetime Nobunaga had made every attempt to eliminate the influence of other Buddhist schools; to that end in 1579 he tricked the Nichiren leaders into publicly swearing not to

[21] In a letter addressed to believers in Sagami and Musashi, cited in Sansom, *A History of Japan 1334–1615,* p. 289.

criticize or attack other religious teachings. He also used his armed forces at the Shingon center of Mt. Kōya in order to keep the rebellious priests in line.[22]

The above account of Nobunaga's attitude toward the feudal power of the Buddhist schools makes more intelligible his turning to the Kirishitan as a counterforce against his adversaries. In 1560 the Jesuits had persuaded the puppet Ashikaga shogun, Yoshiteru, to grant permission for their work in Kyoto, but five years later Yoshiteru was murdered and the Buddhists in turn persuaded the imperial court to expel the Jesuits from the capital. In 1569 Nobunaga reversed the order, so that the Jesuits became free to expand their work throughout Nobunaga's lifetime. He was no doubt aware of the fact that Kirishitan work was successful in the western parts of Japan where the True Pure Land and other Buddhist schools, which did not cooperate with him, had become deeply rooted. With Nobunaga's active encouragement, Kirishitan spread not only among the poor and oppressed but also among the educated and well to do, including high-ranking warriors and their wives. When Nobunaga died, there were 150,000 Kirishitan with two hundred churches. Colleges, seminaries, dispensaries, and other institutions were established, and a good-will mission of the three Kirishitan daimyo of Kyushu (Bungo, Arima, and Ōmura) had gone to the court of Philip II in Madrid and to the Vatican. In 1579 the Jesuit visitor Alessandro Valignano arrived in Japan and advocated a policy of cultural adaptation to reorganize the mission personnel in accordance with the ecclesiastical structure of Zen Buddhist schools in Japan.[23]

---

[22] See *ibid.*, pp. 295–97, and Tamamuro, "Nihon Bukkyō-shi gaisetsu," pp. 177–80. In 1581, 1,383 priests and *hijiri* (unordained ascetics) of Mt. Kōya were beheaded.

[23] See Jennes, *History of the Catholic Church in Japan*, pp. 47–53. Francisco Cabral, then the Jesuit superior in Japan, who had no appreciation of Japanese culture and customs and compelled the Japanese Kirishitan to adopt European manners, naturally questioned Valignano's policies. Cabral was thus relieved of his post and was replaced by Gaspar Coelho. Coelho was made vice-provincial of Japan, which made him the head of a virtually independent vice-province "which, for the time being, had still to rely on the Province of India for material support and new helpers."

Following Nobunaga's death, Toyotomi Hideyoshi continued the policy of eliminating the power of Buddhist groups. In 1585, he destroyed the rebellious priest-soldiers of Negoro and subjugated other religious-political centers such as Kumano, Mt. Kōya, and Tōnomine.[24] However, he astutely permitted the restoration of the Tendai monastic center at Mt. Hiei, allowed the Nichiren sect to preach again, and gave a piece of land for the headquarters of the True Pure Land school in Kyoto—without at the same time allowing them to interfere with his political programs.[25] He was cordial to the Jesuits and valued the service of Kirishitan daimyo and generals under him.[26] So, then, the

---

(Laures, *The Catholic Church in Japan,* p. 107.) In 1588 Pope Sixtus V established the diocese of Funai and appointed Sebastian de Morales as the first bishop of Japan. Incidentally, the good-will mission to the Vatican was a great success for the cause of the Jesuits, for their society was given a monopoly on missionary work in Japan.

[24] Sansom, *A History of Japan, 1334–1615,* p. 343: "His method was simple and effective, for by a mere threat of force, by confiscating weapons in his Sword Hunt and by impounding Kōyasan revenues in the course of his land survey, he frightened the monks into submission and then gained their esteem by returning their estates."

[25] Tamamuro, however, contends that Hideyoshi gave amazingly little to the religious establishments. But the "gesture" was important, both to him and to the recipients. In the case of the erection of the Hōkō temple in Kyoto, he demanded that the daimyo provide materials and the peasants labor, and thus paid practically no money of his own. Moreover, he used this project as an excuse for his Sword Hunt on the ground that the weapons thus confiscated were to be used for nails and other necessary materials of the temple. In so doing, he gave a far-fetched but nevertheless understandable explanation to pious peasants for a measure by which he hoped to prevent the peasant uprisings. (Tamamuro, "Nihon Bukkyō-shi gaisetsu," pp. 182–84.

[26] According to Boxer, Hideyoshi once paid a visit to the Jesuits, and compared Catholic teaching favorably with Buddhism. Hideyoshi told the padre that the monogamous principle of Catholicism alone prevented him from joining the church, "and if you will stretch a point in this, I will likewise become a convert." (Boxer, *The Christian Century in Japan,* pp. 139–40.) This episode, however, should not be taken seriously in evaluating Hideyoshi's own religious beliefs. Although he was very superstitious, and was surrounded by Buddhist priests and ex-priests, Hideyoshi seems to have had almost no religious concern.

Edict of Banishment of Missionaries, which was issued in 1587, was not really enforced until ten years later. His anti-Kirishitan policy was motivated by many factors, including the power struggles of the Kirishitan daimyo, anti-Kirishitan factions among his advisers, pressures from Buddhist leaders who were losing adherents to the new faith, and the internal disunity of the Kirishitan group. When Hideyoshi went to Kyushu during his Korean campaign, he was alarmed at the virtual domination of certain areas by the Portuguese and the missionaries.[27] Unfortunately, Gaspar Coelho, the Jesuit vice-provincial in Japan, led Hideyoshi to believe that he had political influence over the Kirishitan daimyo and even promised to provide two Portuguese ships for Hideyoshi's Korean expedition.[28]

The 1587 Edict of Banishment of Missionaries stated that "henceforward, not only merchants, but anyone else coming from India who does not interfere with the laws of the Shinto and Buddhist deities may come freely to Japan," implying that Hideyoshi was eager to carry on foreign trade without supporting the Kirishitan mission.[29] Only a few missionaries actually left Japan, while the rest of them carried on their work without being molested by the authorities, despite the edict. Furthermore, Franciscans arrived from Luzon in the capacity of envoys from the Spanish governor of Manila, and they too established churches in Japan. The upshot of this was that bitter rivalry and misunderstanding developed between the Jesuits and the Franciscans to the detriment of the total Kirishitan cause.[30] To make matters worse,

[27] *Ibid.*, p. 348. For instance, Nagasaki, which was supposed to be within the Ōmura fief, was in reality "governed by the Jesuits until 1590, when it was brought under Hideyoshi's direct control."

[28] And yet, when Hideyoshi demanded an explanation of why missionaries permitted among the Kirishitan the practices of coerced conversion, the destruction of Buddhist and Shinto buildings, the eating of horses and cows, as well as the Portuguese slave trade involving the Japanese, Coelho had to state that missionaries had no political authority to influence the actions of Kirishitan believers or the Portuguese. See Jennes, *History of the Catholic Church in Japan*, pp. 63–64.

[29] *Ibid.*, pp. 64–65.

[30] *Ibid.*, pp. 80–81.

the captain of a Spanish ship, the *San Felipe*, which was ship-wrecked in 1596 near the Japanese shore, was said to have boasted that the Spanish monarch intended to subjugate Japan through utilizing the Kirishitan.[31] At any rate, Hideyoshi had certain Franciscans and their Japanese Kirishitan helpers, twenty-six in all, crucified early in 1597 at Nagasaki, and ordered all the Jesuits to leave the country.[32] The death of Hideyoshi in 1598, however, terminated the persecution of the Kirishitan.

When Tokugawa Iyeyasu came to power, his policy toward the Kirishitan wavered because of many considerations. His chief preoccupation was with the establishment of the feudal regime on a solid political and economic basis, and he had high hopes for foreign trade. Thus he made concessions to the Jesuits in order to continue trading with the Portuguese, and maintained friend-ship with the Franciscans in order to promote trade with New Spain (Mexico), while he employed an Englishman, Will Adams, who was the pilot of the Dutch boat *De Liefde*, as his adviser in commercial matters and encouraged trade with the Dutch as well as with the English.[33] Iyeyasu never concealed his own dislike for the Kirishitan, and among his advisers were Buddhist priests and Neo-Confucian scholars who shared his religious prejudice. The open antagonism between the Portuguese and the Spaniards, between European Catholics and Protestants, displayed in Japan, did not help the cause of the Kirishitan.[34] Nevertheless, Iyeyasu

[31] This account, however, is not reliable. See Sansom, *A History of Japan, 1334–1615*, p. 374.

[32] In a letter to the Spanish governor of Manila, Hideyoshi explained why Franciscans, who had diplomatic status, were executed. He explained that they had used their diplomatic status as a disguise for missionary work, which was against the law of Japan. He went on to say that if the tables had been turned, so that the Japanese had gone to Spanish territories and preached Shinto, "disquieting and disturbing the public peace and tranquility thereby, would you, as lord of the soil, be pleased thereat? Certainly not; and therefore by this you can judge what I have done." (Boxer, *The Christian Century in Japan*, p. 169.)

[33] See Ilza Veith, "Englishman or Samurai: The Story of Will Adams," *The Far Eastern Quarterly*, V (No. 1, November. 1945), 5–27.

[34] Another sad incident was the "Affair of the *Madre de Deus*." A Japa-nese ship arrived in Macao in 1608, and its sailors provoked a clash with

permitted the Jesuits, the Franciscans, the Dominicans, and the Augustinians to carry on their missionary, educational, and social service activities until 1613. Early in 1614 the edict was issued in the name of the second Tokugawa shogun, Hidetada, but with the sanction of the retired Iyeyasu who still was the real ruler, banning the Kirishitan religion on the ground that it was detrimental to the welfare of the nation and contrary to the teachings of Shinto, Buddhism, and Confucianism.[35] The edict also specified that Buddhist priests should supervise the investigation of the religious behavior of the people, thus making Buddhism a branch of the governmental structure. Immediately, churches were destroyed, missionaries were deported, and Japanese believers were compelled to renounce the faith, and were either persecuted or sent to Manila, Siam, or Macao.[36] In 1614 and 1615, however, the Tokugawa shogunate was destined to have its final showdown with the remnants of the Toyotomi followers, and the persecution of the Kirishitan was temporarily ended.[37]

---

the Portuguese. The sailors were attacked by the Portuguese forces of the acting governor of the city, Andrés Pessoa. The following year, Pessoa arrived at Nagasaki as the captain of the *Madre de Deus,* whereupon the shogunate ordered his seizure. In the end, Pessoa blew up the ship in order to avoid humiliation. See Boxer, "The Affair of the *Madre de Deus.* A Chapter in the History of the Portuguese in Japan," *Transactions of the Japan Society* (London), XXVI (1929), 4–94. Actually, this was one indication of the growing tension between the Japanese and European traders as the result of the increase of Japanese commercial expansion in Southeast Asia. Between 1604 and 1635 the shogunate issued over 350 "Red Seals" (passports for overseas navigation) to Japanese traders and to some foreign residents in Japan. Also, many colonies of Japanese were established in various parts of Southeast Asia about this time. See *ZNBT,* IX, *Edo-jidai,* Part I, pp. 90–119.

[35] For the text of the edict, see Jennes, *History of the Catholic Church in Japan,* pp. 126–28.

[36] On November 7 and 8 high-ranking Japanese Kirishitan and missionaries sailed from Nagasaki. But at least eighteen Jesuits, seven Dominicans, seven Franciscans, one Augustinian, and five diocesan priests managed to remain in Japan.

[37] Although there were Kirishitan followers on the Tokugawa side, there were considerably more of them on the Toyotomi side. The Kirishitan troops fought under banners emblazoned with images of the Cross, of the

In 1616 a stricter edict banning Kirishitan under the penalty of death was proclaimed, and thus the persecution of missionaries and Japanese Kirishitan continued throughout Hidetada's tenure as shogun—the severest being the "Great Martyrdom of Nagasaki" of 1622. Two renegades, Fabian Fukan, an ex-Jesuit brother, and Thomas Araki, an ex-Jesuit priest, cooperated with government officials in the anti-Kirishitan campaigns. Deprived of most clergy, the Kirishitan depended on *kō* (confraternities), such as Sodalities of the Blessed Virgin (established by the Jesuits), Confraternities of the Cord or *Obi-no-gumi* (established by the Franciscans), and Confraternities of the Rosary or *Rozario-no-gumi* (established by the Dominicans),[38] to maintain their solidarity.

In 1623 Iyemitsu became the third shogun, and initiated the most inhuman and brutal measures to stamp out the Kirishitan sect in all parts of Japan. In 1637 the combined factors of religious persecution, merciless oppression, and harsh taxation resulted in the great rebellion of Kirishitan farmers, fishermen, and warriors, together with their women and children, nearly forty thousand in all, at Shimabara, one of the Kirishitan strongholds in Kyushu. Opinions vary as to the role played by the religious factor in this insurrection, however. The first expeditionary forces dispatched by the shogun's order were defeated miserably. Until food and ammunition gave out on April 15, 1638, the Kirishitan men and women, under the command of the seventeen-year-old Masuda (or Amakusa) Shirō, a charismatic figure, withstood the attack of the reinforced shogunate forces, numbering one hundred thousand crack troops, who also utilized the firearms of the Dutch boat, *De Ryp*.[39]

Holy Redeemer, and of Santiago. Understandably, the Kirishitan followers of the Toyotomi hoped that their victory would bring the persecution to an end. Seven priests (two Jesuits, two Franciscans, one Augustinian, and two Japanese clergy) attended the Kirishitan troops on the Toyotomi side. See Jennes, *History of the Catholic Church in Japan*, p. 141.

[38] *Ibid.*, pp. 144–45. How the martyrdoms strengthened the faith of the Kirishitan is well described in Anesaki, *Kirishitan dendō no kōhai*, pp. 656–94.

[39] There were many plots to overthrow the Tokugawa shogunate in

In a way the Kirishitan group followed the pattern of other religious societies, such as the True Pure Land sect and the Nichiren sect, even in their modes of uprising that manifested a peculiar mixture of religious and nonreligious motives and ethos. In this sense the Kirishitan group, even with its universalistic soteriology and European influence, was the last in a series of Japanese "religious societies" that arose in the medieval period. And, just as Oda Nobunaga and other dictators had felt they must destroy the influence of Buddhist groups, Tokugawa Iyemitsu felt compelled to wipe out the Kirishitan group, for he sensed that it might challenge the claim of the feudal regime to be the sole guide for the thought and behavior of the people.

The shogunate, following the Kirishitan uprising in Shimabara, took the extreme measure of closing Japan to all foreign trade,

---

those days, especially by warriors who had been retainers of the daimyo on the Toyotomi side. Many of these masterless warriors (*rōnin*) sided with the insurrection. One of them was Masuda Jimbei, a Kirishitan warrior who had been in the service of the daimyo Konishi Yukinaga. Masuda's son, Shirō (Tokisada) was believed to have superhuman qualities. In 1637 Shogun Iyemitsu was sick and there was a strong rumor that he was dying; at that time, he had no heir. According to Japanese accounts, people observed a strange red color in the sky during the autumn of 1637, and flowers blossomed out of season. Masuda Jimbei and his compatriots came to believe that these strange phenomena were divine signs for them to rise in arms. At that time, a government tax collector took the beautiful daughter of a farmer who could not pay the prohibitive tax, stripped her, and burned her body with flaming torches. Her father and his friends killed the tax collector. (According to another version, the officials of Shimabara invaded a house in the village of Arima where two men, Kakuzō and Sankichi by name, were praying before a holy picture, and after a struggle the officials were killed.) At any rate, the insurgents arose either on the twenty-fifth day of the tenth month according to the Japanese calendar or December 11, according to the Christian calendar (although the Catholic record dates the event six days later than the Japanese account), and then various villages in the neighborhood joined in the rebellion. It is to be noted that some who were not Kirishitan were also involved in the fighting. See Anesaki, *Kirishitan dendō no kōhai*, pp. 698–717; Boxer, *The Christian Century in Japan*, pp. 375–83; Laures, *The Catholic Church in Japan*, pp. 172–74; and Jennes, *History of the Catholic Church in Japan*, pp. 156–59.

with the exception of limited commerce with the Dutch at Nagasaki. The remaining Catholic missionaries and Kirishitan were hunted and tortured, and yet there were some Kirishitan who went underground and preserved their faith stubbornly for generations until the reopening of Japan in the nineteenth century.[40] Nevertheless, the colorful history of the Kirishitan movement came to an end, for all intents and purposes, when the seclusion of Japan was put into effect in 1639.

Neo-Confucianism

The Tokugawa feudal regime, from the time of Iyeyasu, was determined to attain and preserve political as well as social stability. For this purpose the architects of the regime depended heavily on Chinese political norms, for "the Confucian concept of a human order established in harmony with immutable natural principles seemed to justify the rigid social cleavages and political absolutism of the Tokugawa system." [41] Following the example of Toyotomi Hideyoshi, Iyeyasu enforced the division of the populace into four main social classes, namely, the warrior (*shi*), the farmer (*nō*), the artisan (*kō*), and the merchant (*shō*), and restricted the upward mobility of the people within the framework of their prescribed classes. In addition to the above-mentioned four social classes, the Tokugawa system recognized the imperial and courtier families and ecclesiastics as special categories. The shogunate was determined to control the activities of the court and courtiers, and thus in 1615 issued the Ordinances for the Imperial and Courtier Families (*Kinchū narabini Kugeshū shohatto*).[42] The shogunate also regulated the activities of re-

[40] See Furuno, *Kakure Kirishitan*; Laures, *The Catholic Church in Japan*, pp. 181–99; Jennes, *History of the Catholic Church in Japan*, pp. 165–223; and Anesaki, *Kirishitan dendō no kōhai*, pp. 717–820.

[41] Reischauer and Fairbank, *East Asia*, p. 616. See also Sansom, *A History of Japan, 1615–1867*, pp. 69–95.

[42] These ordinances were revisions of the earlier (1613) ordinances for courtiers (*Kugeshū shohatto*). The Tokugawa regime paid nominal respect to the court, but did not permit any interference on the part of the court with practical politics. In 1612 Iyeyasu proposed to arrange a mar-

ligious groups and institutions by means of the Ordinances for Temples (*Jiin hatto*).[43] The backbone of society, according to the Tokugawa regime, was undoubtedly the warrior class.

We may recall that during the medieval period the warriors lived in the countryside and engaged in agriculture directly or indirectly, except when they were called to take arms in the service of their lords. The frequent fighting during the sixteenth century resulted in the development of a class of professional warriors who lived in the so-called castle town which was established by the daimyo. The separation of the warrior class from the rest of the populace became an accepted pattern in the second half of the sixteenth century, and the warriors came to be divided into groups under the direction of group commanders, who in turn were subject to the daimyo through a vertical chain of command. "This was essentially an army type of organization in which there was a minimum identity of family with locality or dependence upon family ties for loyalty." [44] Under the Tokugawa regime, warriors had nothing to do with agriculture or

riage between the Tokugawa and the imperial families. In 1620 his granddaughter, Kazuko, became the consort of the Emperor Go-Mizunoo. At that time, the shogun's retainers were sent to accompany Kazuko, allegedly for the purpose of protecting her safety, but actually to watch and spy on the activities of the court for the shogunate. When Go-Mizunoo retired in 1629, over a disagreement with the shogunate regarding the issue of the imperial prerogatives, Kazuko's daughter was enthroned. This empress, known as Meisei, was the first female to ascend the throne since the Nara period.

[43] The *Jiin hatto* was revised in 1665 and renamed the Ordinances for Temples of All Sects (*Shoshū jiin hatto*), which further integrated the Buddhist priesthood and institutions into the administrative system of the Tokugawa regime, rather than leaving them as a potential menace to the regime.

[44] John Whitney Hall, "Foundations of the Modern Japanese Daimyō," *The Journal of Asian Studies*, XX (No. 3, May, 1961), 325. Hall also observes that both warriors and commoners came to be treated as functional groups and classes. Among the warriors, military ranks such as generals (*karō*), group commanders (*bangashira*), unit commanders (*kumigashira*), officers (*heishi*), petty officers (*kachi*), or foot soldiers (*ashigaru*), came to take precedence over the traditional family-based categories of vassal classification; e.g., cadets (*kamon*) or vassals (*fudai*). See *ibid.*, p. 326.

trade, for they were to serve full time in the military or civil bureaucracy. They were considered to be the daimyo's officers, divided into ranks in ascending order, and paid according to their status. It may be noted in this connection that, while in traditional China the *ju* or the class of educated gentry was considered to be the preserver and transmitter of culture, in Japan under the Tokugawa rule the warrior class was expected to play that role. As early as 1615 the shogunate issued its Ordinances for the Military Houses (*Buke shohatto*), the thirteen general principles governing the life and activities of the daimyo and the warrior class.[45]

Next only to the warrior, the farmer enjoyed prestige during the Tokugawa period because agriculture was considered to be the basis of the national economy, and thus farmers were taxpaying tenants of the daimyo. With improvement in water control and irrigation projects as well as in agricultural methods, agricultural productivity increased considerably during the first half of the Tokugawa period. This may also account for the expansion of rural trade and industry and the rise of a substantial number of educated and well-to-do farmers in the eighteenth century. Undoubtedly there were many poor peasants during the Tokugawa period, but "the upper strata of peasants were in many respects, not least in respect to standard of life, much nearer to the middle ranks of the warrior class than to the majority of peasants."[46] The peace and security established by the Tokugawa regime encouraged the growth of industry and commerce in rural areas as well as in the urban centers. The living standard of artisans and merchants rose correspondingly. The growth of money economy—the use of currency and credit—brought serious disadvantages to the warriors, who depended on feudal agricultural incomes, in contrast to the merchants who were supposed to be the lowest in the social scale. In fact, successful merchants became quite influential, and some of them established large

[45] On this subject, see Tsunoda, *et al.*, *Sources of Japanese Tradition*, pp. 335–38.

[46] Thomas C. Smith, "The Land Tax in the Tokugawa Period," *The Journal of Asian Studies*, XVIII (No. 1, November, 1958), 14.

commercial firms.[47] At the bottom of the social scale were the *senmin* (pariahs), consisting of the *hinin* or "those who were below the four social classes" such as entertainers, executioners, beggars, and brothel keepers; and the *eta*, the Japanese counterpart of the outcastes, who were confined to the ghetto villages of those engaged in the manufacture and sale of such items as leather goods, sandals, and lampwicks. While society was thus stratified vertically, it managed to develop horizontal interhuman relationships within class boundaries.

It has often been pointed out that, unlike the medieval feudal society based on the clan system, society under the Tokugawa regime was based on the household system. Due to the widespread custom of adoption, pseudo-adoption, and the use of fictitious genealogies toward the latter part of the medieval period, "households with the same names" were not always regarded as belonging to the same kinship group. During the Tokugawa period, the three groups—*shinrui* (relatives in the closest sense), *enrui* (distant relatives), and *enja* (literally, related persons)—alone were recognized as kinship groups by law and custom.[48] Such terms as *kamei* (name of the household) and *kaken* (regulations governing the house) referred to those of the household in the narrow sense. The daimyo bestowed names, and usually commoners or nonwarriors were not allowed to use surnames. Among the commoners, especially among artisans and merchants, the custom of "separation of household" (*bekke*) was widely practiced.[49]

[47] For economic structure and development of the Tokugawa period, see Takekoshi, *The Economic Aspects of the History of the Civilization of Japan,* I, 542–55; II, 30–65, 199-566; and III, 1-273.

[48] The category of *shinrui* includes members of the direct line of each household—grandparents, parents, children, and grandchildren plus blood relations of the third degree. Adopted children, stepmothers, and children by concubines were also included in this category. The members of the *shinrui* were usually involved in financial transactions of the household. The term *enrui* refers to the brothers and sisters of grandparents on both sides, grandchildren of brothers and sisters, and children of cousins. The category of *enja* is very ambiguous, often referring to the parents of the household into which one's sons or daughters are adopted.

[49] Usually boys of seven or eight were sent to a merchant's household,

The Tokugawa regime recognized, at least in principle, joint possession of property by husband and wife.[50] The regime also imposed the system of neighborhood units called *gonin-gumi* (the five-man unit), and all the families of each unit were responsible for the welfare and behavior of each member of the households involved.

The foregoing makes it clear that Japanese society under the Tokugawa rule had two foci, namely, the nation (society) and the family (household), both of which were regarded as sacred entities. As such, the nation demanded absolute loyalty, while the family demanded absolute filial piety. It was taken for granted in this connection that the nation was embodied in the figure of the shogun, and the family in the figures of the parents; but should a father oppose the shogun, the children were expected to demonstrate their loyalty by deserting their father. Thus, as Bellah has rightly pointed out, the "religion of filial piety" did not compete with the "religion of loyalty." The former reinforced the latter.[51] Normally, however, nation and family were considered to be in a state of harmony—the relation of these two foci being defined by Neo-Confucianism, which was the official "theology" of the Tokugawa regime.[52]

which was often but not always related to their families, as apprentices (*detchi*) for about ten years or so; after that they became novices (*tedai*). Senior *tedai* were given the rank of chief clerk (*bantō*) and after years of faithful service to the master were given the same trade name and capital to start a branch store. The relationship between the *shuke* (master's household) and *bekke* (branch house) was governed by paternalistic principles for several generations. In many ways, *bekke* were closer than relatives to the *shuke*.

[50] A wife's portion was to be returned to her at the time of divorce, unless she had committed adultery. In order to enter into a marriage contract, the two parties had to get an official go-between; otherwise, the marriage was regarded as *yagō* (literally, a "wild union"). The *yuinō* (token of a tie) was required to be presented by the man's household to the bride's household through the go-between. The warriors and men of higher ranks could not contract a marriage without official sanction. For the commoners, a written notice was expected to be sent to the magistrate by whom the marriage was registered.

[51] Bellah, *Tokugawa Religion*, pp. 81–82.

[52] Naojirō Nishida, *Nihon bunka-shi josetsu*, p. 544.

We are told that Iyeyasu himself eagerly listened to lectures on the *Four Books*, the *Records of the Historian* by Ssu-ma Ch'ien, and the *History of the Former Han Dynasty;* he was also greatly impressed by the example of T'ang T'ai-tsung (r. 627–49), the founder of the T'ang Dynasty in China. "Whatever the subject, he was interested, not in the turn of a phrase or in literary embellishments, but only in discovering the key to government— how to govern oneself, the people, and the country." [53] What Iyeyasu looked for basically was a model for society; and unlike the ancient Japanese who depended on a "heavenly model," he turned to the "Chinese model," based on social gradations for the purpose of political and social harmony. And yet Iyeyasu acquired from the Confucian tradition not a social model as such, but the religious affirmation of an "immanental theocracy," implying that "the order of heaven is not a transcendental substance but is inherent in the conditions of human existence. This is the regulative principle to be recognized and realized." [54] This regulative principle, be it noted, was not law in the Western sense. In the framework of immanental theocracy, "there are only duties and mutual compromises governed by the ideas of order, responsibility, hierarchy, and harmony." [55] These insights were appropriated by the Tokugawa regime as the principles of its social engineering.

It goes without saying that Confucian learning had a long tradition in Japan, for it can be traced as far back as the pre-Nara period. I have also noted earlier that the so-called Neo-Confucianism which arose during the Sung period in China was introduced into Japan during the medieval period by Zen Buddhists. In fact, many Zen masters were also Neo-Confucianists during the fifteenth and sixteenth centuries.[56] It may be useful to quote de

[53] Quotation from *Tōshō-gū go-jikki,* cited in Tsunoda, *et al., Sources of Japanese Tradition,* p. 341.

[54] William S. Haas, *The Destiny of the Mind—East and West,* p. 140.

[55] Escarra, *Le Droit Chinois,* p. 17.

[56] On Neo-Confucianism, see Fung Yu-lan, *A History of Chinese Philosophy,* II, 407–672; Wm. Theodore de Bary, *et al., Sources of Chinese Tradition,* pp. 510–81; and Wing-tsit Chan, "Neo-Confucianism," in MacNair, *China,* pp. 254–65.

Bary's list of characteristics of this school: fundamentalism, restorationism, historical-mindedness, rationalism, and humanism.[57] What is important is to note that in Japan there was a process of transition wherein Confucian scholars (*jusha*) had begun to be emancipated from the Buddhist framework by the turn of the seventeenth century.[58] Inevitably, the seventeenth-century Japanese Neo-Confucianists reacted emotionally against Buddhism, especially its passive quietism. Many of them idealized the "way of the ancient sage-kings" in China. In the words of Ogyū Sorai (1666–1718), "The way of the ancient sage-kings is the highest good. Under the sun, there is no principle more excellent than this one. 'The highest good' is, therefore, the word to praise the way of the ancient sage-kings." [59] The Japanese *jusha* of this period followed the Neo-Confucian school of Chu Hsi (1130–1200), who analyzed and synthesized such concepts as the Great Ultimate, *li* (reason or principle), *ch'i* (material force), human nature, and the mind. The attitude of many Japanese Chu Hsi *jusha* was well exemplified by the statement of Yamazaki Ansai (1618–82): "If I fall into error studying Chu Hsi, I will be in error with Chu Hsi and will have nothing to regret." [60]

There is no question that Confucian scholars made every effort to establish "the way of the ancient sage-kings" in Japan. Their services were in demand both by the Tokugawa shogunate and by the daimyo who were then confronted with the task of developing practical administrative policies. Hayashi Razan (1583–1657), for example, enjoyed unprecedented favor from the

[57] On the exposition of these characteristics, see Wm. Theodore de Bary, "Common Tendencies in Neo-Confucianism," in Nivison and Wright, eds., *Confucianism in Action*, pp. 25–49.

[58] J. W. Hall, "The Confucian Teacher in Tokugawa Japan," in Nivison and Wright, eds., *Confucianism in Action*, p. 271. Even then, Hayashi Razan, the lecturer to the shogun, was "obliged to wear the Buddhist tonsure and take a Buddhist title, in order to retain the favor of Tokugawa Iyeyasu." (*Ibid.*, p. 270.)

[59] Quoted in Nakamura, *The Ways of Thinking of Eastern Peoples*, p. 373.

[60] Nakamura states that "these words of Ansai remind us of Shinran's wholehearted devotion to Hōnen." (*Ibid.*, p. 373.)

shogunate as the adviser to three shoguns and as the founder of an official academy for Chinese culture.[61] Razan's son, Hayashi Gahō (1618–80), was named the first doctor of literature, and his grandson, Hayashi Hōkō (1644–1732), was given the title, *Daigaku-no-kami* (Head of the university), which, incidentally, was handed down to the subsequent heads of the Hayashi family.[62] Understandably, however, there was a basic tension between "the way of the ancient Chinese sage-kings" and the sociopolitical structure of Japan, emerging under Tokugawa rule. In this situation, it was Neo-Confucianism that was reinterpreted and transformed so as to fit into the social structure and political institutions of Japan, rather than the other way around. Thus Hayashi Razan reinterpreted the *li* (reason or principle) of Chu Hsi and equated it with Shinto. "The Way of the Gods is nothing but Reason (*li*). Nothing exists outside of Reason." [63] While Confucian scholars attempted such indigenous reformulations of Neo-Confucianism and worked out philosophical ideals, it was the warrior-administrators who translated philosophical ideals into practical measures for governing the nation. The result was, as Hall rightly points out, that the basic political institutions of the Tokugawa regime actually "owe little or nothing to Chinese models." [64]

This does not imply that Confucian scholarship as such was neglected. On the contrary, under the patronage of the shogunate and some of the daimyo, Confucian studies prospered during the

[61] He was the student of Fujiwara Seika (1561–1619), unofficial adviser to Tokugawa Iyeyasu. In rejecting Buddhist influence, Razan became close to Shinto and stressed the importance of the Shinto communal cult as the basis of the social order. For this reason, he wrote *Honchō Jinja-kō* (A study of Jinja in our nation). His influence on Shinto was slight, but his younger contemporary Yamazaki Ansai, mentioned above, exerted more influence in this respect. Razan also wrote *Honchō Tsūgan* (A historical survey of our nation) with Chu Hsi's *T'ung-chien kang-mu* as his model.

[62] See Tsunoda, *et al., Sources of Japanese Tradition,* p. 354, for a list of Hayashi family leaders.

[63] Nakamura, *The Ways of Thinking of Eastern Peoples,* p. 581.

[64] J. W. Hall, "The Confucian Teacher in Tokugawa Japan," in Nivison and Wright, eds., *Confucianism in Action,* p. 292.

Tokugawa period. There were three main traditions of Confucian studies—the Chu Hsi school (*Shushi-gaku* in Japanese), the Wang Yang-ming school (*Ōyōmei-gaku*), and the school that attempted to return directly to Confucius and Mencius (*Ko-gaku* or *Fukko-gaku*).[65]

The Chu Hsi school was considered the "official" school by the shogunate, and it was actively promoted by the fifth shogun, Tsunayoshi (r. 1680–1709), who established a national Confucian shrine. Some of the Tokugawa's relatives, such as Tokugawa Yoshinao (d. 1650), the daimyo of Owari; Hoshina Masayuki (d. 1672), son of the second shogun, and the daimyo of Aizu; and Tokugawa Mitsukuni (d. 1701), grandson of Iyeyasu, and the daimyo of Mito, were also enthusiastic patrons of the Chu Hsi school. Mitsukuni was instrumental in gathering together able scholars, including Chu Shun-shui (1600–82), a royalist of Ming China then in exile in Japan. Thus developed the tradition commonly referred to as the Mito school.[66] It was the Mito scholars who produced the *Dai-Nihon-shi* (History of great Japan), which eventually provided the theoretical basis for the royalist movement.[67] Some of the famous scholars of the Chu Hsi school were Kinoshita Jun-an (d. 1698), Yamazaki Ansai (d. 1682), Arai Hakuseki (d. 1725), Muro Kyūsō (d. 1734), and Kaibara Ekken (d. 1714).[68] The popularity of the Chu Hsi school is evident from the fact that Yamazaki Ansai alone claimed six thousand disciples.

The Ōyōmei-gaku was, of course, based on the teachings of Wang Yang-ming (1472–1529), the statesman-general who, in rejecting Chu Hsi's view of the *li* (reason or principle), equated the *li* with the mind and interpreted the individual mind as the

[65] See Armstrong, *Light from the East: Studies in Japanese Confucianism*.
[66] See Hammitzsch, *Die Mito-Schule*.
[67] See Webb, "What Is the Dai Nihon Shi?", *The Journal of Asian Studies*, XIX (No. 2, February, 1960), 135–49.
[68] See ZNBT, IX, *Edo Jidai*, Part I, 205–8; Spae, *Itō Jinsai*, pp. 66–70; Tsunoda, *et al.*, *Sources of Japanese Tradition*, pp. 345–77 and 470–79; Hoshino, *The Way of Contentment, Translations of Selections from Kaibara Ekken*; Lloyd, "Historical Development of the Shushi (Chu Hsi) Philosophy in Japan," *TASJ*, XXXIV (1906), 5–80; Anesaki, *History of Japanese Religion*, pp. 270–75; and Graf, *Kaibara Ekken*.

manifestation of the universal Mind. This school was advocated by Nakaye Tōju (d. 1648), Kumazawa Banzan (d. 1691), Miwa Shūsai (d. 1744), Satō Issai (d. 1850), and Ōshio Heihachirō (d. 1837).[69] Moral cultivation of the type based on Wang Yang-ming's concept of the "Prime Conscience" appealed to many Japanese to the extent that Ōyōmei-gaku developed into a pseudo-religious system among warriors as well as among upper-class farmers and merchants. The shogunate did not welcome the development of this school, especially because its thought provided an ethical incentive for social reform.[70] It was not without reason that some of the late Tokugawa reformers, such as Sakuma Zōzan, Yoshida Shōin, Hashimoto Sanai, Yamada Hōkoku, and Saigō Nanshū, came out of the tradition of the Wang Yang-ming school in Japan.

The Ko-gaku (literally, the study of antiquity) was represented by such different types of men as Yamaga Sokō (d. 1685), the

---

[69] See Spae, *Itō Jinsai*, pp. 70–72; Tsunoda, *et al., Sources of Japanese Tradition*, pp. 378–92; Fisher, "The Life and Teaching of Nakae Tōju, The Sage of Ōmi," *TASJ*, XXXVI (1908); Fisher, "Kumazawa Banzan, His Life and Ideas," *TASJ*, Second Series, XVI (1938); and *ZNBT*, X, *Edo Jidai*, Part II, 200–2.

[70] The tradition of Nakaye Tōju was called the *Shin-gaku* (School of the mind). Later, Ishida Baigan also started a school of the mind, which was different from that of Nakaye Tōju. Regarding Ishida Baigan's movement, see Bellah, *Tokugawa Religion*. It is to be noted that the *Ōyōmei-gaku* scholars at Aizu and at Kumamoto were banished by the shogunate's orders in 1683 and 1669, respectively. Kumazawa Banzan, the former warrior turned *Ōyōmei-gaku* scholar, served at one time as chief minister of the fief of Okayama under its daimyo, Ikeda Mitsumasa. The shogunate pressured the daimyo to get rid of Kumazawa, who eventually was kept in custody, even though his influence continued to be felt widely. Satō Issai, a scholar of the Wang Yang-ming school, was compelled to teach the system of Chu Hsi. Satō had several outstanding disciples who were willing to risk their lives for the cause of social and political justice. Ōshio Heihachirō, also known as Chūsai, police officer (*yoriki*) in Osaka, was noted for his integrity. Out of sympathy with the plight of the poor, and disgusted with the corruption of the authorities, Ōshio started the uprising of 1817 in order to take control of the city. His attempt failed, however, and he committed suicide. For the Edict of Prohibition of Heterodox Studies, see Tsunoda, *et al., Sources of Japanese Tradition*, pp. 502–5.

systematizer of the Code of Warriors (*Bushidō*); Itō Jinsai (d. 1705) and his son Itō Tōgai (d. 1736), both moralists and educators; Ogyū Sorai (d. 1728), the political philosopher; and Dazai Shundai (d. 1747), Sinophile and economist.[71] That Yamaga Sokō exerted direct influence on his disciple, Ōishi Kuranosuke, the leader of the famous forty-seven *rōnin* (warriors deprived of their fiefs) who dedicated their lives to the revenge of their daimyo, is well known. The most important thinker of this school, however, was Itō Jinsai, who left a lasting influence through his unique reinterpretation of the Chinese classics.[72]

The real significance of Confucian scholarship in the Tokugawa period, including all three major schools, lay in its activistic temperament. This led the *jusha* (Confucian scholars) to concern themselves with politics, economics, jurisprudence, and other practical aspects of human life. Both the shogunate and the provincial daimyo depended on the *jusha* as moralists, officials, educators, and cultural leaders.[73] In many ways Japanese Confucian scholars dehydrated their own tradition by repudiating the Confucian dualism between reason and matter,[74] and by

[71] See Tsunoda, *et al.*, *Sources of Japanese Tradition*, pp. 393–433; Spae, *Itō Jinsai*, pp. 72–206; and Anesaki, *History of Japanese Religion*, pp. 278–83.

[72] The passage from the Analects, "On the river, the master says, 'What passes away passes thus. It never ceases day or night,'" was usually understood to mean that what passes away never returns. However, according to Itō Jinsai, the river stands for "the virtue of the wise man that is every day made new, and never becomes stagnant." By this interpretation, Jinsai gave a positive meaning to human life and activity. See Nakamura, *The Ways of Thinking of Eastern Peoples*, pp. 431–32.

[73] On this subject, see J. W. Hall, "The Confucian Teacher in Tokugawa Japan," in Nivison and Wright, eds., *Confucianism in Action*, and also a list of *jusha* employed by various daimyo in ZNBT, X, *Edo Jidai*, Part II, 208. See also Abe, "Edo-jidai Jusha no shusshin to shakaiteki-chii ni tsuite," *The Nippon-Chūgoku-gakkai-hō*, No. 13 (1961), pp. 161–75.

[74] Hajime Nakamura points out that most distinctively Japanese Confucian scholars stood for the monism of the material. "Yamaga Sokō, Itō Jinsai and Kaibara Ekken are all monists, believing the material to be the first principle of existence." (*The Ways of Thinking of Eastern Peoples*, p. 432.)

coming too close to Shinto.[75] On the other hand, because of its eclectic spirit and preoccupation with practical morality, Japanese Confucianism was able to contribute a great deal to the development of the Code of Warriors (*Bushidō*),[76] the "Great Learning for Women" (*Onna Daigaku*),[77] and such semireligious movements as the *Shin-gaku* (Mind Learning), founded by Ishida Baigan (d. 1744),[78] and the *Hō-toku* (Repaying the Indebtedness), initiated by Ninomiya Sontoku (d. 1856).[79] It was the conviction of the Japanese Confucian teachers that the manners and etiquette laid down in Confucian writings must be adapted "to the customs of the particular country and the particular place." [80] In achieving this end they were eminently successful. The shogunate believed that the Confucian tradition would provide a system of ethics and models of conduct leading to greater political stability and social harmony among the populace. Ironically, it was the influence of Confucian studies that fostered a historical consciousness among the people and stimulated the revival of Shinto and study of the Japanese classics, all of which tended to undercut the very foundations of the feudal regime.

Buddhism and Shinto under the Tokugawa

Historians often marvel at the fact that the Tokugawa regime managed to keep peace and order in the nation from 1600 till 1867. This indeed was an impressive achievement. If we take a

[75] *Ibid.*, pp. 581–83.

[76] See Sadler, *The Beginner's Book of Bushidō by Daidōji Yuzan* (*Budō Shoshinshū*).

[77] See Sakai, "Kaibara Ekken and 'Onna Daigaku,'" *Cultural Nippon*, VII (No. 4, 1939), 43–56. The *Onna Daigaku*, usually ascribed to Kaibara Ekken, stressed the importance of obedience for a woman—as a child to her father, as a wife to her husband and his parents, and as a widow to her eldest son. A woman was expected to be gentle and chaste, never giving way to passion nor questioning the authority of her elders. See Kaibara Ekken, *Women and Wisdom of Japan*.

[78] The best English source on *Shin-gaku* is Bellah, *Tokugawa Religion*.

[79] See Armstrong, *Just Before the Dawn: The Life and Works of Ninomiya Sontoku*.

[80] Nakamura, *The Ways of Thinking of Eastern Peoples*, p. 582.

closer look at history, however, we find that the Tokugawa rule was by no means so tranquil as might appear to a casual observer. I have earlier characterized the Tokugawa regime as an "immanental theocracy," founded by Iyeyasu, the manifestation of the "Sun God of the East" (*Tōshō*).[81] His successors had to struggle with many complex problems which shook the foundations of the regime from time to time. We have already discussed the Kirishitan uprising and its aftermath during the rule of the third shogun, Iyemitsu. The rule of the fourth shogun, Iyetsuna (1651–79), was marked by disturbances created by the increasing numbers of *rōnin*, the uprising of the Ainu in Hokkaido, great fires in Kyoto and Edo, and eruptions of Mt. Fuji and Mt. Asama, all of which created hardships for the regime and the Japanese people. Iyetsuna's successors, Tsunayoshi (1680–1709), Iyenobu (1709–13), and Iyetsugu (1713–16), exhibited weak leadership, administrative inefficiencies, and fiscal mismanagement. The scholar-statesman, Arai Hakuseki, serving as adviser to the shogunate (1709–15), attempted to tighten the fiscal policy and increase the regime's efficiency, but he was dismissed by the eighth shogun, Yoshimune (r. 1716–45), whose own reform measures failed in spite of his good intentions.[82] Under the tenth shogun, Iyeharu (1760–86), sweeping administrative reform measures were attempted for a while by Tanuma Okitsugu, an able elder (*rojū*), but his policies were reversed by the conservative elders Matsudaira Sadanobu and Mizuno Tadakuni during the rule of the next shogun, Iyenari (1787–1837). The early nineteenth century brought a series of great fires, earthquakes, floods, and famines to various parts of Japan, while

[81] This title was accorded to Iyeyasu by the Tendai abbot Tenkai, and Iyeyasu's mausoleum at Nikkō was named the *Tōshō-gū* (Shrine of the Sun God of the East). See Ogyū Sorai's praise of the "Great Sun God of the East" in Tsunoda, *et al., Sources of Japanese Tradition*, pp. 342–43.

[82] Traditional Japanese historians often praise Yoshimune, who tried to restore sound money and to reform various aspects of the social order, but actually his rule proved to be a failure even before his retirement. "The morale and finances of the military class further deteriorated, and the efficiency of government was again reduced by corruption and economic difficulties." (Reischauer and Fairbank, *East Asia*, p. 623.)

European and American ships began to be seen in Japanese waters.[83] It was the visit of Commodore Matthew Perry in 1853 that compelled the shogunate to face the realities of the world, and thus a new page opened in Japanese history.

Religious development during the Tokugawa period inevitably reflected the social and political growth of the nation. At first Buddhist schools enjoyed the active support of the shogunate. Tokugawa Iyeyasu was reared in the tradition of the Pure Land (*Jōdo*) school which he honored by building the magnificent edifice of the Zōjō-ji and other temples in and around Edo.[84] In addition, Iyeyasu erected the Tō-ei-zan (Mt. Hiei of the east) at Edo's Uyeno hill and appointed the Tendai priest, Tenkai (d. 1643), to be its abbot. (Tenkai was also in charge of temples at Nikkō, and supervised the reprinting of the *Tripitaka*.) Iyeyasu astutely divided the True Pure Land school into two sects.[85] In the edict of 1614 banning Kirishitan, there is a passage that says, "Japan is called the land of Buddha and not without reason. . . . God [kami] and Buddha differ in name, but their meaning is one." [86] In other words, the Tokugawa regime was indifferent to the religious or philosophical differences between Buddhism and Shinto.[87] What concerned the shogunate was how to keep re-

[83] In this situation, as mentioned earlier, Ōshio Heihachirō, a police officer trained in the school of Wang Yang-ming, attempted an ill-fated *coup d'état* in 1837.

[84] He is said to have aspired to become a god to protect the country. He recited the *Nembutsu* during the last years of his life in order to achieve this end. Upon his death, Iyeyasu received the title, *Tōshō Dai Gongen* (the Great Manifestation of the Sun God of the East). See Eliot, *Japanese Buddhism*, p. 306.

[85] Actually, Ōtani Kōju, the abbot of the Higashi Honganji (Eastern temple of the Original Vow), the headquarters of the Eastern sect, and Ōtani Kōchō, the abbot of the Nishi Honganji (Western temple of the Original Vow), the headquarters of the Western sect, were brothers, both sons of the famous Abbot Kennyo.

[86] Eliot, *Japanese Buddhism*, p. 309; and Jennes, *History of the Catholic Church in Japan*, p. 127.

[87] Even today, at Nikkō, the holy place of the Tokugawa family, visitors have difficulty in differentiating Shinto and Buddhist elements, because they are so closely interwoven.

ligious institutions within its political framework. The regime took measures to accomplish this end.

In order to maintain effective control of religious affairs, the commissioners for temples and shrines (*jisha-bugyō*) were appointed both at the shogunate and in each daimyo territory.[88] All temples in the nation were characterized according to sectarian divisions in a pyramidal manner with the *honzan* (central temple) on top, followed by the *honji* (main temple), the *chū-honji* (semi-main temple), the *jiki-matsuji* (direct branch temple), and the *son-matsuji* (branch temple once removed), in descending scale. In this way every temple was subject to another of a higher grade and each religious sect was held corporately responsible for its policies and activities.[89] Furthermore, every household was ordered to become affiliated with a particular Buddhist temple, thus creating a "parochial system" hitherto unknown in the history of Buddhism. To be sure, during the medieval period new Buddhist schools formed religious societies wherein the faithful shared the expense of the maintenance of the temples and the livelihood of the priests. The Tokugawa

---

[88] Both Oda Nobunaga and Toyotomi Hideyoshi had appointed officials to be in charge of religious institutions. Iyeyasu initially appointed two priests, Shōtai and Genkitsu, together with his retainer, Itakura Katsushige. Upon the death of Genkitsu, Sūden, an active anti-Kirishitan Zen priest, replaced him. After 1635, however, only daimyo (at first three, but later the number was increased to five) were appointed *jisha-bugyō*. The shogunate also appointed the *fure-gashira* (literally, "in charge of transmission of messages") from among the leading ecclesiastics of each sect. They were usually abbots of head temples in or around Edo, and served as official go-betweens, transmitting orders from the shogunate to all the temples of their sects. They were also spokesmen for their sects in dealing with the *jisha-bugyō*. Obviously, the *fure-gashira* was not, properly speaking, an ecclesiastical office, but it was an influential one. The vestige of this office, known as the *sō-roku* in the Zen tradition and the *rin-ban* in the True Pure Land tradition today, no longer carries the original meaning. See Tamamuro, "Nihon Bukkyō-shi gaisetsu," in Nakamura, Masutani, and Kitagawa, eds., *Gendai Bukkyo meicho zenshū*, III, 186.

[89] In 1632, and again in 1692, the shogunate ordered all the temples to submit the *hon-matsu-chō* (statement of ecclesiastical affiliation). Those temples which had no affiliation with other temples were demolished.

regime, however, imposed its "parochial system" (*danka-seido*) universally, to the end that every Japanese household had no alternative but to accept nominal affiliation with Buddhism; moreover, its relation to the parish temple (*danna-dera*) was practically frozen. With the prohibition of Kirishitan, every Japanese was ordered to secure a temple certificate (*tera-uke*) to prove that he or she was not a member of the forbidden sect.[90] Such a policy necessitated the existence of a temple in every town and village; thus, while there were only 13,037 temples during the Kamakura era, the number increased to 469,934 during the Tokugawa period.[91] Those sects which grew numerically under the Tokugawa rule were Pure Land, True Pure Land, Nichiren, and Sōtō Zen.

As members of the established religion, Buddhist schools eagerly cooperated with the regime. All Buddhist groups established academies (*dan-rin*) which attracted many aspirants.[92] The religious

[90] Originally, the *tera-uke* was issued only to ex-Kirishitan who gave up their former faith. After the Kirishitan uprising in 1637–38, everybody had to be registered in the religious census (*shūshi-ninbetsu-chō*) and to secure the temple certificate. Accordingly, each temple presented the *uke-ban* (note of certification) on behalf of its *danka* (the household which belongs to the parish). It is also to be noted that the *Kirishitan-bugyō* (commissioners on Kirishitan affairs) in 1640 instituted the inquisition office (*Kirishitan-shūmon aratame-yaku*); those who refused to give up the faith were either tortured or kept in prison (*Kirishitan yashiki*). The fear of the Kirishitan was such that as late as 1687, when the Kirishitan were virtually nonexistent, the shogunate established the *Kirishitan-ruizoku-aratame* (investigation of the relatives of Kirishitan), on account of which the relatives of former Kirishitan "were constantly watched, while the descendants, until the seventh generation for the males and the fourth generation for the females, were kept under the permanent control of the government." See Jennes, *History of the Catholic Church in Japan,* p. 173.

[91] See Tamamuro, "Nihon Bukkyō-shi gaisetsu," p. 185. The figure for temples during the Tokugawa period is, however, not altogether reliable.

[92] The Jōdo school alone established eighteen academies. The Nichiren, the Tendai, the Shingon, the True Pure Land, and the Zen schools maintained their respective academies. One of them, the Takakura academy of the Eastern sect (*Higashi Honganji*) of the True Pure Land had 1,714 students in 1828 and 1,847 students in 1838. (*Ibid.,* p. 191.)

life became formalistic, often stressing the Hinayanistic *vinaya* (disciplines) at the expense of Mahayanistic devotions and practices. There appeared no more originators and charismatic leaders; rather, ecclesiastical leaders, systematizers, and popularizers abounded. The only new sect that emerged during the Tokugawa period was the Ōbaku sect of Zen which was transplanted by the Chinese priest Ingen in 1654. One of his followers, Tetsugen, in 1681 published the Ming edition of the *Tripitaka*. Another Zen priest, Hakuin (1685–1768) of the Rinzai sect, combined profound spirituality with a popular evangelistic style.[93]

On the whole, the material security of Buddhism was had at a price. The role of religion was defined not by Buddhism but by the shogunate. Doctrinal deviation was tolerated but the will of the temporal authority might not be disobeyed. For example, the Nichiren priest, Nichiō (1565–1630), was convinced that it was contrary to his religious convictions to receive the charity and support of non-Nichiren followers. According to this principle of *fuju-fuse* (not receiving from outsiders), Nichiō refused the invitation to cooperate with the first shogun and was promptly banished to Tsushima island. His disciple, Nichikō (1626–98), was also punished, in 1665.[94]

Far more detrimental than persecution to the cause of Buddhism, seen from the religious standpoint, was the moral corruption of the clergy. While some of the clergy, living in richly endowed temples, turned their energy to learning, many took advantage of their semipolitical prerogatives to suppress their helpless parishioners.[95] In some instances, enterprising temples

---

[93] See Hakuin's "Song of Meditation" in D. T. Suzuki, *Manual of Zen Buddhism*, pp. 183–84. On his witty and in a way quite vulgar preaching method, see Nakamura, *The Ways of Thinking of Eastern Peoples*, pp. 592–93. See also Shaw and Schiffer, "Yasen Kanna," *Monumenta Nipponica*, XIII (Nos. 1–2, 1957), 101–27.

[94] Tamamuro, "Nihon Bukkyō-shi gaisetsu," pp. 192–93 and 201.

[95] For example, upon the death of a person, the priest was expected to examine the body, and to confer a posthumous name as he offered prayers for the passage of the deceased to the other world. In some instances, priests refused to perform such funerary rites until they were amply rewarded by the deceased's family. This was especially hard on the poor,

engaged in such questionable activities as the *kai-chō* (revealing
the sacred statues that are ordinarily hidden from people) and
the *tomitsuki* (lot drawing) for money-making purposes, attract-
ing the scorn of the pious laity. The moral and spiritual bankruptcy of established Buddhism inevitably brought criticism and
rebellion from within and without. For example, in the True
Pure Land school, belief developed in *hiji-hōmon* (the secret
transmission of Dharma truth), a cult practiced by pious laymen
in the warehouses of private homes, usually at midnight, without
the presence of priests. Believing that the truth of Shinran was
transmitted to the laity, and not to the clergy who might use it to
their temporal benefit, these lay believers instructed other laymen
and conducted initiations and other rituals. According to their
doctrine, the priests transmitted only an external truth, while
the laity had received the hidden internal truth. With the establishment of Buddhism during the Tokugawa period, these kinds
of beliefs and practices became widespread throughout the
country.[96]

This does not imply, of course, that all Buddhist priests were
looked down upon by the people, nor does it mean that Buddhism
lost its influence on society altogether. There were probably more
saintly priests than corrupt ones, but the undesirable minority
brought a bad name to Buddhism in general. I should not fail to
mention, however, that some of the priests and lay Buddhists
left lasting influences among the people. Take, for example,
Matsuo Bashō (1644–94), a warrior turned poet, who made a
great contribution to *haiku* (short verses) with motifs of utter
simplicity, of what Eliot calls "sympathy with nature." [97] Living

---

but inasmuch as they were the parishioners of a certain temple, they had
no alternative except to accommodate themselves to the unreasonable
claims of the priests. As to the corruption of the clergy, Shaku Ryūgyō
bitterly complained as late as 1866 about priests who were keeping
mistresses, fathering children by nuns, eating meat, drinking, and so on.
See *ZNBT*, X, *Edo Jidai*, Part II, pp. 172–73.

[96] Tamamuro, "Nihon Bukkyō-shi gaisetsu," pp. 193–95. In many ways
the beliefs and rites of the underground Buddhist laity resemble those of
the underground Kirishitan.

[97] Eliot, *Japanese Buddhism*, p. 311. See also the section on "The Haiku

as he did in the unusually flamboyant age of Genroku (1688–1703) that saw the development of the arts and culture among the nonwarrior classes, Bashō reflected the eclectic spirit of his time.[98] Those townsmen who patronized the *jōruri* (dramatic ballads), *kabuki* (classical theater), puppet shows, new kinds of paintings such as *ukiyo-e* (literally, "paintings of the floating world"), and novels had little appreciation for orthodox Buddhist teachings. Conspicuously humanistic and affirmative toward life and the world, these townsmen were nevertheless deeply influenced by Buddhism as well as by Confucianism, as evidenced by their concepts of *giri* (reciprocal obligations) and *ninjō* (humane sentiment), and their implicit belief in the cosmic law of retribution. Their attitude toward established Buddhism, however, tended toward indifference.

Meanwhile, vocal anti-Buddhist sentiment was raised by Japanese Confucian scholars—Fujiwara Seika, Hayashi Razan, Kumazawa Banzan, Yamazaki Ansai, Yamaga Sokō, Itō Jinsai, Ogyū Sorai, and Muro Kyūsō, to name only the most obvious. Some of them had been trained as Buddhists, and their reaction against Buddhism may be characterized as emotional. Others tried, as did Hayashi Razan, to relate the *li* (reason or principle) of Neo-Confucianism in theory with Shinto. There were also some rationalists, not necessarily motivated by adherence to Confucianism or Shinto, such as Tominaga Nakamoto (d. 1746), Nakai Chikuzan (d. 1804), and Nakai Riken (d. 1817), who attacked the corruption and irrationality of Buddhism.[99] As might be expected, one of the significant by-products of the anti-Buddhist trend was increased interest in Shinto.

---

and the Democracy of Poetry in Japan," in Tsunoda, *et al., Sources of Japanese Tradition,* pp. 450–67; and the chapter on "Oku no Hosomichi" (Journey to Ōu), in Kokusai Bunka Shinkōkai, *Introduction to Classic Japanese Literature,* pp. 241–50.

[98] It is interesting to note that Bashō was a contemporary of the priest Keichū, a pioneer in the study of the Japanese classics; Ihara Saikaku, author of the *Ukiyo Zōshi* (Notes on the floating world); and Chikamatsu Monzaemon, often referred to as the Japanese Shakespeare.

[99] See Nakamura, *The Ways of Thinking of Eastern Peoples,* pp. 583–84, and Tamamuro, "Nihon Bukkyō-shi gaisetsu," pp. 202–10.

There were many facets to the so-called renewal of Shinto during the Tokugawa period. Among them, I may cite popular piety, the self-conscious awakening of the Shinto priesthood, the influence of Confucian scholars, and the growth of learning in history and the ancient classics of Japan. Perhaps the best example of the persistent strength of Shinto among the masses appears in the popularity of the Grand Shrine of Ise. In origin, Ise was the clan shrine of the imperial family. During the medieval period, partly in order to counteract the popular movements of new Buddhist schools, the priests of Ise shrine toured the countryside, organizing the *Ise-kō* (devotional associations of the faithful of Ise). Members of this association made it a point to visit Ise at least once in their lifetime. During the Tokugawa period Ise enjoyed a new vogue through the *okage-mairi* (worship to return divine favor) and *nuke-mairi* (unauthorized visit), so that, for instance, in 1705 more than 3,620,000 pilgrims worshiped at Ise during a period of fifty days (between April 9 and May 29).[100] In addition to these devotional movements and practices, there also developed a form of popular Shinto preaching (*Shintō kōshaku*). The cause of Shinto was further aided by the *Shin-gaku* (Mind Learning) movement, founded by Ishida Baigan. Although it was an eclectic system, *Shin-gaku* teachers nevertheless taught the populace to become conscious of their indebtedness to the nation and the kami.[101]

The awakening of the Shinto priesthood came from two sides, the practical and the theoretical. Practically, the Tokugawa regime's order that everyone had to secure a temple certificate (*tera-uke*) was a great shock to the Shinto priests who also were compelled to become nominal Buddhists in order to obey the

---

[100] *ZNBT*, X, *Edo Jidai*, Part II, pp. 175–76. The term *okage* simply means "favor," but in this case it refers to the blessing bestowed by the kami of Ise shrine. When prices went down, or if the harvest were plentiful, people were encouraged to pay thanks to the kami of Ise shrine. The term *nuke-mairi* refers to the pilgrimage to Ise by young men. The *Ise-kō* (devotional association of the faithful of Ise) consisted only of the heads of households. The *nuke-mairi* became in the course of time a form of initiation for young men's groups.

[101] On the spread of the *Shin-gaku* movement, see *ibid.*, pp. 244–48.

law. In this situation, Shinto leaders made repeated petitions both
to the shogunate and to the local daimyo, hoping that Shinto
might be recognized as a legally sanctioned religious sect.[102]
More specifically, they asked permission to have Shinto priests
buried according to Shinto rites on the grounds that the Hayashi family and the daimyo of Mito were allowed to be buried
not according to Buddhist but according to Confucian funeral
rites. The resistance on the part of Buddhist leaders to such arguments drove Shinto leaders to articulate a theoretical formulation
of Shinto as an independent religious system. Two of the Shinto
theoreticians of the seventeenth century were Deguchi (Watarai)
Nobuyoshi (d. 1690) and Yoshikawa Koretaru (d. 1694), both
of whom stimulated the thinking of Yamazaki Ansai (d. 1682),
scholar of the Chu Hsi school of Neo-Confucianism who developed a form of Confucian Shinto known as Suiga Shinto. According to Yamazaki's own claim, "he expounded a doctrine that
had been taught by the Sun Goddess, Amaterasu-Ōmikami, and
communicated through successive kami to her human descendants." [103] What Yamazaki taught in scholarly language regarding
Confucian-Shinto morality, the *Wa Rongo* (literally, Japanese
analects), written in the second half of the seventeenth century,
presented in a more popular style in the form of divine oracles.[104]

Shinto soon found a powerful ideological ally in the school of
national learning, which stressed the philological, historical, and
hermeneutical studies of the Japanese classics. Keichū (d. 1701),
a Buddhist priest, and Kada Azumamaro (d. 1736), lay priest
of Inari shrine of Kyoto, were the pioneers of this movement,
while Kamo Mabuchi (d. 1769), who undertook scholarly research over the *Manyōshū* (Anthology of myriad leaves), an
eighth-century collection of poetry, was the first prominent figure
of this tradition. Mabuchi's disciple, Motoori Norinaga (1730–

[102] See Nagao Nishida, *Nihon shūkyō shisō-shi no kenkyū*, pp. 544–
618.

[103] Holtom, *The National Faith of Japan*, p. 43. See also Sansom, *A
History of Japan, 1615–1867*, pp. 85–87.

[104] See Katō, "A Study of Some of the Oracles and Sayings in the
Warongo or Japanese Analects," *TASJ*, XLV (No. 11, 1918).

1801), devoted many years to the philological and theoretical interpretation of the *Kojiki* (Records of ancient matters) and helped the cause of the *Fukko* (return to antiquity) Shinto movement. Motoori held that "the Japanese and their Shinto, when purged of all foreign accretions and influences, represented the pure, and therefore the best, inheritance of humanity from the divine ages." [105] The last main figure of this tradition was Hirata Atsutane (1776–1843), who was well versed in Chinese philosophy and also familiar with Western knowledge through Dutch. He was, according to Anesaki, "a man of great ability but a bigot of a doubtful character," and his influence had a great deal to do with the anti-foreign movement in the nineteenth century.[106] It is a matter of great interest that, in his attempt to construct a Shinto theology, Hirata depended heavily on the Chinese writings of Jesuits, especially the *T'ien Chu Shih* (True doctrine of the heavenly Lord; 1556 and 1601), by Matthew Ricci, and the *Chi Ko Ta Ch'uan* (Seven books of the seven victories; 1614), by Didacus de Pantoja. In fact, Hirata's work, the *Hongyō Gaihen* (Supplementary compilation of Shinto; 1806), betrays heavy borrowing from three Jesuit books. At any rate, Hirata introduced the notions of creation and eschatology into the framework of Shinto theology, although he modified these concepts in his later years.[107]

The combined effects of the Shinto revival, interest in National Learning, and royalist sentiment advocated by the Mito school of Confucianism, provided the ideological arsenal for those who for a variety of reasons were dissatisfied with the state of affairs in Japan under the Tokugawa shogunate. The decline of the power and prestige of the shogunate was further accelerated by the "threat" of the Western nations that had begun to press Japan to open her doors to foreign trade. By that time the basic contradictions of the feudal regime had become increasingly apparent. While the shogunate still believed in the principle of

[105] Anesaki, *History of Japanese Religion*, p. 308.

[106] *Ibid.*

[107] On the Christian influence on Hirata's theology, see Muraoka, *Zoku Nihon shisō-shi kenkyū*, pp. 321–36.

"immanental theocracy," the political reality no longer supported this principle. For example, some of the powerful daimyo acted very much as though the shogun was little more than an ornamental symbol of a dated political system that was no longer operative. As early as 1829 the daimyo of Mito, Tokugawa Nariaki, started a sweeping reform of his own fief without consultation with the shogunate. Likewise, Mōri Yoshichika (d. 1873), the daimyo of Chōshū (the present Yamaguchi prefecture); Shimazu Shigehide (d. 1835), the daimyo of Satsuma (the present Kagoshima prefecture); and Nabeshima Kanso (d. 1871), the daimyo of Saga (the present Saga prefecture), exercised their authority as independent daimyo in reshaping the policies and administrative structure of their domains. Some of these reform measures violated the traditional religious policies of the shogunate. In this respect, the most extreme change was undertaken in the domain of Mito, which in 1843 abolished 190 Buddhist temples, returned a number of priests to secular life, forbade the Buddhist customs of cremation and the use of posthumous names for the deceased, and encouraged Shinto funeral rites. Furthermore, temple bells were confiscated and recast into cannons, the separation of Shinto from Buddhism was enforced, and those who were not genuine Shinto priests, such as the *Shasō* (Buddhist priests serving in Shinto shrines) and the Mountain Ascetics, were banished from Shinto shrines.[108]

And yet the significant fact is that no one really envisaged the overthrow of the total structure of the feudal regime. What many people realized in Japan during the first half of the nineteenth century was that social, economic, and political realities could no longer be harmonized with the over-all feudalistic framework that had been established in the seventeenth century. The original arrangement of social classes, of the warrior, farmer, artisan, and merchant, was still maintained officially, but the growth of the merchant class tended to tip the scales out of balance. Even within the same class status and power were not necessarily equivalent as is evident in the case of the lower warrior-official,

[108] See Tamamuro, "Nihon Bukkyō-shi geisetsu," pp. 216–18.

who held a minor position but actually exerted considerable influence in the handling of the practical affairs of the domain of the daimyo. It was precisely these alert lower warriors with good education and training who played an important role in bringing about the monarchical rule of the Meiji era. Among the farmers, while the rich peasants continued to prosper, the lot of the poor peasants became worse through heavy taxation, mortgages, exploitation, and famines.[109] We have to bear in mind that farmers during the Tokugawa period, unlike their predecessors in the sixteenth century, were deprived of weapons and lacked sufficient group solidarity to fight effectively against unjust officials or to rebel against the daimyo; even so there were about 1,200 peasant uprisings between the middle of the eighteenth and the middle of the nineteenth centuries. In desperation paupers in big cities, moreover, often attacked the stores of wealthy merchants.[110]

Unfortunately, the shogunate failed to recognize the basic issues involved in these social and economic tensions, and tried to pass over immediate crises either by short-term solutions or by moralistic exhortations advocating the virtues of thriftiness and hard work. Furthermore, the Shogun Iyenari, who headed the regime for fifty-one years, during the crucial period 1787–1837,

[109] During the Tokugawa period there were 154 famines, of which twenty-one were serious and widespread. Among them ten great famines took place in 1619, 1642, 1675, 1680, 1732, 1783, 1784, 1787, 1836, and 1837. After each famine many peasants were compelled to leave their villages to move into towns where they barely survived as paupers, engaged in the lowest types of labor. Their wives, too, worked as kitchen helpers, nursemaids, or doing anything they could find to do. Among the poor the practices of abortion (*mabiki*, literally "thinning out") and of abandoning children became widespread. It is estimated that the famine of 1732 affected 1,600,000 persons and that at least 17,000 died of starvation. After the 1784 famine, Matsudaira Sadanobu estimated that about 1,400,000 peasants left their villages within the period of one year, 1785–86. See Kobata and Wakamori, *Nihonshi kenkyū*, pp. 312–13.

[110] In 1764 nearly 80,000 peasants of Kōzuke and Musashi districts threatened to invade the city of Edo. In 1733 many stores in Edo, such as rice, wine, and corn shops, were attacked by paupers. The inflation of 1787 resulted in similar attacks on stores in ten major cities. See *ibid.*, p. 314.

was notorious for his inefficiency, extravagance, and vanity. His chief accomplishment was that he maintained forty mistresses and sired fifty-five children. As time went on, inevitably the people lost a sense of direction and the nation wavered. Among the intellectuals opinions varied between those who attempted to preserve the residual glory of the Tokugawa regime and those who advocated "reverence for the throne" (*sonnō*). Between were those who wished to "unify the imperial authority and the shogunate" (*kōbu gattai*). All of them came under the influence of Neo-Confucianism, National Learning (*kokugaku*), Shinto, and Dutch Learning (*rangaku*) in different degrees and proportions.[111] Another issue that split the intellectuals of the later Tokugawa period was the question of Japan's relation to the Western nations then pressing her to open her ports to trade. There were those who favored the "opening of the country" (*kaikoku*), while others were adamant in advocating a policy of maintaining seclusion and of "repulsion of foreigners" (*jōi*).[112]

The masses were not particularly excited by such questions as seclusion versus restoration or monarchical rule versus shogunate. Far more important to the majority of the people was their peren-

---

[111] Actually, it was the Shogun Yoshimune who in 1720 permitted the introduction of Dutch and Chinese books, except for those which dealt with Christianity. Two men, Aoki Konyō and Noro Genjō, were ordered by the shogunate to study the Dutch language. Aoki's disciple, Mayeno Ryōtaku (d. 1803) studied anatomy in Dutch at Nagasaki. Mayeno, together with his friends Sugita Genpaku (d. 1817), Nakagawa Jun-an (d. 1886), and Katsuragawa Hoshū (d. 1809), spent four years (1771–74) in translating a Dutch book, *Tavel Anatomia*, and published it with the Japanese title, *Kaitai shinsho* (New anatomy). Sugita Genpaku trained several able Japanese scholars in Dutch learning. Meanwhile, in 1823, P. F. von Siebold, a German physician in the Dutch service, arrived in Japan and taught medicine and ethnology to Japanese students for six years. Among them were such talented young men as Itō Genboku (d. 1871) and Takano Chōyei (d. 1851). In 1838 Ogata Kōan (d. 1863) established an academy of Dutch learning in Osaka and attracted nearly one thousand students. Among them were Hashimoto Sanai (d. 1859), Fukuzawa Yukichi (d. 1901), and many leaders of the Meiji era. See *ibid.*, pp. 318–20. See also Sansom, *A History of Japan, 1615–1867*, pp. 188–92.

[112] See Tsunoda, *et al.*, *Sources of Japanese Tradition*, pp. 591–637.

nial yearning for mundane benefits and the assurance of happiness in the life hereafter. Although every household was registered as a parishioner (*danka*) of a certain Buddhist temple, many people personally wanted more direct contacts with the source of life. It is readily understandable why the magico-religious practices of the *Shugen-dō* (Order of Mountain Ascetics) exerted a great influence among the people.[113] Many of the *yama-bushi* (mountain ascetics) settled in the towns and villages and often married *miko* (shamanic diviners).[114] It was estimated that at the beginning of the Meiji era there were 170,000 *sendatsu* (senior guides to sacred mountains), which meant that a considerably greater number of minor functionaries of the *Shugen-dō* must have been operating in various parts of Japan throughout the Tokugawa period.[115] They provided the masses with incantations (*majinai*), spells, and charms for all conceivable occasions. For example, it became widely believed that one could prevent dog bite if one wrote the ideograph for tiger on the palm of his hand. Among the superstitious people, spirits of all kinds and charismatic persons were feared and venerated. A curious example of this sort of thing was the case of Akiyama Jiun, a merchant and devotee of the Nichiren sect. On his deathbed, after suffering seven years from hemorrhoids, he announced his determination to become a god and save those who might suffer from the same ailment. Shortly after his death he came to be venerated as Jiun Rei-jin, which meant that he was a minor deity; his cult attracted a large number of followers both in Edo and Osaka. Similar cults, centering around charismatic persons, prospered in various parts of Japan.[116]

The founder of the Tokugawa regime was mindful of the need of religious and ideological foundations for feudal society. What Iyeyasu attempted was the establishment of an "immanental

[113] The Tokugawa regime issued the Ordinances for the Mountain Ascetics (*Shugen-dō hatto*) but could not control the internal affairs of this order because of the secretive nature of its organization.

[114] See Hori, *Waga-kuni minkan shinkō-shi no kenkyū*, II, 703–7.

[115] Togawa, *Haguro Yama-bushi to minkan shinkō*, p. 11.

[116] *ZNBT, X, Edo jidai*, Part II, pp. 179–81.

theocracy" with himself as the new savior, but he also depended heavily upon Shinto, Confucianism, and Buddhism to constitute the ethico-religious foundation for the preservation of the political and social order. "Shinto is the way of inner truth and of inner purity," he is remembered as saying. "Confucianism is the way of sincerity, love, and benevolence. Buddhism emphasizes self-lessness and desirelessness, teaching forbearance and compassion." [117] Toward the end of the Tokugawa period, as the prestige of the shogunate declined, and the social and political order began to disintegrate from within, Buddhism became nothing more than a department of the feudal regime, having lost its spirituality. Neo-Confucianism provided many insights, education, ethical principles, and a philosophical basis for Tokugawa Japan, but in the course of time it became transmuted and allied itself with Shinto. The masses, though indifferent to political developments, sensed the lack of that order and coherence which had characterized life in the earlier phase of the Tokugawa rule. In this situation, the age-old shamanistic religious ethos, suppressed for a long time but kept alive in the popular cults of Jizō (Bodhi-sattva Ksitigarbha), Dōso-jin (road-side kami), Binzuru (Pin-dola), Kompira (Kumbhīra), Kishi-mojin (originally an Indian goddess, Hāritī), Benten (Sarasvatī, the Indian deity of riches), and other divinities,[118] erupted in the forms of messianic and healing cults, such as the Kurozumi-kyō, Konkō-kyō, Tenri-kyō, and the Konotabi movement.[119] Some of these popular cults later came to be classified as Kyōha-Shinto (Sect Shinto) by the Meiji government, and as such will be mentioned in the next chapter.

By far the most significant religious development during the latter part of the Tokugawa period was the renewal of Shinto. Shinto, be it noted, was no longer the simple religion of clan and regional kami as was the case in the early period. In the course of centuries it had been nourished and also transmuted by Buddhism, Confucianism, and Taoism, as well

[117] This statement is attributed to Iyeyasu by
in J. W. Hall, "The Confucian Teacher in 1
[118] On these popular divinities, see Eliot, *Japan*
[119] See Anesaki, *History of Japanese Religions,*

Kokugaku (National Learning). Its indifference to doctrinal formulations enabled it to maintain rapport with the masses and their cults, some of which had no organic connection with Shinto. Its indigenous origin and inseparable relation with the imperial clan presented a ready-made alternative for those who were dissatisfied with the ethos of the Tokugawa regime. Nevertheless, it was the Tokugawa regime that provided the ethos and the form of "immanental theocracy" for Shinto that was to play a decisive role in the history of Japan throughout the eras of Meiji, Taishō, and Shōwa until the end of the Second World War. The last Tokugawa shogun officially terminated the feudal regime in 1867, whereupon monarchical rule was restored. By that time Japan had opened its doors to Western nations, and the influence of the modern West was beginning to be felt. Underneath the apparent modernization, however, Japan preserved and even strengthened her affirmation of the principle of "immanental theocracy"—no longer under the shogun, but under the emperor, the legitimate inheritor of the charisma of the imperial office.

CHAPTER V

Modernity, Culture, and Religion

RELIGIOUS ETHOS OF MODERN JAPAN

*(mid-nineteenth century to the
Second World War)*

The modern period of Japanese history had its beginning in the middle of the nineteenth century through the combined pressures of internal and external factors in an intricate combination. The decline of the power and authority of the Tokugawa shogunate, the power struggle among the influential daimyo, the contradictory features of the socioeconomic framework of the feudal system, the general apathy among the populace, the infiltration of Western knowledge, the emotional appeal of the so-called National Learning (*kokugaku*), and the advance of Western powers in the Far East are but a few obvious examples of the many forces that together brought forth a new era in the history of Japan. It was no longer possible or desirable for Japan to maintain her policy of national seclusion; she was destined to chart a new course in the stormy seas of the modern world. And as if to proclaim the coming of a new age, four American "black ships," headed by Commodore Matthew C. Perry, appeared off the shore of Uraga in the summer of 1853.

Before the Dawn

Much has been written about the international as well as the domestic political developments that preceded Japan's decision to open her doors to the rest of the world.[1] It is to be noted in this connection that, while Perry was by no means the only or the first Western envoy who tried to conclude a treaty with Japan, he was the first one who succeeded in this difficult assignment. According to the treaty of 1854, Japan agreed to open two ports to American vessels. This act marked the end of Japan's self-imposed seclusion that had lasted over two hundred years. The real architect of sustained relations between the United States and Japan, however, was Townsend Harris (1804–78), the first American minister to Japan.[2] Following in the footsteps of the

[1] While I cannot cite all the major works dealing with the latter days of the Tokugawa period, I cannot fail to mention Norman, *Japan's Emergence as a Modern State,* and Sansom, *The Western World and Japan.* Others which were helpful in varying degrees are: Akagi, *Japan's Foreign Relations, 1542–1936;* Beasley, *Great Britain and the Opening of Japan, 1834–1858;* Cole, ed., *With Perry in Japan: The Diary of Edward Yorke McCauley;* Craig, *Chōshū in the Meiji Restoration;* Eckel, *The Far East Since 1500;* Fujii, comp. and ed., *Outline of Japanese History in the Meiji Era,* tr. and adapted by Hattie K. Colton and Kenneth E. Colton; Hackett, "Nishi Amane—A Tokugawa-Meiji Bureaucrat," *JAS,* XVIII (No. 2, February, 1959), 213–25; Hani, *Meiji-ishin-shi kenkyū;* Jansen, "Takeuchi Zuizan and the Tosa Loyalist Party," *JAS,* XVIII (No. 2, February, 1959), 199–212; Jansen, *Sakamoto Ryōma and the Meiji Restoration;* Kimura, *Meiji Tennō;* Ōye, *Meiji kokka no seiritsu;* Sakata, *Meiji ishin-shi;* Sakata, ed., *Meiji ishin-shi no mondai-ten;* Van Straelen, *Yoshida Shōin, Forerunner of the Meiji Restoration;* Takekoshi, *The Economic Aspects of the History of the Civilization of Japan,* Vol. III; Wallach, ed., *Narrative of the Expedition of an American Squadron to the China Seas and Japan;* and Yanaga, *Japan Since Perry.*

[2] Sansom rightly points out that the success of Perry's mission was greatly due to financial factors, namely, the emptiness of the shogunate's treasury. "It was chiefly because it was insolvent that it gave way to Perry's pressure in 1853, though this fact was not known to the country at large, and still less to Perry himself, who naturally took full credit for his own diplomatic skill." (*The Western World and Japan,* p. 288.) On Harris, see Griffis, *Townsend Harris;* and Cosenza, ed., *The Complete Journal of Townsend Harris, First American Consul and Minister to Japan.* Harris arrived in Japan in 1856 and carried on difficult negotiations with the shogunate officials in the midst of seemingly insurmountable obstacles. According to Yanaga, "While Harris ably represented his country in dealing with Japan as well as the other powers, he was always supporting the

United States, other powers, such as Great Britain, Russia, the Netherlands, and France, also concluded treaties with Japan.

More important for our purposes is the political and social change within Japan which to be sure was effected largely through Japan's confrontation with Western nations. When Perry appeared on the scene in 1853, Japan was still under the rule of the Tokugawa feudal regime which, since the beginning of the seventeenth century, had maintained, as it were, permanent martial law under the leadership of the samurai class. In the course of time, however, the very success of the regime in preserving domestic peace began to undercut the foundations of the feudal regime itself; consequently, the Tokugawa rulers failed to cope with the social and economic dislocations that inevitably developed. By the middle of the nineteenth century, the once powerful Tokugawa shogunate having lost its grip, many daimyo sensed a need to reform the political structures of the nation. Some tried to strengthen the Tokugawa shogunate in Edo, while others looked toward the imperial court in Kyoto for leadership. Still others envisaged the unification of the shogunate and the imperial court.[3] One of the most pressing problems for Japan in those days was undoubtedly Japan's relation to Western nations.

The controversy between the advocates of "opening of the country" (*kaikoku*) and those of "repulsion of foreigners" (*jōi*) provided an emotional issue that was often used by various factions for other political ends as well. Even among the shogun's immediate circle of advisers opinions were split on the question of how to deal with Western nations. It so happened that the thirteenth shogun, Iyesada (1824–58; shogun, 1853–58) proved to be weak mentally as well as physically. Thus Abe Ise-no-kami Masahiro, the senior minister, had to manage the affairs of the nation in the name of the shogun. He took a conciliatory attitude toward the imperial court, and also attempted to secure the co-

---

Japanese in their dealings with the powers of Europe, especially when the Shōgunate officials were pitted against the shrewd and experienced diplomats of the European nations." (Yanaga, *Japan Since Perry*, pp. 24–25.)

[3] See Sansom, *The Western World and Japan*, pp. 281–97.

operation of such quarrelsome daimyo as the retired Lord of Mito (Tokugawa Nariaki) and the Lord of Satsuma (Shimazu Naria-kira), in order to preserve the political unity of the nation. Abe's successor, Hotta Bitchū-no-kami Masayoshi, on the other hand, convinced of the necessity of opening Japan's doors to the rest of the world, actively tried to persuade the imperial court to approve the treaty with the United States. But the imperial court, which was then strongly influenced by antiforeign factions, was in no mood to endorse the policy of the shogunate.[4] Meanwhile, some of the *fudai daimyō* (hereditary lieges of the Tokugawa family) who were dedicated to upholding the traditional authority of the shogunate, rallied around their spokesman, Ii Kamon-no-kami Naosuke, who now assumed the position of *tairō* or regent. Ii immediately proceeded to conclude treaties with five Western powers in 1858, and sent a Japanese mission to Washington two years later in order to ratify the American treaty in the name of the shogun. Ii's strong measures naturally aroused bitter crit-icism in various quarters, but the determined regent ruthlessly persecuted his opponents and even snubbed the throne. It is a matter of great significance that the most outgoing foreign policy was executed by a man who otherwise espoused the very con-servative values of the traditional feudal society. This colorful and audacious regent of the shogunate met his death at the hands of assassins in 1860.[5]

With the loss of Ii Kamon-no-kami Naosuke's strong person-ality, the morale of the shogunate declined markedly. The con-cocted marriage between Princess Chikako, the younger sister of the Emperor Kōmei (r. 1846–66), and the fourteenth shogun,

[4] One of the thorny issues at that time was the selection of an heir to the shogunate, because the thirteenth shogun had had no male child. Both the Mito branch and the Wakayama (Kii) branch of the Tokugawa family had candidates. The imperial court favored Keiki, son of the retired Lord of Mito, partly because of the royalist sentiment of the Mito leaders, while Ii Kamon-no-kami Naosuke and his associates preferred Keiki's rival who subsequently became the fourteenth shogun. Keiki, how-ever, was destined to become the fifteenth shogun, as we shall see later.

[5] His complex personality emerges in his letters. See Tokyo Daigaku Shiryōhensanjo, *Dai-Nihon ishin shiryō*, Vol. I: *Ii-ke shiryō*.

Iyemochi (shogun, 1858–66) did little to bolster the prestige of the shogunate.[6] Increasingly, the policy of the imperial court hardened under the pressure of antishogunate and antiforeign elements, especially those of the powerful fiefs of Satsuma, Chōshū, and Tosa, as well as some of the politically astute court nobles.[7] Caught between the demands of foreign envoys and the antishogunate sentiment that was erupting in various parts of the nation, the shogunate had to relax some traditional rules and practices, including the system of *sankin kōtai* (alternate residence, by which all the daimyo were required to live alternately in Edo and in their own fiefs). The shogunate also appointed Hitotsubashi Keiki, son of Tokugawa Nariaki of Mito, as guardian of the young shogun. Even then, the shogunate could no longer control the antiforeign activities of some of the leading fiefs, although it was held responsible for the payment of indemnities to foreign powers. Realizing the precariousness of the situation, Keiki went to Kyoto in 1863 on behalf of the shogun in an effort to restrain the extreme antiforeign measures contemplated by those who surrounded the throne. But he was induced, no doubt against his better judgment, to accept the policy of the court instead. Keiki informed the court shortly thereafter that foreign envoys stationed in Japan were prepared to protect their own interests with arms if necessary, and the court upon learning this fact reversed its policy and dismissed the leaders of the extreme antiforeign factions from Kyoto.

The political climate in mid-nineteenth-century Japan was further aggravated by difficult economic conditions. The continued fiscal mismanagement of the shogunate, plus the extraordinary expenses incurred by new demands, such as the construction of

---

[6] This was a desperate effort on the part of the shogunate, of course. There is good reason to believe that the Emperor Kōmei upheld the ideal of collaboration between the court and the shogunate. The court agreed to this marriage on the condition that the shogunate would reverse its foreign policy.

[7] Satsuma is the present Kagoshima prefecture, Chōshū is the present Yamaguchi prefecture, and Tosa is the present Kōchi prefecture. Evidently, after the death of Tokugawa Nariaki (1800–60), the leadership among the royalist groups shifted from Mito to Satsuma.

forts and the purchase of foreign military equipment, had to be compensated for by imposing greater exactions on the farmers and by soliciting forced loans from the merchants. Foreign trade, which at first appeared financially profitable for Japan, soon became a source of financial drain. The lower peasantry, confronted by increased taxes and by the rise in commodity prices, resorted to a series of revolts.[8] Also, as E. Herbert Norman succinctly states, "the economic distress of the lower *samurai*, sharpened by the meteoric rise in prices, threw them into a truly wretched state of penury, deepened their hatred of the *Bakufu* and its foreign policy, and induced them to fasten the responsibility for their troubles on foreign barbarians and their trading operations." [9] No wonder many of the armed insurrections that arose in the 1860s, purporting to be royalist movements, were more basically antishogunate and antiforeign in character and mixed with strong economic motives.[10]

The inability of the shogunate to control the rebellious daimyo, especially the Lord of Chōshū, during the tenure of the fourteenth shogun, Iyemochi, demonstrated the fact that the feudal regime had lost all but the semblance of its residual authority. Following the death of Iyemochi in 1866, his guardian, Keiki, assumed the office of shogun. In this critical moment of history, Léon Roches, then the French minister to Japan, offered assistance to the shogunate, while Sir Harry S. Parkes, the British minister, sided with the forces of Satsuma and Chōshū.[11] To

[8] One of the leading writers in modern Japan, Shimazaki Tōson (1872–1943), published a great novel, *Yoake-maye* (Before the dawn), in which he described the social, economic, and political conditions of Japan during the stormy period between 1853 and 1886. The central figure of the novel is Aoyama Hanzō, a leading citizen in a village along the highway between Kyoto and Edo. In the first half of the novel Shimazaki describes vividly how even humble villagers sensed the whirlwind that shook the foundation of the feudal social order. See Shimazaki, *Shimazaki Tōson-shū*, III (*Gendai Nihon bungaku zenshū*, Vol. LXI).

[9] Norman, *Japan's Emergence as a Modern State*, p. 42.

[10] One of the earliest antishogunate rebellions was called "Ten-chū-gumi" (literally, "A group representing Heaven's punishment"); it arose in Yamato, the present Nara prefecture, in 1863.

[11] It should be noted in this connection that the United States, which

make matters worse, less than twenty days after Keiki became the shogun, the Emperor Kōmei, who was sympathetic with the ideal of *kōbu-gattai* (collaboration of the imperial court and the shogunate), died at the age of thirty-six. In 1867 Mutsuhito (1852–1912), later known as the Emperor Meiji, ascended the shaky throne. Being only fifteen years of age, the new emperor was carefully guarded by certain courtiers and ladies in waiting, while the important decisions were made by a group of advisers. Chief among them was Iwakura Tomomi, a court noble and a close confidante of Nakayama Tadayoshi (1809–88), maternal grandfather of the new emperor.[12] Iwakura proved to be an effective spokesman for the antishogunate elements among the court nobles and samurai in the fiefs of Satsuma and Chōshū. Keiki now realized that he was caught in a network of internal and external problems impossible of solution through the existing structures of society, and surrendered his power to the throne in 1867. Thus ended the feudal regime; monarchical rule was resumed as of January 25, 1868. The city of Edo was renamed Tokyo (Eastern Capital), and the imperial government was established there.

The Meiji Era

With the restoration of direct imperial rule, at least in principle, sweeping changes were introduced by the new regime. The real architects of the Meiji regime were fewer than one hundred relatively younger men, mostly lower samurai but including also a few members of the court nobility, who had been trained in practical politics during the stormy prerestoration decades. "It

initially took the leading role in Japanese affairs, became preoccupied with domestic problems after 1861. Subsequently, Great Britain became the leading power in relation to Japan. For instance, in 1864 Great Britain controlled nearly 90 percent of Japanese trade with Western nations.

[12] The Nakayama family was passionately dedicated to the royalist cause. In fact, Nakayama Tadamitsu, son of Tadayoshi and brother of the Emperor Meiji's mother, was the chief exponent and leader of the armed rebellion called "Ten-chū-gumi," mentioned above. See Kimura, *Meiji Tennō,* pp. 76–78.

was, by a paradox characteristic of the times," says Sansom, "the antiforeign activities of Satsuma and Chōshū that brought to birth a new government dedicated to the fullest extension of foreign intercourse." [13] While the leaders of the new regime were motivated by different purposes, they all realized the importance of developing a modern nation-state with a strong defense system and an industrial economy. Unlike the Tokugawa feudal regime, which had depended heavily on (1) rules of all kinds, regulating the activities of men and women in all walks of life, (2) traditional values and practices at the expense of novelty, (3) a negativistic economic policy, stressing frugality instead of encouraging the financial growth of the nation, and (4) a moralism based on Neo-Confucianism which was oblivious to the development of individual personalities,[14] the Meiji regime adopted the so-called Charter Oath as the guiding force of the nation. The following five articles were announced in the name of the emperor in the spring of 1868:

1. Deliberative assemblies shall be widely established and all matters decided by public discussion.
2. All classes, high and low, shall unite in vigorously carrying out the administration of affairs of state.
3. The common people, no less than the civil and military officials, shall each be allowed to pursue his own calling so that there may be no discontent.
4. Evil (or absurd) customs of the past shall be discarded and justice shall be based on the just laws of heaven and earth.
5. Knowledge shall be sought throughout the world in order to strengthen the foundations of imperial rule.

During the forty-five years of the Meiji Era (1868–1912) Japan indeed was eager to seek new knowledge all over the world.[15] As early as 1870 the government enforced the Regulations for Dispatching Students Abroad, whereby able Japanese students were sent to Europe and North America to acquire up-to-date knowl-

---

[13] Sansom, *The Western World and Japan,* p. 302.

[14] Nishida, *Nihon bunka-shi josetsu,* pp. 536–44.

[15] A very useful "Selected Bibliography on Meiji Japan" is found in Norman, *Japan's Emergence as a Modern State,* pp. 211–22.

edge of medicine, science, law, business, and national defense. "The world was one vast school for them, and they entered it determined to learn only the best in each field." [16] At home the government took the initiative in establishing or introducing Westernized educational institutions (1869), a postal system (1871), a census, military conscription, telegraphic service, and railroads (1872), banks (1873), courts of justice (1875), the patent bureau, a steamship line, and the cabinet system (1885), income tax, electricity, and the Red Cross (1887), a constitution (1889), and parliament (1890). The new regime was most eager to do away with absurd practices of the past, such as the system of barriers, discrimination against the *eta* (untouchables), and the traditions of wearing sword and topknot as well as of sanctioning acts of revenge. Women were encouraged to become educated; the eating of beef, ice cream, and bread was promoted; and social dancing, as well as Western music, was introduced. Even Christianity, the "forbidden religion" during the Tokugawa period, was tolerated.

Notwithstanding these modern or Westernized features and the new system of administration, the Meiji government inherited one significant characteristic of the Tokugawa feudal regime, namely, its "immanental theocracy." This in spite of the fact that the architects of the Meiji regime were passionately antishogunate in principle and in outlook. In a real sense, they were not conscious of their own inner contradictions, because while they envisaged the establishment of a modern nation-state, instinctively they longed for a semidivine nation, a paternalistic and authoritarian state that could, however, utilize the fruits of Western civilization.

The paradoxical character of the Meiji regime may be illustrated by the examples of military conscription and compulsory education. When the throne assumed political authority in 1868, the government had only some 400 soldiers in the imperial guard; otherwise, it had to depend on the military forces of the royalist daimyo. In 1871, 10,000 soldiers were recruited for the

[16] Edwin O. Reischauer, *Japan: Past and Present,* p. 123.

imperial guard from Satsuma, Chōshū, and Tosa. In the following year a universal military conscription ordinance was issued, and it was implemented in 1873.[17] Military conscription was offered, be it noted, as a "gift" from the throne, welcoming all able-bodied males of fully twenty years of age, not only the sons of samurai families but also those of farmers, artisans, and merchants, into the newly created army and navy equipped with Westernized uniforms and weapons. Initially, conscription was very unpopular.[18] But in the course of time military service became an important channel for upward social mobility, so that until the Second World War the peasantry in times of crises often supported the military rather than civilian leaders.

Compulsory education made Japan the first nation in Asia to have a literate populace. Prior to the Meiji Era, education was normally available only to children of the samurai and the elite among the non-samurai classes. The Meiji government established the Department of Education in 1871, and compulsory education was put into effect in 1872.[19] The government also established institutions of secondary and higher education, for both men and women, including schools of commerce, fine arts, military science, teacher's training, music, and other specialized subjects. The entire educational system was designed to meet the needs of the growing nation, that is, the training of a small number of government officials and a large number of technicians. It also aimed at

[17] See Yanaga, *Japan Since Perry*, pp. 112–15.

[18] Children of the former samurai class resented the fact that they were expected to serve in the armed forces alongside the children of farmers, artisans, and merchants. Farmers were not happy to see their sons spend three years in military service away from the farms. The only exemptions permitted were heads of households, heirs, only sons, only grandsons, government officials, students studying abroad, and anyone who could pay 270 yen. Understandably, many of the second, third, or fourth sons tried to become heirs of other households. Some of them left the country, at least officially, as *yōkō-shugyō-sha* (students studying abroad). See Kublin, "The 'Modern' Army of Early Meiji Japan," *FEQ*, IX (No. 1, November, 1949), 20–41.

[19] Toshisuke Murakami and Yoshio Sakata, *Meiji bungaku-shi: Kyōiku-dōtoku-hen*.

providing minimum training in reading and writing for the general populace. From the standpoint of the government, education was a matter of great necessity for the training of faithful and obedient subjects of the empire rather than for the development of individual personalities or participation in a full life. Understandably, the orientation of students toward the "Imperial Way" (*kō-dō*) was considered the fundamental educational goal.[20] The underlying assumption of the "Imperial Way" was that the nation is in essence a patriarchal family with the emperor as its head. It was taken for granted that individuals exist for the nation rather than the other way around. Equally important was the assumption that some men are born to rule while others are to be ruled because men are by nature unequal. Ultimately, education was regarded as a tool of the government, teaching its subjects what to think rather than how to think.

Nevertheless, during the first two decades of the Meiji Era Japan was receptive to the influence of Western thought and civilization, particularly in the government and in private universities, and in educational institutions established by various Christian missionary societies.[21] In this connection, Arnold Toynbee once observed that in the sixteenth century European civilization was rejected by Japan because it was presented primarily as a "strange religion," whereas in the nineteenth century the Western way of life was welcomed by Japan because it was presented as a "strange technology." [22] While there is some truth in this observation, I am inclined to feel that Toynbee oversimplified

[20] When the first *daigaku* (university) was established in 1869, both faculty and students were expected to participate in a semireligious festival in honor of some of the Shinto kami associated with learning, in sharp contrast to the practice of the Tokugawa period which venerated Confucius as the "patron deity of learning" (*gaku-shin*). *Ibid.*, pp. 25–26.

[21] According to Anesaki, "There was never a period in Japanese history when foreign assistance was so welcomed and made use of as in the eighth decade of the nineteenth century." He adds: "The memory of these foreign advisers has been much obliterated, partly wilfully, due to the conservative reaction in the nineties." (Anesaki, *History of Japanese Religion*, p. 350.)

[22] Toynbee, *The World and the West*, p. 54.

the issue. To be sure, the architects of the Meiji regime were preoccupied for the most part with the technological and material aspects of Western civilization. However, the new elite, consisting of young intellectuals in urban areas, could not help but imbibe the spirit of "modernity" that was the driving force of Western civilization. Conspicuous among them were such famous modernists as Fukuzawa Yukichi, Mori Arinori, Nishi Amane, Katō Hiroyuki, and others who formed the *Meiroku-sha* (literally, the "Group of Meiji Six," so called because it was organized in the sixth year of the Meiji Era or 1873). They, and others like them, left lasting influences on the social and intellectual life of the nation.[23] One of the popular songs of the day went:

> Zangiri-atama wo tataite mireba
> Bummei kaika no oto ga suru
>
> If you knock on a head with a short haircut,
> It gives forth: "Civilization and Enlightenment."

What the new elite of Japan sensed in "Civilization and Enlightenment" was the modern European conception of civilization as secularized salvation, signifying "a liberation from the fetters of barbarism just as religion aims at deliverance from the powers of evil."[24] Thus, much as modern Europeans rejected the medieval notion of the state as subservient to the church, Japanese intellectuals during the early Meiji Era reacted emotionally against traditional values and ideologies. They rejoiced in being emancipated from the "immanental theocracy" of the Tokugawa

[23] See Mitsuo Nakamura, "Chishiki kaikyū," and Shimomura, "Meiji no Shakai," both in Shinchō-sha, *Nihon bunka kenkyū*, Vol. XVI; Iyenaga, *Kindai Nihon no shisōka*, pp. 59–84; Anesaki, *History of Japanese Religion*, pp. 350–53; Fujii, *Outline of Japanese History in the Meiji Era*, pp. 39–43; and Kosaka, ed., *Japanese Thought in the Meiji Era*, pp. 49–133. The Meiroku-sha published the *Meiroku zasshi* (Journal of the Meiroku group). During its first year the average circulation of each volume was estimated at 3,200, which indicates how popular this journal was. Fukuzawa was the founder of the Keiō Gijuku, a private university; Mori became the minister of education; Nishi translated Mill's *Utilitarianism;* and Katō became president of Tokyo Imperial University.

[24] W. S. Haas, *The Destiny of the Mind*, p. 296.

feudal period, and envisaged the creation of a new social and political order along the lines of the Western model. In the new Japan, so it was believed, anybody, regardless of his status and class, could attain to a high position, solely on the basis of his ability and merit. Indeed, the motif of *risshin-shusse* (success and advancement in life) was a real gospel for the youth of Japan where social classes had been frozen for so long under the feudal regime.

The Meiji government was also motivated by the motif of *risshin-shusse,* in this case, however, implying "advancing Japan in the family of nations." Thus the government was preoccupied with advancement and progress along the line of national prosperity and defense (*fukoku-kyōhei*)—"more facts, more wealth, more strength, more manufactures, more men, ships, and guns." [25] Realizing how much more advanced the Western nations were than Japan in global competition, Japanese leaders made feverish attempts to catch up with others in the art of international power politics. Soon Japan began to compete with European powers to obtain her share in the exploitation of China. As early as 1874 Japan sent her expeditionary forces to Formosa (Taiwan); she established her sovereignty over Okinawa a few years later.[26] The French occupation of Annam (1884) was followed by Japan's acquisition of Taiwan as a result of the Sino-Japanese War, 1894–95. Japanese advance in the Far East was temporarily halted by the intervention of the three powers (Russia, France, and Germany) in 1895. But in 1900 Japan joined the Western powers in subduing the Boxer Rebellion, and two years later concluded an alliance with Great Britain. Japan's victory in the Russo-Japanese War, 1904–5, made her a great power in Asia, and in 1910 Japan maneuvered to annex Korea.

Such speedy "advancement" for Japan in the game of interna-

---

[25] Sansom, *The Western World and Japan,* p. 313.

[26] In 1880 Japan and China agreed to divide the islands of Okinawa (Ryūkyū), but this division was never actualized. Meanwhile, Japan claimed *de facto* sovereignty over the islands. After the Sino-Japanese War, the issue was decided by default on the part of China. See Yanaga, *Japan Since Perry,* p. 183.

tional politics demanded heavy sacrifices on the part of the people at home. The Meiji regime carefully resisted the temptation of depending on foreign loans which might jeopardize Japan's economic independence. Instead, the government took the initiative in developing various types of industries by exploiting the underpaid labor force. The government turned the industries over to the financial clique (*Zaibatsu*), which subsequently enjoyed a virtual monopoly in finance, industry, and commerce, thanks to its close connections with the political and military leaders as well as with the bureaucrats. What Norman rightly depicts as the characteristics of Japanese capitalism—"the predominant position of state enterprise supported by the financial oligarchy, the retardation of the tempo of industrialization, and the heavy tax burdens on the population, particularly on the agricultural community" [27]— were inevitable consequences of the policies of the Meiji regime.

The dream of Japanese leaders during the Meiji Era was to make Japan a first-class, modern nation-state at any cost as quickly as possible. While the regime was notoriously oblivious to social, economic, and political injustice at home, especially among the lower strata of society, it was extremely sensitive to humiliating clauses in treaties with Western nations, such as those setting aside certain sections of Japan for the exclusive residence of foreigners, and forbidding Japanese courts to prosecute foreign residents. Realizing that these unequal treaties would not be revised until Japanese laws attained the standard of average "civilized" nations in the West, the Japanese government decided to modernize the legal and political institutions of the country. For example, since the traditional anti-Christian policy was found to be a great hindrance to successful treaty revisions, the government, which had no love for Christianity, nevertheless removed in 1873 the edict against Christianity. Partly for the same reason the Constitution was adopted in 1889, and the first Diet was convened in 1890. The government even went so far as to establish a social club, called "Rokumei-kan," where gentlemen and ladies in Western attire could dance and entertain foreign dignitaries.

[27] Norman, *Japan's Emergence as a Modern State*, p. 117.

The last two decades of the Meiji Era witnessed the growth of conservatism and ethnocentric nationalism. The government, which became increasingly bureaucratic, controlled the press and often interfered with the activities of political parties. The arm of the government suppressed socialist and labor movements.[28] Nevertheless, government leaders congratulated themselves on Japan's victory over China and Russia, as well as her annexation of Korea. The apparent success of Japan in the arena of international politics strengthened the Meiji regime's affirmation of the principle of "immanental theocracy," which in turn helped to create a new myth, namely, Japan's divine mission to extend her "Imperial Way" abroad.

From the Death of the Emperor Meiji to the Second World War

The Emperor Meiji, who witnessed in his lifetime the phenomenal growth of Japan from her feudal past to a powerful empire, died in 1912, succeeded by his son, Yoshihito ·(1879–1926), later known as the Emperor Taishō. His reign is referred to as the Taishō Era (1912–26).[29] Yoshihito's poor health, how-

[28] It is to be noted that many of the early leaders of the Japanese socialist movement, such as Abe Isoo, Kinoshita Naoye, Kawakami Hajime, and Katayama Hiromu (Sen), started as Christian socialists, the notable exception being Kōtoku Denjirō Shūsui (1871–1911). Kōtoku later declared himself an anarchist, and was executed together with eleven others in 1911 on the charge of an alleged plot to harm the emperor. While it is difficult to reconstruct accurately the so-called *taigyaku jiken* (incident of great disloyalty) of Kōtoku and others, it is clear that the harsh sentence imposed on them was motivated by the government's effort to wipe out "dangerous" ideologies. On Kōtoku, see Nobutaka Ike, "Kōtoku: Advocate of Direct Action," *FEQ*, III (No. 3, May, 1944), 222–36; Sōgorō Tanaka, *Kōtoku Shūsui: Ichi kakumeika no shisō to shōgai*; and Nishio, *Kōtoku Shūsui*. Equally colorful was the life of Katayama, who eventually left Christianity and embraced Communism. He spent his last years in Moscow and died there in 1933. See Kublin, "A Bibliography of the Writings of Sen Katayama in Western Languages," *FEQ*, XI (No. 1, November, 1951), 71–77.

[29] Monographs on the Taishō Era are not abundant even in the Japanese language, although all books on modern Japan make reference to develop-

ever, necessitated that his son, Hirohito (1901–   ), assume control of the affairs of state as prince regent in 1921. In 1926 Hirohito ascended the throne, and the Shōwa Era began.

The year 1912 was a crucial turning point in the history of
Japan as well as in the history of the world. Across the Pacific
Ocean, Woodrow Wilson took over the presidency of the United
States, which now became a new world power, surpassing many
of the old nations in Europe. In the same year, the People's Revolution overthrew the yoke of the Manchu dynasty in China.
Ironically, the Japanese leaders failed to understand the depth of
the nationalistic aspirations of the Chinese people during the
twentieth century, and continued to follow expansionist policies
in Asia. At home, the army leaders made it impossible for the
Saionji cabinet to stay in power in 1912, and maneuvered to
establish the Katsura cabinet which represented the interests of
the army and the Chōshū clan bureaucrats. Incensed by the
highhandedness of the army, public opinion supported the Federation for the Protection of Constitutional Government, organized by Ozaki Yukio and Inukai Tsuyoshi. The fall of the Katsura
cabinet under public pressure, after less than two months in
office, encouraged the political parties. The increased activities of
the political parties created the political climate which has often
been characterized as the "Taishō Democracy." [30] In retrospect it

---

ments during this interesting period of modern Japanese history. Notable
exceptions are the works of Shinobu, especially his *Taishō seiji-shi* (4
vols.). See also Jansen's review article, "From Hatoyama to Hatoyama,"
FEQ, XIV (No. 1, November, 1954), 65–79. For economic aspects of
this period, see Lockwood, *The Economic Development of Japan: Growth
and Structural Change, 1868–1938*.

[30] It might be well for us to recall that during much of the Meiji Era
political stability was maintained by an uneasy compromise among the
bureaucrats, the financial interests, and the military clique. Rivalry between
the two powerful groups, former members of the Satsuma and the
Chōshū clans, continued within the bureaucracy. Also, the army was
dominated by the Chōshū clan, and the navy by the Satsuma clan. The
creation of the Senate (*Genrō-in*) in 1875 only helped to perpetuate the
influence of the clan oligarchy. Party politics was then still in its infancy
in spite of propaganda by a small group of advocates of popular rights.
Meanwhile, the military clique, especially the army, became increasingly

becomes clear, however, that many party politicians were more concerned with the interests of the financial clique than with the welfare of the general populace.[31] Meanwhile, a new cabinet was organized under Yamamoto Gombei, an influential admiral of the navy and a member of the Satsuma clan. A notorious scandal concerning navy finances brought about the fall of the Yamamoto cabinet, which was succeeded by the Ōkuma cabinet in 1914.[32]

---

powerful after the Sino-Japanese War (1894–95) and the Russo-Japanese War (1904–5). By the turn of the century, the influence of the Senate had increased because it counted among its members such influential figures as Itō Hirobumi, who in 1885 was appointed as the first prime minister, and Yamagata Aritomo, the "father" of the Japanese army. Both Itō and Yamagata, incidentally, belonged to the Chōshū clan. When the Emperor Meiji died in 1912, the cabinet, headed by Saionji Kimmochi, an enlightened nobleman educated in France, was struggling with the solution of difficulties in the national budget. The cabinet turned down the army's request to increase the standing army by two divisions, whereupon Uyehara Yūsaku, the war minister, presented his resignation directly to the throne, bypassing the office of the prime minister. Such an action was considered an illegitimate use of the prerogative of the army, which together with the navy, had access to the emperor as commander-in-chief of the sea and land forces for military matters in times of national crises. Furthermore, the army refused to recommend a successor to Uyehara as war minister. Thus, the Saionji cabinet had to resign. On the eventful life of Saionji (1849–1940) there are many excellent works in Japanese. A recent work —Kimura's *Saionji Kimmochi*—is a useful small book, even though it is very journalistic. See also Bailey, "Prince Saionji and the Popular Rights Movement," *JAS*, XXI (No. 1, November, 1961), 49–63.

It is also to be noted that when Katsura Tarō, a Chōshū man, tried to form his cabinet following the fall of Saionji, the navy, which was dominated by Satsuma men, refused to nominate a minister. Katsura, who had held the position of lord keeper of the privy seal, managed to secure an imperial rescript, ordering Saitō Makoto, the minister of the navy under Saionji, to continue to serve in that capacity. These too obvious schemes on the part of Katsura were bitterly criticized by the public. On Ozaki, see Mendel, "Ozaki Yukio: Political Conscience of Modern Japan," *FEQ*, XV (No. 3, May, 1956), 343–56.

[31] It was well known that the financial cliques, especially the Mitsui *zaibatsu*, offered financial assistance to party politicians in their fight against the army leaders.

[32] To be sure, there was strong resentment on the part of the army leaders against Yamamoto's pro-navy policies. But the immediate cause of the

When the First World War started in 1914, Japan eagerly sided with the Allies on the grounds of her alliance with Great Britain. Japan quickly took over the German sphere of influence in China and in the Pacific. Moreover, taking advantage of the fact that European powers were preoccupied in Europe, the Ōkuma cabinet in 1915 presented the infamous Twenty-One Demands to China.[33] Although strong anti-Japanese demonstrations erupted spontaneously in many parts of China, the government of Yüan Shih-k'ai was too weak to resist the Japanese ultimatum. Ironically, Japan, which was so incensed at unequal treaties between herself and the Western Powers during the Meiji Era, developed into a full-fledged imperialist nation, attempting to dominate China economically and politically. In 1918 Japan participated as one of the victors at the Versailles Conference, where she received most of what she demanded. Japan also was engaged in the ill-fated Siberian Expedition, at first with the Allied Powers but later all alone, due to the insistence of the military clique. The enormous expenditures for keeping troops in Siberia between 1918 and 1922 ended with no gain for Japan, however.

During the First World War the *Zaibatsu* enjoyed unprecedented prosperity, and its political influence increased accordingly.[34] As far as the masses were concerned, the slow rise in

fall of the Yamamoto cabinet was the news of the bribes received by some navy officials from the Siemens Schuckert Company of Germany. This information was revealed in German court proceedings pertaining to a former employee of the Schuckert Company. It is to be noted that Ōkuma Shigenobu, a seasoned politician and the founder of the Waseda University, had the financial backing of the Mitsubishi *zaibatsu*.

[33] For an example of a lame excuse regarding the Twenty-One Demands, see H. Saitō, *Japan's Policies and Purposes*, pp. 130–52. Although the so-called Lansing-Ishii Agreement between the representatives of the United States and Japan in 1917 had some restraining effect on Japan's ambition, it also strengthened Japan's position in Asia, because the United States recognized that "Japan has special interests in China, particularly in the part to which her possessions are contiguous."

[34] The so-called Big Five in the cotton-spinning industry—Kanegabuchi (referred to as Kanebō), Dai Nippon, Tōyō, Ōji, and Fuji—and the Big Five in banking—Mitsui, Mitsubishi, Daiichi, Yasuda, and Sumitomo—

wages could hardly keep up with the rocketing prices. The acute economic imbalance precipitated "rice riots" in many cities in 1918 and a number of serious labor strikes in 1919 and 1920. In fact, the combination of financial difficulties and social unrest toppled the militaristic Terauchi cabinet in 1918. Thus began a period of responsible party government, initiated by Hara Kei (Takashi) of the Seiyūkai, a leading political party.

The party government had to face a series of difficult problems, notably the financial panic of 1920, the steep fall of the stock market in 1922, the great earthquake that almost disrupted the national economy in 1923, and the monetary crisis that necessitated the three-week bank moratorium in 1927. In spite of these difficulties, during the first half of the 1920s the general populace had a taste of a liberal democratic atmosphere.[35] Japan assented to the Five Power Naval Treaty (1921) and disbanded four divisions of the army (1925). It was but natural that young idèalists had high hopes for the League of Nations. Industrial workers organized labor unions, students enjoyed academic freedom, and the whole nation enthusiastically adopted the cinema and baseball.

On the other hand, events during the 1920s also gave impetus to the growth of ethnocentric and fanatic nationalism.[36] In 1922

---

for example, wielded great political power indirectly if not directly. After 1917 no political party could ignore the influence of Nihon Kōgyō Kurabu (The Japanese industry club), which was the association of influential capitalists.

[35] For the liberal, democratic views expressed by some thinkers of this period, see Tsunoda, *et al., Sources of Japanese Tradition,* pp. 718–58.

[36] There were various kinds of patriotic organizations with diverse objectives. Some were promoting the "Imperial Way" at home; others were advocating Japanese aggression into Manchuria, Mongolia, and China. See Tsunoda, *et al.,* pp. 759–805. Probably the best known in the West is the Amur Society (*Kokuryū-kai,* literally, "Black Dragon Society"). Another organization, the Japan Nationalist Society (*Dai Nihon kokusui-kai*), founded in 1919, boasted a membership of over a million in the 1920s. This group grew partly because of its opposition to the untouchables (*eta*), who were demanding their legal rights. The deep-rooted prejudice against the untouchables on the part of the general populace was cleverly utilized by the Japan Nationalist Party.

the League for the Prevention of Communism (Sekka Bōshi-dan) was formed, anticipating the emergence of the Communist party in Japan during the same year. Not content with the mass hunt and arrest of Communists by the government in 1923, the so-called patriots carried on their own zealous campaign against Communism and all other "dangerous, foreign ideologies." [37] It also happened that in 1924 the United States Congress passed a bill excluding further immigration from Japan. The reaction in Japan was immediate and momentous. Two persons committed suicide as a protest against the passage of the bill, the Japanese government presented a formal protest, and the American ambassador to Japan resigned his post. Many Japanese who advocated international cooperation and democratic principles were frustrated. One writer stated: "In the midst of our affliction [meaning the great earthquake of 1923 and its aftermath], the nation that had literally shaken open our gates waved aside a long-standing agreement with us and slammed its gates shut in our faces." [38] Actually, if the United States had decided simply to decrease the number of immigrants from Japan, no problem would have been created. But the exclusion of Japanese immigrants on racial grounds was interpreted as a concrete manifestation of anti-Japanese sentiment on the part of the United States. And the nationalists did not fail to make use of this issue on behalf of their cause. With the formation in 1924 of the National Foundation Society (Kokuhon-sha) through the initiative of Hiranuma Kiichirō, then vice president of the privy council, nationalists gained prestige, and thereby increased their influence among those who began to question the wisdom of international cooperation.

During the second half of the 1920s, or the beginning of the Shōwa Era, the financial situation in Japan turned from bad to

[37] In the midst of the confusion following the great earthquake, ultranationalists spread rumors against Communists, Koreans, etc. It was in this atmosphere that Ōsugi Sakaye, a leftist theoretician, was strangled to death by Amakasu Masahiko, a captain in the army.

[38] Quoted in McWilliams, *Prejudice. Japanese-Americans: Symbol of Racial Intolerance*, pp. 67–68. On the "Exclusion Act," see Konvitz, *The Alien and the Asiatic in American Law*, pp. 22–25.

worse. The Japanese *Zaibatsu* began to lose the China market due to the gradual consolidation of China under the leadership of the Kuomintang. In 1927 the Wakatsuki cabinet, which had maintained a conciliatory China policy, was squeezed out by the combined efforts of the *Zaibatsu*, the bureaucrats, and the Seiyūkai party. The new cabinet was formed by Tanaka Giichi, general of the army and president of the Seiyūkai party. This marked a radical change in Japan's China policy from one of noninterference to one of intervention, as quickly demonstrated by the "Tsinan Affair" and the liquidation of Chan Tso-lin, the *de facto* ruler of Manchuria—both taking place in 1928.[39] Following the defeat of the Tanaka cabinet in the national election in 1929, the Hamaguchi cabinet attempted to reverse its national policy by promising international cooperation, a conciliatory China policy, the solution of chronic depression, and the restructuring of industry in a more rational way. Unfortunately, the effort to promote foreign trade by lifting the gold embargo backfired because of the world-wide depression. The Hamaguchi cabinet also accepted the London Naval Agreement (1930), and for this the prime minister was shot by a fanatic rightist. By this time nationalism had become increasingly fascistic and jingoistic. It was, in the words of Yanaga, "authoritarian, antiparliamentarian, antidemocratic, opposed to disarmament, and suspicious of the League of Nations. It was also a Pan-Asiatic movement, unafraid and unhesitant regarding the use of force." [40]

Events in the nineteen-thirties and early forties are familiar stories. Even if the militarists were aware of the seriousness of the war in Manchuria, which they had started and which they insisted on calling the "Manchurian Incident" and not a war, the

[39] The Tsinan Affair was an inevitable result of the "northern expedition" of the Kuomintang forces that threatened the Japanese sphere of influence along the Tsintao-Tsinan Railway. The provocative attitude of the Japanese army caused strong anti-Japanese sentiment in various parts of China. The death of Chang Tso-lin was considered a mysterious affair until after the Second World War. Incidentally, one of the plotters in this affair was the same Amakasu Masahiko who had earlier strangled Ōsugi Sakaye.

[40] Yanaga, *Japan Since Perry*, p. 495.

general public was unaware that it was only the beginning of a chain of ominous events. Following it came the wholesale assassination of parliamentarians and financiers (1932), Japan's withdrawal from the League of Nations (1933), an attempted *coup d'état* by a group of fanatic young army officers (1936), the Marco Polo Bridge Incident in 1937 that precipitated a full-scale China War, Soviet-Japanese border clashes (1938 and 1939), and Japan's participation in the Tripartite Pact (1940). In 1941 Japan took the fatal step of entering the Second World War.

From the middle of the 1930s, all liberal thinking and expression—whether in religion, philosophy, art, or culture—was condemned under suspicion of being a threat to the Japanese way of life. Freedom of the press, thought, and assembly, as well as freedom of conscience and belief, was violated. Gradually, a sense of "fear" developed among the people, who no longer dared to speak their minds openly, even to close friends. Newspapers, magazines, and radios repeated the same nationalistic slogans. People's thoughts, values, and patterns of behavior, and even the meaning of life, were prescribed and interpreted by militarists and jingoists. To the militarists and ultramilitarists, individuals were nothing more than cogs in the huge machine of the nation. Japan became a great fortress from which war emanated relentlessly until VJ Day, 1945.[41]

[41] There are a number of studies concerning the social, economic, and political development of Japan from the later Taishō Era to the Second World War. The following list of works, helpful though they were in varying degrees, is not meant to be comprehensive. Allen, *Japanese Industry: Its Recent Development and Present Condition;* Bisson, *Japan's War Economy;* Borton, *Japan Since 1931;* Butow, *Tōjō and the Coming of the War;* Byas, *Government by Assassination;* Crowley, "Japanese Army Factionalism in the 1930's," *JAS,* XXI (No. 3, May, 1962), 309–26; Elbree, *Japan's Role in Southeast Asian Nationalist Movements, 1940–45;* Feis, *The Road to Pearl Harbor;* Grew, *Ten Years in Japan,* and *Turbulent Era: A Diplomatic Record of Forty Years, 1904–1945* (2 vols.); Hata, *Nitchū sensō-shi;* Iklé, *Germany-Japan Relations, 1936–1940: A Study of Totalitarian Diplomacy;* Lu, *From the Marco Polo Bridge to Pearl Harbor: A Study,of Japan's Entry into World War II;* Maxon, *Control of Japanese Foreign Policy: A Study of Civil-Military Rivalry 1930–1945;* Moore, *With Japan's Leaders;* Orchard, *Japan's Economic Position: The Progress of*

Culture and Religion

In discussing the cultural and religious development of modern Japan, we have to remind ourselves once again that the transfer of administration from the shogunate to the imperial regime was not such a complete turnabout as it might appear to the casual observer. Many of the economic and political features of the early Meiji Era, for example, can be traced to the 1840s when the shogunate and some of the daimyo were compelled to introduce new measures in order to alleviate financial and political difficulties.[42] In this respect, it might be argued that the architects of the Meiji regime merely tried to "replace an administration already obsolete and declining by a more efficient system of government." [43] On the other hand, the manner in which the transfer of power was achieved had definite implications for the character of the government that was to be established. It is noteworthy in this connection that the establishment of the Meiji regime was not only a "renovation" (*ishin*) that implied the rejection of the past but was also a "restoration of monarchical rule" (*ōsei-fukko*) implying a reversion to the polity of eighth-century Japan. The effort of the Meiji government to maintain a precarious balance between these two contradictory objectives had disastrous consequences in the spheres of culture and religion, to say nothing of the domain of politics.

The first objective of the Meiji regime, "renovation," stressed

Industrialization; Presseisen, *Germany and Japan: A Study of Totalitarian Diplomacy, 1933–1941*; Shiomi, *Japan's Finance and Taxation, 1940–1956*; Storry, *The Double Patriots: A Study of Japanese Nationalism*; A. Morgan Young, *Japan in Recent Times, 1912–1926*, and *Imperial Japan, 1926–1938*.

[42] A very thought-provoking and concise book on the subject is Tōyama's *Meiji ishin*. His critical comments on different approaches to the study of the Meiji Restoration, pp. 1–20, and brief annotated bibliography on the subject, pp. 343–61, deserve special attention. Tōyama demonstrates convincingly why the reforms introduced by some of the daimyo were successful, while those undertaken by the shogunate failed. His narrative explains how the clan oligarchy, especially that of Satsuma and Chōshū, could play such an important role in the political scene during the Meiji Era.

[43] Sansom, *The Western World and Japan*, p. 339.

decentralization of power or "popular rights" (*minken*). This objective was stated in the Charter Oath of 1868: "Deliberative assemblies shall be widely established and all matters decided by public discussion. . . ." The second objective, the "restoration of monarchical rule," stressed the centralization of power or "national rights" (*kokken*).[44] The two ideologies, "popular rights" and "national rights," however, should not be equated with democratic liberalism and absolutistic nationalism, respectively. During at least the first decade or so of the Meiji Era these two ideologies, as well as the two objectives of "renovation" and "restoration of monarchical rule," were not considered necessarily contradictory.[45] The new regime was confident that it was possible

[44] See Maruyama, "Meiji kokka no shisō," in Rekishigaku kenkyū-kai, ed., *Nihon shakai no shiteki kyūmei*. Maruyama points out that the contradictory character of the Meiji regime can be traced to the time when Abe Ise-no-kami Masahiro, the senior minister under the thirteenth shogun (1853–58), took a conciliatory attitude toward the imperial court, and also attempted to survey the views of leading daimyo. Abe, to be sure, was not conscious of the significance, but his policy symbolized both the ideal of "respect for the throne" (*sonnō*) and that of "respect for public opinion" (*kōgi-yoron*). The ideology of "national rights" developed from the ideal of "respect for the throne," while the ideology of "popular rights" developed from the ideal of "respect for public opinion." (See pp. 183–85.) Maruyama also feels that shortly before the Meiji Restoration the lower samurai and politically sensitive noblemen became spokesmen for the masses who had been suppressed by the feudal regime, so that public opinion was represented through these men. Furthermore, the fact that the opening of Japan was forced upon her by external factors drove different factions in Japan to look for a symbol of national unity in the figure of the emperor. See pp. 187–88.

[45] According to Maruyama, the controversy regarding the advisability of the conquest of Korea in 1873 was based on differences not so much in principle as in opinions on timing. Those who were against it were just as nationalistic as those who were for such a venture. In fact, it was the former who were instrumental in sending expeditionary forces to Formosa (Taiwan) in 1874. It was felt by them that sending forces to Taiwan was much less risky than a similar venture in Korea. Maruyama also reminds us that the Genyō-sha, a right-wing movement established in 1881, developed from the tradition of the "popular rights" movement. See pp. 192–97. On the question of the conquest of Korea, which was eventually annexed to Japan, see Conroy, *The Japanese Seizure of Korea, 1868–1910*.

to ... the West and to return to Japan's "p... ... past simultaneously. The emperor himself swore allegiance to the Charter Oath, the most progressive document ever promulgated by the throne, before all the kami of the Shinto pantheon.

Following the ancient Japanese model of "unity of religion and government" (*saisei-itchi*), the Meiji regime in 1868 established the Department of Shinto and issued the Separation Edict, separating Buddhism from Shinto (*shinbutsu hanzen-rei*) on the ground that the Buddhist-Shinto coexistence that had been practiced for nearly ten centuries was contrary to the indigenous Japanese way. In 1869 the status of the Department of Shinto was elevated so that it would supersede that of the Grand Council of State. In 1870 the government issued the Proclamation of the Great Doctrine that was to restore the "way of the kami" (*kannagara*) as the guiding principle of the nation. Accordingly, reversing the Tokugawa system that required all households to register in Buddhist temples, the Meiji government initiated compulsory Shinto registration (*ujiko-shirabe*) whereby every Japanese subject was ordered to enroll in the shrine of the local kami of his residence. Also, rejecting the traditional pattern of funeral services, conducted according to Buddhist rites, the government actively promoted Shinto funeral rites. Meanwhile, the Department of Shinto was replaced in 1871 by the Shinto Ministry. One of the duties of the new department was to conduct a nationwide teaching program centering around three principles: (1) reverence for the kami, (2) the importance of the Law of Heaven and the Way of Humanity, and (3) loyalty to the throne and obedience to the authorities. For this task the department appointed not only Shinto priests but Confucian scholars, Buddhist priests, actors, and professional storytellers (*kōdan-shi, rakugo-ka,* etc.) and, in some instances, even fortunetellers, as moral instructors (*kyōdō-shi*).[46] Such an active effort on the part of the government to promote Shinto, however, encountered resistance and criticism from various quarters. Thus, in 1873, compulsory Shinto

[46] It was reported that there were 7,247 moral instructors (*kyōdō-shi*) in 1874.

registration was abruptly terminated, and more restrained religious policies were adopted.[47]

We have noted earlier that the effort of the Meiji regime to "purify" the religious climate by making Shinto the national religion necessitated the disestablishment of Buddhism through separating it from Shinto. Thus all Buddhist priests who had been connected with Shinto shrines were returned to secular life unless they were willing to be reinstalled as Shinto priests. In 1871 all temple lands were confiscated by government order, and all Buddhist ceremonies that had been performed in the imperial household were abolished. In the following year all the ranks and privileges previously bestowed upon the Buddhist hierarchy were revoked, and the Order of Mountain Ascetics was abrogated.[48] In such a situation, a popular anti-Buddhist (*haibutsu-kishaku*) movement also erupted. The extreme example of government action in separating Buddhism from Shinto was in the Toyama district where the 1,730 Buddhist temples that had existed in 1870 were reduced overnight to seven.[49] Most of the temples were destroyed outright; some were consolidated. While it was not the explicit intention of the government to exterminate Buddhism, some government officials and Shinto priests, assisted by the leaders of the Confucian and the National Learning groups, aroused anti-Buddhist sentiment among the masses. Undoubtedly Buddhism, protected too long by the Tokugawa regime, had been losing its spiritual vitality, and there was widespread discontent on account

[47] The most comprehensive work on religious development during the Meiji Era is Kishimoto, ed., *Meiji bunka-shi: Shūkyō-hen* (English translation: *Japanese Religion in the Meiji Era*).

[48] The government introduced sweeping reform measures for Buddhism in 1872. The name of the True Pure Land sect was changed from Ikkō-shū (Single directed sect) to Shin (literally, "True") sect. The traditional prohibitions against the marriage of Buddhist priests, eating meat, growing hair, etc., were abated. The historic Buddhist priestly practice of "begging" was forbidden, while priests and nuns were permitted to use family names. Each sect or denomination was ordered to appoint a patriarch who was to supervise the activities of his group. See Kishimoto, *Meiji bunka-shi: Shūkyō-hen*, pp. 542–43.

[49] For examples of anti-Buddhist activities, see Kishimoto, *Meiji bunka-shi: Shūkyō-hen*, pp. 165–80.

of the laxity of priestly morals and the highhandedness of Buddhist ecclesiastical organizations.[50]

The foregoing makes it abundantly clear that the Meiji regime, despite its effort to modernize Japan in one sense, inherited from the Tokugawa regime, consciously or unconsciously, the principle of "immanental theocracy." This principle was implemented by the Meiji government's policies in promoting the emperor cult as the most important ingredient of Shinto. For example, in contrast to the practice of holding memorial services for the imperial ancestors according to Buddhist rites, as had been done during the Tokugawa period, the Meiji government erected a Shinto shrine inside the imperial palace in honor of the imperial ancestors and the kami of the Shinto pantheon. Later, a special shrine was established inside the palace for the worship of Amaterasu Ōmikami, the tutelary kami of the imperial clan. The government also established a special shrine in Tokyo for the repose of those who had died for the royalist cause at the time of the Meiji Restoration. This shrine, first named the *Shōkon-sha* (literally, "spirit-invoking shrine") in 1869, was renamed ten years later the *Yasukuni Jinja* (shrine for the pacification of the nation). In 1872 the fourteenth-century royalist, Kusunoki Masashige, was elevated to the rank of kami, and his shrine, called the *Minatogawa Jinja,* was established in Kobe. In the same year the government made all Shinto functionaries as well as some Buddhist clergy "government priests," divided into fourteen ranks. A cult of the Emperor Jimmu, the mythological founder of the nation, was created, and the custom of celebrating the current emperor's birthday (*Tenchō-setsu*) as a semireligious national holiday was instituted. The emperor was no longer just a person who held the charisma of the imperial office. He was elevated to the exalted status of a "living kami"—an eminence which had been claimed but never achieved by ancient Japanese monarchs.[51]

[50] See Tamamuro, *Meiji ishin haibutsu kishaku.*

[51] The title claimed by the throne in the seventh century was *Akitsu-mikami-to Amenoshita-shiroshimesu Yamato-no-Sumeramikoto* (literally, "the living kami, the ruler of the world, and the emperor of the Yamato kingdom"). See Aston, *Nihongi,* II, 197–98.

The "back to the pristine past" movement greatly encouraged the growth of Shinto, but failed to provide the necessary impetus for the establishment of the modern nation-state, which was the second of the twin objectives of the Meiji regime. Outrageous attempts on the part of the Shinto leaders to turn the clock backward were resisted by the modernists, for the mood of the time was not altogether in favor of returning to the past, however important the past might be. In this situation, while Shinto leaders depended solely on the government to promote their cause through political measures, secular intellectuals, as well as some leaders of Christianity and Buddhism, began to take the problem of "modernity" with utter seriousness. Even within the government there were many influential men who promoted Western learning and scientific education in order to create a new society in Japan. Only then, they felt, could Japan compete with the Western powers.

The complex development in education, legislation, culture, and religion during the Meiji Era grew out of the tension and the uneasy compromise that eventually came to be worked out between the "immanental theocracy" and "modernity." It goes without saying that these two elements were essentially irreconcilable. The advocates of the pristine Japanese tradition were motivated by the desire to find the model of society and culture in the past—the way of the kami (*kannagara*). "Back to the Emperor Jimmu!" they cried. The advocates of modernity, on the other hand, placed their faith in the present and future, in the new and the novel. To them the Meiji Era was the beginning of a permanent revolution along the path of enlightenment and civilization (*bummei kaika*). The advocates of both principles, however, shared two qualities, namely, patriotism and utilitarianism, thus a compromise was achieved between them by means of pragmatic, nationalistic principles. How such a compromise was achieved may become evident when we follow the development of education during the early Meiji Era.

When the new regime came into being in 1868 one of its most urgent tasks was the formulation of an educational philosophy and system. Prior to the Meiji Era it was taken for granted that the

Confucian system provided the foundation and framework of education. This assumption was challenged in 1868 by those royalists who were determined to instill the "Imperial Way" in the minds of the youth, and thus there arose a heated conflict between the Confucian teachers (*kangaku-sha*) and the national scholars (*kokugaku-sha*). Around 1870, however, the advocates of Westernized education (*yōgaku-sha*) began to play a dominant role in educational affairs. Their cause was greatly enhanced by the spirit of *bummei kaika*. Probably the most influential among them was Fukuzawa Yukichi (1834–1901), who not only founded a private school based on democratic and utilitarian principles, but also published in 1872–76 a series of pamphlets promoting his iconoclastic ideas about education.[52] Through the initiative of the proponents of Westernized education, the government inaugurated in 1872 a system of universal education, based partly on the French and partly on the American educational systems.[53] The principle behind universal education was clearly stated in the proclamation of the Administrative Council (*Dajō-kan*) as follows: "Each individual is destined to live a happy life by promoting himself in his career. . . . This can be accomplished only by self training, the acquisition of knowledge, and the development of ability; and all this cannot be attained unless one learns and is educated. This is the reason why the school is established." [54] The government also invited many foreign teachers to Japan and sent Japanese students to Europe and American.

The cause of Westernized education experienced a setback after 1881, due to a power struggle in the government. The conservative clan oligarchy felt threatened by the public demand for

[52] Reference to Fukuzawa's *Gakumon no susume* (Encouragement of learning) is made in Anesaki, *History of Japanese Religion*, p. 35, and in Sansom, *The Western World and Japan*, p. 454. See *The Autobiography of Yukichi Fukuzawa* (revised trans., 1960; American ed., 1966); excerpts in Tsunoda, *et al.*, *Sources of Japanese Tradition*, pp. 625–37.

[53] The Japanese government invited an American, David Murray (d. 1905), then a professor at Rutgers College, New Brunswick, New Jersey, to be chief adviser in educational matters between 1873 and 1878.

[54] Quoted in Anesaki, *History of Japanese Religion*, p. 349. A fuller quotation from the same document is found in Nitobe, *et al.*, *Western Influence in Modern Japan*, pp. 34–35.

"popular rights," and maneuvered to squeeze out of the government that year Ōkuma Shigenobu, a cabinet councilor who favored that cause.[55] In this atmosphere the regime attempted to introduce Confucian and nationalistic principles into the educational system. Westernized textbooks were censored, the Confucian classics were made required reading, and the curriculum came under the rigid control of the government. Furthermore, moral teaching (*shūshin*) was stressed as the most important subject in primary education.[56]

To make matters more complex, the clan oligarchy, now securely established in the government structure, changed its policy around the period of 1884–87. The Japanese government, preoccupied with the need to revise the unequal clauses in the treaties with Western powers, attempted to give a new look to the nation by promoting a Westernization policy in order to impress

[55] It is a matter of great interest to note that Saionji Kimmochi, the famous nobleman who had just returned from study in France, became the president of a liberal newspaper, *Tōyō jiyū* (literally, "Asian Liberty"), which advocated popular rights. The cabinet was embarrassed over this, and asked the throne to issue an edict ordering Saionji to resign. Saionji wrote a famous letter to the emperor, stating the importance of the press in parliamentary democracy. He received no reply from the emperor and in the end had to disassociate himself from journalism. His letter is quoted in Kimura, *Saionji Kimmochi*, pp. 49–51. The above incident demonstrates clearly how the oligarchy in power manipulated the throne. Regarding the ouster of Ōkuma, see Fujii, *Outline of Japanese History in the Meiji Era*, pp. 116–25. Ōkuma advocated a party government similar to the English parliamentary system and also the immediate opening of a national assembly. Itō Hirobumi and others, who favored the Prussian system, succeeded in ousting Ōkuma in 1881. This also implied the triumph of the clan oligarchy, an unholy alliance between Satsuma and Chōshū elements. Ōkuma, now out of power, proceeded to organize the Rikken kaishin-tō (Constitutional progressive party), which rivaled the Rikken teisei-tō (Constitutional imperial rule party), an extremely rightist party organized by Itō Hirobumi, Inouye Kaoru, and others. Another important political party was the Jiyū-tō (Liberal party), headed by Itagaki Taisuke. At any rate, the only constructive by-product of the ouster of Ōkuma was that the government had to promise the opening of the national assembly in the year 1890.

[56] See Robert K. Hall, *Shūshin: The Ethics of a Defeated Nation*. For the curriculum change introduced in 1881, see Toshisuke Murakami and Yoshio Sakata, *Meiji bunka-shi: Kyōiku-dōtoku-hen*, pp. 103–8.

foreigners. This policy was adopted not because the government leaders were converted to the values of Western culture, but because the only defense available to them was, in the words of Arnold Toynbee, "to keep the Western intruders at arm's length by learning the 'know-how' of nineteenth-century Western [civilization]." [57] Social dances were sponsored by the government, an orchestra was introduced into the government school of music (*Ongaku-torishirabe-dokoro*), and Westernized hairdos for women were encouraged.[58] Internally, however, the Meiji government returned to the pre-Meiji principle of social stratification. The result was the establishment in 1884 of a peerage, divided into five grades. In the main, the titles were given only to families of the court nobility and of the daimyo. Of the twenty-six titles given to individuals solely on the basis of their meritorious services at the time of the Meiji Restoration, twelve were given to the men from Satsuma and eight to those from Chōshū. In other words, the peerage consisted of the pre-Meiji elite and the new elite, namely, the clan oligarchy.[59] The government also tried to tighten control over the educational system by issuing in 1886 the Primary School Ordinance, the Middle School Ordinance, the Imperial University Ordinance, and the Normal School Ordinances. Through these ordinances, the government attempted to assert the supremacy of the state, while welcoming only those elements of Western knowledge and technology that were useful to Japan. Thus the object of education, according to the Westernized nationalist Mori Arinori, who became the minister of education in 1885, was not the welfare of the pupils but of the country. Sansom rightly observes that the educational reforms undertaken by Mori's leadership, "while in matters of organization following

[57] Toynbee, *The World and the West*, pp. 52–53.

[58] In fact, an association for women with foreign hair styles (*Fujin-sokuhatsu-kai*) was organized. Popular among married women was the *Igirisu-maki* (English style hairdo), while among young girls the so-called Margaret style was common. Also, the traditional custom of married women's dyeing their teeth black, as a symbol of married status, was discouraged. Although the empress gave up this custom in 1875 to set the pattern, as it were, conservative women resisted the change for some time.

[59] See Shimomura, "Meiji no shakai," pp. 46–51.

an Occidental pattern, were reactionary in spirit. . . ." [60] The logical consequences of the compromise, commonly referred to as *wakon-yōsai* (Japanese spirit and Western knowledge)—but in reality implying the supremacy of state rights at the expense of popular rights—was the promulgation of the Imperial Rescript on Education in 1890. In this famous document, which will be discussed later, traditional Confucian and Japanese virtues were exalted as the foundation of education. And, "should emergency arise," so states the Rescript, "offer yourselves courageously to the State; and thus guard and maintain the prosperity of Our Imperial Throne coeval with heaven and earth."

Regarding legislation during the Meiji Era, we need not go into detail, except to point out that the enactment of laws betrayed a similar compromise between "immanental theocracy" and "modernity," or the traditional notion of obligations and Western concepts of rights. Recognizing the fact that Western powers were not going to revise the unequal treaties unless Japan framed new codes, the Meiji government proceeded quickly to adopt various elements of Western jurisprudence. It is readily understandable why in this situation the initial impulse of Etō Shimpei, leading member of the Bureau for the Investigation of Institutions, was that the "French code should not only be translated into Japanese but that it should be adopted *in toto* as our own by simply substituting the word 'Japanese' for the word 'French.' " [61] There were others who were equally enthusiastic for the German or English codes. After years of study and discussion a civil code with strong French elements was accepted in 1890, and it was to go into effect three years later. Likewise, a commercial code with strong German elements was adopted in 1890, and it was to go into effect the following year. Meanwhile, some of the Japanese jurists

[60] Sansom, *The Western World and Japan*, p. 460. It is also significant to note that by the Ordinance of 1887, the graduates of the college of law in the imperial universities were declared qualified to enter government service without the usual civil service examination. The relation between the government bureaucracy and the imperial universities thus became inseparable. Maruyama also observes that a semimilitaristic discipline was introduced into the Normal Schools. See "Meiji kokka no shisō," pp. 201–3.

[61] Nitobe, *et al.*, *Western Influences in Modern Japan*, p. 74.

who had been influenced by English law fought for revision of these codes before they were enforced. The "immediate enforcement" party was defeated in the Diet by the "postponement" party. In the end differences were resolved, and the first three books of the civil code were promulgated in 1896, followed by the promulgation of two other books two years later, while the commercial code was published in 1899. With the adoption of modern jurisprudence, equal treaties were concluded between Japan and other powers by the end of 1897.[62]

Upon closer examination, we cannot help but recognize legal ambiguities involved in the Japanese legal system thus adopted in the 1890s. For example, the civil code, which was in effect until after the Second World War, attempted to uphold both the traditional "household system" and a Westernized "family system." Sansom suggests that the concept of the rights of the individual was alien to traditional Japanese legal thinking and that the jurists had to invent the compound term *"kenri,* made up of *ken,* meaning 'power' or 'influence,' and *ri,* meaning 'interest.' " [63] With the introduction of this new concept, the new civil code made provision that an individual could own, succeed to, or bequeath property as an individual, partly because bonds, stocks, bank deposits, and title deeds had to be registered in the names of individuals. Such a provision marked the rejection of the traditional legal assumptions that individual members of the household had no personal property rights. On the other hand, the new civil code still recognized the house as the legal unit, so that every Japanese was registered either as a head or a subordinate member of a house.[64] The head of the house had the privilege of determining the residence of its members, and conversely he was responsible for the support of its members and for the education of

[62] *Ibid.,* p. 79. For legal developments in Japan after the turn of the century, see pp. 80–84.

[63] Sansom, *The Western World and Japan,* p. 446.

[64] According to the new civil code, the genealogical records of the house were to be kept by the head of the house (Code #987), and the head of the house was not permitted to renounce the headship (#1020). The heir presumptive was not allowed to leave the house (#744), nor could the person who had succeeded to the headship resign it until he could be succeeded by the next head of the house (#752 and #762).

the children. Penalty for violation of these rules constituted grounds for expulsion from the house. Inevitably, the uneasy alliance between the traditional "household system" and the Westernized "family system" in the Meiji code solved some problems but created many more.

Even such a brief survey of educational and legal developments during the early Meiji Era demonstrates how the tension between the two contradictory objectives of the new regime—"renovation" that implied rejection of the past and "restoration" that implied the preservation of and return to the past—was gradually solved by nationalistic, utilitarian principles. Meanwhile, the balance between national rights and popular rights shifted in favor of the former around 1881 with the consolidation of the clan oligarchy that controlled the government bureaucracy. While the advocates of popular rights pushed the cause of constitutional government and forced the regime to call the first Diet in 1890, it was the clan oligarchy, the guardian of the national rights, which drafted the Constitution which was promulgated in 1889. Although the Constitution paid lip service to the rights of the people, it was modeled after the Prussian monarchical autocracy and drew practically no features from the English or French traditions of political philosophy. The prominent notion of the Japanese Constitution was the doctrine of personal rule by the emperor, which meant that in principle the emperor governs the empire as well as reigns. The Constitution provided two organs to assist and advise the throne, namely, the privy council and the ministers of state.[65] The Constitution further stipulated that the exercise of legislative power should require the consent of the Diet.[66]

[65] The significant feature of the Japanese Constitution is that the privy council and the cabinet are placed on an equal footing, so that the former can exert far more influence than might be realized on policy decisions. The doctrine of personal rule by the emperor has been used to rationalize the despotic tendency of the bureaucrats, who manipulated the throne. This doctrine assumes "that the emperor and the people are rival political forces, and that the affirmation of one involves the negation of the other. To recognize too definitely the right of the people to participate in the government would be ignoring the emperor's prerogatives." (Nitobe, *et al.,* *Western Influences in Modern Japan,* p. 261.)

[66] *Ibid.,* p. 264. "The idea in establishing the Diet was to furnish an

The promulgation of the Constitution of 1889 was a clear victory for the bureaucrats who fought for the cause of national rights. Their policy of "Westernization," for the tactical purpose of impressing foreign powers, came under attack meanwhile from two groups of men. The first group, characterized by idealistic nationalism (*Nihon-shugi*), was represented by such influential figures as Kuga Katsunan, Miyake Yūjiro, and Shiga Jūkō, who combined liberal nationalism with a keen sense of social concern. The second group, advocating democratic liberalism (*heimin-shugi*, literally "common people-ism"), was represented by the thought of Tokutomi Sohō. Ironically, the Sino-Japanese War, 1894–95, converted former champions of popular rights into im-(*jiyū*), which was the slogan of the popular rights movement, was perialistic nationalists. In this situation, the cause of liberty taken over by a small group of socialists who began to challenge the bureaucratic government in the name of social justice and pacifism. Another form of resistance, however negative and passive in outlook, against the imperialistic nationalism of the government was the naturalist movement in the domains of literature, poetry, and the fine arts.[67]

As for such conservatives as the National Scholars, Shinto leaders, and Confucian teachers, the growing influence of Western civilization and the rapid development of trade and industry presented causes for alarm not only for the future of the nation but also for their own security. It was but natural, therefore, that they were more than willing to rally behind the bureaucrats who attempted to utilize every means in order to solidify the nation around the throne. Actually, as Sansom once remarked, "it would

---

organ of reference for the emperor in the practical policies of legislation, and not primarily to reflect popular opinion." The Diet Law reads that the Diet is to be composed of the House of Peers and the House of Representatives. It is to be noted that members of the House of Peers were nominated by imperial appointment or by mutual election within each ranking category of (1) members of the imperial family, (2) dukes and marquises, (3) counts, viscounts, and barons, (4) those with distinguished merit and profound knowledge nominated by imperial selection, and (5) payers of large direct taxes relating to land or business (*tagaku-nōzei-sha*). See Fujii, *Outline of Japanese History in the Meiji Era*, p. 244.

[67] See Maruyama, "Meiji kokka no shisō," pp. 204–21.

be difficult to find in the Far East a more pragmatic and utilitarian group than the ruling elite of that time in Japan." [68] And these pragmatic and shrewd bureaucrats welcomed the support of the conservative leaders who affirmed the regime's claim to be the guiding body of the religious, cultural, and political mission of Japan. The religious policy of the Meiji regime was forged under the combined efforts of the conservative leaders of society and the bureaucratic clan oligarchy in their attempt to make legitimate the principle of "immanental theocracy" by elevating Shinto as the national religion. As early as 1872 the regime divided the cultic and religious aspects of Shinto by assigning the former to the Board of Ceremonies and the latter to the Department of Religion and Education. In 1877 the Home Ministry, replacing the Department of Religion and Education, was assigned to administer religious affairs. In 1900 the Home Ministry established within itself the Bureau of Shrines and the Bureau of Religions. Three years later the Bureau of Religion was transferred to the Department of Education, while the Bureau of Shrines remained in the Home Ministry. [69]

The Meiji regime's religious policy in making Shinto the national religion came under attack by the leaders of other religions as well as by secular intellectuals who felt the necessity for freedom in religious beliefs. Also, the Iwakura Mission, which was sent abroad in 1871 in an effort to revise the treaties with Western powers, recommended that the Meiji government adopt a policy of religious freedom in order to impress foreign governments. In this situation, the government conceded to the point of altering its religious policy, as far as its terminology was concerned, while preserving its substance. Concretely, the government reinterpreted Shinto, especially the practice of emperor worship, as a patriotic cult and not a religion. Article 28 of the Constitution, promulgated in 1889, stated explicitly that "Japanese subjects shall, within limits not prejudicial to peace and order and not antagonistic to their duties as subjects, enjoy freedom of religious

---

[68] Sansom, *The Western World and Japan,* p. 466.
[69] These offices were abolished after the Second World War.

belief." At the same time the government banished religious instruction of any kind from all schools, public and private, although "moral teaching, if applicable to all religions, could be given," according to Ordinance 12.

The intention of the Meiji government was clearly twofold. On the one hand, it attempted to satisfy the popular demand for religious freedom by offering a nominal guarantee for it in the Constitution, especially since freedom of religious belief proved to be an important item in treaty revisions with foreign powers. On the other hand, the government continued to allow special privileges to Shinto by creating an artificial concept, "State Shinto," and calling it a cult of national morality and patriotism, applicable to all religions. This strange religious policy was nothing but an ingenious (and dangerous) attempt at superimposing "immanental theocracy" on the constitutional guarantees of religious freedom. What is often forgotten is the simple fact that, despite the "orthodox" interpretations by Shinto and government apologists, "State Shinto" was essentially a newly concocted religion of ethnocentric nationalism. To be sure, it was based on the historic tradition and framework of Shinto, but in this new development—or distortion—of Shinto, the religious autonomy of Shinto was denied. It was the political authority, rather than the religious elite, which determined the policies and activities of State Shinto. In sharp contrast to historic Shinto, which never developed doctrinal orthodoxy and thus remained tolerant of various types of beliefs and practices, State Shinto allowed no deviation from its norm. A learned historian, Kume Kunitake, was expelled in 1892 from the Tokyo Imperial University because of his published article to the effect that Shinto was the survival of a primitive cult.[70] The government was determined to propagate

[70] Ironically, Mori Arinori, a Westernized nationalist, who played a decisive role in shaping the education system, was assassinated by an extreme nationalist on the charge that he had profaned the great shrine at Ise. The fact that such a story was spread widely, and believed by some, indicates that the "Westernized aspect" of Mori did not please conservatives. Sansom writes: "The cause of his murder was summarized in the liberal magazine the *People's Companion* by saying that he fell a victim to the

its gospel of ethnocentric nationalism through various channels, including the army, navy, and educational institutions. In the course of time the clever manipulation of the emperor cult by the bureaucrats, with the wholehearted support of extreme nationalists, exalted the throne in the eyes of the people, while in reality the throne was deprived of its political authority and became nothing but a convenient umbrella for the despotic oligarchy in power.

Let us now examine how various religions in Japan have struggled for their survival under the social, political, and cultural conditions of the modern period.

Sect Shinto and Other Religious Groups

The architects of the Meiji regime who imposed "immanental theocracy" in the form of State Shinto had to take into account, however, the religious aspirations of the masses as well as the internal disunity within the Shinto tradition itself. The net result was a decision on the part of the government in 1882 to divide Shinto into "State Shinto," which was permitted to apply the title *jinja* to its shrines, and "Sect Shinto," which was ordered to use the title *kyōkai* (church) or *kyōha* (sect) for its establishments.

It might be well for us to recall that, prior to the Meiji Era, all religious functionaries were tightly controlled by the Tokugawa feudal regime and that every household in Japan was compelled to belong to a specific Buddhist temple. In this situation religious leaders, assured of status and economic security, tended to ignore the religious needs of the people in the lower strata of society. The dissatisfied masses in turn depended heavily on devotional associations (*kō*) that sponsored among other activities the *okage-mairi* (worship to return divine favor) directed toward prominent Shinto shrines. The masses also turned to magico-religious beliefs and practices for comfort and guidance, aided by mountain ascetics, healers, and various other types of charismatic persons.

---

reactionary thought that he himself aroused." (*The Western World and Japan*, p. 480.)

In a sense, spontaneous religious movements that erupted among the masses during the late Tokugawa period and early Meiji Era were closely related in basic motivation to the phenomenon of peasant uprising (*ikki*).[71] Underlying both phenomena was the motif of *yo-naoshi* (literally, "changing the course of the world"), based on the realization that something had gone wrong in the order of society. Thus, for example, when injustice or too heavy taxation was imposed upon the peasantry by the authorities, the peasants in desperation rose up in arms. But when they sensed the impossibility of rectifying the injustice by means of uprisings, the masses tended to look for solutions for their misfortunes in trance-inducing religious acts, such as the *yo-naoshi odori* (dancing to change the course of the world) which displayed contradictory elements—a strange mixture of frenzy and passivity. It so happened that the last year of Tokugawa rule (1866) was marked by a nationwide peasant uprising. Significantly in 1867 the *ee ja naika* (literally, "any action is all right") dances spread throughout the country.[72] No doubt the oppressed peasants did not understand the political principles involved in the transfer of authority from the shogunate to the throne, but they did expect and hope to be emancipated from feudal burdens and they dreamed of a new order in society that would provide them with certain material benefits. But when they sensed that political change meant nothing more than the replacement of feudal absolutism with an imperial form of absolutism, they turned their attention to spontaneous new religious movements that promised a change in the course of the world. During the nineteenth century a number of such new religions came into being and attracted large numbers of followers among the

[71] See Tōyama, *Meiji ishin,* p. 198.

[72] It was reported that the lucky charms of the Grand Shrine of Ise dropped from the sky in the district of Nagoya in August, 1867. Overjoyed, men and women started dancing madly, forgetting the immediate problems of life. Often men dressed in female kimonos and women dressed in male attire invaded the wealthy homes and demanded food, drink, clothes, and money, saying *"Kore kuretemo ee ja naika* (Why not give us this and that?)." See Tōyama, pp. 187–90.

masses.[73] How to cope with them became a ticklish problem for the Meiji regime.

The Meiji regime also had to deal with the deep-rooted factionalism within the Shinto tradition. As early as 1880 heated controversies arose between the tradition of the Grand Shrine of Ise (Ise-ha) and that of the Shrine of Izumo (Izumo-ha) regarding the kami to be worshiped in the shrines of State Shinto. Both agreed on four kami of the Shinto pantheon mentioned in the *Kojiki,* namely, Ame-no-Minakanushi, Takamimusubi, Kammusubi, and Amaterasu. But those who followed the Izumo tradition insisted that Ōkuninushi, the kami of the Izumo Shrine, should be added to the four kami mentioned above. In this controversy the Izumo school was outmaneuvered by the Ise school, whereupon the followers of the Izumo tradition secured the government's permission to establish themselves as a Sect Shinto denomination called Izumo Taisha-kyō in 1882.[74] In addition to the Izumo Taisha-kyō, the government also recognized the following groups, three of which had come from the Shinto tradition, as Sect Shinto denominations during the Meiji Era.

(1) Shinto Taikyō or Shinto Honkyōku is a loose association of diverse subsects that share belief in the Great Teaching (*Daikyō*) of the kami, commonly referred to as the *kannagara* (the way of the kami). It recognizes no founder.[75] (2) Shinri-kyō (literally, "divine truth religion") considers the hero of Japanese

[73] See Kishimoto, *Japanese Religion in the Meiji Era,* p. 326: "Almost all the new religions which have developed from the time of the Restoration to the present have expressed a desire for 'social reform,' and the number of believers increased quickly after reform became impossible because of political absolutism."

[74] See Mombu-shō chōsa-kyoku shūmu-ka, *Shintō gyōsei enkaku-shi,* p. 85. For a description of the Taisha sect, see Holtom, *The National Faith of Japan,* pp. 199–204, and Bunce, *Religions in Japan,* pp. 134–35.

[75] One of the most important subsects of this group is Maruyama-kyō, founded by Itō Rokurōbei (1829–94). He was adopted by a hereditary *sendatsu* (senior guide to the sacred mountain) family connected with Fuji-kō (Devotional association of Mt. Fuji) which was later renamed Maruyama-kō. After forty years of ascetic training, Itō Rokurōbei became a healer and attracted many followers. See Yuri, *Maruyama kyōso-den.* On Shinto Honkyoku, see Holtom, *The National Faith of Japan,* pp. 190–95.

mythology, Nigi-hayahi-no-Mikoto, as its legendary founder, although Sano Tsunehiko is acknowledged to be its modern reorganizer. This denomination believes in the limitless miraculous power of all the kami in heaven, and teaches respect for the kami and devotion to the nation.[76] (3) Izumo Taisha-kyō, which has been mentioned earlier, considers the Senge family to be in direct succession from the divine ancestor of the people in the Izumo area. Consequently the headship of this denomination is assumed by members of the Senge family. This denomination stresses the importance of correct ceremonies and divination.

The following two are usually considered "Confucianistic" in basic orientation. (4) Shinto Shūsei-ha (literally, "improving and consolidating" religion) was founded by Nitta Kuniteru (1829–1902), who attempted to synthesize Shinto and Confucianism. According to this denomination man receives his body from his parents, but his spirit comes from three kami of the Shinto pantheon, Ame-no-Minakanushi, Takamimusubi, and Kammusubi. These three kami, be it noted, were equated with the *Shang-ti* of the Confucian tradition.[77] (5) Taisei-kyō (literally, "great accomplishment" religion) was founded by a noted samurai, Hirayama Seisai (1815–90). While its doctrines, based on Confucian ethics and traditional Shinto beliefs, are simple, this denomination takes a positive attitude toward science, the arts, and business. Its syncretistic character is evidenced by the fact that its adherents "engage in purification ceremonies, horoscopy, divination, fortune-telling, and rites of meditation, and practice control of breathing." [78]

It is interesting to note that while the following three groups are classified in the category of Sect Shinto, their relationship to classical Shinto is tenuous. Rather, they may be regarded as the heirs of the *Shugen-dō* or "Order of Mountain Ascetics" that blended folk religion and Buddhist elements. (6) Jikkō-kyō (literally, "practical conduct" religion), systematized by Shibata Hanamori (1809–90), and (7) Fusō-kyō (religion of "Fusō,"

---

[76] See Holtom, *The National Faith of Japan*, pp. 195–99.
[77] *Ibid.*, pp. 205–10.
[78] Bunce, *Religions in Japan*, p. 136.

which is a poetically expressed form of the name of Mt. Fuji),
systematized by Shishino Nakaba (d. 1884), developed from
devotional associations (*kō*) centering around the kami who are
believed to reside on top of Mt. Fuji.[79] (8) Ontake-kyō (literally,
"Mt. Ontake" religion), also known as Mitake-kyō, systematized by
a merchant named Shimoyama Ōsuke in 1873, venerates Mt. Ontake, a sacred mountain of the *Shugen-dō*, situated in the southern
part of Nagano prefecture. On this mountain are three shrines:
the Ōmiya (shrine for the great kami), the Wakamiya (shrine for
the young kami), and the Yamamiya (shrine for the kami of the
mountain). While the doctrines of this group are very simple, its
rites are complicated, including the fire-subduing ceremony
(*chinka shiki*), the fire ordeal (*kugatachi shiki*), sacred dancing
(*shimbu shiki*), and various forms of kami-possession.[80]

Of the two so-called Purification Sects, (9) Shinshū-kyō (literally, "divine-learning" religion) was founded by Yoshimura
Masamochi (b. 1839), a descendant of the ancient Nakatomi
family, a hereditary priestly clan. The distinctive tendency in
this group is toward the observation in minute detail of the ancient
Shinto rites as they were before Shinto came under the influence
of Buddhism. Notable among them are various rites of purification and kami-possession. (10) Misogi-kyō (literally, "cleansing"
or "purification" religion), founded by Inouye Masakane (1790–
1849), is syncretistic in its doctrines. It advocates deep breathing
for religious and therapeutic purposes, based on the belief that

---

[79] More specifically, Fusō-kyō is an amalgamation of several *kō* based on
the belief in Mt. Fuji. Originally, members of these *kō* undertook climbing to the top of Mt. Fuji, under the leadership of a *sendatsu*, as a religious
discipline. Gradually, models of Mt. Fuji were established in some parts of
Edo (Tokyo) for those who for a variety of reasons could not undertake
the pilgrimage to the real Mt. Fuji. The cult, based on the pilgrimage to
Mt. Fuji, had adherents in various parts of Japan; it was especially popular
among artisans in Edo. It was Shishino who amalgamated several such
associations and established Fuji Issan Kōsha (Mt. Fuji association),
later renamed Fuji Kyōkai (Fuji church), Shinto Fusō-ha, and Fusō-kyō.
Jikkō-kyō shares many similarities with Fusō-kyō; it considers the climbing
of Mt. Fuji on August 3 as its chief religious act.

[80] See Holtom, *The National Faith of Japan*, pp. 227–31.

deep breathing as well as the loud recitation of magical phrases purify one from mental and physical defilements.

The last three of the Sect Shinto denominations appear to be more "monotheistic" than the rest. They are also the prototypes of "new religions" that developed after the Second World War. (11) Kurozumi-kyō, so named for its founder, Kurozumi Munetada (1780–1850), for example, accepts the eight million Shinto kami officially, but at the same time insists that Amaterasu Ōmikami alone is the absolute god and creator of the universe. It teaches: "One kami is embodied in a million kami, and a million kami are found in one kami." Following the example of the founder, the devotees of Kurozumi-kyō pray to the sun-goddess, Amaterasu, facing the sun in the morning. They believe that by means of breathing exercises cosmic vitality penetrates individual bodies. During his lifetime Kurozumi attracted a considerable number of lower-class samurai in the Okayama district where he lived. After his death this group, then known as Kurozumi-kōsha (Kurozumi devotional association), steadily grew; later it changed its name to Shinto Kurozumi-ha and finally to Kurozumi-kyō.[81] (12) Konkō-kyō (religion of Konkō, which is the name of the kami of this group) was founded by Kawate Bunjirō (1814–83), a peasant in the Okayama district. Konkō or Konjin, also known as Tenchi-kane-no-kami, traditionally considered an evil kami, is said to have appointed Kawate to become the mediator between the kami and humanity.[82] The mediatorship was succeeded to by his descend-

[81] *Ibid.*, pp. 245–56; Hepner, *The Kurozumi Sect of Shinto*; and Thomsen, *The New Religions of Japan*, pp. 61–67.

[82] According to Toshio Ōno, the founder of Konkō-kyō initially venerated various kinds of kami and Buddhist deities. Gradually, he concentrated on Konjin, who was renamed Kane-no-kami and later Tenchi-no-kami. Finally, in 1873, the name of this kami became Tenchi-kane-no-kami. (Ono, "Kyōgishi ni kansuru ichikanken," *Konkō-kyō gaku*, No. 1, 1958, p. 61.) But in order to maintain its status as a Sect Shinto denomination, Konkō-kyō accepted three kami of the Shinto pantheon. "When the sect registered in 1946 in accordance with the Religious Corporations Ordinance, however, these were dropped, and Tenchi-kane-no-kami was listed as the only deity worshipped." (Bunce, *Religions in Japan*, p. 144.) For a general description of Konkō-kyō, see Schneider, *Konkōkyō: A Japanese Religion*, and Thomsen, *The New Religions of Japan*, pp. 69–78.

ants in the male line. (13) Tenri-kyō (divine reason religion) was founded by a charismatic woman, Nakayama Miki (1798–1887) of Yamato (present Nara prefecture). Brought up as a devotee of the Buddha Amida, she married and lived as an ordinary housewife. When she was forty-one, she became kami-possessed under the influence of a practitioner of the *Shugen-dō*. Revelations continued to come to her from a god, known as Tenri-Ō-no-mikoto. Her simple utopian teachings, based on oracles, and shamanistic practices and ecstatic dances attracted peasants who were looking for religious and economic comfort. She shared the antigovernment and antiforeign sentiments of the oppressed peasantry of her time. Miki and her followers were often persecuted by the authorities. At first recognized as a branch of the Yoshida sect of Shinto, this group changed its affiliation to Buddhism in 1880; finally, in 1908, Tenri-kyō was recognized as an independent Sect Shinto denomination.[83]

In addition to the above-mentioned thirteen Sect Shinto denominations, there were also many splinter sects and devotional associations that developed among the masses. Some of them were arbitrarily incorporated as subsects of the recognized Sect Shinto denominations, while others were regarded as *ruiji-shūkyō* or *shūkyō-ruiji-dantai* (pseudo religions, or quasi-religious associations). Despite the government's effort to establish State Shinto as the foundation of the nation, the masses continued to turn to these Sect Shinto denominations and quasi-religious associations for religious leadership. In ethos and polity these groups resembled the Buddhist, Shinto, and Kirishitan "religious associations" that had developed during the medieval period of Japan. Many of them had charismatic leaders whose intense religious experience served as the focal point of the lives of their adherents. Their simple teachings, promising *yo-naoshi*, as well as healing, prosperity, and happiness for individuals, appealed to the oppressed

---

[83] There are many books and articles on Tenri-kyō, both in Japanese and Western languages. See bibliographies in Van Straelen, *The Religion of Divine Wisdom*, pp. 231–35; Thomsen, *The New Religions of Japan*, p. 264; and Offner and Van Straelen, *Modern Japanese Religions*, pp. 283–90.

and superstitious segments of society. Besides, these religious groups provided both a symbol of authority and a sense of belonging which the masses looked for in a time of rapid sociopolitical change.

The government, on the other hand, suspected the very qualities of these religious groups that attracted the common people. Thus the government attempted to draw a clear line of demarcation between State Shinto and Sect Shinto, by means of which the former received various kinds of privileges and financial subsidies from the government, while the latter had to depend on its own initiative in organization, propaganda, and obtaining support. Also, Sect Shinto establishments were not allowed to use the torii, the distinctive form of entrance gate for a shrine.[84] The government was particularly sensitive to the political implications of these religious and quasi-religious movements. For example, the founder of Tenri-kyō, Nakayama Miki, was severely persecuted by the authorities because of her outspoken criticism of the government and the ruling classes which were, in her view, "aligned with foreign capital and were unconscious puppets of the foreign countries."[85] But relentless persecution and tight

[84] According to the ordinance issued in 1888, *kyōkai-kōsha* (devotional associations affiliated with Sect Shinto denominations) and *jinja-fuzoku-kōsha* (devotional associations affiliated with State Shinto shrines) were clearly differentiated. In 1898 teachers and ministers of Sect Shinto denominations were ordered not to teach within the compounds of State Shinto shrines, and in 1904 they were ordered not to participate in the celebration of State Shinto rituals. See Mombu-shō chōsa-kyoku shūmu-ka, *Shinto gyōsei enkaku-shi*, pp. 72 and 115.

[85] Kishimoto, *Japanese Religion in the Meiji Era*, pp. 331–32. It is to be noted, however, that initially Nakayama Miki was hopeful of developing cooperation between her religion and the new government. But the reform of the tax system resulted in greater hardship for the peasantry, so that she proposed financial cooperatives to alleviate their poverty. In 1873 she even performed incantations for rain for the benefit of poor farmers. When the government destroyed her meetinghouse and persecuted her and her followers in 1874, she became very critical of those in power. Indeed, "those who had sought practical solutions in the riotous dances [*ee ja naika* dances] at the end of Tokukawa lost themselves in the Tenri-kyō dances which provided religious inspiration in addition to the promise of practical relief." (*Ibid.*, p. 334.)

control by the government soon compelled Tenri-kyō to reconcile its own god with the Shinto kami, its own cult of the "living god" with the emperor cult, and its various features derived from the tradition of the folk religions with nationalism.[86]

We have noted earlier that the phenomenal growth of Japan after the turn of the century did not improve the lot of the masses. In desperation the peasants and workers resorted to "rice riots" in 1918 and labor strikes in 1919–20, but their efforts were in vain. Sensing that neither modern civilization nor an industrial economy would alleviate their distress, many people turned to messianic or healing religious cults. It was reported in 1924 that there were 98 *ruiji-shūkyō* (quasi religions). The number increased to 414 in 1930, and in 1935 there were over one thousand such quasi-religious cults practicing incantation, divination, fortunetelling, and healing.[87] Important among them were Ōmoto-kyō, Hito-no-michi, Seichō-no-iye, and Reiyū-kai.

Ōmoto-kyō (literally, the religion of "great fundamentals" or "great origin") was based on the "divine oracles" given to a shamanistic peasant woman, Deguchi Nao (1836–1918), during more than twenty years of her kami-possessed life. It was her son-in-law, Deguchi Onisaburō (1871–1948), who systematized the teaching and developed the organizational structure of Ōmoto-kyō. Deguchi Nao was influenced by Konkō-kyō and Tenri-kyō in her youth. Her healing power initially attracted a small number of adherents. Convinced that the divine mystery had been obscured by the ignorance and selfishness of the privileged classes, she boldly announced that, after going through a complete purification, "the Great World shall be changed into the Kingdom of Heaven where Peace reigns through all eternity."[88] Onisaburō

---

[86] One of the secret works of Tenri-kyō doctrine, the *Doroumi-koki*, which contains its own version of the cosmogonic myths, different from the "official" myths accepted by the Japanese government, was eliminated from the doctrinal systems of Tenri-kyō in 1938. Some of the Tenri-kyō theologians concocted nationalistic doctrines instead.

[87] "Taishō shōwa jidai," *ZNBT,* XII, 189.

[88] The "Oracle" was given to her in 1892. (Nao Deguchi, *Scripture of Oomoto,* p. 4.) In the "Oracle" of 1899, we read: "This world is on the verge of collapsing into a muddy field and human beings are on the brink

was more specific when he stated: "Armament and war are the means by which landlords and capitalists make their profit, while the poor must suffer. There is nothing more harmful than war and more foolish than armament." [89] Believers regarded Onisaburō as the *miroku* (Maitreya) or messiah who would establish a new order on this earth. Toward the end of the First World War this cult grew rapidly not only among peasants and people in small towns, but also among government officials and military officers.[90] In 1921 the government arrested Onisaburō and destroyed his "palace" in Ayabe, not far from Kyoto, because the authorities feared that his cult might instigate a rebellion against the throne.

In the 1920s Ōmoto-kyō turned its attention to China, Manchuria, and Mongolia. While it advocated the brotherhood of mankind and interreligious cooperation, especially with Taoist and Lamaist groups in China and the Baha'i group in the West, it also secured the unofficial support of the Japanese militarists who were then plotting to establish Japanese hegemony over the Asiatic continent. In the 1930s Ōmoto-kyō adopted a jingoistic nationalistic line, sponsoring semimilitaristic groups for young men, young women, and adults, for the purpose of "restoring" the Kingdom of God in Ayabe.[91] By the middle of the 1930s Ōmoto-kyō became too powerful even for the nationalistic leaders, and the government arrested Onisaburō and 60 high-ranking

---

of total extinction. . . . That should not happen. Let the peoples of the World repent! For there shall be a Change in the World for the ushering in of a New Age. Be ye ready to work for the salvation of Mankind." (*Ibid.*, p. 6.)

[89] Cited in Shigeyoshi Murakami, *Kindai minshū shūkyō-shi no kenkyū*, p. 152.

[90] Among its influential followers were Akiyama Mayuki, vice admiral of the navy; Ishii Yashiro, colonel of the army; Kishi Kazuta, M.D.; and Taniguchi Masaharu, who later established the Seichō-no-iye cult.

[91] Although herein I refer to this group as Ōmoto-kyō for the sake of consistency, it changed its own designation several times: e.g., Kimmeikai, Kimmei-reigaku-kai, Dainihon-shūsai-kai, Aizen-en. In the 1930s, it called itself Kōdō-Ōmoto (literally, Religion of "Great Fundamentals of the Imperial Way"). Onisaburō also sponsored the Shōwa-shinsei-kai, a nationalistic popular organization, with the cooperation of such prominent ultranationalists as Tōyama Mitsuru, Uchida Ryōhei, and Kikuchi Takeo.

members, and destroyed all the buildings belonging to the sect. Released on bail in 1942, he quietly waited for the end of the Second World War, while his followers continued their activities under cover.

Meanwhile, one of his former disciples, Taniguchi Masaharu (1893–   ), broke away and organized Kōmyō-shisō-fukyō-kai (the association for disseminating illumined ideology), later known as Seichō-no-iye (literally, "the household of growth"), a syncretistic quasi religion. His book, *Seimei-no-jissō* (Realities about life), was widely read among people of all walks of life. In fact, over three quarters of a million copies of this book were sold before 1935.[92] During the Second World War Taniguchi cooperated wholeheartedly with the militarist leaders. Another disciple of Onisaburō, Okada Mokichi (1882–1955), broke away from Ōmoto-kyō in 1934 and established Kannon-kyō (the religion of Kannon or Avalokiteśvara). Notwithstanding the Buddhistic designation thus adopted, Kannon-kyō inherited many features from Ōmoto-kyō. It was renamed Sekai Kyūsei-kyō (the church of world messianity) after the Second World War.[93]

The government authorities looked disfavorably upon the ever-increasing number of quasi religions, and took strong measures to undercut their influences among the masses. For example, Hito-no-michi (literally, "the way of man"), founded by Miki Toku-haru (1871–1938), was compelled to affiliate with one of the Sect Shinto denominations, Fusō-kyō, in order to survive. Soon Hito-no-michi outgrew Fusō-kyō; it boasted 600,000 adherents of its own in 1934. Three years later the government arrested Miki Tokuharu and his son Miki Tokuchika (1900–   ) and ordered the dissolution of the sect on the grounds that Hito-no-michi taught the unacceptable doctrine that Amaterasu was nothing but the sun. This, in spite of the fact that Hito-no-michi, by its

[92] Taniguchi cleverly improved the form of *chinkon-kishin-hō*, a collective cult for becoming kami-possessed, into a more sophisticated *shinsō-kan*, a rite of meditation. Nevertheless, Seichō-no-iye appealed to people as a cult of faith healing.

[93] For the activities of these and other "new religions" after the Second World War, see the next chapter.

own claim, was based on the principles of the Imperial Rescript on Education.[94] It is evident from these facts that the consistent policy of the Japanese government in the modern period, throughout the eras of the Meiji, Taishō, and Shōwa until the end of the Second World War, had been to maintain tight ideological control of the populace, so that all religions and quasi-religious groups —even those which overtly or covertly identified themselves with the Shinto tradition—were not allowed to deviate from the "orthodoxy" defined and enforced by the bureaucratic government.

Buddhism

The complex development of Japanese Buddhism in the modern period cannot be understood without taking into account a series of events and problems that threatened as well as stimulated the Buddhist tradition. In the course of time, external and internal factors elicited a variety of responses from various levels and segments among the Buddhists, so that simple characterizations are bound to miss the total picture. Nevertheless, it is safe to state that the first phase of the Meiji Era was a trying period for Japanese Buddhism in general, especially for its institutional aspects. Historically, Buddhism had in the main enjoyed the favor and support of the ruling class in Japan. Prior to the Meiji Era it enjoyed the prerogatives of a *de facto* state religion, collaborating

[94] Hito-no-michi, like many other quasi-religious cults, had a colorful background. Its founder, Miki Tokuharu, at one time an Ōbaku Zen priest, was originally a member of another quasi religion called Tokumitsu-kyō, founded by Kanada Tokumitsu (1863–1919), an Osaka merchant and a teacher of Ontake-kyō. Kanada advocated the cult of *o-furikaye*, declaring that the sufferings of the people could be transferred by divine mediation to the person of *oshiye-oya* (literally, "the teaching parent," the actual name of the founder of the cult) who vicariously would endure suffering for the people. He adopted the Imperial Rescript on Education as the basis of the doctrine of his group, which maintained a nominal affiliation with Ontake-kyō. His disciple, Miki Tokuharu, claimed to be the true spiritual heir of Kanada Tokumitsu, and called his own cult, which was established after the death of Kanada, Jindō (or Hito-no-michi) Tokumitsu-kyō. It was renamed Hito-no-michi in 1931 and renamed again: the PL Kyōdan (the religion of perfect liberty), after the Second World War.

closely with the Tokugawa feudal regime in its civil administration and thought control. The tables were turned sharply, however, when the architects of the Meiji regime rejected Buddhism in favor of Shinto. Furthermore, as mentioned earlier, the government order separating Buddhism and Shinto (*shinbutsu-hanzen*) precipitated a popular anti-Buddhist (*haibutsu-kishaku*) movement that reached its climax around 1871. As a result a great many temples and monasteries were demolished, a large number of priests and nuns were sent back to secular life, precious treasures were sold or destroyed, and the parochial system was abolished.[95] Confronted by hitherto unknown hardships, Buddhist leaders and adherents reacted in various ways.

Understandably, there were those who reacted to this situation emotionally. On the one hand, some Buddhists, both clerical and lay, experienced a sense of emancipation from their religious upbringing and rejected Buddhism altogether. On the other hand, others reacted violently against the anti-Buddhist movement itself, against Shinto, against Western civilization, against Christianity, and even against the new regime. In some instances Buddhists staged insurrections and riots. For example, in 1873 the Buddhists in the three counties of Echizen (present Fukui prefecture) marched to the office of the prefectural government, carrying bamboo spears with the banner of "Namu-Amida-Butsu," and demanded that the officials agree (1) not to let Christianity enter the prefectural boundary, (2) to allow Buddhist preaching, and (3) not to teach *yōgaku* (Western learning) in the schools. In this case the Buddhist uprising developed into a large-scale peasant revolt, which had to be quelled by government troops.[96]

It is noteworthy that in a time when many were lamenting the loss of the external power, security, and prestige of Buddhism there were men like Shaku Unshō (1827–1909) and Fukuda Gyōkai (1806–88) who were more disquieted by the loss of Buddhism's inner spirit. These men—and there were others like them

[95] For examples of the anti-Buddhist movement, see Taijō Tamamuro, *Meiji ishin haibutsu kishaku*, and Kishimoto, *Japanese Religion in the Meiji Era*, pp. 114–21.

[96] See Kishimoto, *Japanese Religion in the Meiji Era*, p. 123.

—labored against irrational anti-Buddhist movements. They were not merely effective apologists for the Buddhist cause; they were also forerunners of spiritual awakening and reform movements in modern Japanese Buddhism. In the words of Fukuda Gyōkai:

Buddhists regret the *haibutsu kishaku,* but not because temples have been destroyed. . . . It is not because we have lost our government stipend. We grieve before heaven and man that we have lost the Way of the greatest Good. In order to regain the lost Way, and for this reason only, priests should pray for the extension of *dharma* (Buddha's Law) and the prevention of *haibutsu.*[97]

It is especially significant that some of the enlightened Buddhist leaders argued in favor of the separation of religion and state and the principle of religious liberty. The religious vitality of modern Japanese Buddhism owes much to the spiritual awakening that developed during the early Meiji Era.

Side by side with the spiritual awakening, some leaders of Japanese Buddhism during the Meiji Era sensed the need for scholarly endeavor, in both philosophical and philological domains. Indeed, Japanese Buddhism in the modern period was greatly stimulated by its encounter with Western civilization directly or indirectly. As early as 1873 Shimaji Mokurai (d. 1911), a priest of the West Honganji sect, visited the West and India, while Nanjō Bunyū (d. 1927) of the East Honganji sect went to Oxford to study Sanskrit under Max Müller in 1876. It was Nanjō who published in 1883 *A Catalogue of the Chinese Translations of the Buddhist Tripitaka.*[98] Following the examples of these pioneers, a host of able Buddhist scholars continued the scholarly tradition of Japanese Buddhism.[99] One of the most ambitious undertakings was the publication of the *Taishō Tripitaka* (the Taishō edition of the Buddhist *Tripitaka* in Chinese), 100 volumes printed in 1932 un-

[97] Cited *ibid.,* p. 126.
[98] On Nanjō's life, see Iyenaga, *Nihon Bukkyō shisō no tenkai,* pp. 294–315.
[99] See Shōson Miyamoto, "Meiji Bukkyō kyōgaku-shi," *Gendai Bukkyō,* No. 105, *Meiji Bukkyō no kenkyū,* June, 1933 (Tokyo), pp. 18–30.

der the editorship of Takakusu Junjirō (d. 1945).[100] Exposure to European scholarship in Buddhological studies and Western philosophical thought, coupled with increased contacts with other traditions of Buddhism in Asian nations, broadened the horizon for Japanese Buddhists. Emancipated thus from the historic insularity of their own past, Japanese Buddhist scholars attempted not only historical, philological, and doctrinal studies of the Theravada, Mahayana, and Tibetan branches of Buddhism, but also a critical and constructive reexamination of Japanese Buddhism itself. Moreover, rigorous scholarly effort and philosophical inquiries proved to be great assets for the spiritual awakening of Japanese Buddhism. For example, one of the most influential thinkers during the 1890s, Kiyozawa Manshi (d. 1903), combined within himself the influences of Hegelianism and pious devotion to the grace of Amida. Throughout his life Kiyozawa contributed much to the philosophical rejuvenescence of Buddhism. At the same time he "inspired his disciples with a religious ardour combined with calm self-renunciation, and he lived with them in monastic simplicity in the midst of the bustle of Tokyo." [101]

The spiritual and scholarly development of Japanese Buddhism, however, could not be divorced from its institutional dimensions. As stated before, the government in 1870 issued the Proclamation of the Great Doctrine (*Daikyō*), designed to impose Shinto as the guiding principle of the nation. Although the government appointed Buddhist as well as Shinto clergy to be "national priests," the former were overshadowed by the latter. Furthermore, the Zōjō-ji, the famous Pure Land temple in Tokyo, was designated as the training center of the Great Doctrine (*Daikyō-in*). There the statue of Buddha Amida was replaced with the altar of four Shinto kami—Ame-no-Minakanushi, Takamimusubi, Kammusubi, and Amaterasu—while a Shinto gate (torii) was established at the entrance of the temple. The Buddhist clergy who had been ac-

[100] For other publications by Japanese Buddhists, see Kitagawa, "Buddhist Translation in Japan," *Babel: Revue Internationale de la Traduction,* IX (Nos. 1–2, 1963), 53–59.

[101] Anesaki, *History of Japanese Religion,* p. 381. On Kiyosawa's life, see Iyenaga, *Nihon Bukkyō shisō no tenkai,* pp. 316–37.

cepted as "national priests" were expected to wear Shinto ceremonial hats and make offerings to the Shinto kami. Inevitably,
friction arose between Buddhist and Shinto elements, and as the
anti-Buddhist movement began to subside the Buddhist leaders
aspired to be emancipated from Shinto domination. In 1872, a
leading Buddhist, Shimaji Mokurai, then traveling in Europe,
advocated separating "worship" and "government." His position
was supported by Mori Arinori, chargé d'affaires in Washington,
and later by Itō Hirobumi, a cabinet councilor. Consequently,
four branches of the Shin (True Pure Land) sects of Buddhism
were permitted to leave the Great Doctrine movement, and shortly
afterward the entire institution of the Great Doctrine itself was
abolished.[102]

Ironically, the principle of religious freedom, which Buddhist
leaders advocated in order to preserve the independence of their
own faith, was destined to be applied to Christianity—the "forbidden religion" during the Tokugawa period. The political instability in Japan during the 1870s necessitated that the government take a conciliatory attitude toward Buddhism which enjoyed
a residual influence among the general populace. On the other
hand, Christianity appeared to turn the people from the traditional values of Japanese society and to lead them toward such
"Westernized" ideas as the principle of "popular rights" (*minken*)
which was distasteful to the clan oligarchy then consolidating its
power in the government. In this situation, following the government's reluctant withdrawal of the prohibition edict against Christianity in 1873, many Buddhists allied with Shinto, Confucian,
and nationalist leaders in an all-out anti-Christian campaign, which
was called by the Buddhists *haja kensei* (the refutation of evil
religion and the exaltation of righteous religion).[103] After a short-

[102] See Kishimoto, *Japanese Religion in the Meiji Era,* pp. 132–35. The
ill-fated institution of the "national priest" was dissolved in 1884.

[103] The pioneer of this movement was Ugai Tetsujō (d. 1891), a priest
of the Pure Land sect, who wrote many books defending Buddhism against
the anti-Buddhist (*haibutsu kishaku*) movement and criticizing Christianity.
His most famous work was *Shō-ya-ron* (An essay on the ridiculousness of
Christianity), published in 1869. Even Shimaji Mokurai, who advocated
the principle of religious freedom, fought against Christianity, as evidenced

lived government-sponsored artificial Westernization period (1884–
87), a strong nationalist reaction developed with the enthusiastic
cooperation of Buddhist leaders. Probably the most articulate Buddhist spokesman against Christianity during the 1880s was Inouye
Enryō (d. 1919), a priest of the True Pure Land sect. Claiming
to use impartial philosophy—by which he meant, significantly,
Western philosophy—Inouye criticized the "irrationality" of Christianity and praised the "rationality" of Buddhism. His arguments
were based on a simple comparison drawn between the theism of
Christianity and the nontheism of Buddhism. The latter, according to Inouye, was in harmony with Western philosophy and science. However, his so-called impartial comparison of two religions
was motivated by his objections to Christianity, the religion of the
strong Western nations and inseparable from the political structures of these nations.[104]

With the promulgation of the Imperial Rescript on Education
in 1890, Christianity came under greater attack from the nationalists on the grounds that its teaching was contrary to the spirit of
the Rescript, as I shall discuss more fully later. By this time, leaders of the bureaucratic government had come to depend on Confucian, Shinto, and any other systems that might uphold the principle of "immanental theocracy" in order to defend the nation
from the dangerous elements of "modernity." In this situation the
Buddhists "planned to revive their faith by aligning themselves

---

by his book, *Fukkatsu shinron* (New thoughts on the Resurrection), 1875.
Regarding these books see Kishimoto, *Japanese Religion in the Meiji Era*,
p. 148.

[104] "Introduction" of Inouye's *Shinri-kinshin* (The guiding principle of
truth), Vol. I (1886). His other important anti-Christian work was *Bukkyō-
katsu-ron* (Enlivening Buddhism), 2 vols., published in 1887 and 1890.
Concerning these books by Inouye, see Saburō Iyenaga, *Chūsei Bukkyō
shisō-shi kenkyū*, pp. 147–80. Iyenaga examines the philosophical contents
of Inouye's arguments, and concludes that, while Inouye made a valuable
contribution by pointing out the irreconcilability between science and
some elements of Christian teachings, he never applied the same arguments
to some elements of Buddhist doctrines. Actually, Inouye never discussed
the metaphysical dimensions of the two religions in question. Inouye's
Buddhist apologetics reflected the nationalistic aspirations of the people
during the 1880s. See Iyenaga, *Chūsei Bukkyō shisō-shi kenkyū*, pp. 156–58.

with the increasing nationalistic sentiment. They used their hard-won religious freedom . . . to attack Christianity." [105] And in so doing, within the limits of narrow nationalism, Buddhists unwittingly held back the modernization of their religion. [106] Some Buddhists went so far as to oppose the monogamous principle, advocated by a group of Christian leaders, on the ground that it was "un-Japanese." [107] From the Sino-Japanese War (1894–95) onward, the leaders of established Buddhist schools collaborated very closely with ethnocentric nationalism. Even Inouye Enryō, who earlier had claimed to advocate Buddhism from the standpoint of Western philosophy, turned into a spokesman for the Imperial Way. In 1893 he stated that the imperial family is more important than the people, so that filial piety must be subservient to loyalty to the throne. He even applied this hierarchical ethic to the relationship between peasants and landowners. The following year he published an article on "the philosophy of war," which was strongly militaristic in temper. [108] The war effort of Buddhist leaders was appreciated by the government, as evidenced by the case of Ōtani Kōzui, chief abbot of the Nishi-Honganji (one of the True Pure Land sects), who was commended by the emperor for the important role he played in keeping up morale during the Russo-Japanese War (1904–5). [109]

In considering Japanese Buddhism in the modern period, one is struck by the emergence of an active lay leadership. Some leaders advocated the establishment of a new national religion based on a combination of Shinto, Confucianism, and Buddhism. In 1888 Dainihon-kokkyō-daidō-sha (The society for the establishment of the great way [meaning the combination of the three teachings mentioned above] as the national religion of Great Japan) was organized by an influential Buddhist layman, Yamaoka

[105] Kishimoto, *Japanese Religion in the Meiji Era*, p. 146.

[106] *Ibid.*, p. 44. "This was one of the important reasons for the failure of the Buddhist Reformation."

[107] Iyenaga, "Nihon no kindai-ka to Bukkyō," in *Kōza kindai Bukkyō*, II, 16.

[108] *Ibid.*, pp. 19–20.

[109] *Ibid.*, p. 17.

Tesshū (1838–88) and others who were determined to fight against Christianity and Western thought. This society boasted a membership of 35,000 in 1902. Another group of lay Buddhists organized the short-lived Sonnō-hōbutsu-daidō-dan (United movement for revering the emperor and Buddha) in 1889. From the tradition of this movement many social, educational, and philanthropic groups developed later.[110] On the other hand, there were some lay Buddhists who tried to face squarely the problem of "modernity." For example, in 1899 the Shin-Bukkyō-dōshi-kai (Fellowship of new Buddhists) was organized mostly by able young lay Buddhists. This group advocated such aims as the elimination of superstition, anticlericalism, rejection of government interference in religious matters, and the promotion of learning and morality. There were even a few Buddhists in the active socialist and anarchist movements, and some who at least worked closely with members of such movements. Some outstanding Buddhist laymen were also openly critical of the government's policies during the Russo-Japanese War.[111] But, in the main, Buddhists in the modern period eagerly accepted emperor worship as their religious, as well as patriotic, duty.

Following the severe depression in 1908 and the alleged attempt by anarchists to overthrow the government in 1910, the regime in 1912 sponsored the "Conference of the Three Religions," involving representatives of Shinto, Buddhism, and Christianity, in order to secure their cooperation in halting discontent and unrest among the populace. By this time violent anti-Christian sentiment had subsided among Buddhists. When the First World War began, Buddhists organized the Buddhist Society for the Defence of the Nation (Bukkyō-gokoku-dan) and aided the government's

[110] On these two groups, see Kishimoto, *Japanese Religion in the Meiji Era,* pp. 151–52.

[111] The Fellowship of New Buddhists counted among its organizers such influential laymen as Sakaino Kōyō, Takashima Beihō, Kikuchi Kenjō, and Sugimura Sojinkan. The fellowship also had some clerical members, such as Watanabe Kaikyoku. Some Buddhist clergy were also involved in activities that were considered radical. For example, three priests were condemned to death for an alleged attempt to overthrow the government in 1910.

war effort. In the 1920s and 1930s, when Marxism and Communism criticized certain social injustices, Buddhism tended to uphold the *status quo,* preaching the virtues of peace, harmony, and loyalty to the throne. A notable exception was the Youth League for Revitalizing Buddhism (Shinkō Bukkyō seinen dōmei) which was deeply involved in social action; this organization was destined to be dissolved by the authorities in 1937.[112] Jingoists and ultranationalists were then determined to "purify" all religions, including Buddhism. For example, the True Pure Land sect, which traditionally paid highest devotion to Amida, was accused of being irreverent to the Shinto kami. In this situation, some of the Buddhist leaders advocated the so-called Imperial Way-Buddhism (*Kōdō Bukkyō*) and cooperated with the aim of extending the imperial authority both at home and abroad.[113] During the Second World War Buddhism was also exploited by the militarists, especially in connection with the Japanese occupation of the traditionally Buddhist nations in Southeast Asia.

Space does not permit a discussion of the educational, social, and philanthropic works sponsored by Buddhists,[114] as well as the missionary activities undertaken by various Buddhist groups in Hokkaido, Taiwan, Korea, China, Manchuria, and some parts of North and South America.[115] Mention should be made, however, of schismatic groups which arose from the tradition of Buddhism in the modern period; some of them became independent "New Religions" after the Second World War. (1) One of the earliest groups that emerged was Butsuryū-kō (literally, "the association to exalt Buddha"), founded in 1857 by an ex-priest, Ōji Nissen (1817–90). It was primarily a cult of faith healing, and it appealed

[112] Totten, "Buddhism and Socialism in Japan and Burma," *Comparative Studies in Society and History,* II (No. 3, April, 1960), 303.

[113] Regarding the relationship between Buddhism and militant nationalism at home, see Shigemoto Tokoro, "Nichiren no Shūkyō to Tennō-sei Nashionarizumu," in *Kōza kindai Bukkyō,* V, 100–18.

[114] See Fujitani, "Bukkyō to Buraku-kaihō," in *Kōza kindai Bukkyō,* V, 133–50; Ryōshin Hasegawa, "Bukkyō shakai-jigyō ni kansuru kanken," *ibid.,* pp. 151–59; and Pratt, *The Pilgrimage of Buddhism,* pp. 567–95.

[115] Michibata, "Nihon-Bukkyō no kaigai-fukyō," in *Kōza kindai Bukkyō,* V, 177–89.

to the sick and downtrodden. It had a membership of nearly half a million in the 1930s. Being a lay organization, having no priesthood and no temples of its own, this group, which was officially affiliated with one of the Nichiren sects, was for all intents and purposes an independent quasi religion. The influence of Butsuryū-kō left its mark on Reiyū-kai (the association of the friends of the spirit), which will be discussed later. (2) Kokuchū-kai (literally, "the nation's pillar society") was founded by Tanaka Chigaku (b. 1861). At one time he had been a Nichiren priest, but he left the priesthood in order to establish a lay movement based on the teachings of the thirteenth-century Buddhist prophet, Nichiren. His organization changed its name several times, but finally chose the designation Kokuchū-kai. It grew rapidly with the rise of nationalism in the 1890s and the first decade of our century, but declined sharply after the First World War. But through Tanaka's personal influence, many people, including a renowned writer, Takayama Chogyū, once called "the Nietzsche of Japan," rediscovered the relevance of Nichiren's teachings for modern Japan.[116] (3) Remmon-kyō (literally, the "Lotus gate" religion) was founded by Shimamura Mitsu (1831–1914?), wife of a Kyushu merchant. She was both a devout Nichiren follower and a shamanistic diviner. Early in the Meiji Era she started a cultic group that followed the Nichiren tradition together with Shintoistic rituals and the practice of faith healing. This group sought affiliation with Taisei-kyō, mentioned earlier, in order to preserve its own existence, and prospered during the 1880s and 1890s. After the death of the foundress, Remmon-kyō split into two factions, both of which disappeared shortly afterward.

The importance of (4) Reiyū-kai (the association of the friends of the spirit) lies in the fact that it served as the womb for several powerful "New Religions" after the Second World War. Reiyū-kai itself was founded in 1925 through the joint efforts of Kubo

---

[116] Regarding Takayama's spiritual pilgrimage, see Anesaki, *History of Japanese Religion*, pp. 375–79. Anesaki was a close personal friend of Takayama. Incidentally, Anesaki, who was raised in the True Pure Land (Shin-shū) tradition, later became a follower of Nichiren. See Anesaki, *Waga shōgai*, pp. 1–2 and 102.

Kakutarō (1890–1944) and Kotani Kimi (1900–   ). Kubo, originally a carpenter, climbed socially through his contact with officials of the Imperial Household Ministry and became an ardent follower of Nichiren's teachings along the way. His brother's wife, Kotani Kimi, an uneducated peasant woman, turned out to be a shamanistic diviner. Together the two of them enticed Kujō Nichijō, a highborn lady who once had been the abbess of a Nichiren temple in Kyoto, to become the president of Reiyū-kai, which established itself as an independent lay Buddhist movement. Their nationalistic teachings, plus their emphasis on ancestor worship and the practice of divination, attracted a large number of followers before the Second World War. However, during the 1930s several splinter groups, including Risshō Kōsei-kai, which will be discussed later, broke away from Reiyū-kai.[117]

Unlike the four groups above which came out of the Nichiren tradition, (5) the Muga-no-ai (selfless love) Movement derived its inspiration from the teachings of Shinran, the founder of the True Pure Land School of Buddhism, and Leo Tolstoy (1828–1910), the famous Russian novelist and advocate of peace. This movement was established in 1905 by Itō Shōshin (b. 1876) who left the priesthood and founded the Muga-en (Garden of selflessness), a small community of like-minded brethren. Itō's personal influence was felt among pacifists as well as socialists, and he was sympathetic toward the cause of socialism. In the 1930s, however, Itō began to sanction Japanese nationalism, and while his Muga-en still exists in the Aichi prefecture, it has lost the influence and prestige which Itō's movement once enjoyed. (6) Ittō-en (garden of one lantern) may be characterized as a fraternity for primitive communism that derived its original impetus from Shinran and Tolstoy. None of the members of this group is allowed to keep private property, nor to work for profit or the exploitation of others. Ittō-en was founded in 1905 by Nishida Tenkō (1872–   ), whose example of nonpossession and service toward others gradually attracted followers. Believing that the "Universal Light"—the One and Only Light which is the essence of life—would lead all to

[117] On Reiyū-kai, see Thomsen, *The New Religions of Japan*, pp. 109–16; and Offner and Van Straelen, *Modern Japanese Religions*, pp. 91–95.

harmonious relationships based on mutual confidence and selfless service, Ittō-en has carried on its communal life quietly at Yamashina, a suburb of Kyoto. Unfortunately, this group was exploited by the militarists in Manchuria during the 1930s and early 1940s.[118] Ittō-en never claimed to be a Buddhist movement in spite of the Buddhistic influences that are still apparent in it.

There were many other movements that emerged and remained within the Buddhist fold, such as the Young Men's Buddhist Association, the Young Women's Buddhist Association, and various denominational societies for men and women, as well as Buddhist associations for various professions. Fortunately, Japanese Buddhism in the modern period had many able and dedicated leaders, scholars, and reformers who were conscious of the problems presented by "modernity." Nevertheless, the dichotomy between the Buddhist intelligentsia and traditional rural Buddhists was not overcome to a significant degree.

Christianity

The complex developments in international as well as domestic situations in the mid-nineteenth century resulted in the reappearance of Christianity on the modern Japanese scene. Two centuries earlier the Tokugawa shogunate had closed Japan's doors to foreign intercourse ostensibly in order to exterminate the Kirishitan. Throughout the Tokugawa period only the Dutch and Chinese were allowed to carry on limited trade with Japan, for they were considered to be hostile toward Roman Catholicism. During the first half of the nineteenth century, several attempts were made to penetrate Japan, though without success, by Catholic missionaries. Nevertheless, the Société des Missions Étrangères de Paris, whose assigned province was Japan, eagerly awaited the opportunity to reestablish Catholicism in the "forbidden" island kingdom.[119] Meanwhile, Russian Orthodox and various Protestant

[118] On Nishida and Ittō-en, see Anesaki, *History of Japanese Religion*, pp. 400–1; and Thomsen, *The New Religions of Japan*, pp. 221–34.

[119] See Jennes, *History of the Catholic Church in Japan*, pp. 206–9; and Laures, *The Catholic Church in Japan*, pp. 201–6.

churches in Europe and North America were also anxious to send missionaries to Japan as soon as her doors were opened to foreign contact.

It is interesting to note that President Filmore, knowing of the Japanese hatred for Catholicism, instructed Commodore Perry to state that "the United States was not like other Christian countries, since it did not interfere in religion at home, much less abroad." [120] Thus the treaty concluded in 1854 had no reference to religion. Japanese authorities soon recognized the existence of the religious needs of the foreign personnel living in Japan, and thus the 1858 treaty made allowances respecting freedom of worship and the establishment of chapels and cemeteries for foreigners in their concessions. In 1859 Prudence-Séraphim-Barthélemy Girard arrived at Edo as interpreter for the French consul general and as first Catholic chaplain of the foreign community. Soon other Catholic missionaries followed Girard. Also in 1859 the following Protestant missionaries arrived at various treaty ports: J. Liggins and Channing M. Williams of the Protestant Episcopal Church, J. C. Hepburn and his wife of the Presbyterian Church, and S. R. Brown, D. B. Simmons, and G. F. Verbeck of the (Dutch) Reformed Church. They were soon followed by missionaries of other Protestant bodies in both North America and Europe.[121] In 1861 Ivan Kasatkin, ordained as Nicholai, arrived as chaplain to the Russian consulate in Hakodate, Hokkaido. While the religious activities of all these missionaries were officially confined to ministering to foreign residents, many of them, who actually were determined to spread the Christian faith in Japan, spent much time in learning the Japanese language. Some of them translated portions of the Bible as well as devotional literature into Japanese. In the course of time these missionaries came in contact with a number of ambitious Japanese youths who wanted to study foreign languages. There were occasional, secret converts to the Christian faith, even though the shogunate edict

[120] Sansom, *The Western World and Japan,* p. 488.

[121] See Thomas, *Protestant Beginnings in Japan,* pp. 76–79. According to Thomas, there were seven Protestant missionary societies working in Japan in 1872, followed by thirteen new ones during the next decade.

against Christianity was still enforced among Japanese nationals.

The establishment of a Catholic Church in the port city of Nagasaki in 1865 was an important event in the modern history of Catholicism in Japan. The Nagasaki area had been a stronghold of the Kirishitan during the sixteenth and seventeenth centuries, and as might be expected, there were a number of communities of Kakure Kirishitan (Hidden Japanese Roman Catholics), who had secretly kept the faith for two centuries, in and around the city.[122] To them it was an emotional experience to see a new church dedicated to the twenty-six Japanese martyrs of the seventeenth century, and soon they began to visit the priests and to reveal their identity. By the end of 1865 the number of discovered Kirishitan was estimated to be about 20,000.[123] Inevitable conflict with the authorities came in 1867, when leading members of the Kirishitan communities were arrested. It was, however, the last year of the Tokugawa shogunate, which no longer had the determination or the power to exterminate Kirishitan influence.

Following the decline of the shogunate, the new Meiji government that was determined to exalt Shinto adopted a strong anti-Kirishitan attitude. During the first three years of the Meiji Era (1868–70) over three thousand Kirishitan were arrested in Kyushu and many were sent into exile in other parts of Japan, in spite of the protests of foreign diplomats.[124] The government also arrested Ichikawa Einosuke, who taught the Japanese language to an American missionary in Nagasaki, on the ground that he possessed a Japanese translation of some parts of the Bible; he died in jail while awaiting trial. Aroused by these events, the foreign ministers strongly advised the Meiji regime, which was then in-

[122] Furuno, *Kakure Kirishitan*, pp. 45–100.

[123] Jennes, *History of the Catholic Church in Japan*, p. 215.

[124] When the foreign ministers asked for a conference with Japanese authorities, the spokesman of the Meiji regime stressed the principle of the "unity of government and religion" (*saisei-itchi*) which implied that all Japanese nationals were expected to conform to Shinto. Accordingly, "the Christians were persecuted not for the reason that Christianity is an evil religion, but only because it is a foreign religion." The foreign ministers reluctantly agreed that the persecution of Christians was a "political necessity." (*Ibid.*, p. 227.)

tent on treaty revisions, to change its anti-Christian policy.[125] By this time, as noted earlier, some Buddhist leaders also advocated the need for religious liberty—mainly for the purpose of protecting Buddhism from Shinto domination. Under combined pressures from inside and outside, the Meiji regime in 1873 removed the edicts against Christianity.[126] In a strictly legalistic sense, official recognition of Christianity did not take place until freedom of religion was explicitly given by the Constitution of 1889. Nevertheless, with the tacit consent of the government, various branches of Christianity were engaged in active missionary work in the 1870s and 1880s.

As far as the Roman Catholic Church was concerned, the year 1873 marked the end of the persecution of the Kirishitan. Of the Kirishitan who were living in Kyushu at that time, about 14,000 reestablished relations with the priests, while a sizable number of them continued to follow the tradition of the Hanare Kirishitan (separate Kirishitan).[127] The year 1873 also marked the beginning of vigorous Catholic activities under the leadership of Bernard-Thadée Petijean, the bishop. New missionaries were added, Japanese catechists and priests were trained, and institutions of all kinds were established.[128]

---

[125] On the case of Ichikawa, see Sansom, *The Western World and Japan*, pp. 468–69. Iwakura Tomomi, then the most influential statesman, was warned by the American minister that "ill treatment of Christians would affect the friendly relations of the United States with Japan, and when Iwakura shortly afterwards went on his mission to America and Europe he found that the story of Ichikawa was well known in official circles. It was not long after this that the ban upon Christian teaching was removed."

[126] Sansom rightly states: "This order did not specifically cancel the edict against Christianity, but its issue was a convenient and face-saving, if somewhat disingenuous, way of permitting Christian missionary work." (*Ibid.*, p. 442.)

[127] Of the ten thousand inhabitants of the island of Ikitsuki near Hirado, "there are only about 300 Catholics and the rest, with the exception of a handful of pagans, are *hanare*." (Laures, *The Catholic Church in Japan*, p. 228.) Regarding the Hanare Kirishitan in our time, see Tagita, *Shōwa jidai no sempuku Kirishitan*.

[128] Concerning the various activities of the Roman Catholic Church

In 1872 Nicholai of the Russian Orthodox Church moved his headquarters from Hakodate, the port city in Hokkaido, to Tokyo. Convinced from the beginning that the Orthodox Church had to depend on Japanese leadership, Nicholai gathered around him several able converts, including Sawabe Takumaro, a former Shinto priest, and Sakai Tokurei, a former physician.[129] Another Russian priest, Anatoli, joined Nicholai in 1872. Thus the two of them, with the assistance of some Japanese, launched evangelistic and educational programs in Tokyo, Sendai, and Hakodate. In 1875 Sawabe became the first Japanese Orthodox priest, and five years later Nicholai was made bishop.

Meanwhile, the leaders of the various Protestant groups did not remain idle. Initially, the tiny Protestant community in Japan disavowed the evils of denominationalism, as evidenced by the resolution of the first missionary conference in 1872. The so-called Yokohama Church, the first Japanese Protestant Church, established in 1872, was characterized by the same nonsectarian spirit.[130] With the removal of the ban against Christianity in 1873, denominational competition set in, even though some projects such as the translation of the New Testament, completed in 1880, and of the Old Testament, completed in 1888, continued to enjoy interdenominational cooperation. From the beginning, Protestant groups stressed educational work as much as the evangelistic task. There were also ardent Protestants among Westerners employed by the government schools, such as L. L. Janes and William S. Clark.[131] The cause of Protestantism was greatly en-

during this period, see Laures, *The Catholic Church in Japan*, pp. 229–40. In the main, the influence of Catholicism was stronger in Southern Japan. "In 1884 Southern Japan numbered 24,656 Catholics." (*Ibid.*, p. 231.)

[129] In 1871 the membership of the Orthodox Church in Japan was estimated at slightly more than one hundred. It is significant to note that the leaders of the Orthodox Church were "largely intellectuals from among samurai who had supported the Shōgunate." (Kishimoto, *Japanese Religion in the Meiji Era*, p. 183.)

[130] *Ibid.*, pp. 175–83.

[131] Janes, a retired army captain, was invited to teach at the Kumamoto School of Western Learning, which trained samurai youths. In 1875 over thirty of them became Christians under the influence of Janes, and formed

hanced by Niijima Jō, who in 1864 had been smuggled out of Japan, at the risk of his life, and had studied at Andover. Supported by the American Board of Foreign Missions, Niijima, the first ordained Japanese minister, returned to Japan in 1874 and established the Dōshisha School in Kyoto.[132] Two years later, another Japanese pastor, Sawayama Pauro (Paul), returned from America and started his prophetic ministry in Osaka.[133]

Understandably, the Christian movement in modern Japan embodied within itself many problems and contradictions. For the most part, Western missionaries did not differentiate between "Western" and "Christian" values. Also, many of them failed to perceive that they were addressing themselves to one of the most far-reaching sociocultural revolutions, precipitated, to be sure, by the impact of the West. They naïvely hoped that through Christian evangelism and education Western "Christian" culture would displace the traditional "pagan" culture of Japan. "It was not only the eye of faith, but also the eye of the Westerner, who subconsciously lived in the conviction that he could dispose of the destiny of the world. . . ."[134] On the other hand, many of the first-generation Japanese Christian leaders were former samurai or members of the urban gentry. Many of them aspired to "reform Japan through Christianity," which they felt was the spiritual fulfilment of the Meiji Restoration. This conviction drove some of them to

---

the so-called Kumamoto Band. The following year these Christian students from Kumamoto entered the Dōshisha School in Kyoto. Among them were several men who became leaders of the Protestant movement in Japan. Significantly, their Confucian training in the tradition of Wang Yang-ming (Yōmei-gaku in Japanese) provided them with the religious quest which led them to Christianity. (See Kishimoto, pp. 204–9.) Clark, then president of Massachusetts Agricultural College, spent only part of a year in the Agricultural College in Sapporo, Hokkaido. His influence resulted in the formation of the so-called Sapporo Band, a group of Christian students. From this group developed such prominent leaders as Uchimura Kanzō, the founder of the Non-Church Movement, and Nitobe Inazō, a Quaker who later served in the League of Nations.

[132] See Hardy, *Life and Letters of Joseph Hardy Neesima,* and Minoru Watanabe, *Niijima Jō.*

[133] On Sawayama, see Anesaki, *History of Japanese Religion,* pp. 343–46.

[134] Kraemer, *The Christian Message in a Non-Christian World,* p. 36.

educational work and others to political activities. In fact, Kataoka Kenkichi, who later became the Speaker of the House, and Honda Yōichi, who later became a bishop of the Methodist Church, for example, were active both in the Christian movement and in the "popular rights" movement.[135] What characterized these iconoclastic and yet patriotic Christians was their nontheological and ethical tendencies and their unsophisticated biblicism. These Japanese Christian leaders, together with Western missionaries, courageously proclaimed their faith in the midst of almost insurmountable difficulties. But hatred and suspicion of Christianity, nurtured for over two centuries, were not easily driven from the people's minds. Government leaders were determined to impose their own brand of Shinto from above, while Buddhists and others were engaged in anti-Christian campaigns. Besides, Christianity in the nineteenth century was no longer the unrivaled system in the West that it had been during the sixteenth century. The prestige of Christianity was seriously undercut by the "new theology," agnosticism, Unitarianism, and scientific theories.[136] Christian countermeasures to the various forms of criticism were not altogether effective. Instead, increasing emphasis was laid, in the 1880s, on revivalistic movements that aimed at quick conversion of souls. The fact that the churches grew rapidly in numerical strength during the 1880s, however, was a mixed blessing in the long run.[137]

With the promulgation of the Constitution (1889) and of the Imperial Rescript on Education (1890), the "immanental theocracy" of the Meiji regime was firmly established. In this situation,

[135] According to Best, "Unprecedented inroads . . . were made in the countryside as the peasants thought they saw in the Christian emphasis on personal freedom a basis for their struggle in the People's Rights Movement against heavy taxation. . . . More churches were established in the countryside relative to the strength of the church at this time than at any time since." ("Christian Faith and Cultural Crisis: The Japanese Case," *The Journal of Religion*, XLI (No. 1, January, 1961), 21.)

[136] See Schwantes, "Christianity *versus* Science: A Conflict of Ideas in Meiji Japan," *FEQ*, XII (No. 2, February, 1953), 123–32.

[137] On revivalist movements in the 1880s, see Kishimoto, *Japanese Religion in the Meiji Era*, pp. 234–40.

Christianity came under severe attack as an unpatriotic religion. In 1891 Uchimura Kanzō, then lecturer at the First Junior College, refused to bow before the Imperial Rescript; under pressure from the nationalists, he was forced to resign from his teaching position.[138] The spokesman of the anti-Christian camp was Inouye Tetsujirō, then professor of philosophy at the Tokyo Imperial University, who published a book called *Kyōiku to shūkyō no shōtotsu* (A conflict between religion and education) and stressed that the Christian doctrine of universal love was incompatible with the national virtues of loyalty and filial piety taught explicitly in the Imperial Rescript on Education. Soon, nationalists of various kinds joined Inouye in a vigorous anti-Christian campaign, which prompted some Christian leaders to engage in polemics, emphasizing their own loyalty and patriotism.[139] The confused protestations disappeared quickly during the Sino-Japanese War (1894–95). When war broke out, many Christian leaders, having never developed what might be termed a "Christian political philosophy," simply accepted the government's stand and supported the war effort in both the Sino-Japanese and the Russo-Japanese wars. There was, however, a small group of articulate Christian socialists and pacifists. In fact, five of the six founders of the first Social Democratic Party of Japan in 1901 were Christians, and the trade union movement in Japan can also be traced to the Yūai-kai (So-

[138] According to Iglehart, Uchimura did not object to the Rescript, but he did not have time to make up his mind as to how to act in such a situation because "bowing" implied a religious act. "Later he agreed to comply, but it was too late. He resigned from his teaching post, and the impression remained that Christians were disloyal." (Iglehart, *A Century of Protestant Christianity in Japan,* p. 100.)

[139] According to Anesaki, the anti-Christian movement was "not mere chauvinist propaganda but it involved the high aim of bringing back the mind of the nation to the precious heritage fostered by the three religions of Japan." (See his *History of Japanese Religion,* p. 361.) Regardless of the aim involved, polemics turned out to be quite irrational. The only philosopher who stuck to the basic issues of the debate was Ōnishi Hajime (d. 1900). See Saburō Iyenaga, *Kindai Nihon no shisōka,* pp. 113–26. Among the Christian apologists who defended the compatibility of Christianity and patriotism were Honda Yōichi, Yokoi Tokio, Uyemura Masahisa, Kozaki Hiromichi, and a learned Catholic, F. A. D. Lignuel.

ciety of friendly love) organized in 1912 by the Protestant Suzuki Bunji.[140] But, for the most part, Christian leaders in Japan made a passive adjustment to the authoritarian government, and concentrated on the expansion of their respective churches.[141] Christianity was recognized as one of the three major religions and, together with Shinto and Buddhist representatives, Christians participated in the "Conference of Three Religions," sponsored by the government in 1912.[142]

During the First World War and its aftermath the economic imbalance within Japanese society became painfully apparent. As Ernest Best succinctly puts it, the top two percent of Japanese society received ten percent of her total income, while 78 percent of the population, constituting the farmers and working class, lived on one half of the national income. In between was a small middle class which consisted of the technical and managerial group.[143] It was these lesser bureaucrats, technicians, and "Westernized" intellectuals that became the core of the Christian community, especially in Protestant circles, and, as Reischauer points out, "through them the ethics and ideals of Christianity had a much more profound influence on Japanese thought and life than one might assume from the fact that less than 1 per cent of the population became professing Christians." [144] To be sure, there were

[140] Ebisawa, *Gendai Nihon-shūkyō no shi-teki seikaku,* pp. 66–80. It is interesting to note that during the Russo-Japanese War "the still Christian Katayama Sen clasped the hand of the Russian Social Democrat Plekhanov at the Amsterdam meeting of the Socialist International symbolizing its as yet unbroken solidarity." (Totten, "Buddhism and Socialism in Japan and Burma," p. 298.) Regarding Katayama's change from Christian to Communist, see Sumiya, *Katayama Sen.*

[141] A chart giving the expansion of the "Church of Christ in Japan," 1901–11, is given in Kishimoto, *Japanese Religion in the Meiji Era,* p. 288.

[142] *Ibid.,* pp. 299–300. This conference "achieved for Christianity official recognition as one of the three major faiths. But in return for this recognition, the Christians lessened their criticism of the government."

[143] Best, "Christian Faith and Cultural Crisis," p. 24.

[144] E. O. Reischauer, *Japan: Past and Present,* p. 143. Anesaki also notes the Christian influence on the modern Japanese respect for individual personality, sexual morality, and matrimonial relationships. These changes took place because of legal reforms. "Yet without the support of the Chris-

some notable exceptions, such as Kagawa Toyohiko, Suzuki Bunji, and Sugiyama Motojirō, who pioneered various kinds of agrarian reform movements and also actively participated in the labor movement, and Yoshino Sakuzō, Katayama Tetsu, Morito Tatsuo, and Akamatsu Katsumaro, who fought against the authoritarian measures of the government.[145] Nevertheless, the general ethos of the Christian churches in Japan remained predominantly "urban" and "bourgeois." In the 1920s it was not too difficult for Japanese Christians to adjust to the social and political climate of the nation, even though their faith never completely lost its "foreignness," externally or internally. From time to time, when the so-called Christian nations in the West did something contrary to the interests of Japan, such as the passing of the Oriental Exclusion Act by the U. S. Congress, anti-Christian sentiment flared up. By and large, however, the situation was not altogether unfavorable to the normal activities of the Christian churches.

With the beginning of the Manchurian War in 1931 began the state of emergency (*hijōji*) that lasted until the end of the Second World War. Militarists and revolutionary nationalists who rose to power in the 1930s assassinated or intimidated those parliamentarians, financiers, and bureaucrats who did not cooperate with their policy. They were determined to take strong measures in order to establish "a national opinion in which no dissenting voice is heard, by the organization of a great union of the Japanese people," to quote a passage from *Nihon kaizō hōan taikō* (An outline plan for the reorganization of Japan) by Kita Ikki.[146] They further planned "to make East Asiatic people revere the imperial influence by propagating the Imperial Way . . . and to establish the belief that uniting solely under this influence is the one and only way to the external growth and development of East Asia." [147]

---

tian influences the legal reform would not have been so effectively carried through, if not impossible." (Anesaki, *Religious Life of the Japanese People*, p. 90.)

[145] Ebisawa, *Gendai Nihon-shūkyō no shi-teki seikaku*, pp. 84–95.

[146] See Tsunoda, *et al.*, *Sources of Japanese Tradition*, pp. 775–84. The passage quoted is found on p. 776.

[147] *Ibid.*, pp. 804–5. This is a passage from "Draft of Basic Plan for Establishment of Greater East Asia Co-Prosperity Sphere."

Such aims required "domestication" and "reconstruction" of all religions at home so that they might become subservient to the principle of "immanental theocracy," advocated by the ultranationalist regime. Among all religions practiced in Japan, Christianity presented the greatest problem to the government because of its transcendental reference, its claim of universality for its doctrines, and its close ties with the churches in the West. In 1931 several students of St. Sophia University refused to pay homage at the Yasukuni Shrine, Tokyo. Combined pressure from the militarists and Shinto leaders once again exalted the issue of obeisance at the State Shinto shrines as the nonreligious, patriotic duty of all Japanese. Also, militarists engaged in overt anti-Catholic campaigns in some islands of Ryūkyū and in Kagoshima prefecture.[148] In 1936 the Congregatio de Propaganda Fide instructed the papal delegate in Tokyo to the effect that an obeisance at the State Shinto shrine was not to be considered a religious act, and as such could be participated in by Japanese Catholics.[149] In the same year the National Christian Council of the Protestant Churches also publicly accepted the government's interpretation of State Shinto as nonreligious. In 1937 a group of prominent Christians offered a "Christian *norito*" at the Grand Shrine of Ise, asking the Shinto kami to "bring it to pass that the subjects of the empire may quicken and elevate the Japanese spirit as in the Age of the Gods; . . . that they may make the sacred power of the Emperor to shine ever higher. . . ."[150]

In 1936 Japan joined Germany in a so-called anti-Communist pact. This was extended to the Triparte Pact in 1940. At home the Ministry of Education published in 1937 *Kokutai no Hongi* (Fundamentals of our national polity), stressing the unique mission of Japan ruled by a divine emperor.[151] Over two million

[148] See Ebisawa, *Gendai Nihon-shūkyō no shi-teki seikaku*, pp. 98–99.

[149] Kraemer, *The Christian Message in a Non-Christian World*, pp. 403–4.

[150] Quoted in Holtom, *Modern Japan and Shinto Nationalism*, pp. 100–1. See pp. 95–123 for other absurd examples of Christian accommodations during the 1930s.

[151] See Japan. Ministry of Education, *Kokutai no Hongi: Cardinal Principles of the National Entity of Japan.*

copies of this document were eventually circulated to guide the Spiritual Mobilization Movement. Also in 1937 representatives of major religions were called upon to form the Great Unity League of Religions. The Roman Catholics established the National Committee of Catholics for Foreign Propaganda "for enlightening Catholics of other countries in regard to the nation's true aims and motives," while the Executive Committee of the National Christian Council affirmed its "utmost loyalty to Imperial aims, and to accomplish the unity and peace of the Far East, in reverential loyalty to the Imperial Will." [152] Inevitably, consolidation of the Protestant churches was hastened. In 1939 the infamous Religious Organizations Law was enacted in order to place all aspects of the religions under strict government control.[153] In 1940, thirty-four Protestant churches were compelled to form the one "Church of Christ in Japan" (Nihon Kirisuto Kyōdan—commonly referred to as "the Kyōdan") in order to be recognized as a religious organization, the only other Christian body recognized by the Religious Organizations Law being the Roman Catholic Church.[154]

[152] See Iglehart, *A Century of Protestant Christianity in Japan*, pp. 218 and 221.

[153] In proposing the bill, the government stated: "It is regarded as important that the religions prevailing in Japan should foster the idea of our national polity and the spirit of the Imperial Way. . . . For this purpose, it seems necessary to control them." Actually, the first such bill was proposed to the Diet in 1899, but it failed to receive approval "because of the strong opposition of Buddhists, who considered it unfair to treat Christianity on a basis of equality with Buddhism and Shinto." Similar bills proposed in the 1927 and 1929 Diets also failed. See International Institute for the Study of Religions, *Religion and State in Japan*, pp. 70–71.

[154] The Russian Orthodox Church and some smaller Protestant churches, such as the Holiness and Seventh Day Adventist, were not recognized. Part of the Anglican (Episcopal) Church joined the Kyōdan and the remaining part was not recognized. These unrecognized churches were considered "religious associations," subject to the supervision of the local police. The recognized religious organizations, here including Buddhist and Sect Shinto organizations, were tightly controlled by the government in regard to finances, qualifications in ministerial training, and even the faithfulness of the individual members. Later on, all religious organizations were compelled to adopt the "people's ceremony"—a moment of silence with bowed

During the war period the Christian churches as much as other religious groups were exploited by the government as an ideological weapon. Individual priests, ministers, and laymen who did not conform to the aims of the government-sponsored Spiritual Mobilization Movement were jailed, intimidated, or tortured.[155] All religious bodies were expected to send their representatives to the front to comfort the men in the armed forces and also to pray for Japan's victory. The army-dominated Greater East Asia Ministry recruited Catholic and Protestant leaders to interpret Japan's aims to the people in the nations that came within the Co-Prosperity Sphere. In 1944 both the Catholic Church and the Church of Christ joined the Japan Wartime Patriotic Religious Association (Dai-Nihon Senji Shūkyō Hōkoku-kai), in cooperation with Shinto and Buddhist groups. The government even issued, throughout 1944 and 1945, a monthly theme on which all ministers were expected to preach. In those critical years it became very apparent that Christians in Japan, with the exception of some martyrs and prophets, found no other recourse except to succumb to the principle of "immanental theocracy," exemplified by the throne in which both God and Caesar were rolled into one. This unhappy situation lasted until the end of the Second World War.

Confucianism

Lastly, we must not fail to consider the important role played by Confucianism or, more strictly speaking, Neo-Confucianism, in the religious development of modern Japan, in spite of the fact

---

head in memory of the war dead—and the ritual use of the Imperial Rescript on Education in their own religious services. See Iglehart, *A Century of Protestant Christianity in Japan*, p. 248.

[155] See Ebisawa, *Gendai Nihon-shūkyō no shi-teki seikaku*, pp. 106–7. According to Iglehart, the Bureau of Thought Control of the Ministry of Education had "its own powers of punishment for 'subversive thought' paralleling those of the secret police of the Home Ministry in the field of subversive action. Some sixteen thousand individuals during the years 1940 to 1945 were imprisoned by it for suspected disloyal sentiment." (*A Century of Protestant Christianity in Japan*, p. 253.)

that it never claimed to be a religious system. Confucianism served
as an intellectual bridge between the feudal and modern periods;
it also provided the ethical foundations of the "immanental theocracy" of the new imperial regime. Earlier we noted that the Tokugawa shogunate had adopted Neo-Confucianism as the "official
theology" of its sociopolitical engineering, even though it did not
transform society according to the Chinese model. The influence
of Neo-Confucianism was felt strongly in legal institutions and
educational work, and thus it furnished normative principles for
individual and public morality. Japanese Neo-Confucianism, being eclectic in ethos, found no difficulty in allying itself with
Shinto as well as with the "Code of Warriors" (*Bushidō*). The
shogunate was primarily interested in the practical moral teachings of the Confucian tradition and not in its speculative aspects.
Certainly the "dangerous" features of Confucianism, such as the
doctrines of abdication and of righteous rebellion, were abhorred
by the regime. Thus, the primary task of Confucian teachers during the Tokugawa period was to develop a pragmatic hermeneu-
tics to be applied to the interpretation of those elements of the
Confucian tradition that would uphold the given social order and
instill them as moral virtues into the populace.

Following the hierarchical principle, the shogunate originally
had intended to educate only the elite, that is, the children of the
daimyo and samurai who were regarded as the bearers of culture.
But after the middle of the Tokugawa period, the shogunate sanctioned and encouraged the development of private schools called
terakoya (temple schools), supported by well-to-do farmers and
merchants for the education of their boys and girls, and "by the
close of the Tokugawa period 15,862 of these institutions were
reported as in operation." [156] In the main, the "temple schools"

[156] Supreme Commander for the Allied Powers. Civil Information and
Education Section. Education Division. *Education in the New Japan*, I,
21. The teachers at these temple schools were not necessarily Buddhist
priests. Often physicians, *rōnin*, farmers, and merchants who were qualified
to teach the three arts—reading, writing, and the use of the abacus—
served as instructors. See Sakata, ed., *Meiji ishin-shi no mondaiten*, pp.
224–25. For a glimpse of an above-average Confucian training given to
children in the nineteenth century, see Junesay Iddittie, *The Life of*

provided only the minimum of education plus instruction in simple moralistic precepts. Nevertheless, through these schools as well as through semireligious movements such as the Shin-gaku (Mind learning) and the Hō-toku (Repaying the indebtedness) which have been mentioned earlier, the general populace came directly or indirectly under the influence of the Confucian tradition, however distorted it might have been.

As pathological fear of the Kirishitan waned, the shogunate relaxed in 1716 the edicts against foreign (Dutch) learning in order to acquire new and better knowledge in medical and other scientific and technological spheres. With the encouragement of officialdom, the latter half of the eighteenth century witnessed the growth of Dutch learning (*rangaku*).[157] The pioneers of Dutch learning were the intelligentsia of the time, which meant that they had had thorough Confucian training. These men took it for granted that "knowledge" could be divided into two main divisions—the essential and the practical. They never questioned the proposition that Confucian teachings were essential for the moral cultivation of men, whereas what they acquired from Dutch books, covering such Western subjects as medicine and botany, was regarded merely as "practical or real learning" (*jitsu-gaku*). There were some conservative elements in society that reacted emotionally against the Dutch learning, but many Confucianists accepted it on pragmatic grounds. This attitude was succinctly stated by Sakuma Zōzan (1811–64) who advocated the famous motto: *Tōyō no Dōtoku, Seiyō no Gakugei* (Eastern ethics and Western

---

Marquis Shigenobu Ōkuma, pp. 35–36. Incidentally, an exceedingly long novel called *Nansō Satomi hakkenden* (usually translated as "The eight retainers of Satomi"), in nine volumes, was written over a period of twenty-seven years (1814–41) by Kyokutei Bakin. Running through this complicated novel is a theme based on the mixture of the "Code of Warriors" and Confucian morality, stressing the victory of poetic justice. See Kokusai Bunka Shinkōkai, *Introduction to Classic Japanese Literature*, pp. 331–41, and Keene, comp. and ed., *Anthology of Japanese Literature*, pp. 423–28. The fact that such a novel was widely read indicates that there was a sufficient amount of appreciation for Confucian morality among the people.

[157] Sansom, *The Western World and Japan*, pp. 204–5.

science). He and others like him were persuaded that the *li* (reason or principle) taught by Neo-Confucianism and the principle of Western science were one and the same, and it was this Confucian-inspired rationale that enabled the late Tokugawa leaders to reverse their policy of national seclusion. It also provided reasons for the early Meiji leaders to appropriate "wisdom and knowledge" from abroad.

In this connection, we must not overlook the fact that Dutch learning, accepted merely as "practical learning," exerted far greater influence than was originally anticipated. Knowledge of Western geography and economics stimulated some of the Japanese intelligentsia to argue in favor of opening Japan's doors to the rest of the world in order to alleviate the economic distress of the nation.[158] Far more important was the fact that through Dutch learning the spirit of "modernity" was inhaled even by those who were anti-Western. Indeed, the attitude of critical inquiry and the scientific method of investigation that previously had been unknown in the scholarly tradition in Japan began to penetrate not only among scholars of Dutch learning but also among the advocates of Confucian and National Learning as well. In a real sense, the sudden emergence of vigor and vitality in the Mito school of Neo-Confucianism and the Hirata school of Neo-Shinto toward the close of the Tokugawa period may be ascribed to the infiltration of the spirit of "modernity." [159] Not that these schools changed their intellectual contents to any significant degree, but that the scholars of the Mito school and the Hirata school no longer accepted their scholarship as sheer intellectual labor; they were now determined to apply their learning to the practical end of reshaping society and the nation. Significantly, these two schools, despite some basic differences in outlook and motivation,

[158] See Tsunoda, *et al., Sources of Japanese Tradition*, pp. 552–61.

[159] *Ibid.*, pp. 546–47. A significant statement by Hirata Atsutane himself is cited here. Hirata praises the Dutch for their scientific method. Unlike China, Holland does not depend on "superficial conjectures." He goes on to say that "their findings, which are the results of hundreds of people studying scientific problems . . . have been incorporated in books which have been presented to Japan."

agreed on a practical objective, namely the royalist cause. The combined energy of the leaders of these two schools provided the moral and intellectual fervor that guided the national life through its critical transition from the feudal to the modern phase.

Meanwhile, the Western powers that had begun to establish overseas colonial empires in various parts of Asia were extending their influence toward the Far East, so that from the turn of the nineteenth century onward foreign ships began to appear in Japanese waters. Realizing the inadequacy of the traditional Japanese weapons for the protection of Japanese coasts from possible foreign invasions, the feudal authorities turned to the scholars of Dutch learning for practical assistance. In this situation, these scholars shifted their emphasis from medicine, economics, and botany to military science.[160] Following the infamous Anglo-Chinese War, known as the "Opium War" (1839–42), which incidentally was reported to Japan through Chinese and Dutch sources, the shogunate allowed the study of English, French, and German in addition to Dutch. With the transformation of Dutch learning (*rangaku*) into the broader Western learning (*yōgaku*), Japan's intellectual isolation was further broken down. This trend was accentuated by Perry's first expedition in 1853, whereupon the shogunate established a Westernized Naval Academy in 1855

---

[160] According to Sansom, Takashima Shūhan (1798–1866), the pioneer of Westernized military science in Japan, purchased modern weapons from Holland and translated some books on military subjects, and "by about 1840 he had made such progress that he was able to train in Western style two companies of infantry and a battery of artillery and had gained a considerable knowledge of the technical processes in the manufacture of ordnance." (*The Western World and Japan*, p. 249.) Takashima's disciple, Egawa Tarōzayemon (1800–55), opened a school teaching Westernized military science. It was Egawa's disciple, Sakuma Zōzan, a convinced Confucianist, who tirelessly advocated the adoption of Western military methods and influenced such prominent figures as Katsu Awa (1823–1900), first navy minister in the Meiji regime, and Yoshida Shōin (1830–59), who, because of his sense of mission to turn back the Western powers, tried to stow away on one of the American ships under Perry's command in order to study in America. Although he failed in this attempt, he inspired Kido Kōin, Itō Hirobumi, Yamagata Aritomo, and other youths to become leaders at the time of the Meiji Restoration.

and the Bansho shirabe-sho (Office for the investigation of Western books) two years later.[161] Some of the daimyo, such as the lords of Satsuma, Chōshū, Saga, and Echizen, also encouraged Western learning, ostensibly for the purpose of improving their economic situation and defense program. A number of intelligent samurai youths were recruited to study Western learning which was regarded as the only effective weapon to hold back the encroachment of Western nations. Many of these youths thus trained in Western learning became leaders of the new Japan. They were nationalists, grounded in the Confucian tradition, and they were motivated to synthesize "Eastern ethics and Western science" for the benefit of the nation.

With the establishment of the Meiji regime in 1868, the coalition of National Learning (*kokugaku,* that was equated with the Neo-Shinto movement), Confucian learning (*jugaku,* also called *kangaku* or "Chinese learning"), and Western learning (*yōgaku*) came to an end. In the process of creating a new national image, Shinto was clearly in the saddle, for it alone was equipped to exalt the throne as the legitimate heir to the imperial charisma handed down from the sun goddess, Amaterasu. And the architects of the new regime made full use of the Shinto-inspired rationale of the imperial authority for the unification of the nation. They also encouraged Western learning in order to seek knowledge from all over the world toward the end of maintaining national prosperity and defense (*fukoku-kyōhei*). Confucian learning was squeezed out and neglected, or at least so the Confucian scholars felt. Actually, the Confucian tradition was far from being dead. Confucian ethics remained as the only meaningful norm for family and other interhuman relations, and words of Chinese origin which had Confucian connotations were coined to appropriate new ideas introduced from the West.[162] However, Confucianism lost the honors and prerogatives which, as the most influential intellectual tradition, it had enjoyed during the Toku-

---

[161] The Bansho shirabe-sho was renamed the Kaisei-jo in 1863; this school became the nucleus of the Imperial University of Tokyo early in the Meiji Era.

[162] See Nitobe, *et al., Western Influences in Modern Japan,* p. 175.

gawa regime, for many of the early Meiji leaders, notwithstanding their indebtedness to Confucian training during their childhood, turned to Western civilization for intellectual and technological assistance in the task of shaping the course of the nation in the modern world.

If Western influence could have been confined to technological and academic spheres alone, as the Meiji regime had hoped, it would not have caused so much anxiety for the government leaders. If that had been possible, Japan could have developed both a highly centralized hierarchical polity and an efficient, "modern" technological civilization. Instead, Western influence resulted in the emergence of a new intelligentsia that demanded liberty, equality, and human dignity. What the Westernized intelligentsia envisaged was not the kind of technological civilization that was merely to serve the political ends defined by a few men who surrounded the throne, but the kind of civilization that "advances the well-being and dignity of man, since man acquires these benefits through knowledge and virtue," to quote Fukuzawa Yukichi, the spokesman of the modernist movement.[163] It is to be noted that the "virtue," advocated by Fukuzawa, was not the traditional Confucian virtue, based on that hierarchical relationship in which one is expected to know one's place and to fulfill his obligations with diligence, humility, and obedience. Convinced that all men and women were created equal and furnished with the same dignity without distinction, Fukuzawa and others like him instilled the spirit of "modernity" in the minds of youths who were impatient with the traditional values. Although Fukuzawa had had the usual Confucian training in his childhood, he was critical of the Confucian teachings that stressed trust in the words of ancient Chinese sages. He was against any attempt to look for a model of the new society in the past—in the golden days of Yao and Shun. He went so far as to say: "What the ancients achieved is of their time, what we achieve is of our time. Why study the past to function in the present?"[164] The modernists' influence was strongly felt in the educational philosophy of the early Meiji Era, and some of

[163] Quoted in Kosaka, *Japanese Thought in the Meiji Era,* p. 73.
[164] *Ibid.,* p. 74.

them even favored the adoption of Christianity for practical reasons.

The apparent popularity of the modernist movement, especially among the young people in urban areas, aroused fear and resentment among the conservative elements in government circles. The government leaders realized, however, that Shinto, important though it was as the foundation of the new Japan, lacked the intellectual and moral content that was necessary for the nation. Thus, they soft-pedaled anti-Buddhist measures and also sought the alliance of Confucian scholars. Conversely, both Buddhist and Confucian leaders, alarmed at the penetration of "foreign" influence, rallied behind Shinto and the government leaders in their attempt to preserve and strengthen the principle of "immanental theocracy" in the new Japan. However, as we have noted earlier, the government's effort in establishing a new national cult called "Great Teaching or Doctrine" (Daikyō), amalgamating Buddhism and Confucianism within the Shinto framework, was doomed to failure.[165] Thus the government resorted to the ingenious measure of creating State Shinto, which was declared to be nonreligious, over and above all religions which were allowed nominal autonomy.

In this situation, Japanese Confucian leaders also attempted to make a comeback. Unfortunately for them, the Confucian college called Shōheizaka Gakumonjo, which had been supported by the Tokugawa regime, was transformed into the government university in 1868. In the same year a group of Confucianists organized the Shisei-kai (Association of equality of ideas), but it soon declined.[166] Undaunted, the Confucianists established another society called the Shibun Gakkai (Society for the cause of truth), which, in the opinion of a contemporary scholar on modern Japanese Confucianism, was "the most important Confucian organization in Japan in the years from 1880 to 1918."[167] A number of other

[165] One of the cardinal teachings of the *Daikyō* was the Confucian morality of the five relationships.

[166] For a fuller explanation of the name of this society, see Warren W. Smith, Jr., *Confucianism in Modern Japan*, p. 56, n. 53.

[167] *Ibid.*, p. 57. For the activities of the Shibun Gakkai, see pp. 57–63.

Confucian and semi-Confucian organizations also came into being
—the Tokyo Shūshin Gaku-sha (Tokyo society for moral training)
in 1876, the Nippon Kōdō-kai (Japanese association for the teaching of the Way) in 1884, and the Nippon Kokkyō Daidō-sha
(Great association for the establishment of the Japanese national
teachings) in 1888.[168] These organizations were supported by some
of the imperial princes, former court nobles, conservative politicians, and businessmen. While we cannot discuss their activities in
detail, we can safely say that they primarily promoted Confucian
ethics as the moral foundation of the nation. Their initial attempt
at influencing the policies of the Ministry of Education was re-
buffed by those who advocated Westernized education. It was
through the Ministry of the Imperial Household that the Confucianists influenced the throne, as evidenced in the Confucian contents of the Imperial Rescript on Education. In so doing, they
eventually made a decisive impact on the Ministry of Education's
educational philosophy.[169]

The promulgation of the Constitution (1889) and of the Imperial Rescript on Education (1890) are, as Hugh Borton observes,
two sides of the same coin. "That coin was the consolidation in the
socio-political-economic life of Japan of a highly centralized authoritarian form of social organization based upon respect for the
Emperor and the Confucian concept of filial piety. . . . The Imperial Rescript on Education rather than the new Constitution was
the 'new axis of the new order.' "[170] In the Rescript, we read:

Our Imperial Ancestors have founded our Empire on a basis broad
and everlasting, and have deeply and firmly implanted virtue; Our
subjects ever united in loyalty and filial piety have from generation
to generation illustrated the beauty thereof. This is the glory of the

---

[168] *Ibid.*, pp. 64–68. Among the less important were the Rongo-kai (Confucian Analect society) and the Kōshi-kyō-kai (Society for Confucian
teachings); both existed in the 1880s.

[169] On the role played by Motoda Eifu in the preparation of the Imperial Rescript, see Shively, "Motoda Eifu: Confucian Lecturer to the
Meiji Emperor," in Nivison and Wright, eds., *Confucianism in Action*,
pp. 302–33.

[170] Borton, *Japan's Modern Century*, p. 180.

fundamental character of Our Empire, and herein also lies the source of Our Education. Ye, Our Subjects, be filial to your parents, affectionate to your brothers and sisters; as husbands and wives be harmonious, as friends true; bear yourselves in modesty and moderation; extend your benevolence to all; pursue learning and cultivate arts, and thereby develop intellectual faculties and perfect moral powers. . . .[171]

Significantly, the Rescript made no mention of the Chinese sages. Rather, the Confucian virtues are taught as the basic moral principles of Japan, bequeathed to the people of Japan by the imperial ancestors. This implied, however, that Confucian ethical principles had to be completely subordinated to the claims of "immanental theocracy" of the Meiji regime. The transmutation of Confucianism from a semireligious ethical system, based on the teachings of Chinese sages, into an "indigenous" patriotic ethic enabled Japanese Confucianists in the modern period to pontificate on educational and political questions. For example, a noted Confucianist, Inouye Tetsujirō, championed the cause of the anti-Christian movement on the ground that Christianity, being a "foreign" religion, was incompatible with the spirit of the Imperial Rescript on Education.[172] The most conspicuous influence of the Confucian tradition is seen in the "moral teaching" (*shūshin*), a required subject in the primary and secondary schools until the end of the Second World War. The "moral teaching," which was designed to inculcate "Japanized" Confucian virtues and to strengthen faith in the national polity in harmony with the Imperial Rescript on Education, was considered the basis of education so that boys and girls would become first and foremost faithful subjects of the emperor both in time of peace and in time of war.[173] The transmutation of Confucianism meant, however, that Japanese Confucianism lost its prerogatives as an independent semireligious system, comparable to Shinto and Buddhism. Even the Confucian festival,

[171] Official English translation.

[172] Inouye's anti-Christian campaign was noted earlier in connection with Buddhism and Christianity.

[173] For the militaristic spirit that was inculcated through education, see Shigetaka Fukuchi, *Gunkoku-Nippon no keisei*, pp. 212–48.

held at the Confucian temple (*Seidō*) at Yushima, Tokyo, in 1907, was conducted with Shinto-style ritual,[174] and the "Conference of the Three Religions," sponsored by the Japanese government in 1912, invited representatives of Shinto, Buddhism, and Christianity, but none from Confucianism, as such, on the ground that Confucianism was a system of nonreligious ethical teachings that were to be practiced by all Japanese nationals regardless of their religious faith. In this situation, "nonreligious" Confucian ethics and State Shinto, which was propagated by government leaders as a "nonreligious" patriotic cult, developed a new coalition.

Once Japanese Confucianism accepted the premise that Confucian ethics were part and parcel of the indigenous, pristine Japanese heritage, it was easy for Confucian scholars to support the ethnocentric pseudo religion of the state, based on loyalty and filial piety, justifying authoritarianism at home and expansionism abroad. Despite the lofty ethical principles of the Chinese sages, transmitted by the long tradition of Japanese Confucianism, its highest affirmation was now addressed to the throne and to the unique national polity of Japan. The historic Confucian doctrine of *wang-tao* (or *Ō-dō* in Japanese: "Way of true kingship") was reinterpreted in terms of *kō-dō* (the imperial way), and its ethical universalism was transformed into *Nihon-shugi* (Japanese-ism).[175] Ironically, Confucian scholars were not concerned with the new ethical issues that confronted modern Japan; they were more pre-occupied with the preservation of the *status quo* against the encroachment of Western influence, Christianity, and, more basically, of the spirit of "modernity." Even the monogamy advocated by Christians was criticized by a noted Confucianist, Ōtsuki Nyoden (1845–1931), as incompatible with the preservation of the imperial line, for the practice of such a principle might cause the extinction of the imperial house.[176] The Confucianists advocated

[174] See Hiyane, *Nihon shūkyō-shi*, p. 1052.

[175] Toshisuke Murakami and Yoshio Sakata, *Meiji bunkashi: Kyōiku-dōtoku-hen*, pp. 486–98.

[176] See Warren W. Smith, Jr., *Confucianism in Modern Japan*, p. 95. According to Smith, "Ōtsuki concluded that professors and propagandists of the Christian faith were equivalent to national traitors."

the primacy of Chinese studies (*kangaku*) in public school education as the basis for moral learning, and they promoted the moral example of superiors and elders as the answer to social, economic, and political problems. Some of the business leaders who were supporters of the Confucian cause thought that the cultivation of harmony would eliminate conflicts between capital and labor. Bureaucrats cited Confucian classics to reject political democracy in favor of paternalistic authoritarianism as the only system sanctioned by Heaven. Furthermore, socialism, communism, capitalism, and materialism were condemned as the evil products of Western civilization, which according to Japanese Confucianists was doomed to decline. The anti-Western theme of the Japanese Confucianists became more accentuated in the 1930s, especially after the establishment of the Nihon Jukyō Senyō-kai (Japanese Society for the Promotion of Confucianism) in 1934. Accordingly, the Confucianists asserted that Japan was a unique nation that had preserved moral virtues, and that she had as her mission the extension of her moral influence to the rest of the world.[177]

The moralistic rationalization of Japan's aggressive measures in terms of Confucianism was not a novel idea, however. For example, as early as 1895, when Taiwan became a Japanese possession, Japanese authorities portrayed themselves as benevolent and enlightened masters who had the divine commission to emancipate the inhabitants of the island from its state of chaos, ignorance, and misery, and as a gesture to show their good faith they supported Confucian temples in Taiwan. Also, following the annexation of Korea in 1910, Japanese officials encouraged Korean Confucian institutions.[178] It is not altogether clear, however, how effective was the Japanese policy of utilizing Confucianism to ameliorate the natural resentment of the Taiwanese and Koreans toward Japan. When Manchukuo was created by the Japanese militarists in 1931, Japan staged a massive propaganda campaign to the effect that she was assisting the restoration of *wang-tao* (The way of true kingship) under the leadership of Pu Yi, the deposed Manchu

[177] *Ibid.*, pp. 147–66.

[178] *Ibid.*, pp. 166–84, for Japanese policy regarding Confucianism in Korea.

emperor, in this new state.[179] With the outbreak of warfare with China in 1937, and throughout the Second World War, Japanese propagandists in China followed the line that Japan was fighting for the preservation of Oriental culture against the evils of Western influence and Communism, represented by the Kuomintang and the Communists, respectively. The use of the Confucian heritage as an ideological and cultural weapon, however, failed to rally the majority of the Chinese people around the Japanese cause.[180]

In a sense the modern development of Japanese Confucianism was closely related to the development of modern Japan with all her promises and problems. The smooth transition of Japan from her feudal past to the status of a modern state would have been impossible without the guidance of the samurai intelligentsia who were grounded in Confucian learning. It was the Confucian-inspired rationale—that *li* or reason is universal, while knowledge can be divided into "essential" and "practical"—that enabled modern Japan to seek knowledge from the rest of the world, without disturbing the moral fiber of Japanese society. At the same time, it was the same Confucian-inspired rationale that gave encouragement to the strengthening of the particularity and uniqueness of the Japanese heritage. Thus modern Japan was destined to be caught in the grip of two diametrically opposed objectives envisaged by the architects of the Meiji regime. One of them, the reestablishment or restoration (*fukko*) of the ancient system of unity of religion and government (*saisei-itchi*), drove Japan to assert the centrality of State Shinto as the new super religion, ironically declared to be "nonreligious," over all other religious and cultural traditions. However, the second objective, namely, renovation (*ishin*), brought about the introduction, not only of technological and scientific advances, envisaged by the Meiji government, but of philosophical and religious as well as political influences of the modern West.

Caught between these two objectives, the scholars of Confucian-

[179] *Ibid.*, pp. 184–99.

[180] *Ibid.*, pp. 199–223. It is significant to note that the effort of the Kuomintang to guide war-torn China with a modified Confucian ideology was also doomed to failure after the Second World War.

ism, as much as the leaders of Shinto and Buddhism, sided with the conservative reaction against Western influences, against novelty, and against "modernity." They provided the moral and religious fervor for the voice of the past that cried for the preservation of the particular historical experience of the Japanese without any reference to the universal historical experience of mankind. Japanese Confucianism, for example, stressed only those Confucian virtues that were congenial to the social and political order of Japan at the expense of the ethical universalism embodied in the teachings of the Chinese sages. Thus Japanese Confucianists followed an oversimplified formula: that the substance of Confucianism is equivalent to the Japanese spirit and moral heritage, which is anti-Western and antimodern. This formula was, however, reinterpreted under the influence of revolutionary nationalism and militarism, so that Japanese Confucianists, like many leaders of other faiths, accepted the thesis that what is good for Japan is good for Taiwan, Korea, Manchuria, China, and all other nations in Southeast Asia and in other parts of the world. Religions and semireligions were utilized to sanction and support the principle of *hakkō ichi-u* (The whole world under one roof), ruled over by the emperor, regarded as the living kami.[181]

What was taken for granted by Japanese leaders in the nineteenth and twentieth centuries was their ethnocentric belief in the superindividual which was the Japanese nation itself. It was this national affirmation of the underlying religion of "immanental theocracy" that drove Japan down the dreadful and fateful path toward the Second World War.

[181] See Holtom, *Modern Japan and Shinto Nationalism*, pp. 21–23.

CHAPTER VI

Old Dreams or New Vision?

SOME REFLECTIONS ON THE RELIGIOUS SITUATION IN POSTWAR JAPAN

The surrender of Japan to the Allied Powers in the summer of 1945 undoubtedly marked the greatest turning point in the recent history of Japan.[1] The fanatic schemes of the militarists and ultra-nationalists to establish their so-called Co-prosperity Sphere in Asia under Japan's leadership had crumbled. Japan in turn came under the rule of the Allied Powers. In principle, the occupation policy was to be determined by the Far Eastern commission, established by the nations that had participated in the fighting on the Pacific front, and the Supreme Commander for the Allied Powers (SCAP) was expected to consult the representatives of the United States, the Soviet Union, the British Commonwealth, and China—the nations that constituted the Allied Council. In reality, however, the occupation of Japan was conducted almost solely by the United States, and Douglas MacArthur, the first Supreme Commander for the Allied Powers, singlehandedly directed the activities of the Army of Occupation, the headquarters staff in charge of various sections, and a series of military government teams assigned to individual prefectures. Thus, Japan's postwar destiny depended to a great extent on the policies of the United States toward Japan.

During the initial period of the occupation, the American plan aimed at the complete demilitarization of Japan so that she would not become a menace to the peace of the world, and at the estab-

---

[1] See Butow, *Japan's Decision to Surrender.*

lishment of an advanced democracy. In order to achieve these ends, the occupation authorities disbanded the Japanese Imperial General Headquarters, restored political parties, issued what amounted to a "Bill of Rights" removing restrictions on political, civil, and religious liberties, and discrimination on the grounds of race, nationality, creed, or political opinion, and ordered the release of political prisoners. At the same time, all nondemocratic institutions, such as the secret police and other agencies charged with the control of thought, speech, or religion, and with censorship of the press, were abolished. Those who were declared to be "undesirable personnel" were purged from public office,[2] and an International Military Tribunal for the Far East was established to prosecute "war criminals." The first postwar election was held in 1946, and the new, American-inspired Constitution became effective the following year. At the same time, the occupation authorities encouraged the organization of labor unions, and pursued the liquidation of monopolistic combines and the decentralization of economic power and rural land reform, as well as sweeping changes in the educational system. Indeed, as Edwin Reischauer has stated, "the United States, which has usually appeared to be the champion of the *status quo* elsewhere in the world, was clearly a revolutionary force in Japan."[3]

It must be mentioned in this connection that the occupation authorities followed the policy of making as much use of the throne and the bureaucratic government structure of Japan as possible, so that the occupation could be carried out with the least possible expenditure of Allied manpower and resources. This meant, however, that the meaning of the imperial institutions and of the governmental structure had to be redefined in terms of democratic principles. Accordingly, the new Constitution states

[2] U.S. Department of State, *Occupation of Japan: Policy and Progress,* p. 20: "As a direct result of the directives of January 4, 1946, nine out of every ten high officials of the Japanese Government were declared ineligible to hold office, and 120 political organizations were put to the process of dissolution. The Japanese press estimated that 150,000 persons were affected by the directives." On this question, see also Baerwald, *The Purge of Japanese Leaders under the Occupation.*

[3] Edwin O. Reischauer, *Japan: Past and Present,* p. 210.

that "the Emperor shall be the symbol of the state and of the unity of the people, deriving his position from the sovereign will of the people," and that he shall perform only such state functions as are provided for in the Constitution. The wording of the Constitution is equally specific when it declares that "war, as a sovereign right of the nation and the threat or use of force, is forever renounced as a means of settling disputes with other nations. The maintenance of land, sea, and air forces, as well as other war potential, will never be authorized." The Constitution also makes clear that "the Diet shall be the highest organ of state power, and shall be the sole law-making authority of the State," and that "the Cabinet, in the exercise of executive power, shall be collectively responsible to the Diet," while "the whole judicial power is vested in a Supreme Court and in such inferior courts as are established by law." The high ideals and democratic tenets that characterized the new Constitution are succinctly summarized in Article XCIII: "The fundamental human rights by this Constitution guaranteed to the people of Japan result from the age-old struggle of man to be free. They have survived the exacting test for durability in the crucible of time and experience, and are conferred upon this and future generations in sacred trust, to be held for all time inviolate." [4]

Ironically, even before the new Constitution became effective in 1947, American policy began to shift its emphasis from the democratization and demilitarization of Japan to making Japan a strong anti-Communist island fortress in the Pacific. Within Japan the political leaders, who were by and large conservative men from prewar days, tended to welcome the anti-Communist policy of the occupation authority, whereas labor unions, students, peace organizations, and the intelligentsia were alarmed by the possibility that their rights and privileges, guaranteed by the democratic Constitution, might be violated again in the name of anti-Communism. The resentment on the part of the general populace toward the Japanese government, which after all had no recourse but to follow the directions of the occupation authorities, was intensified by the precarious economic situation that inevitably followed the end of

---

[4] For more about the Constitution, see U.S. Department of State, *Occupation of Japan: Policy and Progress,* pp. 117–32.

the war. Understandably, this explosive condition was exploited by the Communists who, incidentally, had been given legal protection by the new Constitution. Dismayed by such an unexpected turn of events, MacArthur resorted to such authoritarian measures as banning the general strike of government employees early in 1947, banning the railway strike in the summer of 1948, and directing the purge of Communist leaders in the summer of 1950.

In a more fundamental sense, the shift of emphasis in the American policy toward Japan reflected changes in the international situation, notably the development of the cold war between the two major powers. In Asia, too, the political situation was greatly altered through the granting of independence to India and Pakistan (1947), the formation of South and North Korean states (1948), the emergence of the Communist state on the mainland of China, and the independence of Indonesia (1949). With the outbreak of the Korean War in 1950, MacArthur assumed, in addition to his duties in Japan, the command of the United Nations' forces in Korea.[5] The extent of hostilities in Korea was such that the attention of the United States became focused "primarily on military developments in Korea rather than on civil reform in Japan," even though the Japanese economy improved markedly on account of American military expenditures.[6] In this situation, both for the protection of Japan from radical Communist influence and also to preserve Japan as an anti-Communist ally of the West, the occupation authorities persuaded the Japanese government to establish a National Police Reserve of 75,000 men, which was later increased to 200,000 and was renamed the Self-Defense Force.[7]

[5] In 1951 MacArthur was replaced by Matthew B. Ridgway. Ridgway was in Japan until after the signing of the Peace Treaty. In 1952 he was replaced as United Nations and United States Commander in the Far East by Mark W. Clark.

[6] E. O. Reischauer, *Japan: Past and Present,* p. 217.

[7] Many people in Japan like to point out that it was the Americans who instituted in 1945 the complete demilitarization, so that Japan might become the "Switzerland of Asia." Until such time as amendment of the American-inspired Constitution takes place, the problem of rearmament will remain a thorny issue, especially since rearmament is such an expensive matter. The military budget has been the favorite target of labor unions, students, intellectuals, pacifists, and religious groups.

Moreover, Japanese trade with America and other nations was resumed in 1950, and in the summer of 1951 the purge orders for most of the so-called undesirable personnel were lifted in order to improve the morale of the nation.[8] On September 8, 1951, Japan signed a peace treaty in San Francisco with forty-eight nations as well as a security pact with the United States. In 1952 an administrative agreement over terms for American bases in Japan was signed, and in 1960 a revised mutual security treaty was signed between the United States and Japan.[9] Since the eleventh session (1956–57) of the General Assembly, Japan has taken an active part in the affairs of the United Nations, too.

The complexity of the postwar situation in Japan is due in part to the fact that external pressures on the island nation come not only from the United States but also from the rest of the world. It must be kept in mind that while Japan, since 1945, has been closely identified with the "Free World," geographically she is destined to remain close to Communist China and Russia. Economically she has to trade with the neutral nations of Asia, if she wants to survive at all. Yet, how to chart her course without alienating one side or the other is an exceedingly difficult problem. For example, Japanese leaders in 1951 held high hopes of developing an economic alliance with the United States in order to reinforce their political and military agreements, and if possible to replace the United States at least partially as a supplier of goods to the less developed nations. The United States, however, assured no favored status to Japan.[10] Realizing that their nation was ex-

[8] In June, 1951, 69,000 persons were depurged, and the following month 14,000 more persons' purge restrictions were lifted. As a result, many conservative politicians and financiers became available again for public office.

[9] The signing of the mutual security treaty caused riots and demonstrations in Japan so extensive that the cabinet of Kishi Nobusuke had to resign.

[10] See Guillain, "Japan's New Phase: Future of Foreign Trade," in *The Manchester Guardian Weekly*, October 18, 1951. He points out that Great Britain reacted very strongly against the idea of a Japanese-American economic alliance. "Washington is keen to reassure the British that the Japanese will not be given *carte blanche* to do as they like and to calm British

pected to take her chances on the international market, many Japanese industrialists questioned the wisdom of her total economic dependence on the "Free World" and began to seek trade with nations in Southeast Asia, with India, and to some extent with Mainland China and Russia.[11] At any rate, with the increase in trade and cultural exchange, Japan will be more and more exposed to influences from various parts of the world. There is, as yet, a deep-rooted fear and suspicion on the part of Asian nations that Japan might become a threat to them again. Only time will tell how soon Japan, with her industrial potential, her huge reservoir of skilled workers, and her advanced technology, will be accepted as a genuine partner among the developing nations of Asia, while maintaining her friendship with the nations in the West.

"Immanental Theocracy" versus Religious Liberty

It was pointed out earlier that, while the architects of the Meiji regime rejected the shogunate, they had even strengthened the principle of "immanental theocracy," inherited from the Tokugawa feudal regime. Their attempt to reconcile the ancient Japanese polity of monarchical rule and the modern technological civilization of the West was implemented in terms of *saisei-itchi* (unity of religion and government), wherein State Shinto—a newly concocted "nonreligious" or "superreligious" cult of national morality and patriotism—was superimposed on nominal constitutional guarantees of freedom of religious belief. The key to this grand scheme was the imperial institution itself. According to the Constitution of 1889 as it affirmed the principle of direct imperial rule, the emperor was declared to be "sacred and inviolable." This implied, on the one hand, that the right of the people to participate in the government was greatly curtailed because of the absolute preroga-

---

fears of a complete and permanent United States control over Japanese industry."

[11] Many Japanese industrialists still remember China as Japan's chief market and source of raw materials before the war. Increasing numbers of Japanese businessmen visit China to promote mutual trade. Even some politically conservative industrialists seem to hold that they can separate economics and politics in regard to Mainland China.

tives of the throne, yet it also meant, on the other hand, that the "sacred and inviolable" emperor could not be held responsible for the management or mismanagement of national affairs. Consequently, actual authority rested neither in the throne nor in the people, but was in the hands of bureaucratic officials and powerful political, military, and financial cliques.

Notwithstanding the legal ambiguity of the nature of imperial rule in the Constitution of 1889, the architects of the Meiji regime depended heavily on the throne to unify the nation. The throne was exalted through imperial edicts, educational institutions, and indoctrination of the military, less as a "political authority" than as a "living kami," in direct descent from the heavenly kami of Japanese mythology, and thus was regarded by some as more dignified than all Shinto and Buddhist divinities.[12] No one was allowed to question the emperor's wisdom or intelligence; he was to be venerated and his birthday was to be observed as a semi-religious national holiday. Even when the emperor happened to be sick or incompetent, the throne as such remained "sacred and inviolable." [13] What was important in accordance with the Imperial Rescript of February 3, 1870, was that "the Heavenly Deities and the Great Ancestress [Amaterasu Ōmikami] established the throne and made the succession secure. The line of emperors in unbroken succession entered into possession thereof and handed it on. Religious ceremonies and government were one and the same (*saisei-itchi*). . . ." [14] The existence and security of the living kami were imperative to an immanental theocratic state. It was he who would have reigned over the world had the ideal of *hakkō*

[12] See Fukuchi, *Gunkoku-Nippon no keisei*, p. 14.

[13] For example, the Emperor Taishō had a serious breakdown in health during his reign. "His speech was affected, and his memory left him, and though his physical functions were normal, his nervous system failed, so that he walked with a dragging step. From this time onwards His Majesty lived chiefly at the imperial villas, the Empress constantly attending him." A. Morgan Young, *Japan in Recent Times 1912–1926*, p. 176. The emperor's son, Hirohito, the present emperor, became the prince regent in 1921.

[14] Quoted in Holtom, *Modern Japan and Shinto Nationalism*, p. 6.

ichi-u (The whole world under one roof) been achieved by the
military forces of his empire.

The above account makes more intelligible why Japanese leaders were determined to safeguard the throne at the end of the
Second World War. During the war, not only the men in the
armed forces but the entire populace were urged to be prepared
to fight for the emperor. Even when the defeat of Japan became
imminent early in 1945, the militarist government advocated the
fanatic motto of *ichioku gyokusai* (one hundred million subjects
together suffer an honorable defeat). What worried Japanese leaders more than the suffering of the people was the security of the
throne and the preservation of the national polity (*kokutai*),[15] so
that the initial offer of surrender was made as a response to the
Potsdam Declaration, "with the understanding that the said declaration does not comprise any demand which prejudices the prerogatives of His Majesty as a Sovereign Ruler."[16] The Allied
Powers in reply made it plain, however, that "from the moment of
surrender the authority of the emperor and the Japanese Government to rule the state shall be subject to the Supreme Commander
of the Allied powers who will take such steps as he deems proper
to effectuate the surrender terms."[17] Although this response caused
heated discussion among Japanese leaders as to whether or not to
surrender, it was the emperor himself who finally decided to
capitulate "unconditionally."

[15] As early as February, 1945, Konoye Fumimaro (or Ayamaro) voiced
his opinion to the throne that it might be wiser to surrender to the Allied
Powers then, for, as far as he could judge, "Public opinion in the United
States and Great Britain has not as yet demanded the transformation of
[Japanese] national polity. . . . From the standpoint of the preservation
of our national polity, we are more afraid of the Communist revolution
that might arise following the defeat than of the defeat itself." Quoted
in Tōyama, *et al.*, *Shōwa-shi*, p. 234. (My translation.)

[16] U.S. Department of State, *Occupation of Japan: Policy and Progress*,
pp. 56–57. The document further states: "The Japanese Government sincerely hopes that this understanding is warranted and desires keenly that
an explicit direction to that effect will be speedily forthcoming."

[17] *Ibid.*, p. 58.

The occupation of Japan, a proud though defeated nation, one which had never been ruled previously by any foreign power, involved many problems, including the important questions of State Shinto, the emperor, and freedom of religion. The "United States Initial Post-Surrender Policy for Japan" instructed General MacArthur to proclaim "freedom of religious worship" promptly on occupation. It also stated: "At the same time it should be made plain to the Japanese that ultra-nationalistic and militaristic organizations and movements will not be permitted to hide behind the cloak of religion." [18] On the other hand, the Supreme Commander was advised to "exercise his authority through Japanese governmental machinery and agencies, including the Emperor," even though the intent of this policy was "to use the existing form of Government in Japan, not to support it." [19] And, indeed, the occupation authorities made "use" of the institution of the emperor for the smooth operation of the occupation program and for the maintenance of national unity and morale. The retention of the emperor, however, gave false encouragement to those Japanese leaders who hoped to see no substantial change in the national polity. Thus, while the cabinet, headed by an imperial prince, Higashikuni-no-miya Naruhiko, immediately following the surrender, advocated the motto of *ichioku sō-zange* (one hundred million subjects together repent), many leaders would have shared the sentiment expressed by Matsui Iwane, the former commander in chief of the expeditionary forces in Shanghai, who said just before his execution as a war criminal: "Looking back, I have no regrets as I meet my death, nor have I anything to feel ashamed of before all creation, or before the gods and Buddha. My deepest regret is that I was unable to realize Sino-Japanese Cooperation and a new life for Asia. . . ." [20] The prime minister still reported to the emperor "with awe and trepidation," and the emperor in

---

[18] *Ibid.*, p. 77. The United States Initial Post-Surrender Policy for Japan was prepared jointly by the Department of State, the War Department, and the Navy Department and approved by the President on September 6, 1945.

[19] *Ibid.*, p. 75.

[20] Hanayama, *The Way of Deliverance*, p. 256.

turn still reported political events to the Grand Shrine of Ise.[21]

The occupation, once started, did not lose much time in destroying the illusions of those Japanese leaders that no substantial change would take place in regard to the internal affairs of the nation. On October 4, 1945, a Basic Directive (Article I), issued by MacArthur, ordered the Japanese government to remove all restrictions on political, civil, and religious liberties. Instantaneously, the notorious "Religious Organization Law," enacted in 1939 and enforced to secure rigid government control over all aspects of religions, was abrogated; and "religious liberty," at least in principle, was proclaimed on December 28, 1945. Stopgap legislation called the "Religious Corporations Ordinance" was put into effect in order to enable Buddhist, Sect Shinto, and Christian groups to retain their judicial capacity.[22]

The principle of "religious liberty," however, did not solve adequately one of the basic religious problems in Japan, namely, the question of State Shinto, officially interpreted as a "nonreligious" cult of patriotism and national morality. The complex issue of State Shinto was therefore dealt with by the occupation forces on December 15, 1945, in the form of the Shinto Directive, prohibiting "the sponsorship, support, perpetuation, control, and dissemination of Shinto by the Japanese national, prefectural, and local governments, or by public officials." This included a specific instruction that all financial support from public funds and all official affiliation with State Shinto institutions be banned. The Directive annulled all forms of "the Religious Functions Order," relating to the State and to the Grand Shrine of Ise, and ordered the elimination of the Shrine Board (*Jingi-in*) of the Ministry of Home Affairs. It also abolished "all public educational institutions whose primary function is either the investigation and dissemination of Shinto or the training of a Shinto priesthood," and prohibited "the dissemina-

---

[21] On November 13, 1945, the emperor reported the "end of war" to the Grand Shrine of Ise, to the Emperor Jimmu's mausoleum at Unebi, Nara prefecture, and to the Emperor Meiji's mausoleum at Momoyama, Kyoto prefecture.

[22] This ordinance was abolished in 1951 when the "Religious Juridical Persons Law" was promulgated.

tion of Shinto doctrines in any form and by any means" in any institution supported by public funds. Furthermore, the Directive prohibited schools supported by public funds from sponsoring visits to Shinto shrines or Shinto ceremonies of any kind, and ordered the removal of miniature Shinto shrines (*kami-dana*) from all offices, schools, institutions, and organizations supported by public funds. Finally, the Directive took pains to explicate the militaristic and ultramilitaristic doctrines that were no longer to be tolerated, for instance, (1) "the doctrine that the Emperor of Japan is superior to the heads of other states because of ancestry, descent, or special origin," (2) "the doctrine that the people of Japan are superior to the people of other lands because of ancestry, descent, or special origin," (3) "the doctrine that the islands of Japan are superior to other lands because of divine or special origin," and (4) "any other doctrine which tends to delude the Japanese people into embarking upon wars of aggression or to glorify the use of force as an instrument for the settlement of disputes with other peoples." [23]

It is significant to note that on New Year's Day of 1946, only two weeks after the issuance of the Shinto Directive by the occupation authorities, an Imperial Rescript was promulgated, reaffirming the "Charter Oath" of the Emperor Meiji, which goes on to state that, keeping in close touch with the desires of the people, the leaders of Japan would govern the new Japan in a thoroughly peaceful way, the officials and the people alike enjoying their own culture and advancing their standard of living. Then, echoing the Shinto Directive, the Imperial Rescript stated: "The ties between us and our people have always stood upon mutual trust and affection. They do not depend upon mere legends and myths. They are not predicated on the false conception that the Emperor is divine and that the Japanese people are superior to other races and fated to rule the world." [24]

The principles of religious liberty, disestablishment of State

[23] The complete text of this directive is found in Holtom, *Modern Japan and Shinto Nationalism,* 2d ed., pp. 215–18.

[24] The text of this rescript is found in the U.S. Department of State, *Occupation of Japan: Policy and Progress,* pp. 135–37.

Shinto, separation of religion and state, and repudiation of the divinity of the emperor were further elucidated in the new Constitution (promulgated on November 3, 1946, and enforced on May 3, 1947). Article 19 states: "Freedom of thought and conscience shall not be violated." Article 20 states: "Freedom of religion is guaranteed to all. No religious organization shall receive any privilege from the State, nor exercise any political authority. No person shall be compelled to take part in any religious act, celebration, rite, or practice. The State and its organs shall refrain from religious education or any other religious activity." Article 89 clarifies another aspect of the same problem: "No public money or other property shall be expended or appropriated for the use, benefit or maintenance of any religious institution or association, or for any charitable, educational, or benevolent enterprises not under the control of public authority." Freedom of conscience, faith, worship, and freedom to form religious associations guaranteed by the new Constitution are applicable to everybody.[25] In this connection, it is to be noted that while State Shinto as such was disestablished, Shinto as a religion was given the same privileges as any other religion.[26] The new Constitution defined the status of the emperor as the symbol of the state and of the unity of the people. As private individuals, the emperor and members of his

[25] In the Constitution of 1899 freedom of religious belief was recognized "within limits not prejudicial to peace and order, and not antagonistic to their duties as subjects." According to the same Constitution (Article 9), the emperor may issue or cause others to issue ordinances necessary for maintaining public peace and order. On this ground, religious belief and activities were often restricted. This type of qualification is not attached to the clause on freedom of religion in the new Constitution.

[26] The Shinto Directive made this point clear. It said: "Private financial support of all Shinto shrines which have been previously supported in whole or in part by public funds will be permitted, provided such private support is entirely voluntary and is in no way derived from forced or involuntary contributions." The Directive further stated: "Shrine Shinto, after having been divorced from the state and divested of its militaristic and ultranationalistic elements, will be recognized as a religion if its adherents so desire and will be granted the same protection as any other religion in so far as it may in fact be the philosophy or religion of Japanese individuals."

family were at liberty to practice any religion of their choice or not to practice any religion at all.

Fortunately or unfortunately, in any part of the world, the question of religion cannot be solved solely by legislation or a constitution. This was particularly true in postwar Japan where the initiative for democratization of the nation came primarily from the occupation authorities, and their intentions were not always understood by those Japanese leaders who did not have an insight into their frame of reference. For example, during the war the Japanese government established the Great Japan Wartime Religious Patriotic Association, consisting of Buddhist, Sect Shinto, and Christian groups. This association was changed into the Religious League immediately after the end of the war. According to Bunce, "all leadership by government officials ceased, but so far as the religions themselves were concerned, wartime leadership remained largely unchanged." [27] It is not surprising, therefore, that religious leaders in Japan tended to interpret such principles as those of religious liberty and of separation of religion and state according to their own preconceptions. Besides, it was not always easy to define sharply complex problems in terms of the letter of the law. In this respect, the ambiguous relationship of the imperial institutions to Shinto has caused many embarrassing problems. As early as November, 1945, when the emperor reported the end of the Second World War to the Grand Shrine of Ise, the question was raised as to who would be the judge as to whether such a visit was an "official" or a "private" act of the emperor. At that time the spokesman for the occupation evaded the issue by commenting: "That's a matter of his own mind." [28] When the emperor visited Ise on June 2, 1952, to report the signing of the Peace Treaty, it was explained as a "private" act of the emperor, but some people suspected that the

[27] Bunce, *Religions in Japan*, p. 43.

[28] Gayn, *Japan Diary*, p. 29. Gayn's account of his conversation with the spokesman of the occupation continues as follows: "Will the State officials be allowed to accompany him?" "Yes, if they travel in their private capacity." "Will they themselves be judges of whether they are officials or private individuals?" "Yes. . . ."

trip was financed by the official funds of the imperial household.[29] A similar problem arose in connection with the funeral, conducted according to Shinto rites, for the Dowager Empress Teimei (d. 1951). While it was not spoken of as a "state ceremony," it was conducted by the officials of the imperial household. Equally controversial was the ceremony of investing the crown prince, held in November, 1952, which was regarded as a "state" function. But according to a government spokesman, "ceremonies which have hitherto been performed in the traditional form of Shinto in front of the imperial sanctuary (*Kashiko-dokoro*) are regarded as His Highness's private functions. . . ."[30]

Another case, not related to the imperial family, may be cited to illustrate the ambiguity that existed regarding the meaning of "religious liberty" in postwar Japan. A few years ago a group of "soldiers" of the Self Defense Force stationed in Niigata prefecture built a small Shinto shrine on the premises of their camp with the permission of their commanding officer. Shortly afterward the higher officials of the Self Defense Force ordered the removal of the shrine on the grounds that such a practice was unconstitutional. This action was protested by the Shrine Association which interpreted Article 20 of the Constitution to mean that the right to perform religious acts was guaranteed to everybody. Therefore, according to the Shrine Association, "the soldiers should have been free to build a shrine and conduct worship." Moreover, it said that "to deny permission to do this to the Self Defense Forces constituted a violation of their religious liberty."[31] The Shrine Association's view on this matter has received strong support from several quar-

[29] See International Institute for the Study of Religions, *Religion and State in Japan*, Bulletin No. 7 (Tokyo, September, 1959), p. 55. According to a public opinion survey conducted in 1953 regarding the prime minister's visit to Ise on his assumption of office, "6.7% regarded this visit as his duty; 50.3% considered it a wise action; 22.6% thought he was free to either go or not to go; 5.9% believed it would have been better if he had not gone; and only 2.2% said he ought not to have gone. About 12% had various other opinions."

[30] Quoted *ibid.*, p. 84.

[31] *Ibid.*, p. 57.

ters,[32] although it has also aroused bitter criticism on the part of many individuals and groups.

While we are in no position to discuss the various issues involved in "religious liberty" at this time, we must acknowledge the fact that this principle was a precious legacy of the Allied occupation of Japan. It must also be noted, however, that "religious liberty" was an important political asset of the occupation authorities in demilitarizing and democratizing Japan, and that as such it provided an ideological basis for the disestablishment of State Shinto and the repudiation of the emperor's divinity. With the shift of emphasis in the policy from that of the democratization of Japan to one of making her an anti-Communist citadel, the occupation authorities began to be more lenient toward those features of Japan which were regarded as "antidemocratic" during the initial period of the occupation in order to improve her economic condition and national morale. Thus, those who were once labeled "undesirable personnel" became again available for public offices, large component units of the *Zaibatsu* combines were left intact in spite of the supposedly trust-busting policy of the occupation, and "the labor unions, which the occupation authorities had so actively built up, were restrained from actions which would cut into Japanese production."[33] Furthermore, the Self Defense Force was established, bypassing the Constitutional principle against rearmament in any form, and the imperial system which was once regarded as the source of the evils of State Shinto was again favored in its humanized and constitutional form.[34] To be sure, State Shinto was disestablished, and the emperor, who is now only the symbol of the state and of the unity of the people, is said to "derive his position from the sovereign will of the people." Thanks to the new Constitution, the people in Japan now enjoy constitutional guar-

[32] See *ibid.*, pp. 37–38.

[33] E. O. Reischauer, *Japan: Past and Present,* p. 214.

[34] Gayn, *Japan Diary,* p. 261: "A direct attack on the imperial system would weaken the democratic elements, and, on the contrary, strengthen the extremists, both Communist and militarist. *The Supreme Commander is, therefore, ordered to assist secretly in popularizing and humanizing the emperor.*" (Original italics.)

antees of freedom of religion and conscience, and even the emperor in his private capacity can participate in any kind of religious worship. Nevertheless, there are some basic ambiguities involved in the practical application of the law, especially in regard to "religious liberty" and "separation of religion and state." For example, as mentioned above, the members of the imperial family and government officials can visit the Grand Shrine of Ise as they have done in the past, and they may very well say that they are exercising their constitutional right of free religious worship. But the fact remains that it is not easy to convince the ordinary people, who have been for so long accustomed to the idea of the state visits of the government officials and the members of the imperial family to the Grand Shrine of Ise, that the emperor, for example, is now "worshipping not as emperor but as a private individual." [35]

Seen from a wider perspective, the significance of the Allied Occupation in 1945 was that it meant the "second opening" of Japan to the rest of the world in her recent history. Only less than a century earlier had Japan reluctantly reversed the traditional policy of self-seclusion. It is to be recalled that the Western powers were then primarily concerned with commercial trade with Japan and not with her domestic affairs, even though their pressure exerted strong influence on the Japanese government's decision to lift the ban against Christianity. Rather, it was the Japanese leaders themselves who were eager to strengthen and enrich the nation by adopting various features of Western civilization. However, sensing the danger that the spirit of "modernity" might undercut the social, cultural, and political foundation of Japan, the architects of the Meiji regime followed the policy of welcoming only those aspects of Western civilization that were useful to them, while maintaining *de facto* "national seclusion" as far as political, ethical, and religious values were concerned. What happened, therefore, was that external aspects of Japan were quickly modernized in order to preserve and strengthen the "immanental theocracy" that was considered the essence of the "unique" national

[35] *Ibid.*, p. 29.

polity. It was this internal, spiritual "seclusion" of Japan that was broken down at the end of the Second World War. State Shinto and the emperor cult were destroyed by the occupation authorities no doubt because of their political rather than their religious implications. Nevertheless, the occupation authorities were destined to play a role of decisive importance in the religious history of Japan.

Religious Freedom and the Boom

On January 1, 1946, MacArthur wrote in his message to the Japanese people: "A New Year has come. With it a new day dawns for Japan. No longer is the future to be settled by a few. The shackles of militarism, of feudalism, of regimentation of body and soul have been removed. Thought control and the abuse of education are no more. All now enjoy religious freedom and the right of speech. . . ." [36] It soon became apparent, however, that it was easier for the occupation authorities to remove the obstacles to freedom by sending directives to the Japanese government than for the Japanese people to exercise those freedoms—given to them as they were, rather than earned by their own efforts. This was particularly true regarding religious freedom.

During the Second World War the Japanese government had enforced the ill-famed Religious Organizations Law (enacted in 1939 and enforced in 1940). Although the thirteen Sect Shinto denominations with 16,467 churches, 126,017 religious functionaries, and 10,407,207 registered adherents were left intact, the fifty-six prewar Buddhist sects were consolidated under government pressure into twenty-eight sects with 77,703 temples, 169,588 priests, and 45,397,053 adherents. The Christian denominations, which had numbered thirty-five in prewar days, were consolidated into two groups—one Roman Catholic and one Protestant—with 1,783 churches, 4,293 clergy, and 277,162 adherents. In other words, only forty-three groups (thirteen Sect Shinto, twenty-eight Buddhist, and two Christian) were officially recognized as religious

[36] His full text is given in U.S. Department of State, *Occupation of Japan: Policy and Progress*, pp. 135–36.

organizations according to the Religious Organizations Law, and these groups came under the administration of the Ministry of Education. All the other religious groups, including those which had refused to join the consolidated Buddhist and Christian groups, as well as newly arisen semi-religious groups, were not regarded as officially recognized religious organizations, and they came under the supervision of prefectural governments. The number of such unincorporated religious groups was 322 in 1938, but it increased to over a thousand toward the end of the Second World War.[37]

With the abrogation of the Religious Organizations Law in December, 1945, the Religious Corporations Ordinance was put into effect to enable religious groups to maintain their juridical capacity. Meanwhile, following the disestablishment of State Shinto which had hitherto been regarded as a "nonreligious" national cult, Shinto—now called Shrine Shinto (*Jinja Shinto*)—began to function as a religion. In February, 1946, a new organization called the Association of Shinto Shrines (*Jinja Honchō,* literally, "central bureau of shrines," referring both to the association and also to the office of the association) was formed, incorporating within it over 80,000 shrines out of a total number estimated to be slightly above 100,000.[38] The Shrine Association now comes under the provisions of the Religious Corporations Ordinance.

[37] See Ministry of Education, *Religions in Japan,* p. 82. Some of these "unrecognized" religious and semireligious groups were discussed in Chapter V.

[38] The Shrine Association was organized by the leaders of the three Shinto agencies that were dissolved—the Association of Shinto Priests (*Dai-Nippon Jingi-kai*), the Research Institute of Imperial Classics (*Kōten-kōkyū-sho*), and the Society for the Veneration of the Grand Shrine of Ise (*Jingū-hōsai-kai*). It is stated that the aim of the Shrine Association is to follow after the Divine Way of the kami, to promote the prosperity of Shinto shrines, to inculcate the eternal laws of ethics, to give thanks for the blessings received from the kami, to observe the virtues of the kami in our daily life, to enhance good customs and manners, and to contribute to the happiness of all mankind. Quoted in Munenori Miyagawa, "The Status Quo of Shinto Shrines," *The Shinto Bulletin,* I (No. 1, March, 1953, Tokyo), 6. In addition to the Shrine Association, there also developed five other smaller associations of Shinto shrines.

Apparently the Religious Corporations Ordinance had been drafted hastily as stopgap legislation by the Religious Affairs Section of the Ministry of Education, even though it was checked by the Religious and Cultural Resources Division (RCR) of the occupation, which was primarily concerned with the principles of religious freedom and separation of religion and state. The period immediately following the end of war was marked by social, cultural, economic, political, and religious confusion. On the one hand, people experienced a certain type of exhilaration upon being emancipated from the oppressive atmosphere of the war period. On the other hand, they were bewildered at the loss of direction and meaning in life, for they sensed that the Japan they had known was crumbling before their eyes. In this situation, many new religious and pseudo-religious cults and groups emerged. For example, one Nagaoka Yoshiko, wife of a sailor, claimed that the spirit of the Sun Goddess, Amaterasu, had left the body of the emperor and had entered her body, and that she—Nagaoka Yoshiko, now known as Jikō-son (Princess of Spiritual Light)—was commissioned to announce the coming of the earthly paradise.[39] She, and many other charismatic persons like her, quickly attracted considerable numbers of followers and established religious corporations. Also, many splinter groups that had been compelled to affiliate with certain Buddhist or Shinto groups took advantage of their religious freedom and declared themselves to be independent religious corporations, so that Sect Shinto, for instance, which had had thirteen recognized denominations before the end of the war, developed into seventy-five groups by 1949.[40] Meanwhile, freedom of religion was interpreted mechanically and literally, and as a

[39] Jikō-son advocated the veneration of the Sun Goddess and the emperor. The fact that the emperor repudiated his own divinity, however, made it possible for her to claim that she was now possessed by the spirit of the Sun Goddess. In her state of kami-possession, Jikō-son predicted the coming of the end of the world and the establishment of a new world order. One of her ardent followers was the famous *sumō* (Japanese wrestling) champion, Futaba-yama, who became an active propagandist of this group.

[40] The Shinto Dai-kyō was split into ten, the Fusō-kyō into twenty-one, the Ontake-kyō into thirteen, and the Shinri-kyō into seven.

result there were in all 742 groups that were incorporated by the Religious Corporations Ordinance.[41] Among them were a number of questionable organizations that claimed to be "religious" in order to receive tax exemptions and other privileges. In order to rectify the confusion and misuse of religious freedom, and also to ensure the preservation of authentic religious liberty, the Religious Juridical Persons Law (*Shūkyō-hōjin-hō*) was adopted in 1951, replacing the loose Religious Corporations Ordinance.

The enactment of the Religious Juridical Persons Law was an important landmark in recent religious development in Japan. While it has its limitations, this law manages to rectify some of the obvious evils that had not been controlled by the previous ordinance, such as profit-making projects operated under the guise of religions. The Religious Juridical Persons Law is divided into ten chapters: (1) General Provisions, (2) Establishment, (3) Administration, (4) Alteration of Regulations, (5) Merger, (6) Dissolution, (7) Registration, (8) Religious Juridical Persons Council, (9) Additional Provisions, (10) Penal Provisions—and "Supplementary Provisions." [42] Running throughout the law are the principles of religious freedom and of separation of religion and state. Also, this law, which is the product of joint efforts of the Ministry of Education, the occupation authorities, and religious leaders of various faiths, seems to take careful account of the peculiarities of the various religious groups and of the realities of the religious situation in postwar Japan. One important result of the adoption of this law was that the number of religious groups was reduced nearly by half.[43]

[41] Of 742 religious corporations, 258 belonged to the Shinto tradition, 260 to the Buddhist tradition, and 46 to the Christian tradition; 178 were miscellaneous groups.

[42] See Woodard, "The Religious Juridical Persons Law," in The Foreign Affairs Association of Japan, *Contemporary Japan* (Tokyo, 1960), pp. 1–84. The English text of the law is found also in this issue.

[43] Of the total number of 379 sects and denominations that came under the provisions of the "Religious Juridical Persons Law," 142 were Shinto groups (with 80,741 shrines; 35,039 churches, and 79,221,216 adherents); 169 were Buddhist groups (with 74,102 temples, 15,961 churches, and 39,720,884 adherents); 38 were Christian groups (with 5,006 churches

Thus far, we have concentrated on the constitutional and legislative framework of the postwar religious situation in Japan. Far more difficult is the assessment of the spiritual vitality of these religious groups and their influence on contemporary Japanese culture and society. In this connection, we have to remind ourselves once again that Japanese religions were destined to share the suffering and agonies of national defeat, as illustrated by the fact that 1,374 Shinto shrines, 2,540 Shinto churches, 4,609 Buddhist temples, and 446 Christian churches were demolished or damaged by the war.[44] A large number of younger religious leaders, both clergy and laymen, were either killed or wounded in action. Those who survived the war, even if they had not actually fought, had to face acute difficulties in making a living as a result of the financial crisis that ensued. Land reform, initiated by the occupation authorities, deprived historic Buddhist temples and Shinto shrines of much of the farm lands that had traditionally provided their economic security. Moreover, the excessive measures undertaken by the government toward national mobilization for the war effort, involving religious groups in numerous ways during the "emergency period" that lasted from 1931 to 1945, had left religious groups virtually impotent in exercising spiritual influence among their adherents. The transition from the period of emergency to the postwar period was further accompanied by the loosening of the social fabric that had been cemented by traditional Confucian morality. After the war religions for the most part lacked leadership and resources to cope with the general apathy and disillusionment of the people. The plight of the religious groups that had existed since before the war was further accentuated by the growing influence of Communism and the emergence of the so-called new religions.

Earlier I touched briefly upon the formation of the Japan Communist party in 1922 and its activities in the 1920s. In those days the Japanese Communists were more effective in social criticism than in practical politics, even though they considered themselves

---

and 576,202 adherents); and 30 were miscellaneous (with 3,476 churches and 3,597,599 believers). Ministry of Education, *Religions in Japan*, p. 82.

[44] *Ibid.*, p. 81.

to be in the vanguard of the farmer-labor movement, destined to revolutionize Japan. They did manage to establish "cells" in some factories, in labor groups, and in trade unions, but their real strength was found among university students and the urban white-collar workers. Following the enactment of the Peace Preservation Law in 1925 Communist activities were suppressed and severe measures were used against their leaders. Nevertheless, Communist influence continued to be felt among left-wing artists and writers. As a part of the proletarian cultural movement, some of the Communist leaders formed the Anti-Religious League in Japan (*Nihon han-shūkyō dōmei*) in 1931. After the decline of the Anti-Religious League in 1934 leftist antireligious activities were with difficulty carried on by members of the Research Group on Dialectical Materialism (*Yuibutsu-ron kenkyū-kai*), but this organization was also disbanded by government order in 1938.[45]

The postwar Communist movement in Japan was greatly aided by the initial policy of the occupation of releasing political prisoners, including 150 seasoned leaders of the prewar Communist movement. Protected by the "Bill of Rights," the Communists started active campaigns among hungry and bewildered people who were desperately looking for immediate and extreme solutions for their problems. Although the Communists won only five of the 466 seats in the House of Representatives in the first postwar election in 1946, they gained thirty-five seats in the 1949 general election. Alarmed by the sudden growth of the Communist party and its sympathizers, the occupation authorities in 1950 purged the leaders of the party, banned the publication of *Akahata* (Red Flag), and took other measures to check leftist growth. Since then the Communist party as such has not made much headway on the Japanese political scene, but Communist influence has not diminished in the trade and labor unions and student groups as well as in various antirearmament and peace movements. Significantly, contrary to the oft-repeated thesis that poverty creates Communists, Communism does not seem to appeal

[45] On antireligious movements by the Japanese leftists, see Akio Saki, et al., *Gendai no shūkyō mondai*, pp. 65–103.

to the poverty-stricken rural population of Japan. Rather, it attracts white-collar workers in urban areas, educators, scientists, artists, and, more particularly, university students who tend "to view the economic and political future of Japan with pessimism and to turn in despair to the supposedly Utopian solutions of Communism." [46] These people are the spiritual heirs of the modernists of the Meiji Era who came under the impact of "modernity" and rejected the traditional religions and cultural values. And just as some of the modernists in the Meiji Era found a new certainty in Christianity, or in science, for that matter, some of their spiritual descendants in postwar Japan find a new certainty in Communism, which to them is an "immanental pseudo religion of materialism." This accounts for their emotional reaction against all kinds of religions, the new as well as the old.

As far as the so-called new religions that mushroomed since the end of the Second World War are concerned, I will discuss them a little later. It should be noted, however, in passing that these "new religions" have old roots, that most of them, despite great variations in doctrinal formulations and cultic practices, share one common feature, namely, a preoccupation with salvation in this world. While their doctrines are far less sophisticated than those of the old established religions, they claim to offer a coherent meaning for life within the framework of their religious communities. As such, they demand full participation on the part of their adherents in a communal organization. Thus, these new religions, as much as Communism, present a serious challenge to the established religions, as we shall see.

Shrine Shinto

The disestablishment of State Shinto in 1945 by means of the Shinto Directive of the occupation authorities opened a new page in the history of Shinto. Government subsidy of Shinto establishments was discontinued, and the farmlands belonging to the shrines were lost under the land reform program. On the other

[46] E. O. Reischauer, *Japan: Past and Present,* p. 265.

hand, all local shrines gained title to their own precincts. These are now incorporated as "religious juridical persons" and are the legal owners of the shrines. In turn they are responsible for the maintenance of the priests and buildings and grounds. Nearly 80,000 shrines agreed to affiliate themselves with the Shrine Association, while 1,000 remained independent. About 250 formed smaller associations, mostly geographical in scope.[47] The transition from State Shinto to Shrine Shinto did not imply, however, that the essential nature of Shinto underwent great change. In the main, the changes took place in the legal and external dimensions, leaving much of the traditional cultic elements more or less intact. For example, the so-called Imperial Household Shinto, that is, the religious rites performed at the three shrines within the imperial palace, continues as ever before, except that it is now supposed to be the private affair of the imperial family. Moreover, the transition from State Shinto to Shrine Shinto did not affect Shinto rites practiced in individual homes. Devout adherents of Shinto still perform their daily ablutions and pay homage at the family shrine as they have always done, and visit their tutelary shrines on special occasions. Furthermore, the country is still dotted with sacred stones, trees, or other objects of popular belief that can scarcely be differentiated from a more general kind of superstition and witchcraft.

Nevertheless, Shrine Shinto as a religion encounters a number of serious problems. First, the traditional *uji-ko* system, based on the notion that those who resided in the vicinity of a shrine were children of the kami of that shrine and thus had an obligation to support it, is breaking down. This is especially true in urban areas.[48] Confronted by hitherto unknown financial difficulties,

[47] See Sokyō Ono, *Shinto: The Kami Way*, pp. 17–19. It is to be noted that these figures refer to the incorporated "juridical persons" and not to the number of separate shrines. In some cases, a number of shrines are jointly incorporated as one religious juridical person.

[48] Usually the *uji-ko* association was identical with such local public associations as the neighborhood group or the block association. Thus, the collection of funds for the shrine virtually was done by the public associations. Although the Shinto Directive technically forbade the public associations to raise funds for Shinto shrines, this principle has been

the shrines now depend heavily on the distribution of paper amulets, voluntary offerings for exorcism and special prayers, and loose offerings from worshipers who flock to them on holidays and festive occasions. Very popular is the paper amulet issued by the Grand Shrine of Ise (*Jingū taima*), over six million of which are distributed throughout the country each year.[49] As to the number of worshipers at various shrines on festive occasions, it dwindled markedly for two years after the end of the war, but since 1948 it has surpassed the prewar figure and has been increasing each year since then.[50] Another noticeable trend is found in the Shinto wedding ceremonies (*Shinzen kekkon*), which have turned out to be an important source of income for the shrines. However, all these promotional ventures, important though they may be for the maintenance of the Shinto institutions, have not contributed to the spiritual awakening of Shinto as a religion.

Second, Shinto faces serious difficulties in formulating its doctrines, in propagating its faith, and in training its priests. Considering the fact that the Meiji Restoration was ignited to a great extent by the "theological" reconstruction of Neo-Shinto, especially in the tradition of Hirata Atsutane, one might be surprised by the lack of theological concern on the part of Shinto leaders in the modern period. On this point, I have already alluded to the fact that the Meiji regime, in establishing what amounted to a newly created superreligious cult called State Shinto, denied the

---

violated in some instances for the simple reason that the *uji-ko* association and the local public associations still overlap.

[49] According to *Tō-shin*, the official organ of the Shrine Association of the Tokyo Prefecture (November, 1959, issue), each *taima* is sold for 50 yen, and two fifths of this amount is turned over to the special fund for the promotion of Shinto (*Shintō kōyō shikin*). Realizing that many modern houses and apartments are not equipped with family shrines (*kami-dana*), the Shrine Association also sells a handy portable box for the purpose of keeping the *taima*. This box (*Hōsai-bako*), which is sold for 100 yen, can be hung on the wall in lieu of the family shrine.

[50] The Kyōdō news agency reported on January 3, 1948, that about 40,000 persons flocked to the Meiji Shrine alone on the first two days of that year. This number was four times greater than the previous year's figure.

religious autonomy of Shinto. In fact, from 1882 till the end of the Second World War, priests of State Shinto were forbidden by law to engage in any form of preaching, for it was the government which formulated the doctrines and dogmas of State Shinto. In the words of a Shinto scholar: "The delay in formulating a theology for contemporary Shrine Shinto is partly due to the 64 years of bureaucratic control of Shinto." [51] This does not imply that there was no theological enterprise whatsoever among Shinto scholars. As early as 1882 the Research Institute for the Imperial Classics (Kōten kenkyū sho, or Kōten kōkyū sho) was established, and in 1890 Kokugakuin University (University for the Study of *Kokugaku* or National Learning) was established. There were other institutes and training schools for priests in Ise and elsewhere. However, scholars of these institutions were preoccupied with the interpretation of the Japanese classics, especially the mythologies contained in them, or the history of shrines, at the expense of philosophical and theological inquiries into the nature of religion, or critical and constructive studies of Shinto doctrines.[52] Since the end of the Second World War various attempts have been made by Shinto thinkers to formulate systematic treatises of Shinto theology.[53] Thus far, however, no definitive work has appeared on the subject.

Equally serious is the problem of the shortage of clergy, as exemplified by the fact that there are today about 21,000 priests for 80,000 shrines. In many cases priests depend on "subpriests," such as village elders and other volunteers, who assist them in the performance of rituals. In order to rectify this situation, Shinto leaders have been trying to recruit able youths and have estab-

[51] Hirai, "Fundamental Problems of Present Shinto," *Proceedings of the IXth International Congress for the History of Religions,* p. 305.

[52] See Toda, "Traditional Tendency of Shintoism and Its New Theoretical Developments," in Japanese Association for Religious Studies, ed., *Religious Studies in Japan,* pp. 229–32.

[53] See Ariga, "Contemporary Apologetics of Shinto," Missionary Research Library, *Occasional Bulletin,* Vol. V, No. 5 (New York, April 22, 1954); Sokyō Ono, *The Kami Way;* and Motohiko Anzu, "The Concept of 'Kami,' " *Proceedings of the IXth International Congress for the History of Religions,* pp. 218–22.

lished training schools for them.[54] But the picture has not yet
improved to any significant degree. Many priests in the countryside have to take on secular jobs in order to augment their
meager incomes. Although Shinto leaders call for an improvement in the relationship between the priests and their parishioners (*uji-ko*), and for an increase in educational and philanthropic works under the auspices of Shinto shrines, Shrine Shinto
as a religion lacks the human as well as the financial resources to
cope adequately with the complex problems of this age of social
change.

Lastly, the most crucial problem that confronts Shinto today is
the ambiguity of its own image. Briefly stated, the Shinto fold
seems to be split between those who regard their faith as one of
the religions in Japan and those who consider it a unique national faith to the extent that it warrants special recognition from
the government. Most adherents of other faiths, secularists, Communists, as well as a small segment of the younger generation
within the Shinto fold, are inclined to hold the first view, whereas
many adherents and leaders of Shinto insist that Shinto alone
has been inseparable from the national life throughout the history
of Japan and that the identification of religion and government
(*saisei-itchi*) has been and always will be the fundamental principle of Shinto. A leading Shinto scholar states: "I think that
this spirit [of the identification of religion and government] has
been given a concrete organized form in the system of State
Shinto; and I also think it understandable that, if this longing
for State Shinto as a system be disappointed, there should be a
demand for its revival in spirit."[55] In a similar vein, a noted
jurist and authority on the Constitution argues that Shinto shrines
are "national institutions, indicating the object of national morality," and should not be regarded simply as institutions of religion.

[54] The most important Shinto institution of higher learning is the Kokugakuin University, located in Tokyo.

[55] Sokyō Ono, "The Contributions to Japan of Shrine Shinto," *Proceedings of the IXth International Congress for the History of Religions,*
p. 391.

He likewise asserts that the emperor is the spiritual symbol of the state, related to the national morality.[56]

The basic ambiguity of the nature of Shinto has raised many thorny issues in the postwar period. A controversial bill was presented to the Diet asking for the redesignation of February 11, the legendary date when the first Emperor Jimmu was supposed to have founded the nation, as National Foundation Day. The Ministry of Education, despite opposition from the Japan Teachers Union, the Japanese Education Association, and a number of other groups and individuals, is in favor of restoring ethics courses not dissimilar from the prewar Moral Teachings (*shūshin*) in public schools. The expenses for the new buildings of the Grand Shrine of Ise, amounting to seven hundred million yen, were collected by the Supporters Association of the Grand Shrine of Ise (*Jingū hōsan kai*), including many government and business leaders. Tokyo authorities encouraged a fund drive for the Meiji and Yasukuni shrines to the extent of 1,270 million yen. In 1957 it was reported that pupils of a certain primary school in Kobe, on a school-sponsored visit to Ise, were required to go through an act of worship at the Grand Shrine. All these attempts to restore some features of State Shinto are receiving strong support from conservative elements in Japanese society.[57] In short, while it enjoys the same religious freedom as all other religions in Japan, Shinto, as a religion, has not been liberated from its own traditions and nostalgia for the days of State Shinto.

[56] See International Institute for the Study of Religions, *Religion and State in Japan*, pp. 32–35.

[57] See Woodard, "The Religious World—Some Random Notes," *The Japan Christian Quarterly*, XXIV (No. 2, April, 1958), 170–72. Woodard also reports that some of these measures are related to the drive to increase pensions for war veterans and the bereaved families of the war dead. In this respect, the Japan Bereaved Families Association (*Nihon izoku kai*), to which 1,800,000 families belong, plays an important role, for it influences nearly 500,000 voters. This association gives strong support to the movement to designate February 11 as National Foundation Day and also to the drive to persuade the government to give special recognition to the Yasukuni shrine.

Buddhism

After the end of the Second World War, Japanese Buddhism, unlike Shinto, was left alone by the occupation authorities, but it confronted many serious difficulties just the same.

Many of the younger Buddhist clergy were dead or wounded, and 4,609 temples had been destroyed or heavily damaged during the war. Acute economic conditions and the policy of religious freedom seriously impaired the traditional ecclesiastical structure of Buddhism, carried over from the Tokugawa period, based on (1) the hierarchical relationship between the main temple (*honzan*) and subordinate temple (*matsuji*), and (2) the fixed relationship between the individual temple and its parishioners (*danka*). It was exceedingly difficult for Buddhist groups to raise money for the reconstruction and repair of temples, since land reform measures deprived many temples of that important source of income. A number of subordinate temples in the countryside suffered from the heavy assessment laid on them by their main temples or denominational headquarters, while they could hardly depend on their poverty-stricken parishioners for additional contributions. Consequently, a large number of clergy were compelled to take on secular jobs to augment their income, and some of them even left the priesthood altogether. For example, in the Fukushima prefecture, 800 out of 1,700 temples had no resident priest.[58] Many temples had to sell or lease parts of their precincts or their forests. Not a few of them started nursery schools or kindergartens partly to provide religious education for children and partly to secure additional income for the maintenance of temples and clergy.[59]

[58] Saki, *et al.*, *Gendai no shūkyō mondai*, p. 188.

[59] According to a survey of the Chisan sect (one of the Shingon denominations) in 1958, only 10 percent of the clergy are supported solely by the contributions of the parishioners; 40 percent of them have to depend partly on the parishioners' contributions and partly on their own income from secular jobs; 50 percent of them receive practically no support from their parishioners. See *ibid.*, p. 191.

The policy of religious freedom was also a serious blow to the anachronistic structures of Buddhist sectarian and denominational organizations. As we mentioned earlier, the fifty-six prewar Buddhist denominations had been consolidated into twenty-eight by the Religious Organizations Law in 1940. The Religious Corporations Ordinance, promulgated in 1945, not only restored some of the fifty-six prewar denominations but permitted the independence of many splinter subsects, so that by 1950 there were altogether 260 Buddhist corporations in existence. It was the Religious Juridical Persons Law, issued in 1951, with its provision for an authentification system, that brought the number of Buddhist groups down to 170. Separatist tendencies inevitably robbed the traditional authority of the main temples and greatly weakened the financial foundations of various denominations. For example, the historic Tendai sect suffered from the fact that all the subsects of the Shugen-dō (Order of Mountain Ascetics) tradition, which had been incorporated into the Tendai sect under the arbitrary religious policy of the Meiji regime, as well as some wealthy establishments, such as the Shitennō-ji of Osaka and the Sensō-ji of Tokyo, broke away and became independent. Equally hard hit was the Shingon sect, which split into ten groups at first; eventually forty-seven new groups emerged from the Shingon tradition.

Obviously, different groups broke away from their main bodies for different reasons. Some of them took the step because of disagreement with their denominational headquarters regarding certain policies, while others were motivated by economic reasons. For example, about 150 temples on the island of Awaji seceded from the Kōyasan Shingon sect in 1958 because they were not willing to pay an assessment imposed by their headquarters. Far more significant was the emergence of a great number of independent associations of lay Buddhists (*Zaike kyōdan*), because of their dissatisfaction with the excessive clericalism and dead weight of old Buddhist institutions. One of the most active lay movements today is the *Zaike Bukkyō kyōkai* (Laymen's Buddhist Society) which holds a lecture series in various parts of

Japan in addition to conducting weekly radio programs and pub-
lishing a monthly journal.[60] It is to be noted in this connection
that while many of these laymen's groups work toward the rejuvenation of Japanese Buddhism from within, some of them,
notably those of the Nichiren tradition, tend to compete with
established Buddhist denominations and are often antagonistic
toward them. As such, some of the new groups that emerged
from the Nichiren tradition are usually classified as "New Religions," and thus will be discussed later under that category.

It is significant to note that Japanese Buddhism in the postwar
period, in spite of social and economic difficulties, has made serious efforts toward rejuvenating itself by modernizing the structures of ecclesiastical institutions, fostering interdenominational
cooperation, and promoting scholarship. Democratization and simplification of the cumbersome administrative systems of the various denominations and sects are, of course, difficult to achieve.
Nevertheless, many denominations have already adopted a system
of election for either the patriarch or the chief administrator.
Laymen are increasingly given responsible positions in the management of denominational or local temple affairs, following the
principle of "unification of clergy and laity" (*sōzoku ittai*).[61] Also,
contradictory as it may sound in view of the separatist tendencies
on the part of many sectarian groups, various kinds of interdenominational agencies and committees have been formed in order
to carry on joint programs in the areas of evangelism, social
service, and religious education. For example, a large-scale "Metropolitan Bon Festival" is held annually at Hibiya Public Hall,
Tokyo, under the auspices of an interdenominational organiza-

---

[60] It is significant that a large number of leading Buddhist scholars, both
clerical and lay, are involved in the activities of this group, which, incidentally, is quite "interdenominational" or "nonsectarian" in character.
Meetings of this group are usually held in lecture halls or other meeting
places and not in temples.

[61] Even in the East- and West-Honganji sects, which have preserved
the system of a patriarchate based on hereditary principles, the actual
administrative authority has been turned over to the *shūmu-sōchō* (administrator of ecclesiastical affairs) who is to be elected by the ecclesiastical
council.

tion called the Buddhist Worshipers Association of Japan (*Nihon Bukkyō sankō kai*).[62] A weekly seminar on Buddhism is sponsored by the Buddhist Culture Research Association (*Bukkyō-bunka kenkyū kai*). An interdenominational *Bukkyo Times*, a weekly publication, now boasts a circulation of over 50,000. Also, the Japan Buddhist Federation sponsors the All Japan Buddhist Conference annually for the purpose of mutual consultation and exchange of ideas among various denominational leaders.[63] Realizing that Buddhism had failed to restrain excessive nationalism and militarism during the war, some Buddhists now take an active part in peace movements. Buddhist leaders have high hopes for the future of the All Japan Buddhist Youth Association, which now has 1,700 local chapters, for they sense that many young people are looking for "a common principle of living based on Buddhism that transcends Communism and Democracy, the two mutually opposing main currents of ideology in the contemporary world."[64]

Earlier I made reference to the prewar development of Buddhist scholarship in Japan stimulated by the pioneering work of such prominent scholars as Nanjō Bun-yū, Anesaki Masaharu, Takakusu Junjirō, Kimura Taiken, Tokiwa Daijō, and Murakami Senshō. It was in 1949 that the Japanese Buddhist Research Association, a prewar organization, was reactivated, and two years later a new organization called the Japanese Association of In-

[62] This great function in Tokyo was held for the first time on an interdenominational basis in the summer of 1941, and has been repeated every year since then. At the 1961 festival, according to a newspaper report, choirs of various Buddhist schools sang Buddhist hymns, Buddhist kindergarten children offered flowers and incense to the Buddha, and the abbot of Zōjō-ji conducted memorial services for all the victims of the China Affair and the Second World War. Among the guests were the ambassadors of Ceylon and Laos and the governor of metropolitan Tokyo.

[63] In 1961 the conference brought together over 1,000 delegates to Sōji-ji, situated at Tsurumi, Kanagawa prefecture. There were two main subjects discussed at the conference—"how to make Buddhist temples more popular" and "the future tasks of Buddhism in Japan."

[64] Mihara, "Buddhism in Japan," *The Mainichi Overseas Edition*, No. 82 (December 20, 1957), p. 1.

dian and Buddhist Studies (*Nihon Indogaku Bukkyōgaku kai*) was organized under the leadership of Miyamoto Shōson in order to promote and coordinate research in various aspects of Indology and Buddhology. This association publishes biannually its official organ, *Journal of Indian and Buddhist Studies*. There are also a number of other scholarly journals on Buddhist studies published by denominational institutions. In the main, prewar Japanese scholarship was primarily concerned with philological analysis of the texts, historical studies of various traditions of Buddhism, and the philosophical explication of basic Buddhist doctrines. There were also some philosophers, such as Nishida Kitarō (1870–1945) and Tanabe Hajime (1885–1962), who depended heavily on Buddhist philosophical insights in their attempt to build their own philosophical systems. All these prewar scholarly traditions have been preserved by postwar Buddhist scholars. Besides, Japanese Buddhist scholars today utilize the methods and insights of psychology, sociology, phenomenology, economics, political science, and symbolic logic in their studies of various aspects of Buddhism. Also, for the first time in the history of Japanese Buddhism, a number of Buddhists address themselves to social, economic, and political issues from the perspective of their own faith.[65] No less significant is the fact that an increasing number of Japanese Buddhist scholars have been invited to teach or give special lectures in Europe, North America, and other Asian nations.[66]

[65] For example, at the Buddha Jayanti, held in Japan in 1959, the following papers were presented: "Buddhism as a System of Social Philosophy," "Buddhism: Its Relation to Industrial Civilization," "The Tragedy of Westernization," "The Role of Buddhism in Modern Civilization—Foundation of Social Activities," "The Buddhist Conception of Peace and the Method of Its Realization," "Buddhism and the Universal History of Philosophy," "Buddhism and the State," "Modern Significance of Buddhism in World Thought," "Economic Thought in Buddhism," "Buddhism in the Age of Science," and "Buddhism and Existentialism."

[66] Suzuki Daisetz (D. T. Suzuki) is well known in Europe and North America as an interpreter of Zen Buddhism to the West. Among other prominent Japanese Buddhist scholars who have been invited to teach or lecture in Western universities are Hisamatsu Shin-ichi, a Zen scholar

The rejuvenation of Japanese Buddhism in the postwar period has been greatly stimulated by the resurgence of Buddhism in other parts of Asia and the formation of the World Fellowship of Buddhists (WFB). A group of Japanese Buddhists attended the first conference of the WFB held in Ceylon in 1950. Its second conference was held in Japan in 1952; this conference attracted 180 Buddhist delegates from eighteen foreign nations as well as 450 Japanese delegates. Japanese Buddhists took an active part in the subsequent conferences of the WFB, held in Burma (1954), Nepal (1956), Thailand (1958), and Cambodia (1961). These conferences provided opportunities for Japanese Buddhists to be exposed to Theravada Buddhist piety, strict monastic discipline, and missionary zeal. Also, Buddhism plays an important role in Japan's relations with other Asian nations. For example, the Burmese Goodwill Mission to Japan was lavishly entertained by a group of leading Japanese Buddhists in 1954. Following the visit of Buddhist delegates from Mainland China in 1955, an organization for the promotion of Buddhist exchange between Mainland China and Japan (Nitchū Bukkyō kōryū kondan-kai) was formed by some Japanese Buddhists. In 1957 a group of leading Japanese Buddhists visited Mainland China to increase mutual understanding between the two nations through Buddhism. In 1958 the Japan Buddhist Federation sent a gift of 810,000 yen in relief funds and some 10,000 pieces of clothing to flood victims in Ceylon. In 1962, commemorating the seventieth anniversary of the introduction of Mahayana Buddhism to North America, a group of Japanese Buddhists visited several key cities in the United States, holding religious symposiums and commemorative ceremonies.

---

and professor emeritus of Kyoto University; Miyamoto Shōson, a scholar of Madhyamika philosophy and professor emeritus of Tokyo University; Masutani Fumio, a leader of the Lay Buddhist Movement and professor in the Tokyo University of Foreign Studies; Ishizu Teruji and Hori Ichirō, both professors of science and religion at Tohoku University; Nakamura Hajime, professor of Indian and Buddhist philosophies at Tokyo University; and Takeuchi Yoshinori, professor of the science of religion at Kyoto University.

Notwithstanding some encouraging signs of modernization, increasing interdenominational activities, respect for scholarship, and growing cooperation with Buddhists in other nations, Japanese Buddhism seems to be caught today between its own past and the demands of the new age. In this connection, a leading Buddhist thinker depicts the five following characteristics as negative qualities of past Japanese Buddhism that have been carried over to modern times: (1) subservience to the political authority and spirit of nationalism, (2) prevalence of magical incantations and other superstitious beliefs and practices, (3) preoccupation with funeral rites and memorial services for the dead at the expense of providing spiritual guidance to the living, (4) lack of doctrinal integrity that leads to compromise with other religions and ideologies, and (5) stress on formalism without equal stress on inner spiritual disciplines.[67] Statistically, according to the report of the Ministry of Education, in 1960 there were 170 Buddhist corporations, with 75,000 temples and other establishments ministered to by 130,000 clergy, and a total of 40,000,000 members. Besides, there are twelve Buddhist universities, over 300 kindergartens, and nearly 300 welfare enterprises of various kinds.[68] Over 700 Buddhist clergy alone have dedicated themselves to work as prison chaplains. Nevertheless, Buddhism as a whole tends to live with a nostalgia for the past. Thus the

[67] Shōkō Watanabe, *Nihon no Bukkyō*, pp. 69–139.

[68] See Mombu-shō, *Shūkyō nenkan* (1961). Buddhist adherents are counted not as individuals but as a household unit of believers. Thus, the figure of 40,000,000 stands for the number of family units. According to Mombu-shō, *Shūkyō nenkan* (1965), the status of Japanese Buddhism is as follows:

Denomination	Number of Sects	Number of Family Units
Tendai	20	2,261,222
Shingon	49	11,567,243
Jōdo, Jōdo-shin, Ji, and Yūzū-nembutsu	27	16,899,289
Zen	23	9,578,446
Nichiren	38	25,917,097
Ritsu	7	577,439
Others	2	167,395

ancient ceremony of blessing the emperor's clothing is still observed annually in Tōji temple in Kyoto,[69] and so-called prayer temples attract huge crowds each year.[70] Many Buddhist leaders are disquieted by the fact that Buddhism is not adequately coping with the issues that confront man in today's world. This may account for the phenomenal growth of "new religions" at the expense of the traditional strength of Buddhism.[71]

Christianity

As for Christianity in Japan, the end of the Second World War marked a period of reconstruction and expansion. During the war 446 Christian churches were damaged and a large number of younger clergy and laymen were lost. Protestant churches, which had put their major efforts into work in urban areas, were hard hit by the bombing of key cities by the Allied forces in 1945. The Roman Catholic church also suffered a heavy toll. For example, the destruction of Nagasaki, a stronghold of Catholicism, alone caused serious hardship to the Catholic church.[72] During the war, the militarist regime had been too clever to allow Christians to become martyrs for their faith, although there were a small num-

[69] This service is said to have originated in the ninth century A.D. for the purpose of praying for protection for the throne, happiness for the people, and good crops. For this ritual a garment of the emperor is sent by the imperial household.

[70] See Kamimura, "Buddhist Worship of the Masses," *Research Tour Papers*, pp. 15–20. According to Kamimura, the three "Prayer Temples" in Tokyo—Asakusa Kannon, Shibamata Taishakuten, and Meguro Fudōsan —every year attract an average 30,000,000; 1,500,000; and 300,000 worshipers, respectively.

[71] International Institute for the Study of Religions, *Religion and Modern Life*, Bulletin No. 5, Part II (November, 1958), p. 29. According to a participant in a round table conference on religion, "the half-death of Buddhism as far as the people are concerned may be due to the fact that the temples give nothing to the people." See also International Institute for the Study of Religions, *Living Buddhism in Japan*, prepared by Yoshio Tamura in collaboration with William P. Woodard.

[72] According to Laures, there had been 121,128 Catholics in Japan in 1941. Of that number, about 10,000 became victims of the war. (Laures, *The Catholic Church in Japan*, p. 246.)

ber of such cases. Rather, the militarists and ultranationalists followed a policy of harassing Christian activities to the point that Christianity, together with other religions, became little more than a patriotic organization with some religious trappings. Thus the initial task for Christianity in the postwar period was as much to undergo spiritual rehabilitation as to undertake the physical reconstruction of its churches and institutions.

The immediate postwar period was also marked by a good deal of interest in Christianity on the part of the general populace, and the Christian groups were determined to take advantage of this atmosphere for the expansion of their work. In this respect Christians benefited a great deal from the constitutional guarantees of religious freedom. Ironically, many people in Japan received the impression, right or wrong, that Christianity received various kinds of support from the occupation authorities, and, as William Woodard has pointed out, MacArthur's "ill-advised effort to promote Christianity was a disservice both to that faith and to the cause of separation of 'church' and 'state.'" [73] Meanwhile, popular enthusiasm for Christianity waned toward the end of the occupation period, partly due to a naïve identification of Christianity with anti-Communist campaigns on the part of some of the Christian leaders and the occupation authorities. The fact that Japanese churches depended heavily on Western churches for their material and human resources did not encourage the growth of initiative among the people. However salutary the motives of the Western churches in helping the Japanese churches, the sheer presence of so many foreign missionaries in Japan tended to emphasize the foreignness of Christianity—a trademark that the Japanese churches could ill afford to have at the time of the restoration of national sovereignty following the occupation period.

Numerically speaking, the Roman Catholic Church and the fundamentalist groups made far greater gains than the older Protestant groups in the postwar period. Among all Christian groups the Eastern (Russian) Orthodox Church suffered the most from the strain of the war period as well as from the tension of

[73] Quoted in Hammer, *Japan's Religious Ferment,* p. 115.

the cold war because of its historic connection with the Moscow Patriarchate.[74] According to an official report in 1964, the Orthodox Church had 48 churches, 56 clergy (including catechists), and 9,194 members.

The Roman Catholic Church has been more effective than other Christian groups in rural work. It has also developed firm bases in the urban centers. The steady growth of Catholicism in Japan may be shown by the fact that while in 1941 it claimed 445 priests (among them 136 Japanese), 234 brothers (132 Japanese), and 1,794 nuns (the majority of whom were Japanese), in 1953 it had 1,048 priests (238 Japanese), 334 brothers (191 Japanese), and 2,954 nuns (2,037 Japanese).[75] According to its official report, in 1964 there were then 1,748 Catholic establishments (churches and monasteries) and 318,941 members. There

[74] The internal strife of the Orthodox Church goes back to the prewar period. It was in 1940 that the Orthodox Church in Japan declared complete independence from the Moscow patriarchate. At that time, Sergius, the archbishop of Tokyo, was compelled to resign, and Iwasawa Heikichi, then professor at the Orthodox Seminary, was elected to take his place. However, anti-Iwasawa factions were so strong that Iwasawa withdrew his candidacy for the episcopate. Instead, Iwasawa recommended Ono Kiichi, head of the administrative office of the Orthodox Church, and Takai Makio, archpriest in charge of the Nagasaki diocese, as two candidates for the episcopate. Ono then proceeded to Harbin, Manchuria, where he was consecrated to the episcopate. However, Ono's leadership was questioned by the anti-Ono factions, and the church suffered from internal disunity during the war. This was one reason why the Orthodox Church was not recognized by the Japanese government under the Religious Organizations Law that was put into effect in 1940. In 1946 those who wanted to restore the historic connection between the Orthodox Church in Japan and the Moscow patriarchate attempted to take over the church under Ono's leadership. The majority of their constituency, however, decided to invite an Orthodox bishop from the United States, whereupon Benjamin, an American Orthodox bishop, went to Japan and served there until he was succeeded by Irenie, another American Orthodox bishop, in 1953. Meanwhile, Michail Zerzenov, an archbishop from Soviet Russia, visited Japan in connection with the Anti-Atomic-Hydrogen Bomb Rally in August, 1957. Following his visit, a group of people who were not happy under the American jurisdiction organized the "Japanese Legitimate Orthodox Church" (*Nihon Seitō Seikyōkai*), under the former archpriest of Nagasaki.

[75] Laures, *The Catholic Church in Japan*, p. 247.

are fifteen dioceses and 218 religious orders. The fact that the Roman Catholic Church still depends on 2,700 foreign personnel presents occasional problems,[76] but in the main its strategy in evangelistic, educational, medical, and other charitable works is well planned and generally effective.[77] The four-hundredth anniversary of the arrival of Francis Xavier, celebrated in 1949, was a great event for Japanese Catholics in the postwar period.[78] In 1960 Doi Tatsuo (Peter T. Doi) became the first Japanese cardinal. The hierarchy has encouraged new experimental programs in evangelism, in the field of church architecture, and in the use of mass communications media. Conversely, an increasing number of laymen are taking active part in the affairs of the church. "In all," says a Protestant observer, "the Roman Catholic Church is carrying on a well rounded program that shows how deeply they are interested in Christianizing this land." [79]

[76] In 1953 Kotani Kimi, spiritual head of Reiyū-kai (The Association of the Friends of the Spirit), was accused of several irregularities regarding financial matters. One of the charges was her unauthorized acquisition of American dollars; she was suspected of having made the transaction through a Catholic priest. See ZNBT, XIII: *Gendai* (Contemporary period) (Tokyo, 1958), 220. In 1959 the Japanese press suspected that a Catholic priest was involved in the mysterious death of a BOAC stewardess. See Mombu-shō, *Shūkyō Nenkan* for 1959, p. 13.

[77] Nielsen, *Religion and Philosophy in Contemporary Japan*, p. 79: "Scores of excellent European scholars, Italian, French, Spanish and German, have been brought to Roman Catholic universities. Protestant scholarship is not as specialized or as much given to research."

[78] For this occasion, the right arm of Xavier, which had been preserved in Rome, was brought to Japan. The solemn mass celebrated on June 12, 1949, in Tokyo attracted 30,000 of the faithful.

[79] William C. Kerr, *Japan Begins Again*, p. 145. The Roman Catholic Church has also penetrated wealthy circles in post war Japanese society. For example, according to *Time* magazine (LXXIII [No. 12, March 23, 1959], 33), at Tokyo's Sacred Heart School, where the present crown princess was educated, "the names of the girls read like a roll call of Japan's wealthiest families," in contrast to the Peers' School, "which is reserved mainly for the descendants of the blue-blooded *kazoku* families." It is curious that despite heavy emphasis on scholarship, the Roman Church in Japan has not produced creative theological thinkers so far. The only exception, perhaps, was Iwashita Sōichi (1889–1940), whose busy

The complex development of Protestant churches in the postwar period becomes more intelligible if we recall the highhanded measures of the militarist government that forced the merger during the war of various denominations into a united "Church of Christ in Japan." The coming of peace brought with it a serious crisis for the internal unity of the United Church, partly because of tensions and disagreements that had not been resolved among various segments within the church and partly because of denominational interests on the part of Western missionary societies that were now called upon to assist in the rehabilitation of the churches they had supported before the war. To be sure, many churches of nearly twenty prewar denominations, including the so-called big three, namely, the Presbyterian, the Methodist, and the Congregational, remained in the United Church, and the Interboard Committee for Christian Work in Japan was formed by various North American churches in order to pool their financial and human resources for the purpose of assisting and cooperating with the United Church in Japan.[80] But the Anglican (Episcopal), the Evangelical Lutheran, the Southern Baptist, and the Nazarene churches, as well as the Salvation Army, the Evangelical Alliance, the Holiness, the Wesleyan Methodist, and some of the Reformed groups left the United Church and became independent bodies again. Moreover, nonecclesiastical bodies, such as the Y.M.C.A., the Y.W.C.A., the Christian Literature Society, and the Bible Society, also returned to their prewar independent status. At the first postwar General Assembly of the United Church, held in 1946, Kozaki Michio became the new moderator. That year also marked the beginning of a three-year evangelistic campaign under the slogan "Christ for all Japan." According to an official report in 1964, the United Church had 1,602 churches and mission stations, 2,644 church workers (pastors and teachers,

---

priestly schedule did not enable him to produce systematic works in the fields of theology and philosophy. See Iwashita, *Shinkō no isan.*

[80] The following churches participated in this cooperative venture: Congregational Christian, Evangelical and Reformed, Evangelical United Brethren, Methodist, Presbyterian U.S.A., Reformed Church in America, Disciples of Christ, and the United Church of Canada.

among whom 286 were foreigners), and 140,343 members.[81]

Statistics of the other major Protestant groups, as of 1964, are as follows: The Anglican (Episcopal) Church, known officially as the Holy Catholic Church in Japan (*Nippon Seikōkai*), had 328 parishes and missions, 425 church workers (among them 54 were foreigners), and 30,836 members.[82] The Evangelical Lutheran Church had 136 churches and mission stations, 165 church workers (among them 61 were foreigners), and 13,411 members. The Church of the Spirit of Jesus (*Iyesu no mitama kyōkai*) has 252 churches, 89 church workers, and 26,821 members.[83] The Baptist Convention had 217 churches, 277 church workers (among them 107 were foreigners), and 15,822 members. The Japan Christian Church had 104 churches, 99 church workers, and 11,863 members. Other groups, such as the Japan Christian (Dutch) Reformed Church, the Seventh Day Adventist, the (Christian and Missionary) Alliance Society, the Evangelical Alliance Mission, the Nazarene Church, the Assembly of God, the Holiness Church, the Salvation Army, and the Free Methodist Church, counted less than 10,000 members each. Some of the splinter sects, such as the Brethren of Christ, the Holy Jesus, the Living Water (*Kassui*), and the Immanuel General Mission groups, are not significant, at least numerically.[84]

[81] The official theological institution of the United Church is the Tokyo Theological College. In addition, the Theology Department of Dōshisha University, the Theology Department of Kansaigakuin University, and the Japan Biblical Seminary are also recognized (*ninka*) by the United Church.

[82] Affiliated with the Anglican Church are such institutions as St. Luke's International Medical Center and St. Paul's University, both in Tokyo; and Momoyamagakuin University and St. Barnabas' Hospital, both in Osaka. The Anglican Church has its own theological college in Tokyo.

[83] Niels Nielsen characterizes this group as a somewhat nationalistic and anti-Western, lower-class organization. Sociologically, this church "represents a Japanese movement akin to the New Religions. It emphasizes faith healing and apparently is not fully orthodox in Christology." (*Religion and Philosophy in Contemporary Japan*, p. 76.)

[84] The Brethren of Christ (*Kirisuto Kyōdai-dan*) and the Immanuel General Mission broke away from the Holiness Church. The Living Water Christian Church (*Kassui Kirisuto Kyōdan*) was organized in 1941 by a

Unique in the Protestant tradition in Japan is the so-called Non-Church (*Mukyōkai*) movement which owes its birth to Uchimura Kanzō (1861–1930).[85] He and his followers attempted to witness for the Christian gospel without ecclesiastical organization and without financial support from Western missionary societies. According to Emil Brunner, the Non-Church movement is most promising not only for Japan, but for all Christianity. In his words: "It is now possible to be a disciple of Christ, to live with Christ, and in fellowship with others to do something in his name—without the necessity of becoming a 'church.' "[86] Others, however, dispute Brunner's exalted evaluation of the movement. Nevertheless, its strong influence among Japanese intellectuals is very significant, considering the fact that most established church groups have made but slight inroads among academic people. Having no stipendiary ministers, the lay Bible teachers of the Non-Church movement present an enduring Biblicism through publications and Bible classes. While Michalson is correct in saying that "the expression of Christianity which prevails in the Non-Church movement is a relatively immature expression,"[87] it was nevertheless an important corrective to the usual approach of established churches in Japan.

One of the important postwar developments in Japan was the influx of foreign missionaries representing churches that had not had contacts with Japan prior to the war, such as the Lutheran Missouri Synod, the Lutheran Brotherhood, the (Swedish) Covenant, the Baptist Bible Fellowship, the Christian Baptist, the

group of disciples of an English evangelist named Baxton. The Holy Jesus Society (*Sei Iyesu Kai*) had close connection with the Living Water Christian Church. These together with other minority groups became independent churches according to the Religious Corporations Ordinance, promulgated in December, 1945.

[85] See Tsunoda, et al., *Sources of Japanese Tradition*, pp. 847–57.

[86] Brunner, "The Unique Christian Mission: The Mukyōkai ('Non-Church') Movement in Japan," in Leibrecht, ed., *Religion and Culture: Essays in Honor of Paul Tillich*, p. 290.

[87] Michalson, *Japanese Contributions to Christian Theology*, p. 124. Incidentally, the membership of the Non-Church group is estimated at hundreds of thousands.

Latter Day Saints of Jesus Christ, the Mennonites, Christian Science, and Jehovah's Witnesses. Indeed, as Nielsen states, "American Christendom must assume responsibility for much of the postwar division [among Protestant Christianity in Japan], since missionary funds from abroad still determine church programs in large measure." [88] It was reported that by 1951 there were over 1,500 foreign missionaries representing 116 churches and boards.[89] The arrival of a large number of missionaries whose theological conviction may be characterized as fundamentalistic resulted in the emergence of many conservative churches and associations, including the Japanese Evangelical Overseas Mission (JEOM), the Evangelical Missionary Association of Japan (EMAJ), the Evangelical Alliance Mission (TEAM), and the New Life League. These fundamentalist churches, with the assistance of their mother churches in North America, have been engaged in a belligerent campaign of mass evangelism. As early as 1959 the number of foreign missionaries affiliated with the Evangelical Missionary Association of Japan was 1,597—four times as large as the number of their counterparts in the United Church. Besides, a small group of forty missionaries is affiliated with the Japan Bible Christian Council. In fact, according to one probably inflated report, "the conservative Japanese constituency numbers 102,900, led by 1,971 licensed and ordained ministers meeting in 1,700 churches. The total number of uncounted adherents . . . is around 101,000." [90]

The older Protestant churches, on the other hand, affiliate themselves with the National Christian Council (N.C.C.), and through it with the World Council of Churches (W.C.C.).[91]

[88] Nielsen, *Religion and Philosophy in Contemporary Japan,* p. 73.

[89] Cited by Vern Rossman in his article, "Churches Face Many Problems as 100th Year Is Celebrated," *The Japan Times,* Nov. 2, 1959, p. 5.

[90] Joseph, "Mass Media Carry Message to Many," *Asahi Evening News,* May 2, 1959.

[91] The members of the National Council of Churches are the United Church of Christ, the Anglican Church, the Evangelical Lutheran Church, the Baptist Convention, the Korean Church in Japan, the Y.M.C.A., the Y.W.C.A., the Women's Christian Temperance Union, the Federation of Christian Social Workers, the League of Christian Nurseries, the Bible Society, and the Education Association of Christian Schools.

The N.C.C. is also a member of the East Asia Christian Council (E.A.C.C.). On the whole, the older Protestant churches suffer from the fact that they still tend to perpetuate their prewar traditions. While there are some promising younger people, by and large the leadership is in the hands of tired men who have lived all their lives in churches guided and supported by Western missionaries and missionary societies, and who still feel emotionally closer to Christians in the West than to their non-Christian neighbors at home. Even Charles Iglehart, who praises Japanese Christians as self-reliant, fully conscious of themselves as being Japanese, acknowledges that the assimilation of Christianity into Japanese life has a long way to go. Although he admits that Christian thinking must widen its base, "from that of the traditional historic formulations of the West to include insights offered by Japan's own greatest truth seekers and spiritual geniuses of the past," [92] he seems to think that such a course will take many more decades, if not centuries.

In 1959 Japanese Protestants celebrated the centennial of the arrival of the first Protestant missionaries in Japan. During the first one hundred years, Protestant Christianity exerted significant influence on Japanese society and culture, and there were some outstanding individual thinkers, theologians, and prophets. Ironically, Protestant Christianity seems to face far more difficult tasks in its second one hundred years. "Congregations tend to remain small, weak and isolated. They draw largely from the educated middle class and have difficulty adequately supporting their pastors. . . . There are churches in 93 percent of the cities of Japan but only in 6 percent of the towns and villages." [93] There are excellent Christian educational institutions, including the newly established International Christian University, and pastors are well educated and dedicated people, even though "theology at times becomes a substitute for life and work, indeed even an escape from reality." [94] Yet Protestants, and also Roman Catholics, for that matter, have not seriously faced such problems as the

[92] Iglehart, *A Century of Protestant Christianity in Japan*, p. 348.
[93] Rossman, "Churches Face Many Problems . . ." *The Japan Times*, Nov. 2, 1959, p. 5.
[94] Nielsen, *Religion and Philosophy in Contemporary Japan*, p. 74.

political order, the economic system, world peace, the family system, and the relationship of Christianity to other religions.[95]

The predicament of Christianity in the postwar period is succinctly stated by a former Communist who is now a Christian. He writes:

Japanese Christianity has had no language with which it could speak directly to the Japanese laborers and masses. In other words, Christianity in Japan has been the property of a few intelligent people. It may not be a mistake to say that Japanese Christianity has been unwilling to get rid of such a *stigma*. Moreover, since the end of World War II Communism has succeeded in winning some of the hearts of the university students and of the intelligentsia, and so the principal basis for Japanese Christianity has partly been destroyed. It may be said that Christianity floats unattached on the surface of present day Japanese society. The fact that a number of Newly Arisen Sects (or *Shinkō Shūkyō*) are getting to the hearts of the masses may be disquieting for those Japanese Christians who deplore the decrease in the number of their believers.[96]

Sect Shinto and New Religions

It has become abundantly clear that the principle of religious freedom has greatly changed the religious situation in Japan in the postwar period. State Shinto has been transformed into Shrine Shinto, which is now incorporated as a religion. With the lifting of governmental control over religious bodies, various subsects and splinter groups that had been incorporated into the major denominations of Buddhism and of Christianity broke away from their parental bodies and declared their independence. Sect Shinto denominations, thirteen in number until the end of the Second World War, also suffered from separatist tendencies in their ranks. Moreover, the postwar period has witnessed the emergence of many new religious cults and movements—some that are Buddhistic or Shintoistic, but many that are syncretistic. According to

[95] See Ariga, "The Christian Mission in Japan as a Theological Problem," *Religion in Life*, XXVII (No. 3, Summer, 1958), 372–80.

[96] Shiina, "The Japanese People and 'Indigenous Christianity,'" *Japanese Religions*, I (No. 2, 1959), 18–19.

an official report in 1963 these "new religions" constitute about half of the total of the 379 religious juridical persons, and the number of their adherents is estimated conservatively at well over ten million.[97]

Among these new religions, some of the most recent ones have already shown signs of decline, while others have become as highly stratified as many of the older religious organizations. The bewildering variety of these new religions is such that it is futile simply to list their names, nor is it easy to classify them according to simple categories, even though there are certain affinities among those that came out of the same tradition—as, for example, among Ananai-kyō, Seichō-no-iye, and Sekai Kyūsei-kyō, whose original impetus can be traced to Ōmoto-kyō, or among Sōka-gakkai, Reiyū-kai, and Risshō Kōsei-kai, which all adhere, at least according to their own claims, to the teachings of the thirteenth-century Buddhist prophet, Nichiren, as I shall explain presently. The Union of New Religious Organizations of Japan (Shin-Nihon-Shūkyō-Dantai-Rengō-Kai, commonly referred to as Shin-Shū-Ren), which was formed in 1951, now has over one hundred member religions.

The perplexing religious development in the postwar period, especially the emergence of so many new religions, inevitably affected the strength and activities of Sect Shinto denominations. I have earlier discussed the pre- and early-Meiji phases of the thirteen denominations of Sect Shinto (Kyōha Shintō), namely, (1) Shintō Taikyō (great teaching of Shinto), (2) Shinri-kyō (divine truth religion), (3) Izumo Taisha-kyō (religion of the Great Shrine of Izumo), (4) Shintō Shūsei-ha (improving and consolidating school of Shinto), (5) Taisei-kyō (great accomplishment religion), (6) Jikkō-kyō (practical conduct religion), (7) Fusō-kyō (religion of Mount Fuji), (8) Ontake-kyō (religion of Mount Ontake), (9) Shinshū-kyō (divine learning religion), (10) Misogi-kyō (purification religion), (11) Kurozumi-kyō (religion of Kurozumi, named after its founder), (12) Konkō-kyō (religion of Konkō, which is the name of the kami),

[97] Ministry of Education, *Religions in Japan*, p. 86.

and (13) Tenri-kyō (divine reason religion). Some of these groups were in a real sense prototypes of the postwar new religions, and as such they have been included in the category of new religions (*Shinkō Shūkyō*) by some writers.[98] Until 1945 the Federation of Sect Shinto (Kyōha-Shintō-rengō-kai) included only the above-mentioned thirteen denominations. However, after the war, many of the subsects of Sect Shinto denominations became independent, so that the number of Sect Shinto groups increased to seventy-five by 1949.[99] Meanwhile, Shintō Shūsei-ha seceded from the federation. On the other hand, Ōmoto (formerly called Ōmoto-kyō, or the "Religion of Great Fundamentals"), which had been classified as a quasi religion before the war, joined the federation of Sect Shinto denominations.

In the main, Sect Shinto denominations, with some notable exceptions, do not seem to be as active and vital as they were before the war. Although most of them seem to maintain their numerical strength,[100] their prestige and influence have been greatly undercut by the aggressive propaganda of the new reli-

---

[98] Offner and Van Straelen, in *Modern Japanese Religions*, include Tenri-kyō in their discussion. Thomsen, in *The New Religions of Japan*, classifies Tenri-kyō, Kurozumi-kyō, and Konkō-kyō as the "old" new religions.

[99] As mentioned earlier, Shintō Taikyō was split into ten, Fusō-kyō into twenty-one, Ontake-kyō into thirteen, and Shinri-kyō into seven.

[100] According to the official statistics of 1964, they are as follows:

(1) Shintō Taikyō	571,610
(2) Kurozumi-kyō	780,106
(3) Shintō Shūsei-ha	51,980
(4) Izumo Ōyashiro-kyō (formerly known as Izumo Taisha-kyō)	2,254,275
(5) Fusō-kyō	198,891
(6) Jikkō-kyō	189,868
(7) Shintō Taisei-kyō	311,810
(8) Shinshū-kyō	519,669
(9) Ontake-kyō	530,414
(10) Shinri-kyō	444,270
(11) Misogi-kyō	114,430
(12) Konkō-kyō	557,084
(13) Tenri-kyō	2,284,656

Mombu-shō, *Shūkyō nenkan* (1965), pp. 262–64.

gions. Partly to offset the encroachment of the new religions, Sect Shinto denominations have been trying to revitalize themselves and consolidate their ranks through expanding their activities in instruction, publication, propaganda, and philanthropy.[101] Some of them, especially those denominations that are related to the veneration of sacred mountains, have been slow to adjust themselves to the new situation in the postwar period. On the other hand, Izumo Ōyashiro-kyō (Taisha-kyō), which by no means has begun to meet the new demands of the modern age, still enjoys popularity among the masses because of the alleged potency of the kami of Izumo in arranging successful and happy marriages. Kurozumi-kyō and Konkō-kyō, which had developed under the shelter of Shinto, promising faith healing and other benefits to the people, are now trying to become modern, independent religions through eliminating the jargon of incantation from their practices and systematizing their doctrines.[102]

By far the most vigorous and successful among the Sect Shinto denominations is Tenri-kyō. As I have said earlier, Tenri-kyō was founded by a charismatic woman, who promised religious and economic comfort to the oppressed peasants toward the end of the Tokugawa period and during the early Meiji Era. In its inception Tenri-kyō was a crisis religion with a message of social criticism, echoing the antigovernment and antiforeign sentiments of the masses. It soon appropriated Shinto elements into its rites, prayers, and doctrines, and was recognized in 1908 as a Sect Shinto denomination. During the 1930s and early 1940s, the doctrines and rituals of Tenri-kyō underwent further changes. The new catechism, published in 1940, entitled the *Detailed Exposition of the Tenri-kyō Doctrine (Tenri-kyō kyōten engi)*, taught the following principles: (1) reverence toward the kami, (2) reverence for the emperor, (3) patriotism, (4) the duty of obeying the law of the universe which is divine wisdom (*tenri*), (5) the importance of the disciplines of morality, (6) purification, (7) the establishment of Tenri-kyō, (8) the benevolence of the kami,

[101] See Iwamoto, "Present State of Sectarian Shinto," *Research Tour Papers,* pp. 21–25.
[102] See Schneider, *Konkōkyō: A Japanese Religion,* pp. 128–45.

(9) the sacred dance, and (10) ease of mind.[103] Tenri-kyō also sent missionaries to Korea, Taiwan, Manchuria, China, and some parts of the Western world.[104] Since the end of the war Tenri-kyō has not only restored its earlier teachings,[105] but has begun to reinterpret the simple message of the foundress in the hope of developing a comprehensive theological system worthy of a modern religion comparable to other world religions.[106] Yet Tenri-kyō has preserved its qualities as a religion of the masses, advocating simple and practical dogmas, faith healing, the practice of pilgrimage to the sacred city, and the offering of physical labor, combined with effective methods of evangelism and a tightly knit ecclesiastical organization. While the rapid expansion of Tenri-kyō has somewhat leveled off, it is still one of the most powerful and influential religious groups in the postwar period. The followers of Tenri-kyō are convinced that salvation extends over all the world from the sacred spot called the *jiba*—the center of the world—situated in the city of Tenri, Nara prefecture. To them, the *jiba* was the cradle of the human race at the time of its crea-

[103] See Van Straelen, *The Religion of Divine Wisdom*, pp. 72–76.

[104] *Ibid.*, p. 72: "According to a very well-known commentator, Hasegawa Nyozekan, it appears that the only people who really worked unselfishly for the people of war-torn China were the Tenri-kyō faithful."

[105] The original teachings of Tenri-kyō are based on: (1) the *Mikagura-uta*, a series of poems composed by the foundress to accompany the divine service; (2) the *Ofudesaki* (literally, the "tip of a writing brush"); (3) the *Doroumi Koki*, usually referred to as the *Koki*, a folksy myth of creation; and (4) the *Osashizu* (literally, the "revealed directions of god"). Thus far, only (1), (2), and (4) have been called the Canons. The *Koki* is yet to be published as a Canon, although Van Straelen gives a brief outline of this document, *The Religion of Divine Wisdom*, pp. 79–86.

[106] Van Straelen noted that Tenri-kyō scholars intensely study Catholic and Protestant theology, and also keep abreast of the latest philosophical and theological publications from the West. "They are extremely fond of Kierkegaard, especially his views concerning man, not in the category of being but in the category of becoming, and they are well acquainted with the works of K. Jaspers and G. Marcel. . . ." (*Ibid.*, p. 21.) The death of Moroi Yoshinori (1915–61) was a great blow to Tenri-kyō. Moroi was a student of mysticism, especially Islamic mysticism; he was also one of the very few creative theologians of Tenri-kyō.

tion, and life at Tenri city is the model of the ideal society which they were commissioned to establish on this earth.

A similar utopian motif lies at the heart of Ōmoto (great fundamentals, previously known as Ōmoto-kyō). I have discussed the checkered history of this group in the previous chapter. Founded originally by a shamanistic peasant woman, the cause of Ōmoto-kyō was greatly enhanced by a charismatic figure, Deguchi Onisaburō, who claimed to establish a new order on earth. Despite Onisaburō's efforts to cooperate with the militarists in the 1930s, Ōmoto-kyō was classified as a quasi religion (*ruiji shūkyō*) and never given status as a recognized Sect Shinto denomination. Furthermore, Onisaburō was convicted of *lèse majesté* and sentenced to life imprisonment. In 1946 Onisaburō, now released, declared the restoration of Ōmoto under the new name, Aizen-en (the garden of divine love). With the death of Onisaburō in 1948, the movement lost its visionary leader. The leadership of the movement, which again took the name of Ōmoto, was succeeded to first by Onisaburō's wife and then by his daughter.[107] The spiritual center of the Ōmoto movement is Ayabe, a town not far from Kyoto.[108] According to the oracle given to the foundress, "Let those who want to know something of the Divine Plan come to Ōmoto at Ayabe, and they shall be given Divine Virtue with which to see the whole world at a glance, and to see everything which shall happen in the world hereafter." [109]

Numerically speaking, Ōmoto has a membership of a little over 134,000 which is less than that of many of the new religious groups that emerged in the postwar period. However, it is significant to note that Ōmoto, like Tenri-kyō, may be regarded as a

[107] Onisaburō's wife, Deguchi Sumiko, led the movement until her death in 1952, whereupon Deguchi Naohi, daughter of Onisaburō and Sumiko, became the leader according to the family constitution that specifies that a woman of the Deguchi family should be the spiritual head of the Ōmoto religion. The administrative head, however, is Deguchi Isao, the son-in-law of Onisaburō.

[108] The headquarters for public relations of Ōmoto is located at Kameoka, which is another town in the Kyoto prefecture.

[109] Deguchi, *Scripture of Oomoto*, p. 5.

model for other newer religions. It embodies within it various elements that make religion a matter of vital concern to large numbers of people in Japan who are looking for a coherent meaning in life and practical guidance in the midst of the uncertainties of the postwar period. For example, Ōmoto adheres to the main features of the indigenous folk religious tradition familiar to the masses, such as charismatic leadership, faith healing, and the practice of kami-possession.[110] Ōmoto also subscribes to the notion of impending cosmic catastrophe, familiar to all Japanese Buddhists. It also guarantees that a new world order will emerge with Ayabe, the new city of god, as the center of the world.[111] Unlike the historic Buddhist notion of *mappō* (the period of the Latter Law) that led the Japanese Pure Land Buddhists in the thirteenth century to the realization of the utter sinfulness of human nature, Ōmoto holds an optimistic view of man and does not recognize sin as an inevitable element in human nature. Furthermore, Ōmoto attempts to commend itself as a universal religion for modern man, advocating world peace and the brotherhood of all mankind. It also utilizes modern scientific and psychological language to present its peculiar mixture of astronomy and astrology, science and pseudo science, medicine and sorcery, salvation and worldly rewards.[112] These features of Ōmoto have been taken

---

[110] The practice of kami-possession in Ōmoto is called *chinkon-kishin,* which was originally a method "by which possessing spirits were identified and exorcised by a mediator after the patient had been brought to what resembled an hypnotic state; the attainment of this state of mind is also referred to as a means of divine communion." (Offner and Van Straelen, *Modern Japanese Religions,* p. 203.)

[111] Significantly, Deguchi Onisaburō claimed to be the *miroku* (Maitreya) or the future Buddha who is to be the master of the new world order.

[112] For example, Ōmoto advocates the following principles as a "scientific approach to God":

1. Observe the true phases of nature, and you think of the substance of the true God.
2. Observe the unerring function of the universe, and you think of the energy of the true God.
3. Penetrate the mentality of the living creature, and you conceive of the soul of the true God.

over almost *in toto* by Seichō-no-iye (the household of growth), Sekai Kyūsei-kyō (the church of World Messianity), and Ananai-kyō (the religion of three and five, meaning the synthesis of the three dimensions—heaven, earth, and man—and the five great religions of the world).

Among the several new religions that derived their original inspiration from Ōmoto, Seichō-no-iye (the household of growth) is the most urbane and sophisticated. In the last chapter we saw how Taniguchi Masaharu (1893–) broke away from Ōmoto-kyō and developed a quasi-religious group of his own before the war. Inheriting a spiritualistic approach from Ōmoto-kyō, Taniguchi improved on it by incorporating insights from Buddhism, Christianity, Freudian psychology, and Christian Science, as well as from the philosophies of Eucken, Bergson, and Hegel. Being a talented and prolific writer, Taniguchi has published numerous books and magazines that serve as the chief means of gaining converts. The most important among his writings is *Seimei-no-Jissō* (The realities of life), forty volumes in all. Also important is *The Divine Education and Spiritual Training of Mankind,* which includes a highly embroidered version of Taniguchi's autobiography.[113] Taniguchi contends on the one hand that all the religions of the world are the same and thus are to be respected; at one time, he even encouraged the Christian to be a real Christian and the Buddhist to be a real Buddhist. On the other hand, he asserts that Seichō-no-iye alone points to the fundamental realities (*jissō*) underlying the teachings of all religions. In a real sense, according to his claim, Seichō-no-iye is a nondenominational or superreligious truth movement addressed both

---

The underlying assumptions of Ōmoto belief are as follows:

1. The prime source of the universe is vitality, which is God.
2. The universe is the manifestation of vitality, or the fragments of God.
3. Man is the chief embodiment of vitality and minister in the government of Heaven and Earth.

(Quoted from The Oomoto Headquarters, *The Oomoto Movement, Its Origin, Aims and Objects,* p. 21.)

[113] Taniguchi's opportunistic life is portrayed in Saki, *et al., Kyōso,* pp. 97–135.

to the adherents of various religions and to nonbelievers. Taniguchi is also critical of established religions on the ground that their teachings cannot be applied to practical life because, in his opinion, they do not understand that now is the time to act. "This realization that now is the time to act turns a religion into practical life. This is Seichō-no-iye. The difference between accomplished religion and the new revelation of Seichō-no-iye is very slight, but this slight difference is extremely important." [114] Nevertheless, Seichō-no-iye has all the earmarks of religion, such as revelation, a founder, sacred scriptures, and adherents, as well as rituals. It is essentially a cult of self-hypnosis by reading the holy writ (Taniguchi's anaesthetic writings) which exalts spirit over matter, sin, and sickness, as well as by participating in a collective cult of meditation (*shinsō-kan*) a rite inherited from Ōmoto-kyō. It is understandable that so many people look toward a charismatic person like Taniguchi, especially because of his claim to cure all diseases, to avert all calamities, and to promise health, prosperity, happiness, and world peace. In spite of, or because of, the looseness of its organizational structure, Seichō-no-iye has developed as one of the most influential new religions since the end of the Second World War.[115]

Sekai Kyūsei-kyō (the church of World Messianity) also inherited much of its doctrinal content from Ōmoto-kyō. Its founder, Okada Mokichi (1882–1955) had suffered from many

[114] Taniguchi, *Divine Education and Spiritual Training of Mankind*, p. 136.

[115] It claims a membership of over 1,400,000. This figure, of course, is based on the list of "subscribers" to Seichō-no-iye literature. A large number of Taniguchi's followers are among the intelligentsia, especially women of the age group between twenty and fifty. It is conceivable that Taniguchi's nationalistic sentiment may be attractive to some people, too. As stated before, he cooperated wholeheartedly with the militarists during the war, advocating loyalty to the throne. "Now the emphasis is not on the Emperor, but upon the 'fatherland' and the national flag. And Seichō-no-iye is one of the Japanese religions which most ardently advocates a 'religious political movement.'" (Thomsen, *The New Religions of Japan*, p. 156.)

kinds of illness in his youth. In addition, he had lost his family business in the great earthquake in 1923. By chance he was exposed to the spiritualism and faith healing of Ōmoto-kyō, and soon became an important figure in the movement. In 1934 he left Ōmoto-kyō and established his own faith healing cult, which came under the oppression of the authorities. After the war Okada's group was incorporated as a religious organization; it took the name of Sekai Kyūsei-kyō in 1950.[116] According to a revelation given to Okada, the god of creation (*sōzō-shushin*) wishes to establish paradise on this earth by eliminating three evils, namely, sickness, poverty, and strife. Okada taught that these evils, like dark clouds, can be eliminated by the divine light, and that the teachers of Sekai Kyūsei-kyō are nothing more than instruments in transmitting the divine light to people.[117] The popularity of this religion seems to derive from its two main features: faith healing and utopianism. It holds that illness can be cured through purifying one's spirit and preaches against the use of medicaments as harmful.[118] It also advocates a natural method of cultivating vegetables and other foodstuffs without the use of fertilizer. Some believers of this group go as far as to refuse vaccination, because they do not acknowledge the existence of bacteria. Similarly, Okada asserted that

[116] When Okada broke away from Ōmoto-kyō, he organized a group called Dai-Nihon Kannon-kai (The Japanese Association of Avalokiteśvara). The authorities objected to his claim to cure diseases on the ground that he had no medical license. In 1947 he restored his religious group and called it Nihon Kannon Kyōdan (Religion of Avalokiteśvara in Japan), which was renamed Meshiya-kyō (Teaching of the Messiah) and again renamed Sekai Kyūsei-kyō.

[117] We are told that Okada Mokichi consecrated some 600,000 sheets of paper which bore the character for "light" in his own handwriting, and handed them out at 1,000 to 1,500 yen apiece. Kazuo Kuroda, "Domains of 'New Gods,' " *The Japan Times*, November 15, 1958.

[118] Fujieda Masakazu, husband of the present matriarch and administrative head of this religious group, claims that all diseases can be cured gradually if not quickly. He says: "At present severe cases of cancer are not healed. It is possible that little by little, as we purify our souls, we will not need doctors." See Fujieda, "The Church of World Messianity," *Contemporary Religions in Japan*, I (No. 4, December, 1960), 33.

poverty, misfortune, and strife can be overcome by spiritual power.[119] Okada's utopianism was based on the belief that the transition from the state of darkness to the state of paradise which had taken place in the spiritual world will soon become apparent in the physical world. Holding that beautiful forms, such as gardens and museums, are appropriate models of the heavenly state, Sekai Kyūsei-kyō has established two miniature paradises—the summer paradise at Hakone and the winter paradise at Atami—both with elegant gardens and exquisite architecture. The art museum at Atami has one of the best collections of the fine arts in Japan. After the death of the founder, his widow, Okada Yoshiko, assumed the leadership of the group until her death in 1962.[120] The present matriarch is Fujieda Itsuki, daughter of the founder. Sekai Kyūsei-kyō boasts a membership of 591,133 as of 1964.

Ananai-kyō (the "Religion of three and five," implying that it synthesizes the teachings of the major religions of the world, including Confucianism, Taoism, Buddhism, Islam, Christianity, Baha'i, the World Red Swastika Society of China, and the Spiritualist Tradition in Japan), deserves brief mention because of its pseudo-scientific approach to spiritualism. Its founder, Nakano Yonosuke (1887–   ), was a disciple of Nagasawa Katsu-

---

[119] It is to be noted that the founder was convinced that his religion could save America. In his own words: "No other nation besides America is today equal to the task of maintaining peace in the world. It is therefore one of the most urgent tasks today to help America improve the health condition of her people. I therefore want to stop the spread of diseases there and to eradicate all of them. . . ." Quoted by Tetsutarō Ariga, "The So-called 'Newly-Arisen Sects' in Japan," Missionary Research Library, *Occasional Bulletin*, V (No. 4, March, 1954), 5.

[120] Shortly before his death, Okada Mokichi was arrested and convicted on charges of tax evasion and graft. Incidentally, he is referred to as Meishu-sama (Enlightened master), and is believed to have ascended to heaven, from where he is still directing the affairs of this world. His widow, Okada Yoshiko, was called Nidai-sama (The second master). She faced many difficult problems, including a couple of scandals caused by the death of members of her flock who were supposed to be undergoing treatment to expel evil spirits. Her daughter, the present matriarch, is called Sandai-sama (The third master).

tate, a Shinto priest who had transmitted the tradition of spiritualism from Honda Chikanori. According to Nakano's own claim, he had a direct encounter with a god, and this religious experience led him to join Ōmoto-kyō.[121] However, he left Ōmoto-kyō in 1949 and established Ananai-kyō. Like Ōmoto-kyō, Ananai-kyō is based on a type of meditation called *chinkon-kishin* (literally, "quieting the soul in order to become the kami"), a cult for becoming kami-possessed. The doctrines of this religion are highly contradictory. One might say, though, that Ananai-kyō is essentially a form of the simple spiritualism common to the Japanese folk religious tradition. To this Nakano added the motif of the approaching end of the world and the coming of a savior. The unique feature of Ananai-kyō is its notion that the will of the kami can be studied in the movement of heavenly bodies. Thus Ananai-kyō has built a number of observatories in various parts of Japan equipped with modern astronomical instruments. It is not likely that Nakano or his associates will be able to synthesize astronomy and religion, but the fact that such a bizarre claim has attracted over 215,000 adherents indicates the confused religious climate of Japan in the postwar period.[122]

Tenshō-Kōtai-Jingū-kyō, commonly referred to as the "dancing religion" (*odoru shūkyō*), is also a typical product of the social and religious confusion that followed the end of the Second World War. Its foundress, Kitamura Sayo (1900–　), was a peasant woman in the Yamaguchi prefecture. In her youth she led a seemingly normal life as a farmer's wife. In 1943 her house caught fire and burned down. This calamity marked the beginning of her spiritual awakening. In 1944 Sayo received the first divine inspiration which convinced her that a Shinto deity, the Heavenly Goddess (*Tenshō-Kōtai-Jingū*), dwelled in her body, whereupon she began to proclaim the coming of a new social order. Her eccentric behavior and her preaching, which took the

---

[121] It is significant to note that Nakano studied spiritualism under Nagasawa together with Deguchi Onisaburō, cofounder of Ōmoto-kyō, and Okada Mokichi, founder of Sekai Kyūsei-kyō. Both Nakano and Okada joined Ōmoto-kyō and worked for some years under Daguchi Onisaburō.

[122] See Thomsen, *The New Religions of Japan*, pp. 143–52.

form of rhythmic singing and dancing, caught the attention of people who were desperately looking for an authority figure with a divine message. Sayo's followers call her Ōgami-sama (Great Goddess), and follow her frenzied religious activities. According to Sayo, the goddess who dwells in her physical body is the same as the God of the Christians and the Buddha. Her oracles are crude and simple, claiming that she and she alone can save humanity. No persons, not even the emperor and high government officials, are spared her merciless condemnation as miserable sinners, or "maggot beggars" and "traitor beggars" as she calls them. She has no use for mundane governments; she refuses to pay taxes and ignores elections.[123] She declares that cemeteries and tombstones are unnecessary. "I have not descended to redeem all human souls," she declares. "I have come to judge the collapsing world and to establish a Heavenly Kingdom. Therefore, I have established policies through which every human being shall choose one of three alternatives: to be punished in public disgrace; to suffer Heavenly capital punishment; or to become an angel. . . ."[124] She is especially critical of organized religions and the medical profession. "I am now creating a world in which churches, temples, idols, and graves will have no place. On the contrary, I will deprive physicians and clerics of their means of livelihood."[125] Because of Sayo's eccentricities many people at first predicted that her religion would attract only a small group of followers. But over 223,000 persons have adopted her dancing religion and they show no signs of deserting her. It is safe to assume that the magnetism of the foundress' charismatic personality will hold them as long as she lives.[126]

[123] When she was arrested for not paying the obligatory quota of crops to the government, she is said to have sung aloud: "Beggars and traitor maggots in neat uniforms are taking on high airs, while the True Redeemer is placed under arrest." Eventually she was released. The district attorney, who had been in charge of her case, became her convert and is now serving as the leader of the Tokyo branch of Tenshō-Kōtai-Jingū-kyō. See Thomsen, pp. 203–4.

[124] Tenshō-Kōtai-Jingū-kyō, *Guidance to God's Kingdom*, p. 7.

[125] Tenshō-Kōtai-Jingū-kyō, *The Prophet of Tabuse*, p. 123.

[126] See Kohler, *Die Lotus-Lehre und die modernen Religionen in Japan*, pp. 98–117.

In sharp contrast to Tenshō-Kōtai-Jingū-kyō that rejects the values of the world, PL Kyōdan (the "PL" stands for "Perfect Liberty") is characterized by its thoroughgoing world-affirming attitude. Earlier I traced the prewar development of this religion, then known as Hito-no-michi (literally, "the way of man"), to another quasi religion, Tokumitsu-kyō, named after its founder, Kanada Tokumitsu.[127] Kanada taught that the sufferings of people could be transferred to him. He affirmed that he would vicariously endure the sufferings of others. This doctrine, called *o-furikaye* (divine mediation that transfers suffering from people to the "teaching parent"), was the basis of Tokumitsu-kyō, to which Kanada added other religio-magical practices derived from Shingon esoterism, Shugen-dō, and folk Shinto. His opportunistic and pragmatic approach to religion attracted many adherents, especially among the merchant class. These features of Tokumitsu-kyō were inherited by Hito-no-michi, founded by Miki Tokuharu (1871–1938).[128] He and his son, Miki Tokuchika

[127] Kanada Tokumitsu (1863–1919) was a contradictory combination of shrewd merchant, engaged in the hardware business, and visionary. Following the example of Kūkai, systematizer of Shingon Buddhism, Kanada practiced austerities in the mountains of Kōya and Katsuragi (the training center of the Mountain Ascetics). He also took training in Ontake-kyō and became a recognized teacher of this religion. He held that the phenomenal world was the manifestation of Mahāvairocana, who, according to him, was also known as the kami of the Grand Shrine of Ise and the kami of the Kumano shrines, or simply as the sun. He astutely adopted the Imperial Rescript on Education as the guiding principle of Tokumitsu-kyō, which was officially founded in 1912. Kanada is venerated as one of the *kakure-oya* (hidden parents) of PL Kyōdan with the posthumous name of Amahito-umiruihiko-no-mikoto.

[128] Miki Tokuharu's own father was a merchant on the island of Shikoku. When Tokuharu was eleven, he was sent to a Zen temple where he spent five years and became a priest. He married and had three children; one of them is Miki Tokuchika, the present patriarch of PL Kyōdan. Miki Tokuharu gave up the priesthood at the age of forty-one and moved to Osaka, where he met Kanada Tokumitsu. In 1916 he became Kanada's disciple. Three years later Kanada died. Miki Tokuharu planted a sacred shrub (*himorogi*) at Tomagahata, the place where his late master had died, and worshiped it every day for five years. His son, Miki Tokuchika, meanwhile, was active in a youth group established for the purpose of composing short poems (*tanka*). Members of this group—young men of the lower

(1900–   ), were arrested in the 1930s and charged with high treason. Hito-no-michi, despite its effort to collaborate with the militarists, was dissolved by government order in 1937. In October, 1945, Miki Tokuchika was released from prison. He renovated Hito-no-michi under the name of PL Kyōdan in 1946.

Much has been written in recent years about the teachings and practices of PL Kyōdan.[129] Its teaching is amazingly simple, based on the theory that "Life is art." It is to be noted that the term "art" is used here in the broad sense, for PL holds that housekeeping, nursing a child, engaging in business, and working in a factory, for example, are as much forms of creative art as are painting a picture, composing a poem, or playing a musical instrument. At the heart of PL teaching is the notion of "ego-phenomena" (*gashō*) or "manifestations of selfishness," referring to those misfortunes, calamities, and sufferings that arise when man forgets God.[130] When "ego-phenomena" appear suddenly, the PL

---

middle class—aspired to experience happiness and beauty through the art of poetry. In 1924 Miki Tokuharu and his son Tokuchika, assisted by Tokuchika's poet friends, proclaimed the establishment of a new religious cult, based on the "revelations" allegedly given to Miki Tokuharu. In order to differentiate the new cult from the teaching of Kanada Tokumitsu, which was known as Shintō Tokumitsu-kyō (the way of the kami as taught by Tokumitsu), Miki Tokuharu called his religion Jindō (or Hito-no-michi) Tokumitsu-kyō (The way of man as taught by Tokumitsu), and registered it as a subsect of Fusō-kyō, one of the thirteen Sect Shinto denominations. The new religion attracted many adherents by teaching practical morality, such as the importance of the family, the virtuousness of women, and loyalty to the throne. Members were given golden statues of the founder to which they could "transfer" all their problems and sicknesses. The phenomenal success of Hito-no-michi frightened the government, which ordered its dissolution in 1937. Miki Tokuharu died the following year. He is venerated as Founder I of PL Kyōdan with the posthumous name of Amamizu-umihi-arawaru-hiko-no-mikoto.

[129] Yashima, *An Essay on the Way of Life*; PL Kyōdan, *Perfect Liberty—How to Lead a Happy Life*; Yashima, *Shosei no shiori*; Yashima, *PL Shoseikun kaisetsu*; Nielsen, *Religion and Philosophy in Contemporary Japan*, pp. 93–99; Thomsen, *The New Religions of Japan*, pp. 183–98; Offner and Van Straelen, *Modern Japanese Religions*, pp. 82–88; and Kohler, *Die Lotus-Lehre*, pp. 68–87. Probably the best study of PL Kyōdan is Bairy, *Japans Neue Religionen in der Nachkriegszeit*, pp. 70–111.

[130] A spokesman of PL Kyōdan states: "Our God is not omnipresent or

believer can request of God that his troubles be transferred to the person of the patriarch, who then will undergo "vicarious suffering" (*tenshō*) for the believer.[131] Actually, "vicarious suffering" is perhaps the oldest, and has been the most persistent, feature of folk religion in Japan. By making this old and familiar motif the central soteriological theme, even though it is expressed in the modernistic language of art, PL Kyōdan appeals to a large segment of the Japanese people, especially those of the lower middle class. It also has an efficient organizational structure, based on a paternalistic scheme, which directs all aspects of PL Kyōdan activities, including management of a huge golf course, classes in the arts and social dancing, training of novices, public relations, and various kinds of educational and philanthropic enterprises. The headquarters of PL Kyōdan is located at Habikino, not far from Osaka, and is frequented by its adherents, now estimated to number over 1,164,000.

Among the new religions that developed out of the Buddhist background, the three most prosperous ones are Reiyū-kai (the association of the friends of the spirit), Risshō-Kōsei-kai (literally, "the society for the establishment of righteousness and friendly relations"), and Sōka-gakkai (society for the creation of values). All three of them acknowledge their dependence on the *Lotus Sutra*, the central scripture of the Nichiren school of Buddhism for their guiding principles. It should be recalled that Nichiren (1222–82) was one of the most charismatic and controversial figures in the religious history of Japan. The school of

---

all-powerful. It may be said that all existence is the body of God. All existence is also the shades and shadows of God. God in PL has no characteristics like human beings. God is 'Law' (*Hō*). The God of PL is like the law of gravitation and has no tangible characteristics." (Yuasa, "PL (Perfect Liberty)," *Contemporary Religions in Japan*, I [No. 3, September, 1960], 29.)

[131] *Ibid.*, p. 26: "Each month there is a meeting in which the believers participate for the purpose of transferring their responsibility to the Patriarch. Prayers are offered there in order to make it possible for the Patriarch to bear responsibility for the sins of the past month. At this ceremony God will bless him and give him strength." This idea of "vicarious suffering" was known earlier as *o-furikaye* in Tokumitsu-kyō and Hito-no-michi.

Buddhism bearing his name developed into a militant, exclusivistic, and nationalistic faith. We earlier pointed out that, in
spite of his antagonism toward the Shingon school (esoteric
Buddhism), Nichiren shared with it the use of the mandala and
the belief in man's redeemability in this phenomenal world. Also,
the fact that he denounced the *Nembutsu* (recitation of Amida's
name) of the Pure Land Buddhists did not prevent him from
developing his own cult of reciting the title of the *Lotus Sutra*.
Living as he did in one of the most turbulent eras of Japanese
history, Nichiren dedicated himself to the establishment of the
great Buddha land in Japan. Many of these characteristics of
Nichiren and his school have been inherited by modern lay
Buddhist associations which had official or unofficial connections
with the Nichiren tradition, such as Butsuryū-kō (the association to exalt Buddha), Kokuchū-kai (the nation's pillar society), Remmon-kyō (the lotus gate religion), and `Reiyū-kai
(the association of the friends of the spirit). These lay associations tended to be anticlerical, and stressed salvation in this world
with various kinds of mundane benefits.

In the previous chapter I pointed out that Reiyū-kai was established in 1925 through the joint efforts of Kubo Kakutarō (1890–
1944), a fanatic lay believer in the *Lotus Sutra,* and Kotani Kimi
(1900–   ), an uneducated housewife with the attributes of a
shamanic diviner. While Reiyū-kai claims to be a lay Buddhist
organization and its rituals are taken from those of the Nichiren
school, its ethos betrays the strong influence of the magico-religious tradition of the masses, as evidenced by the stress on
ancestor cults and the promise of worldly benefits, especially
faith healing. Accordingly, Reiyū-kai regards this phenomenal
world as the arena of man's salvation. Believers are urged to put
their faith not in Buddhas and Bodhisattvas but in the mandala,
the graphic representation of Nichiren's gospel with the title of
the *Lotus Sutra* and the names of Buddhist divinities. To be
sure, it was Nichiren himself who had taught the efficacy of reciting the title of the *Lotus Sutra* for one's salvation; this teaching is accepted by Reiyū-kai. But Reiyū-kai goes farther and
asserts that the saving power of the Buddhas and Bodhisattvas

is concentrated in the mandala, which alone should be worshiped. That is to say, the mandala and the title of the *Lotus Sutra,* as such, have miraculous potencies. Thus, the believer prays: "Namu-Myō-Hō-Renge-Kyō! [Hail, the Lotus of the Wonderful Law] . . . Forgive me for my false mind and misleading thought! . . . Oh, Buddhas and Devas come down, may you guard me! Namu-Myō-Hō-Renge-Kyō!" Furthermore, the believer is taught that he can offer prayers on behalf of his ancestors, for, according to Reiyū-kai, the effect of such a filial act can be transferred to the spirit of the deceased.[132] It is to be noted that Reiyū-kai, being a layman's organization, does not depend on an organized clergy. Instead, lay volunteer teachers form informal local group conferences (*hōza*) for the purpose of instruction, devotion, and mutual encouragement. In addition, Reiyū-kai operates various kinds of philanthropic activities. This is consonant with its teachings that all men are literally "friends of the spirit" (*reiyū*). Currently, Kotani Kimi serves as the president of this group, which claims to have over 4,328,000 members.[133]

Reiyū-kai's emphasis on personal charisma and on easy access to worldly success, plus the absence of a closely knit organizational structure, has made it vulnerable to frequent schisms. Charges of financial corruption and other scandals against the authoritarian and temperamental matriarch, Kotani Kimi, have not helped the

[132] Kotani, ed., *A Guide to Reiyū-kai,* p. 3, cites the following "Merit-Transferring-Prayer": "Forgive all the spirits of my ancestors . . . and of all my family, for their mistakes and misunderstandings, and for all the sins and faults they have committed unintentionally. I read respectfully this holy Sūtra, not through my own ability, but through the merits of Buddhas and Devas. Now as they hear this Sūtra, make their spirits vow to devote themselves to Bodhi."

[133] Although the statistics of Reiyū-kai are not altogether reliable, there is no question about the fact that it was one of the largest new religions in Japan in the postwar period. Incidentally, the main headquarters of Reiyū-kai Kyōdan is located in Tokyo. Kubo Tsuginari, son of the late Kubo Kakutarō, is designated to succeed Kotani Kimi. For more about Reiyū-kai, see Thomsen, *The New Religions of Japan,* pp. 109–16; and Kohler, *Die Lotus-Lehre,* pp. 235–53. A somewhat embroidered personal account of a cofounder is given in Kotani, *Watakushi no shugyō-seikatsu sanjū-gonen.*

cause of Reiyū-kai at all.[134] At any rate, many new groups, such as Hakuai-dōshi-kai (association of universal love), Myōhō-kyō (the religion of the wonderful law), Myōchi-kai (association of wonderful knowledge), Hosshi-kai (association of teachers of dharma), Busshō-gonen-kai (association of praying for Buddha's protection), Tokugyō-kai (association for meritorious deeds), Seigi-kai (association for righteousness), Myōdō-kai (association for the wonderful way), and Risshō-Kōsei-kai, have broken away from Reiyū-kai and claimed independence thus far. Among them, the most important is Risshō-Kōsei-kai.

Risshō-Kōsei-kai (society for the establishment of righteousness and friendly relations)[135] was begun in 1938 by Niwano Nikkyō (1906–   ) and Naganuma Myōkō (1899–1957). Both of them had been active in Reiyū-kai. In his youth, Niwano worked as a clerk in small businesses and eventually became a milk dealer in Tokyo. He was fascinated by astrology, onomancy, and divination, and for a while became a disciple of a certain female shaman.[136] In 1935 Niwano's daughter was cured of illness by an incantation performed by a leading member of Reiyū-kai. This incident marked the beginning of Niwano's career as a voluntary teacher of Reiyū-kai.[137] It so happened that this pious

---

[134] It was mentioned earlier that a charge was brought against Kotani Kimi of securing U. S. dollars illegally. This case was not pressed, however. In 1949 she was accused of not paying her income tax. In 1953 Reiyū-kai was accused of misusing the funds collected for charity; the case was dismissed for lack of sufficient evidence.

[135] It was originally called Dai-Nihon Risshō-Kōsei-kai (Risshō-Kōsei-kai of Great Japan). After the Second World War the organization was renamed simply Risshō-Kōsei-kai.

[136] Niwano was initiated into astrology by his one-time employer, Ishiwara Yoshitarō, who became the first titular head of Dai-Nihon Risshō-Kōsei-kai. Niwano's teachers in onomancy were Kobayashi Seikō and Murayama Keizō; Murayama served as the second titular head of the organization, succeeding Ishiwara. The female shaman who exerted great influence on Niwano was Tsunaki Shōyen, who had a tenuous connection with Shingon Shugen-dō (The order of mountain ascetics which is affiliated with Shingon Buddhism).

[137] Niwano's daughter was cured by Arai Sukenobu, who earlier had joined Reiyū-kai when his own wife had been cured by her faith in Reiyū-

milk dealer came to know Naganuma Myōkō, a housewife who had had an unhappy family life and was afflicted by a serious illness. Niwano persuaded her to join Reiyū-kai and be cured. Although Naganuma Myōkō was skeptical at first, she became a convinced believer when indeed her affliction was healed.[138] She soon became an important member of Reiyū-kai because of her ability to become kami-possessed. Fortunately or unfortunately, Kotani Kimi, the ill-tempered matriarch of Reiyū-kai, did not appreciate the abilities of Niwano and Naganuma. Kotani was especially critical of Niwano's dependence on divination and openly criticized him in a meeting of Reiyū-kai leaders early in 1938. Niwano promptly seceded from Reiyū-kai, and Naganuma followed him. Soon the two of them, together with thirty-odd followers, established Risshō-Kōsei-kai.

The fact that Risshō-Kōsei-kai's secession from Reiyū-kai was not motivated by doctrinal differences might explain the qualitative similarities between the two.[139] There were minor differences, to be sure, but they were differences in emphasis rather than in kind. For example, Reiyū-kai teaches that one's worship should

kai. Arai was well versed in Confucianism and in the study of the *Lotus Sutra;* he tried to synthesize them in terms of filial piety. Eventually Arai broke away from Reiyū-kai and established Kyōshin-kai (association of teaching and faith). His widow, however, later joined Risshō-Kōsei-kai.

[138] Naganuma Myōkō (known as Masa before she took the name of Myōkō) had once been married to a barber in Saitama prefecture and had had a daughter. Her marriage ended in divorce, and her daughter died. She then worked in a noodle shop in Tokyo. Later she married Ōsawa Kunihei, who was fifteen years younger than she was, and they opened a small business of their own. She had a child by this marriage, but the infant died. Being a member of Tenri-kyō, she asked a Tenri-kyō teacher to offer prayers for her recovery from a serious illness, but in vain. In desperation, she listened to Niwano, who pointed out that her illness was caused by the fact that she had neglected the spirits of her ancestors. It was because her illness was cured that she joined Reiyū-kai in 1936. A few years later, she and her husband were separated.

[139] Nor was the secession of Risshō-Josei-kai (The society for the establishment of righteousness and the pure law) from Risshō-Kōsei-kai in 1943 based on doctrinal differences. Thus, these two groups have marked similarities.

be addressed to the mandala itself, whereas Risshō-kai, which reveres the mandala, teaches that one's worship must be directed toward Buddha Sākyamuni who had realized Buddhahood from eternity (*Kuon jitsujō no Shakamuni-butsu*). Also, while Reiyū-kai's rituals are purely Buddhistic, Risshō-Kōsei-kai's rituals blend Buddhist and Shinto elements. As to the objectives, Reiyū-kai emphasizes the repose of the spirits of the ancestors, whereas Risshō-Kōsei-kai stresses the fulfilment of the potentialities of individuals, that is, the attainment of Buddhahood through practice of the way of the Bodhisattva. In other words, according to Risshō-Kōsei-kai, the believer's devotion to the way of the Bodhisattva will benefit the spirits of the ancestors, and not the other way around. For this reason, it teaches the importance of a penitent and obedient mental attitude (*sagaru-kokoro*) which enables one to overcome one's bad habits, suffering, and ignorance. It is through such efforts that a happy family life will be sustained, and righteousness and friendly relations eventually established.

The phenomenal growth of Risshō-Kōsei-kai from a thousand members in 1945 to over a million in 1959 was ascribed to many factors, such as its promise of healing and other worldly benefits, the appeal of Naganuma Myōkō's charismatic personality to women, the organizational genius of Niwano Nikkyō, his appropriation of onomancy and other features of traditional Japanese folk religion, and his emphasis on the family unit.[140] Also effective are the group conferences (*hōza*), in which the directors of local chapters instruct members in religious and personal matters. These are held in Risshō-Kōsei-kai training halls every day of the year. Ironically, this religion, which started as a lay movement to restore the teaching of Nichiren, outgrew the traditional framework of the Nichiren school of Buddhism and broke its affiliation with other Nichiren groups in 1949. By that time, however, Risshō-Kōsei-kai was well established both as a successful new religion and as a potential political force, for it now counted

[140] Thomsen, *The New Religions of Japan,* p. 124: "The name of the applicant is not enough for membership—the names of his parents, of his wife's parents, and a list of the posthumous names of the deceased members of the family must be submitted."

among its adherents the Governor of Tokyo and other prominent citizens. Even then, Risshō-Kōsei-kai, as such, remained inactive politically for a decade. But with Niwano Nikkyō's open declaration in 1959 that he would make a determined effort to establish Buddhist political principles, Risshō-Kōsei-kai began to exert its influence both in local and national elections. It is obvious that no politician can afford to ignore the religious and political impact of Risshō-Kōsei-kai with its two million members scattered throughout Japan.[141]

By far the most controversial among all the new religions is Sōka-gakkai (literally, "The Society for the Creation of Values"), which claims to be a lay organization of the Nichiren Shōshū (literally, "Legitimate School of Nichiren"). Nichiren, be it recalled, had six leading disciples. One of them, called Nikō, became the custodian of the temple at Mt. Minobu in the present Yamanashi prefecture, which was the center of Nichiren's activities toward the end of his life. Indeed, it is Mt. Minobu which has been the most sacred shrine of the Nichiren school from the founder's death in 1282 until the present. However, another leading disciple, called Nikkō (1246–1333), who was unhappy with Nikō's leadership, left Mt. Minobu and established his own temple known as Taiseki-ji (The great stone temple) at the foot of Mt. Fuji.[142] His followers, convinced that Nikkō was the real spiritual heir of Nichiren, called his tradition Nichiren Shōshū, and refused to cooperate with other Nichiren sects. The doctrinal system of Nichiren Shōshū was systematized by Nikkan (1665–1726). Unlike other Nichiren sects, Nichiren Shōshū ignores Buddha Sākyamuni and regards Nichiren alone as the savior who should be the object of worship.[143] Nichiren Shōshū

[141] For general information regarding Risshō-Kōsei-kai, see Thomsen, *The New Religions of Japan,* pp. 117–26; Offner and Van Straelen, *Modern Japanese Religions,* pp. 95-98; and Kohler, *Die Lotus-Lehre,* pp. 253–64.

[142] A tooth said to be one of Nichiren's was brought to Taiseki-ji, where it has been preserved all these years. The official name of the temple is Tahō Fuji Rengezan Taiseki-ji.

[143] According to a spokesman of Sōka-gakkai: "In Sōka-gakkai, Sākyamuni Buddha is not the object of worship. Sākyamuni Buddha is not the

also believes that the wooden mandala, supposed to have been painted by Nichiren, kept at Taiseki-ji, is alone efficacious for the salvation of mankind. Although such beliefs were constructed on flimsy scriptural and/or historical grounds, these disciples have kept fanatical faith with the teachings of Nichiren Shōshū, and have prayed for the time when a national ordination center would be established at Taiseki-ji, which would then become the cathedral of the state religion. However, Nichiren Shōshū remained an insignificant minority until the end of the Second World War.

Meanwhile, something quite unexpected happened, and rejuvenated Nichiren Shōshū. Two frustrated schoolteachers, Makiguchi Tsunesaburō (1871–1944) and Toda Jōsei (1900–58), were converted around 1928 to the teachings of Nichiren Shōshū. Earlier, Makiguchi had advocated a system of education based on value-creating principles and had established the Value Creation Educational Institute (Sōka Kyōiku Gakkai). He insisted on the importance of subjective values for the attainment of happiness, and stressed practical values, namely, gain and profit, together with beauty and goodness, as the goals of education.[144] Maki-

---

Buddha of this present age. Sākyamuni Buddha predicted that in the Latter Days, after a lapse of 2,000 years, his teachings, even the *Lotus Sūtra,* would lose their effectiveness, and that when that time came a *Bodhisattva* by the name of Jōgyō would appear in a country to the east of India. This eastern country could be none other than Japan, and this *Bodhisattva* prophesied by Sākyamuni Buddha could be none other than the great saint Nichiren. Therefore, Sōka-gakkai and the Nichiren Shō sect regard Sākyamuni Buddha as the 'trace Buddha' (*shaku-butsu*) and the great saint Nichiren as their real object of worship. . . . The great saint Nichiren, who is Jōgyō Bosatsu, that is, the savior of the Latter Days, is regarded in substance as the 'original or true Buddha' (*hon-butsu*)." (Takuya Kudō, "The Faith of Sōka-gakkai," *Contemporary Religions in Japan,* II [No. 2, June, 1961], 7–8.)

[144] According to Makiguchi's theory of value, the object of life consists in the pursuit of happiness. And, it is value, and not truth, that constitutes the substance as well as the element of happiness. Just as there are grades in value, so are there many stages and orders in happiness. A life that creates and acquires the maximum value—such is the highest objective of life, and is called the life of Great Good. See the *Mainichi Newspaper,* August 5, 1955, p. 7.

guchi's religious faith provided him with a new passion for carrying out his philosophy of education. However, convinced that Nichiren alone was to be worshiped, Makiguchi and Toda refused to pay homage at the Grand Shrine of Ise, and they were jailed on the familiar charge of *lèse majesté*. Subsequently, Makiguchi died in prison. After the Second World War Toda, who had been released, restored the movement under the name of Sōka-gakkai. He instilled a militant spirit into the organization by inaugurating an unscrupulous and aggressive method of forced conversion (*shaku-buku*). To effect conversion, troops of young men and women were expected to coerce nonbelievers into accepting the Sōka-gakkai faith.[145] Understandably, the activities of Sōka-gakkai had a direct bearing on Nichiren Shōshū, too. The enormous success of Sōka-gakkai is evidenced by the fact that its membership zoomed from roughly 200,000 in 1953 to 4,000,000 in 1959. According to Mombu-shō, *Shūkyō nenkan* (1965), Sōka-gakkai members are listed as adherents of Nichiren Shōshū, which claims to have 14,458,855 members.[146]

[145] See "Sōka-gakkai and the Nichiren Shō Sect (I)," *Contemporary Religions in Japan*, I (No. 1, March, 1960), 55–56: "This method is called *shaku-buku* in Japanese, a term that means, literally, 'to destroy and conquer.' The term occurred originally in the Shōman-gyō, Dainichi-kyō, and other ancient Buddhist scriptures in connection with a parallel term, *shōju*, which means, literally, 'acceptance.' The former term designates intolerant propaganda to produce a forced conversion; the latter a tolerant approach by means of moral suasion. In his writings Nichiren stressed that with *ignorant* men tolerant, moral suasion could be used; but that with *malicious* men it was necessary to use the intolerant method." McFarland reports several incidents of *shaku-buku* and states that in one town "proselytizers often had solicited members through extortion and blackmail and had forced their way into homes to destroy family altars." (H. Neill McFarland, "The New Religions of Japan," *The Perkins School of Theology Journal*, XII [No. 1, Fall, 1958], 15.) See also Kohler, *Die Lotus-Lehre*, pp. 203–35; Saki and Oguchi, *Sōka-gakkai*; Jōdo-Shin-shū Fukyō-kenkyū-sho, ed., *Sōka-gakkai no kentō*; and Tokyo-daigaku Hokkekyō-kenkyū-kai, ed., *Nichiren shōshū Sōka-gakkai*.

[146] Concerning the penetration of Sōka-gakkai among American GIs, see Richard Okamoto, "Japan: A Booming Economy Has Spawned a Militant New Religion with 10 Million Adherents Bent on Dominating the World," *Look*, XXVII (No. 18, September 10, 1963), 24–26.

What is alarming to many observers is the fact that Sōka-gakkai is organized on militaristic and authoritarian principles, so that the whole operation is under the management of a director-general who presumably will exercise enormous power in influencing the future of Japan. For example, the Coal Miners' Union is confronted with the encroachment of Sōka-gakkai. It was estimated in 1957 that approximately 10,000 of the 75,000 unionists affiliated with the Hokkaido regional headquarters of the Federation of Coal Miners were adherents of Sōka-gakkai, while at the Yūbari mines alone the 13,000 union members included an estimated 3,000 believers. It is understandable, therefore, that the Japanese Federation of Coal Miners in its annual congress in 1957 made the following declaration: "Unless some action is taken against the new religions, they will increasingly disrupt the unity of the workers and play into the hands of management. . . ." [147] Equally noteworthy is the significant success of Sōka-gakkai in the political arena. In 1959, in Tokyo alone, Sōka-gakkai's seventy-six candidates for the twenty-three ward assemblies were elected, and their six candidates for the Upper House were also elected. In 1962 Sōka-gakkai's nine candidates won their seats in the House of Councilors, polling more than 600,000 votes for the three members of its slate from among the national constituency. Furthermore, the Kōmei-tō (literally, "fairness society"), consisting of the Sōka-gakkai deputies in the Upper House, now holds the balance of power between the Liberal Democratic party and leftist groups. [148]

Various attempts have been made to analyze the factors that have contributed to the political strength of Sōka-gakkai, although it is too early for us to come to any definite conclusion regarding these matters as yet. It is significant to point out, however, that, according to a recent survey, most of the supporters of the Sōka-

[147] See "Japan's New Church Militant," *Japan Quarterly*, IV (No. 4, October–December, 1957), 415–19.

[148] See Johnson, " 'Low Posture' Politics in Japan," *Asian Survey*, III (No. 1, January, 1963), 17–30; and Moos, "Religion and Politics in Japan: The Case of the Sōka-Gakkai," *Asian Survey*, III (No. 3, March, 1963), 136–42.

gakkai candidates were women whose ages range from twenty to forty, with a few over fifty. For the most part, their average educational level is that of junior high school, and many of them are engaged in manual labor.[149] This class of people, largely neglected by established religions and existing political parties, seems to be looking for religious and political guidance, which some of the new religions are more than willing to provide.

Japanese Religion—Whither?

One of the basic problems in postwar Japan is the rootlessness of the Japanese people. Rightly or wrongly, until the Second World War the Japanese people had a sense of security in their country, in this world, and in the universe. Their sense of security was derived not from any particular doctrine of Shinto, Buddhism, or Confucianism, but from the nebulous but real cosmological orientation that underlay the world view of the Japanese people in the prehistoric and early historic periods.[150] While this cosmic orientation had been submerged through the long history of Japan by the influences of religions and cultures that had been introduced from abroad, it remained at the core of the spiritual culture of Japan, transforming alien influences and naturalizing them. In the words of J. B. Pratt, the Japanese people "have done with Buddhism what they have done with everything else that has been brought them from abroad. They have accepted it simply, humbly, in sincere and almost child-like fashion, and then they have laid the stamp of their own transforming genius upon it." [151] Indeed, it was not any one of the institutionalized religions which gave the Japanese people their sense of destiny and security in this world; it was this underlying cosmological orientation which enabled them to assimilate various alien religious and cultural elements and forms without becoming schizophrenic.

[149] See Ukai, "The Japanese House of Councillors Election of July 1962," *Asian Survey,* II (No. 6, August, 1962), 1–8.

[150] See Chapter I for the characterization of early Shinto as a "cosmic" religion.

[151] Pratt, *The Pilgrimage of Buddhism,* p. 457.

The tragedy of postwar Japan is that the people have lost this fundamental religious orientation. To be sure, the Japanese people experienced serious political crises and religious-cultural disruptions in the past. The penetration of Chinese civilization and Buddhism during the sixth and seventh centuries, the inauguration of the feudal regime toward the end of the twelfth century, the Mongol invasions in the thirteenth century, the arrival of Roman Catholicism in the sixteenth century, the restoration of monarchical rule and introduction of modern Western civilization as well as Protestantism in the nineteenth century were but a few examples of epoch-making events that had far-reaching consequences. Many bloody wars fought among rival groups had devastated the cities and countryside, and more recent engagements, such as the Sino-Japanese War (1894–95), the Russo-Japanese War (1904–5), and the First World War, precipitated social, economic, and cultural dislocations. But never in the history of Japan had she encountered such a traumatic experience as the end of the Second World War.

When Japan surrendered to the Allied Powers in 1945, it was not simply the end of combat. What Japan lost was far more than the divine prerogatives of the throne or the gigantic institution of State Shinto. These were external symbols of something much deeper, that is, the source of the Japanese sense of destiny and security based on a cosmological world view which had been preserved from time immemorial. When the Supreme Commander for the Allied Powers ordered the Japanese government to terminate the sponsorship, support, perpetuation, control, and dissemination of State Shinto, many people outside Japan rejoiced that the end had come to an obscurantist magico-religion, and they praised the courage of the emperor when he repudiated the "false conception" that the emperor is divine. And it may be that today Shrine Shinto, Buddhism, Christianity, and other religions have a real opportunity to grow and develop in an atmosphere of religious liberty that has been guaranteed by the new Constitution. Nevertheless, the fact remains that the Japanese people as a whole have lost their traditional sense of values and of the meaning of history. Such a radical change is not necessarily undesirable. However, it must be recognized that the Japanese people now find themselves off balance and are not certain in which direction they should take the next step. Caught between the free world and the Communist world, and caught between their ancient past and an uncertain future, the Japanese blink and rub their eyes in a world that is changing and moving much too rapidly for their comfort. They cannot even trust their own senses now that their own image of the world has been destroyed. They are sojourners in their own country for the first time in their long history and so they look desperately for some kind of certainty, hope, and faith. This is precisely what the so-called new religions (*Shinkō Shūkyō*) claim to provide—and to a certain degree are succeeding in providing.

Actually, these new religions present nothing new, as far as their religious contents are concerned. Many of them derived their doctrines from Shinto, Confucianism, Buddhism, or Christianity. Their teachings are eclectic and not well systematized, but their simple, direct, and practical beliefs and practices appeal to the masses who do not feel at home with the complex doctrines of established religions. It is important to note, however, that they make full use of group psychology by offering both informal small group meetings and elaborate mass assemblies. Most of them are highly centralized in their organizational structure, utilizing cell group systems as well as incentive plans. A few of them have semimilitaristic disciplines. All of them use modern mass media of communication and have efficient methods of tithing or its equivalent. What gives each of these new religions its distinctive character is the personality of the founder or organizer. Many of these boast unusual spiritual powers in divination, sorcery, incantation, fortunetelling, and healing, which betray the shamanistic roots of their religious orientations. They also have the capacity to attract and maintain rapport with a large number of followers. For the most part, these new religions draw their adherents from the lower middle class, especially middle-aged and older women, although a few of them claim to have some followers among the upper middle class and young people as well.

Opinions vary among scholars as to why so many new religions have mushroomed in Japan since the end of the Second World War. According to a noted historian, "Buddhism *cannot* speak to the new Japanese society; Christianity *does not* speak to it. Japan needs a new religion which combines the good points of Buddhism, Shinto, Christianity, and Chinese ethical teaching." [152] Others attempt to explain the emergence of new religions in terms of the social, cultural, economic, political, and psychological factors that have created the spiritual vacuum in the postwar period. Most observers agree that the rise of new religions signifies the reassertion of the old Japanese folk religious ethos. Indeed, dependence on personal charisma, divination, and exorcism, emphasis on family and communal cohesion, the prevalence of magico-religious cults that promise faith healing and other benefits, and the yearning for a worldly paradise testify to the tenacity of the folk religious tradition. Historically, the masses in Japan, like their counterparts in other parts of the world, have never been concerned with doctrinal minutiae. From time immemorial they have lived close to nature, and they have learned how to cope with the capricious, uncontrollable contingencies of life with the help of shamans, diviners, exorcists, and healers who propitiate the unseen kami and spirits and guide various other aspects of human activities. In the course of time some features of Buddhism, Confucianism, and other religious and semireligious traditions penetrated the world of the masses, but the fundamental meaning of life and the world of the masses remained intact to a significant degree. Only in the last hundred years or so did the masses in Japan begin to sense that their traditional way of life was no longer tenable in the modern age. Yet the tragic fact was that while many advances adopted from Western civilization, such as modern education, industry, and commerce, benefited the elite, these same forms made the life of those in the lower strata of Japanese society harder than before. The anguish of the oppressed masses was barely compensated for by the anticipation of a new political order in Asia which the government

---

[152] This is the opinion of Nakamura Naokatsu, retired Professor of History, Kyoto University; cited in McFarland, "The New Religions of Japan," p. 19.

promised under Japan's leadership. It is understandable, therefore, that the masses greeted Japan's defeat with mixed feelings. While they were relieved of long years of emotional tension and suffering, they also lost the immediate goal of their life. The energy once generated among them for the creation of a new social and political order needed another focus to which it could be redirected. This is, in a sense, what the new religions seem to offer, and this may account for the dynamism exhibited by the new religions.

"Most of the new religions," says a critic, "have something inherently repulsive to the educated mind." This sentiment is shared by many of the intelligentsia and the leaders of established religions. However, leaders of the new religions are seemingly oblivious to such criticism. They scorn the intellectuals for having become mere technicians at the service of the political authorities, and for never having exercised intellectual leadership responsibly for the nation. They are equally critical of the leaders of the older religions for being preoccupied with the maintenance of their temples, lands, etc., without presenting any positive image of future Japanese society. The primary concern of the new religions is how to protect their adherents, especially those who belong to the rapidly growing urban lower middle class, from such evil influences of Western civilization as a high crime rate, juvenile delinquency, an increase in the divorce rate, a lack of discipline at home and in the schools, the irresponsible behavior of the youths who waste their newly found leisure either in moral dissipation or extreme political activities. The leaders of the new religions lament the decline of traditional Japanese mores and morality and, despite their frequent references to democratic slogans, are skeptical of the over-all effect of democracy. Thus they advocate the virtues of the traditional family and group loyalty at the expense of individual dignity. In essence, the new religions are antiintellectual and antimodern. They are also antileftist and anti-Communist in their political outlook. What they present as a positive goal for the future is a peculiar mixture of naïve utopianism, traditionalism, magic, and promises of mundane satisfactions and benefits. But their "paradoxical commitment to reaffirm the old and at the same time to reform it, to repudiate the new and simultaneously to adopt it," to use McFarland's characterization, has a definite appeal to many who are afraid of confronting the uncertainties of postwar Japanese society.[153] Ironically, while these new religions have had men of great business acumen to administer their affairs, they have had virtually no serious philosophical and theological minds to purify and restrain the anaesthetic and hypnotic qualities of the piety of the masses. This may account for the inability of many of the new religions to grasp the complexity of the modern world and their inclination to rationalize ethnocentric nationalism as a form of pseudo theology.[154]

It certainly is a bewildering experience for a historian of religions to be confronted by the crisscrossing trends and forces in the Japanese religious scene in the postwar period. It is, of course, beyond our scope to pass any judgment regarding the relative values and merits of different religious systems. However, at the expense of oversimplification, we can discern three main religious types, each based on its attitude toward the Japanese spiritual tradition throughout her history. The first was exemplified by Confucianism and Buddhism. Historically, Confucianism provided Japan with the most articulate social and political theories as well as individual and social ethics, and Buddhism broadened and elevated the Japanese religious life by contributing cultural forms, metaphysical systems, and soteriological paths. Nevertheless, both Buddhism and Confucianism were so thoroughly indigenized that neither demanded any radical and fundamental reinterpretation of the underlying cosmological world view of the Japanese. Thus there have been Japanese Confucianism and

[153] *Ibid.*, p. 17. McFarland goes on to say: "Such a paradox cannot possibly be directly converted into polity, but it can be resolved in a religious experience and thus become the means of reaffirming an impression of in-group solidarity and the motivation for developing new patterns of group behavior."

[154] For the activities of the Japanese right-wing groups, see Morris, *Nationalism and the Right Wing in Japan: A Study of Post-War Trends.* Some observers are deeply concerned over the alliance that might develop between right-wing nationalism and some of the new religions.

Japanese Buddhism, but the core of Japanese culture has remained intact. In this respect, a statement of Ruth Benedict is pertinent: "It was not Buddhism and it was not Confucianism. It was Japanese—the strength and the weakness of Japan." [155] It must be recognized, of course, that while the Confucian tradition as such has declined in recent years, its influence will remain in various dimensions of Japanese family and social life in the future. Also, Japanese Buddhism since the end of the Second World War has been rejuvenated partly through the recent historical experience of Japan and partly under the influence of the resurgence of the global Buddhist community. Thus Buddhism will continue to exert an important religious influence in Japanese society. One of the greatest problems for contemporary Buddhism seems to be its lack of a vision of history as "a movement in which the new is created and which runs ahead to the absolutely new," to use Tillich's phrase. Unless Buddhism shifts its traditional emphasis, "no belief in the new in history, no impulse for transforming society, can be derived from the principle of Nirvāna." [156]

In sharp contrast to Confucianism and Buddhism, Christianity —here referring to the Roman Catholicism (Kirishitan) of the sixteenth and seventeenth centuries as well as to Catholic, Orthodox, and Protestant forms of Christianity in the last one hundred years—has been more belligerent toward the spiritual tradition of Japan, for Christianity has not been satisfied to become a supplement to existing religious systems. Holding that the universal truth and the path to salvation for all mankind were revealed solely in the Christ event, Christianity has tended to reject not only all the rival religious systems but also the values and meanings of the cultural and historical experiences of the Japanese. Inevitably, the insistence on the universal validity and the transcendental reference of the truth of Christianity tends to make Japanese Christians become uprooted—but not always liberated—from their social, cultural, and spiritual traditions and

[155] Benedict, *The Chrysanthemum and the Sword: Patterns of Japanese Culture,* p. 19.

[156] Tillich, *Christianity and the Encounter of the World Religions,* pp. 72–73.

surroundings. Many Christians lament the fact that today Japan is undergoing "a drastic social and cultural revolution, in the main without the positive benefits of high religion," and they feel strongly that the Christian emphasis on time and history and the importance of the individual is imperative for the revolutionary transformation of Japanese culture and society.[157] But, as Hammer rightly suggests, "if the Christian Church is truly to be present in Japan, and not simply to be a 'caller' at the '*genkan*' (doorway), it must meet with Japanese society." [158] One of the greatest problems for contemporary Christianity seems to be its lack of capacity to take seriously the analysis of human existence and religious insight gained by the historic cultures of Japan, as well as a lack of willingness to enter into the spiritual struggle of the present-day Japanese people.

Third, the religions of indigenous origin, namely, the Shinto and Sect Shinto denominations and the so-called new religions, have to a greater or lesser degree preserved some features of the naturalistic, ethnocentric, and cosmological religious apprehension of the ancient Japanese people. All of them affirm that man is an integral part of a cosmos which is pervaded by the kami or sacred nature. Their optimistic view of the nature of human existence is based on their equation of what they consider "natural" with "original." Accordingly, to them religion offers neither "deliverance" as in Buddhism nor "salvation" as in Christianity, but fulfillment and the perpetuation of human potentialities and vitalities. Also, they subscribe to the view that the "original" model of human society, as portrayed in the myths, existed in the hallowed past of Japan.[159] Traditionally, people in Japan have related themselves to the golden age of the primordial past in two ways. One way was through history, or, to be more exact, the chronicles, which enabled them to trace their ancestries to the age of the

---

[157] See Nielsen, *Religion and Philosophy in Contemporary Japan*, p. 81.

[158] Hammer, *Japan's Religious Ferment*, pp. 118–19.

[159] In the cases of religions of more recent origin, efforts have been made to "mythologize" the life of the founder or organizer, so that he or she is presented as an ahistorical, idealized person.

kami. More important, perhaps, to them were religious festivities and communal rites, because by participating in these rituals and festivities, pilgrimages and holy days, the decisive experiences of their ancestors were reenacted and thus were reactivated in the people's actual experiences.

Historically, such a yearning of the Japanese people to restore the idealized state of the golden days, coupled with the notion of the identity of religion and politics (*saisei-itchi*), has often developed a messianic fervor, especially during political crises. The ethnocentric, messianic restorationism implicit in the indigenous religious tradition of Japan received further stimulus from the apocalyptic notion of Buddhism known as *mappō* (the coming of the age of degeneration of the Buddha's Law) as well as from the "immanental theocratic" motif of Confucianism, as exemplified by the messianic motif of Nichiren's teaching in the thirteenth century and by the emotionally charged restoration movement influenced by the Shinto-Confucian ideologies in the nineteenth century, respectively. Many observers sense the similar ethnocentric, messianic motif in Sōka-gakkai and many other postwar new religions that present the "old dreams" of Japan as the "new visions" of the coming social and political order.

What the future has in store for religion in Japan, no one can predict. It is quite conceivable that other new religions may still emerge and that some of the old ones may decline. We may safely assume, however, that the three types of religious affirmations and approaches which have just been mentioned will survive for many years to come. They will no doubt develop according to their own dynamics, which will inevitably involve certain kinds of conflicts and tensions among them, but they also may influence, transform, and even purify, one another. It goes without saying that religion is not an isolated phenomenon detached from other aspects of human society. Thus the future of religion in Japan will be greatly conditioned by what takes place in the social, political, economic, and cultural spheres, while at the same time religion will also influence the direction of various aspects of Japanese society and culture. And, needless to say, what happens in Japan will have both a direct and an indirect bearing on the future of the rest of the world. Japanese religion—whither? This will remain an important question for historians of religions as well as for others in the second half of the twentieth century.

Chronological Table

Official chronicles of Japan list 28 legendary monarchs. The numbers in parentheses preceding these names, and those of later rulers, indicate the number traditionally assigned to each ruler. The names of fourteenth-century rulers excluded from official listing are preceded by an asterisk.

PREHISTORIC PERIOD

JŌMON PERIOD (5th or 4th millenium to *ca.* 250 B.C.)
Period of fishing and hunting culture. Pottery with *jōmon* ("cord pattern") decoration used.

YAYOI PERIOD (*ca.* 250 B.C.-*ca.* A.D. 250)
Period of gradual blending of Melanesian, Austroasian, Austronesian and northeast Asian cultural influence. System of wet-rice cultivation and the use of bronze, copper, and iron introduced.

A.D. 57   Kingdom of Nu, a principality situated somewhere in the Japanese islands, sends envoy to the Han court in China. (Earliest reference to Japan in a Chinese source.)

200   Fall of Han dynasty in China.

238 or 239   Pimiko, queen of the state of Yamatai (situated probably in the island of Kyushu, Japan), sends tribute to the Wei court in China.

248   Queen Pimiko dies. Her relative, Ichiyo, succeeds her.

TRANSITIONAL OR KOFUN (TUMULUS) PERIOD (*ca.* A.D. 250-*ca.* A.D. 500)

ca. 275-*ca.* 350   Establishment of the Yamato (old name of Japan) kingdom under the authority of the Tennō ("imperial") clan.

Legendary Monarchs

(1) *Jimmu. Known as "The Emperor, the August Founder of the Nation."*

(2) *Suisei.*

(3) *Annei.*

(4) *Itoku.*

(5) *Kōshō.*

(6) *Kōan.*

(7) *Kōrei.*

(8) *Kōgen.*

(9) *Kaika.*

(10) *Sujin. Also known as "The Emperor, the August Founder of the Nation."*

(11) *Suinin.*

(12) *Keikō.*

(13) *Seimu.*

(14) ⎧ *Chūai.*
⎨ *Jingō (or Jingū). The empress who is said to have ruled the nation after the death of Chūai, her husband.*

(15) *Ōjin.*

(16) *Nintoku. Same person as the ruler of Japan recorded in the Chinese sources as San? If so, San is said to have died in 438.*

(17) *Richū.*

(18) *Hansei. Same person as the ruler of Japan recorded in Chinese sources as Chin? If so, he is said to have assumed the throne in 438.*

(19) *Ingyō. Most probably the person known in Chinese sources as Sai, who is said to have died in 462.*

(20) *Ankō. Most probably the person known in Chinese sources as Kō, who is said to have ruled Japan, 462–78.*

(21) *Yūryaku. Most probably the person known in Chinese records as Bu, who reigned in Japan from 478 till the early part of the sixth century.*

(22) *Seinei.*

(23) *Kenzō.*

(24) *Ninken.*

(25) *Buretsu.*

(26) *Keitai.*

(27) *Ankan.*
(28) *Senka.*

367 First envoy arrives in Japan from Paekche (a Korean state).
369 Japanese forces fight against the army of Silla (another Korean state).
391 Japanese forces fight against the army of Koguryō (still another Korean state).
421 The Chinese (Liu Sung) court confers on San the title of Monarch of Japan.
425 San pays tribute to China.
438 Upon San's death, his brother Chin succeeds and pays tribute to China.
443 Japanese ruler, Sai (Emperor Ingyō?) pays tribute to China.
462 Sai dies. His son, Kō (Emperor Ankō?) pays tribute to China.
478 Kō dies. His brother, Bu (Emperor Yūryaku?) pays tribute to China. Chinese court confers on Bu the title of King of Japan and also Generalissimo, not only of Japan but of a large section of the Korean peninsula, as well.

EARLY HISTORIC PERIOD

ASUKA PERIOD (*ca.* A.D. 500-A.D. 710)

(29) *Kimmei (r. 531–71).*
538 (or 552) Introduction of Buddhism into Japan.
562 Silla destroys Mimana, Japan's foothold in the Korean peninsula.
(30) *Bidatsu (r. 571–85).*
(31) *Yōmei (r. 585–87?).*
(32) *Sushun (r. 587?–92).*
587 Umako, chieftain of the powerful Soga clan, destroys his rival, Mononobe no Moriya.
589 Sui dynasty unifies China.
(33) *Suiko (empress; r. 592–628).*
593 Prince Shōtoku (573–621) becomes regent. A Buddhist temple called Shitennō-ji is built at Naniwa (Osaka).
594 Buddhism proclaimed the state religion.
602 Kwalluk, Buddhist priest from Paekche, arrives in Japan, bringing with him books on geomancy, divination, and geography.

604   Seventeen-Article Constitution proclaimed.
607   Japanese envoy sent to the Sui court in China. Building of a Buddhist temple, Hōryū-ji, is commenced.
618   T'ang dynasty established in China.
623   Edict to regulate activities of monks and nuns (Sōni-ryō) proclaimed.
625   Hui-kuan (E-kan in Japanese), Korean priest, transmits the Jōjitsu (Satyasiddhi) and the Sanron (Mādhyamika) schools of Buddhism to Japan.
      (34) *Jomei* (r. 628–41).
630   First Japanese envoy sent to the T'ang court in China.
      (35) *Kōgyoku* (*empress; r. 642–45*).
      (36) *Kōtoku* (r. 645–54).
645   The powerful Soga clan eliminated by a *coup d'état* led by Prince Nakano-ōye (later the Emperor Tenchi) and Nakatomi (later Fujiwara) Kamatari.
      Taika Reform begins.
      (37) *Saimei* (*second accession of Kōgyoku; r. 655–61*).
658   Two Japanese priests, Chitsū and Chitatsu, having studied under Hiuen-tsang, transmit the Kusha (Abhidharma-kosa) school of Buddhism to Japan. First expeditionary forces sent to northeastern Japan to subjugate the Ainu tribes.
      (38) *Tenchi* (r. 662–71; *assumed title officially only in 668*).
666   Japanese priest, Dōshō, transmits the Hossō (Yogācāra) school of Buddhism from China.
668   Silla becomes paramount in Korea.
      (39) *Kōbun* (r. 671–72; *not recognized by some historians*).
      (40) *Temmu* (r. 672–86).
      (41) *Jitō* (*empress; r. 686–97*).
      (42) *Mommu* (r. 697–707).
701   First Confucian festival celebrated in Japan.
701–2   Taihō Reform Code promulgated.

NARA PERIOD (A.D. 710–81)

      (43) *Gemmyō* (*empress; r. 708–15*).
710   Establishment of the first permanent capital at Nara (called Heijō-kyō).
      (44) *Genshō* (*empress; r. 715–24*).
712   *Kojiki* (Records of ancient matters) completed.

713   *Fudo-ki* (Topographical records) commenced.
717   Gyōgi, leader of the shamanistic Buddhists, arrested by order of the government.
720   *Nihonshoki* (Chronicles of Japan) completed.
       (45) *Shōmu* (r. 724–49).
731   Government tolerates activities of the shamanistic Buddhists.
736   The Japanese priest, Gembō, having studied the Kusha (Abhidharmakosa) doctrine in China, returns.
       Kibi-no-Makibi, a Japanese scholar who spent nineteen years in China, introduces Chinese astronomy, mathematics, jurisprudence, music, and calligraphy into Japan.
       Chinese priest, Tao-hsüan (Dōsen in Japanese) transmits the Ritsu (Vinaya) school of Buddhism.
       Indian Buddhist monk, Bodhisena, arrives in Japan.
740   Shen-hsiang (Shin-shō in Japanese), priest from Simala, transmits the Kegon (Avatamsaka) school of Buddhism.
741   Establishment of state-supported official temples (Kokubun-ji) and distribution of the Konkōmyō-kyō (Golden Light sutra) in all the provinces.
745   Gyōgi appointed to the rank of archbishop.
       (46) *Kōken* (*empress; r. 749–57*).
749   Gyōgi dies.
       The ex-Emperor Shōmu takes priestly vows.
752   Dedication of the Great Buddha at Tōdai-ji, Nara.
754   Chinese Vinaya master, Chien-chien (Ganjin in Japanese) arrives in Japan and establishes an ordination hall (*kaidan*) at Tōdai-ji, Nara.
       (47) *Junnin* (r. 757–64).
       (48) *Shōtoku* (*second accession of Kōken; r. 764–70*).
764   Priest, Dōkyō, prime minister.
       Ex-Emperor Junnin banished to the island of Awaji where he was murdered.
766?   *Manyōshū* compiled.
769   Dōkyō attempts to usurp the throne.
       (49) *Kōnin* (r. 770–80).
770   Dōkyō banished (dies in 772).

HEIAN PERIOD (A.D. 781–1191)

       (50) *Kammu* (r. 781–806).
784   Capital moved to Nagaoka.

788 Saicho (Dengyō-daishi; 767–822) founds a temple (the Enryaku-ji) on Mt. Hiei.

791 The Grand Shrine of Ise burns down.

794 Heian-kyō (Kyoto) becomes the capital.

797 *Shoku-Nihongi* (Chronicle of Japan, continued) completed.

800 The court confers the imperial title on the deceased former crown prince Sawara.

805 Saicho founds the Tendai school of Buddhism.
         (*51*) *Heizei* (*r. 806–9*).

806 Kūkai (Kōbō-daishi; 774–835) founds the Shingon school of Buddhism.
         (*52*) *Saga* (*r. 809–24*).

810 Unsuccessful attempt by the ex-Emperor Heizei, supported by Fujiwara Nakanari and Kusuriko, to overthrow the Emperor Saga.

812 Final subjugation of the Ainu.

815 *Shinsen Shōjiroku* (New compilation of the register of families) completed.

816 Kūkai establishes his monastery on Mt. Kōya.

822 Ordination hall (*kaidan*) established at Mt. Hiei.
         (*53*) *Junna* (*r. 824–33*).
         (*54*) *Nimmyō* (*r. 833–50*).

847 Ennin (794–864) transmits Tendai esoterism (*Tai-mitsu*).
         (*55*) *Montoku* (*r. 850–57*).
         (*56*) *Seiwa* (*r. 857–76*).

858 Fujiwara Yoshifusa becomes regent; beginning of *de facto* rule by the Fujiwara oligarchy.
         Enchin (814–91) founds the Miidera branch of the Tendai
         (*57*) *Yōzei* (*r. 876–84*).
         (*58*) *Kōkō* (*r. 884–87*).
         (*59*) *Uda* (*r. 887–97*).

889 Descendants of the Emperor Kammu given the surname of Taira.

894 Termination of sending envoys to China.
         (*60*) *Daigo* (*r. 897–930*).

901 Downfall of the minister of the right, Sugawara Michizane.

905 Anthology of verse, *Kokin-shū* (Collection of ancient and modern verses) compiled.

907 Ex-Emperor Uda goes on pilgrimage to Kumano.
         End of the T'ang dynasty in China.

909 Shōbō, systematizer of the Mountain Priesthood (Shugen-dō) dies.
927 *Engishiki* compiled.
     (61) *Suzaku* (r. 930–46).
930 Fujiwara Tadahira becomes regent.
933 Beginning of conflict between the Miidera and the Enryaku-ji branches of the Tendai school.
935 *Tosa Nikki* (Diary of Ki-no-Tsurayuki) completed.
     Rebellion of Taira Masakado, who called himself the new emperor.
     (62) *Murakami* (r. 946–57).
960 Sung dynasty established in China.
961 Descendants of the Emperor Seiwa given the surname of Minamoto.
     (63) *Reizei* (r. 967–69).
     (64) *Enyū* (r. 969–84).
970 First recorded celebration of a festival to pacify the deceased spirits (*goryō-ye*).
972 Death of Kūya (or Kōya, 903–72), popularizer of devotion to Amida.
     (65) *Kazan* (r. 984–86).
985 Genshin (Eshin sōzu) writes *Ōjō yōshū* (Essentials of salvation).
     (66) *Ichijō* (r. 986–1011).
995 Fujiwara Michinaga (966–1027) becomes *nairan* (deputy of the throne).
1004? *The Tale of Genji* by Lady Murasaki commenced.
     (67) *Sanjō* (r. 1012–16).
     (68) *Go-Ichijō* (r. 1016–36).
1017 Michinaga's son, Yorimichi, becomes *kampaku*.
1019 Fujiwara Michinaga takes priestly vows.
1028 Rebellion of Taira Tadatsune in the Eastern province.
     (69) *Go-Suzaku* (r. 1036–45).
     (70) *Go-Reizei* (r. 1045–68).
1050 Revolt of the Abe family in northern Japan.
1053 Amida Chapel of Byōdō-in, Uji, completed.
1062 Defeat of Abe family by a Minamoto general.
     (71) *Go-Sanjō* (r. 1068–72).
1068 Fujiwara Yorimichi retires from dictatorship.
1069 The emperor attempts to curb Fujiwara power.

(72) *Shirakawa* (r. 1072–86).

(73) *Horikawa* (r. 1086–1107).

1086   Ex-Emperor Shirakawa begins *inzei* (rule by retired monarch); he rules until 1129.

1093   Shirakawa conducts a pilgrimage to Mt. Kimpu, the holy mountain of the Mountain Priesthood (*shugen-dō*).

1095   Armed monks of Mt. Hiei pillage the capital.

1096   *Dengaku* becomes popular. First Crusade in Europe.

1098   Great fire of Kyoto.

(74) *Toba* (r. 1107–23).

1113   Conflict between the Enryaku-ji (Mt. Hiei) and the Kōfuku-ji (Nara).

(75) *Sutoku* (r. 1124–41).

1124   The Golden Chapel of the Chūson-ji completed.

1129   Ex-Emperor Shirakawa dies.

Ex-Emperor Toba's *inzei* begins (lasts until 1156).

1132   Death of Ryōnin (b. 1071), forerunner of Pure Land Buddhists in Japan.

(76) *Konoye* (r. 1141–55).

1142   Fifteen priests of the Kōfuku-ji (Nara) banished to Mutsu province.

(77) *Go-Shirakawa* (r. 1155–58).

1156   The insurrection led by the ex-Emperor Sutoku, Fujiwara Yorinaga, and Minamoto Tameyoshi—called the "Hogen no ran"—occurs.

Taira Kiyomori controls government affairs.

The ex-Emperor Sutoku banished from the capital.

(78) *Nijō* (r. 1158–65).

1158   Beginning of the ex-Emperor Go-Shirakawa's *inzei*; it lasts until 1192.

1159   The insurrection called the "Heiji no ran" occurs.

1160   Branch shrines of Kumano and Hiye—Ima-Kumano and Shin-Hiye—established in Kyoto by the ex-Emperor Go-Shirakawa.

(79) *Rokujō* (r. 1165–68).

1167   Taira Kiyomori becomes *dajō daijin* (chief minister).

(80) *Takakura* (r. 1169–80).

1175   Hōnen (1133–1212) founds the Pure Land (*Jōdo*) sect of Buddhism.

(81) *Antoku* (r. 1180–84).

1181   Taira Kiyomori dies.

(82) *Go-Toba* (r. 1184–98).
1185 Defeat of Taira family by the Minamoto.
Minamoto Yoritomo becomes supreme power.
1191 Eisai (1141–1215) transmits the Rinzai Zen school from China.

MEDIEVAL PERIOD

KAMAKURA PERIOD (1192–1333)

1192 Minamoto Yoritomo founds the Kamakura shogunate.
(83) *Tsuchimikado* (r. 1198–1209).
1198 Beginning of Go-Toba's *inzei.*
Publication of *Senjaku-Hongan-Nembutsu-shū* (Collection of passages on the Original Vow of Amida in which the Nembutsu is chosen above all ways of achieving rebirth) by Hōnen (1133–1212), founder of the Pure Land school.
Publication of *Kōzen-Gokoku-ron* (Propagation of Zen for the protection of the nation) by Eisai (1141–1215), transmitter of the Rinzai Zen school.
1199 Minamoto Yoritomo dies.
1205 Hōjō Yoshitoki becomes the shogun's regent; beginning of Hōjō regency in Kamakura regime.
1207 Hōnen and other Pure Land Buddhists banished from the capital.
(84) *Juntoku* (r. 1210–21).
1212 Hōnen dies.
1215 Eisai dies.
(85) *Chūkyō* (known as *Kujō Haitei; r. three months in 1221).*
1221 The Shōkyū War, initiated by the ex-Emperor Go-Toba against the Kamakura regime.
(86) *Go-Horikawa* (r. 1222–33).
1222 The Kamakura regime banishes three retired monarchs (Go-Toba, Tsuchimikado, and Juntoku) from the capital.
1224 Shinran (1173–1262) founds the True Pure Land school of Buddhism.
1227 Dōgen (1200–53) transmits Sōtō Zen tradition to Japan.
1232 Jōei Shikimoku (Legislation of the Jōei Era) promulgated.
(87) *Shijō* (r. 1233–42).

1238   Great statue of Amida Buddha constructed at Kamakura.
       (88) *Go-Saga* (r. *1242–46*).
       (89) *Go-Fukakusa* (r. *1247–58*).
1253   Nichiren (1222–82) founds the Nichiren (known then as
       the Hokke or Lotus) sect.
       Dōgen dies.
1255   Kakushin founds the Fuke sect of Zen Buddhism.
       (90) *Kameyama* (r. *1259–74*).
1259   Famine and pestilence in Kyoto and many provinces.
1260   Great fire at Kamakura.
       Publication of *Risshō Ankoku-ron* (The establishment of
       righteousness and security of the nation) by Nichiren.
1262   Shinran dies.
1268   Hōjō Tokimune (1251–84) becomes regent (*shikken*) at
       Kamakura.
       Messenger of Khubilai Khan (1215–94) arrives in Japan.
       (91) *Go-Uda* (r. *1274–87*).
1274   First Mongol invasion.
1275   Ippen (1239–89), advocate of Amida cult, founds the Ji sect.
1281   Second Mongol invasion.
1282   Nichiren dies.
1286   Beginning of succession controversy between the Northern or
       Jimyōin (descendants of Go-Fukakusa) and the Southern or
       Daikakuji (descendants of Kameyama) lines of the imperial
       family.
       (92) *Fushimi* (r. *1287–97*).
1287   Beginning of Go-Uda's *inzei*.
       (93) *Go-Fushimi* (r. *1298–1301*).
       (94) *Go-Nijō* (r. *1301–7*).
1302   Kamakura regime bans the activities of the Ikkō (True Pure
       Land) priests.
       (95) *Hanazono* (r. *1308–18*) *Northern or Jimyō'n line.*
       (96) *Go-Daigo* (r. *1318–39*) *Southern or Daikakuji line.*
1321   End of Go-Uda's *inzei*.
1324   Ex-Emperor Go-Uda dies.
1325   Go-Daigo, at the suggestion of Zen master Musō Soseki
       (1275–1351), sends first envoy to China since the T'ang.
       * *Kōgon* (r. *1331–33*)—*Northern line.*
1331   Kamakura regime maneuvers the accession of Kōgon (begin-
       ning of the Northern dynasty).

1333 End of the Kamakura shogunate.
1334 Temporary restoration of direct imperial rule under Go-Daigo. First use of paper currency in Japan.
 * *Kōmyō* (*r. 1336–48*)—*Northern dynasty.*
1336 Kōmyō enthroned with the counterfeit imperial symbols turned over by the Emperor Go-Daigo of the Southern dynasty.

MUROMACHI (OR ASHIKAGA) PERIOD (1338–1573)

 (*97*) *Go-Murakami* (*r. 1339–68*)—*Southern dynasty.*
 * *Go-Kōgon* (*r. 1352–71*)—*Northern dynasty.*
 * *Sukō* (*r. 1348–51*)—*Northern dynasty.*
1338 Ashikaga Takauji becomes shogun. Beginning of the Ashikaga shogunate.
1339 Publication of the *Jinnō-shōtō-ki* (Records of the legitimate succession of the divine sovereigns) by Kitabatake Chikafusa (1293–1354).
 Watarai Tsuneyoshi, advocate of the Ise Shinto school, dies.
 Ashikaga Takauji builds a Zen temple (Tenryū-ji) in Kyoto.
1341 A ship of Tenryū-ji sent to China.
1346 Musō Soseki receives the title of National Teacher (*kokushi*).
1355? Watarai Iyeyuki, a leader of the Ise Shinto school, dies.
1358 Ashikaga Takauji dies. Ashikaga Yoshiakira succeeds as second shogun.
 Hosokawa Yoriyuki becomes the shogun's regent.
 Kōrai (Korea) complains about the activities of Wakō (Japanese marauders).
 (*98*) *Chōkei* (*r. 1368–83*)—*Southern dynasty.*
 * *Go-Enyū* (*r. 1371–83*)—*Northern dynasty.*
1368 Ashikaga Yoshimitsu (1358–1408) becomes the third shogun (rules as shogun until 1394).
 End of the Mongol (Yuan) dynasty and establishment of the Ming dynasty in China.
1369 The Ming court sends messenger to Japan.
1378 Ashikaga Yoshimitsu builds the Muromachi Palace in Kyoto.
 (*99*) *Go-Kameyama* (*r. 1383–92*)—*Southern dynasty.*
1392 Go-Kameyama surrenders imperial prerogatives to the Emperor Go-Komatsu of the Northern dynasty (end of the Southern dynasty). Establishment of the Yi dynasty in Korea.
 (*100*) *Go-Komatsu* (*r. 1383–1412*)—*Northern dynasty.*

1394   Ashikaga Yoshimochi, then nine years of age, becomes the fourth shogun.
1397   The retired shogun, Yoshimitsu, builds the Golden Pavilion (*kinkaku-ji*) in Kyoto.
1401   Ashikaga shogunate requests diplomatic relations with China.
1404   Tally trade (*kangō bōyeki*) begins.
       Peasant uprising (*do-ikki*) in Omi province (followed by similar *ikki* elsewhere).
1408   Yoshimitsu sponsors Nō play; Yoshimitsu dies.
       (*101*) Shōkō (r. 1412–28).
1419   Shogunate terminates diplomatic relations with China.
       (*102*) Go-Hanazono (r. 1428–64).
1435   Mansai (1378–1435), Buddhist priest and adviser to the shogun, dies.
1457   Ōta Dōkan builds his castle at Edo (Tokyo).
       (*103*) Go-Tsuchimikado (r. 1464–1500).
1465   Armed forces of Mt. Hiei attack the Ikkō (True Pure Land) sect's headquarters.
1467   Beginning of the Ōnin War.
1473   Beginning of the uprisings of the Ikkō (True Pure Land) followers (*ikkō-ikki*)—repeated in 1474, 1487, and 1488.
1477   End of the Ōnin War.
1479   Rennyo (1415–99) builds the Hongan-ji (the main temple of the Ikkō sect) at Yamashina.
1481   Ichijō Kanera (1402–81), apologist of Shinto, dies.
1484   Yoshida Kanetomo (1435–1511) advocates Yuiitsu Shinto.
1487–88   Togashi Masachika, Lord of Kaga province, is defeated by the followers of the Ikkō sect.
1489   Great fire in Kyoto; Silver Pavilion (*Ginkaku-ji*) completed.
       (*104*) Go-Kashiwara (r. 1501–26).
       (*105*) Go-Nara (r. 1526–57).
1532   Armed conflicts between the Nichiren and the Ikkō followers in Kyoto.
1541   Oda Nobunaga (1534–82) donates money for the reconstruction of the Grand Shrine of Ise.
1543   Portuguese arrive at the island of Tane (Tanegashima) and introduce gun powder.
1549   Francis Xavier (1506–52) arrives at Kagoshima; beginning of Roman Catholic (Kirishitan) activities.
1551   Xavier leaves Japan.

(*106*) *Ōgimachi* (*r. 1558–86*).

1568 Oda Nobunaga controls the capital.
1571 Oda Nobunaga destroys the Enryaku-ji on Mt. Hiei.
1573 End of Ashikaga (Muromachi) shogunate.

AZUCHI-MOMOYAMA PERIOD (1574–1600)

1576 Oda Nobunaga builds his castle at Azuchi.
1579 Alexandro Valignano, the Jesuit Visitor, arrives.
1580 Abbot Kennyo of Ikkō sect surrenders Ishiyama Honganji to Nobunaga.
1581 Oda Nobunaga orders the killing of the rebellious priests of Mt. Kōya.
1582 Oda Nobunaga dies; Toyotomi Hideyoshi (1536–98) succeeds to power.
1585 Mt. Kōya surrenders to Hideyoshi.
(*107*) *Go-Yōzei* (*r. 1587–1611*).
1587 First persecution of the Kirishitan (Roman Catholics).
1590 Goodwill mission of three daimyo from Kyushu returns from Europe.
1592 First Korean expedition.
1594 Toyotomi Hideyoshi builds his castle at Fushimi.
1596 *San Felipe* incident.
1597 Twenty-six Kirishitan martyred at Nagasaki.
Second Korean expedition.
1598 Toyotomi Hideyoshi dies; Tokugawa Iyeyasu (1542–1616) rises to power.

TOKUGAWA PERIOD (1600–1867)

1600 Victory of Tokugawa in the battle of Sekigahara.
Will Adams, later adviser to Tokugawa Iyeyasu, arrives in Japan.
1603 Tokugawa Iyeyasu becomes the shogun; establishment of the Tokugawa shogunate at Edo.
1605 Tokugawa Hidetada becomes the second shogun.
1608 Hayashi Razan (1583–1657) becomes Confucian tutor to the shogun.
(*108*) *Go-Mizunoo* (*r. 1611–29*).
1614 Anti-Kirishitan edict issued; Takayama Ukon and other Kirishitan banished to Luzon.
1615 *Buke shohatto* (Ordinances for the military houses) issued.

1616 Tokugawa Iyeyasu dies.
1617 Renewed persecution of Kirishitan.
1619 Fujiwara Seika (1561–1619), noted Confucian scholar, dies.
1620 Will Adams dies.
Iyeyasu's granddaughter Kazuko becomes the consort of the Emperor Go-Mizunoo.
1622 The "great Kirishitan martyrdom" of Nagasaki.
1623 Tokugawa Iyemitsu becomes the third shogun.
1624 Spaniards expelled from Japan.
(*109*) *Meisei, or Myōshō* (*empress; r. 1630–43*).
1630 Nichiō, advocate of the Fuju-fuse (not receiving from outsiders) sect of Nichiren school, dies.
1637–38 Kirishitan uprising at Shimabara, Kyushu.
1639–40 Portuguese and other Europeans expelled from Japan.
1640 Kirishitan-bugyō (Commissioners on Kirishitan affairs) appointed.
1641 Seclusion of Japan begins; only Dutch allowed to trade at Nagasaki.
(*110*) *Go-Kōmyō* (*r. 1643–54*).
1648 Tenkai edition of Tripitaka printed.
Nakaye Tōju, Neo-Confucian teacher, dies.
(*111*) *Gosai* (*r. 1654–63*).
1651 Tokugawa Iyetsuna becomes the fourth shogun.
1654 Chinese Zen master Ingen (1592–1673) brings the Ōbaku sect of Zen Buddhism to Japan.
1657 *Dai-Nihon-shi* (History of great Japan) commenced.
1658 Japan refuses Koxinga's request for assistance.
1661 Manchu dynasty established in China.
(*112*) *Reigen* (*r. 1663–87*).
1663 Two hundred and seven Kirishitan of Owari executed.
1665 Chinese emigré Chu Shun-sui (1600–82) settles in Mito.
Jiin hatto (Ordinances for temples) issued.
1680 Tokugawa Tsunayoshi becomes the fifth shogun.
1682 Yamazaki Ansai, scholar of the Chu Hsi school, dies.
1685 Yamaga Sokō, advocate of Bushi-dō, dies.
(*113*) *Higashiyama* (*r. 1687–1709*).
1688–1703 Genroku period, known for unusual exuberance in novels, plays, poems, and paintings.
1690 Englebert Kaempfer, a German in Dutch service, arrives at Nagasaki.

Deguchi (Watarai) Nobuyoshi, Shinto theorist, dies.
Confucian temple moved to Yushima section of Edo.

1691 Hayashi Hōkō (1644–1732) named hereditary head of the state university.
Kumazawa Banzan (b. 1619), Confucian reformer, dies.

1692 Shogun Tsunayoshi gives Confucian lectures to daimyo.

1693 Population of Edo, excluding samurai, astrologers, etc., estimated to be 353,588.

1694 Matsuo Bashō (b. 1644), Haiku master, and Yoshikawa Koretaru, Shinto theorist, die.

1701 Keichū, Buddhist priest and pioneer in National Learning, dies.

1702 Incident of the Forty-Seven *Rōnin*.

1705 Itō Jinsai (b. 1627), Confucian scholar, dies.
Okage mairi (worship to return divine favor) becomes popular.

1708 Giovanni Battista Sidotti (1668–1715), Italian priest, arrives.
(*114*) *Nakamikado* (*r. 1709–35*).

1709 Tokugawa Iyenobu becomes the sixth shogun.
Arai Hakuseki (1657–1725) becomes Confucian consultant to the shogunate.

1712 Tokugawa Iyetsugu becomes the seventh shogun.

1714 Kaibara Ekken (b. 1630), Confucian scholar, dies.

1716 Tokugawa Yoshimune becomes the eighth shogun. Muro Kyūsō (1688–1734) appointed as Confucian consultant to the shogunate. The shogunate relaxes edicts against Western learning.

1724 Chikamatsu Monzaemon, noted playwright, dies.

1728 Ogyū Sorai (b. 1666), Confucian scholar, dies.

1729 Ten-ichi-bō, a notorious *shugen-sha*, executed.

1732 Great famine in the Western provinces caused by locusts.
(*115*) *Sakuramachi* (*r. 1735–47*).

1736 Kada Azumamaro (b. 1669), advocate of National Learning, and Itō Tōgai (b. 1670), Confucian scholar, die.

1739 Russian ships seen in Japanese waters.

1744 Ishida Baigan, founder of the Shingaku movement, dies.
Aoki Konyō (1698–1769) undertakes Dutch learning by the order of the shogunate.

1745 Tokugawa Iyeshige becomes the ninth shogun.

1746 Tominaga Nakamoto (b. 1715), rationalist philosopher, dies.

(*116*) *Momozono* (r. 1747–63).

1757   Sugita Gempaku (1733–1817) studies Dutch surgery.
1760   Tokugawa Iyeharu becomes the tenth shogun.
       (*117*) *Go-Sakuramachi* (r. 1763–71).
1768   Rinzai Zen master Hakuin (b. 1685) dies.
1769   Kamo Mabuchi (b. 1697), Neo-Shintoist, dies.
       (*118*) *Go-Momozono* (r. 1771–79).
1774   Dutch book, *Tavel Anatomia,* translated into Japanese.
1776   Hiraga Gennai succeeds in producing frictional electricity
       machine.
       (*119*) *Kōkaku* (r. 1779–1817).
1786   Tokugawa Iyenari becomes the eleventh shogun.
1787   Matsudaira Sadanobu (1758–1829), leading minister of the
       shogunate, attempts fiscal and social reforms. Imperial palace
       burnt down in the great fire of Kyoto.
1789   Miura Baiyen (b. 1723), rationalist philosopher, dies.
1790   Shogunate issues edict suppressing heterodox learning; Chu
       Hsi school (Shushi-gaku) becomes the official learning.
1795   Shogunate bans the Fuji-kō (devotional association related to
       Mt. Fuji) and the Fuju-fuse sect of Nichiren Buddhism.
1796   *Edo Haruma* (Halma), first Dutch-Japanese dictionary, pub-
       lished.
1798   Motoori Norinaga (1730–1801) completes the *Kojiki-den*
       (Commentary on the *Kojiki*).
1802   *Ezo-bugyō* (Commissioner for Ezo affairs) appointed.
1804   Russian envoy, N. P. Rezanov, arrives at Nagasaki.
1808   Mamiya Rinzō (1780–1844) explores Sakhalin (Karafuto).
       English ship, *H.M.S. Phaeton,* arrives at Nagasaki.
1815   Sugita Gempaku writes *Rangaku-kotohajime* (Beginning of
       the Dutch learning).
       (*120*) *Ninkō* (r. 1817–46).
1817   Kaiho Seiryō (b. 1755), economic and political thinker, dies.
1818   The Englishman Gordon arrives at Uraga seeking trade.
1823   P. F. von Siebold (1796–1866), German physician in the
       Dutch service, arrives at Nagasaki.
1825   Shogunate issues edict to destroy foreign ships.
1829   Fukuoka Mitsugu and other Christians executed. Tokugawa
       Nariaki (1800–60), Lord of Mito, attempts to reform his fief.
1837   Tokugawa Iyeyoshi becomes the twelfth shogun. Financial
       crisis for shogunate caused by great famine. Unsuccessful up-

rising led by Ōshio Heihachirō (1793–1837) American ship *Morrison* driven away from Edo Bay.

1843 Hirata Atsutane (b. 1776), Neo-Shintoist, dies. Anti-Buddhist measures taken in the fief of Mito.

1844 Dutch monarch advises shogunate to open Japan's doors for trade.

(*121*) *Kōmei* (*r. 1846–67*).

1847 Narahashi Soken achieves successful vaccination.

1849 Kurozumi Munetada, founder of the Kurozumi sect, dies.

1853 Tokugawa Iyesada becomes the thirteenth shogun. First Perry expedition.

1854 Perry returns; treaty between Japan and the United States is concluded. Rising Sun flag adopted.

1855 Shogunate establishes School of Western Learning (Yōgaku-sho) which in the following year is renamed Bansho Torishi-rabe-dokoro.

1856 Townsend Harris (1804–78), the first American consul-general, arrives. Ninomiya Sontoku (b. 1787), religious reformer, dies.

1858 Tokugawa Iyemochi becomes the fourteenth shogun. Ii Kamon-no-kami Naosuke (1815–60) becomes prime minister. United States–Japanese Commercial Treaty concluded. Cholera rampant. Shimazu Nariakira (b. 1809), Lord of Satsuma, dies. Three ports—Kanagawa, Nagasaki, and Hakodate—opened for foreign trade. Yoshida Shōin and others executed.

1860 First Japanese mission to the United States dispatched. Ii Naosuke assassinated.

1861 Fukuzawa Yukichi (1834–1901) accompanies Japanese mission to Europe. The Emperor Kōmei's sister, Kazu, marries Shogun Iyemochi.

1862 Nishi Amane (1829–97) and Tsuda Mamichi (1829–1903) sent to Holland to study.

1863 British bombardment of Kagoshima in retaliation for anti-foreign outbursts. Tenchū-gumi, first anti-shogunate armed rebellion, rises in Yamato district.

1864 Bombardment of Shimonoseki by British, American, French, and Dutch warships.

1865 Fukuzawa Yukichi founds a private school (later named the Keiō Gijuku).

1866 Tokugawa Keiki becomes the fifteenth shogun. Satsuma and

Chōshū conclude secret agreement to restore imperial rule.
1867   Tokugawa Keiki surrenders shogun's prerogatives to the throne; end of Tokugawa regime.

MODERN PERIOD

(122) *Meiji* (*r. 1867–1912*).
1868   Meiji Restoration. Charter oath proclaimed. Capital moved to Tokyo.
1871   Feudal domains abolished. Iwakura Mission sent to Europe.
1872   Conscription ordinance issued. Railroad built between Shinbashi and Yokohama.
1873   Meirokusha, composed of modernists, established. Edict against Christianity removed. French jurist, Gustave Émile Boissona de Fontable (1825–1910), becomes legal adviser to Japanese government.
1874   Formosa expedition.
1875   Senate (Genrō-in) and Supreme Court (Daishin-in) established. Niijima Jō (1843–90) founds Dōshisha school in Kyoto.
1876   Sundays declared holidays. Treaty with Korea concluded.
1877   Satsuma rebellion. Tokyo University established.
1878   Ernest F. Fenollosa (1853–1908) employed as a teacher.
1879   Okinawa prefecture established.
1882   Tokyo Semmon Gakkō (later renamed Waseda University) founded.
1884   Yayoi period pottery discovered.
1889   Meiji Constitution adopted.
1890   First Diet convened. Imperial Rescript on Education promulgated.
1894–95   Sino-Japanese War.
1899   Extra-territorialities eliminated.
1902   Anglo-Japanese alliance concluded.
1904–5   Russo-Japanese War.
1907   Six-year compulsory education requirement put into effect.
1910   Annexation of Korea. Kōtoku Shūsui's alleged plot to assassinate the emperor.
(123) *Taishō* (*r. 1912–26*).
1914–18   First World War.
1915   Japan makes the Twenty-One Demands to China.

1918 Siberian expedition. Rice riots. First party cabinet formed by Hara Takashi.
1919 Versailles Peace Conference.
1920 First "May Day" celebrated.
1921 Washington Conference. Crown Prince Hirohito assumes regency on account of Taishō's illness.
1923 Great earthquake of Tokyo.
1924 The Quota Act ends Japanese immigration to the United States.
1925 Universal Manhood Suffrage Law.
(124) Hirohito (r. 1926–).
1928 Communist leaders arrested. Tsinan affair.
1930 London Naval Treaty.
1931 Manchurian "Incident" starts.
1932 Formation of Manchukuo. May 15 incident. Premier Inukai and others assassinated.
1933 Japan withdraws from League of Nations.
1936 Attempted *coup d'état,* known as 2–26 Incident.
1937 Commencement of "China Incident."
1940 Rome-Berlin-Tokyo Axis concluded.
1941–45 Second World War.

POST-SECOND WORLD WAR PERIOD

1945 Douglas MacArthur appointed as SCAP.
1946 New Constitution promulgated.
1947 New Constitution put into effect.
1950 Korean War begins.
1951 MacArthur succeeded by Matthew Ridgeway as SCAP. San Francisco Peace Conference.
1952 End of military occupation of Japan by Allied Forces. United States–Japan administrative agreements; Second General Conference of World Fellowship of Buddhists held in Japan.
1961 World Religionists' Peace Conference held in Kyoto.
1964 Kōmeitō (Political Wing of the Sōka Gakkai) formed.
1965 Second Vatican Council advocates religious liberty.
1966 National Foundation Day (February 11) restored.
1972 Okinawa returned to Japan. Twelfth General Conference of World Fellowship of Buddhists held in Japan.
1981 First Papal visit to Japan.
1985 Prime Minister Y. Nakasone pays official visit to Yasukuni Jinja (Shinto shrine for soldiers dead in wars).
1989 Death of the Shōwa Emperor; beginning of the Heisei era.

Glossary

AMATERASU Ō-MIKAMI   The tutelary kami of the imperial (Tennō) clan. Also known as Ō-hirume-no-kami, she is portrayed in mythologies as the central figure in the heavenly domain. Her grandson, Ninigi, was dispatched to rule Japan, and Ninigi's great-grandson, Jimmu, is regarded as the first legendary emperor. Amaterasu is enshrined in the Grand Shrine of Ise.

AMIDA   Amitābha (the Buddha of Infinite Light) or Amitāyus (the Buddha of Infinite Life), whose abode is the Pure Land (Sukhāvatī).

BAKUFU   The feudal regime; the shogunate government.

BOSATSU   Bodhisattva, a being destined for enlightenment and believed to have vowed to save all beings out of his compassion.

BUMMEI-KAIKA   Civilization and enlightenment.

BUNREI   Dividing the spirit of the kami. Branch shrines may be established from the original shrine of a certain kami to house his spirit as well, and thus the new shrines participate in the power of the original.

BUSHIDŌ   The code of the warrior (*bushi*).

CHINJU-NO-KAMI   A tutelary kami of a definite area or region; in theory different from *uji-gami* (the kami of the clan) and *ubusuna-no-kami* (the kami of the particular locality where one was born). These three kinds of kami cannot easily be differentiated in actual practice.

DAIMYO   A feudal lord.

DAINICHI   The Great Sun Buddha (Mahāvairocana), believed to be the essence of the cosmos in Esoteric Buddhism.

DANKA   A household which supports a Buddhist temple; a parishioner.

DANKA-SEIDO   Buddhist parochial system.

DO-IKKI   Peasants' uprising.

DŌJUKU   A lay assistant in the Japanese Roman Catholic (Kirishitan) tradition.

DŌZOKU   Traditional Japanese kinship system that includes all the branch families (*bunke*) of a certain main family (*honke*).

ETA   Japanese pariahs. The legal distinction between them and others was officially abolished in the nineteenth century. There were 287,111 *eta* recorded in the census of 1871.

FUDOKI   Records of Local Surveys compiled during the Nara period.

FUJU-FUSE   Principle of "not receiving from nonbelievers and not giving," advocated by Nichiō (1565–1630), one of the leaders of the Nichiren school of Buddhism.

FUKKO-SHINTO   The Neo-Shinto Movement, advocated by Motoori Norinaga (1730–1801), Hirata Atsutane (1776–1843), and others, which aimed at a "return to antiquity."

FUKO OR FUGO   A form of compensation, gift, or allowance given to meritorious officials or religious institutions during the Nara period.

GONGEN   A temporary manifestation of Buddha. For example, the Shinto kami of war, Hachiman, was believed to be the manifestation of the third Sun-Buddha Amitābha (the setting sun). In turn, the Emperor Ōjin was regarded as the manifestation of Iwashimizu Hachiman. Later, Tokugawa Iyeyasu was deified and called the manifestation of the Great Sun God (Tōshō).

GORYŌ   Spirits of those who had suffered a violent death, believed to curse the living either by haunting them or inflicting a calamity on them.

GORYŌ-YE   Rituals for the purpose of pacifying the vengeful spirits (*goryō*). Such rituals developed in the ninth century A.D. in Kyoto and gradually spread to the provinces. Significantly, the *goryō-ye* was quite different in form and ethos from the earlier Shinto rituals centering around the kami of the clan.

HAIBUTSU-KISHAKU   Literally, "elimination of Buddha." It refers to the anti-Buddhist movement that arose in the early Meiji Era.

HAJA-KENSEI   Literally, "the refutation of evil (meaning Christianity) and the exaltation of righteousness (meaning Buddhism)." It refers to a Buddhist movement in the late nineteenth century.

HAKKŌ-ICHIU   Literally, "the whole world under one roof." This phrase was used by the Japanese militarists during the 1930s and 1940s as a slogan for the expansionist program.

HAN   A daimyo's realm or fief.

HANARE KIRISHITAN   Literally, "separate Kirishitan," a designation of the Japanese Roman Catholics who refuse to accept the jurisdiction of the Vatican. They are the heirs of those who had preserved their faith while deprived of clergy during the Tokugawa period.

HARAYE OR HARAI   The purification ceremonies of Shinto.

HATTO   Law, ordinance, or prohibition.

HIJIRI   Literally, "holy man," often used to refer to religious persons with some charismatic qualities in contradistinction to leaders of institutionalized religion.

HIMOROGI   An ancient form of Shinto shrine, being a piece of unpolluted land surrounded by evergreens. In the center is a sacred tree.

HIRAKANA OR HIRAGANA   Cursive characters; a form of Japanese alphabet.

HOKKE-IKKI   Armed uprisings of the adherents of the Nichiren school.

HOKKE-SHŪ   A school of Buddhism founded by Nichiren (1222–82) based on the teaching of the *Lotus* (*Sad-dharma pundarīka*) *Sutra;* also known as the Nichiren-shū.

HONGAN   Literally, "original vow," referring to the eighteenth (among forty-eight) vow of Amida, recorded in the *Sukhāvatī-vyūha* (Sutra of the Pure Land), according to which a devotee who relies on the Amida Buddha and repeats his name is assured of rebirth in the Pure Land.

HONGAN-JI   The Temple of the Original Vow; the name of the main temple of the Jōdo-shin-shū (the True Pure Land school). Following the division of this school into two branches in the seventeenth century, both branches have adopted this designation for their respective main temples, the Higashi (Eastern)- and Nishi (Western)-Honganji.

HONJI   Original or metaphysical nature of the Buddha. According to the theory of *honji-suijaku,* the Shinto kami were manifestations (or incarnations, *suijaku*) of the original nature of the Buddha. This theory was advanced to justify the Shinto-Buddhist coexistence pattern known as the *Ryōbu-Shinto* or *Sannō-ichijitsu-Shintō.*

HOSSŌ-SHŪ   The Vijnaptimatrata or Yogācāra school of Buddhism. It was one of the six schools established in Japan during the Nara period.

HŌTOKU   Literally, "Repay the indebtedness," the name of the semi-religious movement initiated by Ninomiya Sontoku (1787–1856).

HŌZA   Literally, "teaching circle," a form of discussion group utilized by some of the new religions for the purpose of religious instruction.

IKKI   An uprising, insurrection, or revolt; e.g., Do-ikki, Hokke-ikki, and Ikkō-ikki.

IKKŌ-IKKI   An insurrection of the adherents of the Ikkō-shū.

IKKŌ-SHŪ   Literally, "single-minded or single-directed sect." The name given to the followers of the True Pure Land (*Jōdo-shin-shū*).

INZEI OR INSEI   The rule of the cloistered ex-emperors who usually delegated only ceremonial functions to the nominally reigning monarchs.

ISE   The seat of the Kōtai jingū which enshrines Amaterasu, the tutelary kami of the imperial clan.

ISE-KŌ   A devotional association of the faithful of Ise, which usually has a village or hamlet as its unit, and sends representatives to worship at the Grand Shrine of Ise from time to time. However, the popularity of Ise was such that sometimes even those who did not belong to *Ise-kō* participated in spontaneous mass pilgrimages to return thanks (*okage mairi*).

ISHIN   Renovation, renewal, or restoration; e.g., Meiji ishin.

IWASAKA   A spot of unpolluted land, surrounded by holy rocks, chosen for the worship of a kami.

JINGŪ-JI   A Buddhist chapel established within the compound of a Shinto shrine.

JINJA   A Shinto shrine.

JINJA HONCHŌ   The Association of Shrine Shinto organized in 1945.

JINJA SHINTO   Shrine Shinto, the post-Second World War name for disestablished Shinto. The heir of the shrines and organization previously known as State (*Kokka*) Shinto. It is now recognized as one of the religions. There are about 100,000 Shinto shrines, and most of them belong to *Jinja honchō*.

JISHA BUGYŌ   Commissioner of temple and shrine affairs during the Tokugawa period.

JI-SHŪ   A school of Amida pietism founded by Ippen (1239–89). It is called the *Ji* (literally, "times") sect, because it follows the custom of singing hymns six times a day.

JIZŌ   Bodhisattva Kṣitigarbha, called Ti-tsang in Chinese. He is believed to stand between this world and the next and to save those on their way to hell.

JŌDO   The Pure Land (*sukhāvatī*), which is Amida's paradise.

JŌDO-SHIN-SHŪ   The True Pure Land school of Buddhism founded by Shinran (1173–1262), also known as the Ikkō-shu.

JŌDO-SHŪ   The Pure Land school of Buddhism founded by Hōnen (1133–1212).

JŌI   Literally, the word means "repulsion of foreigners"; the designation of the anti-foreign movement toward the end of the Tokugawa period.

JŌJITSU   The *Satyasiddhi* school. It was one of the six Buddhist schools established in Japan during the Nara period.

JŌKA-MACHI   "Castle town," that is, the seat of a daimyo.

JŌMON   The name of the earliest phase of the prehistoric period in Japan.

JUNREI   A religious pilgrimage.

JUSHA   A Confucian scholar.

KAIDAN   A Buddhist ordination hall.

KAIKOKU   Literally, "opening the country" as contrasted to *jōi* (repulsion of foreigners).

KAJI-KITŌ   Magico-religious rites and prayers.

KAKURE KIRISHITAN   Hidden Roman Catholics who kept the faith in secret during the Tokugawa period.

KAMI   Although there are many etymological theories regarding this term, there is none that is acceptable to everybody, nor is there an appropriate Western equivalent. It is often translated as god, spirit, or anything that commands the awe and reverence 'of man. It refers to both the "sacred" nature in general and the specific objects of worship in Shinto.

KAMI-DANA   Miniature Shinto shrines, usually kept at home.

KAMI-GAKARI   The state of kami-possession.

KAMPAKU   While this title implies the chief adviser to the throne, historically it meant a *de facto* dictator.

KANGŌ-BŌYEKI   The tally trade.

KANNAGARA   An adverb that modifies actions of the kami. Orthodox Shinto claims to be *kannagara-no-michi* (the way which is in accordance with the will of the kami).

KAN-NUSHI   A head priest of a Shinto shrine.

KEGON-SHŪ   The Avatamsaka school. One of the six Buddhist sects established in Japan during the Nara period.

KIKA-JIN   A naturalized person.

KŌ; KŌ-SHA   These terms refer to both a devotional association and its meetings for the purpose of religious instruction. Many of them are confraternities of laymen and laywomen.

KŌAN   Literally, a "public theme," a paradoxical statement utilized by Zen masters for the spiritual illumination of disciples. Paradoxes are used to dispel ordinary logic.

KŌDŌ   The "Imperial Way" which was advocated by Neo-Shintoists as the ideal principle of polity in Japan.

KŌDŌ BUKKYO   The "Imperial Way" Buddhism which was a nationalistic movement of modern Japanese Buddhism.

KOFUN   Ancient mound; the transitional period between prehistoric and early historic phases in Japan, so called because of large tumuli constructed during this period.

KOGAKU   Also known as *Fukko-gaku*, a branch of Japanese Confucianism that stressed the study of antiquity, that is the teachings of Confucius and Mencius.

KOJIKI   A Japanese classic compiled during the Nara period. It contains myths, legends, and historical accounts, centering around the imperial clan. It is regarded as a semisacred scripture of Shinto.

KOKUBUNJI   A state-supported official Buddhist temple built during the Nara period.

KOKUGAKU   National Japanese learning in contradistinction to *Kangaku* (Chinese or Confucian learning) and *Yōgaku* (Western learning).

KOKUTAI   National polity.

KYŌDAN   Abbreviation of *Nihon Kirisuto Kyōdan* (The Church of Christ in Japan).

KYŌHA SHINTO   Sect Shinto denominations.

KYŌHA-SHINTO-RENGŌ-KAI   The Federation of Sect Shinto denominations.

KYŌKAI   A church, the term used by both the Christian and Sect Shinto groups.

KUSHA   The Abhidharma-kosa school. One of the six Buddhist schools established in Japan during the Nara period.

MAJINAI   A spell or incantation.

MANNYŌSHŪ OR MANYŌSHŪ   An anthology of poetry compiled toward the end of the eighth century. It is often translated as *A Collection of Myriad Leaves*.

MAPPŌ   According to a Buddhist view of cosmic history, there are three periods. The first thousand years was called the period of the "perfect law" (*Sad-dharma, shōbō*); the second thousand years was that of the "copied law" (*Pratirūpa-dharma, zōbō*); and the third thousand years was the period of "degeneration of Buddha's law" (*Paschima-dharma, mappō*). Many leaders of Japanese Buddhism during the Kamakura period took this view of cosmic history seriously and believed they were entering the *mappō* period.

MAREBITO   Also pronounced as *marahito, marabito,* and *marōdo,* this term signifies a "sacred visitor," who visits the world of man from "the other world" (the world of kami) at certain appointed times and seasons. Since a *marebito* is not a kami of the clan or of the region, he is usually given only a minor place as a *marōdo-gami* in an insignificant corner of a Shinto shrine.

MATSURI   Religious ceremonies, rituals, and rites. In popular usage, this term also connotes festivals of various kinds which have lost their religious significance.

MATSURI-GOTO   The affairs of state; government; or political administration. It derives from the word *matsuri,* since political and religious dimensions were regarded as interdependent and interpenetrating in ancient Japan. See also *saisei-itchi.*

MIKKYŌ   Literally, "esoteric doctrines," referring to the esoteric tradition of Buddhism, known variously as *Mantrayāna, Tantrayāna,* or *Vajrayāna.* In Japan there are two main schools of *Mikkyō.* First is the Shingon school, usually referred to as the *Tō-mitsu* (meaning the esoteric tradition of a Shingon temple in Kyoto known as Tō-ji). Second is the esoteric tradition of the Tendai school, referred to as the *Tai-mitsu.*

MIKO   Although there were various kinds of Miko in ancient Japan, they were for the most part female shamanic diviners with charismatic qualities. Even today this type of Miko exists in many parts of Japan. The term is also used to designate a supplementary priestess in Shinto shrines today. These perform sacred dances and assist priests at Shinto rituals.

MIKOTO   A term of respect for a kami, an emperor, or a nobleman.

MI-KOTO   The words of command of a kami, an emperor, or a nobleman.

MIROKU   Maitreya, the Buddha yet to come.

MIYAHITO   Mistresses of the palace.

MONO   Spirits of animals and other "lower" beings.

MONO-TSUKI   The state of being possessed by the spirits of animals or of other beings.

MUJŌ   Transiency or transitoriness; uncertainty; mutability.

MUKYŌKAI   The Non-Church Movement founded by Uchimura Kanzō (1861–1930), a leading Japanese Christian.

NEMBUTSU   Invocation of the holy name of Amida.

NICHIREN-SHŪ   A school of Buddhism founded by Nichiren (1222–82); also known as the Hokke-shū.

NIHONSHOKI or NIHONGI "Chronicles of Japan," compiled during the Nara period.

NŌ PLAY A very symbolic form of Japanese drama that flourished from the fourteenth century onward.

NORITO Words addressed to the kami in the Shinto ceremonies. More specifically, it refers to the ritual passages recorded in the tenth-century book called the *Engishiki*.

ŌBAKU-SHŪ A sect of Zen Buddhism that was transmitted to Japan from China during the Tokugawa period.

O-FURIKAYE The belief in a divine mediation that "transfers" suffering from people to a savior or his human agent.

OKAGE-MAIRI Spontaneous mass pilgrimage to a Shinto shrine to return thanks for the favor bestowed by the kami.

ONMYŌDŌ Yin-yang and Taoist magic.

ŌYŌMEI-GAKU A branch of Neo-Confucianism following the tradition of Wang Yang-ming (1471–1529; his name is pronounced in Japanese as Ōyōmei).

RANGAKU The Dutch (Holland, pronounced in Japanese as *Oranda*) learning.

REIGEN Marvelous efficacy of the kami or the Buddha.

RI Japanese pronunciation of the Chinese word *li*, which means reason or principle.

RINZAI-SHŪ One of the Zen Buddhist schools transmitted to Japan from China by Eisai (1141–1215).

RISSHIN-SHUSSE Success and advancement in life.

RITSU-SHŪ The Vinaya school. One of the six schools of Buddhism established in Japan during the Nara period.

RŌNIN A warrior who is deprived of his fief.

RUIJI-SHŪKYŌ Also known as *Shūkyō-ruiji-dantai;* a pseudo or quasi religion.

RYŌBU-SHINTO As a general term, it refers to the Shinto-Buddhist coexistence pattern that developed in Japan. Specifically, it is the designation of the Shingon-Shinto, which interprets Shinto in accordance with the doctrines of the Shingon school of Buddhism. A similar attempt by the Tendai School of Buddhism is called the *Sannō-ichijitsu-Shinto*.

SAE (OR SAI)-NO-KAMI Also known as Dōsojin; the kami of the road, who is usually worshiped on the village borders, on mountain passes, or by bridges, in order to assure the safety of the traveler or to keep away evil spirits. In the course of time, the function of this kami was taken over by a Buddhist divinity called Jizō.

SAISEI-ITCHI The ancient Japanese idea that religion (*sai*) and government (*sei*) are interdependent and interpenetrating. See *matsuri-goto.*

SAKOKU Closing of the nation to foreign intercourse and trade.

SAMURAI The warrior; also known as *bushi.*

SANRON-SHŪ The Mādhyamika or Sarvasūnyavāda school. One of the six schools of Buddhism established in Japan during the Nara period.

SENDATSU A guide to a holy mountain. See *yamabushi.*

SEMMYŌ Imperial edicts.

SESSHŌ Regent of the emperor.

SHAKU-BUKU A form of forced conversion, practiced by some of the adherents of Nichiren-shū.

SHAMI A Buddhist leader who is not ordained by the official hierarchy.

SHASŌ A Buddhist priest who serves in a Shinto shrine; a common phenomenon in the Shinto-Buddhist coexistence pattern.

SHIKKEN A regent of the shogun.

SHINBUTSU HANZEN Separation of Shinto from Buddhism. This measure was taken by the Meiji regime in other to exalt Shinto as the *de facto* state religion.

SHINGAKU Literally, "Mind-Learning"; a semireligious movement founded by Ishida Baigan (1685–1744).

SHINGON-SHŪ The term Shingon is the Japanese pronunciation of the Chinese term *Chen-yen,* meaning the "true word" (*Mantra*). It is a form of esoteric Buddhism (*Mikkyō*) transmitted to China from India by Subhakarasinha (637–735), Vajrabodhi (663–723), and Amoghavajra (705–74). A Japanese monk, Kūkai, better known as Kōbō Daishi (774–935) transmitted the esoteric doctrine in 806 and established the Shingon-shū. Unlike other schools of Buddhism, esoteric Buddhism believes in a form of cosmo-theism in the sense that Dainichi (Mahāvairocana) is considered the essence of the cosmos. While Dainichi is different from the Buddha Sākyamuni, the latter may be regarded as the former in a mystical sense.

SHINKŌ SHŪKYŌ New religions; the designation of the newly arisen religions in Japan after the end of the Second World War.

SHIN-SHŪ-REN   Abbreviation of Shin-Nihon-Shūkyō-dantai-rengōkai (The Association of New Religions in Japan).

SHUGEN   Mastery of magical power.

SHUGEN-DŌ   The path of acquiring magical power by undergoing austere disciplines in the mountains. It refers to the Order of Mountain Ascetics, a peculiar hybrid of folk beliefs, Shinto, and Buddhism with some elements of the Yin-Yang and Taoistic beliefs.

SHUSHI-GAKU   A branch of Neo-Confucianism following the tradition of Chu Hsi (pronounced in Japanese as Shushi, 1130–1200). The Tokugawa regime adopted Shushi-gaku as its official doctrine.

SHŪSHIN   Morality or ethics.

SHŌBŌ   The period of the "Perfect Law" in the Buddhist cosmic history. See *mappō*.

SHŌEN   A manor.

SHOGUN   A warrior-ruler; generalissimo.

SHŌNIN   A holy man.

SŌHEI   A warrior priest; an armed priest.

SOKUSHIN JŌBUTSU   Becoming a Buddha with one's body during one's earthly existence. This is the goal of the Shingon Buddhist.

SONNŌ   Reverence for the throne; the royalist motto vis-à-vis the pro-Tokugawa party in the mid-nineteenth century.

SŌTŌ-SHŪ   A branch of Zen Buddhism transmitted to Japan by Dōgen (1200–53).

TAIMITSU   Tendai esoterism. See *Mikkyō*.

TAMA   Spirit or soul of the kami and of man. *Ara-mi-tama* is a violent spirit or a spirit that coerces men with power, while *nigi-mi-tama* is a gentle spirit that pacifies men. *Mi-tama-shiro* (the representation of the spirit) or *shintai* (the kami body) is a sacred object through which a certain kami is worshiped. *Tama-shizume* or *chinkon* is a ceremony to prevent the soul from leaving the body. *Tama-yori-hime* is a woman or maiden (*hime*) in whom the *tama* of the kami dwells. *Kuni-tama* is the spirit of the land. Somewhat different is the use of this term as a synonym for "principle," i.e., *yamato-damashii* (the *tama-shii* of *Yamato*) which simply means *Nippon seishin* (the Japanese spirit).

TENDAI-SHŪ   The Japanese pronunciation of the Chinese *T'ien-t'ai* sect, founded by Chih-i or Chih-k'ai (531–97) who advocated the unity of the three truths, namely, (1) all things have no self-nature, (2) all things have provisional existence, and (3) thus, the nature of all things (*dharmas*) is both void (empty) and provisional. Chih-i developed his system based on the *Lotus Sutra* which he considered the culmination of all Buddhist doctrines. This doctrine was transmitted to Japan in 805 by Saicho, better known as Dengyō Daishi (766–822). Saicho attempted to incorporate and integrate monastic discipline, esoteric cults, and Zen (Ch'an) practices into the Tendai system. The Tendai school's attempt to synthesize Shinto and Buddhism is called the *Sannō-Ichijitsu-Shinto*. Shortly after Saicho's death, the "esoteric tradition" (*Tai-mitsu*) became paramount in the Tendai school. See *Mikkyō*.

TENNŌ The emperor.

TERA A Buddhist temple, pronounced *ji* in compound words, i.e., Hōryū-ji, Tō-ji, and Tōdai-ji.

TERA-KOYA A temple school for children.

TERA-UKE A temple certificate required by the Tokugawa regime for every Japanese family in order to prove that its members were Buddhists and not adherents of Roman Catholicism (*Kirishitan*).

TŌ-MITSU The esoteric tradition of the Shingon school. See *Mikkyō*.

TORII A sacred gateway, formed of two upright and two horizontal beams, which is erected in front of a Shinto shrine.

TSUMI Usually translated as "sin," but connotes mental and physical defilements as well as sickness, error, and disaster. According to Shinto, *tsumi* are removed by ceremonial cleansing (*haraye*).

UBASOKU The Japanese pronunciation of *upāsaka* (feminine, *upāsikā*); one who is not a *Bhikkhu* (a member of a monastic order) but who follows the law of the Buddha. In Japan, however, the term *ubasoku* often refers to a charismatic leader who practices semi-Buddhistic and semishamanistic austerities. As early as the Nara period, there were many *ubasoku* ascetics who claimed to have mastered magical power by undergoing austere training at certain mountains. Their tradition devéloped into the *Shugen-dō*. (See *Shugen-dō*.) Later, many *ubasoku* became itinerant preachers, healers, and magicians, travelling from village to village.

UJI The clan.

UJI-BITO Clansman; clansmen.

UJI-GAMI The ancestral or tutelary kami of a particular clan.

UJI-KO Literally "a child of the clan," but refers to one who is regarded as a child of the kami of a clan; as such, it means a parishioner in Shinto.

UJI-NO-KAMI The clan chieftain.

wakō   Literally, "Japanese invaders or marauders," pirates who harassed Korean and Chinese coastal cities during the fourteenth, fifteenth, and sixteenth centuries. Actually, there were a number of Chinese and Koreans who joined such ventures.

wakon-yōsai   Literally, "Japanese spirit combined with Western training," a popular ideal of Japanese intellectuals during the nineteenth century.

yama-bushi   Literally, "one who sleeps in the mountain," a designation of the mountain ascetic of the Shugen-dō tradition.

yamatai   Sometimes pronounced as Yabatai. One of the principalities in Japan during its early historic period.

yamato   The old name of Japan; also the name of the district now known as Nara prefecture.

yamato-e   A form of scroll painting.

yayoi   The name of a section of Tokyo where prehistoric pottery was unearthed. Thus, the name Yayoi was given to the period *ca.* 250 B.C.-A.D. 250 by archaeologists.

yōgaku   Western learning.

yūgyō shōnin   An itinerant holy man; the name given to Ippen (1239–89) and others who traveled from village to village, preaching the simple gospel of the Amida Buddha.

yuiitsu-shinto   A monistic school of Shinto, also known as Yoshida or Urabe Shinto, transmitted since the Heian period in the priestly family called Yoshida. It was systematized by Yoshida Kanetomo (1435–1511), whose goal was the integration of Shinto, Buddhism, and Confucianism within the framework of Shinto. Thus, it is also referred to as Gempon-sōgen-Shinto (fundamental and original Shinto).

yoshi   Good, desirable.

za   Trade guilds that were frequently affiliated with Shinto or Buddhist institutions.

zaibatsu   Plutocracy; the financial oligarchy that developed in modern Japan.

za-nin   Members of the professional guilds.

zen   The *Dhyana* or meditation school of Buddhism that developed in China, known as Ch'an in Chinese or Zen in Japanese. See Ōbaku-shū, Rinzai-shū, and Sōtō-shū.

zōhō   The period of the "Copied Law" in the Buddhist cosmic history. See *mappō*.

Bibliography

WORKS IN WESTERN LANGUAGES

Abegg, Lily. *The Mind of East Asia,* tr. A. J. Crick and E. E. Thomas. London and New York, 1952.

Abegglen, James G. *The Japanese Factory: Aspects of Its Social Organization.* Glencoe, Illinois, 1958.

Ackerman, Edward A. *Japan's Natural Resources and Their Relation to Japan's Economic Future.* Chicago, 1953.

Adams, Charles J. ed. *A Reader's Guide to the Great Religions.* New York, 1965.

Aduard, Baron E. J. Lewe. *Japan: From Surrender to Peace.* New York, 1953.

Aida, Hikoichi. *Kōdōkan Jūdō,* tr. and ed. E. J. Harrison. New York, 1956.

Akagi, Roy Hidemichi. *Japan's Foreign Relations, 1542–1936.* Tokyo, 1936.

Akita, George. "The Meiji Constitution in Practice: The First Diet," *JAS,* XXII (No. 1, November, 1962), 31–46.

Akiyama, Kenzō. *The History of Nippon.* Tokyo, 1941.

Allen, George Cyril. *Japanese Industry: Its Recent Development and Present Condition.* New York, 1939.

———— *A Short Economic History of Modern Japan, 1867–1937.* London, 1946.

———— *Japan's Economic Recovery.* New York, 1956.

Amadei, Emma. "A XVII Century Japanese Embassy Recorded in the Roman Basilica of S. Maria Maggiore," *East and West* (No. 3, January, 1953), 236–38.

Anesaki, Masaharu. *Buddhist Art.* Boston and New York, 1915.

Anesaki, Masaharu. *Nichiren, the Buddhist Saint.* Cambridge, Mass., 1916.

———— *Japanese Mythology* (Vol. VIII of *The Mythology of All Races,* ed. C. J. A. MacCulloch). Boston, 1928.

———— *History of Japanese Religion.* London, 1930.

———— *A Concordance to the History of Kirishitan Missions.* Tokyo, 1930.

———— *Art, Life, and Nature in Japan.* Boston, 1933.

———— *Katam Karaniyam.* Tokyo, 1934.

———— *Religious Life of the Japanese People,* rev. Hideo Kishimoto. Tokyo, 1961.

Anzu, Motohiko. *Shinto as Seen by Foreign Scholars.* Tokyo, 1938.

———— "The Concept of 'Kami,' " *Proceedings of the IXth International Congress for the History of Religions* (Tokyo, 1962), pp. 218–22.

Ariga, Tetsutarō. "The So-called 'Newly-Arisen Sects' in Japan," *Missionary Research Library, Occasional Bulletin,* Vol. V (No. 4, March, 1954).

———— "Contemporary Apologetics of Shintō," *Missionary Research Library, Occasional Bulletin,* Vol. V (No. 5, April, 1954).

———— "Christian Mission in Japan as a Theological Problem," *Religion in Life,* XXVII (No. 3, Summer, 1958), 372–80.

Armstrong, Robert C. *Just Before the Dawn: The Life and Work of Ninomiya Sontoku.* New York, 1912.

———— *Light from the East: Studies in Japanese Confucianism.* Toronto, 1914.

———— *Buddhism and Buddhists in Japan.* New York, 1927.

Asakawa, Kanichi. *The Early Institutional Life of Japan.* Tokyo, 1903.

———— *The Documents of Iriki: Illustrative of the Development of the Feudal Institutions of Japan.* New Haven, 1929.

Aschoff, Angelus. *Catholicism and Shintō in Japan.* (Missionary Academia Studies, Vol. IV, No. 3.) New York, 1946.

Ashida, K. "Japan," in *Encyclopedia of Religion and Ethics,* ed. James Hastings, VII (1914), 481–89.

Aston, William George, tr. *Nihongi: Chronicles of Japan from the Earliest Times to A.D. 697.* 2 vols., London, 1896; 2 vols. in 1, London, 1956.

———— *Shintō: The Way of the Gods.* London, 1905.

———— *A History of Japanese Literature.* New York, 1908.

——— "A Comparative Study of the Japanese and Korean Language," *Journal of the Royal Asiatic Society of Great Britain and Ireland,* Vol. III, Part XI (1879).

Baerwald, Hans H. *The Purge of Japanese Leaders under the Occupation.* (University of California Publications in Political Science, VIII.) Berkeley and Los Angeles, 1959.

——— "Tensions in Japanese Politics: Coal and Korea," *Asian Survey,* III (No. 4, April, 1963), 182–88.

Bailey, Jackson H. "Prince Saionji and the Popular Rights Movement," *JAS,* XXI (No. 1, November, 1961), 49–63.

Bairy, Maurice A. *Japans Neue Religionen in der Nachkriegszeit.* Bonn, 1959.

Baker, Richard T. *Darkness of the Sun.* Nashville, 1947.

Ball, W. MacMahon. *Japan: Enemy or Ally?* New York, 1949.

Ballou, Robert O. *Shintō, the Unconquered Enemy.* New York, 1945.

Batchelor, John. *The Ainu and Their Folklore.* London, 1901.

——— "On the Ainu Term 'Kamui,' " *TASJ,* XVI (1899), 17–32.

Battistini, Lawrence H. *The Postwar Student Struggle in Japan.* Tokyo, 1956.

Beardsley, Richard K. "Japan Before History: A Survey of the Archaeological Record," *FEQ,* XIX (No. 3, May, 1955), 317–46.

——— "Shinto Religion and Japanese Cultural Evolution," in *The Science of Culture,* ed. Gertrude E. Dole and Robert L. Carneiro (New York, 1960), pp. 63–78.

Beardsley, Richard K., John W. Hall, and Robert E. Ward. *Village Japan.* Chicago, 1959.

Beasley, W. G. *Great Britain and the Opening of Japan, 1834–1858.* London, 1951.

———, tr. and ed. *Select Documents on Japanese Foreign Policy, 1853–1868.* London, 1955.

——— *The Modern History of Japan.* New York, 1963.

———, and E. G. Pulleyblank, eds. *Historians of China and Japan.* London, 1961.

Beck, L. Adams. *The Story of Oriental Philosophy.* New York, 1931.

Beckmann, George M. *The Making of the Meiji Constitution: The Oligarchs and the Constitutional Development of Japan, 1868–1891.* Lawrence, Kansas, 1957.

Beers, Burton F. *Vain Endeavor: Robert Lansing's Attempts to End the American-Japanese Rivalry.* Durham, N.C., 1962.

Befu, Harumi, with Edward Norbeck. "Japanese Usages of Terms of Relationship," *SJA,* XIV (No. 1, Spring, 1958), 66–86.

Bellah, Robert N. *Tokugawa Religion.* Glencoe, Illinois, 1957.

———, ed. *Religion and Progress in Modern Asia.* New York, 1965.

Benedict, Ruth. *The Chrysanthemum and the Sword: Patterns of Japanese Culture.* Boston, 1947.

Benl, Oscar. *Die Entwicklung der japanischen Poetik bis zum 16. Jahrhundert.* Hamburg, 1951.

Best, Ernest E. "Christian Faith and Cultural Crisis: The Japanese Case," *The Journal of Religion,* XLI (No. 1, January, 1961), 17–27.

Binyon, Laurence. *Painting in the Far East: An Introduction to the History of Pictorial Art in Asia, Especially China and Japan.* 3d ed. New York, 1960.

Bisson, Thomas A. *Japan in China.* New York, 1938.

——— *Japan's War Economy.* New York, 1945.

——— *Prospects for Democracy in Japan.* New York, 1949.

——— *Zaibatsu Dissolution in Japan.* Berkeley, 1954.

Blacker, Carmen. *The Japanese Enlightenment; A Study of the Writings of Fukuzawa Yukichi.* Cambridge, 1964.

Blakemore, Thomas L. *The Criminal Code of Japan.* Tokyo, 1954.

Blue Cliff Records, see Shaw, R. D. M.

Blyth, R. H. *Zen in English Literature and Oriental Classics.* Tokyo, 1948.

Bohner, Herman, tr. *Jinnō Shōtōki, Buch von der Wahren Gott-Kaiser-Herrschafts-Linie.* Tokyo, 1935.

Borton, Hugh. *Japan Since 1931.* New York, 1940.

———, ed. *Japan.* Ithaca, N.Y., 1951.

——— *Japan's Modern Century.* New York, 1955.

Bowers, Faubion. *Japanese Theater.* New York, 1952.

Bowie, Henry P. *On the Laws of Japanese Painting.* New York, 1951.

Bownas, G. *Japanese Rainmaking.* London, 1963.

Boxer, C. R. *Jan Campagnie in Japan, 1600–1850.* 2d ed. rev. The Hague, 1950.

——— *The Christian Century in Japan, 1549–1650.* Berkeley, Los Angeles, and London, 1951.

——— "The Affairs of the *Madre de Deus,* A Chapter in the History of the Portuguese in Japan," *Transactions of the Japan Society* (London), XXVI (1929), 4–94.

———— "Hosokawa Tadaoki and the Jesuits, 1587–1645," *Transactions of the Japan Society* (London), XXXII (1935), 79–119.

Boyer, Samuel P. *Naval Surgeon: Revolt in Japan 1868–1869*, ed. Elinor and James A. Barnes. Bloomington, Ind., 1963.

Braden, Charles S. *War, Communism and World Religions*. New York, 1953.

Braibanti, Ralph J. D. "Neighborhood Associations in Japan and Their Democratic Potentialities," *FEQ*, VII (No. 2, February, 1948), 136–64.

Briggs, Everett F. *New Dawn in Japan*. New York, 1948.

Brockhaus, Albert. *Netsukes*, tr. M. F. Watty. New York, 1924.

Brower, Robert H. "Formative Elements in the Japanese Poetic Tradition," *FEQ*, XVI (No. 4, August, 1957), 503–27.

———— and Earl R. Milner. *Japanese Court Poetry*. Stanford, 1961.

Brown, Delmer M. *Money Economy in Medieval Japan*. (Far Eastern Association Monograph No. 1.) New Haven, 1951.

———— *Nationalism in Japan*. Berkeley, 1955.

Brumbaugh, T. T. *Religious Values in Japanese Culture*. Tokyo, 1934.

Brunner, Emil. "The Unique Christian Mission: The Mukyōkai ('Non-Church') Movement in Japan," in *Religion and Culture: Essays in Honor of Paul Tillich*, ed. Walter Leibrecht (New York, 1959), pp. 287–90.

Buchanan, Daniel C. "Inari, Its Origin, Development, and Nature," *TASJ*, Second Series, XII (1935), 1–191.

Buckley, Edmund. *Phallicism in Japan*. Chicago, 1895.

Bunce, William K. *Religions in Japan: Buddhism, Shinto, Christianity*. Rutland, Vt., and Tokyo, 1955.

Burks, Ardath W. *The Government of Japan*. New York, 1961.

Butow, Robert J. C. *Japan's Decision to Surrender*. Stanford, 1954.

———— *Tōjō and the Coming of the War*. Princeton, 1961.

Byas, Hugh. *Government by Assassination*. New York, 1942.

Callaway, Tucker N. *Japanese Buddhism and Christianity*. Tokyo, 1957.

Cameron, Meribeth E., Thomas H. D. Mahoney, and George E. McReynolds. *China, Japan and the Powers*. New York, 1952.

Cary, Otis. *A History of Christianity in Japan*. 2 vols. New York and Chicago, 1909.

Casal, U. A. "The Goblin, Fox and Badger and Other Witch Animals of Japan," *Folklore Studies*, XVIII (1959), 1–94.

Casal, U. A. "The Saintly Kōbō Daishi in Popular Lore," *Folklore Studies*, XVIII (1959), 95–144.

Chamberlain, Basil Hall, tr. *Ko-ji-ki*: "Records of Ancient Matters," *Supplement to TASJ*, Vol. X (1882).

———— "The Language, Mythology and Geographical Nomenclature of Japan Viewed in the Light of Aino Studies," *Memoirs of the Literature College*, No. 1 (Tokyo Imperial University). Tokyo, 1887.

———— "Reply to Mr. Batchelor on the Words 'Kamui' and 'Aino,' " *TASJ*, XVI (1888), 33–38.

———— "Essay in Aid of a Grammar and Dictionary of the Luchan Language," *Supplement to TASJ*, Vol. XXIII (1895).

———— *Things Japanese*. London, 1905.

Chan, Wing-tsit. "Neo-Confucianism," in *China*, ed. Harley F. Mac-Nair (Berkeley and Los Angeles, 1946), pp. 254–65.

Chisolm, Lawrence W. *Fenollosa: The Far East and American Culture*. New Haven, 1963.

Clark, Edward M. *The Other Half of Japan*. Harrisburg, Pa., 1934.

Clement, E. W. *A Short History of Japan*. Chicago, 1915.

Clifton, Allan S. *Time of Fallen Blossoms*. New York, 1951.

Coates, Harper H., and Ryūgaku Ishizuka. *Hōnen the Buddhist Saint*. Kyoto, 1925.

Cohen, Jerome B. *Japan's Economy in War and Reconstruction*. Minneapolis, 1949.

———— *Japan's Postwar Economy*. Bloomington, Ind., 1958.

Colbert, Evelyn S. *The Left Wing in Japanese Politics*. New York, 1952.

Cole, Allan B., ed. *With Perry in Japan: The Diary of Edward Yorke McCauley*. Princeton, 1942.

———— *Japanese Society and Politics: The Impact of Social Stratification and Mobility on Politics*. Boston, 1956.

———— *Political Tendencies of Japanese in Small Enterprises*. New York, 1959.

Commission on Christian Education in Japan. *Christian Education in Japan*. New York, 1932.

Conroy, Hillary. *The Japanese Frontier in Hawaii, 1868–1898*. Berkeley, 1953.

———— *The Japanese Seizure of Korea: 1868–1910*. Philadelphia, 1960.

Cornell, John B., and Robert J. Smith. *Two Japanese Villages: Matsunagi, A Japanese Mountain Community; Kurusu, A Japanese*

Agricultural Community. (Center for Japanese Studies, Occasional Papers, No. 5.) Ann Arbor, 1956.

Cosenza, Mario E., ed. *The Complete Journal of Townsend Harris, First American Consul and Minister to Japan.* 2d ed. Rutland, Vt., and Tokyo, 1959.

Craig, Albert M. *Chōshū in the Meiji Restoration.* (Harvard Historical Monographs XLVII.) Cambridge, 1961.

Crawcour, Sydney. "Documentary Sources of Tokugawa Economic and Social History," *JAS,* XX (No. 3, May, 1961), 343–51.

Crowley, James B. "Japanese Army Factionalism in the 1930's," *JAS,* XXI, No. 3 (May, 1962), 309–26.

de Bary, Wm. Theodore. "Common Tendencies in Neo-Confucianism," in *Confucianism in Action,* ed. David S. Nivison and Arthur F. Wright (Stanford, 1959), pp. 25–49.

——, *et al.,* comps. *Sources of Chinese Tradition.* New York, 1960.

Deguchi, Nao. *Scripture of Oomoto.* Kameoka-shi, Kyoto-fu, 1957.

Delplace, L. *Le Catholicisme au Japon.* 2 vols. Malines-Brussels, 1909–10.

Dennett, Tyler. *Roosevelt and the Russo-Japanese War.* Garden City, N.Y., 1925.

des Longrais, F. Joun. *Age de Kamakura: Sources 1150–1333. Archives Chartes Japonaises (Monjo).* Tokyo, 1950.

—— *L'Est et L'Ouest—Institutions du Japon et de l'Occident comparées.* Tokyo and Paris, 1958.

Dettmer, Hans Adalbert. *Die Steuergesetzgebung der Nara-Zeit.* Wiesbaden, 1959.

Dore, R. P. *City Life in Japan: A Study of a Tokyo Ward.* Berkeley, 1958.

—— *Land Reform in Japan.* London, 1959.

—— "The Meiji Landlord: Good or Bad?", *JAS,* XVIII (No. 3 May, 1959), 343–55.

Dorson, Richard M. *Folk Legends of Japan.* Tokyo, 1962.

——, ed. *Studies in Japanese Folklore.* Bloomington, Ind., 1963.

Dumoulin, Heinrich. *Kamo Mabuchi (1697–1769): Ein Betrag zur japanischen Religions- und Geistesgeschichte.* Tokyo, 1943.

—— *Zen: Geschichte und Gestalt.* Berne, 1959.

—— *A History of Zen Buddhism,* tr. Paul Peachey. New York, 1963.

Dürckheim-Montmartin, Karlfried Graf von. *Japan und die Kultur der Stille.* Munich, 1954.

Earl, David. *Emperor and Nation in Japan: Political Thinkers of the Tokugawa Period.* Seattle, 1964.

Eckel, Paul Edward. *The Far East Since 1500.* New York, 1947.

Eder, Matthias. "Figürliche Darstellungen in der japanischen Volksreligion," *FS*, X (1951), 197–280.

———— "Die 'Reisseele' in Japan und Korea," *Folklore Studies*, XIV (1955), 215–44.

———— "Familie, Sippe, Clan und Ahnenverehrung in Japan," *Anthropos*, LII (1957), 813–40.

———— "Shamanismus in Japan," *Paideuma*, VII, Bk. 7 (1958), pp. 367–80.

Elbree, Willard H. *Japan's Role in Southeast Asian Nationalist Movement, 1940–45.* Cambridge, 1953.

Eliade, Mircea. *The Myth of the Eternal Return,* tr. W. R. Trask. New York, 1954.

———— *Patterns in Comparative Religion,* tr. Rosemary Sheed. London and New York, 1958.

————, and Joseph M. Kitagawa. *The History of Religions: Essays in Methodology.* Chicago, 1959.

Eliot, Sir Charles. *Japanese Buddhism.* London, 1935; New York, 1959.

Elisséeff, Serge, and Takaaki Matsushita. *Japan: Ancient Buddhist Paintings.* Greenwich, Conn., 1959.

Embree, John F. *Suye Mura.* Chicago, 1939.

———— "Some Social Functions of Religion in Rural Japan," *American Journal of Sociology,* No. 47 (1941), pp. 284–89.

———— *Japanese Peasant Songs.* (Smithsonian Institution War Background Studies, No. 7.) Philadelphia, 1943.

———— *The Japanese Nation: A Social Survey.* New York, 1945.

Egami, Namio. "Light on Japanese Cultural Origins from Historical Archeology and Legend," in *Japanese Culture: Its Development and Characteristics,* ed. Robert J. Smith and Richard K. Beardsley (Chicago, 1962), pp. 11–16.

Ennin, see Reischauer, Edwin O.

Ernst, Earle, ed. *Three Japanese Plays from the Traditional Theatre.* New York, 1959.

Erskine, William H. *Japanese Customs: Their Origin and Value.* Tokyo, 1925.

———— *Japanese Festival and Calendar.* Tokyo, 1933.

Escarra, Jean. *Le Droit Chinois.* Paris and Peking, 1936.

Fairchild, William P. "Shamanism in Japan," *Folklore Studies*, XXI (1962), 1–122.

Feaney, Robert A. *The Occupation of Japan. Second Phase: 1948–50.* New York, 1950.

Feis, Herbert. *The Road to Pearl Harbor.* Princeton, 1950.

—— *Japan Subdued: The Atomic Bomb and the End of the War in the Pacific.* Princeton, 1961.

Fenollosa, Ernest F. *Epochs of Chinese and Japanese Art.* 2 vols. New York and London, 1912.

Fisher, Galen M. "The Life and Teaching of Nakae Tōju, The Sage of Ōmi," *TASJ*, Vol. XXXVI (1908).

—— "Kumazawa Banzan, His Life and Ideas," *TASJ*, Second Series, Vol. XVI (1938).

Florenz, Karl. *Japanische Mythologie, Nihongi, Zeitalter der Götter.* Tokyo, 1901.

—— *Die Historischen Quellen der Shinto-Religionen aus dem Altjapanischen und Chinesischen Übersetzt und Erklärt.* Göttingen, 1919.

—— "Ancient Japanese Rituals," *TASJ*, XXVII, Part I (1899), pp. 1–112.

—— "Der Shintoismus," in *Die Orientalischen Religionen.* (Die Kultur der Gegenwart, Teil I, Abteilung III, 1; Berlin and Leipzig, 1906), pp. 194–220.

—— "Die Japaner," in *Lehrbuch der Religionsgeschichte*, ed. Chantepie de la Saussaye (Tubingen, 1925), pp. 262–422.

Frank, Bernard. *Kata-imi et kata-tagae: Étude sur les interdits de direction a l'époque Heian.* (Bulletin de la Maison Franco-Japonaise, Nouvelle Série, Tome V, Nos. 2–4.) Paris, 1958.

Frois, Luis. *Die Geschichte Japans, 1549–1578*, tr. from the Portuguese into German by G. Schurhammer and E. A. Voretzsch. Leipzig, 1926.

Fujieda, Masakazu. "The Church of World Messianity," *Contemporary Religions in Japan*, I (No. 4, December, 1960), 24–34.

Fujii, Jintarō, comp. and ed. *Outline of Japanese History in the Meiji Era*, tr. and adapted by Hattie K. Colton and Kenneth E. Colton. Tokyo, 1958.

Fujisawa, Ryōsetsu, tr. and annot. *The Tanni Shō: Notes Lamenting Differences.* Kyoto, 1962.

Fukuzawa, Yukichi. *Autobiography*, tr. Eiichi Kiyooka. Rev. Trans. Tokyo, 1960; New York, 1966.

Fung, Yu-lan. *A History of Chinese Philosophy,* tr. Derk Bodde. 2 vols. Princeton, 1952–53.

Gallagher, Louis J., tr. *China in the Sixteenth Century: The Journal of Matthew Ricci, 1583–1610.* New York, 1953.

Garfias, Robert. *Gagaku: The Music and Dances of the Japanese Imperial Household.* New York, 1959.

Garrott, Dorothy C. *Japanese Youth Faces Life.* Nashville, 1940.

Gayn, Mark, *Japan Diary.* New York, 1948.

Getty, Alice. *The Gods of Northern Buddhism.* Oxford, 1914; Rutland, Vt., and Tokyo, 1962.

Gibney, Frank. *Five Gentlemen of Japan: The Portrait of a Nation's Character.* New York, 1953.

Glacken, Clarence J. *The Great Loochoo: A Study of Okinawan Village Life.* Berkeley, 1955.

Gordon, Marquis Lafayette. *Thirty Eventful Years: The Story of the American Board's Mission in Japan, 1869–1899.* Boston, 1901.

Graf, Olaf. *Kaibara Ekken.* Leiden, 1942.

Grew, Joseph Clark. *Report from Tokyo.* New York, 1942.

——— *Ten Years in Japan.* New York, 1944.

——— *Turbulent Era: A Diplomatic Record of Forty Years, 1904–1945,* ed. Walter Johnson. 2 vols. Boston, 1952.

Grieve, A. J. "Charismata," *ERE,* III, 368–72.

Griffis, William Elliot. *Townsend Harris.* Boston, 1895.

——— *The Religions of Japan: From the Dawn of History to the Era of Meiji.* New York, 1901.

——— *The Mikado: Institution and Person.* Princeton, 1915.

Groot, Gerard J. *The Prehistory of Japan,* ed. Bertram S. Kraus. New York, 1951.

——— "Archaeological Activities in Japan Since August 15, 1945," *American Anthropologist,* L (January/March, 1948), 166–71.

Gropius, Walter, and Kenzō Tange. *Katsura: Tradition and Creation in Japanese Architecture.* New Haven, 1960.

Guillain, Robert. "Japan's New Phase: Future of Foreign Trade," *The Manchester Guardian Weekly,* October 18, 1951.

Gundert, Wilhelm. *Der Schintoismus im Japanischen No-Drama.* Tokyo, 1926.

——— *Japanische Religionsgeschichte: Die Religionen der Japaner und Koreaner in geschichtlichen Abriss darstellt.* Stuttgart, 1943.

Gunsaulus, Helen C. *Japan as Represented in Field Museum of Natural History.* Chicago, 1924.

Gusinde, Martin and Chiye Sano. *An Annotated Bibliography of Ainu Studies by Japanese Scholars.* Tokyo, 1962.

Haas, Hans. *Geschichte des Christentums in Japan.* 2 vols. Tokyo, 1902–4.

———— "Shintoismus," *RGG*, V, 466–70.

Haas, William S. *The Destiny of the Mind—East and West.* London, 1956.

Hachiya, Michihiko. *Hiroshima Diary.* Chapel Hill, 1955.

Hackett, Roger F. "Nishi Amane—A Tokugawa-Meiji Bureaucrat," *JAS*, XVIII (No. 2, February, 1959), 213–25.

Hackin, J., *et al. Asiatic Mythology; A Detailed Description and Explanation of the Mythologies of All the Great Nations of Asia,* tr. F. M. Atkinson. New York, 1963.

Haguenauer, Charles M. *Origines de la civilization japonaise: Introduction à l'étude de la préhistoire du Japon.* Part I. Paris, 1956.

Hakuin Zenji, *see* Shaw, R. D. M.

Hall, John Whitney. *Tanuma Okitsugu (1719–1788): Forerunner of Modern Japan.* Cambridge, 1955.

———— "The Confucian Teacher in Tokugawa Japan," in *Confucianism in Action,* ed. David S. Nivison and Arthur F. Wright (Stanford, 1959), pp. 268–301.

———— "Foundations of the Modern Japanese Daimyō," *JAS*, XI (No. 3, May, 1961), 317–29.

Hall, Robert K. *Education for a New Japan.* New Haven, 1949.

———— *Shūshin: The Ethics of a Defeated Nation.* New York, 1949.

Hambly, Wilfrid D. *Source-Book for African Anthropology.* (Field Museum of Natural History Publications, "Anthropological Series," Vol. XXVI.) Chicago, 1937.

Hamilton, Clarence H. *Buddhism in India, Ceylon, China and Japan: A Reading Guide.* Chicago, 1931.

Hammer, Raymond. *Japan's Religious Ferment.* New York, 1962.

Hammitzsch, Horst. *Die Mito-Schule.* Tokyo, 1939.

Hanayama, Shinshō. *The Way of Deliverance,* tr. Hidco Suzuki, Eiichi Noda, and James K. Sasaki. London, 1955.

———— *Bibliography on Buddhism.* Tokyo, 1961.

Harada, Jirō. *Glimpse of Japanese Ideals.* Tokyo, 1937.

———— *Japanese Gardens.* Boston, 1956.

Harada, Tasuku. *The Faith of Japan.* New York, 1914.

Harada, Toshiaki. "The Origin of Community Worship," in *Religious Studies in Japan,* ed. Japanese Association for Religious Studies (Tokyo, 1959), pp. 213–18.

Harada, Toshiaki. "The Development of Matsuri," *Philosophical Studies of Japan*, Vol. II, comp. Japanese National Commission for UNESCO (Tokyo, 1961), pp. 99–117.

Hardy, Arthur S. *Life and Letters of Joseph Hardy Neesima.* Boston, 1900.

Haring, Douglas, ed. *Japan's Prospect.* Cambridge, 1946.

———— "Japan and the Japanese, 1868–1945," in *Most of the World,* ed. Ralph Linton (New York, 1949), pp. 814–75.

Harootunian, Harry D. "The Economic Rehabilitation of the Samurai in the Early Meiji Period," *JAS,* XIX (No. 4, August, 1960), 433–44.

Harris, Townsend, *see* Cosenza, Mario E.

Harrison, John A. *Japan's Northern Frontier: A Preliminary Study in Colonization and Expansion with Special Reference to the Relations of Japan and Russia.* Gainesville, Fla., 1953.

———— *New Light on Early and Medieval Japanese Historiography.* (University of Florida Monographs—Social Sciences No. 4.) Gainesville, Fla., 1959.

Hattori, Shirō. "The Affinity of Japanese," *Acta Asiatica* (Bulletin of the Institute of Eastern Culture, No. 2; Tokyo, 1961), pp. 1–29.

Hawks, Francis L., *see* Wallach, Sidney.

Haydon, A. Eustace. *Biography of the Gods.* New York, 1945.

Hearn, Lafcadio. *Japan: An Attempt at Interpretation.* New York, 1904.

———— *In Ghostly Japan.* Boston, 1907.

———— *Kokoro: Hints and Echoes of Japanese Inner Life.* Boston, 1927.

———— *Tales and Essays from Old Japan.* Chicago, 1956.

Heaslett, Samuel. *The Mind of Japan and the Religions of the Japanese.* (Religions of the East Series, No. 1.) London, 1947.

Heine-Geldern, R. "Urheimat und früheste Wanderungen der Austronesier," *Anthropos,* XXVII (1932), 561–66.

Hekigan Roku, see Shaw, R. D. M.

Hepner, Charles William. *The Kurozumi Sect of Shinto.* Tokyo, 1935.

Herbert, Zachert. *Semmyō, die Kaiserlichen Erlasse des Shoku-Nihongi.* Berlin, 1950.

Herrigel, Eugen. *Zen in the Art of Archery,* tr. R. F. C. Hull. New York, 1953.

Herrigel, Gustie L. *Zen in the Art of Flower Arrangement,* tr. R. F. C. Hull. Newton Center, Mass., 1958.

Hersey, John R. *Hiroshima.* New York, 1946.

Hewes, Laurence I., Jr. *Japan—Land and Men. An Account of the Japanese Land Reform Program, 1945–51.* Ames, Iowa, 1955.

Hibino, Yutaka. *Nippon Shindo Ron or the National Ideals of the Japanese People,* tr. A. P. McKenzie. Cambridge, 1928.

Hincks, M. A. *The Japanese Dance.* London, 1910.

Hiraga, Gen'ichi. "The Trend of Studies of 'Kirishitan' Literature," *Acta Asiatica* (Bulletin of the Institute of Eastern Culture, No. 4; Tokyo, 1963), pp. 97–113.

Hirai, Naofusa. The Concept of Man in Shintō. Unpublished Master's dissertation, University of Chicago, 1954.

———— "Fundamental Problems of Present Shintō," *Proceedings of the IXth International Congress for the History of Religions* (Tokyo, 1960), pp. 303–6.

Hitchcock, Romyn. "The Ainos of Yezo, Japan," *Report of the U.S. National Museum, 1889–1890* (Washington, D.C., 1891), pp. 429–502.

Holtom, Daniel C. *The Japanese Enthronement Ceremonies.* Tokyo, 1928.

———— *The National Faith of Japan.* New York, 1938.

———— *Modern Japan and Shintō Nationalism.* Chicago, 1943; 2d ed., 1947.

———— "Some Notes on Japanese Tree Worship," *TASJ,* Second Series, VIII (December, 1931), 1–19.

———— "The Meaning of Kami," *Monumeta Nipponica,* III, No. 1 (1940), 1–27; III, No. 2, 32–53; IV, No. 2 (1941), 25–68.

———— "Shintō in the Postwar World," *Far Eastern Survey,* No. 14 (February 14, 1945), pp. 29–33.

———— "Shintoism," in *The Great Religions of the Modern World,* ed. Edward J. Jurji (Princeton, 1946), pp. 141–77.

Honda, H. H., tr. *A Hundred Poems from a Hundred Poets (Ogura-Hyakunin-isshū).* Tokyo, 1948.

Honjō, Eijirō. *Social and Economic History of Japan.* Kyoto, 1935.

Hori, Ichirō. "On the Concept of Hijiri (Holy-Man)," *Numen,* V (No. 2, April, 1958), 128–60; (No. 3, September, 1958), 199–232.

———— "Japanese Folk-Beliefs," *American Anthropologist,* LXI (No. 3, June, 1959), 405–24.

———— "Buddhism in the Life of Japanese People," in *Japan and Buddhism,* ed. The Association of the Buddha Jayanti (Tokyo, 1959), pp. 19–67.

Hori, Ichirō. "Self-Mummified Buddhas in Japan," *History of Religions*, I (No. 2, Winter, 1962), 222–42.

Horioka, Yasuko. *The Life of Kakuzō: Author of the Book of Tea.* Tokyo, 1963.

Hornbeck, Stanley K. *The United States and the Far East: Certain Fundamentals of Policy.* Boston, 1942.

Howell, Richard W. "The Classification and Description of Ainu Folklore," *Journal of American Folklore*, No. 64 (1951), pp. 361–69.

———— "The Kamui Oina: A Sacred Charter of the Ainu," *Journal of American Folklore*, No. 65 (1952), pp. 379–417.

Hozumi, Nobushige. *Ancestor Worship and Japanese Law.* Tokyo, 1913.

Hsu, Immanuel C. Y. "Allied Council for Japan," *FEQ*, X (No. 2, February, 1951), 173–78.

Hubbard, G. E. *Eastern Industrialization and Its Effect on the West.* London, 1935.

Hulse, Frederick S. "A Sketch of Japanese Society," *JAOS*, LXVI (No. 3, July-September, 1946), 219–29.

———— "Convention and Reality in Japanese Culture," *SJA*, IV (Winter, 1948), 345–55.

Iddittie, Junesay (Ijichi, Junsei). *The Life of Marquis Shigenobu Ōkuma.* Tokyo, 1956.

Iglehart, Charles W. *A Century of Protestant Christianity in Japan.* Rutland, Vt., and Tokyo, 1959.

Iino, Norimoto. "Dōgen's Zen View of Independence," *Philosophy East and West*, XII (No. 1, April, 1962), 51–57.

Ike, Nobutake. *The Beginnings of Political Democracy in Japan.* Baltimore, 1950.

———— "Kōtoku: Advocate of Direct Action," *FEQ*, III (No. 3, May, 1944), 222–36.

Iklé, Frank William. *German-Japanese Relations, 1936–40: A Study of Totalitarian Diplomacy.* New York, 1956.

International Institute for the Study of Religions. *Religion and Modern Life* (Bulletin No. 5, Part II). Tokyo, 1958.

———— *Religion and State in Japan* (Bulletin No. 7). Tokyo, 1959.

———— *Living Buddhism in Japan*, prepared by Yoshio Tamura, in collaboration with William P. Woodard. Tokyo, 1960.

———— "Sōka Gakkai and the Nichiren Shō Sect (I)," *Contemporary Religions in Japan*, II (No. 2, March, 1960), 55–70.

Ise-monogatari, see Vos, Fritz.

Ishida, Eiichiro. "The Kappa Legend," *Folklore Studies,* IX (1950), 1–152.

———— "Mother-Son Deities," *History of Religions,* IV (No. 1, Summer, 1964), 30–52.

Ishida, Ichirō. "Zen Buddhism and Muromachi Art," tr. Delmer M. Brown, *JAS,* XXII (No. 4, August, 1963), 417–32.

———— "Tokugawa Feudal Society and Neo-Confucian Thought," *Philosophical Studies of Japan,* ed. Japanese National Commission for UNESCO, V (Tokyo, 1964), 1–37.

Ishida, Takeshi. "Popular Attitudes toward the Japanese Emperor," *Asian Survey,* II (No. 2, April, 1962), 29–39.

Ishimoto, Shidzue. *Facing Two Ways.* New York, 1935.

Iwamoto, Tokuichi. "Present State of Sectarian Shinto," *Research Papers* (Mimeographed for the IXth International Congress for the History of Religions; Tokyo, 1958), pp. 21–25.

Iwasaki, Takeo. "Contemporary Japanese Moral Philosophy," *Philosophy East and West,* VI (No. 1, April, 1956), 69–75.

Jansen, Marius B. *Sakamoto Ryōma and the Meiji Restoration.* Princeton, 1961.

———— "From Hatoyama to Hatoyama" (review article), *FEQ,* XIV (No. 1, November, 1954), 65–79.

———— "Takeuchi Zuisan and the Tosa Loyalist Party," *JAS,* XVIII (No. 2, February, 1959), 199–212.

Japan. Ministry of Education. *Imperial Rescript on Education in Japan* (both original and translation). Tokyo, 1907.

———— *Kokutai no Hongi: Cardinal Principles of the National Entity of Japan,* tr. John Owen Gauntlett. Cambridge, 1949.

———— *Religions in Japan.* 2d ed. Tokyo, 1963.

Japanese Association for Religious Studies (and Japanese Organizing Committee of the Ninth International Congress for the History of Religions), eds. *Religious Studies in Japan.* Tokyo, 1959.

Japanese Classics Translation Committee. *The Manyōshū: One Thousand Poems Selected from the Japanese.* Tokyo, 1940; Chicago, 1941; New York, 1965.

Japanese Joint Organizing Committee of the Ninth International Conference of Social Work. *Social Welfare Services in Japan.* Tokyo, 1958.

"Japanese Music," *Encyclopaedia Britannica* (1962 ed.), XII, 962–63.

Japanese National Commission for UNESCO. *Japan: Its Land, People and Culture.* Tokyo, 1958.

———, ed. *International Symposium on History of Eastern and Western Cultural Contacts.* Tokyo, 1959.

———, comp. *Philosophical Studies of Japan.* 5 vols. Tokyo, 1959–64.

"Japan's New Church Militant," *Japan Quarterly,* IV (No. 4, October-December, 1957), 413–19.

Jennes, Joseph. *History of the Catholic Church in Japan.* Tokyo, 1959.

"Jesus, Society of." *Encyclopaedia Britannica* (1962 ed.), XIII, 9–13.

Jinja Honchō. *Basic Terms of Shintō.* Tokyo, 1958.

Johnson, Chalmers A. "Low Posture Politics in Japan," *Asian Survey,* III (No. 1, January, 1963), 17–30.

Jones, Francis Clifford. *Extraterritoriality in Japan.* London, 1931.

——— *Japan's New Order in East Asia, Its Rise and Fall, 1936–45.* London, 1954.

Jones, S. W., tr. *Ages Ago: Thirty-Seven Tales from the Konjaku Monogatari Collection.* Cambridge, 1959.

Joseph, Kenny. "Mass Media Carry Message to Many," *Asahi Evening News,* May 2, 1959.

Kagawa, Toyohiko. *Christ and Japan.* New York, 1934.

——— *Songs from the Land of Dawn.* New York, 1949.

Kaibara, Ekken. *The Way of Contentment,* tr. Ken Hoshino. London, 1913.

——— *Women and Wisdom of Japan,* tr. S. Takaishi. London, 1914.

Kamimura, Shinjō. "Buddhist Worship of the Masses," *Research Papers* (Mimeographed for the IXth International Congress for the History of Religions; Tokyo, 1958, pp. 15–20.

Kase, Toshikazu. *Journey to the "Missouri."* New Haven, 1950.

Katō, Genchi. *A Study of Shintō: The Religion of the Japanese Nation.* Tokyo, 1926.

——— *What is Shintō?* Tokyo, 1935.

——— "A Study of the Oracles and Sayings in the Warongo or Japanese Analects," *TASJ,* XLV (Part II, 1917), 1–117.

——— "Warongo or Japanese Analects," *TASJ,* XLVI (Part II, 1918), 1–117.

——— "Japanese Phallicism," *TASJ,* I (Supplement), Second Series, 1924.

———— "The Three Stages of the Shinto Religion," *The Japan Christian Quarterly*, III (No. 2, April, 1928), 116–25.

———— "The Naoe Matsuri," *TASJ*, Second Series, VIII (December, 1931), 113–36.

Katō, Genchi, and Hikoshirō Hoshino, tr. and annot. *The Kogoshūi: Gleanings from Ancient Stories*. Tokyo, 1926.

Katō, Genchi, Karl Reitz, and Wilhelm Schiffer, comps. *A Bibliography of Shinto in Western Languages from the Oldest Times till 1952*. Tokyo, 1953.

Kawai, Kazuo. *Japan's American Interlude*. Chicago, 1960.

Kawai, Michi. *My Lantern*. 3d ed. Tokyo, 1949.

Kawamoto, Toshio, and Joseph Y. Kurihara. *Bonsai-Saikei: The Art of Japanese Miniature Trees, Gardens and Landscapes*. Tokyo, 1963.

Kawazoe, Noboru. "The Ise Shrine," *Japan Quarterly*, IX (No. 3, July-September, 1962), 285–92.

Keene, Donald. *The Battle of Coxinga: Chikamatsu's Puppet Play, Its Background and Importance*. (Cambridge Oriental Series, No. 4.) London, 1951.

———— *Japanese Literature: An Interpretation for Western Readers*. London, 1953.

———— *The Japanese Discovery of Europe: Honda Toshiaki and Other Discoverers, 1720–1798*. New York, 1954.

————, compiler and editor. *Anthology of Japanese Literature: From the Earliest Era to the Mid-Nineteenth Century*. New York, 1955.

————, comp. and ed. *Modern Japanese Literature: An Anthology from 1868 to the Present Day*. New York, 1956.

————, tr. *The Old Woman, The Wife, and The Archer: Three Modern Japanese Short Novels*. New York, 1961.

Kerr, George H. *Okinawa: The History of an Island People*. Rutland, Vt., and Toyko, 1958.

Kerr, William C. *Japan Begins Again*. New York, 1949.

Kidder, J. Edward, Jr. *The Jōmon Pottery of Japan*. (*Artibus Asiae* Supplement, Vol. XVII.) Ascona, 1957.

———— *Japan Before Buddhism*. London, 1959.

———— "A Jōmon Pottery Vessel in the Buffalo Museum of Science," *Artibus Asiae*, XV (1952), 11–16.

———— "The Kamegaoka Vessels in the City Art Museum, St. Louis," *Artibus Asiae*, XVI (1953), 198–208.

Kidder, J. Edward, Jr. "Reconstruction of the 'Pre-Pottery' Culture of Japan," *Artibus Asiae,* XVII (1954), 135–43.

Kim, Ha Tai. "Nishida and Royce," *Philosophy East and West,* I (January, 1952), 18–29.

Kindaichi (Kindaiti), Kyōsuke. *Ainu Life and Legends.* Tokyo, 1941.

—— "The Concept Behind the Ainu Bear Festival (Kumamat-suri)", tr. M. Yoshida, *SJA,* V (Winter, 1949), 345–50.

Kirkwood, Kenneth P. *Renaissance in Japan.* Tokyo, 1938.

Kishimoto, Hideo, comp. and ed. *Japanese Religion in the Meiji Era,* tr. John F. Howes. Tokyo, 1956.

—— "Mahayana Buddhism and Japanese Thought," *Philosophy East and West,* IV (No. 3, October, 1954), 215–23.

Kishinami, Tsunezō. *The Development of Philosophy in Japan.* Princeton, 1915.

Kitagawa, Joseph M. "Kaiser und Shamane in Japan," *Antaios,* II (No. 6, March, 1961), 552–66.

—— "The Contemporary Religious Situation in Japan," *Japanese Religions* (Kyoto), II (Nos. 2–3, May, 1961), 24–42.

—— "Ainu Bear Festival (Iyomante)," *History of Religions,* I (No. 1, Summer, 1961), 95–151.

—— "Nuevas Interpretaciones de la Filosofía Budista," *Philosophia* (Mendoza, Argentina), No. 24 (1961), 1–14.

—— "Japan: Religion," *Encyclopaedia Britannica* (1962 ed.), XII, 899–904.

—— "Shinto," *Encyclopaedia Britannica* (1962 ed.), XX, 517–21.

—— "Buddhism and Asian Politics," *Asian Survey,* II, (No. 5, July, 1962), 1–11.

—— "Buddhist Translation in Japan," *Babel,* IX (Nos. 1–2, 1963), 53–59.

—— "Religious and Cultural Ethos of Modern Japan," *Asian Studies,* II (No. 3, December, 1964), 334–52.

—— "The Buddhist Transformation in Japan," *History of Religions,* IV (No. 2, Winter, 1965), 319–36.

—— "Japanese Religion," in Charles J. Adams, ed., *A Reader's Guide to the Great Religions,* New York, 1965.

—— "Japanese Philosophy (Historical)," *Encyclopaedia Britannica,* 1966 ed. (in press).

Knox, George William. *The Development of Religion in Japan.* New York, 1907.

Kohler, Werner. *Die Lotus-Lehre und die modernen Religionen in Japan.* Zurich, 1962.

Ko-ji-ki, see Chamberlain, Basil Hall.

Kokusai Bunka Shinkōkai, ed. *Introduction to Contemporary Japanese Literature.* Tokyo, 1939.

———— *Introduction to Classic Japanese Literature.* Tokyo, 1948.

———— *K. B. S. Bibliography of Standard Reference Books for Japanese Studies with Descriptive Notes,* Vol. IV (Religion). Tokyo, 1963.

Komai, S. "The Okhotsk Culture and the Scythian Culture," *International Symposium on History of Eastern and Western Cultural Contacts,* ed. Japanese National Commission for UNESCO (Tokyo, 1959), pp. 77–79.

Komatsu, Isao. *The Japanese People: Origins of the People and the Language,* Vol. I. Tokyo, 1962.

Konjaku, see Tsukakoshi, Satoshi.

Konvitz, Milton R. *The Alien and the Asiatic in American Law.* Ithaca, 1946.

Kosaka, Masaki, ed. *Japanese Thought in the Meiji Era,* tr. David Abosch. Tokyo, 1958.

Kotani, Kimi, ed. *A Guide to Reiyū-kai.* Tokyo, 1958.

Kozaki, Hiromichi. *Reminiscences of Seventy Years: The Autobiography of a Japanese Pastor,* tr. Nariaki Kozaki. Tokyo, 1933.

Kraemer, Hendrik. *The Christian Message in a Non-Christian World.* London, 1938.

Kublin, Hyman. "The 'Modern' Army of Early Meiji Japan," *FEQ,* IX (No. 1, November, 1949), 20–41.

———— "A Bibliography of the Writings of Sen Katayama in Western Languages," *FEQ, XI* (No. 1, November, 1951), 71–77.

Kudō, Takuya. "The Faith of Sōka Gakkai," *Contemporary Religions in Japan,* II (No. 2, June, 1961), 1–12.

Kuroda, Kazuo. "Domains of 'New Gods,'" *The Japan Times,* November 15, 1958.

Kurzman, Dan. *Kishi and Japan: The Search for the Sun.* New York, 1960.

Labberton, D. van Hinloopen. "The Oceanic Languages and the Nipponese as Branches of the Nippon-Malay-Polynesian Family of Speech," *TASJ,* Second Series, Vol. II (1925).

Lancaster, Clay. *The Japanese Influence in America.* New York, 1963.

Lange, R. "Die Japaner, II. Der Shintoismus," *Lehrbuch der Religionsgeschichte* (3d ed. rev., ed. Chantepie de la Saussaye; Tübingen, 1905), I, 141–71.

Langer, Paul F., and S. Roger Swearinger. *Japanese Communism: An Annotated Bibliography of Works in the Japanese Language with a Chronology, 1921–52.* New York, 1953.

Latourette, Kenneth Scott. *The History of Japan.* Rev. ed. New York, 1957.

Laures, Johannes. *Nobunaga und des Christentum.* (Monumenta Nipponica Monographs, No. 10.) Tokyo, 1950.

————— *The Catholic Church in Japan.* Rutland, Vt., and Tokyo, 1954.

————— *Two Japanese Christian Heroes.* Tokyo, 1959.

Lay, Arthur Hyde. "Japanese Funeral Rites," *TASJ*, XIX, Part III (1891), 507–44.

Lea, Leonora E. *Window on Japan.* Greenwich, Conn., 1956.

Lebra, Joyce C. "Ōkuma Shigenobu and the 1881 Political Crisis," *JAS*, XVIII (No. 4, August, 1959), 475–87.

Lensen, George Alexander. *Russia's Japan Expedition of 1852–1855.* Gainesville, Fla., 1955.

————— *Russia's Push Toward Japan.* Princeton, 1959.

————— "The Orthodox Church in Occupied Japan," *Florida State University Studies,* No. 8 (1952), pp. 93-95.

Lewin, Bruno. *Abriss der Japanischen Grammatik: auf der Grundlage der klassischen Schriftsprache.* Wiesbaden, 1959.

Lloyd, Arthur. *The Wheat Among the Tares: Studies of Buddhism in Japan.* London, 1908.

————— *Shinran and His Work: Studies in Shinshū Theology.* Tokyo, 1910.

————— *The Creed of Half Japan.* London, 1911.

————— "Historical Development of the Shushi (Chu Hsi) Philosophy in Japan," *TASJ*, XXXIV (1906), 5–80.

Lockwood, William W. *The Economic Development of Japan: Growth and Structural Change, 1868–1938.* Princeton, 1954.

Lombard, P. A. *An Outline History of Japanese Drama.* London, 1928.

Longford, Joseph H. "Note on Ninomiya Sontoku," *TASJ*, XXII, Part I (1894), 103–8.

Lowell, Percival. *Occult Japan or the Way of the Gods.* New York, 1895.

Löwith, Karl. "Japan's Westernization and Moral Foundation," *Religion in Life,* XII (1942–43), 114–27.

Lu, David J. *From the Marco Polo Bridge to Pearl Harbor. A Study of Japan's Entry into World War II.* Washington, D.C., 1961.

Luth, Paul E. *Die japanische Philosophie.* Tübingen, 1944.

McCauley, Edward Yorke, see Cole, Allan B.

McCullough, Helen Craig. *The Taiheiki: A Chronicle of Medieval Japan.* New York, 1959.

McEwan, J. R. *The Political Writings of Ogyū Sorai.* (University of Cambridge Oriental Publications, No. 7.) Cambridge, England, 1962.

McFarland, H. Neill. "The New Religions of Japan," *The Perkins School of Theology Journal,* XII (No. 1, Fall, 1958), 3–21.

McGovern, William M. *Introduction to Mahayana Buddhism.* London, 1922.

McNelley, Theodore. *Contemporary Government of Japan.* Boston, 1963.

McWilliams, Carey. *Prejudice. Japanese-Americans: Symbol of Racial Intolerance.* Boston, 1944.

Maki, John M. *Japanese Militarism.* New York, 1945.

———— *Government and Politics in Japan: The Road to Democracy.* New York, 1962.

Malm, William P. *Japanese Music.* Tokyo, 1959.

———— *Nagauta: The Heart of Kabuki Music.* Rutland, Vt., and Tokyo, 1963.

Maringer, J. "A Core and Flake Industry of Palaeolithic Type from Central Japan," *Artibus Asiae,* XIX (No. 2, 1956), 111–25.

———— "Einige faustkeilartige Gerate von Gongenyama [Japan] und die Frage des japanischen Paläolithikums," *Anthropos,* LI (1956).

Marriott, McKim. "Little Communities in an Indigenous Civilization," in *Village India,* ed. McKim Marriott (Chicago, 1955), pp. 171–222.

Martin, Edwin M. *The Allied Occupation of Japan.* Stanford, 1948.

Maruyama, Masao. *Thought and Behavior in Modern Japanese Politics,* ed. Ivan Morris. New York, 1963.

Mason, J. W. T. *The Meaning of Shinto: The Primaeval Foundation of Creative Spirit in Modern Japan.* New York, 1935.

———— *The Spirit of Shinto Mythology.* Tokyo, 1939.

Masunaga, Reihō. *The Sōtō Approach to Zen.* Tokyo, 1958.

Matsumoto, Hikoshichirō. "Notes on the Stone Age People of Japan," *American Anthropologist,* XXIII (No. 1, 1921), 50–76.

Matsumoto, Nobuhiro. *Le Japonais et les langues austroasiatiques.* Paris, 1928.

—— *Essai sur la mythologie japonaise.* Paris, 1928.

—— "Notes on the Deity Festival of Yawatano, Japan," *SJA,* V (Spring, 1949), 62–77.

Matsumoto, Yoshiharu Scott. *Contemporary Japan: The Individual and the Group.* (Transactions of the American Philosophical Society, New Series, Vol. L, Part I.) Philadelphia, 1960.

Maxon, Yale Candee. *Control of Japanese Foreign Policy: A Study of Civil-Military Rivalry, 1930–1945.* Berkeley, 1957.

Mendel, Douglas H., Jr. "Ozaki Yukio: Political Conscience of Modern Japan," *FEQ,* XV (No. 3, May, 1956), 343–56.

Michalson, Carl. *Japanese Contributions to Christian Theology.* Philadelphia, 1960.

Michener, James A. *Japanese Prints: From the Early Masters to the Modern,* with notes on the prints by Richard Lane. Rutland, Vt., and Tokyo, 1959.

Mihara, Shinichi. "Buddhism in Japan," *The Mainichi Overseas Edition,* No. 82 (December 20, 1957), pp. 1–8.

Miki, Fumio. *Haniwa: The Clay Sculpture of Protohistoric Japan,* tr. Roy Andrew Miller. Rutland, Vt., 1960.

Milne, J. "The Stone Age in Japan," *Journal of the Anthropological Institute of Great Britain and Ireland,* X (1881), 389–423.

Miyagawa, Munenori. "The Status Quo of Shintō Shrines," *The Shintō Bulletin,* I (No. 1, March, 1953), 4–6.

Moore, Frederick. *With Japan's Leaders.* New York, 1942.

Moos, Felix. "Religion and Politics in Japan: The Case of the Sōka Gakkai," *Asian Survey,* III (No. 3, March, 1963), 136–42.

Morgan, Kenneth W., ed. *The Path of the Buddha.* New York, 1956.

Morley, James William. *The Japanese Thrust into Siberia.* New York, 1957.

Morris, Ivan. *Nationalism and the Right Wing in Japan: A Study of Post-War Trends.* London and New York, 1960.

—— *The World of the Shining Prince: Court Life in Ancient Japan.* New York, 1964.

——, ed. *Modern Japanese Stories: An Anthology.* Rutland, Vt. and Tokyo, 1962.

Morris, J. "A Pilgrimage to Ise," *Transactions and Proceedings of the Japan Society of London,* VII (1905–7), 248–62.

Morse, Edward S. "Shell Mounds of Ōmori," *Memoirs of the Science Department* (Tokyo Imperial University), Vol. I, Part I. Tokyo, 1879.

—— "Traces of an Early Race in Japan," *Popular Science Monthly,* XIX (1879), 257–66.

Munro, N. G. *Prehistoric Japan.* Yokohama, 1908.

Murao, Shōichi, and W. H. Murray Walton. *Japan and Christ.* London, 1928.

Muraoka, Tsunetsugu. *Studies in Shinto Thought,* tr. Delmer M. Brown and James T. Araki. Tokyo, 1964.

Murdoch, James, and Isoh Yamagata. *A History of Japan during the Century of Early Foreign Intercourse, 1542–1651.* Kobe, 1903; London, 1949.

Nagai, Michio. "Herbert Spencer in Early Meiji Japan," *FEQ,* XIV No. 1, November, 1954), 55–64.

Nagayama, Toshihide. *Collection of Historical Materials Connected with the Roman Catholic Religion in Japan (Kirishitan Shiryō-shū).* Nagasaki, 1924.

Nakai, Gendō. *Shinran and His Religion of Pure Faith.* Kyoto, 1946.

Nakamura, Hajime. *The Ways of Thinking of Eastern Peoples.* Tokyo, 1960.

—— "Basic Features of the Legal, Political and Economic Thought of Japan," *Philosophy East and West: East-West Philosophy in Practical Perspective,* ed. Charles A. Moore (Honolulu, 1962), pp. 631–47.

Nanjō (Nanjiō) Bunyū (Bunyiū), comp. *A Catalogue of the Chinese Translation of the Buddhist Tripitaka.* Oxford, 1883.

—— *A Short History of the Twelve Japanese Buddhist Sects.* Tokyo, 1886.

Natori, Jun-ichi. *Historical Stories of Christianity in Japan.* Tokyo, 1957.

Neumann, Nelly. "Yama no Kami—die japanische Berggottheit," *Folklore Studies,* XXII (1963), 133–366.

Neumann, William L. *America Encounters Japan. From Perry to MacArthur.* Baltimore, 1963.

Nielsen, Niels C., Jr. *Religion and Philosophy in Contemporary*

Japan. (Rice Institute Pamphlets, Vol. XLIII, No. 4.) Houston, 1957.

Nihongi, see Aston, William George.

Nishida, Nagao. " 'Yosashi'—A Fundamental Concept of Japanese Religion," tr. Donald L. Philippi. Tokyo, n.d. (Private circulation.)

Nishida, Kitarō. *Intelligibility and the Philosophy of Nothingness,* tr. and ed. Robert Schinzinger. Tokyo, 1958.

—— *A Study of Good,* tr. V. H. Viglielmo. Tokyo, 1960.

Nishitsunoi, Masayoshi. "Social and Religious Groups in Shintō," in *Religious Studies in Japan,* ed. Japanese Association for Religious Studies (Tokyo, 1959), pp. 219-28.

Nitobe, Inazō. *Bushidō: The Soul of Japan.* New York, 1905.

——, *et al. Western Influences in Modern Japan.* Chicago, 1931.

Nivison, David S., and Arthur Wright, eds. *Confucianism in Action.* Stanford, 1959.

Noma, Seiroku. "Introduction," *Haniwa* (A Catalogue of the Haniwa Exhibition in Four American Museums). New York, 1960.

Norbeck, Edward. *Takashima: A Japanese Fishing Community.* Salt Lake City, 1954.

—— "Pollution and Taboo in Contemporary Japan," *SJA,* VIII (No. 3, Autumn, 1952), 269–85.

—— "Yakudoshi: A Japanese Complex of Supernaturalistic Beliefs," *SJA,* XI (No. 2, Summer, 1955), 105–20.

Norito, see Philippi, Donald L.

Norman, E. Herbert. *Japan's Emergence as a Modern State.* New York, 1940.

—— "Andō Shōeki and the Anatomy of Japanese Feudalism," *TASJ,* Third Series, Vol. II (1949).

Nukariya, Kaiten. *The Religion of the Samurai.* London, 1913.

Numazawa, Franz Kiichi. "Die Weltanfange in der japanischen Mythologie," *Internationale Schriftenreihe für soziale und politische Wissenschaften, Ethnologische Reihe,* Vol. II. Paris and Lucerne, 1946.

—— "The Fertility Festival at Toyota Shinto Shrine, Aichi Prefecture, Japan," *Acta Tropica,* Supplement, XVI (No. 3, 1959), 197–217.

Obata, Kyūgorō. *An Interpretation of the Life of Viscount Shibusawa.* Tokyo, 1937.

Ōbayashi, Taryō. "Die Amaterasu-Mythe im alten Japan und die

Sonnenfinsternismythe in Sudostasien," *Ethnos*, XXV (1960), 20–43.

Offner, Clark B., and Henry van Straelen. *Modern Japanese Religions*. Tokyo, 1963.

Okakura, Kakuzō. *The Book of Tea*. Edinburgh, 1919; Rutland, Vt., 1956.

Okamoto, Richard. "Japan," *Look*, XXVII (No. 18, September 10, 1963), 15–28.

Okladnikov, Aleksei P. "The Role of the Ancient Baikal Region in the Cultural Relations Between East and West," in *International Symposium on History of Eastern and Western Cultural Contacts*, Japanese National Commission for UNESCO (Tokyo, 1959), pp. 141–43.

Ōkubo, Genji. *The Problems of the Emperor System in Postwar Japan*. Tokyo, 1948.

Ōkuma, Count S. *Fifty Years of New Japan*. 2 vols. London, 1909–10.

Olson, Lawrence. *Dimension of Japan*. New York, 1963.

Ōmura, Bunji. *Japan's "Grand Old Man" Prince Saionji, the Last Genrō*. London and New York, 1938.

O'Neill, P. G. *Early Nō Drama, Its Background, Character and Development, 1300–1450*. London, 1959.

Ono, Sokyō. *The Kami Way*. (International Institute for the Study of Religions Bulletin No. 8.) Tokyo, 1959.

—— "The Contribution to Japan of Shrine Shintō," in *Proceedings of the IXth International Congress for the History of Religions* (Tokyo, 1960), pp. 387–92.

Ono, Susumu. "The Japanese Language: Its Origins and Its Sources," in *Japanese Culture: Its Development and Characteristics*, ed. Robert J. Smith and Richard K. Beardsley (Chicago, 1962), pp. 17–21.

The Oomoto [Ōmoto] Headquarters. *The Oomoto Movement, Its Origin, Aims and Objects*. Kameoka, 1950.

Opler, Marvin K. "Two Japanese Religious Sects," *SAJ*, VI (Spring, 1950), 69–78.

Opler, Morris E. "Japanese Folk Beliefs concerning the Snake," *SJA*, I (1945), 249–59.

—— "Japanese Folk Beliefs concerning the Cat," *Washington Academy of Science Journal*, XXXIX (1945), 269–76.

Orchard, John E. *Japan's Economic Position: The Progress of Industrialization.* New York, 1930.

Paine, Robert T., and Alexander Soper. *The Art and Architecture of Japan.* Baltimore, 1955.

Parker, C. K. *A Dictionary of Japanese Compound Verbs.* Tokyo, 1937.

Parker, E. H. "Ma Twan-lin's Account of Japan up to A.D. 1200," *TASJ,* XXII (1894), 35–68.

Paske-Smith, Montague. *Japanese Tradition of Christianity.* Kobe, 1929.

Pettee, James H., ed. *A Chapter of Missionary History in Modern Japan.* Tokyo, 1895.

Philippi, Donald L., tr. *Norito* (A New Translation of the Ancient Japanese Ritual Prayers). Tokyo, 1959.

——— "Songs on the Buddha's Foot-Prints," *Nihonbunka-Kenkyūsho-Kiyō,* No. 2 (1958), pp. 145–84.

Piovesana, Gino K. *Recent Japanese Philosophical Thought 1862–1962.* Tokyo, 1963.

——— "Men and Social Ideas of the Early Taishō Period," *Monumenta Nipponica,* XIX (Nos. 1–2, 1964), 111–29.

PL Kyōdan. *Perfect Liberty—How to Lead a Happy Life.* Tondabayashi, 1958.

Ponsonby-Fane, Richard A. B. *Studies in Shintō and Shrines.* Kyoto, 1942; rev. ed., 1953.

——— *Kyoto, the Old Capital of Japan.* Kyoto, 1956.

——— *History of the Imperial House of Japan.* Kyoto, 1959.

——— *Sovereign and Subject.* Kyoto, 1960.

——— *Vicissitudes of Shinto.* Kyoto, 1963.

Pratt, James B. *The Pilgrimage of Buddhism.* New York, 1928.

Presseisen, Ernest L. *Germany and Japan: A Study in Totalitarian Diplomacy, 1933–1941.* The Hague, 1958.

Priori, Antonio. "Spiritual Aspects and Values of Namban Art (1549–1639)," *East and West,* New Series, XII (No. 4, December, 1961), 241–53.

Rahder, Johannes. *Etymological Vocabulary of Japanese, Korean, and Ainu.* (Monumenta Nipponica Monographs, No. 16). Tokyo, 1956.

——— "The Comparative Treatment of the Japanese Language," *Monumenta Nipponica,* VII (1951), 198–208; VIII (1952), 239–88; IX (1953), 199–257; X (1954), 127–68.

—— "Linguistic Study of the Root 'kon,' " in S. Yamaguchi, ed., *Buddhism and Culture* (Kyoto, 1960), pp. 226–46.

Ramstedt, C. J. "A Comparison of the Altaic Languages with Japanese," *TASJ*, Second Series, Vol. I (1924).

Reichelt, Karl Ludvig. *Truth and Tradition in Chinese Buddhism*, tr. K. V. W. Bugge. Shanghai, 1934.

—— *Religion in Chinese Garments*, tr. Joseph Tetlie. London, 1951.

Reischauer, August Karl. *Studies in Japanese Buddhism*. New York, 1917.

—— *The Task in Japan*. New York and Chicago, 1926.

Reischauer, Edwin O. *Japan: Past and Present*. New York, 1946.

—— *The United States and Japan*. Cambridge, 1950.

—— *Ennin's Travels in T'ang China*. New York, 1955.

——, tr. *Ennin. Diary: The Record of a Pilgrimage to China in Search of the Law*. New York, 1955.

——, and Joseph K. Yamagiwa, tr. *Translations from Early Japanese Literature*. Cambridge, 1951.

——, and John K. Fairbank. *East Asia: The Great Tradition*. (Volume I of *A History of East Asian Civilization*.) Boston, 1958.

Reischauer, Robert Karl. *Early Japanese History*. 2 vols. Princeton, 1937.

Revon, Michel. *Le Shintoisme*. Paris, 1907.

—— "Ancestor-Worship and Cult of the Dead (Japanese)," *ERE*, I, 455–57.

Ricci, Matthew, *see* Gallagher, Louis J.

Rogers, Philip G. *The First Englishman in Japan: The Story of Will Adams*. London, 1956.

Roggendorf, Joseph. *Studies in Japanese Culture*. Tokyo, 1963.

Ross, Floyd H. *Shinto: The Way of Japan*. Boston, 1965.

Rossman, Vern. "Churches Face Many Problems as 100th Year is Celebrated," *The Japan Times*, November 2, 1959, p. 5.

Sadler, Arthur L. *The Maker of Modern Japan: The Life of Tokugawa Ieyasu*. London, 1937.

—— *The Beginner's Book of Bushidō by Daidōji Yuzan (Budō Shoshinshū)*. Tokyo, 1941.

Saitō, Hiroshi. *Japan's Policies and Purposes*. Boston, 1935.

Sakai, Atsuharu. "Kaibara Ekken and 'Onna Daigaku,' " *Cultural Nippon*, VII (No. 4, 1939), 45–56.

Saniel, Josefa M. *Japan and the Philippines, 1868–1898*. Quezon City, 1963.

────── "The Mobilization of Traditional Values in the Modernization of Japan," in R. N. Bellah, ed., *Religion and Progress in Modern Asia* (New York, 1965), pp. 124–49.

Sansom, Sir George B. *Japan: A Short Cultural History*. New York, 1931; rev. ed., 1962.

────── *The Western World and Japan*. New York, 1950; rev. ed., 1962.

────── *A History of Japan to 1334*. Stanford, 1958.

────── *A History of Japan, 1334–1615*. Stanford, 1961.

────── *A History of Japan, 1615–1867*. Stanford, 1963.

────── "The Imperial Edicts in the Shoku Nihongi (700–790 A.D.)," *TASJ*, Second Series, I (1924), 5–39.

────── "Nichiren," in *Japanese Buddhism*, by Sir Charles Eliot (London, 1935), pp. 416–31.

Sasaki, Gesshō. *A Study of Shin Buddhism*. Kyoto, 1925.

Sasaki, Ruth Fuller. "A Bibliography of Translations of Zen (Ch'an) Works," *Philosophy East and West*, X (Nos. 3–4, October, 1960-January, 1961), 149–66.

Satomi, K. *Japanese Civilization: Its Significance and Realization, Nichirenism and the Japanese National Principles*. London, 1923.

Satow, E. M. "The Shinto Shrines of Ise," *TASJ*, I (1874), 99–121.

────── "The Revival of Pure Shin-tau," *TASJ*, III, Part I (Supplement, 1875; rev., 1882), 1–87.

────── "The Mythology and Religious Worship of the Ancient Japanese," *The Westminster and Foreign Quarterly Review*, New Series, LIV (1878), 27–57.

────── "Ancient Japanese Rituals," *TASJ*, VII, Part I (1879), 97–132; IX (1881), 182–211.

Saunders, E. Dale. *Mudrā: A Study of Symbolic Gestures in Japanese Buddhist Sculpture*. New York, 1960.

────── *Buddhism in Japan*. Philadelphia, 1964.

────── "Japanese Mythology," in *Mythologies of the Ancient World*, ed. Samuel Noah Kramer (Garden City, 1961), pp. 409–42.

Scalapino, Robert A. *Democracy and the Party Movement in Pre-War Japan: The Failure of the First Attempt*. Berkeley, 1953.

Schiffer, Wilhelm. "New Religions in Postwar Japan," *Monumenta Nipponica*, XI (No. 1, April, 1955), 1–14.

Schneider, Delwin B. *Konkōkyō: A Japanese Religion*. Tokyo, 1962,

Schull, William J. "The Effect of Christianity on Consanguinity in Nagasaki," *American Anthropologist*, LV (January-March, 1959), 74–88.

Schurhammer, Georg. *Shin-To, the Way of the Gods in Japan (According to the Printed and Unprinted Reports of the Jesuit Missionaries in the Sixteenth and Seventeenth Centuries)*. Leipzig, 1923.

Schwantes, Robert S. "Christianity *versus* Science: A Conflict of Ideas in Meiji Japan" (Religion and Modernization in the Far East: A Symposium, I), *FEQ*, XII (No. 2, February, 1957), 123–32.

Schwartz, W. L. "The Great Shrine of Idzumo," *TASJ*, XLI (Part 4, October, 1913), 493–681.

Seidensticker, Edward. "Japan: Divisions in Socialism," in *Revisionism: Essays on the History of Marxist Ideas*, ed. Leopold Labedz (New York, 1962), pp. 363–73.

Seki, Keigo. *Folktales of Japan*. Chicago, 1963.

Shaw, R. D. M., tr. *The Blue Cliff Records: The Hekigan Roku*. London, 1961.

――― *The Embossed Tea Kettle: Orate Gama and Other Works of Hakuin Zenji*. London, 1963.

Shaw, R. D. M., and Wilhelm Schiffer, tr. Hakuin, "Yasen Kanna, 'A Chat on a Boat in the Evening,'" Preface and Part I, *Monumenta Nipponica*, XIII (Nos. 1–2, 1957), 101–27.

Shiina, Rinzō. "The Japanese People and 'Indigenous Christianity,'" tr. Sakaye Kobayashi, *Japanese Religions* (Kyoto), I (No. 2, 1959), 18–21.

Shinoda, Minoru. *The Founding of the Kamakura Shogunate, 1180–1185, with Selected Translations from the Azuma Kagami*. New York, 1960.

Shiomi, Saburō. *Japan's Finance and Taxation, 1940–1956*, tr. Shōtaro Hasegawa. New York, 1957.

Shively, Donald H. "Motoda Eifu: Confucian Lecturer to the Meiji Emperor," in *Confucianism in Action*, ed. David S. Nivison and Arthur F. Wright (Stanford, 1959), pp. 302–33.

Shoku Nihongi, see Snellen, J. B.

Shorrock, Hallam C., Jr. "The Church of Christ in Japan (Nippon Kirisuto Kyōdan)," *International Review of Missions*, XLI (April, 1952), 193–201.

Silberman, Bernard S. *Japan and Korea: A Critical Bibliography.* Tucson, 1962.

———, ed. *Japanese Character and Culture.* Tucson, 1962.

——— *Ministers of Modernization: Elite Mobility in the Meiji Restoration, 1868–1873.* Tucson, 1964.

Slawick, Alexander. "Kultische Geheimbunde der Japaner und Germanen," *Wiener Beitrage zur Kulturgeschichte und Linguistik* (Salzburg-Leipzig), IV (1936), 675–764.

——— "Zur Etymologie des japanischen Terminus *marehito* 'Sakraler Besucher,'" *Wiener Völkerkundliche Mitteilungen,* Second Yearbook, No. 1 (1954), pp. 44–58.

Smith, Munroe. *A General View of European Legal History and Other Papers.* New York, 1927.

Smith, Robert J., and Richard K. Beardsley, eds. *Japanese Culture: Its Development and Characteristics.* Chicago, 1962.

Smith, Thomas C. "The Land Tax in the Tokugawa Period," *JAS,* XVIII (No. 1, November, 1958), 3–19.

Smith, Warren W., Jr. *Confucianism in Modern Japan: A Study of Conservatism in Japanese Intellectual History.* Tokyo, 1959.

Snellen, J. B., tr. "Shoku Nihongi: Chronicles of Japan Continued, from 697–791 A.D.," *TASJ,* Second Series, XI (1934), 151–239; XIV (1937), 209–79.

Spae, Joseph John. *Itō Jinsai.* (Monumenta Serica Monograph, Vol. XII.) Peiping, 1948.

——— "The Catholic Church in Japan," *Contemporary Religions in Japan,* IV (No. 1, March, 1963), 3–78.

Steiner, Kurt. "The Revision of the Civil Code of Japan: Provisions Affecting the Family," *FEQ,* IX (No. 2, February, 1950), 169–84.

Stoetzel, Jean. *Without the Chrysanthemum and the Sword: A Study of the Attitudes of Youth in Post-War Japan.* New York, 1955.

Storry, Richard. *The Double Patriots: A Study of Japanese Nationalism.* London, 1957.

Supreme Commander for the Allied Powers (SCAP). Civil Information and Education Section. Religion and Cultural Resources Division. *Religions in Japan.* Washington, D.C., 1948.

——— Civil Information and Education Section. Education Division. *Education in the New Japan.* 2 vols. Washington, D.C., 1948.

Suzuki, Daisetz Teitarō. *Manual of Zen Buddhism.* Kyoto, 1935; New York, 1960.

———— A Miscellany of the Shin Teaching of Buddhism. Kyoto, 1949.

———— Essays in Zen Buddhism. Series I–III. London, 1950–53.

———— Studies in Zen Buddhism. London, 1955.

———— Zen and Japanese Culture. New York, 1959.

———— Zen and Japanese Buddhism. Tokyo and Rutland, Vt., 1958.

Swan, Peter C. An Introduction to the Arts of Japan. New York, 1958.

Swearinger, Rodger, and Paul Langer. Bibliography of Japanese Communism. New York, 1950.

———— Red Flag in Japan. Cambridge, 1952.

Taeuber, Irene B. The Population of Japan. Princeton, 1958.

Taiheiki, see McCullough, Helen Craig.

Tajima, Ryūjun. Étude sur le Mahāvairocana-Sūtra. Paris, 1936.

———— Les Deux grands mandalas et le doctrine de l'ésotérisme Shingon. Tokyo, 1959.

Takahashi, Takeichi, and Junjō Izumida. Shinranism in Mahayana Buddhism and the Modern World. Los Angeles, 1932.

Takakura, Shinichirō. The Ainu of Northern Japan: A Study in Conquest and Acculturation, tr. and annot. John A. Harrison. (Transactions of the American Philosophical Society, New Series, Vol. LI, Part IV.) Philadelphia, 1960.

Takakusu, Junjirō, tr. I-Tsing: A Record of the Buddhist Religion as Practiced in India and the Malay Archipelago. Oxford, 1896.

———— The Essentials of Buddhist Philosophy. Honolulu, 1947.

Takekoshi, Yosoburō. The Economic Aspects of the History of the Civilization of Japan. 3 vols. New York, 1930.

Takeuchi, Yoshinori, "Shinran's Religious Philosophy." (Mimeographed lecture notes, Columbia University, 1962.)

Taniguchi, Masaharu. Divine Education and Spiritual Training of Mankind. Tokyo, 1956.

Tanni Shō, see Fujisawa, Ryōsetsu.

Tatsui, Matsunosuke. Japanese Gardens. Tokyo, 1934.

Taut, Bruno. Houses and Peoples of Japan. Tokyo, 1937.

Tenrikyō, The Headquarters of. A Short History of Tenrikyō. Tenri, Nara-ken, 1956.

Tenshō-Kōtai-Jingū-kyō. The Prophets of Tabuse. Tabuse, 1954.

———— Guidance to God's Kingdom. Tabuse, 1956.

Thomas, Winburn T. Protestant Beginnings in Japan. Tokyo and Rutland, Vt., 1959.

Thomsen, Harry. *The New Religions of Japan*. Tokyo and Rutland, Vt., 1963.

Tillich, Paul. *Christianity and the Encounter of the World Religions*. New York, 1961.

Toda, Yoshio. "Traditional Tendency of Shintoism and Its New Theoretical Developments," in *Religious Studies in Japan*, ed. Japanese Association for Religious Studies (Tokyo, 1959), pp. 229–32.

Torii, Ryūzō. "Études archéologiques de la Mandchourie meridionale," *Journal of the College of Science* (Tokyo Imperial University), Vol. XXXVI (1915).

———— "Études archéologiques des Ainu des Iles Kouriles," *Journal of the College of Science* (Tokyo Imperial University), Vol. XLII (1919).

Totten, George O. "Buddhism and Socialism in Japan and Burma," *Comparative Studies in Society and History*, II (No. 3 April, 1960), 293–304.

Toynbee, Arnold. *The World and the West*. New York and London, 1953.

Trewartha, Glenn Thomas. *Japan: A Physical, Cultural and Regional Geography*. Madison, 1945.

Tsuchiya, Kyōson. *Contemporary Thought of Japan and China*. London, 1927.

Tsugaru, Fusamaro. *Die Lehre von der japanischen Adoption*. Berlin, 1903.

Tsukakoshi, Satoshi, tr. *Konjaku: Altjapanische Geschichten aus dem Volk zur Heian-Zeit*. Zurich, 1956.

Tsunoda, Ryūsaku, tr. *Japan in the Chinese Dynastic Histories*, ed. L. Carrington Goodrich. South Pasadena, 1951.

————, Wm. Theodore de Bary, and Donald Keene. *Sources of Japanese Tradition*. New York, 1958.

Tucker, Henry St. George. *The History of the Episcopal Church in Japan*. New York, 1938.

Uchimura, Kanzō. *How I Became a Christian*. Tokyo, 1913.

Ui, Hakuju. "A Study of Japanese Tendai Buddhism," *Philosophical Studies of Japan*, Vol. I, ed. Japanese National Commission for UNESCO (Tokyo, 1959), pp. 33–74.

Ukai, Nobushige. "The Japanese House of Councillors Election of July 1962," *Asian Survey*, II (No. 6, August, 1962), 1–8.

Umehara, Suyeji. "Ancient Mirrors and Their Relationship to Early

Japanese Culture," *Acta Asiatica* (Bulletin of The Institute of Eastern Culture, Tokyo), No. 4 (1963), pp. 70–79.

Underwood, A. C. *Shintoism: The Indigenous Religion of Japan.* London, 1934.

U.S. State Department. *Occupation of Japan: Policy and Progress.* (Publication No. 2671, Far Eastern Series 17.) Washington, D.C., n.d.

Uyehara, Cecil H. *Leftwing Social Movements in Japan: An Annotated Bibliography.* Tokyo and Rutland, Vt., 1959.

Van Straelen, Henry. *Yoshida Shōin: Forerunner of the Meiji Restoration.* Leiden, 1952.

—— *The Religion of Divine Wisdom.* Kyoto, 1957.

Veith, Ilza. "Englishman or Samurai: The Story of Will Adams," *FEQ,* V (No. 1, November, 1945), 5–27.

Visser, Marinus Willem de. *The Bodhisattva Ti-Tsang (Jizō) in China and Japan.* Berlin, 1914.

—— *Ancient Buddhism in Japan.* 2 vols. Paris, 1928–35.

—— *The Bodhisattva Akasagarbha (Kokuzō) in China and Japan.* Amsterdam, 1931.

Vogel, Ezra. *Japan's New Middle Class: The Salary Man and His Family in a Tokyo Suburb.* Berkeley and Los Angeles, 1963.

Von Mehren, A. T., ed. *Law in Japan: The Legal Order in a Changing Society.* Cambridge, Mass., 1963.

Vories, William Merrell. *Ōmi Brotherhood in Nippon.* Kobe, 1934.

Vos, Frits. *A Study of the Ise-monogatari with the Text according to the Den-Teika-hippon and an annotated translation.* 2 vols. The Hague, 1957.

Voss, Gustav, and Hubert Cieslik, tr. *Kirishito-ki und Sayo-Yoroku: Japanische Dokumente zur Missionsgeschichte des 17. Jahrhunderts.* Tokyo, 1940.

Wach, Joachim. *Sociology of Religion.* Chicago, 1944.

Waley, Arthur, tr. *The Tale of Genji.* 2 vols. Boston, 1935.

—— *The Real Tripitaka.* New York, 1952.

Wallach, Sidney, ed. *Narrative of the Expedition of an American Squadron to the China Seas and Japan, under the Command of Commodore M. C. Perry, Compiled at His Request and under His Supervision by Francis L. Hawks.* New York, 1952.

Ward, Robert E. "The Commission on the Constitution and Prospects for Constitutional Change in Japan," *JAS,* XXIV (No. 3, May, 1965), 401–29.

Warner, Langdon. *The Enduring Art of Japan*. Cambridge, 1952.

Watanabe, Shōzaburō. *The Common Origin of the Japanese and Korean Languages*. Tokyo, 1910.

Watsuji, Tetsurō. *A Climate: A Philosophical Study*, tr. Geoffrey Bownas. Tokyo, 1961.

Webb, Herschel. "What is the Dai Nihon Shi?" *JAS*, XIX (No. 2, February, 1960), 135–49.

—— *Research in Japanese Sources: A Guide*. New York, 1965.

Weber, Max. *The Sociology of Religion*, tr. Ephraim Fischoff. Boston, 1963.

Wedemeyer, A. *Japanische Frühgeschichte*. Tokyo, 1930.

Wheeler, Post. *The Sacred Scriptures of the Japanese*. New York, 1952.

Whymant, A. Neville J. "The Oceanic Theory of the Japanese Language and People, *TASJ*, Second Series, Vol. III (1926).

Williams, Harold S. *Tales of the Foreign Settlements in Japan*. Tokyo and Rutland, Vt., 1958.

Wilson, Robert A. *Genesis of the Meiji Government in Japan 1868–1871*. (University of California Publications in History, Vol. LVI.) Berkeley and Los Angeles, 1957.

Woodard, William P. "The Religious World—Some Random Notes," *The Japan Christian Quarterly*, XXIV (No. 2, April, 1958), 170–75.

—— "The Religious Juridical Persons Law," in *Contemporary Japan*, ed. The Foreign Affairs Association of Japan (Tokyo, 1960), pp. 1–84.

Wright, Arthur F. "The Formation of Sui Ideology, 581–604," in *Chinese Thought and Institutions*, ed. John F. Fairbank. (Chicago, 1957), pp. 71–104.

Yajima, Suketoshi. "Dutch Books on Science and Technology brought to Japan in XVII and XIX Centuries," *Archives internationales d'histoire des sciences*, VI (January-March, 1953), 76–79.

Yamabe, S., and L. Adams Beck, tr. *Buddhist Psalms* [of Shinran Shōnin]. London, 1921.

Yamagiwa, Joseph K., tr. "Ō-Kagami" ("The Great Mirror"), in *Translations from Early Japanese Literature*, by Edwin O. Reischauer and Joseph K. Yamagiwa (Cambridge, 1951), pp. 271–374.

—— and Edwin O. Reischauer, tr. "Tatsumi Chūnagon Monogatari" ("The Tales of Tatsumi Chūnagon"), in *Translations from*

Early Japanese Literature (Cambridge, 1951), pp. 139–267.

Yamakami, Sōgen. *Systems of Buddhist Thought.* Calcutta, 1912.

Yamamoto, Kōshō. *The Private Letters of Shinran Shōnin.* Tokyo, 1956.

Yanaga, Chitoshi. *Japan Since Perry.* New York, 1949.

Yanaihara, Tadao. *Religion and Democracy in Modern Japan.* Tokyo, 1948.

Yashima, Jirō. *An Essay on the Way of Life.* Tondabayashi, 1950.

Yawata, Ichirō. "Prehistoric Evidence for Japanese Cultural Origins," in *Japanese Culture: Its Development and Characteristics,* ed. Robert J. Smith and Richard K. Beardsley (Chicago, 1962), pp. 7–10.

Yazaki, Takeo. *The Japanese City: A Sociological Analysis,* tr. David L. Swain. Rutland, Vt., and Tokyo, 1963.

Young, A. Morgan. *Imperial Japan 1926–1938.* New York, 1938.

——— *Japan in Recent Times 1912–1926.* New York, 1940.

Young, John. *The Location of Yamatai: A Case Study in Japanese Historiography, 720–1945.* (The Johns Hopkins University Studies in Historical and Political Science Series, Vol. LXXV, No. 2.) Baltimore, 1957.

Yuasa, Tatsuki. "PL (Perfect Liberty)," *Contemporary Religions in Japan,* I (No. 3, September, 1960), 20–29.

Zürcher, E. *The Buddhist Conquest of China.* 2 vols. Leiden, 1959.

WORKS IN JAPANESE

Abe Yoshio. "Edo-jidai jusha no shusshin to shakai-teki-chii ni tsuite" (Social status of Confucian scholars in the Edo period), *Nippon-Chūgoku-Gakkai-hō,* No. 13 (1961), 161–75.

阿 部 正 雄 「江戸時代儒者の出身と社会的地位について」

(日本中国学会報　第十三集)

Aiba Shin. *Fuju-fuse-teki shisō no tenkai* (Development of the ideology of non-receiving and non-giving). Tokyo, 1961.

相 葉 伸　不受不施的思想の史的展開

Akamatsu Toshihide. *Kamakura Bukkyō no kenkyū* (A study of Buddhism during the Kamakura period). Kyoto, 1932.

赤 松 俊 秀　鎌倉仏教の研究

―――― *Shinran*. Tokyo, 1962.

親　鸞

Akiyama Hanji. *Zenke no shisō to shūkyō* (Thought and religion of the Zen Buddhists). Tokyo, 1962.

秋 山 範 二　禅家の思想と宗教

Anesaki Masaharu. *Kirishitan shūmon no hakugai to sempuku* (Persecution and underground movement of the Kirishitan sect). Tokyo, 1925.

姉 崎 正 治　切支丹宗門の迫害と潜伏

―――― *Kirishitan kinsei no shūmatsu* (The end of the prohibition of the Kirishitan). Tokyo, 1926.

切支丹禁制の終末

―――― *Kirishitan dendō no kōhai* (The rise and decline of Kirishitan missionary work). Tokyo, 1930.

切支丹伝道の興廃

―――― *Kirishitan hakugaishi-chū no jinbutsu jiseki* (Personages and episodes in the persecution of the Kirishitan). Tokyo, 1930.

切支丹迫害史中の人物事蹟

―――― *Kirishitan shūkyō bungaku* (The religious literature of the Kirishitan sect). Tokyo, 1932.

切支丹宗教文学

―――― *Hokke-kyō gyōja Nichiren* (Nichiren, the practitioner of the Lotus Sutra). Tokyo, 1933.

法華経の行者日蓮

―――― *Shōtoku Taishi no taishi risō* (Prince Shōtoku's ideal of the great man). Tokyo, 1944.

聖徳太子の大士理想

―――― *Waga shōgai* (My life). Tambaichi, Nara-ken, 1951.

わが生涯

Anzu Motohiko. *Shintō to saiki* (Shinto and its rituals). Tokyo, 1940.

安津素彦　神道と祭祀

―――― *Shintō gairon* (An outline of Shinto), Vol. I. Tokyo, 1954.

神道概論　上篇

Aoyama Michio. *Nihon-kazoku-seido no kenkyū* (A study of the Japanese family system). Tokyo, 1947.

青山道夫　日本家族制度の研究

Aruga (or Ariga) Kizayemon. *Nihon kazoku-seido to kosaku-seido* (The family and tenancy system in Japan). Tokyo, 1943.

有賀喜左衛門　日本家族制度と小作制度

―――― "Nihon no iye" (The family in Japan), in Nihon Jinruigaku-kai, ed., *Nihon minzoku* (The Japanese people) (Tokyo, 1952), pp. 154–84.

「日本の家」

（日本人類学会編　日本民族）

Asano Kenshin. *Shakai shūkyō to shite no Bukkyō* (Buddhism as a social religion). Tokyo, 1934.

浅野研真　社会宗教としての仏教

―――― *Nihon Bukkyō shakai jigyō-shi* (A history of Buddhist social work in Japan). Tokyo, 1935.

日本仏教社会事業史

Ashikaga Enjutsu. *Kamakura Muromachi jidai no Jukyō* (Japanese Confucianism during the Kamakura and Muromachi periods). Tokyo, 1932.

足 利 衍 述　　鎌倉室町時代之儒教

Bamba Masatomo. *Nihon Jukyō-ron* (On Japanese Confucianism). Tokyo, 1939.

万 羽 正 朋　　日本儒教論

Bukkyō Daigaku. *Hōnen shōnin kenkyū* (A study of Saint Hōnen). Kyoto, 1961.

仏 教 大 学　　法然上人研究

Bukkyō Gakkai, ed. *Hasshū-kōyō kōgi* (Lectures on the main tenets of the eight Buddhist schools). Kyoto, 1954.

仏 教 学 会　　八宗綱要講義

Bukkyō Shakai-gakuin, ed. *Shinkō ruiji shūkyō hihan* (A critical study of the new pseudo religions). Tokyo, 1936.

仏教社会学院　　新興類似宗教批判

Bukkyō shigaku (The journal of Buddhist history). Tokyo, 1949–

仏 教 史 学

Bukkyō-shi-gakkai, ed. *Nihon Bukkyō no chiiki-hatten* (A study of the geographical development of Japanese Buddhism). Kyoto, 1961.

仏教史学会編　　日本仏教の地域発展

Bussho Kankōkai. *Dai Nihon Bukkyō zensho* (Complete collection of Japanese Buddhism). 151 vols., Supplement, 10 vols. Tokyo, 1913–22.

仏 書 刊 行 会　　大日本仏教全書

Chiba Sakaye. *Yoshikawa Shintō no kenkyū* (Studies in Yoshikawa Shinto). Tokyo, 1939.

千 葉 栄 吉川神道の研究

Chikuma Shobō. *Bukkyō-bungaku-shū* (A collection of Buddhist literature). Tokyo, 1962.

筑 摩 書 房 仏教文学集

Chūgai Nippō Henshū-kyoku, ed. *Jinja to shūkyō hihan* (A critique of shrines and religion). Kyoto, 1930.

中外日報編輯局 神社と宗教批判

Dai Nihon Keishin-kai. *Dai Nihon jinja-shi* (Studies on shrines in Japan). 4 vols. Tokyo, 1933.

大 日 本 敬 神 会 大日本神社志

Daitō Shuppansha. *Kokuyaku issai-kyō wakan senjutsu-bu* (Complete collection of Buddhist scriptures translated into Japanese). Tokyo, 1962.

大 東 出 版 社 国訳一切経和漢選述部

Date Mitsuyoshi. *Nihon shūkyō-seido shiryō ruiju-kō* (Collection of historical source materials on Japanese religious institutions). Tokyo, 1930.

伊 達 光 美 日本宗教制度資料類従考

Doi Chūsei, *et al. Nihongo no rekishi* (A history of the Japanese language). Tokyo, 1957.

土 井 忠 生 日本語の歴史

Ebina Danjō. *Kokumin-dōtoku to Kirisuto-kyō* (National morality and Christianity). Tokyo, 1912.

海 老 名 弾 正 国民道徳と基督教

Ebisawa Arimichi. *Kirishitan-shi no kenkyū* (A historical study of Kirishitan). Tokyo, 1942.

海老沢有道　切支丹史の研究

—— *Kirishitan tenseki sōkō* (The Kirishitan literature). Tokyo, 1943.

切支丹典籍叢考

—— *Kirishitan no shakai-katsudō oyobi Namban igaku* (The social works of Kirishitan and the European medicine). Tokyo, 1944.

切支丹の社会活動及南蛮医学

—— *Gendai Nihon-shūkyō no shi-teki seikaku* (Historical characteristics of contemporary Japanese religions). Tokyo, 1952.

現代日本宗教の史的性格

Egami Namio. "Nihon Minzoku: Bunka no genryū to Nihon kokka no keisei" (The Japanese people: Development of Japanese culture and formation of the Japanese nation), *Minzokugaku kenkyū* (Journal of ethnology), XIII (No. 3, 1949).

江上波夫　日本民族文化の源流と日本国家の形成
　　　　　（民族研究）

——, *et al.,* "Nihon kodai kokka no keisei" (Formation of the early Japanese nation), *Tōyō bunka* (Oriental civilization), No. 6 (September, 1951).

日本古代国家の形成（東洋文化）

Enoki Kazuo. *Yamatai-koku* (The Yamatai nation). Tokyo, 1960.

榎一雄　邪馬台国

Etō Sokuō. *Shūso to shiteno Dōgen zenji* (Dōgen as the founder of a sect). Tokyo, 1938.

衛藤即応　宗祖としての道元禅師

Fujiki Kunihiko. *Heian jidai no kizoku no seikatsu* (The life of the aristocracy during the Heian period). Tokyo, 1960.

藤 木 邦 彦　平安時代の貴族の生活

Fujisawa Morihiko. *Shinwa densetsu-hen* (Myths and legends). (Vol. I of *Nihon Minzokugaku Zenshū.*) Tokyo, 1961.

藤 沢 衛 彦　神話伝説篇 (図説日本民俗学全集)

Fujitani Toshio. "Bukkyō to Buraku-kaihō" (Buddhism and the liberation of social outcastes' villages), in *Kōza kindai Bukkyō* (Essays on modern Buddhism), V (Kyoto, 1961), 133–50.

藤 谷 俊 雄　「仏教と部落解放」

　　　　　　　(講座近代仏教　第 5 巻)

Fujiwara Ryōsetsu. *Nembutsu shisō no kenkyū* (A study of the nembutsu ideology). Kyoto, 1957.

藤 原 凌 雪　念仏思想の研究

Fukihara Shōshin. *Nihon yuishiki-shisō-shi* (A history of the ideation-only theory in Japan). Kyoto, 1944.

富 貴 原 章 信　日本唯識思想史

Fukuchi Shigetaka. *Gunkoku-Nippon no keisei* (Formation of the militaristic Japanese nation). Tokyo, 1959.

福 地 重 孝　軍国日本の形成

Fukuda Gyōyei. *Tendai-gaku gairon* (An introduction to the study of Tendai Buddhism). Tokyo, 1954.

福 田 堯 穎　天台学概論

Fukui Kōjun. "Shōtoku taishi no denki ni tsuite no Shinagaku-teki kōsatsu" (A sinological study of the biography of Prince Shōtoku), *Nippon-Chūgoku-Gakkai-hō*, No. 2 (1950), pp. 105–17.

福 井 康 順　「聖徳太子の伝記についてのシナ学的考察」

　　　　　　　(日本中国学会報)

Fukuo Takeichirō. *Nihon kazoku-seido-shi* (A history of the Japanese family system). Tokyo, 1948.

福尾 猛市郎　日本家族制度史

Funagasaki Masataka. *Nihon shomin shūkyō-shi no kenkyū* (A study of the history of folk religion in Japan). Kyoto, 1962.

舟ヶ崎 正孝　日本庶民宗教史の研究

Furukawa Tetsushi. *Kinsei Nihon shisō no kenkyū* (Studies in modern Japanese thought). Tokyo, 1948.

古 川 哲 史　近世日本思想の研究

———, ed. *Nihon shisō-shi* (History of Japanese thought). Tokyo, 1954.

　　日本思想史

Furuno Kiyoto. *Kakure Kirishitan* (The hidden Kirishitan). Tokyo, 1959.

古 野 清 人　隠れキリシタン

Furuta Shōkin. *Nihon Bukkyō shisō-shi* (History of Japanese Buddhist thought). Tokyo, 1960.

古 田 紹 欽　日本仏教思想史

——— *Hakuin,* Tokyo, 1962.

　　白 隠

Futaba Kenkō. *Kodai Bukkyō shisō-shi kenkyū* (A study of early Japanese Buddhism: Ritsuryō and Anti-Ritsuryō Buddhism in early Japan). Kyoto, 1962.

二 葉 憲 香　古代仏教思想史研究

Haga Hideo. *Ta no Kami* (Agricultural deities: The rituals of rice production in Japan). Tokyo, 1959.

芳賀 日出男　田の神

Hanayama Shinshō. *Shōtoku Taishi gyosei Hokke giso* (Prince Shōtoku's commentary on the *Lotus Sutra*). 2 vols. Tokyo, 1931–33.

花 山 信 勝　聖徳太子御製法華義疏

Hani Gorō. *Meiji-ishin-shi kenkyū* (A historical study of the Meiji restoration). Tokyo, 1956.

羽 仁 五 郎　明治維新史研究

Harada Toshiaki. *Kodai Nihon no shūkyō to shakai* (Ancient Japanese beliefs and society). Tokyo, 1948.

原 田 敏 明　古代日本の信仰と社会

———— *Jinja* (Shrines). Tokyo, 1961.

神 社

Hasebe Kotondo. "Akashi-shi-fukin Nishiyagi saishinsei—zenki sui-sekishutsudo jinrui yōkotsu no genshisei ni tsuite" (On the dating of the human bones discovered in the prehistoric site at Nishiyagi near the city of Akashi), *Jinruigaku zasshi*, Vol. LX, No. 1 (July, 1948).

長 谷 部 言 人　「明石市附近西八木最新世前期堆積出土人類腰骨の
原始性に就いて」(人類学雑誌)

———— "Ezo," in Nihon Jinruigaku-kai, ed., *Nihon minzoku* (The Japanese people) (Tokyo, 1952), pp. 130–45.

「蝦夷」(日本人類学編　日本民族)

Hasegawa Ryōshin. "Bukkyō shakai-jigyō ni kansuru kanken" (One view regarding Buddhist social work), *Kōza kindai Bukkyō*, V (Kyoto, 1961), 151–59.

長 谷 川 良 信　「仏教社会事業に関する管見」
(講座近代仏教 5)

Hasegawa Yūjirō. *Konkō-kyō gaikan* (An outline of the Konkō-kyō). Tokyo, 1931.

長谷川雄次郎　　金光教概観

Hashikawa Tadashi. *Gaisetsu Nihon Bukkyō-shi* (An outline history of Japanese Buddhism). Kyoto, 1958.

橋　川　正　　概説　日本仏教史

Hashimoto Minoru. *Nihon Bushidō-shi* (A history of Japanese *Bushidō*). Tokyo, 1940.

橋　本　実　　日本武士道史

Hata Ikuhiko. *Nitchū sensō-shi* (A history of war between Japan and China). Tokyo, 1961.

秦　郁　彦　　日中戦争史

Hattori Shirō. *Nihongo no keitō* (Lineage of the Japanese language). Tokyo, 1959.

服　部　四　郎　　日本語の系統

Hayashi Rokurō. *Kōmyō kōgō* (The empress Kōmyō). Tokyo, 1961.

林　陸　郎　　光明皇后

Hazama Jikō, *Nihon Bukkyō no tenkai to sono kichō* (The development of Japanese Buddhism and its main tenets). 2 vols. Tokyo, 1953.

硲　慈　弘　　日本仏教の展開とその基調

Higo Kazuo. *Nihon shinwa kenkyū* (A study of Japanese mythology). Tokyo, 1938.

肥　後　和　男　　日本神話研究

——— "Nihon kodaishi e no kanken" (A view of the prehistory of Japan), *Minzokugaku kenkyū* (Journal of ethnology), Vol. XIV (No. 2, December, 1949).

「日本古代史への管見」（民族学研究）

———— *Nihon shinwa no rekishi-teki keisei* (Historical development of Japanese myths). Tokyo, 1958.

日本神話の歴史的形成

Hiraizumi Chō. *Chūsei ni okeru sha-ji to shakai tono kankei* (The relations between society and religious institutions during the medieval period of Japan). Tokyo, 1926.

平　泉　澄　　中世に於ける社寺と社会との関係

Hiraoka Jōkai. *Tōdai-ji no rekishi* (A history of Tōdai-ji). Tokyo, 1961.

平　岡　定　海　　東大寺の歴史

Hirata Kanichi. *Shintō no hongi to sono tenkai* (The fundamental doctrine of Shinto and its development). Kyoto, 1959.

平　田　貫　一　　神道の本義とその展開

Hirata Toshiharu. *Yoshino-jidai no kenkyū* (A study of the Yoshino period). Tokyo, 1943.

平　田　俊　春　　吉野時代の研究

Hiyane Yasusada. *Nihon shūkyō-shi* (A history of religion in Japan). Tokyo, 1925.

比 屋 根 安 定　　日本宗教史

———— *Nihon Kirisuto-kyō-shi* (A history of Christianity in Japan). 5 vols. Tokyo, 1938–40.

日本基督教史

———— *Shūkyō-shi* (History of religion). (Vol. XVI of *Gendai Nihon Bummei-shi* [History of modern Japanese civilization].) Tokyo, 1941.

宗教史（現代日本文明史）

Hori Ichirō. *Nihon Bukkyō-shi-ron* (Essays on the history of Japanese Buddhism). Tokyo, 1940.

堀　　一　　郎　　日本仏教史論

——— *Yugyō shisō: Kokumin-shinkō no honshitsu* (Yugyō: An essay on the fundamental characteristics of national beliefs). Tokyo, 1944.

遊行思想　国民信仰の本質論

——— *Minkan shinkō* (Folk beliefs). Tokyo, 1951.

民間信仰

——— *Waga-kuni minkan-shinkō-shi no kenkyū* (A study of the historical development of Japanese folk beliefs). 2 vols. Tokyo, 1953–55.

我が国民間信仰史の研究

——— *Nihon shūkyō no shakai-teki-yakuwari* (The social role of Japanese religion). Tokyo, 1962.

日本宗教の社会的役割

——— *Shūkyō-shūzoku no seikatsu-kisei* (Conditioning factors for religion and custom). Tokyo, 1963.

宗教習俗の生活規制

Hosokawa Kameichi. *Nihon jōdai Bukkyō no shakai-keizai* (The social economy of ancient Japanese Buddhism). Tokyo, 1931.

細　川　亀　市　　日本上代仏教の社会経済

——— *Jiryō shōen no kenkyū* (A study of manors owned by Buddhist temples). Tokyo, 1934.

寺領荘園の研究

Hōzōkan. *Kōza kindai Bukkyō* (Essays on modern Buddhism). 6 vols. Kyoto, 1961–63.

法　蔵　館　　講座近代仏教

Iba Takashi. "Bukkyō ongaku" (Buddhist music), in Tsuji Sōichi, *et al., Shūkyō ongaku* (Religious music) (Tokyo, 1933), pp. 169–211.

伊　庭　孝　「仏教音楽」(辻荘一　その他　宗教音楽)

Ichimura Kisaburō. "Nihon kenkoku-irai no nensū ni tsuite" (A study of the dating of the foundation of Japan), in *Takigawa hakase kanreki kinen ronbun-shū* (Collection of essays in honor of the 60th birthday of Dr. Takigawa), Vol. II: *Nihon-hen* (Volume on Japan) (Uyeda, Nagano-ken, 1957), pp. 367–89.

市 村 其 三 郎　「日本建国以来の年数」

(滝川博士還暦記念論文集　日本史篇)

Igarashi Chikara. *Heian-chō bungaku-shi* (A history of the literature of the Heian period). 2 vols. Tokyo, 1937–39.

五 十 嵐 力　平安朝文学史

Ikawa Jōkei. *Hōnen-shōnin-den zenshū* (The complete collection of the biographies of Saint Hōnen). Osaka, 1952.

井 川 定 慶　法然上人伝全集

Imai Takuji. *Heian-jidai nikki bungaku no kenkyū* (A study of diaries of the Heian period). Tokyo, 1957.

今 井 卓 爾　平安時代日記文学の研究

Imayeda Aishin. *Zen-shū no rekishi* (History of Zen Buddhism). Tokyo, 1962.

今 枝 愛 真　禅宗の歴史

Inaba Keishin. "Ippen Shōnin no shisō ni tsuite" (A study of Ippen Shōnin's thought), *Nihon Bukkyō shigaku* (Historical study of Japanese Buddhism), II (No. 2, April, 1943), 60–75.

稲 葉 慶 信　「一遍上人の思想について」

(日本仏教史学　第二巻　第二号)

Inaba Shūken. *Kyōgyōshinshō no shomondai* (Various problems of the *Kyōgyōshinshō*). Kyoto, 1962.

稲 葉 秀 賢　　教行信証の諸問題

Inouye Kaoru. *Nihon kodai no seiji to shūkyō* (Politics and religion in ancient Japan). Tokyo, 1961.

井　上　薫　　日本古代の政治と宗教

—— *Gyōgi* (Saint Gyōgi). Tokyo, 1962.

行　基

Inouye Mitsusada. *Nihon Jōdo-kyō seiritsu-shi no kenkyū* (A historical study of the development of Pure Land Buddhism in Japan). Tokyo, 1956.

井 上 光 貞　　日本浄土教成立史の研究

—— *Kizoku bunka no keisei* (Formation of aristocratic culture). Tokyo, 1960. (*Zusetsu Nihon rekishi,* 2.)

貴族文化の形成（図説日本歴史 2 ）

—— *Nihon kokka no kigen* (Origin of the Japanese nation). Tokyo, 1960.

日本国家の起原

Inouye Tetsujirō. *Nihon Shushigaku-ha no tetsugaku* (The philosophy of the Chu Hsi school in Japan). Tokyo, 1905.

井 上 哲 次 郎　　日本朱子学派之哲学

—— *Waga kokutai to kokumin-dōtoku* (Our national polity and national morality). Tokyo, 1925.

我が国体と国民道徳

Ishida Eiichirō. *Momotarō no haha* (Mother of Momotarō). Tokyo, 1956.

石 田 英 一 郎　　桃太郎の母

Ishida Ichirō. *Jōdo-kyō bijutsu* (The art of the Pure Land school). Kyoto, 1956.

石 田 一 良　浄土教美術

—— *Chōnin bunka* (Culture of the townsman). Tokyo, 1961.

町人文化

Ishida Jūshi. *Jōdo-kyō kyōri-shi* (History of the doctrines of Pure Land Buddhism). Kyoto, 1962.

石 田 充 之　浄土教教理史

Ishida Mosaku. *Shakyō yori mitaru Nara-chō Bukkyō no kenkyū* (A study of Buddhism of the Nara period based on the copied scriptures). Tokyo, 1930.

石 田 茂 作　写経より見たる奈良朝仏教の研究

—— *Tōdai-ji to kokubun-ji* (Tōdai-ji and provincial state temples). Tokyo, 1959.

東大寺と国分寺

Ishii Kyōdō. *Jōdo no kyōgi to sono kyōdan* (Doctrines and ecclesiastical organizations of the Pure Land school). Tokyo, 1931.

石 井 教 道　浄土の教義と其の教団

Ishikawa Ken. *Sekimon Shingaku-shi no kenkyū* (Studies in the history of the Shingaku movement). Tokyo, 1938.

石 川 謙　石門心学史の研究

Ishimoda Tadashi. *Chūsei-teki sekai no keisei* (The formation of the medieval world). Tokyo, 1946; 4th ed., 1950.

石 母 田 正　中世的世界の形成

Ishizu Teruji. *Tendai jissō-ron no kenkyū* (A study of the Tendai doctrine of reality). Tokyo, 1947.

石 津 照 璽　天台実相論の研究

Itō Mikiharu. *Inasaku-girei no ruikeiteki kenkyū* (A typological study of rice rituals). Tokyo, 1963.

伊 藤 幹 治　　稲作儀礼の類型的研究

Iwashita Sōichi. *Shinkō no isan* (The legacy of faith). Tokyo, 1941.

岩 下 荘 一　　信仰の遺産

Iyenaga Saburō. *Chūsei Bukkyō shisō-shi kenkyū* (Studies in the intellectual history of medieval Buddhism). Kyoto, 1947.

家 永 三 郎　　中世仏教思想史研究

——— *Jōdai Bukkyō shisō-shi kenkyū* (A historical study of early Buddhist thought in Japan). Tokyo, 1950.

上代仏教思想史研究

——— *Nihon dōtoku-shisō-shi* (A history of ethical thought in Japan). Tokyo, 1954.

日本道徳思想史

———, ed. *Nihon-Bukkyō shisō no tenkai* (Development of Buddhist thought in Japan). Tokyo, 1956.

日本仏教思想の展開

——— *Nihon bunka-shi* (A history of Japanese civilization). Tokyo, 1959.

日本文化史

——— "Nihon no kindai-ka to Bukkyō" (Modernization of Japan and Buddhism), *Kōza kindai Bukkyō* (Essays on modern Buddhism), II (Kyoto, 1961), 7–35.

「日本の近代化と仏教」

（講座近代仏教　第 2 巻　歴史編）

———— *Kindai Nihon no shisōka* (Some modern thinkers in Japan). Tokyo, 1962.

近代日本の思想家

———— *Nihonjin no shisō no ayumi* (The intellectual development of the Japanese people). Tokyo, 1962.

日本人の思想の歩み

Iyanaga Teizō. *Nara-jidai no kizoku to nōmin* (Aristocracy and peasantry during the Nara period). Tokyo, 1956.

弥 永 貞 三　奈良時代の貴族と農民

Izui Hisanosuke. "Jōdai Nihongo ni okeru boin-soshiki to boin-keitai" (The vocal system and vocal interchanges of eighth-century Japanese), in *Miscellanea Kiotiensia* (Kyoto, 1956), pp. 989–1020.

泉 井 久 之 助　「上代日本語における母音組織と母音交替」

(京都大学文学部五十周年記念論集)

Jōdo-shin-shū fukyō-kenkyū-sho, ed. *Sōka-gakkai no kentō* (An analysis of *Sōka-gakkai*). Kyoto, 1961.

浄土真宗布教研究所　創価学会の検討

Kakogami Eryū. *Shin-shū-gaku no kompon mondai* (Fundamental problems of the study of Shin Buddhism). Kyoto, 1962.

神 子 上 恵 竜　真宗学の根本問題

Kambayashi Ryūjō. *Kōbō Daishi no shisō to shūkyō* (The thought and religion of Kōbō Daishi). Tokyo, 1934.

神 林 隆 浄　弘法大師の思想と宗教

Kanda Hideo. *Kojiki no kōzō* (Structure of the *Kojiki*). Tokyo, 1959.

神 田 秀 夫　古事記の構造

Kaneharu Isamu. *Shōtoku Taishi kyōgaku no kenkyū* (A study of the doctrine of Prince Shōtoku). Kyoto, 1962.

金 治 勇　聖徳太子教学の研究

Kaneko Daiyei. *Nihon Bukkyō-shikan* (An interpretation of Buddhist history in Japan). Tokyo, 1940.

金 子 大 栄　日本仏教史観

Kasahara Kazuo. *Ikkō-ikki* (The uprising of the Ikkō sect). Tokyo, 1959.

笠 原 一 男　一向一揆

――― *Shin-shū ni okeru itan no keifu* (Genealogy of heresies in Shin Buddhism). Tokyo, 1962.

真宗における異端の系譜

Katayose Masayoshi. *Konjaku monogatarishū-ron* (Essays on the Konjaku *monogatari*). Tokyo, 1944.

片 寄 正 義　今昔物語集論

Katō Genchi, comp. and ed. *Shintō shoseki mokuroku* (A bibliography of Shinto). 2d ed. Tokyo, 1943.

加 藤 玄 智　神道書籍目録

Katō Totsudō. *Minkan shinkō-shi* (A history of Japanese folk beliefs). Tokyo, 1925.

加 藤 吐 堂　民間信仰史

Katsuno Takanobu. *Sōhei* (Warrior priests). Tokyo, 1959.

勝 野 隆 信　僧 兵

――― *Hiei-san to Kōya-san* (Mt. Hiei and Mt. Kōya). Tokyo, 1959.

比叡山と高野山

Kawasaki Yasuyuki. *Kizoku bunka no seijuku* (The growth of the aristocratic culture). Tokyo, 1960. (*Zusetsu Nihon rekishi*, 3.)

川 崎 庸 之　貴族文化の生熟 (図説日本歴史3）

Kazuye Kyōichi. *Nihon no mappō-shisō* (The ideology of the latter law in Japan). Tokyo, 1961.

数 江 教 一　　日本の末法思想

Kimura Ki. *Meiji Tennō* (Emperor Meiji). Tokyo, 1956.

木　村　毅　　明治天皇

———— *Saionji Kimmochi*. Tokyo, 1959.

西園寺公望

Kindaichi Haruhiko. *Nihongo* (The Japanese language). Tokyo, 1957.

金 田 一 春 彦　　日本語

Kindaichi Kyōsuke. *Kokugoshi keitō-hen* (Historical lineage of the Japanese language). Tokyo, 1938.

金 田 一 京 助　　国語史系統編

————, *et al.* "Nihongo no keitō ni tsuite" (On the lineage of the Japanese language), *Kokugogaku* (Studies in the Japanese language), No. 5 (February, 1951).

金 田 一 京 助　　「日本語の系統について」

その他　　　　（国語学　第五輯）

———— "Ainu bunka to Nihon bunka tono kōshō" (Cultural contacts between the Ainu and the Japanese), *Nihonbunka-Kenkūjo-Kiyō* (Transactions of the Institute for Japanese Culture and Classics [Tokyo]), No. 2 (March, 1958), pp. 16–39.

金 田 一 京 助　　「アイヌ文化と日本文化との交渉」

（日本文化研究所紀要　第二輯）

Kishimoto Hideo, ed. *Meiji bunka-shi: Shūkyō-hen* (Meiji cultural history: Section on religion [Vol. VI]). Tokyo, 1954.

岸 本 英 夫　　明治文化史　6　宗教編

Kitao Nichidai. *Nichiren monka jūippa kōyō* (An outline of the eleven branches among the adherents of Nichiren). Kyoto, 1935.

北 尾 日 大　　日蓮門下十一派綱要

Kiyohara Sadao. *Shintō-shi* (A history of Shinto). 8th ed. Tokyo, 1942.

清 原 貞 雄　　神道史

Kiyono Kenji. "Nihon sekki-jidai jinrui" (Stone age peoples of Japan), in *Seibutsugaku kōza* (Studies in biology). Tokyo, 1930.

清 野 謙 次　　「日本石器時代人類」(生物学講座)

———— *Nihon minzoku seisei-ron* (Development of the Japanese people). Tokyo, 1937.

　　　日本民族生成論

———— *Kodai jinkotsu no kenkyū ni motozuku Nihon jinshuron* (A theory about the Japanese race based on the study of archaic human bones). Tokyo, 1949.

　　　古代人骨の研究に基く日本人種論

Kobata Atsushi, and Tarō Wakamori. *Nihonshi kenkyū* (A study of Japanese history). Tokyo, 1958.

小葉田淳　和歌森太郎　　日本史研究

Kobayashi Kenzō. *Gendai Shintō no kenkyū* (A study of contemporary Shinto). Tokyo, 1956.

小 林 健 三　　現代神道の研究

Kobayashi Yukio. "Yayoishiki doki no yōshiki kōzō" (Styles of the Yayoi period wares), *Kōkogaku hyōron* (Review of archeology), Vol. I, No. 2 (1935).

小 林 行 雄　　「弥生式土器の様式構造」
　　　　　　　(考古学評論)

———— "Jōdai Nihon ni okeru jōba no fūshū" (The custom of horse-back riding in the early period of Japan), *Shirin* (Historical studies), Vol. XXXIV, No. 3 (July, 1951).

「上代日本における乗馬の風習」

(史林)

———— "Kofun-jidai bunka no seiin ni tsuite" (Some factors that contributed to the formation of the tumulus period culture), in Nihon Jinruigaku-kai, ed., *Nihon Minzoku* (Japanese race) (Tokyo, 1952 and 1961), pp. 113–29.

「古墳時代文化の成因について」

(日本人類学会編　日本民族)

———— *Nihon kōkogaku gaisetsu* (An outline of Japanese archeology). Tokyo, 1961.

日本考古学概説

Kokugakuin Daigaku Nihon Bunka kenkyū-sho, ed. *Shintō rombun sō-mokuroku* (A comprehensive catalogue of articles on Shinto). Tokyo, 1963.

国学院大学日本文化研究所編　　神道論文総目録

Kondō Yoshihiro. *Kodai shinkō kenkyū* (A study of ancient beliefs). Toyko, 1963.

近 藤 喜 博　　古代信仰研究

Kotani Kimi. *Watakushi no shugyō-seikatsu sanjū-gonen* (The thirty-five years of my spiritual training). Tokyo, 1958.

小 谷 キ ミ　　私の修業生活三十五年

Kōyasan Daigaku Mikkyō-kenkyūkai, ed. *Kōbō Daishi no risō to geijutsu* (The ideal of Kōbō Daishi and the arts). Kōya-san, 1948.

高野山大学密教研究会　　弘法大師の理想と芸術

Kozaki Hiromichi. *Kokka to shūkyō* (State and religion). Tokyo, 1913.

小 崎 弘 道　国家と宗教

Kubo Tokutada. *Kōshin-shinkō no kenkyū* (A study in the Kōshin belief). Tokyo, 1961.

窪 徳 忠　庚申信仰の研究

Kubota Shōbun. *Bukkyō shakai-gaku* (Buddhist sociology). Tokyo, 1962.

久 保 田 正 文　仏教社会学

Kudō Eiichi. *Nihon-shakai to Purotesutanto dendō* (Japanese society and Protestant missions). Tokyo, 1959.

工 藤 英 一　日本社会とプロテスタント伝道

Kurabayashi Shōji. "Kyūtei-girei no kōzō" (The structure of the imperial palace rituals), *Nihonbunka-kenkyūsho-kiyō* (Transactions of the Institute for Japanese Culture and Classics), No. 8 (March, 1961), pp. 156–302.

倉 林 正 次　「宮廷儀礼の構造」
　　　　　　　（日本文化研究所紀要　第八輯）

Kurita Hiroshi. *Jingi shiryō* (Historical materials on Shinto). 4 vols. Tokyo, 1926–27.

栗 　 田 　 寛　神祇資料

Kuwata Tadachika. *Kizoku bunka kara Buke bunka ye* (From the aristocratic culture to the warrior culture). Tokyo, 1960. (*Zusetsu Nihon rekishi,* 4.)

桑 田 忠 親　貴族文化から武家文化へ
　　　　　　　（図説日本歴史　4 ）

———— *Hōken bunka no keisei* (Formation of the feudal culture). Tokyo, 1960. (*Zusetsu Nihon rekishi, 5.*)

封建文化の形成

(図説日本歴史 5)

Manabe Kōsai. *Jizō bosatsu no kenkyū* (A study of Bodhisattva Ksiti-garbha). Kyoto, 1960.

真 鍋 広 済　　地蔵菩薩の研究

Maruyama Masao. *Nihon seiji shisō-shi kenkyū* (A study in the history of Japanese political thought). Tokyo, 1952.

丸 山 真 男　　日本政治思想史研究

———— *Nihon no shisō* (Japanese thought). Tokyo, 1961.

日本の思想

Masutani Fumio. *Shinran Dōgen Nichiren.* Tokyo, 1956.

増 谷 文 雄　　親鸞　道元　日蓮

———— *Nihonjin no Bukkyō* (Buddhism of the Japanese people). Tokyo, 1960.

日本人の仏教

Matsuda Kiichi. *Kirishitan no kenkyū* (A study of Kirishitan). Osaka, 1953.

松 田 毅 一　　キリシタンの研究

Matsumaye Takeshi. *Nihon shinwa no shin-kenkyū* (A new study of Japanese mythology). Tokyo, 1960.

松 前 健　　日本神話の新研究

Matsumoto Hikohachirō. "Nihon senshi jinrui-ron" (A view of the prehistoric peoples of Japan), *Rekishi to Chiri* (History and geography), Vol. III, No. 5 (1919).

松 本 彦 七 郎　　「日本先史人類論」

　　　　　　　　　（歴史と地理）

Matsumoto Nobuhiro. *Nihon shinwa no kenkyū* (A study of Japanese mythology). Tokyo, 1946.

松 本 信 広　　日本神話の研究

―――― *Nihon no shinwa* (Myths of Japan). Tokyo, 1956.

　　　　日本の神話

―――― "Shinwa no seikaku" (The nature of Japanese myths), in *Jōmon Yayoi Kofun jidai* (The Jomon, Yayoi, and Kofun periods) (Tokyo, 1956), pp. 304–10. (*Zusetsu Sekai bunkashi taikei*, 1.)

　　　　「神話の性格」

　　　　（図説日本文化史大系　Ⅰ　縄文　弥生　古墳時代）

Matsumoto Rōyei. *Kōbō Shinran Nichiren*. Tokyo, 1919.

松 本 露 影　　弘法　親鸞　日蓮

Matsumura Takeo. *Nihon shinwa no kenkyū* (A study of Japanese mythology). 4 vols. Tokyo, 1955–58.

松 村 武 雄　　日本神話の研究

Matsuno Junkō. *Shinran—Sono shōgai to shisō no tenkai katei* (Shinran: his life and the developmental process of his thought). Tokyo, 1959.

松 野 純 孝　　親 鸞

―――― "Kamakura Bukkyō to josei" (Kamakura Buddhism and women), *Journal of Indian and Buddhist Studies*, X (No. 2, March, 1962), 648–60.

　　　　「鎌倉仏教と女性」

　　　　（印度学仏教学研究　第十巻　第二号）

Michibata Ryōshū. "Nihon-Bukkyō no kaigai-fukyō" (Overseas evangelical works of Japanese Buddhism), in *Kōza kindai Bukkyō,* V (Kyoto, 1961), 177–89.

道 端 良 秀 　（日本仏教の海外布教」（講座近代仏教）

Mikami Tsugio. "Nihon kokka bunka no kigen ni kansuru futatsu no tachiba—Tennō-zoku wa Kiba-zoku ka" (An essay on two views of the origin of Japanese culture—with reference to the question as to whether or not the imperial clan was the "horseback riding tribe"), *Rekishi hyōron* (Studies in history), Vol. IV, No. 6 (June, 1950).

三 上 次 男 　「日本国家　文化の起原に関する二つの立場」
　　　　　　（天皇族は騎兵族か）
　　　　　　（歴史評論　第四巻　第六号）

Mikasa no Miya Takahito (H.I.H. Prince Takahito Mikasa), ed. *Nihon no akebono* (The dawn of Japan). Tokyo, 1959.

三 笠 宮 崇 仁 　日本のあけぼの

Mishina Shōyei. *Kenkoku shinwa ronkō* (Essays on the myths of the founding of the nation). Tokyo, 1937.

三 品 彰 英 　建国神話論考

Miyaji Harukuni. "Inari-shinkō no ichi-kiban" (Background of Inari worship), *Nihonbunka-kenkyūsho-kiyō* (Transactions of the Institute for Japanese Culture and Classics), No. 9 (October, 1961), pp. 58–84.

宮 地 治 邦 　「稲荷信仰の一基盤」
　　　　　　（日本文化研究所紀要　第九輯）

Miyaji Naokazu. *Jingi-shi taikei* (An outline history of Shinto cults). Tokyo, 1941.

宮 地 直 一 　神祇史大系

Miyamoto Hiroto. "Tsugumo kaizuka-jin no basshi fūshū ni tsuite" (Some notes on the custom of pulling teeth in reference to the human body unearthed at the shell mound of Tsugumo), *Jinrui-gaku zasshi* (Journal of anthropology), Vol. XL, No. 5 (1925).

宮 本 博 人　「津雲貝塚人の抜歯風習に就て」

　　　　　　　（人類学雑誌）

Miyamoto Shōson. "Meiji Bukkyō kyōgaku-shi" (A history of Buddhist doctrinal studies during the Meiji era), *Gendai Bukkyō* (The contemporary Buddhism [Tokyo]), No. 105: *Meiji Bukkyō no ken-kyū* (A special issue for the study of Meiji Buddhism) (June, 1933), pp. 18–30.

宮 本 正 尊　「明治仏教教学史」

　　　　　　　（現代仏教：明治仏教の研究）

――――, ed. *Bukkyō no kompon shinri* (The fundamental truth of Buddhism). Tokyo, 1956.

　　　　仏教の根本真理

――――, et al. *Indo-tetsugaku to Bukkyō no shomondai* (Collected studies on Indian philosophy and Buddhism [In honor of Professor Ui Hakuju upon his 60th birthday]). Tokyo, 1953.

　　　宮本正尊　その他　　印度哲学と仏教の諸問題

Miyata Toshihiko. *Kibi-no-Makibi*. Tokyo, 1961.

宮 田 俊 彦　吉備真備

Miyazaki Eishū. *Nichiren-shū-shi kenkyū* (A study of the history of the Nichiren school), Vol. I. Tokyo, 1950.

宮 崎 英 修　日蓮宗史研究

Mochizuki Shinkyō. *Bukkyō daijiten* (Buddhist dictionary). 5 vols. and appendix. Tokyo, 1931–36.

望 月 信 享　仏教大辞典

Mombu-shō. *Shūkyō nenkan* (Yearbook of religion). Tokyo, 1961 and 1965.

文　部　省　　宗教年鑑

Mombu-shō Chōsa-kyoku Shūmu-ka. *Shintō gyōsei enkaku-shi* (A history of the administration of Shinto). Ge-no-Jō, n.d. (Mimeographed.)

文部省調査局宗務課　　神道行政沿革史 (下の上)

Mori Kanshō. *Sangōshiiki kōgi* (An interpretation of the *Sangōshiiki*). Kōya-san, 1941.

森　寛　紹　　三教指帰講義

Mori Katsumi. *Kentō-shi* (Envoys to China). Tokyo, 1959.

森　克　己　　遺唐使

Morimoto Rokuji. "Yayoishiki doki ni okeru nisha" (Two kinds of Yayoi period wares), *Kōkogaku* (Archeology), Vol. V, No. 1 (1934).

森　本　六　爾　　「弥生式土器に於ける二者」 (考古学)

Morioka Kiyomi. *Shinshū kyōdan to Iye-seido* (The True Pure Land sectarian community and the family system). Tokyo, 1962.

森　岡　清　美　　真宗教団と「家」制度

Moroto Sojun. *Hōnen-shōnin no gendaiteki-rikai* (A modern interpretation of Saint Hōnen). Kyoto, 1964.

諸　戸　素　純　　法然上人の現代的理解

Munakata jinja fukkō kisei kai, ed. Munakata jinja-shi (History of Munakata shrine), Vol. I. Tokyo, 1961.

宗像神社復興期成会　　宗像神社史 (上巻)

Murakami Shigeyoshi. *Kindai minshū shūkyō-shi no kenkyū* (A study of the recent historical development of folk religion). Tokyo, 1958.

村 上 重 良　　近代民衆宗教史の研究

Murakami Toshio. *Shugen-dō no hattatsu* (The development of the order of mountain ascetics). Tokyo, 1943.

村 上 俊 雄　　修験道の発達

Murakami Toshisuke, and Sakata Yoshio. *Kyōiku-dōtoku-hen* (Section on education and morality). (*Meiji bunkashi* [Meiji cultural history], Vol. III.) Tokyo, 1955.

村 上 俊 亮
　　　　　　　明治文化史　教育道徳編
坂 田 吉 雄

Muraoka Tsunetsugu. *Nihon bunka-shi gaisetsu* (An outline history of Japanese culture). Tokyo, 1939.

村 岡 典 嗣　　日本文化史概説

———— *Nihon-shisōshijō no shomondai.* (Important problems in the history of Japanese thought). Tokyo, 1957. (*Nihon Shisōshi kenkyū*, Vol. II.)

　　　日本思想史上の諸問題（日本思想史研究　Ⅱ）

———— *Norinaga to Atsutane* (Norinaga and Atsutane). Tokyo, 1957. (*Nihon Shisōshi kenkyū*, Vol. III.)

　　　宣長と篤胤（日本思想史研究　Ⅲ）

———— *Shintō-shi* (A history of Shinto). (*Nihon Shisōshi kenkyū*, Vol. I.) Tokyo, 1956.

　　　神道史（日本思想史研究　Ⅰ）

———— *Zoku-Nihon-shisōshi-kenkyū* (A study of the history of Japanese thought [continued]). Tokyo, 1939.

　　　続日本思想史研究

—————— *Zōtei-Nihon-shisōshi-kenkyū* (A study of the history of Japanese thought). Rev. ed. Tokyo, 1940.

増訂日本思想史研究

Murata Masashi. *Nambokuchō-ron* (Essays on the southern and northern dynasties). Tokyo, 1959.

村 田 正 志　　南北朝論

Naganuma Kenkai. *Nihon shūkyō-shi no kenkyū* (Studies in the history of Japanese religion). Tokyo, 1928..

長 沼 賢 海　　日本宗教史の研究

Nakamura Hajime. *Tōyō-jin no shii-hōhō* (The ways of thinking of eastern peoples). 2 vols. Tokyo, 1948.

中 　村 　元　　東洋人の思惟方法

Nakamura Kokyō. *Tenrikyō no kaibō* (A critical diagnosis of the Tenrikyō). Tokyo, 1937.

中 村 古 峡　　天理教の解剖

Nakamura Mitsuo. "Chishiki kaikyū" (Intellectual class), in Shinchō-sha, *Nihon bunka kenkyū* (Studies in Japanese culture), Vol. VI. Tokyo, 1959.

中 村 光 夫　　「知識階級」

（新潮社　日本文化研究　6）

—————— , *et al. Kindaika to dentō* (Modernization and tradition), in *Kindai Nihon shisō-shi kōza* (Studies on the development of modern Japanese thought), Vol. VII. Tokyo, 1959.

中村光夫　その他　　近代化と伝統

（近代日本思想史講座　7）

Naoki Kōjiro. *Nihon kodai kokka no kōzō* (The structure of the early Japanese state). Tokyo, 1958.

直 木 孝 次 郎　　日本古代国家の構造

───── *Jitō Tennō* (The Empress Jitō). Tokyo, 1960.

持統天皇

Naora Nobuo, "Harima no kuni Nishiyagi kaigan kōsekisō-chū hakken no jinrui ihin" (On human remains discovered in the prehistoric site along the seaside of Nishiyagi in the province of Harima), Parts I and II, *Jinruigaku zasshi* (Journal of anthropology), Vol. XLVI, Nos. 5 and 6 (1931).

直 良 信 夫　　「播磨国西八木海岸洪積層中発見の人類遺品」

（人類学雑誌）

Nihon Jinruigaku-kai, ed. *Nihon minzoku* (The Japanese people). Tokyo, 1952.

日本人類学会　　日本民族

Nishida Nagao. *Nihon shūkyō-shisō-shi no kenkyū* (A study of the history of religious thought in Japan). Tokyo, 1956.

西 田 長 男　　日本宗教思想史の研究

Nishida Naojirō. *Nihon bunkashi josetsu* (Introduction to the cultural history of Japan. Tokyo, 1942.

西 田 直 二 郎　　日本文化史序説

Nishio Yōtaro. *Kōtoku Shūsui*. Tokyo, 1959.

西 尾 陽 太 郎　　幸徳秋水

Nishitani Keiji. *Sekai-kan to kokka-kan* (A world view and a view of the nation). Tokyo, 1941.

西 谷 啓 治　　世界観と国家観

———— *Nihirizumu* (Nihilism). Tokyo, 1949.

ニヒリズム

Nishitsunoi Masayoshi. *Nenjū gyōji jiten* (A dictionary of annual festivals). Toyko, 1961.

西角井正慶　年中行事辞典

Numazawa Kiichi (Franz K. Numazawa). "Tenchi wakaruru shinwa no bunkashi-teki haikei" (Cultural background of the myth concerning the separation of heaven and earth), *Academia*, I (1952), 4–20.

沼沢喜一　「天地分るる神話の文化史的背景」(アカデミア)

Ōba Iwao, "Jōdai saigishi to sono iseki ni tsuite" (Prehistoric places of worship and their remains), *Kōkogaku zasshi* (Journal of archaeology), Vol. XX, No. 8 (1930).

大場磐雄　「上代祭祀阯と其の遺蹟に就いて」

（考古学雑誌　第二〇巻　第八号）

———— "Nihon ni okeru ishi-shinkō no kōkogaku-teki kōsatsu" (An archeological study of stone-worship in Japan), *Nihonbunka-ken-kyūsho-kiyō* (Transactions of the Institute for Japanese Culture and Classics), No. 8 (March, 1961), pp. 1–26.

日本における石信仰の考古学的考察」

（日本文化研究所紀要　第八輯）

Ōbayashi Taryō *Nihon shinwa no kigen* (Origins of Japanese myths). Tokyo, 1961.

大林太良　日本神話の起原

Ogasawara Haruo. "Chūsei Ise-Shintō no shisō" The theory of medieval Ise-Shinto), *Nihonbunka-kenkyūsho-kiyō* (Transactions of the Institute for Japanese Culture and Classics), No. 2 (March, 1958), pp. 80–143.

小笠原春夫　「中世伊勢神道の思想」

（日本文化研究所紀要　第二輯）

Oguchi Iichi. *Nihon shūkyō no shakai-teki seikaku* (Social characteristics of Japanese religion). Tokyo, 1953.

小 口 偉 一　　日本宗教の社会的性格

Oka Masao, *et al. Nihon minzoku no kigen* (The origin of the Japanese people). Tokyo, 1958.

岡正雄　石田英一郎　江上波夫　八幡一郎　　日本民族の起原

Okamato Kenji. *Jingō Kōgo* (The Empress Jingō [or Jingū]). Tokyo, 1959.

岡 本 堅 次　　神功皇后

Ōkubo Toshiaki. *Nihon bunka no kindaika* (Modernization of Japanese culture). Tokyo, 1961. (*Zusetsu Nihon rekishi, 7.*)

大 久 保 利 謙　　日本文化の近代化

　　　　　　　（図説日本歴史　7 ）

Ono Seiichiro, and Shinshō Hanayama, eds. *Nihon Bukkyō no rekishi to rinen* (The history and ideology of Japanese Buddhism). Tokyo, 1940.

小 野 清 一 郎

花 山 信 勝　　日本仏教の歴史と理念

Ōno Susumu. *Nihongo no kigen* (Origin of the Japanese language). Tokyo, 1957.

大 　野 　晋　　日本語の起原

Ōno Tatsunosuke. *Nichiren.* Tokyo, 1958.

大 野 達 之 助　　日 蓮

Ono Toshio. "Kyōgishi ni kansuru ichi-kanken" (One view regarding the history of [Konkō] doctrine), *Konkō-kyō gaku* (The journal of the Konkō-kyō [Konkō, Okayama]), No. 1 (1958) pp. 60–77.

小 野 敏 夫　　「教義史に関する一管見」

　　　　　　　（金光教学　Ⅰ）

Origuchi Shinobu. "Tokoyo oyobi Marebito" (The world of eternity and the sacred visitor), *Minzoku* (Folklore [Tokyo]), IV (No. 2), 1–62.

折 口 信 夫　「常世及びまれびと」(民俗)

Ōta Ryō. *Nihon jōdai ni okeru shakai-soshiki no kenkyū* (The Japanese social system in the early period). Tokyo, 1929.

太　田　亮　日本上代に於ける社会組織の研究

Ōyama Kōjun. *Shin-Butsu kōshō-shi* (A history of the interaction between Shinto and Buddhism). Kōya-san, 1944.

大 山 公 淳　　神仏交渉史

Ōye Shinobu. *Meiji kokka no seiritsu* (Formation of the state in the Meiji era). Tokyo, 1959.

太 江 志 乃 夫　　明治国家の成立

Rekishi-gaku kenkyūkai, ed. *Nihon shakai no shiteki kyūmei* (An Historical analysis of Japanese society). Tokyo, 1949.

歴史学研究会(編)　　日本社会の史的究明

Saiki Ariyoshi, ed. *Jingi zensho* (Complete works on Shinto). 5 vols. Tokyo, 1906–8.

佐伯有義(編)　　神祇全書

——— *Dai Nihon jingi-shi* (A history of Shinto in Japan). Tokyo, 1914.

　　　大日本神祇史

Saitō Yuishin. *Jōdo-kyō-shi* (A history of Pure Land Buddhism). Tokyo, 1927.

斎 藤 唯 信　　浄土教史

Sakata Yoshio. *Meiji ishin-shi* (A history of the Meiji restoration). Tokyo, 1960.

坂 田 吉 雄　　明治維新史

Sakata Yoshio, ed. *Meiji ishin-shi no mondaiten* (Problems in the history of the Meiji restoration). Tokyo, 1962.

坂田吉雄 (編)　明治維新史の問題点

Sakazume Nakao. "Hennenjō yori mitaru kaizuka (Gaisetsu)" (Shell mounds viewed from the study of chronology), in Nihon jinruigaku-kai, ed., *Nihon minzoku* (The Japanese people) (1952), pp. 58–82.

坂 詰 仲 男　「編年上より見た貝塚」

　　　　　　　　　(日本人類学会編　日本民族)

Saki Akio, Takashi Inui, Iichi Oguchi, and Eiichi Matsushima. *Kyōso* (Founders of [new] religions). Tokyo, 1955.

佐木秋夫　等　教　祖

―――, and Iichi Oguchi. *Sōka Gakkai*. Tokyo, 1957.

　　佐木秋夫　小口偉一　創価学会

―――, Yuiichi Homma, Gembō Hoshino, Shūken Suzuki, and Kyōtoku Nakano. *Gendai no shūkyō mondai* (Religious problems of today). Tokyo, 1959. (*Nihon shūkyō-shi kōza* [Studies in Japanese history], 4.)

　　佐 木 秋 夫　等　現代の宗教問題

　　　　　　　　(日本宗教史講座　第四巻)

Sakisaka Itsuo, ed. *Nihon shakaishugi-undō-shi* (A history of the Japanese socialist movement). Tokyo, 1955.

向坂逸郎 (編)　日本社会主義運動史

Sakurai Tokutarō. *Nihon minkan-shinkō-ron* (A study of folk beliefs in Japan). Tokyo, 1958.

桜 井 徳 太 郎　日本民間信仰論

Sano Yasutarō. *Tsurezure-gusa shinkō* (New lectures on the *Tsurezure-gusa*). Tokyo, 1947.

佐 野 保 太 郎　徒然草新講

Sasaki Nobutsuna. *Jōdai bungakushi* (A history of ancient literature). 2 vols. Tokyo, 1935–36.

佐々木信綱　上代文学史

Satō Tokuji. *Bukkyō no Nihonteki tenkai* (The Japanese development of Buddhism). Tokyo, 1936.

佐藤得二　仏教の日本的展開

Sekai kōkogaku taikei (*SKT*) (Encyclopedia of world archeology). 16 vols. Tokyo, 1959–62.

世界考古学大系　（平凡社）

Seki Akira. *Kika-jin* (The naturalized peoples). Tokyo, 1956.

関　晃　帰化人

Seki Giichirō, ed. *Nihon jurin sōsho* (Series of Japanese Confucian writings). 6 vols. Tokyo, 1927–29. Second series, 4 vols. 1930–33.

関儀一郎（編）　日本儒林叢書

Sekiguchi Shindai. "Tendai shikan no seiritsu to sono tenkai" (The formation of *T'ien t'ai shih-kuan* [*Samatha Vipasyana*] and its development), in Miyamoto Shōson, ed., *Bukkyō no kompon shinri* (The fundamental truth of Buddhism) (Tokyo, 1956), pp. 841–70.

関口真大　「天台止観の成立とその展開」

　　　（宮本正尊編　仏教の根本真理）

Sekiyama Naotarō. *Kinsei Nihon jinkō no kenkyū* (Studies in the demography of recent periods in Japan). Tokyo, 1948.

関山直太郎　近世日本人口の研究

Sekki-jidai-bunka kenkyukai, ed. *Nihon sekki-jidai sōgō bunken mokuroku* (A comprehensive bibliography on Japan's prehistoric period). Tokyo, 1958.

石器時代文化研究会　日本石器時代綜合文献目録

Shimaji Daitō. *Tendai kyōgaku-shi* (The development of the Tendai doctrine). Tokyo, 1929.

島 地 大 等　　天台教学史

Shimazaki Tōson. *Shimazaki Tōson-shū* (Collected works of Shimazaki Tōson), Vol. III. Tokyo, 1957. (*Gendai Nihon bungaku zenshū* [Collected works of contemporary Japanese literature] 41.)

島 崎 藤 村　　島崎藤村集（現代日本文学全集）

Shimizudani Kyōjun. *Tendai no Mikkyō* (Esotericism of the Tendai tradition). Tokyo, 1929.

清 水 谷 恭 順　　天台の密教

Shimmi Kiichi. *Kakyū-shizoku no kenkyū* (A study of lower-class warriors). Tokyo, 1954.

新 見 吉 次　　下級士族の研究

Shimmura Izuru. *Nihon Kirishitan bunka-shi* (A history of Kirishitan culture in Japan). Tokyo, 1942.

新　村　出　　日本吉利支丹文化史

Shimomura Fujio. "Meiji no shakai" (Society during the Meiji era), in Shinchō-sha, *Nihon bunka kenkyū* (Studies in Japanese culture), Vol. VI. Tokyo, 1959.

下 村 富 士 男　　「明治の社会」
　　　　　　　　（新潮社　日本文化研究　第六巻）

Shinobu Seisaburō. *Taishō seiji-shi* (Political history of the Taishō era). 4 vols. Tokyo, 1951–52.

信 夫 清 三 郎　　大正政治史

Sugihara Sōsuke. "Iwajuku no kyūsekki" (Stone implements discovered in Iwajuku), *Kagaku Asahi* (Asahi science), Vol. X, No. 7 (July, 1960).

杉 原 荘 介　　「岩宿の旧石器」（科学朝日）

Sukeno Kentarō. *Kirishitan no shinkō seikatsu* (The religious life of the Kirishitan). Tokyo, 1957.

助 野 健 太 郎　　キリシタンの信仰生活

Sumiya Mikio. *Katayama Sen*. Tokyo, 1960.

隅 谷 三 喜 男　　片山潜

Suzuki Hiromichi. *Heian-makki monogatari no kenkyū* (A study of novels of the late Heian period). Tokyo, 1960.

鈴 木 弘 道　　平安末期物語の研究

Suzuki Hisashi. "Sagami Hirasaka Kaizuka (sōki-Jōmon-shiki iseki) no jinkotsu ni tsuite" (Notes on the human bones unearthed at the shell mound at Hirasaka in the Sagami district—considered as remains of the early Jōmon period), *Jinruigaku zasshi* (Journal of anthropology), Vol. LXI, No. 3 (1950).

鈴 　 木 　 尚　　「相模平坂貝塚（早期縄文式遺跡）の人骨について」
　　　　　　　　　（人類学雑誌）

Tagita Kōya. *Shōwa jidai no sempuku Kirishitan* (Hidden Kirishitan in the Shōwa era). Tokyo, 1954.

田 北 耕 也　　昭和時代の潜伏キリシタン

Takagami Kakushō. *Mikkyō gairon* (An outline of esoteric Buddhism). Tokyo, 1938.

高 神 覚 昇　　密教概論

Takagi Hiroo. *Shinkō shūkyō* (New religions). Tokyo, 1958.

高 木 宏 夫　　新興宗教

——— *Nihon no shinkō shūkyō* (New religions in Japan). Tokyo, 1959.

　　　　日本の新興宗教

Takagi Hiroo. *Sōka-gakkai to Risshō-kōsei-kai*. Tokyo, 1960.

創価学会と立正校成会

Takahashi Kenji. *Dōho dōken no kenkyū* (Study of bronze spears and swords). Tokyo, 1925.

高 橋 建 自　銅鉾銅剣の研究

Takahashi Takashi. *Sakanouye-no-Tamuramaro*, Tokyo, 1959.

高　橋　崇　坂上田村麻呂

Takahashi Tomio. *Ō-shū Fujiwara-shi yon-dai* (The four generations of the Fujiwara family in the northwest). Tokyo, 1958.

高 橋 富 雄　奥州藤原氏四代

Takamine Hiroshi. *Kokugo ga sesshushitaru Bukkyō bunkà* (Buddhist culture adopted into the Japanese language). Osaka, 1944.

高　峰　博　国語が摂取したる仏教文化

Takarada R. *Sangōshiiki kanchū* (A brief commentary on the *Sangōshiiki*). 2 vols. Kyoto, 1885.

宝 田 蘭 若　三教指帰簡註

Takeda Chōshū. *Sosen sūhai* (Ancestor worship). Tokyo, 1957.

竹 田 聴 洲　祖先崇拝

Takeda Yūkichi. *Kojiki setsuwa-gun no kenkyū* (A study of classification of the Kojiki myths). Tokyo, 1954.

武 田 祐 吉　古事記説話群の研究

Takeoka Katsuya. *Nihon shisō no kenkyū* (A study of Japanese thought). Tokyo, 1940.

竹 岡 勝 也　日本思想の研究

Takeuchi Yoshinori. *Kyōgyō shinshō no tetsugaku* (Philosophy of [Shinran's] *Kyōgyō shinshō*). Tokyo, 1941.

武 内 義 範　教行信証の哲学

Tamaki Hajime. *Nihon kazoku-seido hihan* (A critical study of the Japanese family system). Tokyo, 1935.

玉　城　肇　日本家族制度批判

—— *Nihon kazoku-seido-ron* (An essay on the Japanese family system). Kyoto, 1953.

日本家族制度論

Tamamuro Taijō. *Meiji ishin haibutsu kishaku* (The anti-Buddhist movement at the time of the Meiji restoration). Tokyo, 1939.

圭 室 諦 成　明治維新廃仏毀釈

—— "Nihon Bukkyō-shi gaisetsu" (A brief history of Japanese Buddhism), in Hajime Nakamura, Fumio Masutani, and J. M. Kitagawa, eds., *Gendai Bukkyō meicho zenshū* (Modern Buddhist classics), III (Tokyo, 1960), 3-237.

「日本仏教史概説」

（中村元　増公文雄　J.M.北川編

現化仏教名著全集　第八巻　日本の仏教）

Tamura Enchō. *Hōnen shōnin den no kenkyū* (A study of the biography of Hōnen). Kyoto, 1956.

田 村 円 澄　法然上人伝の研究

—— *Nihon Bukkyō shisō-shi kenkyū: Jōdo-kyō-hen* (A study of the history of Buddhist thought in Japan: The Pure Land sect). Kyoto, 1959.

日本仏教思想史研究　浄土教篇

Tamura Yoshio. "Nihon Tendai honkaku-shisō no keisei-katei" (The process of development of the concept of original enlightenment in Japanese Tendai Buddhism), *Journal of Indian and Buddhist Studies,* X (No. 2, March, 1962), 661–72.

田 村 芳 朗　「日本天台本覚思想の形成過程」

　　　　　　　（印度学仏教学研究　第十巻　第二号）

Tanaka Takeo. *Wakō to kangō bōyeki* (Japanese marauders and the tally trade). Tokyo, 1961.

田 中 健 夫　倭寇と勘合貿易

Tanaka Yukio. "Chikuzen Okitsugū no sekisei mozōhin" (Stone models [of boats, etc.] unearthed at Okitsu shrine in Chikuzen), *Kōkogaku zasshi* (Journal of archeology), Vol. XXV, No. 2 (1935).

田 中 幸 夫　「筑前沖津宮の石製模造品」

　　　　　　　（考古学雑誌）

Taniguchi Masaharu. *Seimei no jissō* (Realities of life). 40 vols. Tokyo, 1937.

谷 口 雅 春　生命の実相

Toganoo Shōun. *Mandara no kenkyū* (A study of mandala). (*Toganoo zenshū* [Collected works of Toganoo], Vol. IV.) Kōya-san, 1958.

栂 尾 祥 雲　曼荼羅の研究

Toda Jōsei. *Shakubuku kyōten* (A canon of winning converts). Tokyo, 1951.

戸 田 城 聖　折伏教典

Togawa Anshō. *Haguro Yama-bushi to minkan shinkō* (The mountain ascetics of the Haguro sect and folk beliefs). Tsuruoka-shi, Yamagata-ken, 1950.

戸 川 安 章　羽黒山伏と民間信仰

Tokoro Shigemoto. "Nichiren no shūkyō to Tennō-sei nashionari-zumu" (Nichiren's religion and the imperialistic nationalism), in *Kōza kindai Bukkyō* (Essays on modern Buddhism), Vol. V (Kyoto, 1961), pp. 100–18.

戸 頃 重 基 　 「日蓮の宗教と天皇制ナショナリズム」

　　　　　　　　（講座近代仏教　第五巻　生活編）

Tokyo-daigaku Hokkekyō-kenkyū-kai, ed. *Nichiren-shōshū Sōka-gakkai* (Nichiren-sho sect and Sōka-gakkai). Tokyo, 1962.

東京大学法華経研究会編　　日蓮正宗創価学会

Tokyo-daigaku shiryō-hensanjo. *Dai-Nihon ishin shiryō* (Restoration documents of Japan): *Iike shiryō* (Documents of the Ii family), Vol. I. Tokyo, 1959.

東京大学史料編纂所　　大日本維新史料　井伊家史料

Tōma Seita. *Nihon minzoku no keisei* (Formation of the Japanese race). Tokyo, 1951.

藤 間 生 大 　 日本民族の形成

Torii Ryūzō. "Kita Chishima ni sonzai suru sekki-jidai iseki-ibutsu wa somo-somo nani-shuzoku no nokoseshi-monoka" (Which ethnic group left the stone age remains now found in the Northern Kuriles?"), *Tōkyō Jinruigaku zasshi* (Tokyo journal of anthropology), Vol. XVII, No. 187 (1901).

鳥 居 竜 蔵 　 「北千島に存在する石器時代遺跡遺物は抑も何種族

　　　　　　　の残せしものか」

　　　　　　　（東京人類学会雑誌　第十七巻　第一八七号）

———— "Nihon sekki jidai minshū no joshin shinkō" (Prehistoric Japanese belief in female deities), *Jinruigaku zasshi* (Journal of anthropology), Vol. XXXVII, No. 11 (1922).

　　　「日本石器時代民衆の女神信仰」

　　　（人類学雑誌　第三十七巻　第十一号）

Torii Ryūzō. "Gojin sosen yūshi-izen no dankon sonhai" (Our prehistoric ancestors' phallic cult), *inruigaku zasshi* (Journal of anthropology), Vol. XXXVIII, No. 3 (1923).

「吾人祖先有史以前の男根尊拝」
　　　　(人類学雑誌　第三十八巻　第三号)

———— *Yūshi izen no Nihon* (Japan before history). Tokyo, 1925.
有史以前の日本

Tōyama Shigeki. *Meiji ishin* (The Meiji restoration). Tokyo, 1951.
遠 山 茂 樹　　明治維新

————, Seiichi Imai, and Akira Fujiwara. *Shōwa-shi* (A history of the Shōwa era). Tokyo, 1959.
　　遠山茂樹　今井清一　藤原彰　　　昭和史

Tsuda Sōkichi. *Jindai-shi no kenkyū* (A study of the divine age). Tokyo, 1924.
津 田 左 右 吉　　神代史の研究

———— *Kojiki oyobi Nihonshoki no kenkyū* (A study of *The Ancient Matters* and *The Chronicle of Japan*). Tokyo, 1930.
　　古事記及日本書紀の研究

———— *Jōdai Nihon no shakai oyobi shisō* (Society and thought of early Japan). Tokyo, 1933.
　　上代日本の社会及び思想

———— *Nihon no Shintō* (Shinto of Japan). Tokyo, 1949.
　　日本の神道

Tsuji Zennosuke. *Nihon Bukkyō-shi* (A history of Japanese Buddhism). 11 vols. Tokyo, 1944–53.
辻 善 之 助　　日本仏教史

———— *Nihon bunka-shi* (A history of Japanese culture). 11 vols. Tokyo, 1949–53.

日本文化史

Uda Toshihiko. *Norito jiten* (A dictionary of Shinto liturgical prayers). Tokyo, 1963.

莵　田　俊　彦　　祝詞辞典

Ui Hakuju. *Zenshū-shi kenkyū* (A study of the history of Zen Buddhism). 3 vols. Tokyo, 1939–43.

宇　井　伯　寿　　禅宗史研究

———— *Nihon Bukkyō gaishi* (An outline history of Japanese Buddhism). Tokyo, 1951.

日本仏教概史

———— *Bukkyō kyōten-shi* (A history of Buddhist scriptures). Tokyo, 1957.

仏教経典史

Umeda Yoshihiko. *Jingi-seidoshi no kisoteki kenkyū* (A basic inquiry into the history of Shinto institutions). Tokyo, 1964.

梅　田　義　彦　　神祇制度史の基礎的研究

———— *Nihon shūkyō seido-shi* (A history of religious institutions in Japan). Kyoto, 1962.

日本宗教制度史

Umehara Suyeji. "Jōdai no koshiki-fun ni tsuite" (Notes on tumuli of the early historic period), in Nihon jinruigaku-kai, ed., *Nihon minzoku* (The Japanese people). Tokyo, 1952, pp. 100–12.

梅　原　末　治　　「上代の古式墳に就いて」

（日本人類学会編　日本民族）

Umezawa Isezō. *Ki-gi hihan* (A critical study of the *Kojiki* and the *Nihonshoki*). Tokyo, 1962.

梅沢伊勢三　　記紀批判

Uyeda Masaaki. *Nihon jōdai kokka seiritsu-shi no kenkyū* (A historical study of the formation of the early Japanese nation). Tokyo, 1959.

上田正昭　　日本上代国家成立史の研究

―――― *Yamato-takeru-no-mikoto* (Prince Yamato-takeru). Tokyo, 1960.

日本武尊

Uyehara Yashitarō. *Shoki no Hongan-ji* (The *Hongan-ji* during its early period). Kyoto, 1933.

上原芳太郎　　初期の本願寺

Uyemura Seiji. *Jimmu tennō* (The Emperor Jimmu). Tokyo, 1958.

植村清二　　神武天皇

Wakamori Tarō. *Shugen-dō-shi kenkyū* (A study of the history of the order of mountain ascetics). Tokyo, 1943.

和歌森太郎　　修験道史研究

―――― *Chūsei kyōdōtai no kenkyū* (A study of social solidarity groups during the medieval period. Tokyo, 1950.

中世協同体の研究

―――― *Yamabushi* (Mountain ascetics). Tokyo, 1964.

山伏

――――, ed. *Nihon bunka no akebono* (The dawn of Japanese civilization). Tokyo, 1960. (*Zusetsu Nihon rekishi,* 1.)

和歌森太郎（編）　　日本文化のあけぼの

（図説日本歴史　1）

———— *Taishū bunka no jidai* (The age of mass culture). Tokyo, 1961. (*Zusetsu Nihon rekishi,* 8.)

大衆文化の時代

（図説日本歴史　8）

Washio Junkei. *Kamakura bushi to Zen* (The warriors of the Kamakura period and Zen Buddhism). Tokyo, 1936.

鷲尾順敬　鎌倉武士と禅

———— *Nihon Bukkyō bunka-shi kenkyū* (A study of the Buddhist cultural history in Japan). Tokyo, 1938.

日本仏教文化史研究

Watanabe Ichirō. *Chōnin bunka no seisei* (Development of townsman culture). Tokyo, 1961. (*Zusetsu Nihon rekishi,* 6.)

渡辺一郎　町人文化の生成

（図説日本歴史　6）

Watanabe Minoru. *Niijima Jō.* Tokyo, 1959.

渡辺実　新島襄

Watanabe Shōichi. *Nihon kinsei dōtoku-shisō-shi* (A recent history of moral thought in Japan). Tokyo, 1961.

渡辺正一　日本近世道徳思想史

Watanabe Shōkō. *Nihon no Bukkyō* (Buddhism in Japan). Tokyo, 1960.

渡辺照宏　日本の仏教

Watanabe Yosuke. *Azuchi-jidai-shi* (A history of the Azuchi period). Tokyo, 1956.

渡辺世祐　安土時代史

Watsuji Tetsurō. *Nihon seishin-shi kenkyū* (A study of the spiritual history of Japan). Tokyo, 1926.

和 辻 哲 郎 　 日本精神史研究

———— *Sakoku: Nihon no higeki* (National seclusion: the tragedy of Japan). Tokyo, 1950.

鎖国　日本の悲劇

———— *Nihon rinri-shisō-shi* (A history of Japanese ethical thought). 2 vols. Tokyo, 1959–61.

日本倫理思想史

Yamada Yoshio. *Hirata Atsutane.* Tokyo, 1943.

山 田 孝 雄 　 平田篤胤

————, *et al.*, annots. *Konjaku monogatari shū* (Tales of long ago), Vol. III. Tokyo, 1961. (*Nihon koten bungaku taikei* [Encyclopedia of Japanese classical literature] 24.)

今昔物語集

（日本古典文学大系）

Yamakawa Chiō. *Hokke shisō-shi-jō no Nichiren shōnin* (Saint Nichiren in the history of the lotus ideologies). Tokyo, 1934.

山 川 智 応 　 法華思想史上の日蓮上人

Yamakawa Uichi. *Jingi jiten* (A dictionary of Shinto). Tokyo, 1924.

山 川 鵜 市 　 神祇辞典

Yamamoto Isao. *Dengyō Daishi.* Tokyo, 1935.

山 本 勇 夫 　 伝教大師

Yanaihara Tadao. *Uchimura Kanzō to tomo-ni* (With K. Uchimura). Tokyo, 1962.

矢 内 原 忠 雄 　 内村鑑三とともに

———, ed. *Sengo Nihon shōshi* (A short history of post-war Japan). 2 vols. Tokyo, 1958–60.

矢内原忠雄 (編)　戦後日本小史

Yanagita Kunio. *Shintō to minzokugaku* (Shinto and folklore studies). Tokyo, 1943.

柳　田　国　男　　神道と民俗学

——— *Yamamiya-kō* (A study of mountain shrines). Tokyo, 1947.

山宮考

——— "Tama-yori-hime-kō" (Some reflections on Tama-yori-hime), in his *Imōto no chikara* (The power of the sister) (Tokyo, 1953), pp. 51–76.

「玉依姫考」

(妹の力)

——— *Nihon no matsuri* (Festivals of Japan). Tokyo, 1953.

日本の祭

———, general ed. *Minzokugaku jiten* (A dictionary of folklore studies). Tokyo, 1951.

柳田国男　監修　　民俗学辞典

———, and Origuchi Shinobu. "Nihonjin no kami to reikon no kannen sono hoka" (The Japanese views on kami, soul, etc.), *Minzokugaku kenkyū* (Journal of ethnology), Vol. XIV (No. 2, September, 1949).

柳田国男　折口信夫 (対談)

　　　　　　「日本人の神と霊魂の観念　そのほか」

　　　　　　(民族学研究)

Yashima Jirō. *Shosei no shiori* (A handbook of the way of life). Osaka, 1950.

八 島 二 郎　処生の栞

———— *PL shoseikun kaisetsu* (An exposition of the PL way of life). Tokyo, 1952.

PL処生訓解説

Yasunaga Bentetsu. *Ita-honzon gisaku-ron* (The spuriousness of the wooden object of worship). Tokyo, 1956.

安 永 弁 哲　板本尊偽作論

Yazaki Takeo. *Nihon toshi no hatten katei* (Developmental process of Japanese cities). Tokyo, 1962.

矢 崎 武 夫　日本都市の発展過程

Yokota Kenichi. *Dōkyō*. Tokyo, 1959.

横 田 健 一　道 鏡

Yoshimura Shigeki. *Inzei* (Cloistered rule). Tokyo, 1958.

吉 村 茂 樹　院 政

Yūki Reimon, *et al.,* eds. *Nihon no Bukkyō* (Buddhism in Japan). Tokyo, 1958. (*Kōza Bukkyo* Series, V.)

結城令聞(編)　日本の仏教
　　　　　　　(講座仏教　5)

Yūki Sazuku. *Bukkyō-rinri no kenkyū* (A study of Buddhist ethics). Kyoto, 1962.

遊 亀 教 授　仏教倫理の研究

Yuri Jun'ichi. *Maruyama kyōso-den* (A biography of the founder of Maruyama-kyō). Kawasaki-shi, 1955.

柚 利 淳 一　丸山教祖伝

Zusetsu Nihon bunkashi taikei (Illustrated encyclopedia of Japanese cultural history). 13 vols. Tokyo, 1956–58.

図説日本文化史大系〔小学館〕

1. *Jōmon Yayoi Kofun jidai* (The Jōmon, Yayoi, tumulus periods).

   縄文　弥生　古墳時代

2. *Asuka jidai* (The Asuka period).

   飛鳥時代

3. *Nara jidai* (The Nara period).

   奈良時代

4. *Heian jidai* (The Heian period), Part I.

   平安時代〔上〕

5. *Heian jidai* (The Heian period), Part II.

   平安時代〔下〕

6. *Kamakura jidai* (The Kamakura period).

   鎌倉時代

7. *Muromachi jidai* (The Muromachi period).

   室町時代

8. *Azuchi Momoyama jidai* (The Azuchi Momoyama period).

   安土桃山時代

9. *Edo jidai* (The Edo period), Part I.

   江戸時代〔上〕

10. *Edo jidai* (The Edo period), Part II.
    江戸時代（下）

11. *Meiji jidai* (The Meiji era).
    明治時代

12. *Taishō Shōwa jidai* (The eras of Taishō and Shōwa).
    大正昭和時代

13. *Gendai* (The contemporary period).
    現　代

Zusetsu Nihon minzokugaku zenshū (Collected works on Japanese folklore illustrated). 8 vols. Tokyo, 1961.
図説日本民俗学全集（藤沢衛彦）

Zusetsu Nihon rekishi (Illustrated history of Japan). 8 vols. Tokyo, 1960–61.
図説日本歴史（中央公論社）

Zusetsu sekai bunkashi taikei (Illustrated encyclopedia of cultural history of the world). 27 vols. Tokyo, 1959–61.
図説世界文化史大系（角川書店）

Index

Abe family, 53

Abe Ise-no-kami Masahiro, 179, 200*n*

Abe Isoo, 191*n*

Abe-no-Kiyotsugu, 48

Abe-no-Nakamaro, 54*n*

Adams, Will, 145

Administrative Council, 205

"Affair of the *Madre de Deus*," 146*n*, 154*n*

Agata-no-Inugai Michiyo, 29*n*

Agricultural College, Sapporo, 241*n*

Aichi prefecture, 235

Aizen-en, *see* Ōmoto-kyō

Aizu, 157, 158*n*

Akamatsu Katsumaro, 245

Akamatsu Mitsusuke, 99*n*

Akira-keiko, 49*n*

Akiyama Jiun, 174

Akiyama Mayuki, Vice Admiral, 223*n*

Alliance Society (Christian and Missionary), 302

Allied Council, 262

Allied Powers (1914–1918), 194

Allied Powers (1941–1945), 262, 269, 332

Amakasu Masahiko, 196*n*, 197*n*

Amaterasu, or Amaterasu-Ōmikami (Sun Goddess), 8, 10*n*, 17*n*, 43, 100, 169, 216, 219, 224, 228, 253, 268, 280; Shrine of, 33*n*, 203

Ame-no-Minakanushi, 216, 217, 228

American Board of Foreign Missions, 241

Amida, 33, 43, 113, 114–15, 117–18, 120–21, 220, 227, 228, 233; cult of, 58, 60, 73–85 *passim*, 104–5, 113

Amur Society, 195*n*

Ananai-kyō, 307, 316–17

Anatoli, Father, 240

Anesaki Masaharu, 293

Ankō, 9.

Anglican Church, 247*n*, 301–2

Annam, 189

Anti-Atomic-Hydrogen Bomb Rally, 299*n*

Anti-Religious League, 283

Antoku, Emperor, 52

Aoki Konyō, 173*n*

Arai Hakuseki, 157, 161

Arai Sukenobu, 324*n*, 325*n*

Araki, Thomas, 147

Arima, 142, 148*n*

Ashikaga family, 95–96

Ashikaga era, 126, 131–32

Ashikaga Takauji, 86, 95–96

Ashikaga Yoshiakira, 96

Ashikaga Yoshimitsu, 96, 97, 106

Ashikaga Yoshimochi, 106*n*

Ashikaga Yoshiteru, 142

Ashiwara, 57*n*

Asuka, 23

Asuka era, 22–30 *passim*

Asuka temple, 33

Ato Ōtari, 48*n*

Augustinian missionaries, 146